POLEMICS
AND
PROPHECIES

1967–1970

By I. F. Stone

A NONCONFORMIST HISTORY OF OUR TIMES

POLEMICS AND PROPHECIES

1967–1970

I. F. STONE

LITTLE, BROWN AND COMPANY

BOSTON   TORONTO   LONDON

973.92
587p

Library of Congress Cataloging-in-Publication Data

Stone. I. F. (Isidor F.), 1907–
    Polemics and prophecies, 1967–1970.

    (A nonconformist history of our times)
    Includes index.
        1. United States — Politics and government — 1963–1969.
    2. United States — Politics and government — 1969–1974.
    3. Vietnamese Conflict, 1961–1975 — United States.
    4. World politics — 1965–1975.   I. Title.   II. Series:
    Stone, I. F. (Isidor F.), 1907–   Nonconformist
    history of our times.
    E846.S77   1989   973.92   89-12125
    ISBN 0-316-81763-5 (HC)
    ISBN 0-316-81747-3 (PB)

MV PA

Published simultaneously in Canada
by Little, Brown & Company (Canada) Limited

PRINTED IN THE UNITED STATES

For my sister Judy

*The author wishes to thank Gerry Bruck, Jr.
for his devoted efforts in selecting
and editing this collection.*

Contents

Part VI Disarmament: A Century of Futility

Part VII That Barroom Brawl with the Lights Out Revisited

Part VIII Endless War

Part IX The Mideast

Part X Pax Americana

Part XI 'It Wasn't for Lack of Spies . . .'

Part XII The Streets

AUTHOR'S PREFACE

A Word about Myself

I am, I suppose, an anachronism. In an age of corporation men, I have been an independent capitalist, the owner of my own enterprise, subject to neither mortgager nor broker, factor nor patron. In an age when young men, setting out on a career of journalism, must find their niche in some huge newspaper or magazine combine, I have been a wholly independent newspaperman, standing alone, without organizational or party backing, beholden to no one but my good readers. I am even one up on Benjamin Franklin — I have never accepted advertising.

The majority of the pieces collected in this volume are from a four-page miniature journal of news and opinion, on which I was a one-man editorial staff, from proofreader to publisher. This independence, like all else, had its price — the audience. My newspaper reached a relative handful, but the 5,000 readers with whom I started grew to more than 70,000 in nineteen years. I was in the black every one of those years and paid off the loans which helped me begin, without having to appeal to my readers or to wealthy friends to keep going. I paid my bills promptly, like a solid bourgeois, though in the eyes of many in the cold-war Washington where I operated I was regarded, I am sure, as a dangerous and subversive fellow.

I have been a newspaperman all my life. In the small town where I grew up, I published a paper at fourteen, worked for a country weekly and then as correspondent for a nearby city daily. I did this from my sophomore year in high school through college, until I quit in my junior year. I was a philosophy major and at one time thought of teaching philosophy, but the atmosphere of a college faculty repelled me.

While going to college I was working ten hours afternoon and night doing combination rewrite and copy desk on the *Philadelphia Inquirer*, so I was already an experienced newspaperman making $40 a week — big pay in 1928. I have done everything on a newspaper except run a linotype machine.

I had become a radical in the twenties while in my teens, mostly through reading Jack London, Herbert Spencer, Kropotkin and Marx. I became a member of the Socialist Party and was elected to the New Jersey State Committee of the Socialist Party before I was old enough to vote. I did publicity for Norman Thomas in the 1928 campaign while a reporter on a small city daily, but soon drifted away from left-wing politics because of the sectarianism of the left. Moreover, I felt that party affiliation was incompatible with independent journalism, and I wanted to be free to help the unjustly treated, to defend everyone's civil liberty and to work for social reform without concern for leftist infighting.

I was fortunate in my employers. I rarely, if ever, felt compelled to compromise with my conscience; even as an anonymous editorial writer I never had to write something I thought untrue. I worked for a succession of newspaper people I remember with affection: J. David Stern and his editor Harry T. Saylor on the *Camden Courier-Post*, the *Philadelphia Record* and the *New York Post*; Freda Kirchwey of *The Nation*; Ralph Ingersoll and John P. Lewis of the newpaper *PM*; Bartley Crum and his editor Joseph Barnes of the short-lived New York *Star*; and Ted O. Thackrey of the *New York Post* and the New York *Daily Compass*. Working for them was a wonderfully rewarding experience and I learned much from all of them. From 1932 to 1939 I was an editorial writer on the *Philadelphia Record* and the *New York Post*, then strongly pro–New Deal papers. In 1940 I came to Washington as Washington Editor of *The Nation* and have been here ever since, working as reporter and columnist for *PM*, the New York *Star*, the *New York Post* (for a short interval) and the New York *Compass*. When the *Compass* closed in November 1952 and no congenial job seemed likely to open up, I decided to launch a four-page weekly newsletter of my own.

I succeeded because it was what might be called a piggy-back launching. I had available the mailing lists of *PM*, the *Star* and the *Compass* and of people who had bought my books. For a remarkably small investment, in two advance mailings, I was able to get 5,000 subscribers at $5 each. I was my own biggest investor, but several friends helped me with loans and gifts. The existence of these highly selective mailing lists made it possible to reach what would otherwise appear to be needles in a haystack — a scattered tiny minority of liberals and radicals unafraid in McCarthy's heyday to support, and go on the mailing lists of, a new radical publication from Washington. I am deeply grateful to them.

It speaks well for the tradition of a free press in our country that even in the heyday of McCarthy it was possible for me to obtain my second-class mail permit without trouble. I had then been working in Washington for twelve years as correspondent for a succession of liberal and radical papers. I had supported Henry Wallace in 1948. I had fought for the civil liberties of Communists, and was for peace and coexistence with the Soviet Union. I had fought the loyalty purge, the FBI, the House Un-American Activities Committee, and McCarran as well as McCarthy. I had written the first magazine article against the Smith Act, when it was first used against the Trotskyites in 1940. There was nothing to the left of me but the *Daily Worker*.

Yet I was able to get second-class mail privilege without a single political question. I encountered old-fashioned civil service courtesy and political impartiality in the post office, and the second-class mail privilege when I started was my bread and butter. The difference between the second-class rate and the cheapest third-class rate was the equivalent of my salary.

My idea was to make the *Weekly* radical in viewpoint but conservative in format. I picked a beautiful type face, Garamond, for my main body type, and eschewed sensational headlines. I made no claim to inside stuff — obviously a radical reporter in those days had few pipelines into the government. I tried to give information which could be documented so the reader could check it for himself. I tried to dig the truth out of hearings, official transcripts and government documents, and to be as accurate as possible. I also sought to give the *Weekly* a personal flavor, to add humor, wit and good writing to the *Weekly* report. I felt that if one were able enough and had sufficient vision one could distill meaning, truth and even beauty from the swiftly flowing debris of the week's news. I sought in political reporting what Galsworthy in another context called "the significant trifle" — the bit of dialogue, the overlooked fact, the buried observation which illuminated the realities of the situation. These I often used in "boxes" to lighten up the otherwise solid pages of typography unrelieved either by picture or advertising. I tried in every issue to provide fact and opinion not available elsewhere in the press.

In the worst days of the witch hunt and cold war, I felt like a guerilla warrior, swooping down in surprise attack on a stuffy bureaucracy where it least expected independent inquiry. The reporter assigned to specific beats like the State Department or the Pentagon for a wire service or a big daily newspaper soon finds himself a captive. State and Pentagon have large press relations forces whose job it is to herd the press and shape the news. There are many ways to punish a reporter who gets out of line; if a big story breaks at 3 A.M., the press office may neglect to notify him while his rivals get the story. There are as many ways to flatter and take a reporter into camp — private off-the-record dinners with high officials, entertainment at the service clubs. Reporters tend to be absorbed by the bureaucracies they cover; they take on the habits, attitudes and even accents of the military or the diplomatic corps. Should a reporter resist the pressure, there are many ways to get rid of him. If his publisher is not particularly astute or independent, a little private talk, a hint that the reporter seems irresponsible — even a bit radical — "sometimes one could even mistake him for a Marxist" — will do the job of getting him replaced with a more malleable man.

But a reporter covering the whole capital on his own —

particularly if he is his own employer — is immune from these pressures. Washington is full of news — if one story is denied him he can always get another. The bureaucracies put out so much that they cannot help letting the truth slip from time to time. The town is open. One can always ask questions, as one can see from one of my "coups" — forcing the Atomic Energy Commission to admit that its first underground test was detected not 200 miles away — as it claimed — but 2600 miles away. This is the story of how I got that story — one example of what independent news gathering can be like.

The first underground test was held in the fall of 1957. The *New York Times* report from the test site in Nevada next morning said the results seemed to confirm the expectations of the experts: that it would not be detected more than 200 miles away. But the *Times* itself carried "shirttails" from Toronto, Rome and Tokyo saying that the shot had been detected there. Since the experts (viz. Dr. Edward Teller and his entourage at Livermore Laboratory, all opposed to a nuclear test ban agreement) were trying to prove that underground tests could not be detected at a distance, these reports from Toronto, Rome and Tokyo piqued my curiosity. I did not have the resources to check them by cable, so I filed the story away for future use.

Next spring, Stassen, then Eisenhower's chief disarmament negotiator, testified before the Humphrey Disarmament Sub-committee of the Senate that a network of stations a thousand kilometers (or 580 miles apart) could police a nuclear test ban agreement and detect any underground tests. Two days after his testimony the AEC issued its first official report on the Nevada explosion for publication the following Monday. This said that the Nevada underground explosion had not been detected more than 200 miles away. The effect was to undercut Stassen's testimony. If the Nevada blast could not be detected more than 200 miles away then a network of stations 580 miles apart would not be able to police an agreement. I recalled the *New York Times* report of the previous fall, dug it out of a basement file and telephoned the AEC press office. I asked how the AEC reconciled its statement in the report

about to be released that the blast was not detected more than
200 miles away with the reports from Rome, Tokyo and
Toronto the morning after that it had registered on seismo-
graphs there. The answer was that they didn't know but
would try to find out.

In the meantime I decided to find me a seismologist. By
telephoning around I learned there was a seismology branch in
the Coast and Geodetic Survey, where I duly found a
seismologist and asked him whether it was true that Tokyo,
Rome and Toronto had detected the Nevada underground
blast. He said that he did not believe the claims of these three
foreign stations but he showed me a list of some twenty U.S.
stations which he said had certainly detected it. One of these
was 2600 miles north of the test site in Fairbanks, Alaska,
another was 1200 miles east in Fayetteville, Arkansas. I copied
the names and distances down. When he asked why I was so
interested, I said the AEC was about to release a report for the
following Monday claiming that the explosion was not detected
more than 200 miles away. When he heard the AEC angle, he
became less communicative. I had hardly got back to my office
when the phone rang; it was the AEC press relations man. He
said "We just heard from Coast and Geodetic. There must be
some mistake. We'll reach Nevada by teletype in the morning
and let you know." When the Joint Committee on Atomic
Energy later investigated the incident, the AEC claimed it was
an "inadvertent" error. No agency in Washington — not even
State Department or Pentagon — has a worse record than the
AEC for these little "errors."

No bureaucracy likes an independent newspaperman.
Whether capitalist or communist, democratic or authoritarian,
every regime does its best to color and control the flow of news
in its favor. There *is* a difference here and I'm grateful for it.
I could not operate in Moscow as I do in Washington. There
is still freedom of fundamental dissent here, if only on the
edges and in small publications.

For me, being a newspaperman has always seemed a cross
between Galahad and William Randolph Hearst, a perpetual

crusade. When the workers of Csespel and the 1956 Hungarian Revolution put a free press among their demands, I was thrilled. What Jefferson symbolized for me was being rediscovered in a socialist society as a necessity for good government.

I believe that no society is good and can be healthy without freedom for dissent and for creative independence. I have found among the Soviets kindred spirits in this regard and I watch their struggle for freedom against bureaucracy with deepest sympathy. I am sorry, when discussing our free press with them, to admit that our press is often almost as conformist as theirs. But I am happy that in my own small way I have been able to demonstrate that independence is possible, that a wholly free radical journalist can survive in our society. In the darkest days of McCarthy, when I often was made to feel a pariah, I was heartened by the thought that I was preserving and carrying forward the best in America's traditions, that in my humble way I stood in a line that reached back to Jefferson. These are the origins and the preconceptions, the hopes and the aspirations, from which sprang the pieces that follow.

I. F. STONE

PART I

When Two
Equals One

WHO ARE THE
DEMOCRATS?

The two-party system is like those magic black and white squares which look like a staircase at one moment and a checkerboard the next. Sometimes the two parties seem very distinct and sometimes they seem very much alike. This is one of those periods in which they look very much alike, whence the growing disillusion with the two-party system itself. The twin problems of retreat from empire abroad and of conciliating the black revolt at home call for changes of attitude and policy more fundamental than any we have faced since slavery.

The differences between the two parties just aren't that fundamental. To examine the past and nature of the Democratic party, which has normally been the party of change and reform, is to doubt its capacity to cope with the twin crises of our time. In the days of Franklin D. Roosevelt, unlike those of Grover Cleveland, it seemed easy to tell Democrats from Republicans. When we look back on the New Deal now, from the perspective of our present needs, the difference does not look as sharp as it did then. The rhetoric of American political controversy has never prized understatement, and the strategy of the rich has been to scream so loudly at the slightest diminution of their privileges that the sheer decibel count gives the poor the satisfying illusion that a revolution is going on. So it was with the Roosevelt Revolution. When the clamor died down and the smoke of battle began to lift, the Bastilles were still standing.

If one were trying to explain the American two-party system to a visitor from a different political planet, let us say a citizen of a Soviet one-party state, the simplest way to begin would be to say that both American parties were capitalist parties. The difference between them has been that generally the Republicans have represented the interests of the big property-owners; the Democrats, the small. But both are equally devoted to private property. After five years of Lyndon Johnson, it may be hard to recall that in the Administrations of FDR and Harry Truman the Democrats were tormented by the accusation that they were crypto-Communist. If a Soviet visitor asked hopefully whether it was true that in those days the leadership was secretly inspired by Lenin, one would have to explain that such charges must be taken in the same sense as when oppositionists within a Communist state are denounced as agents of capitalism. This is the universal poetic license of political controversy. When the Democrats are most heatedly accused of interfering with free enterprise, it usually turns out that all they have been doing is trying to slow up the rate at which the big fish of business have been swallowing the little ones.

Any division of the two parties between big property and small requires many qualifications. Big landowners dominate the Democratic party in the Southern states, which are still pretty much one-party systems; small farmers are the backbone of the Republican party in the Midwest and the rural Northeast. There are also big businessmen in the Democratic party and small businessmen in the Republican. Indeed, Babbitt—the archetype of the Republican standpatter—was a small businessman, from the Midwest, let it be noted. It is often said that American politics stops at the water's edge; it also stops at the oil well's mouth. The same big oil companies which dominate the Republican party in New York and Philadelphia also dominate the Democratic party in Houston and Oklahoma City. Depletion allowances are as sacred as the Stars and Stripes.

Wisely managed corporations diversify their political portfolios by giving to both parties, though not so generously to the Democrats. In a famous incident during a Federal investigation of the Sugar Trust in the 1890's, a sugar magnate—or tycoon, as we now say—was asked about the extraordinary impartiality shown in the benefactions he showered equally on both parties. "The American Sugar Refining Company," he replied genially, "has no politics of any kind. . . . Only the politics of business."

This helps explain why few big businessmen flee the country when the Democrats, as in the 1948 Truman campaign, wage anti-big business campaigns so ferocious as to make Soviet citizens tremble lest the directors of General Motors end up digging uranium in the Far North of an American Siberia. Truman, in a famous speech to farmers at Dexter, Iowa, a few weeks before the 1948 election, sounded like a latter-day Robespierre. "The Wall Street reactionaries," he said in prose as sharp as any guillotine, "are not satisfied with being rich . . . they are gluttons of privilege . . . cold men . . . cunning men. . . . They want a return of the Wall Street economic dictatorship." But when this *enragé* won, the stock market barely yawned.

The style of politics has changed. Trouncing big business, which proved sure-fire stuff two decades ago, has gone out of fashion. We are in a new Era of Good Feeling, in which both parties—and both wings of both parties—share a trusting faith that any problem can now be solved by enlisting private enterprise—so long as it is sufficiently subsidized from public funds. The cynical may wonder whether this is not just another way of buying the acquiescence of the wealthy in social reform by arranging that they make a profit on that, too. Here is a sample of the new rhetoric, as practiced by a present-day radical Democrat:

I do not think we have many real grievances to be urged against bigness in business today. . . . Some Americans hark back before the days of the managerial revolution, back to the days of the "robber barons." But this country and its economy have matured spectacularly since the trust-busting days. . . . The big businesses of bygone generations did, indeed, act in a pattern of savage repression of competition. And current revelations of price-fixing [perish the afterthought!] and other price-holding practices do not help to ease a strong historical suspicion of the motives of great corporations on the part of government

leaders, small businessmen and others. . . . [But] the pluralistic economy of the 1960's bears little resemblance to the economy of the turn of the century that brought forth the first great
trust-busting era. . . . It is high time that the traditional hostility between the intellectuals on the one hand and management
on the other was ended. Doctrinaire thinking has no place . . .
[etc.].

Alert readers may already have recognized the prose style—
as bland as marshmallows, richly garnished with fashionable
literary and political clichés[1]—of Hubert Humphrey. The
quotation is from his last book as a Senator, *The Cause Is
Mankind*. So statesmanlike had he become by 1964, even before his maturing four years as Lyndon Johnson's Vice
President.

Harry Truman was an unsuccessful haberdasher while
Humphrey has been stigmatized, somewhat snobbishly, because of his family business, as "a drugstore liberal."[2] On

[1] Often misconstrued, as in the reference to the managerial revolution.
Apparently Humphrey did not get beyond the title of James Burnham's
book.
[2] Robert Sherrill and Harry W. Ernst, *The Drugstore Liberal* (New
York: Grossman, 1968).
From *The New York Review of Books*, September 26, 1968:

To the Editors:
In I. F. Stone's essay "Who Are the Democrats?" [August 22] he says,
"Harry Truman was an unsuccessful haberdasher while Humphrey has
been stigmatized, somewhat snobbishly, because of his family business, as
'a drugstore liberal' "—and, as his footnote indicates, he bases the second
half of that sentence on the title of the book I co-authored, *The Drugstore Liberal*.
Shucks, I thought everyone would be familiar with the old saying,
"He's a drugstore cowboy," meaning no cowboy at all; and I thought
everyone would understand that I was just playing on this to say that
Humphrey isn't much of a liberal. The title is only accidentally related to
the fact that Humphrey owns a drugstore—a happy accident, however,
which I hoped would add some humor to the title and therefore to a topic
that is too often painfully dull. In any event, while there are few things
I would not do to show my regard for Mr. Stone, permitting him to in-
flate his reputation as an unsnobbish democrat at my expense is not one
of them.

Robert Sherrill

I. F. Stone replies:
Sorry, that was dumb of me.

the eve of a new nominating convention, it may be useful to recall that the great heroes of the party of the common man have not been of lowly origin. Its four outstanding Presidents were all of the Gracchus type, upper-class leaders of lower-class upsurge. All the Democratic revolutionaries—as their fond followers hailed them—were men of comfortable fortune and privileged position. Jefferson and Roosevelt were landed aristocrats. Jackson—the only one of them born in poverty—amassed a fortune in land and slaves, in shrewd alliance with the haves against the have-nots of the frontier. The kind of early hardship Wilson knew was of the genteel and socially secure variety that afflicts the sons of ill-paid Presbyterian ministers in well-to-do Southern small towns.

Except for Jefferson, all were originally of rather conservative views, and none was ever as radical as he sounded. Even Jefferson, as Richard Hofstadter observed in his perceptive *The American Political Tradition*, confined "the generous and emancipating thoughts for which his name is so justly prized" almost entirely to his private correspondence. To their overwrought political opponents, all four seemed to be traitors to their class, reckless leaders of the angry dispossessed. But unlike the Gracchi, none of them ever nourished the tree of liberty with more than a few drops pin-pricked from the privileged, who bleed easily. They were revolutionists only in an inflated and metaphorical sense.

Jefferson affirmed the equality of man but never tried to extend the right to vote beyond the propertied minority. Jackson was the symbol rather than the leader of the Jacksonian Revolution; its battles for universal white manhood suffrage and free public education were won before he became President. Wilson, like Teddy Roosevelt, began by being disdainful of the progressive tide they both later rode to fame and power. The measure of Wilson's New Freedom—how glamorously our liberal patent medicines have been labeled!—is that its principal surviving monuments are the Federal Reserve System and the Federal Trade Commission. The former, after all the attacks upon "the Money Trust" which led up to it, merely rationalized our central banking system. The latter, which was to protect the country against the abuses of big business, long ago degenerated into a toothless watchdog.

Though Utopian socialism had as great a vogue among American intellectuals before the Civil War as Communism did before the Second World War, and the American Socialist party was a living force before and for a decade after the First World War, socialistic ideas—as distinct from specific reforms which the Socialists were first to advocate —never penetrated the Democratic party. Even Roosevelt, who was ready to try anything to get the country out of the Great Depression, stopped short at the socialistic. Early in his Administration there was some agitation "to put idle hands and idle machines together"; there was an attempt to do just this in an idle Ohio mattress factory. I can remember my disappointment as a young editorial writer on one of the few pro-New Deal newspapers in the country when the project was so quickly nipped in the bud that it seems to have disappeared from the history books. Production for use—a forgotten phrase—was taboo. The Roosevelt Administration preferred to make jobs by "leaf-raking" and public works rather than disturb production for profit. FDR's celebrated pragmatism ended where the profit system began. His successors show no disposition to go beyond it.

The Democrats, as the party of the agrarian and small property-owner, and of the urban machines based on the proletarian immigrant, have tended to be readier for social reform than the Republicans, but not beyond the framework of the capitalist system. Indeed, the Democrats are super-sensitive to attack as "soft on communism." This is often a major determinant of what they will do in foreign and domestic policy. But the record is full of anomalies. Wilson began the non-recognition policy the Republicans applied to the Soviet Union. Roosevelt broke the diplomatic embargo and extended recognition to Moscow.

Should increased international tension or domestic turbulence bring a flare-up of our characteristic American anti-Communist paranoia, it is hard to tell which party would be first to pander to it. It was the liberal Democrat Wilson who sent Eugene Debs to jail in World War I and the conservative Republican Harding who pardoned him. The first American witch hunt after the Russian Revolution was launched by Wilson's Attorney General A. Mitchell Palmer. But it was the Republicans who revived the Red mania as a political tactic early in the Great Depression under the now forgotten Hamilton Fish, the first sniffer-outer of what came to be known later as "un-American activities." Right-wing Democrats and Republicans carried this on as a weapon against the New Deal and, with covert help from J. Edgar Hoover, revived it again as soon as the Second World War ended.

The purpose was to smear the period of Democratic dominance (in the ugly words later used by Eisenhower's unscrupulous Attorney General, Herbert Brownell) as "twenty years of treason." The Democratic reaction was an attempt to run at one and the same time with the hounds of anti-Communism and the hares of Jeffersonian liberalism. Truman instituted a loyalty purge within the government which put a premium on mediocrity and cast a pall of fear on the capital long before Joe McCarthy. His Smith Act prosecution of the Communists was begun in 1948 as a weapon against the Henry Wallace third-party movement. But his Attorney General, Tom Clark, opposed the repressive Mundt-Nixon bill, and Truman himself vetoed it as an effort at thought control in a message which was in the great tradition of Jefferson's opposition to the Alien and Sedition laws.

Panicky Senate Democratic liberals, among them Humphrey and Morse, had tried to block this bill with a substitute which was in some ways worse—a bill setting up detention camps in time of war or national emergency for persons suspected of being potential spies or saboteurs. This monstrosity marked the debut in American legislation of the idea that a man might be jailed not for something he did but for something it was thought he might do. The right-wingers cheerfully tacked this on to their own bill where-upon these liberals turned about and voted to support the President's veto of the entire measure. But a Congress under the influence of the anti-Red sentiment stirred by the Korean war passed it over Truman's veto. Thanks to this law, America some day may see concentration camps used against black or white radicals.

Humphrey's civil liberties record during this and the McCarthy period followed the standard Democratic pattern. He made occasional speeches against McCarthyism but was himself a junior McCarthy in purging the Farmer-Labor party of Minnesota and investigating the labor movement, particularly the United Electrical Workers, for communistic influence. The high-watermark of Humphrey's cowardice as a liberal, or defensive hysteria as an anti-Communist, was set in 1954, when with the same group of Senate liberals (this time including John F. Kennedy[3]), Humphrey sponsored the outlawry provisions of the Communist Control Act of 1954. These set up standards so sweeping for determining who was a Communist that Humphrey, Morse, and the other sponsors could have been declared Communists too. It was a Republican, John Sherman Cooper, who made the one principled speech against this nonsense, and it was Kefauver who cast the lone vote against it.

Humphrey, as the current villain of the antiwar forces, is being blamed for all this, but his record is no worse than that of Wayne Morse, their current hero, or of many other good liberals like the late Herbert Lehman. They made a shabby record during Joe McCarthy's heyday; it was a Republican Administration and a group of Senate conservatives who finally did McCarthy in. But Humphrey's record has a rich flatulence characteristic of the man; he never does anything by halves, and has a genius for making a fool of himself. "I am tired," he said in 1954, "of reading headlines

[3] He had voted with Nixon in the House to override Truman's veto of the Mundt-Nixon bill and had since been elected to the Senate.

about being a leftist." So in the Senate that year we find him
deploring the disbandment of his own little labor witch
hunt subcommittee, offering to make its files available to
Joe McCarthy, declaring that "rooting out Communist infiltration . . . is priority business" and boasting that his
Communist outlawry amendment would force every Senator to stand up and be counted. "We are going to lay the
issue on the line," he exulted, "and not on the fringes."

When the Eisenhower Administration, as well as many
of Humphrey's old ADA friends, objected that outlawry
would be unconstitutional, Morse chortled gleefully, "It
now appears that the White House thinks the Senator from
Minnesota is a little too hard on the Communists." Morse
had lent his prestige as a constitutional lawyer to the Humphrey bill, and still boasts—to show his own political purity
—that he once helped father a bill to outlaw the Communists. This whole episode reached its comic climax when
Humphrey told the Senate that a man "does not have to become a member of the Communist party to express unorthodox ideas. Let him become a member of other parties, or of
the Republican or the Democratic party, if he wants to express unorthodox ideas." Someone should have unfurled a
travel-style poster in the Senate chamber at the close of that
speech, "Join the GOP and overturn the world."

Marx in his *Eighteenth Brumaire* said history was a form
of politics. A corollary needs, however, to be added. The
larger the ingredient of politics, the poorer the quality of
the history. This is particularly true when the historical estimates reflect immediate rather than long-range political
considerations. Judgments made in the heat of a presidential
campaign are bad enough; those molded by the passions of a
campaign for the nomination are worse. Four years ago in
the pages of this same *New York Review* I poked fun at
Humphrey's inflated rhetoric and his attempts to ingratiate
himself with businessmen, but welcomed as a liberal victory
Johnson's choice of Humphrey as running mate. Eugene
McCarthy then appeared only as a moribund Senate liberal
who had played ball with the oil interests on the Senate Fi-

nance Committee and was the choice of Texas Governor
Connally. Goldwater was the menace; Johnson was not
only the lesser evil but the hope of peace. Humphrey's
more distant past, like Morse's, was forgiven because of the
part Humphrey had played in the fight for a nuclear test
ban, for disarmament, for civil rights, indeed for almost
every social reform measure of the preceding eight years.

Had McCarthy become Vice President, Humphrey might
today be the hero of the peace forces. The reversals of
mood and ideology required, despite the record we are
now emphasizing, would have been no greater than those
which occurred in the case of Robert F. Kennedy, or
Wayne Morse, or of the Americans for Democratic Action,
when that organization of homogenized and certified anti-
Communist liberals—which Humphrey helped to found—
turned against the war and Humphrey himself. Ambition,
conviction, recognition of objective circumstance, may be
more powerful than past position and any desire for con-
sistency. Who for that matter would have dreamed a year
ago that Allard K. Lowenstein could hoist that most lacka-
daisical of all the Senate Democratic liberals, Eugene Mc-
Carthy, onto a white horse?

The historian has the good fortune to begin after fate has
given him the outcome; he can then decide according to his
political philosophy the factors which made it "inevitable"
—no word ever more richly deserved the disparagement of
inverted double commas. The man who must write before
we know what will happen can only rework past history to
fit the outcome his heart fears or desires. Wisely operated
oracles, as far back as Delphi, knew that their only safety
was in ambiguity. But voters and those who presume to advise them face an inescapable test—the need to pick from
two usually ambiguous choices. Which brings us back to
the magic squares of the American two-party system, and
why this system sometimes seems to be government by rou-
lette. You put down your money but you never really
know what you're going to get.

The war. The war. The war. It ruined Johnson. And

Johnson ruined Humphrey. And a Humphrey-Nixon choice this time may ruin the American political system. The hardest part of my pre-convention assignment is to assess the history of the Democratic party and the nature of its seemingly all but certain candidate in the light of the war, and the overwhelming need to end it.

The first thing to be said about the war is that it has become the overriding issue because we are unable to win it. Our past is littered with Vietnams, small countries on which we have worked our will in the name of anti-Communism and, before Communism, of liberty. But the deeds arouse little protest when (as Lady Macbeth urged) done quickly. Johnson was as arrogant in the Dominican Republic, Dulles and the CIA as unscrupulous in Guatemala, but neither brought any widespread revulsion. Our national conscience did not twinge until the military situation hurt. Vietnam would be no issue if the Diem dictatorship had succeeded, if Kennedy's "advisers" had been enough to subdue the revolt against it, if Johnson's bombing of the North had worked, or if Westmoreland's strategy could have gone on to the point where there were no more Vietnamese left, and we could be sure we didn't have to start body-counting the Chinese, too. If the Viet Cong go on causing us enough trouble, any President will have to make peace because victory isn't worth what it would cost, and the wider risks it would entail. This is why John F. Kennedy to his credit drew back twice on Cuba. So we co-exist with Communism 90 miles off Key West but decline to compromise with it 9,000 miles from California. To the fresh eye, the frontiers of freedom must seem downright whimsical.

The second thing to be said is that successful wars, especially if short and profitable, are popular. When Lincoln as a Whig Congressman opposed the Mexican war, the result was his defeat for reelection. Pulitzer and Hearst made circulation, McKinley won reelection, and Teddy Roosevelt earned his glamorous reputation with that "splendid little war" against Spain which marked the debut of American imperialism in the Far East. The Philippines were our first Vietnam in Asia, Aguinaldo the first Ho Chi Minh we encountered; there was no lack of enthusiasm when we set out, in the slogans then current, to "help our little brown brother," and if he rejected that help to "civilize 'em with a Krag." The Krag was the M-16 of the time. An Anti-Imperialist League sprang into action between 1898 and 1900. But a new book[4] which has gone neglected shows that its leaders were upper-class conservatives and liberal gentlemen like Godkin of *The Nation*. Perhaps this study of the first American anti-imperialist movement has attracted so little attention during the current anti-imperialist agitation because in this it runs so counter to political clichés. The popular side was pro-imperialist.

A lot of nonsense has to be cleared away if we are to chart a fresh course. We Americans are neither the benefactors we think ourselves nor the devils our enemies see in us. Most peoples at some time in their history are expansionist and the expansion is always carried on in the name of some benevolent mission. The Czars found this in Pan-Slavism, the Kaiser in *Kultur*, the French in their *mission civilatrice*, and the British in the white man's burden, which was heavy with loot from the darker continents. Revolutionary movements, whether religious or secular, are particularly expansionist. From Mohammed to Mao their leaders have felt the urge to bestow the new faith as widely as possible, if necessary by the scimitar or gun.

Among the smaller peoples, our current victims, the Vietnamese, themselves rank high on any scale of aggressive imperialism. Their acquisition of the Mekong delta, which they took from the Khmers, goes back only to the eighteenth century, and Black Nationalists who see the Vietnam war as whitey vs. colored should speak to the darker-skinned Montagnards, the dispossessed "nigras" of the Vietnamese peninsula.

Among the big peoples we rank high as land-grabbers.

[4] Robert L. Beisner, *Twelve Against Empire—The Anti-Imperialists: 1898–1900* (New York: McGraw-Hill, 1968). I recommend it highly.

We pushed to the Pacific and took half of Mexico as our Manifest Destiny, reluctantly abandoned our designs on Canada, dominated the rest of the hemisphere in the name of Pan-Americanism, set out to make the world safe for democracy under Wilson, and are now rigging elections as far away as Southeast Asia in the name of self-determination. Nations, like gases, tend to expand until stopped and contained by countervailing forces they cannot overcome. We may be headed for containment by China.

Another obstacle to clear thinking is the myth that the people are inherently peaceful. This is part of the democratic ideology. It was born on the eve of the French Revolution, and survived proof to the contrary furnished by the fresh enthusiasm of the Revolutionary and Napoleonic armies. In our own country the Democrats as the popular party have been expansionist from the beginning. They were the agrarian party, and hungered for more land. It was mercantile and capitalist New England which was cold to the War of 1812, even though the war was presumably fought for free maritime commerce; the planters of the South saw the war as a way to solidify their hold on the Floridas while the farmers of the Northwest wanted to annex Canada. The Monroe Doctrine, that first monument of naïve North American imperialism, was a Democratic party accomplishment.

The secret of this unilateral declaration of a protectorate over the hemisphere was that Canning's original proposal for a joint Anglo-American declaration would have included a self-denying ordinance, pledging both powers to seek no territorial aggrandizement. When Monroe consulted Jefferson as the party's greatest living elder statesman, the latter replied, "Do we wish to acquire to our own confederacy any one or more of the Spanish provinces? I candidly confess that I have ever looked on Cuba as the most interesting addition which could be made to our system of States." [5] Jefferson would have accepted Canning's

[5] See p. 98 of the J. Reuben Clark Memorandum on the Monroe Doctrine published by the State Department in 1930 as Secretary of State

invitation, though with this imperialist regret. Calhoun, too, was ready "even if it should pledge the U.S. not to take Cuba or Texas." But the prevailing view embodied in the Monroe Doctrine only barred the transfer of any territory in the Western Hemisphere to a *European* power. Though all this was done in the name of making the Western Hemisphere safe for freedom, we declared our neutrality as between Spain and the colonies in revolt against her. Secretly we often favored Spanish rule.

In the Clark memorandum (see footnote five) the State Department for the first time disclosed instructions sent to our Minister to Madrid in 1829 urging Spain to keep control of Cuba. Bolívar's liberating armies were freeing the slaves and "the sudden emancipation of a numerous slave population . . . could not but be very sensibly felt upon the adjacent shores of the United States." The Vietnamese war is in the pattern set by our relations with Latin America: in the name of liberty, we supported first foreign and then native oligarchies.

On one refreshing occasion our unctuous pretensions were abandoned for plain talk. When Cleveland's Secretary of State warned Britain to keep hands off Venezuela in 1895, he interpreted the Monroe Doctrine with a frank imperial arrogance even Lyndon Johnson in his most brash private moments could hardly equal:

Today [Secretary Olney warned Britain] the United States is practically sovereign on this continent and its fiat is law upon the subjects to which it confines its interposition. Why? It is not because of the pure friendship or good will felt for it. It is not simply by reason of its high character as a civilized state, nor because wisdom and justice and equity are the invariable characteristics of the dealings with the United States. It is because in addition to all other grounds, its infinite resources combined with its isolated position render it master of the situation and practically invulnerable as against any or all powers.[6]

Stimson moved toward a Good Neighbor policy. The documents there printed for the first time from the Department files are the best antidote to the mythology of the Monroe Doctrine.

[6] The Clark Memorandum, p. 159.

Five years after Olney's note, the Democratic party for the first time in its history did indeed campaign against McKinley in 1900 on an anti-imperialist platform, but they were "at a disadvantage," as Robert Beisner's study of the anti-imperialist movement shows, "because they had bellowed for war in 1898 as loudly as anyone." William Jennings Bryan, the party's foremost anti-imperialist leader, "first volunteered to fight in Cuba, then declared himself an opponent of expansion, and finally urged Senate approval of the peace treaty" by which we annexed the Philippines and set out on the course we are still pursuing, of trying to make the Pacific as much a *Mare Nostrum* as the Atlantic or the Caribbean. Indeed our Navy's ambition is to control all the seven seas, and all the Eurasian outlets to them, from the Bosporus to the Formosan straits. Only the rhetoric of anti-Communism keeps us from seeing that no nation in history has ever had such grandiose imperial pretentions, such *hubris, chutzpah*, or brass.

The choice now is between disengagement and disaster. To scale down these colossal ambitions is the first necessity of American politics. But the retreat from empire, as the experience of other great nations has shown, is traumatic. There could be no poorer choice than Humphrey for that task. The first requirement is to disown Johnson's war, and Humphrey cannot disentangle himself, even if he would, from his association with it. Humphrey's nomination would ratify, while McCarthy's would rebuke, the decisions which put U.S. combat troops again on the mainland of Asia. The second count against a Humphrey choice is that his is the very type of spurious liberal evangelism which has provided idealistic cover for our effort to dominate the world. McCarthy's more astringent and sophisticated views offer some hope of a change. We need to recover our cool.

A third count against Humphrey is that he has given no reason to believe that he is any more ready than Johnson to negotiate a compromise in Vietnam. He went far beyond mere loyalty to Johnson when he told *U.S. News & World Report* (May 27), "If Nixon and Humphrey should be the candidates in the general election, I don't think our views of the war would be far apart." This is a war Nixon has wanted us to fight since 1954. Humphrey told students at St. Paul last May 27 we ought to be willing to stay at the conference table "in Paris for months, and if necessary for years, until a satisfactory solution was reached."

This is in accord with the Johnson strategy of defusing anti-war protest with the talks, keeping the fighting at a level the public will tolerate and hoping that somehow we can restore a non-Communist South Vietnam, like South Korea, in our sphere of influence. Humphrey's speech of July 12, supposedly designed to chart a foreign policy of his own, sounds remarkably like the same Johnson-Rusk cracked record. On the one hand Humphrey says, as they do, that "we are not the world's policeman," but on the other hand we must be prepared to fulfill mutual defense commitments where others "violate frontiers and foster local turmoil" as, though he did not say so, in Vietnam. So we are back where Johnson started. Nowhere here is there the necessary recognition that we may only make "local turmoil" worse by the magnitude and clumsiness of our intervention. This is the beginning of wisdom, but Humphrey is a long way from it.

The psychological and institutional obstacles to a retreat, not just from Vietnam but from the future Vietnams that a Pax Americana makes unavoidable, are so great as to make one doubt its possibility. A new President must face up to a military bureaucracy so huge that its weight in the scales of policy is almost insuperable. It is not that the Pax Americana policy has made such a huge machine necessary. It is that the existence of the machine, and all the careers and interests which depend upon it, require continuance of the Pax Americana. We are the prisoners of this machine, which must find work commensurate with its size to justify its existence. The magnitude of the monster is indicated by the growth of the military budget from $12 billion just before the Korean war only eighteen years ago to its current $80 billion and the $102 billion recently requested of Secretary

Clifford by the Joint Chiefs of Staff. This is like trying to keep a dinosaur as a household pet. It will eat us out of house and home. But only McCarthy has even touched on this subject.

The psychological obstacles are as great. The average man approaches the problem of war with simple reactions of anxiety and threatened virility thousands of years old. There is a strong movement for peace, but there is also a strong contingent of cavemen among us, and it is hard to see which is the majority; the same people often belong to both categories. Reagan and Wallace speak for large constituencies, too. In Vietnam as in Korea the Democrats *have* kept the wars limited while Reagan, like MacArthur before him, speaks for a Republican right wing which thinks the whole business can be ended in no more time than it takes to go from the seventeenth to the eighteenth hole by dropping a bomb on Peking and another on Moscow.

The two urgent issues are the Vietnamese war and the black revolt. Both require solutions for which we are poorly conditioned. One is to give way in Vietnam to a Communist, though also nationalist, tide. The other is to deal with the aspirations of the blacks, and the other poor, which can only be met by fundamental changes, a real redistribution of income from haves to have-nots, and an intervention of the State deeper and more far-reaching than anything America has ever known before. The only party less prepared for this than the Democrats, though not much less so, is the Republican party.

The issues, however, are beyond that unspoken ideological consensus within which the two-party system operates. The Democratic party, unlike the Republican, has some legitimate claim to being the party of "the people." But the people for whom it speaks turn out on closer examination to be middle-class owners of property, white-collar workers, or the organized working class. The urban and rural poor, and all but the thin upper strata of the blacks and our other "colored" minorities, are not really a part of its constituency.

They are outside "the people" in whose name it claims to speak. Unfortunately for revolutionary theorists, the more fortunate, those with something to lose, are the overwhelming majority. The poor, white and black, are but a lower fifth of the population. Should the Democratic party move too far in the direction of taking them in, and serving their interests, it is likely to lose much of its white and skilled-worker followers to the Republican party. It is this which makes the Democratic party look so unsatisfactory to the black radicals and the New Left, a purveyor of half measures rather than fundamental change. But in this the party faithfully reflects a majority constituency, and in this sense it is truly *representative*.

The new radicals generally are unwilling to face up to this reality. They prefer to believe that there is something wrong with the party, or with something called "the system," or that society is sick, rather than admit that what they are revolting against is the majority itself. To admit that would be too difficult and too untactful a break with the dominant ideology of democracy. Black nationalist separatism is fantasy based on despair but in one respect it is more realistic than the New Left, for in proposing separation it recognizes that what it is combating is the white majority and not some clique, conspiracy, or perverse ruling elite which has somehow led "the people" astray. In a democratic society it is always assumed that the people are good, as in theology it is always assumed that God is good. Evil is an accident, or the work of the devil. When large numbers of ordinary men commit some outrage against humanity, it is tacitly assumed that somehow they are not part of "the people."

That myth, the Common Man, is the theoretical sovereign of democratic society, and when he turns up in a racist mob or a typical veterans' organization, ideology literally turns off our vision. Democratic political stereotypes remain stalwartly non- and pre-Freudian because you can't win elections by telling voters they themselves are at fault. It is easier to let them off the hook by blaming some abstraction. Adam's sins are still attributed to some serpent which crept into the Garden. It is the nature of the white majority, and of man, that brings the two-party system to the verge of breakdown when faced with the need to swallow a military defeat and to tax the whites for the benefit of the blacks. The danger is that the white majority may choose instead to follow a simplistic demagogy which advocates as the way out a get-tough policy at home and abroad. Against that darkening backdrop, McCarthy is a wan hope.

August 22, 1968
*New York Review**

---

* Those selections not specified as taken from *The New York Review of Books* appeared in *I. F. Stone's Bi-Weekly*.

PARTY OF THE RICH
AND WELL-BORN

The Republican party began as, and is again, a minority party. It originated as a third party in 1854, when the slavery issue was splitting the Democrats and the Whigs. It is, according to Dr. Gallup, really a third party again today. In 1940 a poll of between-election leanings showed that 42 percent identified themselves as Democrats, 38 percent as Republicans, and 20 percent as independents. When Gallup repeated the same poll in the fall of 1967, there were more independents than Republicans. The Democrats still held at 42 percent but the Republicans had dropped to 27 and the independents risen to 31 percent.

Neither party can win without this floating independent vote, but the Republicans must get more of it than the Democrats. It is indicative that the only two men to be elected President on the Republican ticket in the last forty years had not been identified with the party when they entered politics. Herbert Hoover had been a strong Wilsonian while Eisenhower only four years before had been wooed

by the ADA. Both Hoover and Eisenhower won because
their appeal was wider than the party's. To paraphrase
Sholom Aleichem, it's hard to be a Republican in American
politics, a real one that is.

The statistics would seem to show that in 1968 the best
way to elect a Republican President would be to pick a candidate who looks and sounds as little like a Republican as
possible. By that standard the candidate least likely to succeed would seem to be Richard Nixon; the one who best
fills the bill would be John Lindsay. The Republicans
would do best if they went underground, with a crypto-
Republican candidate who could if necessary swear that he
had never really carried a party card.

This is as extraordinary a reversal as may be found in
American history. From 1860 until 1932—a space of sev-
enty-two years, more than two generations—only two
Democrats were elected President, Cleveland and Wilson.
All the others were Republican. A flood of election-year
books seeks to explain or change this history. Most of them
are as dull as the party itself; except in the days of Lincoln
and Teddy Roosevelt, the Republicans have always been the
duller of the two parties. The best books I have found in
this tidal wave of ephemera are George H. Mayer's *The
Republican Party 1854–1966*, a new edition brought up to
date of a book which first appeared in 1964, and Milton
Viorst's *Fall From Grace: The Republican Party and the
Puritan Ethic*. The former is a definitive and scholarly
work, astringently realistic but rather plodding in style, as
if the author himself couldn't help getting bored by his subject; the latter is short and lively, a swift and engaging synthesis of the work in the field, including Mayer's, but with
many fresh insights—Viorst shows real gifts as an historian.

The myths about the Republican party these two books
explode were exploded a generation ago by Charles Beard
in his moving and stately *Rise of American Civilization*.
Mayer and Viorst depict the Republicans as the party of
business and of the WASP. Viorst tries to make the story a
little more interesting by linking the party with the Puritan
ethic, though it is hard to tell where Puritanism ends and

plain acquisitiveness begins. This is no novel thesis. The surprise is that at this late date it should be attacked as "outrageous" and "audacious" by a Republican newspaperman who is a Washington correspondent. In the Washington *Post*, Robert D. Novak called Viorst a "super-liberal" and accused him of overlooking the party's left wing! [1]

In some periods of their history and on some issues, the two parties seem indistinguishable. Foreigners often fail to tell them apart, and Americans in some periods have spoken of them as Tweedledum and Tweedledee. Both parties are loose coalitions, warring multi-party systems, held together by habit and convenience. An operative definition of the Republican party is that it is the one which doesn't have a left wing, but only an occasional, slight and passing protuberance left of center, like a La Guardia or a Wayne Morse. Herbert Hoover, on his return from Europe in 1920 to enter politics, announced that he objected "as much to the reactionary group in the Republican party as to the radical group in the Democratic party." One cannot imagine his reversing this language and attacking the radicals in the Republican party. The last time the Republicans had a faction which could properly be termed radical was a century ago during Reconstruction. The only Republican President whom Wall Street ever regarded as a dangerous fellow was Teddy Roosevelt. In 1904, running against a conservative Democrat, Judge Alton B. Parker, the mercurial and demagogic Teddy sounded incendiary, even if his assaults on "malefactors of great wealth" were largely verbal. In retrospect the first Roosevelt, with his cult of war and masculinity, his imperialist adventures in Latin America and his naïve racism, sounds less like a radical than a premature Fascist, an American Mussolini before his time.

The men who practice politics and those who write about them are two different breeds. The former are concerned with power, and with interests and ideas as means to achieve it. The latter tend to overemphasize the ideas with

[1] Novak collaborates on a syndicated column which sometimes seems to specialize in uncovering hidden left-wing influences nobody else had noticed.

which the scramble for power is rationalized. Our party system calls for treatment by an anthropologist. It is a form of sport, especially a spectator sport. It is a variant of what William James sought when he called for a moral equivalent of war; the party system is an easy way of working off aggressive instincts. It resembles gang warfare, in that it is a means by which the bold and power-hungry, recruiting a handful of followers, can rule the territory they have staked out and enjoy the combat for dominion against rival gangs. They hand out favors and sell protection. Politics is also a form of business; the same division of labor which produces bankers and bus drivers also produces politicians and office holders.

Perhaps the American two-party system seems less mysterious when one observes that traces of two parties can be found in almost all societies, though in one-party dictatorships you may have to look for the other party in jail or concentration camps. The purges in the hierarchies of the communist states reflect the fact that even these One-and-Only parties are really two. Common to all societies are the same two types, the hards and the softs, the standpatters and the reformers, those who believe in coercion and those who believe in persuasion, those who think stability is best preserved by holding fast to the past and those who would bend a little with changing events and aspirations. The Democrats may waver but the Republicans stand with the former in all these pairs.

From the standpoint of interests and classes, the American two-party system may be seen as a division between the more and the less favored, the older stock and the newer immigrant, the businessman and the farmer, the creditor and the debtor, the employer and his workman. The Hamiltonians, the Federalists, the Whigs, and the Republicans appear as the spokesmen for the former, the anti-Federalists, the Jeffersonians, and the Democrats as the spokesmen for the latter. The big money has favored the former but also bought influence in the latter. But it is the Jeffersonian and Democratic strain which has constantly widened de-

mocracy and in periods of hard times responded to the
needs of the poorer elements. The welfare state is the creation of the Democrats and the bane of the Republicans.
This is no small difference.

The Republican party was born of the slavery issue as a
sectional party after slavery split both the existing national
parties, the Democrats and the Whigs. Most farmers—except for a rich handful, who tended to be Whig—were
Democrats until the free soil dispute split the free farmer
from the slave farmer. The two could not exist side by side.
When the Kansas-Nebraska Act and the Dred Scott decision destroyed the Missouri Compromise and threw open all
the Western lands to colonization by slave holders, the
Democratic party split. The Western farmer became a Republican. He remained a Republican out of inertia and filial
piety until the twenties, when hard times hit the Farm Belt
and Republican Presidents vetoed three different attempts
to give the farmer forms of crop control which would be
the equivalent for him of the protective tariff for manufacturers. These vetoes were to give the West to the Democrats and the New Deal.

To say that the Republican party was born of the slavery
issue is not to say that it began as a crusade against slavery.
This is a myth Mayer and Viorst easily dispose of. "At no
point in its anti-slavery campaign," Viorst writes, "was
there any sign that the Republican party was moved by any
compassion for the black man." On the contrary, as Viorst
points out, "In the Republican constitution of Kansas,
adopted by the Yankees in the heat of the anti-slavery campaign, free Negroes were forbidden even to enter the
State." Illinois banned Negro immigration by a two-to-one
margin in a popular referendum. From Ohio to California,
in all that free soil territory, Negroes were excluded from
voting. The Republican press in the Northwest, Viorst
relates, "proudly supported the politics of what it called
with much precision, 'the white man's party.' "

The story is one the black, or Afro-American, must read
with despair. The abolitionists were almost as hated in the

North as in the South. The two predecessor parties of the
Republicans, the Liberty and the Free Soil parties, though
they concentrated only on keeping slavery out of the
Western territories, were handicapped, Mayer writes, because "they could not sell the moral arguments for the containment of slavery." The Republican party succeeded by
soft-pedaling the issue of slavery altogether and concentrating on economic issues which would attract Northern businessmen and Western farmers.

"Perhaps the temper of the Republican convention"
which nominated Lincoln "can best be established," Viorst
relates, "by noting that the delegates baldly rejected a proposal to endorse from the Declaration of Independence the
statement that 'all men are created equal.'" Later they reversed themselves "but only after a bitter fight on the convention floor." The platform, with its equivocation on slavery and its espousal of protective tariffs, free homesteads,
and internal improvements, "abundantly demonstrated that
the Republican party had safely made the shift from a coalition held together by the fear of slavery to one united by a
common vision of material gain."

Lincoln, the Great Emancipator, looked to the radicals of
his time—as he begins to look to ours—as the Great Equiv-
ocator. The American Anti-Slavery Society, in comment-
ing on his nomination, saw it as "a convenient hook
whereon to hang appeals at once to a moderate anti-slavery
feeling and to a timid conservatism." Ambition had led him,
Viorst notes, "to align himself with the Whigs, 'the better
people' of the community, rather than the Democrats, the
party of the Southern poor." He became a Republican after
1856. His philosophy of the fluid society "captured the essence of middle class Republicanism." Lincoln summed this
up when he said, "I don't believe in a law to prevent a man
from getting rich. It would do more harm than good. So
while we do not propose to war upon capital, we do wish to
allow the humblest man an equal chance to get rich with
everybody else."

Privately Lincoln felt an abhorrence for the oppression

of the Negro but in public he found it expedient to take an evasive position. In the Douglas debates he denied that he had ever favored "the social and political equality of the white and black races." Viorst completes his portrait of Lincoln by saying, "It is probable that he was at least a step ahead of the Republican party generally in his sympathy for the Negro as a human being. But on one point he was in firm accord with the Republican position. Lincoln would by no means risk war to free the slaves." It was only "the shells which fell on Fort Sumter" which "ended the equivocation." Today's racial turmoil springs from the fact that the Negro was a side issue in a conflict between two classes of propertied white men, the Southern planter on one side and the Northern businessman and farmer on the other.

Lincoln's humanity, imperishably expressed, lifts him beyond detraction. But his compassion was mostly for white men, and only a little for black. "After years of fighting," Viorst writes with painful justice, "he remained faithful to the view that the Negro was less a human being than a divisive factor between the sections." He had no desire "to envenom further the hatred between North and South by emancipating the slaves." His attitude seemed if anything, Viorst goes on, "to have hardened over the course of the war." He spoke of black men "as of a military commodity, of no more intrinsic importance than cavalry horses."

The radical Republicans themselves saw the Negro as an instrument. Viorst quotes a speech by Sumner of Massachusetts in which that radical Senator warned that only through the vote of enfranchised black men "can you save the national debt from the inevitable repudiation which awaits it when recent rebels in conjunction with Northern allies [Democrats] once more bear sway. He is our best guarantee. Use him." The radicals' objective, Viorst writes, "was to make the Negro into a tool, not into a productive, self-reliant human being." Without land the Negro could not attain full citizenship. There was talk for a time "of confiscating major rebel estates for the distribution of parcels among the Negroes, but the Republicans were too

devoted to the sanctity of private property." The conflict
ended with the Negro half serf, half free. We are only now
beginning to pay for the full consequences.

Those sins of the fathers have set our teeth on edge. Suddenly those half-forgotten battles during Reconstruction
over "forty acres and a mule" loom up as the one immediately relevant episode in the dreary and familiar annals of
the party. The years which stretch from Grant to Eisenhower—two victorious and easy-going generals, only dimly
aware of what was going on around them in the White
House—are years of smugness and enrichment. Nothing
more fully discloses the nature of the "party of Lincoln"
than the fact that the Negro made his greatest advances
under the Democrats, and that Franklin D. Roosevelt,
Truman, Kennedy, and Johnson recruited him into the
same party with the Southern white supremacist. Political
history shows few stranger alliances.

The corollary may be a Republican return to power as
the whiter of the two white men's parties. For the first time
the GOP may become the party of the working-class white
and the non-WASP. Recently Richard Nixon envisioned
himself as the leader of a new coalition made up of "the
Republicans, the New Liberals, the New South and the
black militants." No other candidate has gone into so splendid a trance. The "new coalition" will more likely turn out
to be a coalition of white against black.

The Republican party has always seen itself as the party
of the self-made man. Usually nobody is readier to step on
those below him than the man who made it upward on his
own. The psychology of the self-made man now finds its
counterpart in the psychology of whole classes who think
they made it on their own—so why can't the Negro?
Whether they join the Republican party or not, the urban
white working class, the second and third generation of non-
WASP immigrants who have hitherto been Democrats because they felt like underdogs, are acquiring the Republican
outlook with success and turning rightward in reaction
against the rising revolt of the Negro. Their movement up-

ward from proletarian slums to mass-produced suburban villas, their fear of Negro violence and their aversion to Negro neighbors may make them Republican for the first time in their history. The white American working class had been split historically by the prejudices of the native Yankee against the foreign immigrant, whether Irish or East European. The Know-Nothings were the Birchite wing of the first Republicans. The immigrants, while hostile, like white workers generally, to the free Negro and the Abolitionist, stayed with the Democrats as the party which welcomed the new arrival. White workers may now close ranks against the black.

Thus the GOP's failure to reconstruct the South in 1868 and set the Negro wholly free may pave the way for its return to power in 1968. If so this will be the prelude to fresh disasters. It will only demonstrate again the GOP's utter incapacity for any task that requires social revolution. It can no more carry out basic changes at the expense of the well-to-do than an elephant can fly.

With the end of the Civil War, its brief flirtation with idealism was ended. Big business rose to undisputed dominance. The Republican party was its instrument. Politics became secondary to acquisition. Business made the fundamental decisions, helping itself liberally to the public lands and public treasury in the Hamiltonian tradition while recommending laissez-faire and rugged individualism to the worker and farmer it exploited. That era ended in 1929 with the Great Depression, but the mentality of that earlier period not only lives on beneath the surface of the welfare state but is showing signs of revival in the current emphasis among Democrats and Republicans alike on the need to "enlist" free enterprise in the war against poverty.

Babbitt is making a comeback. Viorst quotes from Sinclair Lewis a speech by that archetypal Republican small-town businessman of the twenties to show "how little the Puritan-social-Darwinian ethic had changed after more than a half century of wear." Babbitt angrily tells his children, "The first thing you got to understand is that all this uplift and flipflop and settlement work and recreation is nothing in God's world but the entering wedge of socialism. The sooner a man learns he isn't going to be coddled, and he needn't expect a lot of free grub . . . the sooner he'll get on the job and produce, produce, produce. That's what this country needs." That is indistinguishable from Goldwater or Reagan.

Neither Nixon nor Rockefeller is quite so naïve, but both share the belief that somehow "free enterprise" can again be our salvation, cleaning up the slums and making jobs for the poor, with subsidies and tax benefits from the public treasury. So for that matter does Bobby Kennedy, at least at times and in some sections of the country. Suburbia, with no desire to be taxed for the benefit of the poor and blacks, sees this as a painless way out.

But there is no painless and certainly no profitable way to correct a century of plunder and neglect. A whole spectrum of problems from the slum to air and water pollution was created by giving free rein to free enterprise to make a buck any way it saw fit. Those conditions are not going to be corrected by the same entrepreneurial forces which created them. These exhortations to business to create jobs recall Hoover's pathetic exhortations to business during the Great Depression. Bank presidents are built to resist evangelism. There has been no rush to invest money in Watts or Harlem, and in Washington in the wake of the latest ghetto riots it's suddenly hard even to get insurance in lily-white neighborhoods. There is no more sensitive plant than the buck. The party of business is even less likely than the Democrats to engage in such heretical observations. Not less but more public funds and social planning are required. Unfortunately the white middle class is not in the mood and that mood is determining the minstrelsy of this presidential campaign.

Rockefeller would no doubt appear in Novack's eyes as the "Republican left wing" that Viorst perversely overlooked. But there is no sign of a different tune from Rockefeller. On the contrary he has just discovered that no ideological barrier divides him from Reagan, the TV Tarzan of Republican politics. In foreign policy, Rockefeller has just suggested that we take over the protection of a whole arc of Asia from Iran to Japan, as if we did not already have enough trouble in Vietnam. He is as imperialist as Teddy Roosevelt; counter-insurgency and the Green Berets had their origin in the Rockefeller reports of the 1950's from which the Kennedys borrowed them. In domestic policy Rockefeller is giving ever more emphasis to "crime in the streets," notably, as Sidney E. Zion of the *New York Times* has just shown in *Ramparts* for June 15, 1968, in the shape of a program extraordinarily insensitive to constitutional safeguards, complete with wiretapping and allowing the police to stop-and-frisk, enter without knocking, and shoot-to-kill. So the Grand Old Party from right to "left" is firmly united again.

Recent events have magnified the occupational hazards of prophecy. The only surprise would be if there were no more surprises ahead. Something like a race is on between bigotry and apathy. The latest Gallup poll as this is written shows an almost equal loss of faith in both parties. The answers to the question which party could best handle our problems show that the largest number, 42 percent, see no difference or have no opinion. Thirty percent now think the Republicans would do best, only 28 percent the Democrats. The general lack of enthusiasm for any of the candidates reflects this same mood, compounded of the disillusion created by Johnson's peace promises in 1964—how believe anyone after that?—and an instinctive feeling that the issues raised by the Negro revolt are beyond solution by normal politics. But even Lyndon Johnson may stir nostalgia after four years of Nixon, or a combination of Rockefeller and Reagan. The Republicans are even less prepared than the Democrats to deal with the debacle of American imperialism in Southeast Asia and the beginning at home of racial war.

June 20, 1968
New York Review

A GRACEFUL PATSY
AGAINST A DIRTY
FIGHTER?

We have ourselves a candidate against Lyndon Johnson in the Democratic primaries but unless he picks up steam he's not going to set any voters on fire. Senator Eugene McCarthy was supposed to be the main attraction at the Conference of Concerned Democrats in Chicago last week-end. But his speech—like the one he delivered a few weeks earlier before SANE's national meeting in Chicago for labor leaders against the war in Vietnam—fell flat. He has wit, charm and grace. But he seems to lack heart and guts. This may seem a strange thing to say of the only Democrat willing to step out and challenge Johnson for the nomination. Unfortunately it seems to be true. Watching him at the press conference here at which he launched his candidacy, one began to wonder why he was running at all. A certain cynicism and defeatism seems basic to the man. This is no way to embark on a fight. His hero, Adlai, was a Hamlet. McCarthy gives one the uneasy feeling that he doesn't really give a damn.

The dreadful thing about presidential campaigns is that they make liars of us all. We join up, and stop saying what we think, for the good of the cause. I suppose I'll be swept up in this same kind of nonsense myself. But at least at the beginning a few honest words may be useful. We have to support McCarthy. A poor showing in the primaries for McCarthy will be a poor showing for peace. But he's also got to support us. And himself. It's no easy matter for a politician to challenge the head of his party. It may be political suicide. To embark on so risky an undertaking half-heartedly is the worst possible policy. The only safety lies in shooting the works. There's no other way to a long-shot victory and anyway that's the way to enjoy a wonderful, even if losing, battle in a good cause. If McCarthy couldn't evoke enthusiasm from dissident laborites and dissident Democrats just dying for a new hero to cheer—how's he going to do out in the sticks? Where the audiences are cold? Or half hawk? Or just curious?

One purpose of the intra-party fight against Johnson, as McCarthy and Bobby Kennedy have been saying, is to restore the faith of youth in normal politics and—as they might put it privately—"get them off the streets." McCarthy's going to have to do a lot better than he has so far if he's going to make much of a dent among the disaffected youth and Negroes—though at least he, unlike Bobby, is willing to lay his political future on the line to fight the war. What has to be improved first of all is how McCarthy says it. He just doesn't transmit any sense of passion. Secondly what he does say isn't good enough. The Chicago speech was full of insincere hokum. A sample: "John Kennedy set free the spirit of America. The honest optimism was released." McCarthy doesn't believe it, so why say it? And poor Adlai reduced to the role of Kennedy's UN errand boy would have been surprised to learn that his ideas were revived by Kennedy. Where? At the Bay of Pigs? We would also be glad to spare some of McCarthy's fancy quotes at Chicago from Péguy on Dreyfus and Toynbee on the Punic wars for a little more clarity on Vietnam. It's Ho, not Hannibal, who concerns us now.

McCarthy is remarkably unclear about Vietnam. The Chicago speech showed lazy staff work when he invoked the names of Eisenhower and Bradley among those who had warned us against a land war in Asia—although these two dippy old duffers only a few days before were calling for an invasion of North Vietnam! Most revealing of all were his answers at the Washington press conference. Little attention was paid these by the press because (1) the chief interest seemed to be in politics and personality and (2) most of the Washington press corps is for—or indifferent to—the war.

These answers are pretty appalling. The clearest and simplest appeal McCarthy can make is to say that Johnson broke his 1964 pledges and has adopted more and more of Goldwater's policies. That is true. Everybody can understand it. It's effective. Indeed there's little else he needs to say. But, McCarthy went on to say, "I'm not going to talk about that in the campaign." That one remark really tells the whole story. Is he going to run a cream-puff campaign against as tough and dirty a fighter as Lyndon B.?

McCarthy will stir no enthusiasm if he goes around being a graceful patsy. One of the main functions of the campaign is to educate the electorate and to prepare the way for wiser policies. One main line is evident and needs to be hammered on over and over again. The choice is not between isolationism and internationalism. It's between wasting our blood and wealth in the attempt to enforce a Pax Americana or becoming a loyal member of the United Nations. Somebody has to say out loud that we can't take over the white man's burden in the new Kennedy-era guise of Green Berets and counter-insurgency. Over and over again somebody must say clearly, as the way to peace, "stop the bombing" and "negotiate a coalition government" in South Vietnam.

It is Johnson strategy to ignore the fact that U Thant and others have said over and over again that talks will follow if the bombing ends. McCarthy's reply on bombing was all fuzz. It is also Administration strategy to distract attention from the fact that the new NLF program offers a viable compromise solution. I suspect McCarthy's never even seen it. He needs to do some hard thinking and fresh study if he's to be effective. His most alarming reply was on containment of China. There he said we didn't need Vietnam because we now have a new base in Thailand! That is, a second Vietnam, simmering on the burner?

We enlist in McCarthy's army but we intend to keep stirring up mutiny until the General stops yawning.

December 11, 1967

THE CANDIDATE LEAST LIKELY
TO MAKE PEACE

The question raised by Governor Rockefeller's four-stage plan for peace in Vietnam is whether you can sell the Brooklyn Bridge a second time to the same sucker. Essentially it asks Ho Chi Minh again to call off the war and withdraw his men on the same promise of free elections later. The Rockefeller plan is the 1954 Geneva settlement all over again. Once Ho withdrew his forces after 1954, he had no leverage to make us keep the Geneva promise of elections and reunification. He would be in an even weaker position this time, militarily and politically.

Under the devious wording of the Rockefeller plan, Ho would withdraw all his forces but we would not withdraw all of ours. As he withdrew his forces, we would withdraw "the bulk" of ours. "The small U.S. forces left in Vietnam," the Rockefeller plan says, "would be confined to fixed installations as long as North Vietnam carries out its commitments." [1] Thus an undetermined number of U.S. troops would remain in bases around the country. These forces would not leave until after the elections. Only our side would have the means of enforcing the terms of the settlement. U.S. troops could move into action from their bases on any violation, real, imagined or contrived.

The Rockefeller plan is as lopsided politically. In the 1954 agreement there was no restriction on those who could participate in the promised elections. We decided not to hold the elections because we knew that Ho and the Communists would win. One way to prevent such a victory this time would be to exclude the Communists. The Rockefeller plan says the NLF will be "guaranteed participation in the political life of the country" only when it "ceases

[1] See text *Washington Post*, July 14.

guerrilla operations and agrees to abide by the democratic process." That means the guerrillas would have to give up their arms and then satisfy the governing authority in the South that they would "abide by the democratic process" before they could campaign and vote. This governing authority under the Rockefeller plan would be left to the existing regime in Saigon, with its rigged Constitution and its repressive election laws under which Communists and "pro-Communists" are excluded.

What does the phrase—"to abide by the democratic process"—in the Rockefeller plan mean? Saigon has long had an "open arms" program for Communists and other NLF members who defect. When the Saigon military in charge of the defector camps are convinced the VC have renounced their past views, they are set free to participate in the normal life of the country. Does Rockefeller mean any more than this? In a *U.S. News & World Report* interview June 24, 1968, Rockefeller was questioned about an earlier proposal to broaden the base of the Saigon government. "Are you talking," he was asked, "about bringing in the Viet Cong or the National Liberation Front?" "No," was his answer, "I said democratic elements and I do not consider the Viet Cong a democratic element."

Additional light is thrown on what Rockefeller has in mind by his newly published campaign book, *Unity, Freedom & Peace: A Blueprint for Tomorrow*. In it he says we should "accept in South Vietnam's political life any group that seeks its objectives through the political process, rather than by pursuing them by force *or subversion*" (my italics). On ABC-TV's *Issues and Answers* July 14, the day after his new plan was released, Rockefeller put forward the same formula again. He said the Viet Cong could participate in the election "if they agree to drop military action and subversion." You can stop military action by a cease-fire but how do you stop "subversion"?

At one time Rockefeller said he would accept even a Viet Cong government in South Vietnam if it was the result of truly free elections. Now he says the Viet Cong cannot take part in elections until they give up "force and subversion." What is subversion? The New Deal was constantly attacked as subversive. Even the ADA was labeled subversive during the witch-hunt years of the forties and fifties. In Saigon subversion is anything which threatens the domination of the military junta and the landlord-gentry class. It took a Saigon court only 23 minutes the other day to find the leaders of the new middle-class "Alliance of National, Democratic and Peace Forces" guilty of subversion *in absentia*, and condemn them to death for it. If the NLF has to satisfy the Saigon regime that it has given up "subversion" before it can participate in the political process, it may have to wait a long time.

In the 1954 agreement there was a provision that no one was to be persecuted for the part he had played in the struggle against the French and their puppets. Diem violated it and sparked the rebellion when he began to throw many of the former Viet Minh fighters into concentration camps. This time there would be no guarantee that the Viet Cong, after laying down their arms, might not end up in jail again because they had not convinced the Saigon regime that they had sincerely given up "subversion." Thieu and Ky couldn't have thought up a cuter peace offer.

Nelson Rockefeller is as tricky as Nixon and as glib in his liberalism as Humphrey. For a quarter of a century he has been, if anything, more consistently and ferociously dedicated than either to the cold war and its anti-Communist obsessions. Of all the candidates he is the one least likely to draw back from our costly effort to become the policeman of the world. His position on civil rights is liberal—it could hardly be otherwise to get anywhere in the politics of New York—but liberals fool themselves if they think he would cut down military expenditure for social reconstruction. No major figure in American politics has worked harder than Rockefeller to push ever higher the billions we allocate to the Pentagon. To woo the Kennedy forces and exploit peace sentiment, Rockefeller has reluctantly and belatedly been persuaded to coo like a dove. But his whole record spells hawk.

No one can be more surprised than Eisenhower to hear Rockefeller trying to sound like a peace candidate. During the last Republican administration, Eisenhower was not cold warrish enough for Rockefeller and they split because Rockefeller did not think he was spending enough on the armed forces. In June, 1960, Rockefeller refused to join other Republican Governors in supporting Nixon as Eisenhower's successor. Rockefeller issued an almost hysterical statement at the Governors' conference in which he said we faced a "national catastrophe" unless we quickly stepped up our military efforts. Rockefeller had been urging an increase of at least $3 billion a year in the military budget. He did not come out for Nixon until the latter at a secret meeting in July agreed to support the demand for bigger arms expenditures. "There must be no price ceiling," said the joint statement which sealed their bargain, "on America's security."

Eisenhower in his memoirs, *Waging Peace*, said this statement "seemed somewhat astonishing, coming as it did from two people who had long been in administration councils and who had never voiced any doubt—at least in my presence—of the adequacy of America's defenses." Eisenhower noted that the Pentagon's budget had risen from "less than $12 billion before the Korean war under the Democrats to more than $41 billion in 1960." He pointed to the new supersonic jets of the Air Force and the "revolutionary new submarine-borne Polaris missiles" of the Navy as solid evidence of increased military strength. He related that after Rockefeller's "catastrophe" statement in June, 1960, Eisenhower dryly told a meeting of Congressional leaders at the White House, "I suspect that Rockefeller has been listening too closely to half-baked advisers."

One of those "half-baked advisers" was Dr. Edward Teller. He was the one scientist on the panel which, under Nelson's chairmanship, wrote the famous Rockefeller

Brothers Report on "International Security: The Military Aspect" in 1958. This was a blueprint for a U.S. role as world policeman in the nuclear age. The Strangelovian touch of Dr. Teller was exquisitely visible in the report's most wondrous sentence. "Very powerful nuclear weapons," it said, "can be used in such a manner that they have negligible effects on civilian populations." Such was the Pied Piperism Rockefeller was prepared to follow. The report called for the complete reorganization of the armed forces. One innovation charted the course to a whole series of Vietnams. It called for mobile forces "tailored to the gamut of possible limited wars which may range from conflicts involving several countries to minor police actions." These limited war forces "may require a highly complicated weapons system *including nuclear weapons*" (my italics). This readiness to use nuclear weapons in limited wars anticipated Goldwater by six years; though Goldwater suggested nuclear weapons in Vietnam for defoliation purposes only, not—as the Rockefeller report did—for combat.

Two years before the NLF was organized in 1960, Rockefeller was ready for intervention in Vietnam. "Our security can be imperilled," his report warned in 1958, "not only by overt aggression but also by transformations which are made to appear, insofar as possible, as not aggression at all." Greece, it said, "has furnished one example, Vietnam another." The report invented the phrase "non-overt aggression," i.e., an aggression of which there is no proof in overt acts, only a hunch that something bad is going on. Interventionism never developed a more useful, if paradoxical, doctrine. The report asked us to "realize that non-overt aggression presents issues which are deliberately and intrinsically unclear" and to recognize that "to ask for certainty in these situations is a recipe for inaction." This implies that we must be ready to resolve any doubts in favor of intervention. There is an occult quality about the phrase "non-overt aggression" which recalls the demonology of the cold war and the witch hunt years in their most virulent phase.

The fact is that Rockefeller has always been more comfortable with the cold war liberal Democrats than with the
conservative Eisenhower-type Republicans. His "liberalism" is the same mixture of social demagogy at home and
military intervention abroad which has characterized Democratic policy from Truman to Johnson and Humphrey.
Rockefeller can claim to be the original cold warrior. He
boasts in his new book that he was called anti-Russian and
pro-Fascist when he fought successfully at the UN organiz-
ing meeting in San Francisco in 1945 to admit Fascist Argentina to membership over Molotov's objections—and
those of men on our side as diverse as Secretary of State
Hull and Walter Lippmann. This signaled the first efforts
to use the new organization as an anti-Soviet bloc. Rockefeller also boasts of the part he played in the adoption of
Article 51 of the Charter, which allowed for "regional
groupings" within the UN. Originally it was represented as
an effort to preserve the Monroe Doctrine but it led to the
very development the United Nations was intended to
avoid—the breakup of the world into hostile military blocs.
Rockefeller now boasts that it was Article 51 which four
years later made the formation of NATO possible. Article
51 also laid the basis for SEATO.

It is not surprising that in his new book the President for
whom Rockefeller expresses the greatest admiration is Truman. Rockefeller admires Truman because he "decided to
reverse President Roosevelt's policy of accommodation
with the Kremlin, decided to terminate World War II by
dropping two atomic bombs on Japan, [and] decided to
contain Soviet expansion into the Mediterranean by offering the Truman Doctrine to Greece and Turkey." In foreign policy Rockefeller has always felt more at home with
the Democrats. Much of the military program sketched out
in the Rockefeller report of 1958 was implemented by the
Kennedy Administration: one of Kennedy's first acts was to
send Congress a special message boosting military spending;

by fiscal 1962 it was $10 billion more than Eisenhower's 1960 figure of 41 billion. Since, of course, it has been doubled by the Vietnamese war. But Kennedy wasn't belligerent enough for Rockefeller. Rockefeller attacked him for suggesting that we give up Quemoy and Matsu; these tiny Chinese offshore islands seemed to Rockefeller "of tremendous significance" to "the defense of freedom." He criticized Kennedy for not being more aggressive in Laos and Vietnam, accused the new President of mishandling nuclear defenses in "several secret exchanges of letters" with Khrushchev and after the Bay of Pigs wanted him to make another attempt to topple Castro. He was for intervention in the Congo to prevent a Communist takeover during the scare created by poor Lumumba's effort at independence.

Rockefeller is incautious enough in his new book to give himself high marks for courage because he was dubious about the nuclear test ban agreement Kennedy negotiated. He wanted assurances that the treaty "does not prohibit the use of nuclear weapons to repel aggression anywhere" and that the Kennedy Administration—rather than use the treaty as a first step toward broader disarmament measures, as was hoped at the time—would "take every feasible step to preserve the ability of our military establishment to deter and defeat Communist aggression against free peoples everywhere." Like his scientist mentor Dr. Teller, Rockefeller feared nothing so much as a détente. In this he saw eye to eye with the military. It is in keeping with this record that Rockefeller in a chapter on "Fiscal Integrity" in the new book nowhere suggests any cut in military expenditures or in the escalating costs of the Vietnamese war. He says we will have to "discipline ourselves to set clear priorities and to make hard choices" which will demand "rare political courage." But he lacks the courage to specify what are the hard choices he would make if elected. His whole record shows that for him military strength comes first, and that military strength is not merely defense but a capacity for intervention anywhere in the world.

It is not strange that Rockefeller's admiration for Johnson comes through in the new book. He praises Johnson's "self-sacrifice" in renouncing renomination and sees it as a "courageous" step toward "the ending of our own, increasingly malignant controversy between 'hawks' and 'doves' and a long step toward the restoration of national unity." His only criticism is that Johnson's "peace overtures to North Vietnam were launched in a manner to stir concern among our friends in Southeast Asia who now feel themselves directly menaced." He sets out to correct this. He writes:

I would warn our adversaries not to 'overreact' to our current discomfiture in foreign relations. In commencing our new quest for honorable peace in Vietnam, we are expressing a sober reassessment, not seeking peace at any price. At stake in this judgment is not only peace in Vietnam but the chances of peace in Asia, the Middle East and the whole world. Our adversaries ought not to conclude that we will be unable to devise an effective strategy against their 'wars of national liberation,' i.e., subversion, or that other peoples less weakened than the South Vietnamese will not rise up against incursion and intrusion.

These opaque phrases could have come as easily from Rusk or Johnson. They suggest no more than a tactical retreat. If the military have their way, the retreat will be no more than enough palaver at Paris to keep the home front quiet until after the election when they can go on with the war undisturbed. Rockefeller speaks of a "sober reassessment" but there is no hint that this would extend to the wisdom of our involvement in land and civil wars in Asia, much less to the idea of trying to impose a Pax Americana. On the contrary Rockefeller in a speech in Philadelphia on May 1 unveiled a grandiose vision of a new regional grouping under American leadership which would ensure "economic progress and political stability" for all the Asian "hundreds of millions living in the great crescent from Japan throughout India to Iran." This is a sure way to more and bigger than Asian Vietnams.

July 22, 1968

THE GOP CONVENTION
WAS NOT WITHOUT
ITS CHEERING ASPECTS

From a Marxist-Leninist point of view, the Republican convention was clearly a victory for the working class. A poor boy grew up to defeat a Rockefeller for the Republican nomination. Those massed millions in last-minute TV and newspaper advertising failed utterly to overcome a militant armed with the correct political line. His proletarian loyalties were so little affected by success that he at once planned to celebrate by visiting Moscow and discussing his future plans in the Kremlin. He was unfortunately dissuaded by nervous bourgeois advisers.

Another cheerful way of looking at the convention is to notice how firmly the party has committed itself to turning power back from Washington to the state and local governments. If anything happens to Nixon after his election, the Presidency will be turned over to a man who only six short years ago had reached eminence no higher than leadership in the Kiwanis Club and the Parent-Teacher Association in a suburb of Maryland, ranking somewhere in the rural hierarchy between a deputy sheriff and a duly elected dogcatcher. The Republicans have proven again that in America anybody is liable to become President.

The convention was a humbling affair altogether for us ethnics. It was hard to listen to Goldwater and realize that a man could be half Jewish and yet sometimes appear to be twice as dense as the normal gentile. As for Agnew, even at a convention where every speech seemed to outdo the other in wholesome clichés and delicious anticlimaxes, his speech putting Nixon into nomination topped all the rest. If the race that produced Isaiah is down to Goldwater and the race that produced Pericles is down to Agnew, the time has come to give the country back to the WASP's.

TV is ruining the two-party system. Mayor Daley is smart to keep that electricians' strike going through the Democratic convention. The advantage of a national primary would be to shield the American public from too intimate a view of its politicos at work and play. It would take a comic genius to duplicate some of the ideas Republican speakers came up with. We remember with special pleasure that passage in Ivy Baker Priest's nominating speech for Ronald Reagan in which she said, "We cannot afford the status quo." The only real sense we could get out of that remark in that upper bracket assemblage was that maybe some delegates were falling behind in the payments on their yachts. We had always assumed that the status quo was something Republicans could never have too much of. Another oratorical banana peel was dropped by Agnew, whose style of delivery reminds us strongly of W. C. Fields. In nominating Nixon, he quoted his hero as saying, "Right now change rules America. It is time for America to rule change." This sonorous tidbit sounded as if Nixon were casting himself as a modern Canute. The GOP has been trying for years to hold back the tides.

August 19, 1968

WHEN A TWO-PARTY SYSTEM BECOMES A ONE-PARTY RUBBER STAMP

When a country is denied a choice on the most burning issue of the time, the war in Vietnam, then the two-party system has become a one-party rubber stamp. This is the first and essential point to be made in the wake of the Dem-

ocratic and Republican conventions. The Establishment
and the military have locked the ballot boxes. If the results
are an intensified alienation among the youth who must
fight this war, an increase in resistance to the draft, a rise in
street demonstrations and violence, this is the cause and not
some occult conspiracy. The real conspiracy was the one
which wove together Eisenhower's last inflammatory message to the Republican convention with the iron control
Johnson and Daley exercised over the Democrats. Both parties, both candidates, have been drafted. The Pentagon has
won the election even before the votes are cast.

The second thing which needs to be said is that the country owes a debt of gratitude to the tatterdemalion army of
Yippies, hippies and peaceniks—and to their leaders David
Dellinger, Tom Hayden and Jerry Rubin—who frightened
the Establishment into such elaborate security precautions
in Chicago. They made opposition to the war visible. The
special barbed-wire fences around the Amphitheatre which
turned "Stalag '68" into the favorite joke of the Convention, the system of electronically checked passes so intricate
that it led to a whole series of angry clashes with the delegates themselves, the vast concentration of police, National
Guardsmen and troops, as if in preparation for a revolution,
dramatized for the whole world to see that there was something indelibly undemocratic about this Democratic convention.

Of course security precautions were justified. The Secret
Service, the FBI and the Chicago police had a right to be
fearful of what might happen, especially if Johnson himself
had turned up, and this was the grim eventuality I believe
they had in mind. But the question not to be lost sight of is
why for the first time in American history a convention and
a President required so much protection.

This was the scandal it proved impossible to hide and this
is why the police were so brutal in dealing with the cameramen and the reporters. They *were* the main enemy of the
proceedings, the eyes and ears of the country, the unwelcome witnesses of the rigging within the Convention and

the repression without. Johnson and Daley, alike in so many ways, are alike in their obsessive animosity to the press. Daley's big and beefy police seemed to crack the skulls of the TV and press reporters with a special gusto and as if given free rein by their masters. Their conduct was in its own way a resounding tribute to the First Amendment. It also gave middle-class whites a taste of the police brutality which is an old story to blacks.

The convention was a triumph of what the Russian Communists would call "democratic centralism," that submission of "the lower organs of the party to the higher" which they are reimposing in Prague. The delegates chosen were less representative of the party rank-and-file than of the party machines, and the committees were even less representative than the delegates. A Citizens' Committee, to include respected retired jurists, ought to be formed to take testimony from delegates, demonstrators and the police on the whole question of how this convention and the protests against it were handled. It would show I believe that security was used as a way to control the convention. If assassination plots were as thick as Daley and the police now claim—and Humphrey idiotically echoes them—then it is strange that no attempts were made, no shots fired, no bombs thrown. For in the crowded hallways of the main hotels including the Hilton, it would have been easy for an assassin to take a potshot at any one of the candidates. There security was poor.

On the other hand, at the Amphitheatre, guards were used to harass McCarthy and McGovern delegates. The opposition on the floor was hamstrung by lack of phone communications and by the arbitrary and arrogant rulings that Carl Albert as Chairman applied to any attempt to protest. The Johnson steamroller stopped the effort of the Humphrey forces to put a slightly milder face on the pro-war Vietnam plank. Not the slightest deviation was allowed. Johnson and Daley are masters of meticulous detail,[1] accus-

[1] A sample: In Chicago, unlike Miami, reporters with credentials did not get assigned seats as usual at conventions. This seemed odd. We

tomed to rule their kingdoms with an iron hand. So it was
that a convention strikingly cool—despite its unrepresentative majority—to any mention of Johnson's name was forced
to wear his brand in the platform plank on Vietnam and the
choice of Vice President. A candidate who might have pla-
cated blacks and antiwar delegates was Fred Harris of
Oklahoma. But he was the vice chairman of the Kerner
commission, whose report Johnson disliked. Johnson and
Daley preferred a safe and bridle-broken liberal like Muskie
of Maine (Johnson put a saddle on him long ago), with an
appeal to Chicago's Polish Americans and an "ethnic" off-
set to Agnew.

To wander in Lincoln Park among the hippies and Yippies, to drop in on the headquarters of the New Left demonstrators, to talk at random with the youths in Grant Park
and the streets was to feel that in revulsion against the war
the best of a generation were being lost—some among the
hippies to drugs, some among the radicals to an almost hysterical frenzy of alienation. There were a few among them I
am sure who sought deliberately by taunts and obscenities
to provoke a confrontation with the police, but far more
were driven to angry resistance by Daley's unwillingness to
let them sleep in Lincoln Park and to grant permits for
peaceful demonstrations and parades. These would have let
off steam and been far easier to police than crowds which
felt their elementary rights were being trampled. Even Joseph J. Lefevour, president of the Chicago lodge of the Fraternal Order of Police, in the middle of a press conference
called to defend police tactics, admitted (*Chicago Tribune*,
August 30), "Most of the kids in the parks," i.e., Lincoln and
Grant parks, "have been orderly. They've obeyed our orders and joked with us. But then their leaders work them up
to fever pitch and disappear, leaving the kids to take the
consequences." But could they have been worked up "to

---

learned the reason why on the night of the balloting for nominees and the
final session, when I and many other reporters were unable to get into
the top galleries supposedly reserved for us because they were packed by
Daley goons from the Sanitation Department.

fever pitch" without the brutal nightly sweeps at curfew
time in Lincoln Park, and the indiscriminate and sadistic
way the police beat and tear-gassed not only peaceful demonstrators in Grant Park but onlookers behind the police's
own barricades in front of the Hilton?

Daley has long run a one-party state in Chicago, with
just that combination of brutality, social welfare handouts
and cooperation with big business which is also the essence
of Johnson's own conception of personal government. The
way Humphrey has stepped out as Daley's apologist, even
after the climactic raid on the McCarthy headquarters in
the Hilton, is an index of what we can expect from a Humphrey Administration, of what he means by law and order,
and of what lies behind his platitudinous evangelism. Another index—to be forgotten at our peril—was his appearance before the Catholic War Veterans on the eve of the
convention when he threw away a moderate prepared
script and delivered a warmongering address. These two
events have finally decided for me that Humphrey is no
lesser an evil than Nixon. A vote for Humphrey is a vote
for Johnson's war and Daley's police state tactics.

I confess that I do not know what to do politically at this
juncture. The three main ways open are Allard Lowenstein's effort eventually to take over the Democrats, Marcus
Raskin's attempt to form a New Party, and the New Left's
call to go into the streets. To meet the crises of race and
war which confront the country, time and patience, faith in
persuasion, are required. But how preach these virtues to a
youth who may be called up any day for the army? The
war is destroying our country as we are destroying Vietnam. Hate and frenzy are poor substitutes for political
thinking, yet the *enragés* among the youth, with their ro-
manticism about guerrilla war, may set the tune for the
whole country. A handful may provoke the government to
such overreaction as to polarize the country between ex-
tremes.

The New Left and even its moderate allies are still operating in a fog of misconceptions. The main one is that "the
people" are against the war. The people on the contrary are

confused and divided. To say that the streets "belong to the people," as Tom Hayden has, is to overlook those people who feel the streets belong to them, too, for the ordinary business of their lives. "Let that party," Raskin said to the Democrats the other day in calling for a New Party, "be the party of the cops, the military, the big city bosses and the non-people." There are an awful lot of "non-people." The need is for dialogue, not monologue, to win them over. If law and order really break down, if democratic processes are abandoned, it is we of the Left, the antiwar forces and the intellectuals who will be the first to suffer. To play with revolutionary talk and tactics as the New Left is doing, when there is no revolutionary situation, is to act as the provocateurs for an American fascism.

The deeper tragedy lies in the increasing abandonment of nonviolent tactics by black and white dissenters alike. To howl down those with whom we differ, to use obscenities instead of arguments, to abandon persuasion for direct action, to dehumanize the other side with cries of "pigs" and worse is to embark on a game the rightists are better equipped to play, and to set examples which American Storm Troopers may some day apply to us. Hate is still the main enemy of the human race, the fuel that heats the furnaces of genocide. How build a better world by relapsing into primitive and sanguinary habits?

September 9, 1968

WHY HUBERT IS AS
TRICKY AS DICKY

It is a delusion to believe that Humphrey is not saying what we want him to say on Vietnam because he is afraid of Johnson. Humphrey's whole record, not just as an anti-Communist on the home front, but on Southeast Asia, leaves

little reason to believe that he would have a different position on the Vietnam war even if freed from Johnson's influence. Humphrey's enthusiasm for American intervention in
Southeast Asia goes back to 1950, when he welcomed Truman's decision to give financial aid to the French and to
their puppet emperor, Bao Dai. When the French were
criticized for not sending troops to Korea, Humphrey defended them on the ground that they were already "fighting for freedom in Indochina." Humphrey was second only
to Nixon in readiness for U.S. involvement. When Nixon
proposed sending American troops into Indochina before
the Geneva conference in 1954, Humphrey was not prepared to go that far, though he told the Senate on April 19
of that year that he thought Nixon's famous off-the-record
speech to the American Society of Newspaper Editors was
"very responsible, considered, mature and intelligent." The
entente cordiale between them far antedates the current
campaign, which is being fought like a gentlemanly boxing
match.

Humphrey *is* a prisoner of the Johnson Administration
and perhaps even more so of the labor movement, his only
organized support outside the party machines. George
Meany is if anything even more hawkish on the war than
Johnson, as Meany was more hawkish than Eisenhower.
Humphrey would take all the enthusiasm out of Meany's
support if he were to shift over on Vietnam. But the essential reason that Humphrey holds back is that he has always
believed in the war, and in the necessity of creating a bulwark in Vietnam against Communist expansion into Southeast Asia. It is indicative that the highly unfair and twisted
attack made on him by Allan Ryskind of *Human Events*,
the organ of the far rightists, in a newly published book,
Hubert, is unable to pin on him any dove-like statement
about the Indochina war. "This is our great adventure,"
Humphrey declared expansively in a talk less than a year
ago to the U.S. embassy staff in Saigon, "and a wonderful
one it is." No one has been more gung ho about this war
than Hubert Humphrey. Eisenhower and Kennedy as well

as Johnson had his support as the escalation continued and the U.S. stakes grew.

The Salt Lake City speech has to be read against this consistent record. Its major disappointment, from the standpoint of the peace movement, does not lie in Humphrey's tricky position on the bombing halt: the fact that like Johnson he links it to reciprocal concessions and goes further than Johnson has in explicitly stating that the bombing would be resumed if we were dissatisfied with the other side's conduct ("bad faith"). This is not unconditional cessation. More important is that Humphrey shows no readiness whatsoever for any political compromise in the peace negotiations themselves. Essentially he, like Johnson and Thieu, call on the other side to lay down its arms and accept "free elections" under South Vietnam's rigged Constitution. Humphrey in no way departs from the clichés of Johnson and Rusk: the view of the war as purely an aggression from the North; the pretense that land reform is going on when South Vietnam's oligarchic legislature, representative of the landlord class and not the peasantry, has already overwhelmingly rejected it; and the old will-o'-the-wisp—that the South Vietnamese army will soon be able to take over the main burden of the war. Without a fresh view of the past and the present, the way cannot be cleared for a political settlement and a genuinely representative government in South Vietnam. This is what Johnson does not want and there is no reason to believe that Humphrey or Nixon is any readier for it than he is.

Humphrey repeated that stupefying nonsense about how on March 31 Johnson "sacrificed his own political career in order to bring negotiations that could lead to peace." Every day makes clearer that just the opposite is the case. Johnson freed himself from the pressures of politics in order to carry on the war. His line has hardened. His latest appointment of a U.S. representative to the UN shows that he no longer bothers to try and fool public opinion at home and abroad by naming men like Goldberg or Ball who are or appear to be doves. Goldberg was himself the victim of Johnson; he really thought the President wanted peace when he stepped down from the Court to go to the UN. Ball's reputation as a dove has always been overblown, and his attack on U Thant for advocating an end of the bombing showed how little reality there was behind the gossip that he was the dove-in-residence of the State Department. I myself never thought his dissent on the war much more than a reflection of his fear that we were paying too much attention to Asia at the expense of his old clients in the Common Market. But of his successor, Russell Wiggins, there is no doubt. Though a liberal in domestic affairs, Wiggins made the editorial page of the *Washington Post* a faithful echo of the Johnson-Rusk line on Vietnam. Johnson no longer needs to pretend.

I am just back from a few days in Paris, where I had a look at the stalemated Paris peace talks. For the newsmen, it is like covering a glacier, except that glaciers sometimes move an inch or so a year. The line of the other side seems to have hardened with our own. There is less emphasis on the *Alliance* as a bridge to the South Vietnamese middle class and a political compromise; the NLF is back in the center of discussion. Apparently Hanoi was preparing last March to make so explicit an offer on peace talks if the bombing ended as to put Washington squarely on the spot. Johnson outflanked Hanoi by making his own offer of a limited bombing pause first. It was a skillful ploy, not a serious proposal, and Washington was surprised when Hanoi accepted it. My impression is that Hanoi did so because of pressure from its own allies. My impression from our own side is that the reason we do not stop the bombing altogether and begin substantive talks is because we have no real negotiating position ready except a Korean solution, i.e., the surrender of the other side. There is a lot more fighting ahead before serious negotiations can be envisaged. The lull is over and the NLF spokesmen exude a quiet confidence.

The outlook is bleak. In South Vietnam, the jails are full of Buddhists and of other non-Communist peace elements. At home it is as foolish to rely on Nixon for peace as on

Humphrey. Johnson has already shown what he thinks of Humphrey in arranging for Marvin Watson to campaign for him. At lunch in Paris some North Vietnamese asked me to explain the election and the two-party system. I said it was a triumph of the dialectic. It showed that two could be one and one could be two, and had probably been fabricated by Hegel for the American market on a subcontract from General Dynamics. The North Vietnamese are Marxists with a sense of humor, but none of us was really laughing.

October 7, 1968

PART II

'Saigon Afire Now...'

THE MONSTER
WITH LITTLE BRAIN
AND NO HEART

Two words sum up the beginnings of our military campaign to subdue the Mekong Delta. One is futility and the other brutality. The first invasion, launched with a tremendous air and naval bombardment, and an equally sensational splurge of publicity, was Operation Dockhouse V. It has just fizzled out. "The ten-day sweep," a sentence buried in the AP's daily military roundup from Saigon admitted (Washington *Star*, January 16, 1967), "proved unproductive." This force of 4,000 U.S. and South Vietnamese Marines could claim no more than 21 Viet Cong killed and 14 captured "during 10 days of slogging through thigh-deep delta mud 68 miles south of Saigon" (*New York Times*, January 17). That is an average of two VC killed a day. We'd like to see McNamara's cost effectiveness figures on this operation. U.S. intelligence must be pretty dismal if such a vast panoply of power was brought to bear in an area where nobody seemed to be around. A companion invasion a few days later 10 miles away by South Vietnam's 9th Division was also preceded by a huge outpouring of firepower and ballyhoo. A detachment of reporters and cameramen were on the heavy missile cruiser *Canberra* as it poured high explosive shells for an hour and a half into the landing area. One of them wrote (*Washington Post*, January 10), "It sounded like a thunderstorm with lightning striking every few minutes." Since nothing more has been heard of that invasion, obviously its results weren't anything to boast of either. Any time the Pentagon runs out of the glamorous names it gives these operations, we'd suggest a code name

suited to this combination of monstrous power with dim intelligence. Why not Operation Dinosaur?

While the Marines were still chasing phantoms in Operation Dockhouse V, 30,000 U.S. troops launched Operation
Cedar Falls, the biggest of the war, against the so-called
Iron Triangle. The name was another triumph for our military men, who seem nowadays to be graduates of Madison
Avenue rather than West Point. The name conjures up the
impregnable fortress. It was another area where the troops
met more peasants than guerrillas. It is or was a fertile 60-
mile-square area of forest, paddy fields, orchards and rubber
plantations long dominated by the Viet Cong under tacit
agreements with French rubber companies and local offi-
cialdom. By the end of the fifth day, U.S. infantrymen had
"fired their rifles only occasionally" and "one intelligence
officer" found it necessary to explain that "he thought it
unlikely that more than 100 enemy soldiers were ever in the
target areas at one time" (*New York Times*, January 13).
But 10,000 peasants live there. It was decided that they were
all "at least passive Vietcong" (*same*) and must be uprooted
and resettled and the whole area razed. To make 10,000
peasants homeless in order to get at 100 guerrillas is the idiot
arithmetic of this war, guaranteed to create 10 new rebels
for every one we kill or capture.

Imagine 30,000 Chinese troops uprooting Iowa villagers
to save them from Republicanism and you get some idea of
how likely this is to win—as our sentimental generals say—
the hearts of the people. This operation in the Iron Triangle
was pictured by the London *Sunday Times* (January 15) in
all its mindless technology. Its correspondent flew over the
scene with the engineer colonel in command. "Below us a
22-ton armored bulldozer named 'Hogjaws' leads a clearing
column on a compass course through the jungle," he cabled.
"Above Hogjaws a 'talkout' helicopter circles, broad-
casting through loudspeakers a tape-recorded message calling on the Vietcong to surrender. Hogjaws is leading a column of two tanks, four 14-ton bulldozers and 12 armored
personnel carriers. As the bulldozers clear a wide road

across the Triangle, the colonel says, 'We are developing a new style of jungle warfare here—we remove the jungle.' " This is not warfare. It's a demolition job.

While bulldozers destroy the jungle, the rubber trees, the rice paddies and the villages, fire rains down on the area from the skies. In seven days, Major General de Puy, commander of the First Infantry Division, had requested and received more than 660 air strikes in support of his troops (*New York Times*, January 15). There were 12 thunderous raids by B-52s and "30 artillery batteries with upward of 130 cannon had been hammering" the area all week (*New York Times*, January 14). It was in this heavy artillery fire that eight American soldiers were killed and 34 wounded, the fourth case of accidental artillery shelling of his own men among the troops General de Puy commands.[1] The South Vietnamese military man who is the province chief told the London *Sunday Times* man he was delighted with the progress of the operation. "The big thing," he said, "is that the Iron Triangle will never threaten Saigon again—within two weeks it will be a big bare field." This recalls that earlier pacification campaign described by Tacitus. We cannot forbear quoting again his familiar condemnation of his fellow Romans, "When they make a wilderness, they call it peace." So do we in the Mekong Delta.

The strategy of the campaign now unfolding is simple and repulsive. An anonymous general explained it to a correspondent in South Vietnam months ago. Mao Tse-tung, in his book on guerrilla war, says the guerrilla lives among the people like a fish in water. "We're going to dry up the water," was how this general put it. We're going to remove the people, and make the area in which the guerrillas have hitherto lived, literally unlivable. This is what we see in the Iron Triangle campaign. Peter Arnett, the AP's prize-winning correspondent, described the process unforgettably in a dispatch published in many Sunday papers January 15: "Burning homes, crying children, frightened women,

[1] This brought to 400 the number of our own troops killed by U.S. bombs and shell-fire, otherwise so surgically precise in avoiding civilians.

devastated fields, long lines of slowly moving refugees." He said it "brought back memories of the resettlement of thousands of peasants during the era of the late Ngo Dinh Diem." That, too, was supposed to "pacify" the countryside. The refugees were herded into camps without latrines or water. "On arriving at the camp," Reuters reported (*Washington Post*, January 15), "a few of the peasants spat in disgust but most were glad to escape the bombs and the defoliation chemicals sprayed from the air." An American official commented complacently, "They don't love us but their attitude is improving." As Lyndon Johnson said in his State of the Union message, "They know that it is possible for them to choose their own national destinies—without coercion."

January 23, 1967

THE FRAUD WITH
WHICH BOMB RESUMPTION
WAS EXCUSED

The principal excuse for resuming the bombing of the North will turn out, when the full truth is available, to be a fraud. President Johnson said he had "no alternative but to resume full-scale hostilities" because North Vietnam had used the four-day Têt truce for "major resupply efforts of their troops in South Vietnam" rather than to seek a peaceful settlement. In London Prime Minister Wilson went even further and told the House of Commons next day that "the massive southward movement of troops and supplies in the North . . . threatened to create a severe military unbalance." Neither Saigon nor Washington had claimed that troops as well as supplies had been moved south, much less that the movement was such as to create a "severe military unbalance." This would have been too silly an exaggeration for our military to venture. Even if we loaned McNamara and the Seventh Fleet to Hanoi, it couldn't change the military balance of power in the South—in four days yet! Harold Wilson was the foremost victim—and the most far-out echo—of a U.S. propaganda campaign.

This campaign was initiated by Secretary Rusk at his press conference February 9, the second day of the truce. He said, "We have seen large numbers of boats and other vessels dashing south along the coast of North Vietnam to resupply their forces *in the southern part of North Vietnam* and in the demilitarized zone" (my italics). He declared this "indicates that it is their intention to continue the operation." Few stopped to notice that the Secretary did not say the supplies were crossing the 17th parallel. Nor did anyone ask whether supply was a violation of the truce, especially when it occurred on North Vietnam's own territory. The Secretary's remark that the North was resupplying troops in the DMZ was not true. Raymond R. Coffey of the *Chicago Daily News* Service cabled from Saigon next day that "for all the road, sea and air traffic sighted in the North, U.S. officials acknowledge that they still do not have any reports of men or materiel moving into the demilitarized zone of South Vietnam [*sic*]. The farthest south any traffic has been sighted is around Dong Hoi, 20 miles or so [it's closer to 40—IFS], above the zone." [1] But for every reader who saw Coffey's dispatch there were millions who got the intended picture of the Communists crassly violating the truce to move massive supplies across the border. *Time,* for example, said (February 17) that Hanoi used the truce "for reinforcement and replenishment of its troops below the 17th parallel. Army trucks rumbled down canopied jungle trails into South Vietnam and cargo vessels sped down the

[1] This passage was omitted from the dispatch as published in the *Washington Post* February 11. A reader sent me a clipping from the Toronto *Star* February 11 which ran the full dispatch.

coast with impunity. . . ." Like an orchestra leader striking his baton, the Secretary of State had launched a theme that was to be repeated and amplified from Washington and Saigon to prepare the public mind for a resumption of the bombing.

The day after Rusk's press conference, State Department spokesman Robert McCloskey was asked whether supply activities were a violation of the truce. He replied coyly that he did not want to get into that "since I don't have sufficient information to specify what are violations and what are not violations in the technical sense." When one correspondent recalled that elements of the U.S. 9th Infantry Division "began to debark during either the Christmas or the New Year's truce this past time around" and asked whether that was a truce violation, McCloskey answered, "I can't say yes or no." Like Rusk, McCloskey created the impression that this was a violation without saying so explicitly, since that would have been palpably untrue. It was not until the end of the truce that the AP ticker carried a story from Bob Gassaway in Saigon saying that both sides had "agreed only to refrain from staging offensive operations" but "retained the right to continue the movement of supplies." One has to be pretty gullible to believe that Rusk and McCloskey did not know this all the time.

According to the Coffey dispatch from Saigon we have already quoted, "while questioning North Vietnam's activity, U.S. military authorities also were trying to quietly ignore the U.S. movement of men and supplies that has continued all through the cease-fire." Coffey reported that the first full day of the truce "a new one-day record of 2,762 tons was set for cargo delivered by air to units in the field." He said the daily Air Force communiqué had in the past routinely listed the volume of cargo and passengers carried. But the day after the Rusk press conference—the day the U.S. military in Saigon first issued its sensational charge that supply missions in the North were "five times the normal"— the figures on cargo and passengers carried were missing from the daily Air Force communique. "When asked for the figures and why they were missing," Coffey reported, "an Air Force officer said the top U.S. headquarters command had 'told us not to' release them." When Coffey finally got the figures "they showed that U.S. planes—not counting truck and ship movements at all—carried 7,042 tons of supplies and more than 17,000 men during the first three days of the cease-fire."

The most vivid glimpse of U.S. supply efforts was printed in *Le Monde* (February 12–13) that week-end. It said:

While the American services report a considerable intensification of road, rail, river and coastal traffic in North Vietnam, press correspondents Friday were able to verify, on the road from Saigon to Tay-Ninh, that American supply missions had also been able to profit from the Têt truce to increase the resupply of troops in combat rations and munitions. Long files of trucks belonging to the military transport companies were stretched out along this Northwest road. They were protected by tanks and by helicopters flying along at treetop level. In the town of Tay-Ninh itself, huge trucks and tractors were hauling loads of shells for 105-mm and 155-mm cannons to American units established on the outskirts of the Vietcong's Zone C.

This did not appear in the U.S. press but R. W. Apple, Jr., cabled from Saigon February 12 in the *New York Times* of the same date, that while U.S. briefing officers said resupply efforts in the North "called into question the good faith of the North Vietnamese high command" and "asserted that the allies had made no move to take advantage of the truce"—

Correspondents in the provinces north and northwest of Saigon said, however, that the highways were much more crowded than usual with U.S. convoys. Officers in the American First Infantry Division and 25th Infantry Division confirmed that they were moving extraordinary amounts of food, fuel and ammunition to forward positions."[2]

[2] It may be that troops were also moved during the truce. The weekly casualty report issued February 16 in Saigon "also showed," according to a summary in the *Washington Post* February 17, "an addition of 2,000 U.S. troops, bringing the total in Vietnam as of February 11, to 412,000."

But before the truth had thus begun to leak out, the U.S. press was treated to a tidal wave of misrepresentation about what was going on in the North. The day after Rusk's press conference, the U.S. military in Saigon pulled out all the stops. Their propagandistic purpose was faithfully mirrored in the night lead from Saigon by Alvin B. Webb, Jr., on the UPI wire February 10. He cabled that "U.S. scout planes and ships Friday reported helplessly watching North Vietnam take advantage of a 4-day truce to build up their forces with massive supplies," and "American sources said the Communist 'saturation push' has all but killed hopes of extending the cease-fire." The military didn't want the cease-fire in the first place, and were afraid Johnson might somehow be drawn into peace talks. It was not surprising that U.S. officials "added," according to Webb, that "any hopes for extending the truce to allow for peace talks" had "vanished in the dust of the Communist supply convoys." One commander became so alarmed, Webb reported, "that he urged American planes break off their cease-fire 'stand-down' and immediately resume bombing the flood of North Vietnamese ships, trains [this was the only dispatch I saw that implied the trains were again running down the North Vietnamese panhandle] and trucks ferrying arms to South Vietnam's Communist guerrillas." One could almost see the guerrillas waving happily from the ferry slips as the boats came in.

The figures given out in Saigon on February 10 produced headlines that the North Vietnamese were pouring 35,000 tons of supplies "southward" [but still, as few paused to realize, in *North* Vietnam]. The UPI that morning in its enthusiasm even said the barges and the "trucks stacked up at enemy infiltration routes . . . could handle up to 70,000 tons of supplies" but the figure on which the military settled was 35,000. By the time Saigon had to put it in writing this was reduced to 25,000 with many qualifications. But the

---

That was the third day of the truce. The same communique, according to the AP ticker February 16, showed that South Vietnamese forces declined that week by 3,000. They seem to desert faster than we can replace them.

press generally showed a happy capacity for ignoring the fine print. The traffic was declared to be five times heavier than "normal" but nobody stopped to point out that "normal" has been a condition of constant bombardment in which trucks and ships dared only move under cover of darkness. No American dispatch that I saw raised the question of how the military could be so sure that none of the truck and ship loads carried civilian supplies. There are 17 million people in North Vietnam and perhaps two million live in the area between the 17th and 19th parallels. Keeping them supplied under bombardment cannot be easy. Could it be that *none* of this was food and fuel for civilians? The only dispatch I saw which touched on this point was in the London *Times* February 11. Its man in Saigon said the military "conceded" (apparently when he asked them) that "some of the supplies could be for civilians." "Quite a few people after all," he noted dryly, "live in the southern 'panhandle.' However," he added, "American sources are 'persuaded' they are mostly military."

The Pentagon press office claimed it knew no more than was contained in the communiqué when I tried to raise these and other questions about the figures. The communiqué claims the sighting of 2,200 trucks, though admitting nervously in two places that there may have been duplication. North Vietnam has been getting trucks from Soviet bloc sources, but that is still a lot of trucks. Total U.S. truck *and* bus exports to all of Europe East and West in 1965 was 2,752.

Most of the Soviet trucks are two and a half tons—so I learned at second hand from government sources here—some are four tons. How did military intelligence estimate their loads? In the U.S., where single trucks go as high as 15 tons, the average load per truck carried in 1965 (Motor Truck Facts, 1966) was only 2.65 tons. If they average two tons per load in North Vietnam they are doing miraculously well. This would mean 4,400 tons carried by those 2,200 trucks. Let us make it 5,000 tons to even it off. This still leaves 20,000 tons to be accounted for.

The communiqué says about 1,570 vessels were spotted between the 17th and 19th parallels but admits that 600 were "moving north," while "approximately 970 were observed moving south." Obviously ships heading north were not carrying supplies for the guerrillas in the South. So this leaves 20,000 tons to be carried by 970 vessels. Let us round this off to 1,000 vessels, which means 20 tons per vessel. But from all I can learn most of the vessels in Vietnam are sampans which do well if they carry 500 pounds or a quarter ton. They would have to make 80 round trips in four days to deliver 20 tons. Not even MACV in Saigon claimed these sampans had speedboat motors with which to scurry up and down the 100 miles between Dong Hoi and Vinh that fast.

It turned out in addition that waterborne supply was hampered by bad weather and heavy seas. When the truce ended the U.S. command admitted there had been a "considerable decline" in the southward movement of North Vietnamese supplies but did its best to hide the cause. "This could mean," the AP from Saigon said the military explained (*St. Louis Post-Dispatch*, February 12), "that with extra munitions [nobody had turned up proof of munitions at all] piled up on the border [nor that any shipments had actually been spotted at any border], President Ho Chi Minh's regime did not want its trucks and boats exposed unnecessarily—loaded or empty—after Sunday's dawn" when the truce ended. It was only in William Tuohy's dispatch from Saigon next day in the *Los Angeles Times* that I learned "the level of waterborne shipments down the coast of North Vietnam decreased because of high surf."

Between the high surf and the tall tales, the truth was easily lost to sight. The U.S. military—with the State Department and the White House—have never pulled off a more successful Operation Brain Wash.

February 27, 1967

THE MENDACITIES GO MARCHING ON, TRUCE OR NO TRUCE

The U.S. used the Têt truce in Vietnam to bring up supplies for the biggest ground operation of the war. This is the truth hidden from the American public, which is still being fed the myth that massive supply operations in North Vietnam gave Johnson no alternative but to resume his bombing. The brain-washing that afflicts most Americans was deliciously summed up by a cartoon in the *Montreal Star*. This showed two U.S. officers beside a huge battleship being loaded with troops while cranes swung tanks aboard overhead. One officer says to the other, "Just watch those Congs use the truce for a big buildup."

In last week's issue we exposed the fraudulent campaign about a huge and illegal supply buildup in the North. No sooner had we gone to press than it was announced February 23 that some 30,000 troops had launched "Junction City," a giant search-and-destroy operation against the Viet Cong Zone C in Tay Ninh Province, the biggest yet in this war. Readers will recall that last week we quoted an *Agence France Presse* dispatch from Saigon in *Le Monde* (February 12–13) which described the "long files" of military trucks stretched out during the truce on the road from Saigon to Tay Ninh and the loads of shells for 105-mm and 155-mm cannons being hauled to American units on the edge of Zone C. When the offensive was unleashed from there the following week *AFP* in *Le Monde* (February 25) reported that this offensive "had been prepared during the Têt truce." Not one word of this has appeared in the U.S. press. I managed to break through the Iron Curtain that shelters government propaganda here by making available advance proofs of last week's issue to *The Guardian* in London and Manchester which printed a résumé of our story under a four-column headline on page one, Friday, February 24. This produced so many queries from London that the Pentagon that day was forced to issue a denial, which appeared on the UPI wire but was printed only in London. It isn't much of a denial and it embodies a new falsehood.

The Pentagon denies that it ever charged that the North Vietnamese were violating the truce by their supply activities (all north of the 17th parallel so far as our own reconnaissance observed it) and that it never denied that we were using the truce for movement of supplies, too. Literally this may be so. But the White House, the State Department and the Pentagon certainly did their best to create a contrary impression without explicitly stating a falsehood. Indeed its spokesmen continue to foster that false impression. Senator Russell repeated this myth when debate opened in the Senate February 23 on the supplemental Vietnamese war appropriation. Arthur Goldberg in Tokyo went even further. Three days after the Pentagon issued its denial here, Goldberg was repeating the same myth in Tokyo (*New York Times*, February 28) and adding a new embellishment: he claimed a violation not only of the truce but of the Geneva accord, though even our military did not claim that supplies had actually been spotted crossing the 17th parallel!

It is frustrating to feel so powerless as these myths go marching on. I feel as if I were being smothered under a blanket. The new falsehood in the Pentagon reply was in its smug assertion that all the truce meant to us was higher wages for longshoremen since we have air and naval supremacy "and have no need of a truce of any kind to move supplies." Let us put aside for a moment the Double-Think character of this remark, which implies that any time our bombing of the North stops it is somehow not cricket for people there to breathe freely and move around normally, while the cessation lasts. The hidden falsehood lies in the fact that while we do dominate the air and the sea, we do not dominate the roads in South Vietnam. "Normally"—to use the word our military applies to the constant bombing of the North—we cannot move supplies on most of the roads in the South without a heavy investment of armor and troops.

In the truce, supply was not a violation by either side. To fire upon a convoy (or an air strip) was a violation of the truce. It was therefore easier and less costly for us to move on the roads (and far less dangerous to land and drop supplies upcountry).[1] Tay Ninh has been an air supply area. It is much more costly and difficult to move heavy supplies by air, especially when small air strips ("normally" subject to enemy fire) limit landings to helicopters and the smaller cargo planes. To get from Saigon to Tay Ninh city on the edge of Zone C one goes about forty-five miles northwest on Route 1 and then about thirty-five miles north on Route 22 to Tay Ninh. Few Americans are foolhardy enough to venture very far out of Saigon on Route 1 even by day without a military escort, and fewer still on Route 22, where peasant and commercial traffic—as our military admits—pay road fees to the Viet Cong. Helicopters and tanks protected the trucks which went up those roads during Têt, but they didn't have to fear the kind of traps, ambushes or blocks of "normal" times.

When Saturday's *Le Monde* (February 25) reached me Sunday with its reference to the use of Têt by U.S. forces to prepare the "Junction City" operation, I called this to *The Guardian*'s attention. It published this in London Monday morning. As a result there were questions from Laborite backbenchers in the Commons that day, notably by Sidney Silverman, James Davidson and Michael Foot. Foot asked the Foreign Minister whether the new offensive had not been made possible in part by resupplying during the truce. But this and similar questions drew evasions rather than denials from the foreign minister, George Brown. All this, too, was blacked out in the U.S. press. No one reported either the questions or the answers and it was only by telephoning London that I was able to learn about it in time for this issue. Here the initiation of naval shellfire, river mines

[1] This may explain the sharp increase in air cargo during Têt which we also reported last week.

and artillery barrages across the parallel is accompanied by
the usual escalation in mendacity. Mr. Johnson summoned
an impromptu press conference to deny that these new
moves constituted escalation at all. He said he wouldn't describe them as *any* kind of step-up because, as he said, "I
wouldn't want to put my credibility in doubt." Nobody
had the temerity to suggest this was a maidenhead he had
lost a long time ago.

March 6, 1967

HOW TV AND PRESS
WERE LED TO REHASH
THOSE TÊT SUPPLY LIES

Just how uncritical, and indifferent to the truth, most of the
press, TV-radio and magazines are, was demonstrated again
by the results of the briefing the Pentagon held March 17
on the eve of the Guam conference. Thirty-two reconnaissance photos and charts (hitherto shown only privately to
equally gullible Congressmen) were released. News stories
and TV-casts thereupon rehashed the myth that we had to
resume the bombing of the North because the Communists
took advantage of the truce for massive resupply to their
troops in South Vietnam. "How Reds Cashed In On Bombing Pause" (*U.S. News & World Report*, March 27) was a
typical headline.

We were not invited to the briefing but were able next
day to see the text and the photos at the Pentagon. Few
reporters seem to have examined either carefully. The heading itself was a giveaway. It said "Briefing by Defense

Spokesman on Tết Resupply Activities *Within* North Vietnam" (my italics). It did not allege a violation of the truce nor deny that we had stepped up supplies during Tết, too. No claim was made, and no photos showed, that supplies had been observed crossing the 17th parallel. The nearest point of heavy supply activity was at Quang Khe, "about 55 miles north of the demilitarized zone." Trucks were shown moving "toward Mugia Pass" but none actually in the pass, which is supposed to be the entrance to the "Ho Chi Minh" trail in Laos.

Perhaps in response to critical analyses like those in this *Weekly*, the Pentagon briefing for the first time admitted, "some of this activity was believed to be associated with the redistribution of food and other non-military products required by various segments of the economy," and to "military forces stationed in that general area of *North* Vietnam" (my italics). No military supplies were identified in any of the photos and caption of the ninth photo said of the "containers, baskets, boxes and bags . . . clustered near the shoreline" that "many of the bags and baskets presumably contained food . . . and other non-military products." It added, "It must be emphasized that this was not all bound for South Vietnam." These admissions were not mentioned in any news stories or TV-casts we saw.

Originally the press was told the North moved 35,000 tons "southward" during the truce. Now the Pentagon scaled this down to 23,000 tons. It appeared from chart number 25 that this 23,000 was "estimated" from "a detailed analysis" of "photographic and visual sightings." Just how the estimate was made was not explained.

Chart number 32 said, "the largest logistic resupply effort ever detected" took place during Tết. This sounded pretty sensational until the figures were examined. Chart number 25 said 1,400 water craft were sighted during the truce, "an average of 350 craft per day or twenty-eight times the daily norm." This puts the "daily norm," i.e., under bombing and shelling, at an average of twelve and a half ships per day.

Traffic "normally" must be almost dead if that is all the ships we sight a day along two hundred thirty miles of coastline between Haiphong and the DMZ.

A second figure claimed "sightings of 2200 trucks," an average "of 550 per day, or twenty-two times the daily norm." That makes the "daily norm" only twenty-five trucks—in a country of 17 million people! This figure gives one some idea of the economic strangulation imposed by our bombing and blockade. The surprise is not that the North took advantage of the truce—as we did in the South—to speed up supplies, but that the volume observed was so small.

March 27, 1967

THEY'D DO ANYTHING
FOR THE PEASANT
BUT GET OFF HIS BACK

On the eve of the Guam conference, Vice President Humphrey delivered a speech to the National Farmers Union in Oklahoma. Nothing better attests the phoniness of Johnson's talk at Nashville and Guam about our "pacification" and "revolutionary development" programs in South Vietnam. For Humphrey, an American liberal speaking to the most progressive of the three big farm organizations in this country, devoted a third of his speech to Vietnam without mentioning the issues most vital to its people, 85 percent of whom are peasants.

The fundamental problem of land reform was not mentioned once. Neither was the problem of the exorbitant rents which absentee landlords continue to exact despite laws more than a decade old which were supposed to limit them to 25 percent of the rice crop. To speak as Humphrey did of the desire to become "free citizens rather than virtual serfs" without mentioning the conditions which keep them serfs marks a new stage in Humphrey's degeneration. He even had the effrontery to quote Tolstoy's famous remark about regimes which are willing to do anything to lighten the peasant's burden except get off his back. That exactly describes the alliance of landlord and militarist we are imposing by force on South Vietnam, and seek only to hide behind a façade of new elections rigged like last year's to keep out any elements not satisfactory to landlord and general. Our "revolutionary development" program is designed to prevent the development of that revolution in distribution of the land we were supposed to have promised Vietnam's landless at the Manila conference. Like everything else in Johnson's program, it must be read in reverse, as the opposite of what it seems to mean.

It will not escape the sharp-eyed that the final communiqué at Guam, instead of repeating the Manila promise of land reform, which implies land for the landless, refers vaguely to "reform of land policies and tenure provisions." This implies only some improvement in the conditions of sharecroppers and tenants. This, too, has been talked of for months without results. It is the scaling down even of the promises which is significant. Equally so is the appointment of Robert W. Komer as the President's No. 2 man for Saigon. Komer was for fourteen years a CIA man before he became assistant to McGeorge Bundy under Kennedy. Last March he was named Johnson's $30,000-a-year assistant for "peaceful reconstruction" in South Vietnam. Six months later he turned in a report on rural progress so spurious in its optimism that even Johnson seemed to be embarrassed by it and denied that "pacification" was going anywhere near so well. The impression Komer has created in Washington and Saigon is of an abrasive opportunist. His razzle-dazzle style of operation accords perfectly with Johnson's own which, ever since he called Diem "the Churchill of Asia" in 1961, has been to lay it on with a shovel. The self-delusion which has marked official reports on Vietnam since our involvement began may now be expected to reach ecstatic heights with Komer in charge. If he's an example of CIA training, the Agency must be run by retired circus press agents.

Next to land reform, the main question is political liberty. Among the urban middle class, this was the chief source of dissatisfaction with the Diem dictatorship. "We do not seek to impose our political beliefs upon South Vietnam," Johnson said grandiloquently at Nashville. "Our Republic rests upon a brisk commerce in ideas." [1]

But the last elections in Vietnam, for the Constituent Assembly, were held reluctantly and only to quiet Buddhist agitation. There was freedom neither of party organization nor of nomination, nor of the press. Two reactionary parties, the Dai Viets and the NQQVD, one an old stooge of the Japanese and the other of the Kuomintang, were the only ones allowed to operate. Ky promised that for seven days before the election there would be freedom of the press—but he never kept that promise. It is a black mark for American journalism that no reporter seems to have raised the question of a free press with either Johnson or Ky during the Guam conference.

How do you have a free election without a free press? When will the censorship be lifted on the Saigon papers? The most independent English-language paper in Saigon, *The Guardian*, was suspended last December after only a few months of publication when its editor dared question the official story of how Tran Van Van, Ky's chief civilian rival for the Presidency, was murdered. Its managing editor, Ton That Thien, was seen, and his cry of anguish "We have become a nation of thieves and beggars" heard, on the vivid CBS documentary about Saigon March 14. His life is believed in danger. His friends are trying to get him an invitation to America. Why does no reporter raise the question

---

[1] A brisk commerce in standardized ideas—those who have nonconformist views to offer are lucky to get precarious stalls on the edges of the market-place.

of his fate and the future of the press with Ky and Johnson? Nothing could bring the ideals of America into greater disrepute among Asian intellectuals than the contrast between our constant talk of defending freedom and our complacent acquiescence in the total absence of a free press.

The chief question raised by the Guam conference is why it was held at all. The first natural reaction is to dismiss it as another publicity stunt were it not for the fact that originally there were no plans to include Ky or the other South Vietnamese leaders; that sounded as if something serious were afoot. Or could this merely have been another instance of Johnson's frenzied desire for "action"?

March 27, 1967

THE MINDLESS MOMENTUM OF
A RUNAWAY MILITARY MACHINE

The central thesis of General Westmoreland's debut on the home front is the oldest alibi of frustrated generals—they could have won the war if it hadn't been for those unpatriotic civilians back home. This was how the Kaiser's ex-generals consoled themselves over their beers after World War I and this was the soothing syrup the French generals spooned up after Dienbienphu. But the former lost the war despite all their monocled splendor because they invited exactly what they had always told themselves they ought to avoid—a war on two fronts, against France and Russia at the same time. The latter lost because their perpetual talk of how they were really winning, when year after year they were losing the finest cadres of the French officer class in the Indochinese morass, finally made the French people realize their generals were first-class liars and their dirty little colonial war not worth the cost. Both cases provide obvious parallels to our own predicament, headed as we are for that major war on the Asian mainland we were always told to avoid, and led by generals who have claimed to be winning ever since 1961, and still claim it, though, as Westmoreland also said, they see no end in sight! We wonder what kind of logic they teach them at West Point.

The heart of General Westmoreland's opening speech at the AP luncheon came when he said the enemy was "discouraged by repeated military defeats" but hanging on because "encouraged by what he believes to be popular opposition to our efforts in Vietnam." One does not need to be a military expert to question this assessment. From the enemy point of view, they are doing far better than they had a right to expect. An undeveloped nation of 30 million people with little industry of its own has defied the world's greatest military power for six years. The rebels have grown from a handful to a formidable army despite (or perhaps because of) the constant step-up in our bombardment North and South. In recent months a whole series of enormously expensive and glamorously named U.S. military sweeps have done little but tear swaths in the jungle. While our casualties have risen sharply, the enemy has managed to elude us, and to strike back at times and places of his own choosing. We are switching troops from the Mekong Delta to handle a swiftly deteriorating military situation in the northern part of South Vietnam. It is no secret that Westmoreland wants more troops and that we are going to need a limited mobilization to get them. Add the billion-dollar losses of our air war, and the growing difficulties of the no longer almighty dollar, as the mounting costs of this "little war" undermine it, and ask yourself whether the other side may not feel downright exuberant, indeed overconfident.

Let us put the case in the most hard-boiled terms. The United States can win this war in Vietnam *if* it is prepared to put in a million men, or more, and then to slug it out patiently year after year until the guerrillas are worn down.

It can win if it deliberately de-escalates the firepower and meets the guerrillas on their own terms, in close combat, instead of alienating the entire population with indiscriminate artillery and airpower. A nation of 30 million cannot defeat a nation of 200 million if the bigger nation cares enough to pay the price of victory and has the patience to pursue it. The key is *patience,* and patience is what the United States lacks. It is not just the signs of popular opposition to the war which encourage the other side. It is the visible impatience. Even our hawks don't like the war and want to get it over with as quickly as possible. For us the war is a nuisance. For them the war is a matter of life-and-death. They are prepared to die for their country. We are prepared to die for our country too—if it were attacked—but not for the mere pleasure of destroying theirs. This is why they have the advantage of morale, and for this General Dynamics cannot provide a substitute.

Self-deception has been the characteristic of our leadership in this war from its beginning. Self-deception is still the key to Westmoreland's presentation. Even after so many years he still refuses to recognize the popular roots of the Vietnamese rebellion. He prefers to see it as something essentially artificial and imposed, which Hanoi can turn off with some magic spigot. First we were going to end the war by bombing Hanoi, but now that we'll soon be running out of meaningful targets in the North, we are in effect promised a quick victory if only we can bomb Berkeley into submission. The general who couldn't defeat the enemy abroad now returns to take it out on the *peaceniks* at home. Our country, he says, is founded on debate. But now, though we may be blundering toward a world war, we are told that debate is treasonable. The greatest issue in our country's history must be decided by momentum and default. Our generals would like to suppress peace sentiment here as they do in Saigon. Free discussion is to be made suspect.

A "high government source" told an equally anonymous *Baltimore Sun* (April 21) reporter (we suspect it was Johnson himself talking to his friend Philip Potter) that the U.S. had to avoid the buildup of a war psychology at home and conduct the Vietnamese war "rather coldly" because our power is so "beyond comprehension" that we mustn't let it get out of hand "if the Northern Hemisphere is not to go up in smoke." This is the awful truth a solemn joint session of Congress ought to hear. Yet Johnson is doing what his better judgment tells him not to. Westmoreland is stepping up war fever at home while abroad the wraps are taken off Hanoi, Haiphong and the Mig air bases in a way which brings nearer that final confrontation with China and perhaps also the Soviet Union. As Senator McGovern told a *Washington Post* reporter (April 26) after a brilliant and courageous Senate attack on the growing war madness, "They [i.e., Johnson and the generals] are really going for broke." As the fog of war closes in, and the drums beat louder, which is patriotism, which is love of country, to fall silent or to try and speak some sobering word?

May 1, 1967

IF DADDY KEEPS AT IT, LUCI, ONE DAY YOU WON'T WAKE UP

The President's now famous "World War III" bedtime remark to his daughter, Luci, deserves closer examination. The story has been circulating in the press corps on an off-the-record basis for months. Mr. Johnson has told it so often that it is surprising it did not get into print sooner. It seems to have become one of his favorite anecdotes. One can understand a worried President telling his daughter the night of the first air raids in the immediate vicinity of Hanoi and Haiphong, "Your Daddy may go down in history as having unleashed World War III," adding, in case that was not enough to get her attention, "You may not wake up tomorrow." But it is hard to understand the mentality that can tell and retell the story as if it were some kind of creditable escapade. A James Reston column November 4, 1966 quoted Johnson as saying he had been on tranquilizers since his heart attack in 1955. If this is how lightly Johnson risks a world war, the rest of the country had better start taking them too.

The most extraordinary aspect of this affair has gone unnoticed. The day after the remark to Luci, Johnson flew out to Omaha for a speech in which he told the people of this country, "Peace is more within our reach than at any time in this century." This should add a few miles more to that credibility gap. Ever since Johnson made his first major escalation in February, 1965, by beginning the bombing of the North, there have been repeated hints in the press that Hanoi and Haiphong were to be left alone because Peking or Moscow or both might intervene if the capital and the main port of North Vietnam were smashed. It has been impossible to ascertain if these hints reflected discreet warnings from the Russians and Chinese or discreet reassurances from Washington. Now we learn from the Luci anecdote that Johnson, in authorizing air strikes for the first time within the immediate vicinity of Hanoi and Haiphong, felt that he was risking World War III. The country was neither consulted nor advised on the gravity of that step. On the contrary, it was deceived. The only sense in which it could truthfully be said that peace was then "more within our reach than at any time in this century" was if those air raids had set off a full-scale nuclear confrontation between the U.S. and USSR and with it a peace of extinction.

The only charitable explanation is that when Johnson spoke of peace that day in Omaha and again at Des Moines, he meant the surrender of the other side and had been sold the idea by the Joint Chiefs of Staff that these bombings were worth the risk because they offered a quick victory. The June 29 raids opened three weeks of savage attacks on

the oil installations in and around Hanoi and Haiphong.
The briefings in Saigon and the press conference held by
Secretary McNamara the day they began created the im-
pression that this was a swift and easy way to dry up North
Vietnam's aid to the guerrillas. McNamara said the raids
were ordered "to counter a mounting reliance by North
Vietnam on the use of trucks and powered junks to facili-
tate the infiltration of men and supplies into South Vietnam." Triumphant headlines appeared next day over the
Navy's claim that two miles from the center of Haiphong
its fliers had hit installations representing 40 percent of
North Vietnam's oil storage capacity and 95 percent of its
tanker-unloading capacity and left them 80 percent destroyed. From these first headlines one would have imagined
that henceforth only a trickle of light arms transportable by
bicycle and foot would reach the South while the economic
life of the North would be crippled.[1]

Now almost a year later, it is clear that the sequel of these
raids was a sharp escalation in the volume and size of the
arms and ammunition supplied. There has been an extraordinary increase in the firepower of the guerrillas. SAM's
have appeared as far south as the demilitarized zone, where
they recently shot down a Skyhawk jet and forced suspension of B-52 flights in that area; the B-52 flies too low and
too slowly to evade the SAM. The 140-mm rocket made its
appearance in the attack on the Danang air base last February and on May 12 as far south as Saigon, where it was used
in the attack on Bien Hoa air base. There six Americans were
killed, one hundred wounded and twenty-nine planes destroyed or damaged. American casualties are increasing.
The number of both guerrilla and conventional clashes
seem to have risen and the so-called "pacification" has had
to be shifted to U.S. military control to save it from collapse. The South Vietnamese have failed to provide secu-

[1] Few noticed, however, that eight days later reconnaissance photos
showed 70 percent of the installations were still in operation (*Facts-on-
File*, July 7). These sober revisions never seem to catch up with the
original claims in this fallaciously precise numbers game.

rity: as against 25 attacks all last year on "pacification" teams there have been "more than 300 attacks this year on pacification teams and more than 500 team members have been killed or wounded" (Raymond Coffey from Saigon in *Chicago Daily News*, May 5). These CIA-trained teams have the job of "rooting out" suspected subversives in the villages; it is easy to imagine the injustice they commit and the hatred they sow.

What all this spells is the coming end of the politically comfortable war Johnson has so far waged—a war without special taxes or wage and price controls, a war of one-year tours of duty, fought by the less fortunate of our society, white and Negro, while the junior executive types of the politically powerful Reserve forces have escaped a call-up. Now the military forces are crying out for more troops or "we'll be here forever," as Hanson Baldwin's anonymous source put it in the *New York Times*, May 17. Here again it is worth looking back at the events of last June 29. Again there is the temptation to "go for broke" in one big new plunge, then at the oil resources of the North, this time perhaps to shut off Haiphong harbor altogether, again at the risk of a confrontation with Russia—anything rather than face the reality of a long, painful war of attrition on the ground against resolute guerrillas. Again Johnson would rather gamble on World War III than face elections next year with a country awakened to the painful costs.

McNamara said June 29 in announcing the new step-up in air raids that one of the purposes was to punish the North for continuing its attempt "to subvert and destroy the political institutions of the South." This is the myth that leads to disaster. If this is not a rebellion but a conspiracy and an invasion, why limit the punishment to North Vietnam? Why not hit at the sources in China and Russia? Why not make it painful for the Kremlin? The theory of the war as an external conspiracy which can be shut off like a faucet leads straight to a confrontation with Moscow. This is the inescapable logic of the Johnson-Rusk-McNamara theory of the war. This is the reason for the fresh outcries in the

Senate. This is why U Thant warns that we may be in the
first stages of World War III. This is why the Pope spoke
in anguish at Fatima. Desperation, impatience, the oversim-
plification of a complex struggle are leading Johnson
straight to a confrontation that would put world civilization in jeopardy.

May 22, 1967

NONE SO BLIND AS
THOSE WHO WILL NOT SEE

A new stage in the Vietnamese-American tragedy began
with the arrests of Dr. Spock, the Reverend Coffin and the
three other leaders of the draft resistance movement. We are
headed for escalation—in repression at home and in war
abroad. The two are the obverse sides of the same process.
There is an historic fitness in the coincidence of the arrests
with the Johnson Administration's campaign to fuzz, confuse and elude the possibility of peace talks opened up by
Hanoi's public declaration that talks "will," rather than
"could," follow an end of U.S. bombing. Our favorite
headline of the period was in the *Baltimore Sun*, January 6,
1968. It said, "U.S. Hunting Signs Hanoi Seeks Peace. Admits Its World-Wide Search Is Without Success." Johnson
and Rusk are cultivating myopia. They wouldn't be able to
see a peace talk offer if Ho Chi Minh brought it personally
to the White House West Gate.

The Administration's search for "assurances" before end-
ing the bombings in a pantomime for the naïve. In a local
New York TV program (WNBC, January 7), Edwin
Newman asked William P. Bundy, Assistant Secretary of
State for Far Eastern and Pacific Affairs, "Now would I be

correct in deducing from what you said, that if we had an assurance there would be no increase in the movement from North to South [i.e., of troops and supplies] that that would be sufficient for us?" To which Bundy replied cryptically, "Well, that's an illustration . . . one good illustration." Newman never got a chance to interrupt Bundy's slippery loquacity long enough to ask just how many "illustrations" would be required before we would agree to talk. Fulbright cut through the fog by telling the AP (*New York Post*, January 9), "The Administration is only interested in surrender."

From the Administration's point of view the alarming reactions to Hanoi's offer were not those which came from friendly and neutral capitals urging us to negotiate but from the U.S. embassy in Saigon. The fear there is that any real possibility of peace talks would lead to the collapse of the South Vietnamese government. Its leading figures would make plans to follow their bank accounts into exile while the lesser men would begin to make their own deals with the NLF. Johnson escalated the war in 1965 by putting U.S. ground troops into the South to avoid a military collapse. The escalations of 1968 will be aimed to prevent a political collapse. The bombings of Russian and Chinese ships in Haiphong harbor, the air attacks on Yunnan from across the Laos border, the itch for hot pursuit into Laos and Cambodia, and the plans for an "Inchon landing" across the DMZ into North Vietnam are the familiar symptoms of that "politics of escalation" with which the Johnson Administration has countered every opportunity for peace talks in the past.

Johnson prefers a wider war to a compromise peace. Only wider war can hide from public view how quickly his pumped-up campaign of optimistic forecast has collapsed. The successful attacks all over the country on U.S. and South Vietnamese outposts and airfields, up to the very outskirts of Saigon and Danang, show how very far the enemy is from military exhaustion. Politically the Saigon government is falling apart even without peace talks. The rigged elections gave the Catholic minority a dominant position in both houses of the new legislature and seemed to assure the military junta a built-in pro-war majority. But the rejection by both houses of the military decree drafting eighteen-year-olds shows how sick of the war even this once die-hard sector of Vietnamese opinion has become. The basic shift was plainly signaled when Saigon's Catholic clergy called for an end of the bombing and assailed the corruption in the regime. A Buddhist-Catholic alliance against the war is now shaping up, and even the labor movement—largely created by the CIA—is swinging against us with the police attacks on the electrical workers' strike in Saigon.[1] The regime's mass base is dwindling to the handful of last-ditch patriots who own the brothels and the bars.

The war this year will become more than ever an American war, and our army more plainly than ever an occupying force. Escalation will require more troops, and perhaps even the dangerous step—already rumored here—of bringing in Chinese troops from Formosa, a step which would inflame Vietnamese opinion and create more tension with mainland China. Indeed the military campaign for "hot pursuit" into Cambodia and Laos seems designed as a roundabout way to force such dangerous expedients and partial mobilization. We are already short of troops to deal with the swarm of attacks all over the country and to shore up the collapsing effort at "pacification." Any serious efforts at "hot pursuit" across the border would soon force Johnson to provide more troops even if it meant higher draft calls and mobilization of reserves in an election year. *U.S. News & World Report* estimated (December 11) that the Cambodian sanctuaries could be "cleaned out" with three U.S.

---

[1] An AP dispatch we saw only in the Washington *Star* January 12 said six labor leaders were arrested by the police as they left a bargaining session with government officials in Saigon. Tran Quoc Buu, chairman of the Vietnamese Workers Federation, predicted the arrests would lead to a general strike by its 300,000 members. "How can we fight against the Communists under these conditions?" he told the AP. "We lose all right to fight against the Communists when things like this happen." Until now Buu and his unions have been faithful creatures of the U.S.

divisions. But to get three more divisions would require a step-up in the draft at home. This means more draft resistance and an intensified struggle in the Negro ghettoes. To shut the door on peace abroad is to invite more racial conflict at home. This is the direction of Johnson's policy and this is the larger dimension of the unfolding tragedy. . . .

January 22, 1968

SAIGON AFIRE NOW—
WILL IT BE WASHINGTON
IN APRIL?

It is no longer necessary to argue the mendacity of our leaders and the incompetence of our military. Mr. Johnson has assured us that the successful surprise attack on 100 South Vietnamese cities and towns was really a Viet Cong defeat; if they suffer a few more such defeats, we'll be lucky to settle for a coalition government in Hawaii.[1] No nation ever had the misfortune to be led by a bigger team of clowns than those whom Johnson and Rusk, and Westmoreland and Bunker put through their daily capers in Washington and Saigon; their body counts alone are enough to make Bob Hope jealous: these seem to be based on an extension to warfare of installment credit principles—count now, kill later.

[1] Sir Robert Thompson, who ran Britain's successful anti-guerrilla campaign in Malaya and was head of the British Advisory Mission in South Vietnam from 1961 to 1965, wrote of these attacks in the London *Sunday Times* February 11, "In terms of guerrilla and mobile warfare, Gen. Vo Nguyen Giap has achieved a master stroke in South Vietnam and has greatly enhanced his reputation—if such a thing were possible—as an outstanding general and victor of Dien Bien Phu."

We still don't know what hit us. The debris is not all in Saigon and Hué. The world's biggest intelligence apparatus was caught by surprise. Our No. 1 Whiz Kid, the retiring Secretary of Defense McNamara, capped his record of misjudgments on Vietnam by preparing a final defense "posture" statement in which he reported "a drop in [Viet Cong] combat efficiency and morale"! The day he read this report to the Senate Armed Services Committee the Viet Cong made their nationwide raids. Neither under Japanese nor French occupation were the rebels ever able to stage such widespread and coordinated attack. Yet we have 500,000 troops in the country as compared with the 60,000 of the French; our Army is incomparably better supplied with firepower and airpower; and for three years we have been bombing the North so heavily that every town and city except Hanoi and Haiphong is in ruins.

When the bodies are really counted, it will be seen that one of the major casualties was our delusion about victory by airpower: all that boom-boom did not keep the enemy from showing up at Langvei with tanks. Three years of interdiction by airpower and the rebels are steadily better equipped; the days when they depended on weapons captured from our side are long over. Another casualty is the reputation of Westmoreland and our Joint Chiefs of Staff. On TV Westmoreland and Wheeler began to look more and more pathetic as they clung to those inflated body count box scores which only they still take seriously. It is as if they mistake the art of warfare for the demolition and extermination business. Giap is proving that superior military and political skill can win over vastly superior firepower, i.e., brain power over bulk. This is what did in the dinosaur.

Two events during the uprising were deadly. They will never be forgotten as symbols the world over of what the Pax Americana really means for the people we claim to be protecting. One occurred at Bentre after it was shelled "regardless of civilian casualties," as the ordinarily unemotional AP reported February 7, "to rout the Vietcong." A

U.S. major explained, "It became necessary to destroy the town to save it." This will go down in the history books as typical of our whole Vietnamese campaign. The whole country is slowly being burnt down to "save it." To apply scorched-earth tactics to one's own country is heroic; to apply it to a country one claims to be saving is brutal and cowardly. Everywhere we call in artillery and air strikes rather than fight it out hand-to-hand with the guerrillas; this has been characteristic of our intervention from the beginning and this is the secret of why the rebellion grows ever stronger. It is we who rally the people to the other side.

The other incident took place at Khesanh where we turned away not only civilian refugees but allied forces fleeing the fallen camp of Langvei. We not only refused them shelter but disarmed them before driving them away. The best account was a magnificent on-the-spot piece of journalism by Newbold Noyes in the Washington *Star* February 11. The decision was based, it is clear, on two motives. One was an unwillingness to share precious supplies, but had they been Americans our men would have shared their last crust to give them shelter. The other was the suspicion that there might be Viet Cong among them. How can one fight a successful war when mistrust of one's own allies is so deep? Colonel Lownds, the commander at Khesanh, acted only after consulting higher quarters and was in agony over the decision. "This thing," he told Noyes, "can come back to haunt me—all of us. If these people say when the chips were down, after getting us to fight for you, you wouldn't protect us, then the whole civic action business here goes down the drain." The truth is that when the chips are down we feel that the "gooks" (or whatever the similar term of the moment) are expendable. To the darker peoples everywhere this incident will sound (fairly or unfairly) like "whitey" all over again. Don't think it won't rankle.

The idea that we Americans are a superior race, and are justified in using any means of mass killing to save American lives, will be the argument for using tactical nuclear weapons in defense of Khesanh. It is this racial angle above all which would make it madness for us to add nuclear weapons to the suffering we have already imposed on the Vietnamese people. Let just one "little" tactical nuclear weapon be used at Khesanh and the moral devastation will be beyond calculation. It will stir race hate among the colored peoples everywhere; they will feel that again they and not whites are the guinea pigs of these terrible weapons. The Chinese will bank this away as moral capital for the day when they can wage nuclear war on us. At home the awful split among our own people will be vastly deepened. The alienation among the youth and for every American of conscience will be beyond anything we have yet experienced. By far the strongest reason for getting out of this Vietnamese war as soon as possible is because sooner or later it will carry us to that fatal step, that crime against mankind.

It is time to stand back and look where we are going. And to take a good look at ourselves. A first observation is that we can easily overestimate our national conscience. A major part of the protest against the war springs simply from the fact that we are losing it. If it were not for the heavy cost, politicians like the Kennedys and organizations like the ADA would still be as complacent about the war as they were a few years ago. A second observation is that for all the poppycock about the Vietnamese war clashing with our past traditions, we have long been an imperialistic people. The Truman Doctrine and the Johnson Doctrine are only extensions of the Monroe Doctrine, new embodiments of that Manifest Destiny to which our expansionists appealed in a less cautious day. Bolívar once said that we plagued Latin America in the name of liberty; today we do it to a growing sector of the world. Everywhere we talk liberty and social reform but we end up by allying ourselves with native oligarchies and military cliques—just as we have done in Vietnam. In the showdown, we reach for the gun.

And this I fear is what we are going to do at home in dealing with the rising threat of a Negro revolt. We could be in the first stage of what Mao has envisaged—a worldwide colonial uprising against American power, accompanied by a complementary and similar rising of blacks in the racial colonies that our ghettoes have become. It is foolish to dismiss Mao's vision because the guerrilla movements in Latin America and Africa have so far proven unsuccessful and because most Negroes still want only to be accepted fully as fellow Americans. These facts give us time to save our country but only if that time is utilized wisely and quickly. So long as the war goes on it must deepen racial bitterness at home and abroad, because colored peoples are the victims and because colored men make up so disproportionately large a share of our own combat troops while the cry rises to save the white boys from the draft for the graduate schools. And the longer the war goes on the less money we have for the giant tasks of social reconstruction at home. We put $2 billion into the French attempt to hold Indochina. We have spent $65 billion since 1954 on our own. This year the war will easily cost $30 billion. The new "defense" budget has already burst its seams with the *Pueblo* affair, and it was already $80 billion. These stupendous sums are the counterpart of the precious time and energy we waste.

Now Martin Luther King announces a new march on Washington for April. Negro moderates regard it as the last gasp of the nonviolent movement. If it fails, they see race war in our cities. Dr. King, as always, is playing it by ear. He is a mystic. He has no concrete program. He has no clear aim except the full emancipation of his people. The nearest thing to a concrete objective is the Conyers bill, which would spend $30 billion—the cost of one year in Vietnam—for the rehabilitation of our slums and the human beings twisted by life in these urban jungles. That bill hasn't a chance in this atmosphere. The whole trend is to cut rather than to increase welfare expenditures. The emphasis is on repressing crime in the streets, which translates into repressing the Negro. Johnson gave in to that trend by calling in his crime message for enactment of a federal inciting-to-riot bill, which the Administration liberals have fought for two years. The Attorney General, like the new report on the Newark "riots," has stressed that these racial convulsions are due to misery, not conspiracy. But we are moving inexorably to the club, the gun and the jail, to a Vietnam at home.

Troops are being trained to fight urban guerrillas. GI's in Vietnam are being offered discharge 90 days early if they join an urban police force back home. Dr. King promises nonviolence but he also projects a vast sit-down to bring Washington to a standstill unless it prepares to give the Negro what he wants. If he fails, more Negro youth will turn to the revolutionary way. The chances of avoiding some outburst of violence during those April demonstrations will grow slimmer the longer they last. Some shooting, even accidental, may anger even Washington's apathetic Negro population and set off racial fighting here and by chain reaction in other cities. To move toward the end of the war, to show a readiness to spend for reconstruction at home instead of devastation abroad, would change the whole atmosphere. Must we wait until the fires that rage in Saigon set Washington ablaze too?

February 19, 1968

PART III

'...Will It Be Washington in April?'

THE FIRE HAS
ONLY JUST BEGUN

The assassination of Dr. Martin Luther King, Jr., was the occasion for one of those massive outpourings of hypocrisy characteristic of the human race. He stood in that line of saints which goes back from Gandhi to Jesus; his violent end, like theirs, reflects the hostility of mankind to those who annoy it by trying hard to pull it one more painful step further up the ladder from ape to angel.

The President and the Washington establishment had been working desperately up until the very moment of Dr. King's killing to keep him and his Poor People's March out of the capital; his death, at first, promised to let them rest in peace. The masses they sang were not so much of requiem as of thanksgiving, that the nation's No. 1 Agitator had been laid to rest at last. Then a minority of his own people, and not all of them the ignorant and the hungry, celebrated his memory with an orgy of looting while black radicals and New Leftists hailed the mindless carnival as a popular uprising. Since the liquor stores were the No. 1 target, it might sourly be termed the debut of Marxism-Liquorism in revolutionary annals. Those among his own people who sneered at his nonviolent teaching as obsolete now seized upon his death as a new excuse for the violence he hated. Thus all sides firmly united in paying him homage.

Dr. King was a victim of white racism. Its record encourages such murders. Dr. King was only the most eminent in a long series of civil rights victims. The killers are rarely caught, even more rarely convicted; the penalties are light. The complicity, in this case, may go further. It is strange that the killer was so easily able to escape when the motel in which he was killed was ringed with police; some came within a few moments from the very direction of the fatal shot. Violent anti-Negro organizations like the Klan have their cells in many police forces. The Memphis police had shown their hatred in the indiscriminate violence with which they broke up Dr. King's march a week earlier. The Attorney General should be pressed to include the Memphis police in his investigation of the slaying.

Though Dr. King was the greatest Southerner of our time, few Southern political leaders expressed any sorrow over his passing. Most, like Stennis of Mississippi, ventured no more than antiseptic and ambivalent condemnation of *all* violence. In the House on April 8 the few Southerners who spoke deplored the riots more than the killing. The one exception was Representative Bob Eckhardt of Texas, who dared call Dr. King "my black brother." Privately many white Southerners rejoiced, and their influence was reflected in the scandalous failure to declare a holiday in the District the day Dr. King was buried. Though stores closed, government offices were open and Negro mailmen delivered the mail as usual. This is still, despite its black majority, a Southern-ruled town; it shuts down on Washington's birthday, but not Lincoln's.

The most powerful of the District's absentee rulers, Senator Robert C. Byrd (D. W. Va.), went so far as to imply in a Senate speech April 5, that Dr. King was to blame for his own death. Byrd said those who organize mass demonstrations may "in the end . . . become themselves the victims of the forces they set in motion." While Dr. King "usually spoke of nonviolence," Byrd went on smugly, "violence all too often attended his action and, at the last, he himself met a violent end." This should make Byrd the South's favorite criminologist.

Byrd is the Senator to whom the blacks of Washington must come for school and welfare money. As chairman of the Senate Appropriations subcommittee on the District of Columbia budget, Byrd wields far more power than the city's figurehead Negro "Mayor." He has used this key position to block liberalization of welfare rules not only in the District but in the country, since the federal government can hardly apply elsewhere rules more liberal than those he will allow in the District. Byrd has become the national pillar of the "man in the house" rule. This, as the report of the Commission on Civil Disorders protested, makes it necessary for the unemployed father to "abandon his family or see them go hungry." In this sense not a few of the child looters in our gutted ghettoes can trace their delinquency straight back to Robert C. Byrd.

For whites who live like myself in almost lily-white Northwest Washington on the very edge of suburbia, the ghetto disorders might have taken place in a distant country, viewed on TV like Vietnam (which it begins to resemble), or as a tourist attraction on a visit in the bright spring sunshine before curfew to the sullen and ruined ghetto business districts. It was not until five days after the trouble started that two young soldiers turned up for the first time to guard our own neighboring shopping center—"as a precautionary measure," they explained—and tape appeared on its liquor-store windows. Even sympathetic and radical whites found themselves insulated from what was going on not just by the military cordons but even more by an indiscriminate black hostility. Even some liberal and leftist families with children moved out of integrated neighborhoods on the edge of the ghetto in apprehension. These were our first refugees from black power.

Nothing could be more deceptive than the nationwide mourning. Beneath the surface nothing has changed, except perhaps for the worst. The President has called off his address to a joint session indefinitely. His Senate Majority Leader, Mansfield, warns the Congress not to be "impetuous" in reacting to the disorders. How fortunate we should be if all our dangers were as remote as this one! The new civil rights bill, if it passes, is more likely to bring new evils in its anti-riot provisions than reform in housing.

In Washington, as in most cities hit by black violence, the police and the troops have been on their best behavior to the point where business spokesmen are complaining that there has been too much leniency in dealing with looters.

For once, to the Administration's credit, lives have been put ahead of property. Had police and soldiers begun to shoot, the killings would have become a massacre and the riots a black revolution. As it is, in Washington at least, the black community has been grateful for the protection afforded it. But this leniency is unlikely to survive when and if white rather than black areas begin to go up in smoke. There is little time left for the big multi-billion-dollar program which alone can rehabilitate the hopeless and bitter generation of blacks that racial discrimination and the slums have bred. Whites still think they can escape the problem by moving to the suburbs, and as long as they think so, nothing will be done. There are already 55,000 troops in our 110 scarred cities—more than we had in Vietnam three years ago. Already the police talk of guerrilla war. If it comes, a half million troops will not be enough to contain it. A looting suspect told one reporter at a police station here, "We're going to burn this whole place. It might take years but we'll do it." This is the agony of a lost race speaking. If we cannot respond with swift compassion, this is the beginning of our decline and fall.

April 15, 1968

BILLIONS FOR MISSILES AND PENNIES FOR POVERTY

The day the poor were driven out of Resurrection City was the day the Senate voted to approve an anti-missile system. Monday June 24 deserves to go down in history for its symbolic significance. Congress turned a flinty banker's face to the poor but took the first step toward the deployment of an ABM (anti-ballistic missile) network which could cost more than their most utopian demands. The first installment for Sentinel, the "thin" one, is $5 billion. The total cost of the big one the military-industrial complex wants can easily run to $50 billion. Even that is only the beginning. For the ABM will set off a new spiral in the arms race, as each side builds more missiles to overwhelm the other's anti-missiles, and then more anti-missiles to counter the new missiles. "And at the end of it all," as Nelson of Wisconsin told the Senate that day, the U.S. and the Soviet Union "will be right back where we started, except out of pocket $50 to $100 billion."

While the chief lobbyist of the poor, the Reverend Ralph David Abernathy, went to jail, the lobbyists of the military-industrial complex celebrated their biggest victory. The ABM will prove to be our most wasteful handout. But the lobbyists who sold this bill of goods did not have to live in shanties or confront police lines on their way to the Capitol. The clients of the welfare state ought to get acquainted with the clients of the warfare state. The decision to go ahead with the ABM, the *Congressional Quarterly* said in a special study May 24 of the military-industrial complex, will benefit more than 15,000 companies including such major defense contractors as General Electric, General Dynamics and Thiokol-Chemical. One brokerage firm told its customers last summer that the day Congress approved the ABM was "the day they will shake the money tree for electronic companies." In the last quarter of 1967, after Johnson overruled McNamara and approved the Sentinel, seventy-five mutual investment funds "sold $90 million in other stock holdings [the *Congressional Quarterly* report says] and invested the proceeds in electronics."

The ABM is the latest breakthrough in the arms race, and it is time to recognize the arms race for what it is—the socialism of the rich. It is the welfare system which supports some of our richest corporations. The physicist Ralph Lapp, who did so much to arouse the country to the fallout danger in the campaign against nuclear testing, has provided the best overall view of what the ABM and the arms race really mean in his new book, *The Weapons Culture*. The spokesmen for the poor should use it as ammunition. Dr. Lapp observed that the so-called free enterprise system "has been distorted into a kind of 'defense socialism,' in which the welfare of the country is permanently tied to the continued growth of military technology and the continued stockpiling of military hardware." Dr. Lapp estimates that since World War II the U.S. has spent about one trillion dollars—1,000 billions or 1,000,000 millions—on armament! The program has fallen like manna on the country-club set and—with the related space program—created a whole new generation of millionaires. We could have cleaned up every slum and solved every racial and social problem with a fraction of the money, thought and energy which went into military hardware, most of it already junked as obsolete.

Solidarity Day brought a vast throng to Washington and half a dozen Establishment phonies hastened to address it from the Lincoln Memorial. But no occasional upsurge of benevolent feeling, much less spurious oratorical generalities about poverty, is going to change the allocation of resources between those who grow rich on weaponry and those who decay on welfare. The swift liquidation of Resurrection City once the visitors had departed was the reflection of a more permanent solidarity among those who fatten on the waste of national income. Those poor shanties the police destroyed were the first signs, we hope, of a widening and continued struggle against the inhumanity and the irrationality of our spending policy. During the House debate June 26 which ended with sharp cuts in the welfare budget, a typical Iowa Republican opponent of the poverty program said the country did not have "money to throw away . . . on this type of luxury" while a tightwad on the Democratic side (Flood of Pennsylvania) cried, "What do you want? Diamonds? What are you going to use for money? Cigar store coupons?" But when it comes to the war machine and the space program the billions flow freely.

Mrs. Green of Oregon protested that this same Congress

had voted $4 billion for the space program. "That means," she said, "we are willing to spend more dollars for outer space than we are willing to spend in total amount of tax dollars for the education of fifty million boys and girls in our elementary and secondary schools." But education, unlike the race for the moon, does not rain dollars on Houston, Texas. "It makes me heart-sick," Mrs. Green cried, "to see my nation spending in one day in Vietnam more than the total amount of increase I am requesting that affects two million teachers and the quality of education for fifty million boys and girls." It is not only the blacks nor only the poor who suffer from the huge allocations to the war and space machines. It is the quality of American life. Urban blight and pollution could be ended permanently for what that war in Vietnam has cost us. Abernathy's little army has been fighting a battle for all of us.

Resurrection City is supposed to have been a mess. I found it inspiring. It reminded me of the Jewish displaced persons' camps I visited in Germany after the war. There was the same squalor and the same bad smells, but also the same hope and the same will to rebuild from the ashes of adversity. To organize the hopeless, to give them fresh spirit, to set them marching was truly resurrection. If much went wrong, that was to be expected; what was miraculous was that so much could be accomplished with the supposed dregs of our society. Disorganization is hardly a novelty in Washington; you can find it everywhere from Capitol Hill to the Pentagon. The striking thing about Resurrection City is that there was so much genuine non-racialism. The organizers have been given very little credit for bridging a gap everyone deplores. The Reverend Ralph David Abernathy is not the first man of God to be ridiculed and jailed. The wry humor of the poor he led was summed up for me by that touching sign on one of the mule wagons: "Don't Laugh Folks," it said, "Jesus Was A Poor Man." It would be tragic if their voices were so easily smothered.

The skewed vision which afflicts the respectable in our society was beautifully summed up in the outburst of con-

cern for the twenty-three skinny mules that finally made it
to Washington. The first edition of the *Washington Daily
News* June 28 carried across its front page a picture of a
mule in clover with a caption saying that the mules had been
moved to pasture land in Columbia, Maryland, "where the
meadows go for $8000 an acre and their next-door neighbors
are $15,000 show horses and $20,000 stallions. 'They're
going to be treated better than any mules in the history of
muledom,' one bountiful lady says." What of the poor hungry human mules who balked at their heavy burdens?

When the Vietnamese war causes inflation, the poor bear
the burden in the shape of higher living costs; they eat less.
When higher taxes are imposed and the budget cut to save
the dollar from inflation, the poor pay again in the shape of
fewer jobs and reduced welfare. And now that there is hope
the Vietnam war may be ending and more funds available to
help them, the Under Secretary of the Treasury tells a
Town Hall audience in Los Angeles June 25 that he doubts
the end of the war will bring any sizable reduction in the
military budget. Mr. Barr estimated that "a cessation of hostilities would result in great pressures to rebuild stock in
military supplies and equipment to a more acceptable level."
He informs us that "We have been fighting this war on a
very, very lean [only $80 billion!] budget." How dare the
poor be so obstreperous when the Pentagon is so hungry?

July 8, 1968

THE MASON-DIXON LINE
MOVES TO NEW YORK

On my way into New York City from La Guardia, the taxi-
driver told me that his daughter, after a first year as teacher

in a black ghetto, had transferred out to Long Island in despair. "The children were wonderful," he said. "The trouble was the parents." An hour later at lunch a Jewish schoolteacher from Brooklyn complained of the black children in her mathematics class for slow learners, but said the black parents, when she called on them for help, were without exception not only cooperative but grateful. But teacher and taxi-driver agreed in blaming Mayor Lindsay, though just for what was not clear. Indeed very little in New York's crisis is clear, perhaps because the real motivations are kept hidden as shameful. More and more people, particularly among the striking teachers, and in the Jewish community, are flailing about in hysteria. A sample: I asked the Brooklyn schoolteacher just what was the issue in the strike. She replied with appalling simplicity, "Anti-Semitism." How do you win a strike against anti-Semitism? By circumcising all gentiles and turning Black Muslims into Black Jews? "What does Mr. Shanker want?" the mayor asked in a similar vein in a radio interview next day. "For the police vans to come into the [Ocean Hill-Brownsville] community, arrest them and send them to New Jersey?" Is the Exodus to be re-enacted, this time with a black cast?

The plain truth is that John V. Lindsay is in trouble because he suddenly finds himself the Mayor of a Southern town. The Mason-Dixon line has moved north, and the Old Confederacy has expanded to the outer reaches of the Bronx. Even without this tide of racism, it would take a genius with two heads to govern the city successfully. Some of its basic problems are universal. One is size. Another is bureaucracy; the educational bureaucracy has entrenched itself in a maze of regulations beyond effective public control. A third is poverty; by next year one of every eight New Yorkers will be on relief. The city is choked with automobiles and people. Even if all eight million were a multiple birth from the same mamma, they would aggravate the hell out of each other. But in New York, as elsewhere, those of a different color, whether black or Puerto Rican, are no longer willing to accept second- or third-class citizenship submissively. They are pushing upwards into the better jobs and the sunnier places. In New York, the world's biggest Jewish city, this has created a special problem—a confrontation between blacks and Jews. This is rapidly turning Lindsay into the world's most down-trodden WASP.

The defeat two years ago of his proposal for a civilian review board to hear complaints against the police was the first disturbing signal in what had been the most liberal city in the country. New York's lower-middle-class whites were reacting like their counterparts elsewhere. In the struggle over schools the fears have now spread to liberal teachers hitherto sympathetic to the civil rights movement. Conflicts in the ghetto with Jewish landlords and storekeepers were relatively easy to contain. But the teachers' strike has churned up fears in an educational establishment that Jewish teachers and principals have dominated for a generation. Now that black unrest seems to threaten union standards and their jobs they are reacting like less liberal and less intellectual "ethnic" groups. The teachers' union is moving closer to the benighted old-line A.F.L. craft unions. A formidable anti-black coalition is shaping up. One of its victims may be the good name of the Jewish community.

If this great city is to be saved from race war, more Jewish intellectuals are going to have to speak up in ways that their own people will resent, just as white Southerners resented those who spoke up for the Negro. The teachers' union is exaggerating, amplifying and circulating any bit of anti-Semitic drivel it can pick up from any far-out black extremist, however unrepresentative, and using this to drive the Jewish community of New York into a panic. Albert Shanker and the teachers' union are exploiting natural Jewish fears of anti-Semitism in order to win the community's support for the strike and for its major objective, which is to prevent effective decentralization and community control of the school system. Unless more Jewish leaders speak up in public and say what they do in private, this manufactured hysteria may prove a disaster for both the black and the Jewish communities. Peoples, like generals, tend to be obsessed by their last war. To hear some New York Jews talk one would think the America of 1968 was the Germany of 1932. They do not see that they themselves are caught up in the backlash which is creating in Wallace the nearest American counterpart to Der Fuehrer, that they are joining the rednecks, that the danger lies in white racism not black. The latter is despairing and defensive; the former holds the potential of a new Nazism in its effort to maintain white supremacy. It would be eternally disgraceful were Jews this time to be among the Brown Shirts.

To visit the black-controlled schools which have stirred such forebodings on both sides of the controversy is like waking from a nightmare. I spent Friday, October 25, in the Ocean Hill-Brownsville district, observing classes and talking with teachers and principals in JHS 271 and its intermediate school neighbor, IS 55, and the visit was therapeutic. It was a day without pickets and I saw only one policeman. The atmosphere was incredibly different from what I had been led to expect. I found black and white teachers, Jewish and gentile, working together not just peacefully but with zest and comradeship. The cleanliness and the neat clothing of the children reflected well on the homes from which they came. The classes were orderly. There was none of that screaming by teacher against pupil, and among the children, which is common in most New York schools. I felt at the end of the day that the racial and union issues were terribly overblown and that the real concern within the embattled district was simply to create effective schools. I saw no reason why this could not be reconciled with proper union standards and I felt it would be a tragedy if this experiment in community control were shut down.

I watched Mrs. Naomi Levinson teach an English class full of eager black children. I read some of the touching poems and essays they had produced. "It's the first time in my eight years as a teacher," she told us proudly, "that I have been allowed to use unconventional teaching methods." I talked with another teacher, Leon Goodman, whose face lit up with pleasure when he explained the new methods of teaching science he was allowed to apply. "We get them to think rather than simply to copy down abstractions from the blackboard." Both impatiently denied that they had encountered any anti-Semitism.[1] I sat in on a teacher-team conference of five English teachers, three black, two white, one of the whites a delicate-featured blonde WASP, the other an intense and dark-eyed Jew. The two whites were volunteers. One of them had brought a bongo drum into the classroom to use with the reading of Vachel Lindsay's incomparably rhythmic "Congo" as a way to awaken the children to the wonders of poetry. The atmosphere of this mixed group was wholly devoid of any racial self-consciousness or tension. One felt their pleasure in working together. In the corner of one classroom we watched a young black teacher with a group of children who took turns at reading "The Prince and the Pauper." On the blackboard was the assignment, "Write a story about something that went wrong in a person's life" and next to it in a row there were the helpful hints, "No money. Sickness. No food. No light. No home. No friends. No job." The words telescoped the familiar annals of the ghetto.

The only racialism, if it can be called that, was in the evidence of efforts to awaken black pride. There were some vivid watercolors produced in a new painting class and exhibited in a hallway as "Soul on Paper." Another hallway blackboard had "Black Is Beautiful" written not only in French and Spanish but in Greek, Hebrew, Punjabi, Swahili, Arabic and Esperanto. One room's walls were covered with pictures and clippings variously headed "Religion, Statesmen, Musicians, Scientists, Inventors, Diplomats" showing black achievement in these fields.

In the classroom where Leslie Campbell, an African gown over his normal clothes, teaches Afro-American Studies, there were posters showing "Our Homeland" and "Our Proud and Glorious Past." They reminded me of

[1] About three-fourths of the non-striking teachers in Ocean Hill-Brownsville are white and about one half of these are Jewish.

Zionist posters in many Jewish Sabbath schools. There were
also posters of "The Proud Look" and "Black Pictures of
Christ." Campbell after class was friendly and open. He described himself as a black nationalist revolutionary but said
he found himself very much in a minority on the faculty.
"Most of my black colleagues," he said, "are simply educa-
tionists," though they agree on African studies for its psychological value. The other teacher of Afro-American
Studies at JHS 271, Alan Kellock, turned out to be a young
white man who has studied in Egypt and Ghana and is finishing a doctorate in African history for the University of
Wisconsin. He said he had encountered no racial prejudice
in Ocean Hill-Brownsville. What purpose did he see in
Afro-American history courses? "To get the black children
to feel they are worthwhile people. To give them a sense of
identity and dignity." Kellock obtained his teaching license
last summer. He feels JHS 271 is the most promising place
to teach in the entire city.

David Rogers, in his blockbuster of a new book, *110 Liv-
ingston Street: Politics and Bureaucracy in the New York
City School System*, quotes an authoritative earlier professional study of the city's schools by Strayer and Yavner.
"The greatest failing of the schools today," they found as
he did, "is the failure to use the creative ability of teachers."
When I read this afterwards, I understood the enthusiasm I
had found in the two schools I visited. I had thought of
community control as a kind of lesser evil, a way of appeasing black dissatisfaction. I did not realize what a dead hand
the bureaucracy has fastened on the schools and how much
could be done just by lifting it. "Not many teachers come
into the system sour," said Percy Jenkins, the Virginia-born
Negro who is now principal of IS 55, "but they don't stay
long without becoming sour. The kids come in with lively
minds but by the fourth grade they too have lost interest."
Jenkins himself, a graduate of West Virginia State College,
had been in "the system" 15 years and risen to assistant
principal before he was chosen to head IS 55 in this commu-
nity-control experiment. "What you see here," one white

teacher explained later, "is a function of the principal, of the fresh directions he maps out and of the commitment brought to this experiment by young liberal arts college volunteers with new ideas."

I spoke with Rhody McCoy, the head of the district; with his assistant, Lloyd Hunter; with the principal of JHS 271, William H. Harris, and with his white assistant principal, John Mandracchia. I have never met a more devoted group of people. All of them are harassed and overworked but sustained by a combination of desperation and joy, desperation because they fear the experiment may soon be wiped out under union pressure, joy in a chance to demonstrate in the little time they have what community control could accomplish. They are enlightened men; one forgets all the nonsense of black and white in talking with them; color vanishes. They fear black extremism as much as white misunderstanding. *And their focus is on the child.*

That cannot be said of their opponents. The child, whether black or white, seems to be the forgotten bystander in the teachers' strike. The union's rallying cry is "due process," i.e., for teachers, and its concern is their tenure. Its alliance is not with the parents for better education but with the employing bureaucracy for the maintenance of their common privileges. The "due process" issue they have raised is a monumental bit of hypocrisy. The best analysis of it may be found in the report by the New York Civil Liberties Union, *The Burden of Blame*. The unsatisfactory teachers were *transferred*, not discharged, and transfers normally are made without hearing or charges; the teachers prefer it that way, to keep their records free from blemish.

The real problem is how to keep teachers *in* ghetto schools. The Board of Education regulations are designed to discourage teachers from fleeing them. The contractual procedures between the Board and the union limit the teacher's freedom to transfer. "Yet," the civil liberties union reported, "in Ocean Hill-Brownsville, the UFT sought to ignore all these procedures and claimed the right for unlimited numbers of teachers to transfer out at will for the duration of the experiment, to abandon the experiment for as long as it continues and then to be free to return, presumably when 'normal' conditions had been reinstated. . . . Significant numbers of teachers did leave . . . Months later, when the Ocean Hill-Brownsville Local Governing Board attempted to exercise a similar unilateral right of transfer, the UFT cried foul."

The Board of Education's notions of "due process" are as one-sided. I have read the full text of the decision handed down by Judge Francis E. Rivers as trial examiner in the case of the transferred teachers. It is by no stretch of the imagination the vindication it appears to be in the headlines.

The hearing, by screening out all but professional witnesses, and barring not only parent testimony but that of para-professional school aides, and by applying strict rules of evidence unsuited to administrative procedures, managed to acquit the teachers without any real exploration of the charges against them.

The Board of Education is past master at manipulating regulations and procedures to achieve the ends it seeks. The Rogers book shows how hard it is even for teachers and principals to find out how it operates. Only a Kafka could do justice to the murk it generates. In a column on due process in the *New York Post* October 24, Murray Kempton provided an incisive glimpse of these operations in the proceedings now underway against four JHS 271 teachers accused of threats, or acts of terror, against attempts to reinstate the transferred teachers. Their attorneys were forbidden to see the reports on which the charges were based. When one attorney asked, "Do you proceed under any rules and regulations?" the reply was "We do not." After all this talk about due process, Kempton commented, "we suddenly discover that in this system there is no protection for anybody except the conscience and good-will of the Superintendent."

All bureaucracies are secretive, none more so than the New York Board of Education. The Rogers book is an eye-opener, particularly in its account of how desegregation was sabotaged by the Board. It did not work, Rogers concludes, "because the bureaucracy and the staff made them fail." It was out of the frustration created by the failure of integration that black and Puerto Rican parents turned to community control. This, too, is being sabotaged by the Board and by the union. They fear the loss of power and privilege if democracy is substituted for bureaucracy. They have the support of all the unions which do business with the educational system, a billion-dollar business. The New York trade union movement, like its educational establishment, has been a stronghold of white supremacy. This is where and how the racial issue arises, and the Jewish community is being enlisted because teaching has been a Jewish preserve in New York as it was once an Irish Catholic preserve. If community control is crushed, the racial struggle will take on more violent and hateful forms to the detriment of both the black and Jewish communities.

The Jews, as the more favored and privileged group, owe the underprivileged a duty of patience, charity and compassion. It will not hurt us to swallow a few insults from overwrought blacks. It is as right to invoke the better Jewish tradition against Jewish bigotry as to invoke the better American tradition against white racism. The genocidal threat, if any, in this situation lies in the slow death and degradation to which so many blacks and Puerto Ricans are doomed in our slums. To wipe out the slums and help save their occupants would be the truest memorial to those who died in Auschwitz. When an idealistic young Mayor and the Rabbi who tried to defend him are howled down in a synagogue, it is time for the slap that can alone bring hysterics to their senses. Lindsay was saying "a Jewish philosopher—" when he was forced to leave. The philosopher he was about to quote was Spinoza. He, too, was thrown out of the synagogue in his time. We ought to have better sense today.

November 4, 1968

NIXON ABOUT TO
ABOLISH HUNGER
"FOR ALL TIME"—AGAIN

On the problems of the poor, as on everything else, the
Nixon Administration flounders about like a ship with a
broken rudder. In its first months, the word went out that
there would be no food stamp program. Then last May
[1969] a day before Secretary of Health, Education and
Welfare Finch and Secretary of Agriculture Hardin were to
appear before the Senate's McGovern Committee on Hunger, the Administration decided it would be too embarrassing to let them go up on the Hill empty-handed. So Nixon
sent Congress a food stamp message. The rhetoric had a
high caloric content:

That hunger and malnutrition should persist in a land such as
ours is embarrassing and intolerable. . . . Millions of Americans are simply too poor to feed their families properly. . . .
Something like the very honor of American democracy is at issue. . . . The moment is at hand to put an end to hunger in
America itself for all time.

To the hungry this must have sounded like the Prophet
Elijah landing with a mandate from Heaven. But the program didn't match the advertising copy. It fit Senator Mon-
dale's capsule history of the food stamp program. He said
the government "keeps authorizing dreams and appropriat-
ing peanuts." Though "the moment" was "at hand" to "put
an end to hunger . . . for all time," Congress is still waiting for the Administration to send up a bill. Even the nig-
gardly Senate Agriculture Committee has reported out a
food stamp bill better than Nixon's proposals, and it will be
among the main items of business when the Senate recon-
venes. Senator McGovern has a bill in (with 31 co-

sponsors) which would expand our meager food stamp program to five times its current size. By failing to send Congress a specific legislative proposal, the White House is delaying action in food stamps altogether.

The confusion has been compounded by the President's new message on welfare. Two-thirds of all persons on relief are in dependent families. "For dependent families," Nixon said in his welfare message, "there will be an orderly substitution of food stamps by the new direct monetary payments." The food stamp program he outlined last May would apply only to single persons or childless couples. But, according to an analysis by the National Council on Hunger and Nutrition, if food stamps are eliminated this will cut welfare standards for 87 percent of those in dependent families. Nixon said his program would be "a leap upward for many thousands of families that cannot care for themselves." This would be true only for those living in Alabama, Florida, Mississippi, South Carolina and Texas. Even with a reasonable amount of state supplementation, four-fifths of those in dependent families will end up with less to eat under Nixon's latest program to end hunger.

The principle of a national standard and the principle of a minimum welfare guarantee represent steps forward but the ballyhoo[1] had best be muted until the fine print is available in a legislative proposal. It is not a guaranteed minimum income. "A guaranteed income," Nixon said, "would undermine the incentive to work." Every welfare recipient under Nixon's plan "must also accept work or training provided suitable jobs are available, either locally or at some distance if transportation is provided." At what rate of pay and under what conditions Nixon has yet to answer.

Nixon's New Federalism, in turning over employment training to the states, threatens to reinforce old forms of oppression. In the related field of vocational training, the

---

[1] *U.S. News & World Report* called the proposals "so revolutionary" as to create unrest in Congress while *Newsweek* said they were "so sweeping that even some of his Republican Cabinet officers were left gasping for conservative breath."

states have made a poor record. In welfare administration, most of the states and localities have been unsympathetic to the poor, especially the minorities. "If you feed 'em," one Southern county commissioner told a McGovern committee staff member, "they won't work." Would such officials force welfare recipients to take substandard jobs at substandard wages under threat of removal from the welfare rolls? Could this be used to undermine wage rates? To break strikes, particularly those pitiful stirrings of the unskilled and the unorganized at the rural level?

Nixon has often said it was dangerous to raise hopes that could not be fulfilled. His welfare program violates this favorite precept. Both the poor and the well-to-do taxpayers are in for disillusionment. He promised "a complete replacement" of the present welfare system with its humiliations, but the minimums he proposes are so low that the state welfare systems, snoopers and all, must remain in existence to supplement them. "A measure of the greatness of a powerful nation," he grandiloquently began his welfare message to Congress, "is the character of the life it creates for those who are powerless to make ends meet." How could he then without blushing offer a $65-a-month minimum to the aged, the blind and the disabled? And even less than that to dependent families—$500, or little more than $40 a month, for each adult; $300, or $25 a month, for each child? In what hovel without running water can you feed, clothe and house a family on that income level?

The $1600 minimum is based ultimately on the Agriculture Department's "economy" diet of $1200 a year for a family of four. Any mother who can perform the miracles of cooking, buying and storage this requires should have no trouble obtaining an executive job in industry. The biggest disappointment is invited by Nixon's promise in Madison Avenue prose to replace welfare with "workfare." The AFL-CIO's George Meany, in an unusually sharp criticism of Nixon's plan, pointed out that "contrary to popular conception, the nation's welfare rolls today cover fewer than 100,000 able-bodied men." Even with far more day-care, it is doubtful that enough working mothers can be drawn off relief to make more than a five percent dent in the relief rolls (500,000 off 10,000,000). As for his aid to working fathers paid below the poverty level, a minimum wage of $2 an hour for a 40-hour week would bring them out of poverty faster. Why should the taxpayer subsidize the substandard employer?

September 9, 1969

THE REAL MEANING OF NIXON'S JUDICIAL PHILOSOPHIES

In the general condemnation of the President's outburst over the Carswell rejection, one point seems to have been rarely made, if at all. When Nixon spoke of the right of the South and "its legal philosophy" to be represented on the Supreme Court, few commentators observed that this only referred to the white South. Of the 50 million Southerners, about 10 million are black. For them, the Haynsworth and Carswell appointments, far from being representative, were an affront. The "legal philosophy"—as Nixon so pretentiously called it—of these two mediocre Southern judges is only white supremacy, as reflected in their foot-dragging on civil rights.

It is a very serious matter for the country that in this time of racial crisis, we have a President for whom 10 million Southern blacks are invisible, politically non-existent. This is far less excusable in a northern president than it is in the average white Southerner. Nixon's predecessor, Lyndon Johnson, whatever his other faults, never showed such a blind spot to blacks, though a Southerner, nor to Mexican-Americans, though a Texan. On the contrary, he named the first Negro Judge to the Supreme Court. Johnson would never dare imply, as Nixon did in his statement protesting Carswell's rejection, that the South had a regional philosophy different from the rest of the country's. There is, after all, only one basic American philosophy, as expressed in the Declaration and the Constitution, and imposed on a rebellious South by the Civil War. It is a little late in the day to dignify racial inequality as an alternative American philosophy with a right to a seat on the Supreme Court, and more than strange to watch a Republican President march to the strain of Dixie.

There is today another white South which the President also ignores. It may be a minority white South, but when you add its numbers to the blacks and other minorities of color, it is big enough to elect a Yarborough in Texas and to lead the recent (and integrated!) Democratic state convention in South Carolina to reject a "freedom of choice" school plank. Indeed there are few places left in the South where a candidate for public office can treat blacks as politically non-existent. To act as if the South were still lily-white and monolithic, to key one's whole strategy opportunistically to Wallace, is to undermine that growing, more thoughtful white minority in the South *and on its courts.* When Nixon says the Senate would not accept a Southern nominee he is really saying that it will not accept the only kind of nominee which serves his short-sighted strategy. To nominate a judge like Frank M. Johnson or Elbert Tuttle or Bryan Simpson from the Southern federal bench (as the Reverend Ralph Abernathy suggested here the other night) would not fit into Nixon's plans because this would please the blacks and the non-bigoted whites, and give *their* South another representative, alongside Black and Marshall. The issue is not sectionalism but Nixon's effort—as Reverend Abernathy so well said—"to revive a dead order." Instead of building on a coalition of enlightened whites and blacks, Nixon is playing to the white mob. There could be no greater disservice to our country, no more serious violation of his oath of office.

Nixon's other complaint was that Haynsworth and Carswell were rejected because of "their philosophy of strict construction of the Constitution—a philosophy that I share." This also will not stand up under closer examination. Hugo Black is a "strict constructionist"—he applies the Bill of Rights and other constitutional guaranties strictly. Nixon and Mitchell are the loose constructionists. Most crime, especially of violence, has always been a state and local police matter. What could be a looser construction of the Constitution than to bring them under federal control, as in their recent proposals on dynamiting? In the past three generations liberals have used the commerce clause to make possible all kinds of social reform. Nixon and Mitchell are using it to create a federal police, and to police not only criminals but the transportation of ideas across state lines, as in the prosecution of the Chicago Seven.

When the Supreme Court recently held seven to one that the double jeopardy clause of the Constitution forbids a state to prosecute an acquitted man a second time on substantially the same evidence, who was construing the Constitution strictly—the majority or the lone dissenter, a Nixon-style "strict constructionist," his Chief Justice Burger? Or let us take a favorite proposal of the Nixon-Mitchell era, preventive detention. What could be a looser construction of the Constitution than to hold a man in jail before trial because you think he might commit some other crime in the meantime? You have to construe the Constitution with extraordinary looseness, in fact you have to ignore its guaranties of fair trial and bail, to arrive at any such result.

Yet the Administration has a bill in Congress to allow preventive detention in federal cases involving "violent" crimes. It is trying to slip the same proposal through Congress this year in the District of Columbia crime bill "by hiding it under a misleading title." The quotation is from a speech by a Southern strict constructionist, Ervin of North Carolina. He called the attention of the Senate April 8 to a study made by the National Bureau of Standards for the Law Enforcement Assistance Administration of the Department of Justice. This showed how spurious were Attorney General Mitchell's arguments for preventive detention.

Mitchell claimed that "the pre-trial release of potentially dangerous defendants constitutes one of the most serious factors in the present crime wave." But the study showed that only five percent of those originally charged with a violent crime are rearrested for another violent crime—*arrested*, notice, not proven guilty and convicted. Ervin said the Nixon Administration was ignoring one of the most meaningful conclusions of the study. He said it "clearly shows that speedy trial alone would eliminate almost completely the small number of crimes committed by persons on bail." He told the Senate, "Our task is not to enact an unconstitutional and unwise preventive detention law but to insure that the constitutionally guaranteed right of speedy trial for all criminal suspects becomes a reality." He accused the Administration of using "the law-and-order slogan" to justify a "fundamental negation of America's constitutional traditions."

Behind Nixon's talk of the philosophy of strict construction, as behind his talk of the philosophy of the South, is plain and simple white middle-class prejudice. Preventive detention means putting blacks in jail more easily. His strict constructionism is only a legislative device for restricting the rights of the blacks and the poor generally, as when Chief Justice Burger dissented from a recent decision holding that welfare payments could not be cut off without first granting the recipients a formal hearing. The Nixon-Mitchell-Burger philosophy is to give fewer rights to the disadvantaged. It is the philosophy of the smug, the unsympathetic rich and the Southern white supremacist. That is the kind of majority outlook he hopes to create on the Supreme Court, whether by appointing mediocrities from South or North.

April 20, 1970

PART IV

Nixon: The Evil of Banality

SO WHAT'S A LITTLE
ISAIAH BETWEEN FRIENDS?

The Nixon inaugural must have set a record for the number of invocations. We counted four before Nixon took the oath and one afterward. Indeed it might be said there were six, for Nixon's own inaugural address was in the same genre, so much so that at one moment when our attention wandered we thought Billy Graham had been elected President. From Nixon's first reference to "the majesty of this moment" to the peroration in which he urged us to build a "cathedral of the spirit," we realized we were hearing a Golden Treasury of the pulpit's most venerable purple phrases. The ministry lost what the country has gained.

Isaiah is our favorite prophet. Ordinarily we would have been pleased when Nixon let it be known that he would take the oath of office on a Bible with its pages open to Isaiah. But we could not forget that Johnson—who could also sound like Billy Graham—started out by leaning heavily on Isaiah, too. His favorite quotation, particularly in his campaign against Goldwater, was Isaiah's "come, let us reason together" but it fell into disuse after he began bombing North Vietnam. Nixon chose that page of Isaiah in which the Prophet spoke of beating swords into ploughshares. This would be heartening if Nixon's speeches on the need for bigger arms spending during the campaign, and his choice for Secretary of Defense, did not seem to suggest that we might have to beat ploughshares into swords. Melvin Laird hasn't been spending his years on the House Appropriations defense subcommittee trying to sell the armed services on Isaiah. Laird has written about a Strategy Gap. Nixon has spoken about a Security Gap, a Submarine Gap and an armament Research Gap. Perhaps it would be safest to put this Isaiah incident down to a Rhetoric Gap, like the

Gospel Gap which enables Billy Graham to denounce materialism—as he did at the Inaugural—while remaining a favorite spiritual back-scratcher of the pious rich.

We would be more impressed with the peaceful sentiments expressed in the Nixon inaugural if they had not become standard fare. Kennedy and Johnson, too, spoke evangelically in their inaugurals of the terrible power of the new weaponry, the need for peace and for diversion of resources to human need. Then they added a "but" about remaining strong, and this—if strength can be measured in more arms—was serious. "Let us cooperate," Nixon said, "to reduce the burden of arms. . . . But to all those who would be tempted by weakness, let us leave no doubt that we will be as strong as we need to be. . . ." Kennedy, too, made the same pledge and then in almost the same words added, "We dare not tempt them with weakness." Kennedy proceeded to step up the arms race and Nixon is pledged to do the same. Nixon announces an era of negotiation as Johnson promised "we will be unceasing in the search for peace." In less than two months he was bombing North Vietnam. Henry Cabot Lodge was then his special adviser and soon to be Ambassador in Saigon, as he will now be Nixon's at the Paris talks. Though the objective circumstances have changed, the parallels are not reassuring.

Our Presidents at their inaugurals have all come to sound like card-carrying members of the Fellowship for Reconciliation. It's easier to make war when you talk peace. They make us the dupes of our hopes, as the newspaper headlines the morning after the inaugural about Nixon's "sacred commitment" attest. Johnson, too, snowed the country with a similar performance when he went up on Capitol Hill for a last boast-in and sob-in among his old cronies, those aged pygmies in aspic, preserved from reality by the gelatinous mutual flatteries which fill the Congressional Record. They are all g-r-e-a-t statesmen, like Lyndon and Sam and Gerry and what's-his-name. The surprise was not the last performance of Johnson-playing-Lionel-Barrymore-playing-Lyndon, but the fact that he got away with it; the press by and large acted like sob-sisters in the 1890's covering a society ball to help the poor. Amid the sniffles no one was so uncouth as to peep into Johnson's fantastic exaggerations, like his claim to be spending $68 billion "for such things as health and education" the next fiscal year. More than $35 billion of this is normal expenditure from social security, where the government takes in more from the lower brackets than it pays out, and the munificence is attested by Johnson's proposal to raise the minimum from $55 to $80 *a month*, just enough to keep a beneficiary from dying too visibly.

Johnson, too, talked of peace, but it will be years before we stop paying all the costs—fiscal and social—of his Vietnam war. He said it was "imperative . . . to resist inflation." But it wasn't imperative enough for him to impose taxes on the profits his war inflation created in the upper brackets. The poor and the black will now pay with unemployment to fight that inflation, as they paid disproportionately with their lives to fight his war. He, too, talked of the need "to scale down the level of arms among the superpowers" so that "mankind" could "view the future without fear and great apprehension." But he may have set off a new spiral when he approved the "thin" anti-ballistic missile. And new arms for a fantastically overarmed nation take first priority in his final budget.

In the masterly flim-flam of budgetary accounting, the new estimates gloss over the fact that the war this year will cost $3 billion more than we were told before. A $3.4 billion decline is promised next year (largely due to the saving on planes and explosives if we continue to stop bombing the North). *But* the savings are already whisked away in a $4 billion increase in arms expenditures in the year beginning July 1. Total military spending will be $81.5 billion, nosing past the peak of World War II—how's that for Isaiah!

The poverty program remains just short of $2 billion but arms research and development will go up $850 million to a total of $5.6 billion, including work on such new goodies as missiles which can be hidden on the ocean floor. There's not a gap Nixon mentioned that the Johnson military budget does not fill—a "new generation" of missiles (how beautifully they breed!) with multiple warheads, five squadrons of new FB-111 bombers (to keep Fort Worth and General Dynamics prosperous), $2.4 billion to give the Navy three fast new nuclear attack submarines, the quiet variety which won't disturb sleep in the ghettoes. There is more money for the Air Force's advanced bomber. Just to make sure we don't run out of new Vietnams there's three-quarters of a billion this year and a billion next for those overpriced C5A carrier planes which can get troops fast to any new trouble spot and millions more for three of those Fast Deployment Logistics ships which will take the place of foreign bases and have heavy equipment ready for the troops when the C5A's get them there. Even a submissive and somnolent Congress several years running has turned down the DPL's as an engraved invitation to more trouble, but Johnson's budget asks Congress to come and reason together with him again about the item.

No wonder this is a smooth transition. It's practically one continuous performance, and better than ever for the Pentagon. So what's a little Isaiah between friends?

January 27, 1969

UNCLE SAM'S CON MAN BUDGET

It's fortunate for the U.S. government that it is not subject to the SEC. Any corporation which filed annual financial reports like the new federal budget would run afoul of SEC accounting requirements designed to protect the investor.

Let us begin with the claim that it now has a surplus instead of a deficit. If a present-day conglomerate had among its subsidiaries an insurance company, and set up its overall annual accounts in such a way as to make it appear that the legal reserves of its insurance company were available to meet a deficit in its other business operations, that conglomerate would soon find itself hailed into court by the SEC or its own stockholders. Nixon's claim of a $5.8 billion surplus for the coming 1970 fiscal year is based on just such fiction. It is achieved by lumping the surpluses in the government's trust funds with the deficit in its normal operations. Johnson did the same thing in January when he unveiled his 1970 budget and claimed a budget surplus of $3.4 billion. The main source of both claims to a surplus lay in the huge social security funds, the government's public insurance business. These and other trust funds are segregated by law and not usable for any other purpose.

When Johnson presented his budget, Senator Williams of Delaware pointed out that the Johnson calculations of a surplus for both fiscal 1969 and 1970 were based on the existence in 1969 of a $9.3 billion and in 1970 of a $10.2 billion surplus in these trust funds. "Under the law," Williams told the Senate, "no Administration and no Congress can divert these trust funds to defray the normal operating expenses of the Government." Williams said that if this bit of deceptive accounting were eliminated, it would be seen that Johnson had a deficit of $6.9 billion instead of a surplus of $2.4 billion in fiscal 1969 and a deficit of $6.8 billion instead of a surplus of $3.4 billion in 1970. Senator Williams told me after Nixon's budget revisions were made public that all his criticism of Johnson's budget was equally applicable to Nixon's. Nixon's claimed $5.8 billion surplus for 1970 was really a deficit of $4.4 billion if the trust fund reserves were deducted.[1]

Of course this method of federal accounting has been

[1] Williams also criticized Johnson for failing to include in the 1970 budget a $2.7 billion Commodity Credit loss which the government must pay sooner or later. Nixon, too, brushed this same item under the table. To carry on the same metaphor, $2.7 billion is quite a crumb.

going on for years and of course it accurately measures the net impact on the economy of federal collections and payments from the standpoint of inflation. In earlier days this was called the "national income account" as distinguished from the administrative budget. But the administrative budget is the better index to the government's fiscal solvency, since a deficit in normal operations does not become visible in the consolidated cash account or "unified budget" until the deficit has grown so large that it even wipes out the surplus in the trust funds. The danger signal blinks later in the "unified budget." Earlier budget messages used to give both the consolidated account *and* the administrative budget. But though the basic 1970 budget presentation takes four separate volumes which total 2,012 pages (and weigh, even in paperback, seven pounds), there is no place in it where one can find the administrative budget. Why admit that the operations of the government are still in the red, if you can make it look as if they are in the black? The $10.2 billion surplus in the trust funds helps to dampen inflation but it is not available to buy bombs for B-52's or to feed the hungry.

The "unified budget" has another effect. It understates the extent to which the war machine eats up public revenues. The first chart in the budget message purports to show that 41 cents of every dollar in expenditure goes to the military. But if the trust funds of the government are separated from the rest of its activities, then the military share is about 55 cents. The sums Americans pay into social security trust funds for unemploment, old-age and other insurance are no different in this sense from the sums they pay private insurance companies. There is no more reason to lump public insurance than private insurance funds with the general revenues of the government in measuring the impact of military expenditures.

The way to begin to see the real fiscal impact of the war machine is to begin with the memorandum line on page 526 of the main budget volume where "receipts by source" are shown. This discloses that of $198 billion in receipts, $51 billion is in trust funds. This leaves available for the general purposes of the government $147 billion. If you next turn to the table on "budget outlay by function," you will find $81.5 billion for national defense. So national defense takes 55 percent of this $147 billion. Then if you look more closely you will see near the foot of the expenditure table $2.8 billion for civilian and military pay increases. The Pentagon's share of that, for its employees in *and out* of uniform (the Pentagon employs nearly one-half of all the *civilian* employees in the government) is $2.5 billion. When that additional pay item is added, the total for national defense is $83 billion, or better than 56 cents of every dollar available. That is a third (actually 36 percent) more than the 41 cents shown in the first budget chart.[2]

At the same time, lumping the trust funds with the general revenues exaggerates the government's contributions to health and welfare. Johnson boasted that outlays for health and welfare in his 1970 budget would be $55 billion, "which is 28 percent of federal outlays . . . more than double the level prevailing in 1964" when his War on Poverty was launched. But $42.9 billion of this was to come "from self-financed trust funds for retirement and social insurance and Medicare." So almost four-fifths of this benevolent munificence was from the beneficiaries. Only the difference, $12.1 billion, represents outlays from the general revenues. That is about 8 percent, not 28 percent.

While the government was to pay $42.9 billion from these insurance and health trust funds, it would collect a total of $45.8 billions in fiscal 1970, or almost $3 billion

[2] I can remember when a feature of the annual federal budget presentation was a chart showing how much was absorbed by past, present and future wars. This added military expenditures, veterans' benefits and interest charges, the last item because past wars are the real reason for the public debt. These three items in the 1970 budget total more than $106 billion and will take more than 70 percent of the general revenues. Secretary Laird said the other day that much of the Soviet Union's space activity was really military. This is also true of our space program. The funds spent on rocket boosters to reach the moon also improve the technology of mass murder by intercontinental ballistic missile. If space is added to the other three items, the total is $110 billion, or almost 75 percent of the $147 billion available.

more than it paid out. This addition to the surplus in the trust funds is, of course, anti-inflationary, for it cuts down purchasing power, but this is purchasing power at the bottom of the economic pyramid, taken from those least able to pay. Regarded as taxation, social security deductions from payroll represent a savagely regressive—and, unlike so many income taxes, inescapable—form of taxation. I can remember, when social security legislation was first being drafted in the early days of the New Deal, writing editorials proposing—as did other liberals and radicals—that it be financed out of income taxes so as to create a more equitable distribution of wealth, taking funds from the top of the pyramid to ease poverty at the bottom. The Social Security system adopted, which we still have, essentially takes from the poor what it gives them, and gives less than it takes.

The Welfare System and the War on Poverty were admissions that social security was abysmally inadequate. But Johnson's War on Poverty was made to look far more extensive than it was, and Nixon's revisions use the same deceptive computations. "Our 1970 Revised Budget," says a Budget Bureau statement of April 14 [1969], "involves *a 10 percent increase over FY '69 in spending for the poor* [italics in the original]. This reflects our deep commitment to the under-privileged." The Budget Bureau statement did not explain, however, that this also represented a cut of $300 million in Johnson's poverty recommendations for fiscal 1970—nor that much of this bloated estimate is padded out with normal payments from social security.

Johnson claimed he would spend $27.2 billion on "Federal Aid to the Poor." Nixon out of that "deep commitment" revised this downward to $26.9 billion. The biggest item in Johnson's, as in Nixon's Federal Aid to The Poor compilation (at page 47 of the main budget message volume) is $13.5 billion for "income assistance." My curiosity was piqued by a discrepancy of almost $10 billion between this item and a passage at pages 42–3 of the *Budget in Brief*. This said that federally aided public welfare would in fiscal

1970 provide assistance to a monthly average of 10 million individuals at a total cost of $7 billion. "The federal share," it said, "was $3.7 billion." When I asked the Budget Bureau where the rest of the claimed figure of $13.5 billion came from, I got this compilation (in millions):

600	administrative expenses
6,300	old-age pensions
400	R.R. retirement pensions
500	unemployment insurance
2,100	Veterans Administration[3]
$9,900	Total

The figures given me were "rounded" and so the final totals do not quite match, but this $9.9 billion of "padding" explains how that $3.7 billion in federal welfare income assistance was made to look like $13.5 billion.

It is fortunate that few people on welfare spend their spare time reading the federal budget. It would foment riots. The Budget Bureau "press kit" for Nixon's revisions of the 1970 budget says these involve "hard choices" and are part of the Nixon Administration's "concern for the poor." Nixon added $300 million for dependent children but squeezed $200 million of this out of a projected increase in our pitifully low old-age pensions. "For the aged," the same Budget Bureau explanation says, "a 7 percent social security cost-of-living increase is included in the revised 1970 budget." It does not explain that this is a revision *downward* from the 10 percent increase recommended by Johnson, nor that Nixon also shelved Johnson's proposal to increase the minimum from $55 a month to $80 a month. There are two million Americans—believe it or not—now expected to enjoy retirement on $55 a month! Instead of getting a $25 raise to $80 a month, they will only receive the general 7 percent increase, though I was told this would be

[3] The Budget Bureau, when I asked what the Veterans Administration had to do with the War on Poverty, explained that 80 percent of veterans' pensions, 75 percent of veterans' survivors' pensions and 20 percent of other veterans' benefits had been counted as "Federal Aid to The Poor" in the Johnson table!

"rounded off" so that instead of a mere $3.85, they would get $4 or $5 a month more. This could bring them up to $60 a month. Thanks to the Administration's concern for them, moreover, the revised legislation "includes liberalization of the social security retirement test" allowing them to earn more outside income without having it deducted from their pensions. The liberalization turns out to be $120 a year, about $2 a week,[4] and raises the ceiling on allowed earning to $36 a week! What a *dolce vita*!

Roughly a billion each was cut out of social security and out of the military budget by Nixon. This symmetry of sacrifice is deceptive. Before anyone starts dropping pennies into cups for the Pentagon, I would like to lift the curtain on another murky corner of the budget. To evaluate the Nixon military "economies" you have to go back for another look at the Johnson budget for 1970. This projected a drop of $3.5 billion in the costs of our "Southeast Asia operations." This was to be our first dividend of the road to peace, the money to be saved principally by ending the bombing of the North. Johnson in making up his budget could have allocated this $3.5 billion to welfare or to the rebuilding of the cities. Instead Johnson's budget allocated $4.1 billion more to military spending *unconnected with the Vietnam war*. This accounts for the fact that in his 1970 budget the cost of national defense rose by more than half a billion dollars over 1969 despite the projected $3.5 billion drop in the costs of the Vietnam war.

This favored treatment of the military machine has to be seen against the background of a figure revealed in the Nixon revisions. His revised budget estimates for fiscal 1969, which ends next June 30, disclose that $7.3 billion had to be squeezed out of the normal civilian and welfare opera-

[4] The liberalization will allow a maximum of $1800 a year without deductions. By comparison retired professional military men (20 years service) are allowed under the Dual Compensation Act of 1964 to fill Civil Service jobs paying up to $30,000 and still collect their full pensions, a privilege not given other veterans. Under the new pay raise this will mean retired army officers can draw up to $50,000 a year in Civil Service pay and pensions.

tions of the government in this fiscal year to meet the expenditure ceilings imposed by Congress as a condition for voting the 10 percent surtax. This squeeze over and above the original 1969 budget was made necessary by an unexpected rise in certain "uncontrollable" items exempt from mandatory ceilings. *The biggest uncontrollable item was the Vietnam war which cost $3 billion more in fiscal 1969 than had been budgeted for it.* So all kinds of services were starved in 1969 to meet the swollen costs of Vietnam in fiscal 1969. Yet when a $3.5 billion drop in Vietnam war costs were projected for fiscal 1970, the amount saved was allocated not to the depleted domestic sector but to the growth of the war machine.

Nixon's cut of $1 billion in military outlays can only be evaluated properly if you first start by observing that it was *a cut in a projected $4.1 billion increase* in military spending. The cut came out of a lot of fat, whereas the cut in health, education and welfare, and domestic services, came close to the bone and gristle. The second point to be made about the military cuts is that they represent no real overhaul of the bloated military budget. Robert S. Benson, former aid to the Pentagon Comptroller, showed (in the March issue of *The Washington Monthly*) how easily $9 billion could be cut out of military spending without impairing national security. But the three main "economies" cited by the Nixon backgrounders are sleight-of-hand. One is "lower consumption of ammunition in Vietnam." This looks optimistic in view of the enemy offensive and our own search-and-destroy missions; as in other years, this may be one of those preliminary underestimates which turn up later in a supplemental request for funds. The second "saving" comes out of the shift from Sentinel to Safeguard, but the reduction in fiscal 1970 will be at the expense of larger ultimate costs. Indeed, while the Nixon estimates show that Safeguard will ultimately cost $1.5 billion more, McGraw-Hill's authoritative DMS, Inc., service for the aerospace industry puts the final cost $4.3 billion higher, or a total of $11 billion without cost overruns (which DMS expects). The third "economy" cited is $326 million saved (as a *Washington Post* editorial noted tartly April 3) by "postponing procurement of a bomber missile (SRAM) that doesn't yet work." Like all else in the Nixon Administration, the budget revisions represent feeble compromises which give the military machine priority over the growing urban, racial and student crises.

May 5, 1969

SAME OLD FORMULAS, SAME TIRED RHETORIC

In an exchange of toasts at the White House last month, the Australian Prime Minister drew an implied comparison between Lincoln and Nixon. Walt Rostow, too, used to get Lyndon Johnson's juices flowing in the morning by telling him he was just like Lincoln. The Australian got so carried away that he ended up by demonstrating his native talent with the boomerang. If Lincoln had not persevered against the Copperheads and the Horace Greeleys, Mr. Gorton explained, there would today be "a slave autocracy in the South . . . But there would have been no United States." Since Lincoln and the North were trying to reunite the country by force of arms ("aggression") against the wishes of the Southern states for independence ("self-determination"), Mr. Gorton's flattery was clearly beginning to rebound. The more he went on the more it sounded like a toast to Ho Chi Minh.

Mr. Gorton's analogy invites elaboration. If John Brown had succeeded in raising a slave revolt, if the North had helped the rebels, and if England had intervened on the side of the slaveholders (as the Tories later wanted to), the situation would have been comparable to the Vietnamese war. Suppose further that England, tired of a costly distant conflict, had proposed that all "non-Southern" forces withdraw, thus putting Lincoln's Unionist armies in the same "foreign" category as Britain's. Suppose the slaves were asked to lay down their arms while the slaveholders kept their army intact, and trust to "free elections" under a vague promise of international supervision but with the slaveholder regime still in power. Suppose that regime in Richmond were filling the jails with spokesmen for poor white, non-slaveholding and pro-peace elements while Britain—heavily arming this regime in preparation for its own troop withdrawal—piously insisted that its only purpose was to give the South the right of self-determination. That is where Nixon stands today.

For those who wonder just what Nixon was up to in his May 14 peace proposals, the Nixon-Gorton visit offers another source of illumination. Except for New Zealand, with its 150 token soldiers, Australia is the only white country which has put troops beside our own in the effort to revive the white man's burden in Asia. The war is almost as unpopular in Australia as here, and Gorton's opposition—the Labor party—led the protest demonstrations which greeted Ky two years ago in Australia. The conservative coalition Gorton heads was Johnson's faithful junior partner. Gorton was here only a week before Nixon's Vietnam speech. If Nixon were contemplating any real departure in policy, he would be leaving Gorton out on a limb. It would be necessary to prepare Australian public opinion. But nothing in their exchanges reflected any change in policy; they spoke as simple-mindedly as Johnson of their joint effort "to help South Vietnam preserve its independence."

Those who are working themselves into euphoria by wishful exegesis of what Nixon did *not* say in his May 14 address would be wise to pause a moment over what Nixon and Gorton did not say in their exchanges a week earlier. These, as expected, attracted little attention in this country, and did not have to take American peace sentiment into

account.[1] The Nixon farewell statement, which Gorton
said was framed with his agreement and served as a final
communiqué, spoke of their talks on "Vietnam and regional
security." A continued U.S.-Australian protectorate over
Southeast Asia was implied. Nixon welcomed, and promised to support, Australia's decision to keep troops in Ma-
laysia and Singapore when the British leave two years
hence, forever ending the Kipling era east of Suez. But not
a single word was said about the negotiations in Paris, or the
hope of a turn toward peace.

Nixon, like Johnson, is playing for time. His May 14 address strongly recalls Johnson's at Johns Hopkins in April
1965. Johnson deluded many people into believing that he
was moving toward peace at the very moment he was committing the first U.S. combat troops to the South. The only
remarkable thing about the Nixon address is that at one
point he seemed to be pulling his own leg. When Nixon
said "repeating the old formulas and the tired rhetoric of
the past is not enough," he seemed to be setting himself up
for the cartoonists. If I were running the Secret Service I
would find out who wrote that and take him down to the
White House cellar for interrogation under the bright
lights. For as Senator Gore showed in a devastating analysis
on the Senate floor May 20, the speech was full of old formulas and tired rhetoric picked up almost verbatim from
Johnson and Rusk. Even Nixon's titillating hints about free
elections and a neutral South Vietnam were also uttered, as
Gore found, in almost the same words by Rusk in 1966.
The parallels with Johnson sound as if Nixon was down on
the ranch. If this weren't politics, it would be plagiarism.

The speech is so tricky it has everybody confused except
Henry Kissinger. "Proponents leak stories that the President is sending subtle signals to the Reds that he'd let them
share in a new Saigon government as part of a peace package," the *Wall St. Journal* said May 23. "Opponents warn
this would bring the 'disguised defeat' Nixon had vowed

[1] Indeed the only place the texts are available is in the *Weekly Compilation of Presidential Documents* for May 19.

not to accept. White House aides insist no decision has been made." Never have there been so many hints with so little substance.

You can read in Chalmers Roberts in the *Washington Post* (May 18) that silence gives consent and that what Nixon didn't say May 14 really means he is ready to accept even an interim coalition government. This was "spelled out by persons in a position to know," Roberts wrote ecstatically. But gravitation being what it is, what goes up must come down, and he added a *but*— "The U.S. cannot accept settlement terms which would turn the South over to the Communists and make a mockery of the years of American and South Vietnamese bloodletting." The only sure non-mockery, it would seem, is to maintain in power the same oligarchy we have imposed on the South for 15 years.

On the other hand you may read in David Lawrence (May 21) that the Nixon Administration has "at last" decided that it will not tolerate the continuance of heavy attacks and is not ruling out drastic reprisals which "could mean the resumption at any moment of the bombing of North Vietnam and even a blockade of Haiphong harbor." Obviously the White House is handing out different lines of poop. Richard Wilson (Washington *Star*, May 21) reports jubilantly that before Nixon went on TV May 14 he gave an extemporaneous résumé to his top-level officials. They not only applauded but "there was no doubt what they were applauding." The main emphasis was on "not quitting" and on Nixon's "unpleasant options" if Hanoi does not accept mutual withdrawal. These include "a massive fire-bomb raid to destroy Hanoi." We'll put 'em back in the Stone Age yet. Senator Hugh Scott, the GOP whip, dropped hints of the same kind after Senator Kennedy—in the wake of "Hamburger Hill"—attacked the bloody nonsense of charging up any hill a well dug-in enemy baits for U.S. attack.

In the blizzard of hints, there is also a preview of what Nixon may say to Thieu on Midway June 8. It is hinted that if one reads the fine print closely one will see that Sai-

gon holds a secure veto over the international supervisory
body to verify withdrawals "and for any other purpose
agreed upon between the two sides." The elections, too,
would be held under "agreed procedures" and agreed
means the agreement of the Thieu regime. While Nixon
takes the high road, Thieu will have the low, and when domestic opinion gets tired of seeing the Reds reject Nixon's
"generous" offers, the iron will be hot and the Pentagon
hopes it can strike again.

June 2, 1969

MIDWAY TO
A NGUYEN VAN NIXON ERA

Two decades ago Karl Mundt and Richard Nixon were
comrades in arms on the House Un-American Activities
Committee. Long before Joe McCarthy, they were our
foremost practitioners of McCarthyism. When Nixon said
at Beadle State College in South Dakota on his way to Midway, "In public life, we have seen reputations destroyed by
smear . . . We have heard . . . sly voices of malice,
twisting facts" he was providing a perfect description of
their own activities in those years. A satirist, seeking savagely to caricature America, could not have done better
than Nixon preaching the virtues of a free society at a ceremony dedicating a library named for Mundt. The only time
Mundt ever came close to a book was to see whether or not
it might have been written by a Red. Their main achievement was the creation, for the first time in our history, of
an official agency designed to police public thinking. Their
Mundt-Nixon bill, fathered up a dark alley by the U.S.
Chamber of Commerce, was fought as unconstitutional by

conservative leaders of the American bar and opposed by Tom Clark, then Attorney General. It was vetoed by President Truman as an attempt at "thought control."

Thanks to the anti-Red hysteria which marked the early months of the Korean war, Congress passed it over his veto. It created a Subversive Activities Control Board—the very name is redolent of Inquisition rather than free society—but Supreme Court decisions have left it an empty shell. It was supposed to set up a blacklist of Reds, to force them to put a Scarlet Letter label on their publications and broadcasts, and to deny them the right to travel abroad. All these efforts have been struck down as unconstitutional. The SACB is a ghostly reminder of the fascistic ideas which were written into American law under the guise of fighting Communism. Mundt and Nixon were a long way from Jefferson in those years. There is little reason to believe them much closer today, when Nixon has appointed three heroes of the witch-hunters to key posts: Burger, the defender of "faceless informer" testimony, to be Chief Justice; Roger Robb, the prosecutor of J. Robert Oppenheimer, to the Court of Appeals for the District of Columbia; and Otto Otepka, the pet State Department stool pigeon of congressional inquisitors like Eastland, to a $36,000-a-year job on the Subversive Activities Control Board. It may be no accident that Nixon's little lecture on freedom never once mentioned the Bill of Rights.

Nixon had to find a very out-of-the-way college to get away with a commencement address which claimed for itself "the honesty of straight talk" without saying a word about the war. He also had to be a long way from nowhere to get away with his description of black demands for open admission to such schools as New York's City College. "Instead of seeking to raise lagging students up to meet the college standards," Nixon said, "the cry now is to lower the standards to meet the students. This is the old familiar self-indulgent cry for the easy way." This was extraordinarily insensitive. Whatever its merits, the demand for open enrollment for graduates of ghetto high schools is hardly a form of self-indulgence. On the contrary it reflects the desire of the blacks fortunate enough to be in college to open the doors wider to the less fortunate, and to force better teaching in ghetto high schools. The C.C.N.Y. proposals, for example, are only a more modest variant of the open enrollment to all high school graduates which exists in many state colleges.[1] It was unfair so to misrepresent black demands in that faraway lily-white forum. If "passionate concern," as Nixon said, "gets nowhere without dispassionate analysis," it was his obligation to speak soberly of his own plans for higher education. But that would have gotten him back to the war, and the whole web of lies would come apart if one strand were treated honestly.

Nixon's commencement address next day at the Air Force Academy was another example of his tendency to sound like Billy Graham while practicing the below-the-belt in-fighting he perfected in the House of Representatives. The real issues now raising a storm in Congress over military spending and military power cannot be seriously discussed with a man who talks of "unilateral disarmers" and "neo-isolationists." This is the old smear-and-run tactics of the old Nixon. The speech was low demagogy, full of *non sequiturs* and floosy historical analogies. But what it said is clear enough. Nixon is determined to pursue the course of the Pax Americana. This means no reduction in military spending or military power, and it reveals, as in a lightning flash, how illusory it is to expect any move toward disarmament from this Administration. He speaks rather of "control of arms" and only "in the context of other specific moves to reduce tension around the world." That is the old Dulles dream of forcing political concessions as the price of arms negotiations.

The Air Force speech is the best key to the charade on Midway Island. A President who believes that the U.S. must be the world's policeman is headed for more Vietnams, and is unlikely (as he said) to accept a "disguised defeat" in getting out of this one. The token withdrawal,

[1] Including, as I learned by phone, Beadle State itself.

which may prove to be largely support or kitchen troops, is aimed to appease and mislead opinion at home. The best guide to the realities lies in the astringent comments of the two Senators closest to the military. Russell said the withdrawal of 25,000 men "is of no great significance" and "will not substantially reduce American casualties." Stennis said he had no "high hopes" that the South Vietnamese army would soon be able to take over the war. If Nixon has his way we may keep troops in Vietnam indefinitely, as we have in Korea and Western Europe, to man "the frontiers of freedom."

This is the meaning of Pax Americana, and if it leads to unrest at home, he is ready for it. "We have the power to strike back as need be," he said at Beadle State. "The nation has suffered other attempts at insurrection." Though he proclaims an era of negotiation abroad, he is preparing for confrontation at home. That helicopter spraying 50 pounds of CS gas indiscriminately over campus demonstrators, nearby elementary schools and hospital facilities in the Berkeley People's Park clash may be a preview of what can be expected elsewhere. Reagan, the National Guard and the police treated fellow Americans with the mindless and mechanical brutality we mete out in Vietnam. We are beginning to repeat here all the errors we made there. Nixon is as little responsive to his opposition as Thieu is to his. Thieu returned from Midway so emboldened that he held a press conference threatening that anyone who even advocated a coalition with the NLF would be "severely punished." Instead of spreading freedom to Vietnam, Nixon may soon be reducing it here. Instead of de-Americanizing the war, we are beginning to Vietnamize America. We may be moving toward a Nguyen Van Nixon era, combining the worst of both regimes.

June 16, 1969

NIXON IN THE FOOTSTEPS OF
POPEYE'S ELDER STATESMAN

A President with troops scattered around the globe can always find some excuse for action "to protect them." The successful assertion of Congressional authority over the war-making powers of the President is not a constitutional problem. The real problem to which Congress and the country should address themselves lies in the nature of our foreign policy and the size of our military establishment. As long as we have navies on every sea, bases on every continent, Green Berets for intervention and C-5A's for swift intercontinental transport, the chances of stumbling into new Vietnams and Cambodias—or worse—will remain high.

This basic question was hardly touched upon in the Senate debate over the Cooper-Church amendment. The rationale for the expansionist course we have been pursuing since the Truman Doctrine was put by one of Nixon's Republican supporters, Senator Clifford P. Hansen of Wyoming. He said World Wars I and II had taught us the "hard lesson" that we had to maintain an active role in keeping the peace "or we will be forced to fight big wars." To pull out of the war in Southeast Asia, *or anywhere else that the President thought our involvement necessary*, "would be," Hansen said, "to abdicate our responsibilities as a great nation and as a force for justice and liberty." This is the basic premise of our disastrous involvement in Indochina but it was not challenged. The supporters of the Cooper-Church amendment were too busy splitting enough constitutional hairs to muster a majority.

The real lesson of the two world wars was just the opposite. The lesson was that no single power, or combination of powers, was strong enough to keep the peace, that only a world organization could save mankind from a fresh catastrophe. It was this realization which led to the League of Nations and afterward to the United Nations. If the UN fails, it is unlikely that mankind will have another chance. These vital truths are receding from public consciousness. When the UN held its twenty-fifth anniversary on June 26 in San Francisco, neither the President nor the Secretary of State put in an appearance or bothered to send a message. This was the first anniversary not addressed by an American President. Truman, Eisenhower and Johnson each honored the UN's birthday. This may well be dismissed as hypocrisy but at least the sinners turned up in church. This time the affair was ignored. Even in the rebellious Senate no one marked the occasion. U Thant's anniversary address was hardly noticed in the press, though its insight and humanism shine like secular Gospel beside the inanities and evasions of Nixon's efforts to represent his Cambodian search-and-destroy operation as an Indochinese Stalingrad.

In his TV interview on Cambodia, Nixon conjured up the danger of a "rampant isolationism" if we were forced out of Indochina. A President who says he fears isolationism ought to be a supporter of the UN. But when people like Nixon speak against isolationism they are not advocating internationalism. What they fear is a revulsion against militarism and imperialism. The Pax Americana is the "internationalism" of Standard Oil, Chase Manhattan and the Pentagon. Nixon is, it is true, trying somewhat to cut down American commitments abroad under irresistible fiscal pressures, White House briefers speak of abandoning our world policeman role, but the alternative they offer is not a revitalized UN but the so-called Guam Doctrine. This is imperialism by proxy. We may be on the verge of imposing quotas against the Orient's low-wage textiles but we are eager to buy its low-wage soldier-power. The Guam Doctrine will be seen in Asia as a rich white man's idea of fighting a war: we handle the elite airpower while coolies do the killing on the ground.

Unfortunately, faith in victory by airpower and combat-by-coolie is so deeply ingrained in American thinking that it was sometimes hard to tell doves from hawks in the Cooper-Church debate. "The argument has been made," Cooper said, "that our amendment scuttles the Guam Doctrine." He said its purpose was merely to require Congressional approval before extending the doctrine to Cambodia again. "Nothing in the Cooper-Church amendment," Church assured the Senate, "would prevent Asians from helping Asians." He called this "a viable and valid cause." Helping is quite a euphemism for what we have been getting Asians to do to each other. Church said the amendment would not prevent the Thais or the South Vietnamese from fighting "for the Lon Nol government." It would merely require prior Congressional approval for "the kind of undercover arrangements that were used to make it so profitable for Thailand, South Korea and the Philippines to send their forces to Vietnam." It may sound to Asians as if the doves merely wanted to drive a harder bargain for their services.

The Cooper-Church restrictions on U.S. airpower over Cambodia may also prove too subtle for the Oriental mind. The amendment does not prohibit U.S. bombing of Cambodia nor U.S. close air support of South Vietnamese or Thai forces *in* Cambodia. It only forbids "direct" air support to Lon Nol's forces. The word "direct" was added on motion of Senator Jackson (D. Wash.). It was foreshadowed by Secretary Laird's earlier explanation that while we were only going to bomb enemy supply lines in Cambodia, Lon Nol troops who just happened to be in the same area might derive "ancillary benefits" from it. No Secretary of Defense has shown a finer genius for semantics.

The Guam Doctrine may be traced back to that elder statesman, Wimpy, in the Popeye comic strip. Wimpy in a crisis always manfully suggests, "Let's you and him fight." In trying this out on Asia, Nixon hardly pays a compliment to the astuteness of its ruling classes, the world's oldest merchants. They were taking customers tenderly to the cleaners in their bazaars when the progenitors of Anglo-American civilization were still painting themselves a bright baby blue. The first time we tried Wimpy-Nixon statecraft was in

China. There the Asians on our side ended by making business, not war. They sold whole armies to the Asians on the other side and retired with the swag to Taiwan. SEATO's latest meeting, like that of "free Asia" in Djakarta a few weeks earlier, indicates no rush to man the Cambodian "frontier of freedom." Indonesia, the pride and joy of our anti-Communists, flatly turned down Pnom Penh's request for arms. SEATO's final communiqué "expressed understanding" for Lon Nol's appeal. The Thais are waiting to see how much we are willing to pay. If the price isn't high enough, they'll come to terms with China. To them this may not seem to be the fate worse than death we proclaim it. Japan deals with China. So does Burma. No Chinese planes, after all, are devastating Asia. Mao's Little Red Book doesn't look as scary as a B-52. Why be an American-style anti-Communist if you can't make an honest buck on it?

"The prospect suddenly loomed," Nixon said in his formal report explaining his latest *incursion*, "of Cambodia's becoming virtually one large base area for attack anywhere into South Vietnam along the 600 miles of the Cambodian frontier." What happens when that prospect suddenly looms up again? This is the question he never answered in his TV interview. Do we go back in, bomb Hanoi, invade the North or commit some larger folly? The least Congress can do is pass the McGovern-Hatfield bill and set a firm date on our withdrawal from the Indochinese morass. Not enough Asians are going to fight Asians for us even if the price is right.

July 13, 1970

PART V

The Menace of Militarism

McNAMARA AND
THE MILITARISTS

The catchword most often associated with Robert S. Mc-Namara's seven years as Secretary of Defense was "systems analysis." Yet the greatest deficiency in his book, *The Essence of Security*, which brings together his most important public papers during those years is his incapacity for analyzing systems, though of another order. No one would guess from these antiseptic pages that there are such things as militarism, or a military-industrial complex, or just plain politics, and that they represent *systems*, i.e., inescapable relationships which affected the problems McNamara faced in the Pentagon and the decisions he made.

McNamara voices all the stereotypes of liberal humanitarianism, but he keeps them free from the grime of reality. He argues for wider public knowledge and participation in defense problems, and says we must not be frightened away by their complexity. But the only complexity with which he deals is the minor one of weaponry. He omits the other and greater social complexities in which decisions of weaponry are enmeshed. He reminds one of a mid-Victorian novelist writing without mention of sweat or sex.

Let me cite two simple but fateful decisions—one at the very threshold, the other at the end of his stewardship. Both sharply raised the tempo of the arms race, and involved—as he himself admits—billions of wasted dollars without in any way adding to national safety; indeed, they magnified the dimensions of peril. One was his surrender to Kennedy on the missile gap, the other was his surrender to Johnson on the anti-ballistic missile. Both represented the victory of politics over reason, and of military-industrial interests over real considerations of security. An informed public would have been a powerful ally against both decisions; and McNamara tried in some degree to marshal it. But how can an effective opinion be created if men as able as McNamara are squeamish about telling the full truth?

There is a striking difference between this farewell message by the ablest civilian manager our military establishment ever had and those of our two greatest soldier presidents. That difference in the end may prove a disservice, outweighing all the managerial and budgetary reforms with which McNamara is credited. Washington in his Farewell Address warned against the danger to liberty in "an overgrown military establishment," and Eisenhower provided a graphic new term for an old problem when he warned against the "military-industrial complex." These two warnings provide fundamental insights into basic institutional dangers, and the warnings were given weight because they came from such honored military men.

But McNamara after seven years of wrestling with the military bureaucracy nowhere even uses the term or touches on the meaning of militarism as a social phenomenon. On the contrary, he is so blind to the intrinsic nature of military establishments and the mentality they develop that he advocates new social missions for the Pentagon, particularly in education! He seems unaware of the social consequences when he proposes to apply on a larger scale at home those "civic action" military programs we have helped to launch in Latin America. "Quite apart from the projects themselves," he says of this Latin experience, "the program powerfully alters the negative image of the military man as the oppressive preserver of the status quo." This is public relations, not social engineering. It may change the image in glossy North American publications, but not the reality in Latin America.

McNamara seems unaware that the fruit of all this civic action our Marines began to launch a half century ago has been a succession of Neros like Somoza, Batista, and Trujillo. The same tough-guy types and the same authoritarian temperaments are bred by our own—and every—military establishment. It does not speak well for McNamara that after so many turbulent years of close association with these men McNamara seems to have missed the point. This master of quantification seems poorly equipped for factors which escape measurement—like the quality of men and institutions. His proposal that the Pentagon move into social problems has now been taken up by his successor, Clark Clifford, a better political operator but without McNamara's enormous energy and grasp of detail. In a speech September 26 [1968] Clifford said he had asked his aides to draw up for the new administration plans under which the military services could help "in alleviating some of our most pressing domestic problems." This is the road to Argentina and Peru.

The most striking example of McNamara's shortsightedness in this area lies in his attitude toward the concept of the military-industrial complex. A certain complacency, perhaps conceit, leads McNamara to gloss it over. Several years before Eisenhower launched the famous phrase, Lieutenant General James M. Gavin, after his retirement in 1958 as Chief of Research and Development in the Pentagon, touched on the fierce pressures the arms manufacturers, with their allies in Congress and the military, are able to exert. In his book *War and Peace in the Space Age*, he said it took "the judgment of Solomon and no little political fortitude" to resist them. McNamara seems so confident that he possessed both that, in a farewell newspaper interview he gave the Associated Press (Washington *Star*, February 4, 1968), he dismissed the dangers against which Gavin warned. His interviewer, Saul Pett, asked McNamara whether he shared Eisenhower's concern about the military-industrial complex. "I don't," McNamara replied, "as long as the Secretary of Defense operates as he should, examining all the factors of a problem and making decisions on his own analysis, regardless of the pressures applied to him." [1] The reply is not re-

[1] McNamara's successor has taken a step further in the process of dulling public awareness. "I am convinced today, after six months in this office," Secretary of Defense Clifford said complacently on September 26, "that the dangers General Eisenhower warned against were real dangers. But I am also convinced that they have been avoided through

ally responsive. It does not touch on the problem—the pressures which *prevent* the Secretary from operating "as he should."

The military-industrial complex has been a reality ever since war, in the latter part of the last century, became big business. It made its debut in the naval rivalry which enriched steel and shipbuilding companies in England and Germany and helped to bring on World War I. The power of the military-industrial alliance has grown with the cost of armaments and the magnitude of military spending since World War II. It is embodied in a network of trade associations that link the defense industries to the Pentagon. Like many of the corporations themselves, these organizations are staffed by a multitude of retired generals and admirals. Their pressures distort military decision and national policy. No doubt McNamara overcame these pressures in many intra-mural controversies, as in the shelving of the nuclear powered airplane, the Skybolt missile, the RS-70 supersonic bomber, and the Dynasoar program. But from an overall point of view, the military-industrial complex never had it so good as in the McNamara years. Eisenhower's last military budget was $44 billion; McNamara's last was almost twice that amount. The monster fattened even as McNamara strove mightily to keep its nose clean in public. It might even be said that he saved it from its own excesses. He was more its nursemaid than its master.

If the President backs the Secretary of Defense, McNamara asked his AP interviewer in what was intended to be a clincher, "how can the military-industrial complex get to

the checks and balances of our governmental system." This soothing bit of banality came in an address to the National Security Industrial Association, perhaps the most powerful single component of the armament lobby, and in the midst of many signs that the military-industrial complex was riding higher than ever, including Clifford's own abandonment, on *Meet The Press*, September 29, of McNamara's long effort to make the country understand that the concept of nuclear superiority was meaningless. One would be tempted to say that the sky's the limit now on the arms race, if the skies of space were not the very scene of its coming intensification.

him?" He said he was backed by both Kennedy and Johnson, as no doubt on many occasions he was. But he did not mention their failure to back him in two of his most momentous decisions. It was the political power of the military-industrial complex operating through the Presidency, which forced McNamara against his better knowledge and judgment to acquiesce, when he took office, in the costly fraud of the "missile gap," and which also forced him, as he left office, to participate in the nonsense about building a "thin" anti-missile defense against China. Yet nowhere in the index nor in the chaste pages of *The Essence of Security* is there any reference to the military-industrial complex. The nearest that McNamara comes to this indelicate fact of life in the Pentagon is when he writes, "Every hour of every day the Secretary is confronted by a conflict between the national interest and the parochial interests of particular industries, individual services, or local areas." This is flutteringly vague. No one would guess from that pallid little sentence, or anything else in the book, what enormous pressures the arms lobby can generate or the major occasions on which they overwhelmed McNamara himself. Yet to repeat the phrase McNamara chose as title of his book, "the essence of security" lies not so much in any external enemy as in controlling these interests and the momentum of the arms race from which they profit. This is what we most need defense against.

It may be urged on McNamara's behalf that these are official speeches in which he could not afford to be wholly candid. But so were Washington's and Eisenhower's. In any case the excuse implies that the Secretary was unable, as a prisoner of forces stronger than himself, to tell the whole truth. But this excuse attests to the power of the institutional forces whose potency he disparages. Now that he is out of the Pentagon, he could have touched upon them in a preface, but perhaps the admission would have been too much for his pride. McNamara is at bottom a bright schoolboy who hates to have anything less than A-plus on his report card; his idealized image is the No. 1 Whiz Kid. To admit the realities would be to admit that he was not wholly capable of mastering them.

The fact is that McNamara arrived in Washington an innocent country lad from the bucolic simplicities of the automobile business. He seemed never to have heard that dirty eight-letter word *politics*. He discovered on reading the secret reports when he took office that there was no missile gap, and proceeded in all fresh innocence and enthusiasm to tell this to the press as if it were glad tidings, as indeed it was or should have been. Had he done a little systems analysis of the kind which comes easily to politicians who never heard of computers, he would have realized that he was stepping into a complicated situation in which the facts and the truth were minor considerations. He was giving aid and comfort to the enemy, i.e., the Republican party. McNamara's press conference put Kennedy's new Secretary of Defense squarely behind Eisenhower, who had declared only three weeks earlier in his last State of the Union message, "The 'bomber gap' of several years ago was always a fiction, and the 'missile gap' shows every sign of being the same." It also undercut one of Kennedy's principal campaign themes, and, as any sophisticated observer would surmise, threatened to upset a network of understandings between the Democratic party and the aviation lobby, "contracts"—as the politicians say—whence many campaign contributions had flowed.

The roof fell in on McNamara. Next day Pierre Salinger told the press that he was speaking with Kennedy's approval in terming McNamara's finding "absolutely wrong." It is a pity there is no record of what went on between Kennedy and McNamara. The latter must have been startled to discover that in Washington facts counted for so little; his discovery, after all, was far from sensational. Even my little *Weekly*, in an issue which went to press a week before the McNamara backgrounder (which was restricted to a select few) had called attention to evidence that there was no missile gap, including a report by Britain's Institute of Strategic Studies. This credited Russia with only thirty-five ICBM's, as against the 400 to 500 figure given in the exuberant leaks to the press from Air Force Intelligence and the aviation lobby. Perhaps the facts marshaled by McNamara in a White House showdown explain why Kennedy himself, the day after Salinger's "absolutely wrong," scaled down his own rebuke to "premature." But six weeks later in his first budget message to Congress, Kennedy unabashedly declared, "It has been publicly acknowledged for several years that this nation has not led the world in missile strength," and launched a huge missile buildup, though authoritative figures from the outgoing Republicans showed we were not only ahead in long-range missiles but had ten times as many vehicles (missiles and bombers) capable of reaching Russia with nuclear weapons as Russia had capable of reaching the U.S. Now in his new book McNamara lifts the curtain just a little on that farce and ever so gingerly calls it a mistake. This is in the chapter based on his San Francisco speech of September, 1967, which was supposed to be sensationally candid. McNamara said of that 1961 decision:

Our current numerical superiority over the Soviet Union in reliable, accurate and effective warheads is both greater than we had originally planned and much more than we require. How this came about is a significant illustration of the intrinsic dynamics of the nuclear arms race. . . . In 1961 when I became Secretary of Defense, the Soviet Union had a very small operational arsenal of intercontinental missiles. However, it did possess the technological and industrial capacity to enlarge that arsenal very substantially. . . . We had to insure against such an eventuality by undertaking a major buildup of our own Minuteman and Polaris forces. . . . But the blunt fact remains that if we had had more accurate information about *planned* [my italics] strategic forces, we simply would not have needed to build as large a nuclear arsenal as we have today. . . . I am not saying that our decision in 1961 was unjustified; I am saying that it was necessitated by a lack of accurate information.

This apparent candor covers a network of deceptions. If the reader will go over McNamara's passage carefully, he will see that he not only admits there was no missile gap but admits he knew it at the time. He falls back on the excuse that we had no "accurate information" on what the Soviets *planned* in the way of *future* production. But that is not how the Kennedy Administration told it at the time. The public was told that we were behind; that there *was* a missile gap. Ralph Lapp, in his penetrating new book *The Weapons Culture*, puts it plainly when he writes, "There was no missile gap but it was not politically expedient to admit this fact. Instead, the myth was perpetuated and the arms race accelerated." Kennedy, "having campaigned on a missile gap platform apparently found it politically necessary to commit the nation to more missiles than Mr. McNamara believed to be enough for strategic deterrence." All this was due to the power of the military-industrial complex, which Lapp's book explores and whose potency McNamara denies.

The inadequacy of McNamara's account becomes more striking if one checks back on those given in Sorenson's *Kennedy* and Schlesinger's *A Thousand Days*. The former says that the U-2 flights disclosed that Khrushchev's first ICBM had proven "too costly, too cumbersome and too vulnerable a weapon for mass production," and that he had settled "for a very few of these missiles" while he tried to develop a better ICBM. Schlesinger writes that while the "missile gap" had "withered away" by the time the first Kennedy budget was prepared, it nevertheless provided for more missiles than did the extensive program already launched under Eisenhower. Schlesinger says "the White House staff . . . wondered whether the new budget was not providing far more missiles than national security required." He is protective of Kennedy and blames McNamara for the increase. Schlesinger says that McNamara

did not believe that doubling or even tripling our striking power would enable us to destroy the hardened missile sites or missile-launching submarines of our adversary. But he was already engaged in a bitter fight with the Air Force over his effort to disengage from the B-70, a costly high-altitude manned bomber rendered obsolescent by the improvement in Soviet ground-to-air missiles. After cutting down the original Air Force missile demands considerably, he perhaps felt that he could not do more without risking public conflict with the Joint Chiefs and the vociferous B-70 lobby in Congress. As a result, the President went along with the policy of multiplying Polaris and Minuteman missiles.

This shift of blame to McNamara strains one's credulity. But what it adds up to is that Kennedy and McNamara built more missiles than they thought we needed in order to appease the Joint Chiefs and the aviation lobby for the cancellation of the B-70. This is a very different decision-making process than that portrayed by McNamara in the Pett interview and in *The Essence of Security*. "The blunt fact," to use McNamara's phrase, is that it was not lack of accurate information, nor in this case "the intrinsic dynamics of the arms race," but the dynamics of the political system and the military-industrial complex which led us to overbuild.

Another point and another revelation is in order before we leave this McNamara account of what happened. McNamara went on to another misleading half-disclosure:

Furthermore, that decision in itself, justified as it was, in the end could not possibly have left unaffected the Soviet Union's future nuclear plans . . . the Soviet reaction is in part a reaction to our own buildup since the beginning of the 1960s. Soviet strategic planners undoubtedly reasoned that if our buildup were to continue at its accelerated pace, we might conceivably reach in time a credible first-strike capability against the Soviet Union. That was not, in fact, our intention. . . . But . . . the result has been that we have both built up our forces to a point that far exceeds a credible second-strike capability.

This is only half the story. The whole story is that, after the U-2 incident, the Russians knew that we knew the truth about the missile gap. They hoped the new Administration would not unleash a new phase in the arms race by acting as if there were a missile gap. They tried to open talks with the new Administration on this problem but met with what may have sounded to them like nuclear double-talk. We owe this revelation to another passage (page 301) in Schlesinger's *A Thousand Days*. McNamara's account has to be read against Schlesinger's:

> The Soviet Union watched the arrival of the new administration with marked interest. Khrushchev, who had given up on Eisenhower after the U-2 incident and the collapse of the Paris summit in May, 1960, seized several opportunities to semaphore his hopes for Kennedy. His messages to Harriman and others after the election were followed by a Pugwash meeting on disarmament in Moscow in December [1960]. . . . Walt Rostow and Jerome B. Wiesner, who were among the Americans at the Moscow meeting, saw V. V. Kuznetsov of the Soviet Foreign Office. . . . In the course of their talk Kuznetsov mentioned the campaign furor about a "missile gap" and suggested that, if the new administration went in for massive rearmament, it could not expect the Russians to sit still.

So Kennedy and McNamara knew at the time they made their decisions that they were choosing between the appeasement of military-industrial pressures at home and a chance to avert a sharp and costly step-up in the arms race with the Russians. The American public may have been in the dark but both sides understood the cost entailed if the new Administration gave in to the missile gap propaganda. This again is very different from the picture drawn by McNamara.

Rostow's reply to the Russians, as reported by Schlesinger, must have made the Russians feel that we took them for fools. "Rostow replied," Schlesinger writes, "that any Kennedy rearmament would be designed to improve the stability of the deterrent, and the Soviet Union should recognize this as in the interests of peace; but Kuznetsov, innocent of the higher calculus of deterrence as recently developed in the United States, brusquely dismissed the explanation." It is hard to know whether Schlesinger wrote this tongue-in-cheek. The "higher calculus of deterrence" must have seemed to Kuznetsov sheer cant, a highfalutin new synonym for the low arithmetic of domestic arms-lobby politics, which was threatening to develop a U.S. first-strike capacity rather than a stable deterrent. This, and not the lack of accurate information, is why both sides find themselves with far more destructive capacity than they need. McNamara's account is far from being as candid as it appears to be.

This is even more true when McNamara comes to discuss the ABM, the anti-ballistic missile. The definitive and final word on the missile-to-shoot-down-a-missile was said by General Omar Bradley in a little-noticed and undeservedly forgotten speech he made at St. Alban's[2] in Washington, in 1957. "Missiles will bring anti-missiles," General Bradley predicted, "and anti-missiles will bring anti-anti-missiles" until this "whole electronic house of cards" collapses; the only way out is "accommodation in a world split by rival ideologies" even if at the cost of "such sacred traditions as absolute national sovereignty." McNamara's argument against the ABM is on a less lofty plane. It is in the realm of hardware rather than philosophy. McNamara argues that the enemy may easily overwhelm our batteries of anti-missiles by adding to the number of attacking missiles or the number of warheads they carry. Both sides would step up their missiles and anti-missiles in this mad arithmetic and still find themselves where they started. McNamara's powerful presentation of this argument may be found in Chapter Four, as reprinted from his San Francisco speech against the ABM.

But if the text of the speech as delivered is compared with the text reprinted as Chapter Four of the book, one finds that the book omits—almost as if he were ashamed of it and preferred to forget it—that portion of the speech which embodied his backdown under pressure from Johnson, and his acquiescence in a "thin" ABM system, ostensibly aimed only at China. That portion of the speech has been rele-

[2] The only place the text was ever published was my *Weekly* of November 18, 1957.

gated to an appendix, which includes the admission in the original speech, "The danger in deploying this relatively light and reliable Chinese-oriented ABM system is going to be that pressures will develop to expand it into a heavy Soviet-oriented ABM system. We must resist that temptation firmly." The advice seems ironic from a man who had just succumbed to the first step away from his own better judgment and in the direction of a new and destabilizing chapter in the nuclear arms race.

Few readers of the McNamara book will realize that Chapter Four is the relic of a retreat from the very argument it presents and a surrender to the pressures of the military-industrial complex. These had been building up for years. In 1959, Eisenhower rejected a recommendation by the Joint Chiefs of Staff that the U.S. build an anti-ballistic missile defense. The wisdom of that rejection had been underscored by McNamara himself only nine months before his backdown. On January 23, 1967, at the annual Senate "military posture" hearing, he testified that if Eisenhower had gone ahead with that ABM system, the Nike-Zeus, in 1959, at an estimated cost of $13–$14 billion, "most of it would have had to be torn out and replaced, almost before it became operative, by the new missiles and radars of the Nike-X system." The lesson he tried to drive home was, "By the same token other technological developments in offensive forces over the next seven years may make obsolete or drastically degrade the Nike-X system as presently envisioned." A few weeks later, to emphasize the point, the Defense Department disclosed that the U.S. had spent $20 billion since World War II on missile systems never completed or out of service because of obsolescence. Their military value was nil but the social waste and the private profit were enormous.

In that portion of the San Francisco speech which remains in Chapter Four, McNamara cites the fact that the science advisers of Eisenhower, Kennedy, and Johnson, and the directors of research and engineering at the Pentagon under his secretaryship and those of his two Republican predecessors had all advised against the deployment of an ABM system. They all saw in it "a senseless spiral upward of nuclear arms." But in 1967 Nixon and the Republicans in Congress, allied with the Joint Chiefs of Staff, were pressing an ABM gap against the Democrats as the Democrats and the military had pressed a missile gap against the Republicans six years earlier. Johnson gave in to that pressure. Ralph Lapp in his book says of this what McNamara should have said in his: "If a U.S. president authorizes a $5-billion Sentinel system to protect himself from Republican charges of failing to insure the nation's security, then one might just as well junk all the elaborate systems of defense analysis that we possess."

It is these systems on which McNamara's reputation is based. He betrayed them by acquiescing in the ABM in 1967 as he acquiesced in the missile gap buildup in 1961. This man, who prides himself on objective considerations of cost-effectiveness and at the same time tries hard to live by liberal precepts, could have ended his term in office with honor by resigning on the ABM issue, as he might have resigned on the even more compelling issue of the continued bombing of North Vietnam. But Vietnam, his most traumatic experience and the scene of his most disastrous misjudgments, is barely mentioned in passing. The noblest effort of his career, his testimony of August 25, 1967 before the Stennis subcommittee of the Senate, in which he cogently argued the case against the bombing of the North, is not even included in his book, again as if he would like to forget it and to have it forgotten. McNamara is capable of writing that worldwide student unrest springs from "the fear that somehow society, all society—East and West—has fallen victim to a bureaucratic tyranny of technology that is gradually depersonalizing and alienating modern man himself." How inspiring an example he might have set if he had himself defied this "bureaucratic tyranny" and resigned in protest against the bombing of the North, or the decision to embark on the ABM, with all the fateful consequences

against which he himself warned! If loyalty to the bureaucratic and political team is to outweigh loyalty to mankind,
what hope can there be? Certainly nothing McNamara can
possibly do at the World Bank can begin to match what he
might have done by a resignation on either or both of these
issues.

The elaborate reasons McNamara gives in the appendix
as to why it is all right to build a "thin" system against
China though not a big one against Russia are a subterfuge.
The advocates of an ABM regard the decision to build a
"thin" $5-billion defense as the entering wedge for a big
one which will cost from $40 to $70 billion. The idea of an
ABM defense against China is best judged by comparing
our nuclear power with theirs. "Our alert forces alone
carry more than 2,200 weapons" averaging more than one
megaton apiece, McNamara disclosed in the San Francisco
speech. As against this nuclear armada, the debates in Congress have revealed that our intelligence believes that by the
mid-seventies the Chinese may have four or five intercontinental missiles! The best reply to McNamara's Chinese argument was the comment of Senator Russell, who favors a
big ABM. "The Chinese are not completely crazy," he said.
"They are not going to attack us with four or five missiles
when they know we have the capability of virtually destroying the entire country. . . . I don't like people to think that
I am being kidded by this talk of a defense against a Chinese
nuclear attack."

The ABM will prove the biggest military-scientific gravy
train yet. A few days after the San Francisco speech, announcing that we would build the "thin" ABM against
China, Senator Clark of Pennsylvania called the Senate's attention to what happened in the stock market. He said the
story was there. "Where is the ABM money going to go?
Raytheon, up 4⅛ to 91⅛ on Monday, September 18, the
day of the McNamara speech; Aerojet General, up 4⅝ to
33¼ on the same day. Strong rising trends have been just
as visible in other major ABM contractors—Thiokol, Martin
Marietta and Sperry Rand. The vast new defense pork lunch

wagon—maybe the biggest ever—has begun to roll, and the investors on the stock market know it." The money needed "to rebuild our cities and heal the wounds in our society," Clark protested, "is being drained off to build Armageddon instead." These are the realities one will not find in McNamara's book.

November 7, 1968
New York Review

ON NATIONAL DEFENSE, SPACE AND FOREIGN POLICY, THE NEW GOP PLATFORM READS AS IF WRITTEN BY GENERAL DYNAMICS FOR A NEW ARMS RACE

All political platform-writers cultivate amnesia. This beneficial affliction is evident in that portion of the new Republican platform which deals with National Defense. "All the world was respectful," it says, "of America's decisive strategic advantage over the Soviets achieved during the Eisenhower Administration." On the contrary, the Eisenhower Administration was accused by the Democrats and the aviation lobby of allowing first a bomber gap and then a missile gap to develop. Both turned out to be figments of the armament salesman's imagination. But eight years ago the Democrats were accusing the Republicans of endangering national security by falling behind in the arms race. This time the Republican platform makes the same accusation against the Democrats. Kennedy called Eisenhower's term in office "years of the locust" in which "we obtained economic security at the expense of military security." This time the Republicans charge that "advanced military research and development have been inhibited and stagnated by inexpert, *cost-oriented* administrators" (my italics).

One difference between 1960 and 1968 is that we were then spending some $40 billion plus at the Pentagon while this year it will be $80 billion plus. This year's requests by the Joint Chiefs of Staff, before Secretary Clifford pared them down, was $102 billion.

But the Republicans do not think those who administer the military budget ought to be "cost-oriented." It is they who now talk of "gaps." Though the Democrats are spending twice as much as did the Republicans, the Democrats are accused of "frittering away superior military capabilities" by "standing still" and "enabling the Soviets to narrow their defense gap, in some areas to outstrip us, and to move to cancel our lead entirely by the early seventies." The Republicans picture the Navy saddled with "second-best weaponry" (the TFX), submarine improvements delayed while "the Soviets have proceeded apace," anti-submarine warfare "left seriously inadequate, new fighter planes held up and new strategic weaponry left on the drawing boards." In the platform plank on science, they also "deplore the failure of the Johnson-Humphrey Administration to emphasize the military uses of space." The Republicans "regard the ability to launch and deploy advanced spacecraft as a military necessity." The platform reads as if written by General Dynamics.

The Republican concern for the military is again evident in the platform plank on a healthy economy. The Republicans say "such funds as become available with the termination of the Vietnam war *and upon recovery from its impact on national defense* will be applied in a balanced way to critical domestic needs and to reduce the heavy tax burden" (my italics). The first priority will be to rebuild our "starved" armed forces. In our July 8, 1968 issue we called attention to a series of Johnson Administration speeches which tried to prepare public opinion for the news that even if the Vietnamese war ended there would be little money available for domestic needs because the money would be needed by the military to cope with backlogs of delayed weapon improvements and depleted inventories. Did not the Under Secretary of the Treasury on June 25 explain that the military had been fighting the Vietnam war "on a very, very lean budget?" Only after these military needs are met will the Republicans apply what is left, if anything, "in a balanced way" to "critical domestic needs" and to "reduce the heavy tax burden." The suffering poor will be helped equally with the suffering rich, but only after our suffering military has been taken care of.

In its special study last May 24 of the military-industrial complex, *Congressional Quarterly* reported, "One Pentagon source told *CQ* that any increment over $40 billion in the post-Vietnam defense budget will be purely due to pressures by the military-industrial complex rather than to the defense needs of the nation." *Congressional Quarterly* in that same study said, "Several highly placed Administration and industry sources said cuts totalling $10 to $15 billion could be made in the defense budget while retaining or improving the current level of national security." That saving alone would be enough, according to a report made some weeks ago to Governor Rockefeller, to scrap our present welfare system and initiate a system of guaranteed minimum income for the poor. But the platform's long and lachrymose platform plank on the poor says not one word about any income guarantee. On the poor, the Republicans are "cost-oriented."

One paragraph in the foreign policy plank endorses "limitation" of arms provided there are "trustworthy guarantees" against violation. But a major section of the national defense plank is devoted to specific areas in which the Republicans would step up the arms race. They want to build more missile-armed nuclear submarines and to stimulate military research in an effort to find "major innovations" in weaponry. They pledge "to assemble the nation's best diplomatic, military and scientific minds for an exhaustive reassessment of America's worldwide commitments and military preparedness." There is no sign, however, of any retreat from a Pax Americana. In a passage of the foreign policy plank which sounds exactly like Rusk, the Republicans say, "We do not intend to conduct foreign policy in such a way as to make the United States a world policeman." But the very next sentence, again exactly like Rusk, says, "However, we will not condone aggression or so-called 'wars of national liberation.' " In the plank on Vietnam the party does express its concern over "hastily extemporized undeclared wars which embroil massive U.S. Army forces thousands of miles from our shores" but the solution favored seems to be the use of more airpower. For the next sentence says, "It is time to realize that not every international conflict is susceptible of solution by American *ground* forces" (my italics). Our colonial cops will travel in B-52's.

If there is any doubt about the GOP's commitment to Pax Americana, Nixon made it clear at his August 6 Miami Beach news conference when asked whether he now thought the Vietnam war unwinnable, "I do not think that the war is not winnable and I should state further that I certainly do not seek the Presidency for the purpose of presiding over the destruction of the credibility of the American power throughout the world." This paraphrases Churchill's famous last stand for British imperialism.

August 19, 1968

———

A GOLDWATER
TO HEAD THE PENTAGON

As show business, Nixon's introduction of his Cabinet was shallow and banal. He himself seemed like a bush-league Ed

Sullivan. No less than 10 times the TV audience was assured that there was some mysterious "extra dimension" enveloping what seemed to be a random assortment of the kind of businessmen to be met at any Rotary Club luncheon; the only extra dimension visible in their records was the size of their bank accounts. This is another Cabinet of millionaires. At first glance the weakest appointment was Nixon's law partner, John Mitchell, to be Attorney General. At a time when that office requires the deepest insights, we get an Attorney General who has spent his professional career as a municipal bond expert! The best appointment was that of William P. Rogers to be Secretary of State; the most alarming, that of Melvin R. Laird to be Secretary of Defense. Unfortunately Rogers, who was a first-rate Attorney General under Eisenhower and gave us some of the best federal judges ever to sit in the South, knows next to nothing about foreign affairs, while Laird is all too well equipped to be effective at the Pentagon in terms of his own outlook. He is a more competent and less open Goldwater. The prize in the Nixon package has gone to the military-industrial complex. . . .

Nixon has tried to create the image of a non-ideological Cabinet; he has called his Cabinet "pragmatic centrists." The man he would put in the Pentagon is no centrist. His legislative score for 1967 was rated at 100 percent by the U.S. Chamber of Commerce, 85 percent by the conservative Americans for Constitutional Action, and 7 percent by Americans for Democratic Action; he is liberal on health legislation. "A steely and shrewd politician . . . at the center of our largest conservative apparatus," was the summation of the National Committee for an Effective Congress.

Neither is Laird a pragmatist. I was wrong last week in saying that he would be as surprised to be called a practitioner of geopolitics as Babbitt would have been to be called a guru. This small-town Wisconsin lumber dealer is quite at home with the swamis of the cold war. His one book, *A House Divided: America's Security Gap* (Henry Regnery, 1962), warms up to a climax in which he calls Christianity and communism irreconcilable but says, "positivism, not communism, is the philosophical virus that causes our paralysis." In his native Marshfield, Wisconsin, just using such words in public would be enough to mark a man down as suspect. "It is a profound lesson of history," Laird writes in a peroration worthy of his fellow Presbyterian, John Foster Dulles, one of Laird's heroes, "that as any nation increases its dedication to materialistic, positivistic criteria at the expense of dependence upon God and the truths beyond history, that nation has begun its downward course." This deep-seated opposition to materialism does not keep Laird from worrying about "the present profit squeeze" nor from suggesting as mandatory "a major overhaul of the tax system," by which he means a shift from income to more direct taxes, i.e., from the rich to the poor, who are presumably better adapted to a less materialistic way of life.

The book carries a modest acknowledgment "for able editorial and stylistic assistance" to Karl Hess, who surfaced to fame two years later as Goldwater's ghost writer. The "strategy gap" the book seeks to fill is the lack of an offensive posture. The book suggests that the U.S. take the initiative, among other places (1) in ridding Cuba of communism, (2) in any future East German or Hungarian uprising, and (3) in effecting "the unification of Germany." A Pentagon chief with such aims will rarely have a dull moment. These are high-wire examples of the brinkmanship Laird so admires in Dulles. The basic axiom of the book is "better dead than Red," though expressed in the fruitiest and most full-bodied Goldwaterite prose. "Is the fact that more lives are involved in decisions today," Laird asks in sententious reference to nuclear war, "sufficient in itself to make the condition of life [i.e., liberty] second to the primacy of biological preservation?" The answer, in the finest tradition of extremism in the defense of liberty, is "no." This overreadiness for the ultimate sacifice was considered too dangerous for the White House in 1964. It would be no less dangerous in the Pentagon today.

At his Pentagon press conference Friday, December 13,[1] when a reporter asked, "May I read some of your words back to you from your book?" Laird replied, "I was afraid someone might do that." The words read back to him were that "the credible announcement of first-strike initiative is the sole way to effective disarmament discussions with the Soviet Union." Laird claimed this was the thesis not only of his book but of a report concurred in six years ago by all the members of the House Defense Appropriations subcommittee, on which he has served since 1953. He said that was "written in a period of confrontation. We are now in a period of negotiations, and I think that that should be considered as we face the future."

Yet Laird doesn't seem to be facing the future very differently now than then. The ability, if necessary, to take the nuclear initiative and strike first is implicit in the insistence on nuclear "superiority" which is a central theme not only of the book but of Laird's major expositions of defense policy since and indeed of the Nixon campaign. The Nixon task force report on National Security made the maintenance of nuclear superiority its main recommendation. It assailed "the euphoric hope" that peace could be reached by replacing superiority with parity. It said the U.S. "must be prepared to crush all *threats* to the peace with force if required" (my italics) including nuclear weapons. This implies first strike and preventive war. Negotiation in this context becomes another form of dictation through intimidation.

The full significance of the Laird appointment becomes clearer if one goes back and has a fresh look at the kind of men on the task forces which prepared Nixon's position pa-

[1] In his book (p. 134) Laird cites as an example of Khrushchev's "mastery of the psychological techniques of political warfare" his announcement that a 50-megaton bomb would be set off on Halloween eve." He thus became the first American statesman to discover that the Kremlin so finely tuned its moves to exploit the superstitious twinges of the West (perhaps as an echo of the Pumpkin Papers in the Hiss case?). We hope no brooder over a crystal ball in Moscow finds in the day and date chosen for Laird's first Pentagon press conference a similarly ingenious way to frighten the U.S.S.R.

pers on defense and foreign policy. These were heavily weighted with the military and apocalyptic rightists. The task force on national security "was made up primarily," *Congressional Quarterly* noted in a study December 4 which predicts a sharp rise in military spending under Nixon, "of military and civilian officials associated with the 'massive retaliation' doctrine of the 1950's and members of Congress who favor a 'tough' military line." Many of them are men whom Laird salutes as his mentors in his book—Admirals Arleigh Burke and Arthur Radford on the defense task force, and on the foreign policy task force Professor Robert Strausz-Hupé of the University of Pennsylvania and Professor Gerhart Niemeyer of Notre Dame, both mighty Druids in the dark forests of geopolitics. Other kindred spirits on the defense task force were Craig Hosmer, Dr. Edward Teller's faithful mouthpiece on the Joint Congressional Committee on Atomic Energy, and Senator Tower of Texas. On the foreign policy task force, just to keep it from slipping too far left, were also Robert Amory, who lost his job as deputy director of the CIA in the wake of the Bay of Pigs; Robert C. Hill, who distinguished himself as Eisenhower's last Ambassador in Mexico by indiscreet relations with the right-wing *Sinarquistas;* Professor David N. Rowe of Yale, and Walter Judd. The last two have been as stalwart as Mao himself, though on the other side, in resisting revisionism in America's China policy.

These task forces and their composition do not fit that mask of moderation the Nixon public relations strategy has fashioned for his debut. Any idea that the work of these Republican troglodytes on defense and foreign policy can be dismissed as a mere campaign exercise will be dispelled by a closer look at Laird's record, his book and his associations. He is one of them. Along with Henry A. Kissinger, the new White House foreign affairs expert, and Kissinger's deputy, Richard V. Allen, Nixon's foreign affairs expert during the campaign, they belong to a closely knit mutual admiration society. The accolade from Kissinger's colleagues of the Harvard liberal establishment on his appointment as Nixon's mentor has served to distract attention from his less well-known but more significant ties with these right-wingers. Laird's book is complimentary in its references to Kissinger, as it is to Niemeyer and Strausz-Hupé. Laird told the Washington *Star* in a full-length interview December 18 that in 1964, as chairman of the Republican platform committee, "he relied more heavily on the views of Henry Kissinger than those of Barry Goldwater," while Allen in an interview with the *New York Times* December 14 disclosed that during the Nixon campaign he "maintained discreet contact with Dr. Kissinger, then foreign policy adviser to Governor Rockefeller." Such political dexterity must be close to genius.

Laird in his book also acknowledges the inspiration of David M. Abshire, who, with Allen, edited a huge 1,000-page right-wing symposium on *National Security: Political, Military and Economic Strategies in the Decade Ahead* (Praeger: 1963) for the Georgetown Center for Strategic Studies and the Hoover Institution on War, Revolution and Peace. Allen himself moved from the first to the second and is now on leave to the White House. The volume carries an introduction by another of Laird's heroes, Admiral Burke. Among the contributors are Kissinger and such seers as Herman Kahn, Edward Teller, Senator Jackson and Walt Rostow. When Allen three years later published a study for the American Bar Association, *Peace or Peaceful Co-Existence?*, Laird praised it in the *Congressional Record* (August 26, 1966) as proving "conclusively" from a study of 3,000 Communist documents (no less!) that co-existence was only a more deceitful way of seeking world domination through "a many-pronged offensive." This is back to the bogeyman view of the fifties. Laird, Kissinger and Allen will prove a formidable team in fashioning foreign policy.

Whether prongs or tentacles, Laird sees them everywhere. His world-view, like that of Niemeyer and Strausz-Hupé, is equally compounded of demonology and melodrama. During the hearings on the fiscal 1966 budget in March, 1965, when the bombings of North Vietnam had just begun, Laird told McNamara (page 121, Part 3 House appropriations hearings), "I think there is a good possibility that we will have a breakout under Communist pressure in some other place in the world within the next six or seven weeks. It seems that the Communists operate this way. At the time of the missiles to Cuba, Red China attacked India. At the time of the Bay of Tonkin, that incident, when we were completely diverted on the situation taking place in the Vietnamese war, the Communist-backed rebels marched and took over Stanleyville [in the Congo], which was a very strategic place." It takes a wide-angle vision to link together in one cosmic plot the Cuban missile crisis, the Indo-Chinese border war, the Tonkin Gulf bombings and the rebellion in the Congo.

Had Laird been Secretary of Defense in the past eight years, history might have been very different. He thinks we should not have backed away at the Bay of Pigs. He sees Rostow as naive, Rusk as soft and McNamara as a positive menace. He believes President Kennedy made a cardinal mistake when he said we would never strike first. He advocates a policy of nuclear reprisal along the lines of "a policy called 2X" which he says Dulles considered in the fifties. This would involve a steady escalation in nuclear reprisal to "the point at which the cost to the enemy would outweigh the gain" and show him that aggression was "unprofitable." Though an opponent of McNamara's cost-effectiveness approach, Laird seems to have a touching faith that such reprisals would lead an enemy calmly to sit down and balance gains against losses and decide that crime doesn't pay, like a businessman soberly contemplating a poor investment.

Something of this approach is evident in Laird's own shift away from support of Johnson in the Vietnam war. Laird began to lose enthusiasm after Johnson in the Johns Hopkins speech announced a readiness to negotiate. Laird has no faith in the Saigon regime and believes the Communists will take over if our troops pull out. This is also the view of the Joint Chiefs of Staff, who would like (from distant echoes we have picked up) to keep a garrison force of U.S. troops there indefinitely. They may find Laird easy to convince. Laird warns in his book that past mistakes have been due to our failure to listen to the military in political discussions. He describes the military as "highly intelligent citizens with a broad grasp of our military potential and future needs . . . well-equipped to make meaningful recommendations for policy." There is no trace in this description of that astringent eye required to keep the military within bounds.

Not to examine Laird's views and record fully in the hearings and the confirmation debate would be a gross neglect of senatorial duty. If the appointment cannot be blocked, at least the country should be put on notice as to what it may expect. Laird at one point suggested in the House that the Peace Corps be renamed the Freedom Corps because "freedom is the important issue" and "mere survival under peace is not the important message we wish to deliver to the world." To confirm Laird as Secretary of Defense is to risk the likelihood that in the next four years the Pentagon's course will be set on higher goals than "mere survival."

December 30, 1968

NIXON AND THE ARMS RACE: THE BOMBER BOONDOGGLE

The No. 1 question for the new Nixon Administration is what it will do about the arms race. If it opts for higher military spending, the consequence will be intensified social conflict. If the new President's policies in office follow his campaign pledges, the decision has already been made. Nixon has begun by promising to perpetuate one of McNamara's greatest errors and to undo his greatest accomplishment. The error is that miscarriage of an airplane, the TFX, now known as the F-111, which has already cost the country several billion dollars. His accomplishment was to make the country realize that at a certain point in the awful arithmetic of nuclear power, superiority in weapons became meaningless.

In his Security Gap speech over CBS on October 25, Nixon said that one of his major aims would be to "correct its [the Pentagon's] over-centralization" in order to give greater weight in decision-making to the military as against the top civilians. "I intend to root out the 'whiz kid' approach, which for years," Nixon said, "has led our policies and programs down the wrong roads." But he is following McNamara down his most costly wrong road, just when the military have been proven right and the top civilians wrong, and indeed—as we shall see—on the one issue where the "whiz kids" sided with the military against McNamara. On the other hand, Nixon has set out, in the search for nuclear superiority, to follow the military down a dead-end path where the military are demonstrably wrong and the "whiz kids" are demonstrably right. To examine these two divergent courses is to see the trouble which lies ahead, on many different levels, for the new Administration and the country.

Let us begin with the TFX and with the speech Nixon made November 2 at Fort Worth, Texas. Fort Worth is where General Dynamics builds the TFX or F-111, the plane that was the focus of the longest and bitterest controversy of McNamara's years in the Pentagon. "The F-111 in a Nixon Administration," the candidate said at Fort Worth that day, "will be made into one of the foundations of our air supremacy." This pledge, which received too little attention, may prove to be the biggest blooper of the campaign, and the beginning—if Nixon tries to keep that pledge—of the biggest fight between the Nixon Administration and the very forces he might have counted on for a honeymoon, the Senate conservatives who specialize in military policy and who were most critical of McNamara in the

TFX affair. It is startling that a man as cautious as Nixon should have made so unqualified a pledge to a plane which has become a tragic joke.

Last May, when the Senate Appropriations subcommittee on the Department of Defense was holding hearings on the budget for the fiscal year 1969, the Chairman, Senator Russell of Georgia, booby-trapped the Air Force Chief of Staff, General McConnell, with what appeared to be an innocent question on this plane, the F-111:

SENATOR RUSSELL: Would it be a very serious matter if one of these planes were recovered by any potential enemy in a reasonably good condition?

GENERAL MCCONNELL: Yes, we have quite a few things in it that we would not want the enemy to get.

SENATOR RUSSELL: That is mainly electronic devices.

GENERAL MCCONNELL: That is true of practically all the aircraft we have.

SENATOR RUSSELL: Of course the Russians got a B-29 when they were one of our allies. They fabricated a great many of them as nearly comparable to the B-29's as they could. I was hoping if they got a F-111 they would fabricate some of them as near ours as they could and see if they had as much trouble as we did. It would put their Air Force out of business.[1]

Neither General McConnell nor his civilian superior Air Force Secretary Harold Brown dared say one word in reply to Senator Russell's cruel jibe.

Russell's sardonic view of the F-111 is shared on both sides of the aisle in the Senate. On October 3, Senator Curtis of Kansas, a senior Republican, a member of the Aeronautical and Space Sciences Committee, delivered a devastating attack on the F-111 in the Senate, in which he said McNamara's "obstinacy" in producing the F-111, "will be a major problem that the new Administration must face." Just one month later Nixon began to face it by pledging himself at Fort Worth to make this plane "one of the foundations of our air supremacy."

[1] Senate Appropriations Committee Hearings on the 1969 Defense Department budget, Part I, Department of the Air Force, p. 103. Released September 19, 1968.

Either Nixon and his staff do not read the newspapers, much less the *Congressional Record* and the hearings, or Nixon like McNamara is determined to override military judgment and keep the billions flowing into General Dynamics for this jinxed plane. The difference is that when McNamara overrode the military, it was difficult for outsiders to judge so complex a technological controversy—especially when so many of the facts were still classified. Newspapermen like myself, who start with a strong bias against the military, assumed that McNamara was probably right. But 1968 is the year when the F-111 finally went into combat; the results have led many people inside and outside Congress to look at the old controversy with a fresh eye.

Nixon's reckless pledge was the only bright spot for the F-111 in the year 1968. The latest, 1969, edition of *Jane's Aircraft*[2] says succinctly,

The 474th Tactical Fighter Wing at Nellis [Air Force Base, Nevada] was the first to be equipped with the F-111As [the Air Force version of the F-111]. Six aircraft from Nellis arrived at the Takhli base in Thailand on 17 March 1968 and made their first operational sorties over Vietnam on 25 March. Two were lost in the next five days.

The foreword, which went to press later, says "Three of the first 8 F-111A's dispatched to Vietnam were lost in a matter of weeks and the type was grounded shortly afterwards." No mention was made of these losses by Secretary of the Air Force Brown when he read his prepared statement to the Senate appropriations defense subcommittee in executive session last May 6. On the contrary, he said the F-111 "is proving, in its tests and operational units, to be an outstanding aircraft." By then three of the original six had been lost, as may be seen from the following colloquy, where the reader will notice Secretary Brown's squeamish reluctance to use the word "lost":

SENATOR RUSSELL: How many of these have we sent over to Southeast Asia?

2 John W. R. Taylor, ed., *Jane's All the World's Aircraft, 1968–69* (New York: McGraw-Hill), p. 279.

SECRETARY BROWN: We sent six and have sent two replacements.

SENATOR RUSSELL: You have lost three, so you have five?

SECRETARY BROWN: There are five there now.

SENATOR RUSSELL: Do you have any information on these three that were lost? Do you know whether any of them fell into the hands of the North Vietnamese to be sent to Moscow along with all the secret equipment of the Pueblo?

GENERAL McCONNELL [Air Force Chief Staff]: No, sir.[3]

In his Senate speech of October 3, Senator Curtis disclosed, "Thus far, 11 F-111 aircraft have crashed with a number of fatalities." He revealed that the wings were broken off one plane during a "static ground test" just six weeks before the first six planes were deployed to Southeast Asia, and that the week before his Senate speech another F-111A had crashed during a training flight owing to "a fatigue failure in the wing carrythrough structure."

If rightists treated Nixon and the Defense Department the way he treated the State Department in the days when he was a practicing witch-hunter, a proposal to make such a plane, with such a record, a foundation stone of American air supremacy would have been adduced as proof positive that the Pentagon had been infiltrated with Red and pinko saboteurs.

Last January the British Royal Air Force canceled its order for 50 F-111K's. In March Congress ordered work stopped on the F-111B's, the version for the U.S. Navy. On October 7, Senator Symington followed Senator Curtis with a speech suggesting that production of the F-111's for the Air Force also be stopped: he said that "the series of crashes in the past five months" makes it doubtful that it will ever prove to be "a truly reliable airplane" and declared that its future should "receive highest priority upon convening of the new Congress."

The strangest discovery which turns up in studying Nixon's pledge at Fort Worth is that he and his staff were either unaware of, or ignored, his own famous "position pa-

[3] Senate 1969 Defense Appropriations Hearings, *op. cit.*, pp. 102–3.

pers." The one on "Research and Development: Our Neglected Weapon," [4] which was made public in May, 1968,
says of the F-111:

The effort to transform the TFX (F-111) into an all-purpose
all-service aircraft has created serious problems. Against military
advice, the F-111 was selected as a superior, yet economical,
weapons system . . . The aircraft were to cost approximately
$2.4 million each. Now they are priced at more than $6 million
each . . . In view of the recent decision that the F-111B, the
Navy version, is unacceptable, and a substitute aircraft be initiated, the final cost of the program will increase enormously
coupled with years of delay. The program has resulted in the
Air Force having a new aircraft that does not meet the original
requirements . . . The F-111B has been found unacceptable
and the F-111 Bomber version does not meet Air Force requirements for an advanced bomber in the 1970 time frame.

Nixon devoted one of his main campaign speeches to "the
research gap." The Fort Worth speech showed his own research gap. Did he and his staff fail to read their position
papers? Another of these papers, "Decisions on National
Security: Patchwork or Policy?" is also in conflict with his
Fort Worth speech. That paper says "a notable example"
of how the top civilians overrode military judgment in the
McNamara years was the original award of the contract for
the F-111. "The contractor unanimously recommended by
both the military analysts and the Weapons Evaluation Systems Group," it says, "was rejected." The rejected bidder
was Boeing. The contractor McNamara chose was General
Dynamics. Nixon at Fort Worth affirmed the same choice.

We are not dealing here with a minor item. General
Dynamics is the country's biggest weapons producer. A Defense Department press release of November 18 on the nation's top 10 defense contractors showed General Dy-

[4] All these position papers have been reprinted in a one-volume com-
pilation, *Choice for America: Republican Answers to the Challenge of
Now*, published July, 1968, by the Republican National Committee, 1625
Eye St. N.W., Washington 20006.

namics as No. 1. In the fiscal year ending last June 30, it received $2.2 billion in arms contracts, or 5.8 percent of the total awarded in those 12 months. More than 80 percent of the firm's business comes from the government. The TFX represented the biggest single plum in military procurement. The original contract was for 1,700 planes at a total cost of $5.8 billion, or about $3 million per plane. These figures have since skyrocketed. This year, before the Navy contract was cancelled, the Pentagon admitted the cost of the Navy version would be $8 million apiece and of the Air Force version $6.5 million. As usual these, too, were understatements. Senator Curtis disclosed that the contractor's cost information reports put the average cost of the Navy plane at $9.5 million and that internal budgeting projections at the Pentagon put the Air Force plane at $9.1 million each. The original contract would have run up in the neighborhood of $15 billion.

Even with the cutbacks, more than $6 billion has already been spent and at least between $3 and $4 billion more "will be added in succeeding years," Senator Curtis said, "if present Defense Department plans are carried to completion." If Nixon keeps his word, they *will* be completed, perhaps expanded. But if he tries to do so, he will almost certainly find himself embattled with the Air Force buffs in Congress. For Curtis, Symington, Russell, and McClellan speak for a group of Senators who feel that the Air Force has been starved and stunted while all this money has been wasted on the TFX. We are in the presence of a wide-open split not only between the proponents of General Dynamics and Boeing respectively but within the Air Force and the whole military-industrial complex.

History is repeating itself, and it is the history of subordinating military efficiency to moneyed and political pressures. The only difference is that Nixon will find it harder than did McNamara to hide the realities, now that the F-111 has finally begun to fly—and fall. When the Kennedy Administration took over, General Dynamics was drifting close to receivership. It lost $27 million in 1960 and $143

million in 1961. *Fortune* magazine in January and February
of 1962 published a fascinating two-part story of its misjudgments and its business losses by Richard Austin Smith.
Smith said its losses on its civilian plane business had been so
disastrous that its working capital had dropped below the
minimum required by its agreement with its bankers and
that if the bankers had not reduced the minimum this "tech-
nically could have started the company down the road to
receivership." Smith wrote that the output of the General
Dynamics plant at Fort Worth in 1962 would be half what
it was in 1961. *Fortune* said, in its strangulated prose, that
General Dynamics would have to shut down its facilities
"unless it gets contract for joint Navy-Air Force fighter."
This was the TFX.

The TFX contract saved General Dynamics in 1962.
The cancellation of the F-111 could ruin it in 1969. The
effect of cancelling the Navy version of the plane was already reflected in a third quarter deficit, as of September
30, 1968, amounting to $1.51 a share compared with a net
profit of $1.13 a share in the third quarter of 1967. *Moody's
News* showed General Dynamics had to write off $39.6
million in contracts in 1968 as against only $12 million in
1967. Its net after taxes for the first nine months of 1968,
after allowing for sales of assets which made the accounts
look better than they otherwise would have, was only $9
million as compared with $36 million for the same period
the previous year.

Standard & Poor's Outlook, October 7, 1968, said the
stock of General Dynamics was "a speculation in the success of this F-111 program" and that "the most important
price determinant over the near term will be developments
in this trouble-plagued F-111 program." *The Value Line*,
October 18, said, "Since our July review the ever-sensitive
stock market has sold these shares down to a two-year
low." It said that if the problems of the F-111 were not
soon resolved, it was "vulnerable to further procurement
cutbacks." This was the bleak outlook two weeks before
Nixon's speech at Fort Worth. McNamara saved General

Dynamics in 1962. Nixon promised on November 2 to save it again.

McNamara's error on the TFX is worth close study because it shows the diminishing relationship between military procurement and genuine considerations of defense. It demonstrates the growing extent to which procurement is determined by military-bureaucratic and industrial considerations. The prime determinants were to save the largest company in the military-industrial complex financially and to appease the bomber generals, who simply will not admit that their expensive toys have grown obsolete. Billions which could do so much for poverty are squandered to maintain these favorite Pentagon clients on the military relief rolls in the lush style to which they have become accustomed.

General Dynamics, behind its glamorous front, is almost as much a creature of the government as the Air Force. In 1967 some 83 percent of its sales were to the government. *Moody's* observes of the huge Fort Worth establishment, where Nixon gave so much solace to this peculiar form of free and private enterprise, that the "plant, including most machinery and equipment, is leased from the U.S. government." The chief asset of General Dynamics seems to be its ability to wangle contracts out of the Pentagon.

The error in the TFX affair occurred on three levels, which have had varying degrees of attention, in inverse ratio to their importance. McNamara was wrong—so events seem to have proven—(1) in giving the TFX contract to General Dynamics instead of Boeing, (2) in insisting that the same basic plane be adopted for the diverse needs of the Air Force and Navy, and (3) in surrendering to the pressure of the Air Force for a new bomber and the Navy for a new missile weapons system to meet a nonexistent Soviet bomber threat just so they could go on with their expensive bomber game.

The first, the least important, got the most attention in

earlier years, since it promised Republican and conservative Democratic critics of the Kennedy and Johnson Administrations a scandal. But the shock of the Kennedy assassination cut short the McClellan committee investigation. A key figure was Roswell Gilpatric, a corporation lawyer who has done two tours of duty at the Pentagon, the first as Under Secretary of the Air Force in 1951–53 and again as Deputy Secretary of Defense in 1961–64, returning on each occasion to the famous Wall Street law firm of Cravath, Swaine and Moore, with which he has been associated since 1931. Through Gilpatric's efforts the firm became counsel for General Dynamics in the late fifties, and Gilpatric has combined his law work with activity in foreign and military policy in the Council on Foreign Relations and as a member of the Rockefeller Brothers Special Study project, which called for a sharp increase in military expenditures in January, 1958. In 1960 he was named as adviser on national security affairs by Kennedy during his campaign for the Presidency and after the election became Deputy Secretary of Defense, No. 2 man to McNamara at the Pentagon. There he played a major role in awarding the TFX contract.

General Dynamics has always been adept at having friends at court. It chose for its president in the fifties a former Secretary of the Army, Frank Pace. The $400-million losses of its Convair division during his incumbency make one wonder whether his chief qualification for the job was that he knew his way around Washington. Similarly it did not hurt General Dynamics to have its ex-counsel as No. 2 man in the Pentagon while it was fighting for the contract which could alone save it from receivership. Nor was General Dynamics hurt by the fact that Fred Korth, whom the Kennedy Administration had for some unfathomable reason made Secretary of the Navy, was a Fort Worth, Texas, banker, a past president of the Continental Bank, which had loaned money to General Dynamics, "and that Korth had kept an active, though not a financial, interest in the activities of this bank" [5] while in public office.

[5] Robert J. Art, *The TFX Decision* (Boston: Little, Brown, 1968), p. 4.

Korth told the McClellan committee "that because of his peculiar position he had deliberately refrained from taking a directing hand in this decision [within the Navy] until the last possible moment." [6] But it was "the last possible moment" which counted. Three times the Pentagon's Source Selection Board found that Boeing's bid was better and cheaper than that of General Dynamics and three times the bids were sent back for fresh submissions by the two bidders and fresh reviews. On the fourth round, the military still held that Boeing was better but found at last that the General Dynamics bid was also acceptable.

It was at this last moment that the award was made to General Dynamics. The only document the McClellan committee investigators were able to find in the Pentagon in favor of that award, according to their testimony, was a five-page memorandum signed by McNamara, Korth, and Eugene Zuckert, then Secretary of the Air Force, but not—interestingly enough—by Gilpatric. Senator Curtis charged in his Senate speech on October 3, that some months after the contract was announced in November, 1962, "a team of experts was assembled in the Pentagon to review the designs . . . The experts were directed to find strong points for General Dynamics and weak points for Boeing so the decision could be defended in Senate hearings."

During the McClellan committee hearings in 1963, Senator Ervin of North Carolina focused on another angle to this contract when he said to McNamara, "I would like to ask you whether or not there was any connection whatever between your selection of General Dynamics, and the fact that the Vice President of the United States happens to be a resident of the state in which that company has one of its principal, if not its principal office." The reference of course was to Lyndon Johnson, to Texas, and to Fort Worth. McNamara answered, "Absolutely not." [7] In the dissolute atmosphere of Washington there were few to believe such political virginity possible. When General Ac-

[6] *Ibid.*, p. 5.
[7] *Idem.*

counting Office investigators asked McNamara how he
came to override military judgment, "The Secretary said
that, after finding the Air Force estimates inadequate for
judging the cost implications of the two proposals [i.e.,
General Dynamics' and Boeing's], he had made rough
judgments of the kind he had made for many years with the
Ford Motor Company." The most charitable comment is
that the TFX, then, proved to be the Edsel of his Pentagon
years.

Under normal circumstances one would have expected
all this to be aired in the 1968 campaign. But the military-
industrial complex plays both sides of the political fence,
and the defense contractors are an easy source of campaign
funds. Nixon not only kept silent but pledged himself to the
very same plane. The same cynical charges made behind the
scenes about the original TFX contract will no doubt be
made again about Nixon's reaffirmation of it. The first
point in favor of General Dynamics was and is its financial
weakness. Boeing, with a better record for engineering and
on costs, is in good shape; half its business is commercial, a
testimony to its reputation. Why let the weaker company
go down the drain? The TFX affair illustrates the survival
of the unfittest in the military-corporate jungle.

The second point in favor of General Dynamics was and
remains political. General Dynamics is in Texas, a swing
state with twenty-four electoral votes, and its biggest sub-
contractor on the F-111, Grumman, is in New York with
forty-five electoral votes. Boeing would have produced the
plane in Kansas, with eight votes, which go Republican anyway, and in the state of Washington with nine. Nixon's
November 2 pledge shows that any major new plane must
show it can fly successfully through the electoral college.
Nixon's pre-election speech at Fort Worth recalls two
other comparable appearances there, one *opera buffa*,
one tragic. The former occurred on December 11, 1962, a
month after General Dynamics won the TFX contract,
when Johnson made a triumphant visit to the plant at Fort
Worth and was greeted by union members waving banners

which said "LBJ Saved the Day" and "We're Here to Say Thanks to LBJ." [8] The other was the morning of November 22, 1963, a few hours before he was assassinated, when President Kennedy addressed a rally in Fort Worth and paid tribute to the TFX as "the best fighter system in the world." [9] For Johnson and Kennedy, as for Nixon, in the TFX contract electioneering and defense were inextricably mingled.

A key word in the TFX controversy was "commonalty." McNamara wanted a plane which could be used by the Air Force and the Navy in common. With the cancellation of the contract for the Navy's version of the F-111, the battle for commonalty between the two services was lost. But Nixon's pledge on the F-111 shows that commonalty still exists in defense politics. For Republican as well as Democratic administrations, what is best for General Dyamics is best for the country.

This mention of "commonalty" brings us to the other two misjudgments involved in the TFX decision. One was to try to build one plane for many diverse Air Force and Navy missions. The other was to counter a Soviet bomber threat which does not now exist and is unlikely ever to come into being. With these misjudgments [10] we come to technological details which must become part of public knowledge if we are to understand the expensive and nightmarish nonsense in which the arms race has engulfed us.

President-elect Nixon, as we have seen, pledged himself to "root out 'the whiz kid' approach" to national defense. As it happens, the "whiz kids" were as opposed to the TFX as generals and admirals were to the idea of trying to build a

[8] Fort Worth *Star-Telegram*, December 12, 1962, quoted in McClellan Committee hearings on the TFX, Part X, p. 2658.

[9] *Public Papers of the Presidents: John F. Kennedy 1963*, p. 887.

[10] I venture to speak so dogmatically not only because of what has happened this year to the F-111, but because among men at the Pentagon devoted to McNamara I have found no one who does not feel the TFX was a mistake.

common plane for both services. "Pressure within the Defense Department for a single sophisticated multimission aircraft [using the new swing-wing design] came from the Office of Defense Research and Engineering, which .was headed in the early 1960s by Harold Brown, the present Secretary of the Air Force," *Congressional Quarterly* reported last February 16. "Although the concept was opposed by the young systems analysts that Defense Secretary McNamara had brought with him to the Pentagon, they were not then in a position to conduct a running battle with Brown. At the time the Office of Systems Analysis was subordinate to the Pentagon comptroller, which was one level below Brown." Nixon to the contrary, this mistake might not have been made if the "whiz kids" had had more influence.

McNamara had been trying to cut down duplication in supplies among the three services, a source of enormous waste, and he accomplished substantial savings in this field. His critics in Congress say privately that to an automobile man, accustomed to mounting various kinds of cars on much the same chassis, the idea of using the same "chassis" in military planes must have seemed a natural. Indeed to an outsider there seems to be little reason why the same plane should not be used by the various services for the same type of mission. Why—for example—can't the Air Force and the Navy use the same dogfighter?

The trouble in the case of the TFX or F-111 is that the Air Force and the Navy had such diverse missions to be performed by the common plane on which McNamara insisted. It is being built for a tactical fighter, a long-range strategic bomber, a reconnaissance plane, and—until the Navy contract was canceled—a new weapons system, a plane carrying a new type of missile.

The Navy wanted the plane to be light enough for a carrier but big enough to carry a special missile—the Phoenix —and a big load of radar equipment. Its Naval mission would be to loiter hour after hour over the fleet to protect it from a nuclear supersonic bomber attack; the radar would enable the plane to detect an incoming plane and hit it with the missile far enough away so that the fleet would be safe from nuclear blast and radiation. The Air Force wanted the plane to be able to fulfill a very different mission. It was to be able to fly at supersonic speed under the radar defenses around the Soviet Union and then, after unloading its nuclear bombs on target, make altitude swiftly enough to elude not only enemy ack-ack or fighter planes but the effects of the nuclear blast it had set off. To fit one plane to two such diverse purposes would seem to require the ingenuity of a Rube Goldberg. This particular mistake has been thoroughly debated, since it serves intra-service animosity. There's nothing the Navy hates worse than losing a battle to the Air Force.

A second level of misjudgment, the most basic of all, has hardly been discussed at all, at least in public. Here one is led to question the good sense of both the Air Force and the Navy. The Navy is still as full of bomber admirals as the Air Force is of bomber generals. They started the bomber gap nonsense in the fifties and still suffer from the obsessions which the arms lobby exploits so skillfully. "In the early 1950's we were told the Russians were going to build thousands of supersonic bombers," Senator Symington commented ruefully last May during the Senate hearings on the 1969 defense budget. "They did not build any long-range bombers of that type." [11] Symington was himself once the captive and spokesman of those inflated fears, as he was several years later of the "missile gap" campaign, which he later helped to expose as fraudulent.

In the hearings last April on "The Status of U.S. Strategic Power," which reflected the views and fears of those who favor a bigger arms budget, Chairman Stennis said of the present Soviet bomber fleet, "I have never looked upon these bombers as a serious threat to the U.S. unless we just let our guard down completely. They are the same old bombers, the Bear and the Bison." These are the subsonic bombers whose appearance in Moscow in the fifties set off the

[11] 1969 Senate Defense Appropriations Hearings, Part V, p. 2664.

bomber gap scare. The Russians just aren't spending money on long-range supersonic nuclear bombers when the same delivery job can be done so much more cheaply and quickly by missiles.

When Stennis's Preparedness Subcommittee of Senate Armed Services filed its report October 4 on the U.S. Tactical Air Power Program, it said, "The F-111B [i.e., the Navy version of the F-111 armed with the Phoenix missile—IFS] was designed primarily for fleet air defense against a Soviet supersonic bomber. But that threat is either limited or does not exist." Yet the Navy, having got rid of the F-111B, is planning its new VFX-1 to carry a Phoenix missile for use against the same non-existent supersonic Soviet bomber attack. The Navy insisted in the fiscal 1969 hearings that the Phoenix-armed plane "is the only system that provides the Navy with an acceptable level of Fleet Air Defense for the 1970–80 era, particularly for any missile threat against the fleet." [12]

This assumes that the Soviets will play the game our way and build the supersonic nuclear bombers the Phoenix is designed to counter. In chess, when one sees the other side concentrating his forces in one sector, one attacks in another. But our Joint Chiefs of Staff do not seem to play chess. *Congressional Quarterly*, which has good sources in the Pentagon, reported last May 3 that many Navy aviators were hostile to both the F-111B and its successor, the VFX-1 project, for a Phoenix-armed plane. It quoted a Pentagon source as saying the whole program was based on a false premise. It said Soviet doctrine envisioned the use of fighters, submarines, and missile-launching patrol boats instead of nuclear supersonic bombers for attacks on carriers and battleships. Obviously an attack would come where the other side can see we are least prepared. The Phoenix is likely to prove not only a waste of funds but an impediment to genuine defense by concentrating on a threat which does not exist now and is not likely to exist later.

[12] *Ibid.*, Part IV, p. 1426.

The main Air Force mission for the F-111 is a reflection of the same bomber delusions, but on a larger scale. To see this in perspective one must step back and observe that we now have three major ways of destroying the Soviet Union. One is the ICBM, the intercontinental ballistic missile. The second is the submarine-launched nuclear missile, the Polaris. The third is the intercontinental bomber force of the Strategic Air Command. Any one of these three forces can itself deliver much more than the 400 megatons which Mc-Namara estimates would destroy three-fourths of the Soviet Union's industrial capacity and 64 million people, or one-third its population.

Of the three mega-murder machines, the only one which can be stopped is the bomber fleet. It's an expensive luxury, a toy on which the bomber generals dote, and which the aircraft industry is only too happy to supply. High-flying bombers cannot get through the Soviets' radar and SAM (surface-to-air) missile defenses. So the F-111 is designed to duck low under Soviet radar defenses, drop nuclear bombs, and make a high, fast getaway, all at supersonic speeds. The basic argument against the F-111 is that if we ever want to hit major targets in the Soviet Union, we would do so with missiles which can reach their targets in thirty minutes with fifteen-minute warning time instead of planes whose flight and warning time would be measured in hours. If we tried to use bombers first, they would only warn the enemy and provide plenty of time for retaliatory missile strikes against our cities. If these bombers were to be used for a second strike *after* a Russian attack on us, the bombers (if any were left) would arrive hours after the missiles, and there would be little if anything left to destroy anyway. The intercontinental bomber is a surplus and obsolete deterrent but one and one-third billion dollars is allocated to the F-111 in the fiscal 1969 budget, much of it for these bombers.

But this is not the end of this expensive nonsense. The

military always assumes that the enemy will do what we do, that anything *we* produce *they* will produce. This is sometimes but not always true. The geographical and strategic situation of the Soviet Union is not the same as that of the United States; this dictates differences in weapons systems. In addition—no small consideration—the country which is poorer and has fewer resources to waste will be more careful in its expenditures. But we always estimate that the enemy will spend as prodigally as we do. This is how the bomber and missile gap scares originated. So we are spending billions to "keep ahead" of Soviet bombers and bomber defenses. We are also assuming that the Soviets will be as silly as we are and also build a fleet of F-111's to "get under" our radar defenses. So Congress has already embarked on another multi-billion-dollar program of building new radar "fences" and new types of interceptor planes to deal with these hypothetical Soviet F-111's.

To make all this plausible, the Air Force does its best to hide from the Congress the true facts about the Soviet air force. Twice during the past year Senator Symington, who feels that the billions spent on this bomber are diverting funds which could more sensibly be spent on new fighter planes, has asked Pentagon witnesses for the numbers of the various Soviet bombers. "Do you believe," he asked Dr. John S. Foster, Jr., Director of Defense Research and Development, "that the Soviet Union poses a serious bomber threat to the United States today?" The answer was "Yes, Senator Symington, I do." Symington replied incredulously, "The Soviets have not built a bomber for years, except the Blinder—and the latter's performance is not as good as the B-58 which we abandoned. In spite of that we now have to spend billions of dollars defending against bombers also."

He then asked Dr. Foster to supply the Appropriations Committee with the numbers of each type of Soviet bomber. The numbers were deleted by the censor.[13] But if one turns to McNamara's final statement in the same hear-

[13] See p. 2362, 1969 Defense Department Budget Hearings, Part IV.

ings[14] he gives the number of Soviet intercontinental bombers as 155, as compared with our 697. These Soviet bombers are mostly the old subsonic Bear and Bison bombers, neither of which could possibly duck under U.S. radar defenses in the way the F-111 is supposed to duck under the Soviet Union's.

Even the report on *The Status of U.S. Strategic Power* filed last September 27 by the Senate's Preparedness Subcommittee under Senator Stennis, which argues for larger arms expenditures, says, "There is no evidence that the Soviets are proceeding with the development of a new heavy bomber and, should they elect to develop one, it is probable we would see indications of the program three to four years before the aircraft becomes operational."

To counter this, the Air Force sophists have come up with a new argument. When Senator Symington asked Dr. Foster, as head of Pentagon research and development, why they were planning new types of bomber defense against non-existent types of Soviet planes, Dr. Foster replied, "discouragement of Soviet aspirations to develop a more advanced bomber." [15] But why spend billions to discourage the Soviets from building a bomber they show no signs of building anyway?

Another favorite reason often used by the Air Force may be found in Air Force Chief of Staff General McConnell's presentation to the Stennis hearings on strategic power last April. "A bomber force," the general said, "causes the Soviets to continue to develop bomber defenses rather than concentrating their expenditures just on missile defenses." [16] *So we waste money to make them waste money.* Though we are richer, this may be worse for us than them, because our planes are far more elaborate and expensive.

Since the Air Force thus admits that there is no sign as yet of a new supersonic Soviet bomber able to penetrate

[14] *Ibid.*, Part V, p. 2718.
[15] *Ibid.*, p. 2719.
[16] "Status of US Strategic Power," Preparedness Investigating Subcommittee of the Senate Committee on Armed Services, 90th Congress, 2nd Session, April 30, 1968, Part II, p. 169.

our existing defenses, why does it go on talking of a Soviet bomber "threat"? As usual, it turns out that this simple word has an unexpected meaning in the special language developed at the Pentagon. This prize item of military semantics may be found in the testimony of Air Force Secretary Brown to these same Stennis committee hearings. Dr. Brown was explaining to the committee that if Soviet anti-aircraft defenses were improved and we had to build in additional "penetration aids" to get past more efficient radar devices, we would have to build bigger bombs than we now have. "Otherwise," he said, "we will find ourselves carrying many penetration aids and comparatively few weapons." Dr. Brown went on to say there was "general agreement" at the Pentagon that such an advanced U.S. bomber "probably will be needed at some time in the future" but just when would depend on "how fast and far the Soviet threat is likely to evolve." Then he explained, "By threat here we are principally talking about Soviet defenses against bombers." [17]

The threat, in other words, is not that they might be able successfully to attack us with their bombers but that they might build up their anti-bomber defenses to the point where we might not be able to attack them successfully with *our* bombers! It would be only a short step from this to defining aggression as the building of defenses to discourage an enemy attack.

The *reductio ad absurdum* is in a passage I found in the fiscal 1969 defense budget hearings before the House Approriations Committee. Mahon of Texas, the able chairman of the defense subcommittee, was questioning Air Force officials about the Soviet bomber menace. Here is the colloquy which spills the whole and final truth about this costly nightmare:

MR. MAHON: Officials of the Department of Defense have not indicated to this committee that they think the Soviets will go very strong on the manned bomber. They will rely principally on the ICBM. Is that right?

[17] *Ibid.*, p. 179.

GENERAL McCONNELL [Air Force Chief of Staff]: That is the consensus.

MR. MAHON: The Air Force has a little different view?

GENERAL McCONNELL: [Deleted by censor].

MR. MAHON: [Deleted by censor].

GENERAL McCONNELL: [Deleted by censor].

MR. MAHON: How long have the Soviets had, Secretary [of the Air Force] Brown, to develop a follow-on[18] bomber?

SECRETARY BROWN: They have had ten years.

MR. MAHON: Have you seen any evidence?

SECRETARY BROWN: I see no evidence of it, Mr. Chairman. The Air Force view is at least as much a view that "they ought to have one" as it is "they will have one." [19]

Billions in contracts for new bombers and new bomber defense are threatened should the Russians stubbornly persist in not building a new bomber force. In extremity perhaps Congress might be persuaded to add the Soviet Union to our foreign aid clients and give them an advanced bomber force to keep the U.S. aircraft business strong and prosperous. Or General Dynamics and the other big companies in the military-industrial complex might pass the hat among themselves and buy Moscow a new bomber. Should those old obsolete subsonic Bears and Bisons stop flying altogether, it would be a catastrophe for Fort Worth, a form of economic aggression in reverse. Ours—the rich man's strategy—is to make the Russians waste their resources by wasting ours. Theirs—the poor man's strategy—might be to strike a mortal blow at the arms business here by cutting their own expenditures to the minimum the balance of terror requires.

Nothing so terrifies the military-industrial complex as this notion of a *minimum* deterrent, as we shall see when we analyze Nixon's pledge to restore that crucial notion of "nuclear superiority," about which McNamara had finally succeeded in making the country see a little sense.

January 2, 1969
New York Review

[18] Air Force lingo for a new bomber.

[19] House Appropriations Committee Hearings on the Fiscal 1969 Defense Budget, Executive Session, February 26, 1968, Part I, p. 751.

NIXON AND THE ARMS RACE: HOW MUCH IS "SUFFICIENCY"?

The annals of the Nixon Administration, in so far as arms are concerned, must begin, like the Gospel of John, with The Word. But Nixon has changed The Word at the very outset. In the campaign it was "superiority." At his first press conference this was changed to "sufficiency." The two words seem to move in different directions. One implies an endless arms race. The other seems to promise that at some point we will have enough. . . .

Sufficiency was the Eisenhower Administration theme in fighting off the demands for higher defense spending from the military and its industrial allies. Is Nixon, faced with budgetary problems and an unstable dollar, coming back to it now? That is the question which will soon be answered by his decision on the anti-ballistic missile and by the results of the review he has ordered of the military budget, which is due the latter part of March.

The shift from "superiority" to "sufficiency" may prove to mean little or nothing. But the shift, even if only semantic, offers new leverage to the peace movement. For it raises the question of how much armaments is enough, and it raises it on the highest level and in the broadest forum. When the new President himself adopts the term "sufficiency," he invites public discussion of the military budget in the simplest and most graphic terms. How much is enough? If Secretary Laird has his way, the budget review will find present military appropriations *in*sufficient. Perhaps the peace movement ought to set up a public hearing board of its own to take testimony from experts on this problem of "sufficiency" and publish both the testimony and the final report. In what follows we will try to give a preliminary sketch of the military monster.

The real word for America's nuclear arsenal is not sufficiency but lunacy. When the Rathjens report says "the
strategic forces of both sides are too large," that is the
understatement of the millennium. Briefly, we have three
and one-half times as many nuclear warheads as the Soviet
Union, and ten times as many as we need—not just to
"deter" but to destroy it. The first figure is from Clark Clifford's final posture statement on the fiscal 1970 budget
(page 42) last January 15. This says we can launch 4,200
warheads with our ICBM's, Polaris submarines, and bombers, while the Soviet Union can launch 1,200. The second
figure is from a table (page 57) of McNamara's final posture
statement for the fiscal 1969 budget dated January 22 of last
year. This for the first time gave figures on the number of
1-megaton warheads (one megaton = 1,000,000 tons of
TNT) needed to wreck the Soviet Union. The *maximum* is
400.

As McNamara explains, "Further increments would not
meaningfully change the amount of damage because we
would be bringing smaller and smaller cities under attack."
McNamara figures this would kill 74 million people, or
more than three times the total Soviet losses in World War
II, and destroy 76 percent of Soviet industry. Give or take
any reasonable number for error, this is no longer war as
man has ever known it before, but instant cremation. Sev-
enty-four million people will be "only" 30 percent of the
Soviet population in 1972, the year to which this table is
projected. But a footnote (page 52) of an earlier McNamara posture statement in January, 1967 still applies to these
estimates of lethality. The footnote explains that they cover
only "prompt" deaths from blast and fallout—"they do not
include deaths resulting from fire, storms, disease, and general disruption of everyday life." So add to the immediate
deaths any number for the slow deaths, and then ask yourself again how much is enough? What is sufficiency?

The assumption behind these computations is as distant

from human realities as the numbers. Never has so much precision been attached to so much spurious rationality. The assumption is that war is a kind of game on which nations embark after consulting a computer to see who would come out ahead. Not the least dangerous aspect of our war machine is that it is based on so fallacious a theory as to why and how wars occur. Starting from so abstract and mechanistic an axiom, the planners have developed a series of corollaries which seem designed to confuse not only us but even our computers.

The first corollary is that if it looks to the attacker as if the damage to himself in any war would be "unacceptable," he will be "deterred." The second corollary is that the way to confront your enemy with "unacceptable" damage is to have an "assured destruction capability," which you can impose on him in a "second strike" of retaliation if he attacks first. The third is that to do this you need a nuclear arsenal which is so large and so invulnerable that the enemy cannot destroy it—or enough of it—in a first strike to save himself from destruction in return. The fourth and final corollary is that you have to keep building more and better weapons to be sure of maintaining that second-strike capacity. This is what keeps the nuclear rat race going. Those who work within the military bureaucracy are doomed to serve its purposes. The proliferation of doctrine furthers the proliferation of armaments. The finely spun concepts of deterrence and second strike give a rational appearance to an essentially irrational process, the mindless multiplication of weaponry.

The arms race is based on an optimistic view of technology and a pessimistic view of man. It assumes there is no limit to the ingenuity of science and no limit to the deviltry of human beings. Thus so-called "conservative" military planning assumes the best of the enemy's laboratories and the worst of his intentions. It seeks to ensure against all possible contingencies, like an insurance salesman selling protection against the possibility of blizzards in the tropics.

The proliferating corollaries of deterrence having conditioned us to mega-weapons and mega-deaths, the sheer numbers of nuclear weaponry no longer surprise us. They numb and comfort. When Clifford reports that we have 4,200 deliverable warheads as compared with the Soviets' 1,200, we are instinctively cheered to hear that we are so far "ahead." No one any longer asks where they would be "delivered" or how many times we might find ourselves killing the same peasant woman and her cow. Such talk is "old hat." It is hard to realize that less than a decade has passed since a one-time Chairman of the Joint Chiefs of Staff like General Maxwell Taylor could argue that 200 missiles would be a sufficient minimum deterrent. It is odd to be reminded by General LeMay himself in his new book[1] that "as few as 17 large-yield Soviet ICBM's could severely damage the 17 densely populated urban complexes in the United States that contain over one-third of our population."

By the same calculation, three large-yield U.S. ICBM's could destroy Moscow, Leningrad, and Kiev while thirty much smaller ones could wreck the Soviet Union's thirty other cities with a population of 500,000 or more. Surely this should be enough deterrence. LeMay himself proceeds by a series of splendid non sequiturs to prove that this means we need more missiles! He goes on to say, "The Soviets have 40 ICBM's for each U.S. urban complex. The U.S. on the other hand, to cover some 175 dispersed Soviet cities, would need 7,000 missiles to provide the same ratio of 40 per target. Yet we plan to have only 1,054 from now on." If one large-yield Soviet ICBM is enough to damage severely a whole U.S. urban complex, why do they need 40? And why do we need 40 each for every one of 175 Soviet cities, though 175 gets us down to places like Kirovsk, half the size of Hiroshima (about 100,000) which we destroyed with a "primitive" A-bomb so small (less than 20 kilotons) we no longer consider that size a strategic weapon?

[1] General Curtis E. LeMay, *America Is in Danger* (Funk & Wagnalls, 1968), p. 88.

Our 4,200 warheads average out—to adopt LeMay's
standard—to twenty-four each for those 175 Soviet cities.
But apparently this is insufficient. We are on the verge of
expanding the number of warheads eightfold, and soon
after, ten- or twelvefold. A table appended to McNamara's
last posture statement (page 214) shows that during the
eight years in which he presided over the Defense Department we spent over $68 billion on our strategic forces.[2]
And now we are told, in effect, by McNamara himself, that
it is not enough! [3] Our weapons have to be MIRVed.

The acronym stands for Multiple Independently Targeted Reentry Vehicle. The subject has long been a deep
secret. It was first described publicly by Secretary McNamara, when he said in his final posture statement on January
22 of last year, "Now, in the late 1960's, because the Soviet
Union *might* [the italics were McNamara's] deploy extensive ABM defenses, we are making some very important
changes in our strategic missile forces. Instead of a single
large warhead, our missiles are now being designed to carry
several small warheads and penetration aids, because it is the
number of warheads, or objects which appear to be war-

[2] For the morbid it is worth adding that despite this vast nuclear
arsenal we also allocated more than $190 billion to our general purpose
forces during the same eight years. The total assigned in those eight years
to "defense" (surely it deserves quotation marks in this context) was more
than $500 billion or half a trillion dollars!

[3] At the same time McNamara warned, " 'Superiority' is of little significance. For even with . . . any 'superiority' realistically attainable, the
blunt, inescapable fact remains that the Soviet Union could still effectively
destroy the United States, even after absorbing the full weight of an
American first strike. . . . Under these circumstances, surely it makes
sense for us both to try to halt the momentum of the arms race which
is causing vast expenditures on both sides and promises no increase in
security" (pp. 52–53, final posture statement, 1969 budget). In a similar
vein Clifford warned in his final posture statement for fiscal 1970 (p. 49),
"We stand on the eve of a new round in the armaments race with the
Soviet Union, a race which will contribute nothing to the real security
of either side while increasing substantially the already great defense burdens of both." No such sentiments have ever been expressed by their successor, whose book, *America's Strategy Gap: A House Divided*, is a
Goldwaterite "better dead than Red" manifesto.

heads [i.e., the so-called "penetration aids"—IFS] to the
defender's radars, that will determine the outcome in a con-
test with an ABM defense."

Last August, sixteen MIRV's were tested successfully for
the first time in an ICBM, the Minuteman, and in an underwater ballistic missile, the Poseidon, which will replace Polaris. A vast expansion in the number of our warheads is
now under way. McNamara's final budget set in motion the
conversion of 31 of our present 41 Polaris-carrying submarines into carriers of Poseidon. The remaining 10 are of a
type it would be too expensive to convert; it would be
cheaper to replace them with new Poseidon submarines.
The number of warheads the Poseidons can carry is still
classified. The number generally given is 10 warheads per
missile, though I have been told by one informed source
that the Poseidon can carry as many as 14.

Each Polaris sub now carries 16 Polaris missiles, or a total
for the fleet of 656 missiles, each with one warhead. But as
Poseidons replace the Polaris on 31 ships—with a total of
496 missiles—and if each Poseidon missile can carry 10 warheads, that is a total of 4,960 warheads. In addition we are
replacing Minuteman I and Minuteman II, our main intercontinental ballistic missiles, with Minuteman III, which
will also be MIRVed. Again the figures are classified but it
is generally believed that each Minuteman III will carry
three warheads.

In his final posture statement McNamara projected for the
period 1969–73 a nuclear missile force made up of:

> 1,000 Minutemen
>   496 Poseidons
>   160 Polaris
>   54 Titans
> ———
> 1,710 missiles

This was the same size as our nuclear missile force last September when we estimated our own nuclear long-range
missile force at 1,710 and the Soviet's at 945. But MIRVed
up, this would become, in warheads:

3,000 Minutemen
4,960 Poseidons
  160 Polaris
   54 Titans
_____
8,174 warheads

This would change the disparity in nuclear missile warheads from less than two-to-one in our favor (1,710 to 945)
to almost nine-to-one (8,174 to 945). It would mean we
could aim several of our missiles at each one of theirs, threatening a possible first strike. To see how this expansion of nuclear power must look to the other side we need only read a
passage in Clark Clifford's final posture statement last January, and substitute U.S. where he said Soviets. "It is quite
evident," Clifford wrote, "that if the Soviets achieve greater
accuracy with their ICBM's, together with a MIRV capability, our land-based strategic missiles will become increasingly vulnerable to a first strike."

The most alarming aspect of this vast expansion of American striking power, as seen from the other side, must be the
fact that it is accompanied by a new propaganda campaign
designed to make the U.S. feel insecure—to sell the idea that
all this still is not enough. A new numbers game is being
played similar to the ones which accompanied the bomber-
and missile-gap campaigns. Its principal spokesman is the man
Nixon picked to be Secretary of Defense, Melvin R. Laird.
Through him and its multifarious lesser mouthpieces, the
military-industrial complex is trying to make it appear that
new "gaps" are developing, one in strategic offensive
power, the other in anti-ballistic missiles, and that these
threaten to change the balance of power and to create what
Nixon in the campaign melodramatically called a "survival
gap," a phrase he may regret if he should now seek to hold
the military budget down.
This new campaign focuses first of all on the sharp increase in the number of Soviet ICBM's in recent years. The

latest U.S. intelligence estimates, as given by Clifford in January, credit the Soviet Union with a steep increase in ICBM's in two years: from 250 in mid-1966 to 570 in mid-1967 to 900 in September, 1968, as compared with the 1,054 ICBM's we have had since we decided to freeze their numbers at that level in November, 1964.

It is possible that by next fall the Soviets will actually have more ICBM's than we do. By focusing simplistically just on these numbers, a new wave of near-hysteria may be whipped up. But ICBM's are not the only component of the strategic forces. And numbers are not the only thing that counts. The cryptic remark with which Clifford followed this revelation is a good starting point for assessing the realities. "We have been anticipating for some time," Clifford reported, "a Soviet deployment of a solid-fuel ICBM. We now believe the deployment of such a missile has started, although at a relatively slow rate." These quiet words light up an extraordinary technological missile gap in our favor. Liquid-fuel missiles are obsolete. They take about fifteen minutes to load, and they are so full of valves and controls, the chances of a misfire are high. The solid-fuel missile can be fired in less than a minute. We have only fifty-four liquid-fuel ICBM's left in our arsenal, the huge Titans, still useful as big city-killers, though vulnerable to a first strike. We began to phase out the liquid-fuel Atlas and to deploy the solid-fuel Minuteman as far back as the autumn of 1962. It is startling to learn that we only now "believe," in Clifford's words, that the Soviets have begun to deploy a solid-fuel missile of their own, though "at a relatively slow rate." "Their new solid-fuel ICBM," Clifford added (page 46), "appears to be no better than our earliest Minuteman missiles, first deployed in fiscal 1963." Fiscal 1963 began July 1, 1962. U.S. intelligence estimates of Soviet power are not given to understatement. If that is the best the intelligence men can say, the lag is serious indeed.

The fact is that during the past six years we have not only replaced all our liquid-fuel Atlases with solid-fuel Minutemen but introduced two new and improved models of Minuteman; the missile industry, like the automobile, believes that the way to maintain sales is to get the customer to trade in his old car every few years for a new model. Our present force consists of 600 Minuteman I's and 400 Minuteman II's, and the Minuteman III—with MIRV, i.e., multiple warheads—is already being phased in.[4]

To go from Minuteman I to Minuteman III, as we have seen, is to increase the number of warheads by at least three for the same number of missiles. Even the Senate group closest to the Pentagon in outlook, the Preparedness Subcommittee of Senate Armed Services under the chairmanship of Stennis, said in its report last September 27:[5]

Instead of an increase in numbers of missile launches, we have planned to meet the greater and still growing Soviet threat by qualitative improvements such as *Poseidon, Minuteman III, MIRVs,* increased accuracy, penetration aids and silo hardening. *The Joint Chiefs themselves have not recommended a quantitative increase in missiles to meet the current threat* [emphasis added].

The numbers game is discounted on this more sophisticated level of discussion. What the Joint Chiefs ask, says the Stennis report, is not more missiles but "the phasing in of an advanced ICBM, which they believe would provide for the modernization [a lovely word, in two or three years a missile model is already "ancient"—IFS] of the force while increasing our total missile throw weight. Technical improvements which the Joint Chiefs foresee include better warhead design and increased reliability, survivability, penetrability and accuracy." What the Stennis report might have added, but doesn't—the Pentagon does not like to mention the subject—is that more "throw weight" would presumably make it possible for the new ICBM to carry more warheads than Minuteman III, further multiplying our striking power.

[4] *Status of U.S. Strategic Power. A Report by the Preparedness Subcommittee of the Senate Armed Services Committee,* 90th Congress, 2nd Session, September 27, 1968, p. 11.
[5] *Ibid.,* pp. 11-12.

If we MIRV, the Soviets will eventually MIRV their missiles, too. In the letter submitting his report to the full Armed Services Committee, Senator Stennis says, "Of major importance in the strategic nuclear field, are the apparently well-documented press reports that the Soviets have flown a multiple re-entry vehicle. This compounds our concern. . . ." But these "press reports" apparently were not "well-documented" enough to be confirmed in this year's posture statement. In any case we are several years ahead in this technological breakthrough and have already begun to deploy Poseidons and Minuteman III's.

Lest it stupefy the reader, we will touch only in passing on two other components of the nuclear equation in strategic offensive forces which the new numbers game omits— the intercontinental bomber (we have 646, or four times the Soviet fleet of 150), and the underwater missiles carried by nuclear submarine. We have 656 missiles (in process of being MIRVed, as we have seen, into ten times as many warheads) as against the Soviets' forty-five. When all these numbers and the technological factors are added in, the imbalance is so great that it makes talk of a new missile gap— even if the Soviets pass us in the number of ICBM's—a colossal deception. The gap in our favor is enormous.

Much the same holds true of the strategic defensive. It is true that the Russians have already built some elements of an anti-ballistic missile system around one city, Moscow, while we have yet to deploy our Sentinel at all. But their ABM system is already obsolete, and it would be to America's advantage if the Russians wasted scarce resources in deploying it. "Their GALOSH ABM system," Clifford reported in January, "resembles in certain important respects the Nike-Zeus system which we abandoned years ago because of its limited effectiveness." It is the same system Eisenhower wisely vetoed when the Joint Chiefs recommended its deployment in 1959. Even the Stennis report (page 10) says, "The fact that it has not been deployed at other cities probably indicates that Soviet officials have reservations about its effectiveness."

Perhaps they are at last readier to learn from our experience than the present advocates of the Sentinel ABM system in this country. "Had we produced and deployed the NIKE-ZEUS system [which GALOSH resembles] proposed by the Army at an estimated cost of $13 to $14 billion," Deputy Secretary of Defense Cyrus Vance told a Senate inquiry[6] two years ago, "most of it would have had to be torn out and replaced almost before it became operational, by the new missiles and radars of the NIKE-X system. *By the same token, other technological developments in offensive forces over the next . . .* [deleted by Pentagon censor] *years make obsolete or drastically degrade the NIKE-X* [Sentinel] *system as presently envisioned*" (my italics).

Even here our planned ABM program is many times the size of the Soviets'. They are wasting money putting an already obsolete system around one city. We are on the verge—if we go ahead with Sentinel—of wasting many times that amount by deploying a soon-to-be-obsolete "thin" ABM system big enough to give a dubious "area defense" to the whole country and "point defense" to more than a dozen cities. Even in folly, we may insist on being "ahead."

Even before the Russians finish deploying GALOSH around *one* city, we are preparing a further expansion of striking power big enough to overwhelm a much more extensive and up-to-date Soviet ABM when and if they deploy one. Such is the endless see-saw of the nuclear arms race.

In any discussion of "sufficiency" it is essential to take a close look at what our military thinks sufficient. To see the dimensions of the expansion projected for the next four years it is necessary to go back to McNamara's final posture

---

[6] *U.S. Armament and Disarmament Problems. Hearings before the* [Gore] *Subcommittee on Disarmament of Senate Foreign Relations,* February 3 to March 3, 1967, 90th Congress, First Session, p. 58.

statement of last year and read the section entitled "Capability Against the 'Highest Expected Threat' in the NIE." The NIE stands for the National Intelligence Estimates. These are agreed upon by the U.S. Intelligence Board (of twelve separate intelligence agencies, no less!). The Board provides a range of estimates as to Soviet power in the next few years. A McNamara footnote explains (page 57) that the "highest expected threat" is actually higher than anyone really expects, since this "is actually composed of the upper range of NIE projections for *each* element of the Soviets' forces" (italics in original). That is, strategic missiles, missile-armed submarines, and bombers. "In many cases," the footnote continues, "these represent alternatives and it is highly unlikely that all elements would ever reach the top end of the quantitative range simultaneously. Therefore, the 'highest expected threat' is really a greater threat than that projected in the NIE."

With that in mind, the reader may be prepared more fully to grasp the stupendous multiplication of our retaliatory power sketched by McNamara when he says,

Even if the Soviet strategic forces by 1972 reach the higher end of the range of estimates [these are classified—IFS] projected in the latest NIE's and even if they were to assign their entire available missile force to attacks on our strategic forces (reserving only refire missiles and bomber-delivered weapons for urban targets), about one-half of our forces programmed for 1972 would survive and remain effective.

Then McNamara says,

If the Soviets expand the Moscow ABM defense and deploy the same or a similar system around other cities at the highest rate projected [again the figures are classified—IFS] in the latest NIE's, about three-quarters of our surviving weapons would detonate over their targets.

Apparently—though McNamara does not say so explicitly—some 1,600 1-megaton warheads could under those circumstances reach their target. That is four times the 400 1-megaton warheads we mentioned earlier as enough to

wreck the Soviet Union. Here McNamara inserts the table
to which we earlier referred. It purports to show Soviet
population and industry destroyed in such an attack in
1972, assuming a total Soviet population of 247 million, of
whom 116 million would be urban. This is the horrendous
table:[7]

			INDUSTRIAL CAPACITY DESTROYED
WARHEADS	FATALITIES		
1-mt	millions	%	%
100	37	15	59
200	52	21	72
400	74	30	76
800	96	39	77
1200	109	44	77
1600	116	47	77

We see in this table that even if only 100 warheads got
through it would destroy 59 percent of Soviet industry and
kill 50 percent more people in one blow than the Nazis did
in the four years of World War II. If the Soviet Union
published a table of this kind we would accuse them of trying to terrorize us into giving up the nuclear arms race altogether.[8]

As if to pile horror on horror, McNamara added, "Even
if the Soviets deploy a substantial number of [additional]
ABM interceptors by 1972 our strategic missile forces alone
could still destroy more than two-fifths of their total popu-

[7] Line in original because, as McNamara explains, "beyond 400 . . .
would not meaningfully change the amount of damage."

[8] A more than adequate substitute is provided—with majestic objectivity—by McNamara himself in a table on p. 64 showing the number of
fatalities on both sides in the event of an "all-out strategic exchange" in
the mid-1970's. This shows that even if the U.S. built up offensive and defensive forces to a maximum so-called Posture B, including an anti-missile
defense, which he says would probably end by costing $40 billion, the
Soviets, by a maximum program of their own, adding MIRV's and penetration aids, plus 550 mobile ICBM's, could kill 90 million Americans even
if we struck first! Mobile ICBM's, constantly moving around on vehicles, would be almost impossible for an enemy to target.

lation (more than 100 million people) and over three-quarters of their industrial capacity." What an arsenal we must be building up!

McNamara goes on to explain that "these results, of course, reflect the decisions we have taken in recent years to enhance the future capabilities of our 'Assured Destruction' forces." These, he says, include (1) the replacement of Polaris by Poseidon with MIRV's, (2) improved missile penetration aids, i.e., chaff and decoys to confuse the radars which set in motion the other side's ABM's, (3) an increase in the planned number of Minuteman III ICBM's with MIRV's, (4) development of new small re-entry vehicles "to increase substantially the number of warheads or penetration aids which can be carried by a single missile," and (5) "the development and production of SRAM's for our strategic bombers." This last is an acronym for Short Range Attack Missiles. These would enable our intercontinental bombers to stop short of Soviet bomber defenses and fire nuclear missiles into Soviet territory.

In addition to the SRAM, the Air Force has begun a campaign for a new weapon system called SCAD (see the *New York Times*, February 5). These add a new horror to our alphabetical military nightmares. SCAD stands for Subsonic Cruise Armed Decoy. These are small pilotless but nuclear-armed aircraft which could be launched from a carrier plane toward enemy targets from beyond the Soviet Union's defense perimeter. One enthusiastic planner was quoted as saying, "SCAD does for bombers what the multiple warhead does for missiles—it makes the enemy's defense problem virtually impossible." It would take a new and larger intercontinental bomber to carry SCAD's, and this is what the Air Force hopes for. The cost, of course, will be in the billions.

In the meantime SCAD is one of ten "Advanced Development Projects" for which Clifford asked almost a quarter billion dollars in additional research and development funds in the new fiscal 1970 budget. One of these is a new ABM

to succeed Sentinel and a new "Underseas Long-Range
Missile System" in case Soviet anti-submarine capability becomes a threat to Polaris and Poseidon. Another is an Ocean
Engineering project which may take us one step further toward the new idea of hiding ICBM's under the ocean floor.
The armed forces also have not yet given up the idea of
using the MOL (the Manned Orbital Laboratory) as a step
toward weapons in space, despite an international treaty
against it. This, dear reader, only skims the surface of what
is on the drawing boards and in the laboratories; we have
only touched the highlights of the unclassified material on
strategic weapons. We have not even touched the plans in
the works for counter-insurgency, which promises new
Vietnams, or such goodies as new bacteriological and chemical weapons.

For the military, there will never be "sufficiency."

I would like to make three grave observations in conclusion.

(1) With MIRV, we are entering a new period of darkness. The U-2 and the SAMOS satellite dissipated the missile gap nonsense because we could actually see and count
how many ICBM's the other side had. There is no way to
see from afar, or to be sure, just how many MIRV's there
are on each missile. This may bring us back to that atmosphere of panicky conjecture and exaggeration so useful to
the arms lobby and the military.

(2) The deployment of an ABM will make each side
fearful lest the other venture a first strike, calculating that
the ABM, if improved sufficiently and buttressed by fallout
and blast shelters, may cut down casualties to an "acceptable" level. Each side will become more fearful of adventur-
ism on the other.

(3) MIRV's open a new era in the arms race, and raise
the threat of a first-strike capacity. If one side can, by
MIRV's, obtain, let us say, a tenfold advantage over the
other, it may have enough to destroy the other's missiles—

or think it has. This will take the balance out of the "balance of terror."

McNamara implies that the MIRV was developed as an answer-in-advance to a Soviet ABM. But there is evidence that MIRV was first developed to provide capacity for a first or preemptive strike. At last year's Senate hearings on the fiscal 1969 military budget, Senator Mansfield put a series of questions to Dr. John S. Foster, Jr., whom Laird has retained as the Pentagon's Director of Research and Engineering. These have gone almost unnoticed but deserve close attention. Question No. 10 asked, "Is it not true that the U.S. response to the discovery that the Soviets had made an initial deployment of an ABM system around Moscow and possibly elsewhere was to develop the MIRV system for Minuteman and Polaris?" The unexpected answer was:[9]

Not entirely. The MIRV concept was originally generated to increase our targeting capability rather than to penetrate ABM defenses. In 1961-62 planning for targeting the Minuteman force it was found that total number of aim points exceeded the number of Minuteman missiles. By splitting up the payload of a single missile [deleted] each [deleted] could be programmed [deleted] allowing us to cover these targets with [deleted] fewer missiles. [Deleted.] MIRV was originally born to implement the payload split-up [deleted]. It was found that the previously generated MIRV concept could equally well be used against ABM [deleted].

In 1961–62 our strategic force was far greater than the Soviet Union's. If we then sought a MIRV in order to cover more aim points, this could only have been for a counterforce or preemptive strategy. That was the time when McNamara, as shown by his famous Ann Arbor speech of June 16, 1962, was moving in that direction. "For a short time," General LeMay says in his new book, *America Is in Danger* (page 269), "I thought we had convinced Mr.

[9] *Senate Appropriations Committee Hearings on the Department of Defense Budget for Fiscal 1969*, 90th Congress, 2nd Session, Part 4, p. 2310. All the deletions are in the original, as made by the Pentagon's censors.

McNamara, but I soon learned how wrong we were. To be successful, such a counterforce strategy requires a clear nuclear superiority because it takes more than one missile to destroy another." MIRV, by increasing the number of warheads manyfold (Dr. Foster admitted to Mansfield), might soon give us in the neighborhood of 10,000 warheads, in place of our present 1,700 or so single-headed missiles.

At present the U.S. has three strategic forces, each of which is big enough to strike a mortal blow at the Soviet Union even if the other two were destroyed in a first strike. If we add SCAD's to our bombers and MIRV's to the Minuteman and to the nuclear submarine (Poseidon), we will have what must begin to look from the other side, with its present level of forces, like three separate strategic forces, *each with a first-strike capacity*. The MIRV is incomparably more unsettling to "the balance of terror" than the ABM. The MIRV is the great leap forward of the nuclear arms race. McNamara put it very quietly in this colloquy before the House Appropriations Committee hearings last year on the 1969 military budget:[10]

MR. MAHON [D. Tex., chairman of the committee]: I am concerned lest the Soviet Union make some kind of "quantum jump" in the development of their strategic forces. . . . Is it your view that neither the United States nor the Soviet Union in the next few years will come up with an entirely new weapon which will outmode present weapons?

SECRETARY MCNAMARA: I think it extremely unlikely. There will be continued development in such weapons. The true significance of more recent developments are obscured somewhat by the fact that they did not involve as dramatic a *physical* change as took place between the bomber and the missile. I, myself, do not agree with your statement that there are not changes going on today as important in terms of strategic capability as those that occurred between the bomber and the missile. *The fact is that the destruction capability between the Atlas and the Poseidon or between the Atlas and Minuteman III, in my opinion, was substantially more than between the B-52* [our last intercontinental bomber] *and the Atlas* [our first intercontinental missile] [my italics].

[10] *Op. cit.*, Part I, pp. 251-2.

Such are the incredible dimensions projected for our military machine. Unless some new agreement puts an end to the endless spiral and proliferation of new weapons and anti-weapons, it will devour an ever-increasing share of the material and scientific resources on both sides and make war, should it come, many times more destructive. . . .

March 27, 1969
New York Review

THE WAR MACHINE
UNDER NIXON

In government the budget is the message. Washington's heart is where the tax dollar goes. When President Nixon finally, and very tardily, presented his first budget proposals in mid-April in a mini-State of the Union message, he said, "Peace has been the first priority." But the figures showed that the first concern of the new Administration, as of the last, was still the care and feeding of the war machine.

Only Nixon's style had changed. "Sufficiency" rather than "superiority" in nuclear armaments remained the new watchword. But in practice it was difficult to tell them apart. Administrations change, but the Pentagon remains at the head of the table. Nixon's semantics recalled John F. Kennedy's eight years earlier. The Eisenhower Administration had waged battle for four years against the bomber gap and the missile gap with the slogan of "sufficiency." "Only when our arms are sufficient beyond doubt," was Kennedy's elegant riposte in his inaugural, signaling a new spiral upward in the arms race, "can we be certain without doubt that they will never be employed." The rhetoric was fresh but the idea was no different from John Foster

Dulles's "position of strength." This is the *plus ça change* of American government and diplomacy. It emerged intact after Nixon's first three months in office, too.

At a press conference four days after his budget message, Nixon said again that "sufficiency" in weaponry was "all that is necessary." But a moment later he was clearly equating it with nuclear superiority. He said he didn't want "the diplomatic credibility" of a future President in a crisis like that over Cuba's missiles "impaired because the United States was in a second-class or inferior position." A press corps obsessed with the latest plane incident off North Korea did not pause to consider the implications. Was "diplomatic credibility" to be measured in megatons? Were we preparing again to play a thermonuclear game of "chicken," to see who would blink first at the prospect of instant incineration? Was this not the diplomacy of brinkmanship and the strategy of permanent arms race?

No correspondent asked these questions, and Nixon did not spell out the inferences. His tone was softer, his language more opaque, than that of the campaign, but the essential "security gap" theme had not changed. The main emphasis of Nixon's first months in office, the main idea he tried to sell the country, turned out to be that it was in mortal peril of a Soviet first-strike capacity. The new Administration sought to overcome a mounting wave of opposition to the ABM, and to the military generally, by ringing the bells of panic.

True, the Secretary of State often seemed to deny the perils the Secretary of Defense painted. Which was the party line? It was indicative that when visiting editors were given a press kit on the ABM April 7, with a covering letter on White House stationery signed by Herbert G. Klein as Nixon's "Director of Communications," the only thing new in that kit, the only news it contained, *and the one bit on which nobody commented*, was the "document" the Administration had chosen as the first item. It was a reproduction of a column in which Joseph Alsop three days earlier had exuberantly portrayed the "grim" (a favorite Alsop word) dangers of a first strike from Laird's new monster, the Soviet SS-9. The leading journalistic pied piper of the bomber gap and the missile gap had been enlisted by the new Administration to help it to propagate a new gap. If the White House stationery and the Klein signature were not enough to make Alsop's nightmare official doctrine, the reproduction of the column carried at the bottom of the page this imprimatur: "Prepared under the direction of the Republican National Committee, 1625 Eye St. N.W., Washington, D.C." The candor was dazzling.

The Budget Bureau fact sheets which accompanied Nixon's spending proposals sought to create the impression that on the military budget, as on so much else, Nixon in power was reversing the course set by Nixon on campaign. "Military and military assistance programs account for 1.1 billion (27 percent) of the $4.0 billion outlay reduction [for fiscal 1970]," said one fact sheet, "and $3.0 billion (55 percent) of the cut in budget authority." But, as we shall see, while the cuts in domestic civilian programs proved all too real, those in the military budget were either dubious or deferrals.

There was in the Nixon budget one complete and dramatic about-face—on the FB-111. Six months earlier, just before the election, at Fort Worth, where General Dynamics was building this new strategic bomber, Nixon had promised to make the F-111 "one of the foundations of our air supremacy." Now it was put permanently on the shelf. Procurement of the bomber was cut back sharply for fiscal 1969, which ended June 30, and abandoned altogether for fiscal 1970. Only the F-111D, the Air Force fighter version of this plane, was to stay in production a while longer.

Thus *finis* was soon to be written to the career of the multipurpose, multiservice plane originally known as the TFX, one of McNamara's most costly misjudgments. But on this, as on almost every other item of apparent economy in the Nixon-Laird revisions of the Pentagon's budget, the few hundred millions saved in fiscal 1969 and 1970 were linked to commitments which would cost literally billions more in the decade ahead. Every short step back hid another leap forward in expenditures.

The TFX was McNamara's effort to stall off the drive of the bomber generals to commit the country to an entirely new manned bomber in the missile age. He gave them the FB-111, the bomber version of the TFX, instead. Laird reduced FB-111 procurement in fiscal 1969 by $107 million and eliminated altogether the planned outlay of $321 million in fiscal 1970. But he then added $23 million for fiscal 1970 to speed "full scale engineering" of the new intercontinental bomber AMSA (Advanced Manned Strategic Aircraft) for which the Air Force and the aviation industry have been lobbying for years. "The FB-111," Laird told the Senate Armed Services Committee March 15, in an echo of the lobby's arguments, "will not meet the requirements of a true intercontinental bomber and the cost per unit has reached a point where an AMSA must be considered to fill the void."

It will be quite a void. The cost overruns, which had more than doubled the price of the FB-111, now became the excuse for going ahead with a far more expensive bomber. The net saving of $405 million in fiscal 1969 and 1970 ($107 plus $321 minus $23 million) will commit the country to a new plane which Senator Proxmire told the Senate April 22 will cost at least $24 billion during the next decade. Such illusory economies place heavy first mortgages on the future in favor of the military and at the expense of social needs.

Even so, there was hidden in the F-111 cutback a $200 million consolation prize for General Dynamics. The formal budget document[1] carried an increase of $155.7 million for "Production of F-111D at minimum sustaining rate related to FB-111 cancellation." I was puzzled by this reference to a "sustaining rate." What was being "sustained"— military needs or General Dynamics?

[1] House Document No. 91-100, 91st Congress, First Session. *Reductions in 1970 Budget Requests. Communication from the President of the United States*, p. 17.

I found a fuller explanation when *Aviation Week & Space Technology* arrived for May 5. It said the revised Nixon procurement plans for General Dynamics F-111D provided $599.8 million for aircraft "plus $56 million for advance procurement and $71.4 million to cover excess costs generated in fiscal 1968." It said the total of $727.2 million "represented a sharp increase over original fiscal 1970 plans of $518 million." Indeed this is an increase, though *Aviation Week* did not say so, of $209.2 million rather than the $155.7 specified in the budget message.

The increase had been approved by Deputy Defense Secretary David Packard—a director of General Dynamics until his Pentagon appointment—to counterbalance a cut of $320.9 million in the FB-111 program. It would "enable General Dynamics to retain its present production facilities." Not only did thirteen of these fighter planes crash in their twenty-six months of operations[2] but Senator Curtis of Kansas, in a comprehensive Senate speech last October 3, said they were not maneuverable enough as fighters. They are effective only as tactical bombers against enemy forces like those in Vietnam, which have no air cover of their own. Yet the government was not cutting back on its original plan to buy 331 of these F-111D's.

This is only one of many examples in the budget of how easily the Nixon Administration finds millions for such dubious military purposes but not for urgent social needs. The $200 million consolation for General Dynamics is the same amount—a very inadequate amount—Nixon set aside in his budget message for riot-devastated cities. Nixon got a lot of publicity out of his order to give this urban program priority, but it didn't have enough priority to be a $200 million addition to the budget. It was just deducted from the meager amounts already available for other urban purposes.

Those who still look for the "shape" of the Nixon Administration are bound to remain bewildered. Shape is another

[2] AP in Omaha *World Herald*, March 7, 1969.

word for policy, and policy requires the substitution of decision for drift. The campaign promised decision from one direction, the right. The situation requires decision from another direction, which might be called the left. Nixon turns out to take his stand—though that is too strong a word—in the middle of makeshift compromises. Whether on electoral reform or tax reform or poverty, feeble and inadequate half-measures are the rule. This shapelessness is the shape of the new Administration.

Hand-to-mouth decisions are standard in all governments, and inertia is basic in politics as in physics. But drift is only safe in quiet waters; to let inertia have its way in stormy seas is to risk disaster. Richard Nixon in the sixties is beginning to resemble Calvin Coolidge in the twenties, when the country kept cool with Cal, just before going over the brink with the stock market crash and the Great Depression.

To let inertia reign in the American government is also to let the military dominate. The sheer size of the military establishment, its vast propaganda resources and its powerful allies in every business, locality, and labor union affected by the billions it spends every year, gives it momentum sufficient to roll over every other department and branch of the government. In the absence of a strong hand and hard choices in the White House, the Pentagon inevitably makes the decisions.

But there is more than default, and more than meets the eye, in the military budget. The readiest source of campaign funds and political support for nomination and election as President lies in the military-industrial complex. It is also the most skillfully hidden source. I suspect that the 1968 campaign, like the 1960, was preceded by deals which called for a buildup in military procurement. This would help to account for the steep increase in appropriations by the Kennedy Administration despite its discovery on taking office that the "missile gap" did not exist.[3]

[3] Carl Kaysen, who was Kennedy's Deputy Special Assistant for National Security Affairs, has given us more precise figures than I have ever

The two plums the military-industrial complex most wanted on the eve of the 1968 campaign were the ABM and AMSA, a new advanced strategic bomber. In 1966 the Armed Services Committees of both houses recommended extra funds to speed both projects. A Congress still comatose on military matters dutifully voted the money. But McNamara refused to spend it. Johnson made two moves during the following year which cleared the way for both projects. In September, 1967 he forced McNamara to swallow the bitter pill of advocating a "thin" ABM system in which the Secretary of Defense clearly disbelieved. Two months later Johnson made the surprise announcement—as much a surprise to McNamara as to the press—that he was shifting the redoubtable Pentagon chief to the World Bank. That cleared the way for AMSA, too, and with both projects it also cleared the way for the 1968 campaign.

As late as January, 1968, in his last posture statement as Secretary of Defense, McNamara was still fighting a rearguard action against AMSA. He argued that the principal problem lay in the growing sophistication of Soviet air defenses. "Repeated examination of this problem," he told Congress, "has convinced us that what is important here is not a new aircraft but rather new weapons and penetration devices."

AMSA began to inch forward when Clifford replaced McNamara. In Clifford's first posture statement last January, he struck a new note when he declared the FB-111 would be too small to carry the new weapons and penetration devices McNamara had in mind. One wishes one knew

---

seen before in the chapter on "Military Strategy, Military Forces and Arms Control" in the Brookings Institution symposium, *Agenda For The Nation* (Doubleday, 1969). He wrote (pp. 562–3) that the decisions of 1961 and 1962 by Kennedy "called for the buildup by 1965 of a U.S. strategic force of nearly 1,800 missiles capable of reaching Soviet targets; somewhat more than a third were to be submarine-launched. In addition, some 600 long-range bombers would be maintained. *This was projected against an expected Soviet force of fewer than a third as many missiles and a quarter as many bombers capable of reaching the United States"* (italics added). The "overkill" was worth billions to the aviation and electronics industries.

more about this, since it seems unlikely that McNamara
would have overlooked so simple a point. While Clifford
said "we are still uncertain whether a new intercontinental
bomber will be needed in the 1970s," he more than doubled
the research and development funds for AMSA, increasing
them from $30 million in fiscal 1969 to $77 million in fiscal
1970, "to keep the program moving."

The Nixon-Laird revisions two months later went further. They not only added $23 million more for AMSA but
authorized the Air Force to move into the engineering
phase, the last stage in R and D before procurement. "Now,
after a very careful review," Laird told the Senate Armed
Services Committee March 27, "we have decided to cut off
the FB-111 program . . . and concentrate our efforts on
the development of a new strategic bomber, AMSA." General Dynamics, which lost out when Nixon phased out FB-
111, will be one of the bidders on AMSA.

ABM and AMSA together could spell $100 billion in elec-
tronic and aviation contracts in the years ahead. AMSA itself may prove a bigger gamble and a far more costly error
than the TFX. *Space/Aeronautics* for January published a
special issue plotting future trends in strategic warfare. It
pointed out some of the pitfalls which may lie ahead for
AMSA. About eight years elapse between concept definition and actual production in developing a new bomber.
But Pentagon intelligence has never been able to come up
with estimates of enemy threat valid for more than two or
three years. "Thus," this Conover-Mast publication for the
aerospace industry concluded, "there is no way of telling,
the critics of AMSA claim, whether we would be committing ourselves to a system we really need or to what will
end up as an immensely costly mistake."

The survey admitted that AMSA would be "less vulnerable than the B-52 and perform better," but added philo-
sophically that "in a nuclear exchange time is too important
an element for bombers to have any real effect." In other
words even the fastest bomber may have no targets left
after the far swifter missile exchange is over. One firm intel-

ligence forecast emerged from the survey. "If AMSA is built," *Space/Aeronautics* said, "it will probably be our last strategic bomber. Once the present generation of Air Force commanders is gone, the top-level manpower will not be there to produce the sort of pressure that has kept AMSA alive for so long." Once the bomber admirals are dead, the clamor for a new bomber will die out, too. But the last fly-by will cost plenty.

AMSA is only one of many new military projects hidden in the new 1970 budget which will add billions to the future costs of government. "The present inflationary surge, already in its fourth year," Nixon said in his April 14 message, "represents a national self-indulgence we cannot afford any longer." But the principal beneficiaries of that indulgence are the military and their suppliers. And they seem to be exempt from anti-inflationary measures.

Fully to appreciate what the military is getting one has to begin with a disclosure made in the Budget Bureau's presentation of Nixon's budget revisions. Nixon had to squeeze $7.3 billion out of the normal civilian and welfare activities of the government in fiscal 1969 in order to meet the expenditure ceilings imposed by Congress when it enacted the 10 percent surplus income tax. This reduction over and above Johnson's budget for fiscal 1969 was made necessary by certain "uncontrollable" items. An example is the interest on the public debt, which rose by $300 million. But the biggest uncontrollable item, ten times that much, or $3 billion, was an increase in Vietnam war costs over and above those originally estimated by Johnson.

So all sorts of civilian services during the current fiscal year have had to be pared to meet the unexpected increase in the cost of the Vietnam war. Now let us couple this revelation about the 1969 budget with a basic decision made by Johnson in the 1970 budget. In that budget Johnson for the first time, on the basis of his decision to end the bombing of the North, which was very costly, and perhaps in expectation of less combat on the ground in the South,[4] forecast the first sharp cutback in Vietnam war costs. This was estimated as a saving of $3.5 billion during fiscal 1970.

This was to be the country's first "peace dividend." But instead of applying this $3.5 billion in the 1970 budget to starved civilian and welfare services, or to reduction of the deficit, Johnson added this $3.5 billion *and $600 million more* to the money available for the Pentagon to spend on procurement and activities other than those connected with the Vietnam war. *The total increase in the non-Vietnamese military budget as projected by Johnson was $4.1 billion more, even though he estimated the Vietnam war was going to cost $3.5 billion less.*[5] In his April 14 message, Nixon said of our domestic needs, "What we are able to do will depend in large measure on the prospects for an early end to the war in Vietnam." The Johnson 1970 budget projected the first slowdown but proposed to use the savings entirely for military expansion. Nixon went along with that decision.

From the Pentagon's point of view there could not have been a smoother transition than the shift from Johnson to Nixon. Nixon revised Johnson's social and welfare programs downward but left his military budget essentially untouched. It read like the handiwork of the Johnson who

---

[4] According to a little-noticed press release by Senator Stephen M. Young (D. Ohio), a member of the Senate Armed Services Committee, which has access to much information otherwise secret, Johnson had originally planned a cutback of troops in Vietnam. Young asked Nixon to recall two divisions before July and more later with an announcement, "We have accomplished our objectives in Vietnam. Our boys are coming home." Young said Johnson had decided on a similar announcement last year but was talked out of it by the Joint Chiefs of Staff.

[5] Since I have been challenged on this "peace dividend" by some colleagues, and others have wondered by what elaborate computation I arrived at it, I give the source, p. 74 of *The Budget of the US Government for Fiscal 1970.* It says, "As shown in the accompanying table outlays in support of Southeast Asia are anticipated to drop for the first time in 1970—declining by $3.5 billion from 1969. This decline reflects changing patterns of combat activity and revised loss projections. *Outlays for the military activities of the Department of Defense, excluding support of Southeast Asia, are expected to rise by $4.1 billion in 1970, to provide selected force improvements*" (my italics).

was the ally of the military and the armament industries as chairman of the Senate Preparedness subcommittee during the fifties. Johnson's last defense budget was not only the highest ever sent Congress—$81.5 billion as compared with the World War II peak of $80 billion in fiscal 1945—but laid the basis for a huge expansion in spending during future years. It gave the go-ahead signal to a wide variety of projects the armed services had long desired.

Nixon had campaigned on a "security gap," but Johnson left few if any gaps to fill. "The number of new programs spread through the new defense budget," *Space/Aeronautics* commented in its February issue, "is astounding in comparison with the lean years from fiscal 1965 to 1969." Among them were $400 million for "major developmental activity on no fewer than six new aircraft" and—biggest item of all—an increase of $1.64 billion to a total of $2.85 billion for the Navy's surface ship and submarine building program. Arms research and development was boosted $850 million to a total of $5.6 billion, including work on such new monsters as missiles which can be hidden on the ocean floor.

This farewell budget also put Nixon in a bind. As *Space/Aeronautics* pointed out in that same editorial, if Nixon tried to cut back appreciably on the Johnson budget, he would open himself to "security gap" charges. On the other hand, "If he doesn't defer or cancel at least some of them, and if the war in Vietnam cannot be brought to an honorable close some time next year, he will face a crushing arms bill in fiscal 1971, when many of these starts begin to demand more money." That was the risk Nixon and Laird preferred to take.

Nixon claims to have cut $4 billion from 1970 outlays, and taken $1.1 billion, or 27 percent, from the military. Critics have protested that he took $3 from civilian needs for every $1 he took from the military. But even this is illusory.

From another point of view, even if we accept the Nixon cuts at face value, the military will have $3 billion more in fiscal 1970 for non-Vietnamese war purposes than it had in fiscal 1969. We have seen that Johnson budgeted a $3.5 billion cut in Vietnam war costs for fiscal '70 and then added $4.1 billion to the military budget for projects unconnected with the Vietnam war. If you deduct Nixon's $1.1 billion from that $4.1 billion, the Pentagon is still ahead by $3 billion.[6] If Nixon had applied the whole projected saving of $3.5 billion on Vietnam to civilian use or deficit reduction, the fiscal 1970 total for national defense would have been reduced to $97,499 million. All Nixon did was to *cut the Johnson increase* by a fourth. Even this may turn out to be—at least in part—a familiar bit of flim-flam. Since 1965, when Johnson began to bomb the North and take over the combat war in the South, almost every annual budget has underestimated Vietnamese war costs. These have had to be covered later in the fiscal year by supplemental appropriations. The under-estimate in fiscal 1969, as we have seen, was $3 billion. The fiscal 1970 budget is running true to form.

The biggest "economy" item in the Nixon military budget is $1,083.4 million, which is attributed to "reduced estimates of ammunition consumption rates." [7] Just how much of the estimated $1.1 billion "saving" in outlays for fiscal 1970 will be the result of lower consumption of ammunition in Vietnam was not made clear. The $1,083.4 million is given as a net reduction of obligational authority in fiscal 1969 and 1970. It is one of the three main items in that

[6] Even that understates the case. Down near the bottom of the budget outlays table of the Nixon revisions is $2.8 billion more for "civilian *and military* pay increases" (my italics). Laird in his April 1 presentation said this would add $2.5 billion but failed to make clear whether this was for the whole government or only for Pentagon civilian and military employees—almost half the civilian employees of the government work for the Pentagon. Clifford in his 1970 statement gave a figure of $1.8 billion for Pentagon pay increases but did not make clear whether this included the civilian employees. So pay raises will add between $1.8 billion and $2.5 billion to this $3 billion figure.

[7] See page 17 of House Document No. 91–100, 91st Congress, First Session.

$3 billion cut in obligational authority for fiscal 1970 which make it possible for the new Administration to claim that 55 percent of the total cut in obligational authority for 1970 ($5.5 billion) came from the military. Obligational authority is not necessarily or entirely translated into actual outlays during the fiscal year in which it is granted.

This projected cut in the rate of ammunition consumption is in addition to Johnson's projected cut of $3.5 billion in Vietnam war costs. Though Laird does not blush easily, even he seems to have been embarrassed by this particular "economy." "To be perfectly frank," said Laird, who rarely is, when he first broached this item to the House Armed Services Committee on March 27, "I think the ammunition consumption rates for Southeast Asia are based on rather optimistic assumptions, particularly in view of the current Têt offensive." Yet, under pressure from the White House to show more economy, the optimism rose sharply in the next four days. The following table shows the change in estimated savings for ammunition and its transportation in millions of dollars in those four days:

	March 27	*April 1*
Ground Munitions	−$380	−$460
Ammo. Transport	− 34.4	− 34.4
Air Munitions	− 417.9	− 511.9
Ship Gun Ammo.	− 47.1	− 77.1
TOTAL CUTS	879.4	1,103.4

These figures are for total obligational authority for fiscal years 1969 and 1970. Perhaps the Administration hesitated to make public its actual outlay estimates for these two years, since they may easily turn out to be higher rather than lower, and may have to be met later in the year by a supplemental appropriation. Between March 27 and April 1 Laird boosted the estimated reduction in total military outlays for fiscal 1970 from "about $500 million" to $1,113 million. Most of the increased "economy" seems to have come from this ammunition item.

There are several indications in the official presentations

themselves which lead one to think Laird was right to be queasy. The original 1970 budget projected consumption of 105,000 tons a month in ground munitions through December, 1970. Actual consumption in January was given as 96,000 tons, but that was before the recent enemy offensive got under way. The consumption of ammunition must have risen sharply with the fighting in February, March, and April, but when I asked the Pentagon for the monthly figures since January, I was told they could not be given out. "We can only say," an official spokesman told me, "that the Secretary's projections are being borne out." If that is true our troops must have been meeting enemy attacks with switchblades.

Another indication—how I love tracking down these liars!—appears in what we know about the volume of bombs dropped on South Vietnam and Laos since we stopped bombing the North. The Pentagon's own figures on total tonnages dropped show little change. Total tonnages dropped in September and October last year, before the bombing of the North stopped, were almost 240,000. Total tonnage dropped in January and February of this year, when it was dropped only on Laos and South Vietnam, was more than 245,000. There was an increase of 5,000 tons. That increase makes the estimate of a saving of more than a half billion dollars in air munitions for fiscal 1969 and 1970 look very phony indeed.

Laird himself said consumption of air munitions was rising. On March 27 he told the House Armed Services Committee that while consumption had been estimated at 110,000 tons per month for the twenty-four months from January 1969 to December 1970—that doesn't sound like much deescalation ahead, at least in the air!—"actual consumption is now running at about 129,000 tons per month." Yet he projected a saving of $42.5 million on air munitions in fiscal 1969 and $375.4 in fiscal 1970. When he got back to the committee four days later, he placed actual consumption even higher, at 130,000 tons a month, but also projected higher savings! Now he was to save $89.5 million on air munitions in fiscal 1969, or twice the figure four days earlier, and $442 million for fiscal 1970, an increase of $47 million over the earlier estimate. Yet Laird said he saw "no indication that consumption will decline by very much during the next twelve-to-eighteen months." How then were expenditures on air ammunition to be lower than expected when the tonnage of bombs dropped was running higher than expected? Non-Euclidean geometry is not half so exotic as Pentagon arithmetic.

The ammunition figures for Vietnam are stupendous. The original Johnson-Clifford budget in January projected the cost of ammunition in Vietnam during fiscal 1970 at $5.2 billion. This expenditure of shot and shell over Vietnam is two-and-a-half times the total 1970 revised Nixon budget of $2 billion for the Office of Economic Opportunity (down $132 million), and more than twice the revised elementary and secondary education outlay for 1970 which he set at $2.3 billion (down another $100 million).

After this razzle-dazzle on ammunition, the next largest item of military saving in the Nixon-Laird budget revisions is the ABM. Let us return to the formal document sent Congress by the President. There on page 17[8] are given "principal changes in 1970 budget authority resulting from 1969 and 1970 Defense program changes." The second largest of these is $994 million for "reorientation of the antiballistic missile program to the new Safeguard system." This and the ammunition item make up almost $2.1 billion of that $3 billion cut in military obligational authority on which the new Administration commends itself.

A businessman in financial difficulties who thought up such savings for his stockholders would soon be in jail for embezzlement. The "reorientation" of Sentinel into Safeguard may reduce spending in fiscal 1970 but only by add-

[8] House Document No. 91-100. Reductions in 1970 Appropriations Request. Communication from the President . . . together with details of the changes. 91st Congress, First Session.

ing at least $1.5 billion and possibly $5.5 billion more in the next few years. This is an expensive rebaptism or, better, if we consider the phallic significance of these monsters, recircumcision. Nixon had an easy way out of the ABM fight if he wanted one. He could have announced that like Eisenhower he had decided to keep the ABM in research and development until he was sure it would not be obsolete before it was deployed.

If he had been a little more daring and a little less beholden to the military-industrial complex, he might have cut billions[9] from the military budget immediately by offering a freeze on all new deployment of strategic defensive and offensive missiles, if the Russians did likewise, as a preparation for strategic arms negotiations. This would not only save at least $5 or $6 billion in the new fiscal year but ensure our present nuclear superiority and fully guarantee against first-strike nightmares.[10]

Nixon chose instead a tricky stretch-out. This offered some reductions in the new fiscal year, as compared with Johnson's ABM proposal, but at the expense of higher costs later. This ingenious compromise made it possible to offer an apparent saving to the taxpayer *and* larger eventual orders to the electronics and missile industries. This not only fulfilled the Administration's promise of New Directions but enabled it to move in opposite directions at the same time. Johnson's Sentinel was estimated to cost $5.5 billion, Nixon's Safeguard from $6.7 to $7 billion, or $1.5 billion more. This may prove another official underestimate. An

[9] The Johnson budget for 1970 placed the expenditure for strategic forces at $9.6 billion as compared with $9.1 in 1969 and $7.6 in 1968. Much of this is for deployment of new weaponry.

[10] "Such a freeze," Senator Percy declared in a speech April 17, "should be acceptable to the Defense Department. Secretary Laird has testified that our missiles on land and under the seas as well as our long-range bomber force present an overwhelming second-strike array. If a freeze—fully verifiable by both nations through satellite reconnaissance as well as other intelligence sources—is put into effect, the U.S. deterrent will remain credible into the foreseeable future." But if the deterrent remains credible, what will the poor missile salesmen do?

authoritative service, which covers all developing major weapons and aerospace systems for industrial and governmental subscribers, places the total cost of Safeguard much higher.

This is DMS, Inc. (Defense Marketing Service), a ten-year-old service now a part of McGraw-Hill. I had never heard of it until an anonymous reader sent me a reproduction of its report on Nixon's Safeguard. I checked with its Washington office by telephone and was given permission to quote it. Its detailed analysis places the total cost of the system at $11 billion and ends by warning that "in a program as complex as Safeguard, historical experience indicates costs in the long run are likely to be considerably higher." When Senator Cooper put the DMS analysis into the *Congressional Record* May 8, he noted that it did not include "about $1 billion AEC warhead costs." This would bring the total cost of Nixon's Safeguard past $12 billion.

The DMS report notes that we have already spent $4.5 billion on the ABM from fiscal 1956, when the Army started the Nike-Zeus program, through fiscal 1968, and that the research efforts which made Nike-Zeus obsolete before it could be deployed are still going on, at a cost of $350 to $500 million annually. "A number of new concepts as well as hardware," the report said, "are currently under investigation." These threaten Safeguard with obsolescence too. "Preliminary research," DMS said, "has pointed the way toward the following types of advances." One was radars of much higher frequency, so the interception "would be made with either a much smaller nuclear warhead or even a conventional high explosive charge." Another was a new third stage for Spartan, so the missile could fly out at greater ranges and "maneuver through a cloud of decoys to find and destroy the real warhead." A third—most expensive of all—was "defensive missiles carried either in ships or large aircraft deployed closer to the enemy's launching sites."

We give these details to show that in embarking on the

ABM we are embarking on a wholly new sector of the arms race with a high rate of obsolescence to gladden the hearts of the electronics companies and of AT&T, whose Western Electric has long been the main contractor. The reader should note that the three advances cited in the DMS report are relatively simple and foreseeable developments. All kinds of "far-out" possibilities are also being investigated. The secret hope which lies behind all this Rube Goldberg hardware is that some day somebody will turn up a perfect ABM defense and thus enable the possessor to rule the world because a power so armed can threaten a first strike, knowing it will be immune to retaliation.

The most candid expression of this viewpoint was made by Senator Russell during the defense appropriations hearings in May of last year. "I have often said," Senator Russell observed, "that I feel that the first country to deploy an effective ABM system and an effective ASW [antisubmarine warfare] system is going to control the world militarily." [11] This control of the world, however, may be on a somewhat reduced basis. Six months later, during the Senate's secret session on the ABM (November 1, 1968), Senator Russell admitted, "There is no system ever devised which will afford complete protection against any multiple firing of ballistic missiles . . . we will have no absolutely foolproof defense, I do not care how much money we spend on one, or what we do." Senator Clark replied that casualties would be so high as to destroy civilization "and if there are a few people living in caves after that, it does not make much difference." To which Russell made his now famous rejoinder, "If we have to start over again with another Adam and Eve, I want them to be Americans and not Russians" (*Congressional Record*, E9644, November 1, 1968). Thus we would at last achieve an unchallengeable Pax Americana! And thus the ABM turns out to be another variant of the military's unquenchable dream of an Ulti-

[11] Department of the Army, Senate Hearings, Department of Defense Appropriations for fiscal 1969, 90th Congress, Second Session, Part II, page 868.

mate Weapon, to leap some day like a jackpot from a slot machine if only they go on pouring money into R and D.

I would ask the reader's indulgence for one more foray into the labyrinthine depths of the Pentagon budget. Deeper knowledge of these recesses is necessary if we are ever to hunt down and slay the dragon. I want to deal with the next largest source of the Nixon military "economies." These involve deferrals of expenditures amounting to about $480 million. Most critical comment has been content to note that mere deferral of spending is not real economy, since what is saved in fiscal 1970 will be spent later. There is a more important point to be made. These deferrals, if closely examined, provide additional proof of how recklessly and wastefully the Pentagon dashes into production before full testing and evaluation have been completed, before it knows, in other words, that these expensive weapons will work. We will see how much pressure it takes to make the Pentagon admit this elementary error.

To grasp the full significance of these so-called "economies" of Nixon and Laird we must see them against the background of revelations by two Senators, one the leading pillar of the military in the Senate establishment, Senator Russell, the other a former Secretary of and long-time spokesman for the Air Force who has turned against the military-industrial establishment, Senator Symington.

During the secret debate on the ABM last November 1, Russell told the Senate one of the "most serious mistakes" he had ever made as Chairman of the Armed Services Committee, which passes on all military requests for authorization, and as chairman of the Senate subcommittee, which passes on all defense appropriations, "was in allotting vast sums to the Navy for missile frigates before we knew we had a missile that would work on them." He said "we built missile frigates, we built missile destroyers and missile escort ships" on the basis of "unqualified" testimony of "everyone in the Department of Defense and in the Navy" that effective missiles were being developed. "It probably cost the taxpayers," Russell said, "$1 billion, because they have had to rebuild those missiles three times."

A more comprehensive statement of the same kind was made to the Senate by Symington on March 7 of this year. He put a table into the *Congressional Record* (at page S2464 that day) which showed how much had been spent in the past sixteen years on missiles which were no longer deployed or never had been deployed, because of obsolescence. The total was fantastic. Symington gave the names, the expenditures, and the life-span of each missile. The total cost of those no longer deployed was $18.9 *billion*, and the cost of those which were abandoned as obsolete or unworkable *before* deployment was $4.2 billion. The total was $23 billion. Imagine what those wasted billions could have done for our blighted cities!

Symington's table was introduced to underscore his point —buttressed by past testimony from McNamara—that the ABM would soon be another monument to this kind of expensive obsolescence. Another inference to be drawn from this table is how many billions might have been saved if the Pentagon had not rushed so quickly into these miscarriages. Behind the glamorous names which flashed through the appropriations hearings and the ads in the aeronautical and military trade journals—Navaho, Snark, Dove, Triton, and even Plato (what did he do to deserve *this* honor?)—lies an untold story of beguiling missile salesmanship and drunken-sailor procurement methods. It might be worth billions in future savings if a Congressional investigating committee really dug up the full story and its lessons.

The need for such an investigation becomes plain if one examines the funny thing which happened to SRAM (acronym for short-range attack missile) on Secretary Laird's way to and from the budget forum on Capitol Hill between March 27, his first appearance before the House Armed Services Committee, and his second appearance on April 1, just four days later. SRAM is one of the new missiles which have been under development. It is supposed to be mounted on a bomber so it can be rocketed into enemy territory from a position more than a hundred miles away from the enemy's defense perimeter. The idea is to circumvent the enemy's defenses by stopping the bomber out of their range and lobbing the missiles over them.

SRAM has had several predecessors, all expensive, of course; it is not a simple contraption. The predecessors appear in Senator Symington's table. Crossbow, Rascal, and Skybolt were earlier attempts at a stand-off missile; they cost a total of $962.6 million before they were abandoned prior to deployment. Hound Dog A, which cost another $255 million, is another missile in the same family which is no longer deployed. SRAM is very different in capability, range, and complexity. SRAM is intended to do for the bombing plane what penetration aids do for the ICBM. SRAM is supposed to carry all kinds of devices to confuse the radars of the enemy defense.

When Laird appeared before the House Armed Services Committee on March 27 he referred, without further explanation, to "delays experienced in the SRAM development production program." The original Johnson-Clifford budget last January for fiscal 1970 called for the modification of all seventeen B-52 squadrons of series G and H at a total cost of about $340 million to enable them to carry SRAM. The "modification kits," as Laird described them, were to be bought from Boeing "at a total cost of about $220 million," and it was planned to buy kits for twelve squadrons in 1970, leaving the rest to be modified in 1971. Laird proposed to save $30 million in fiscal 1970 by equipping only ten squadrons in 1970 and the remaining seven in 1971. He said "This change will give us a smoother program."

But the White House and the Budget Bureau, desperate for ways to cut, put pressure on the Pentagon, and four days later Laird was back before the Armed Services Committee. Now instead of $30 million he proposed a deferral of the SRAM program amounting to $326 million. It now appeared that he had been less than candid with the committee. The cryptic references to "delays" turned out to be quite an understatement. He came forward with new changes in the SRAM program, all of them—he explained —"related to the difficulties encountered in the development of this Short Range Attack Missile." Now it was not "delays," but "difficulties."

Laird went on to quite a revelation. "We have now reached the conclusion," he told the committee, "that procurement of operational missiles should be deferred until the test program conclusively demonstrated that they will work as intended." So "we have deleted most [but not all!] of the missile procurement funds" from fiscal 1969 and 1970, for a total cut in the two years of $153 million.

Then he proposed to defer not only the missiles but the modifications designed to enable the B-52's to carry them. "Inasmuch as we do not know when operational missiles will be available," Laird said, "we have also deferred all special SRAM modification work on the B-52's and FB-111's." The total net deferral—after adding $17 million to R and D for "a greater portion of the overhead cost" (another consolation fee?)—was to be $326 million.

This shows how much pressure it takes to squeeze the fat out of the military budget, and a little more candor out of the Pentagon. Why didn't Laird tell the committee on March 27 what he revealed on April 1? But for the extra pressure, the Pentagon would have gone on with procurement of the SRAM before knowing whether it would work, and with modification of the strategic bombers to carry the missiles before it was sure that it would have the missiles. What if further testing modifies the missile, and this requires a change also in the kits which modify the planes to carry these missiles? Why risk the waste of millions?

The SRAM story raises similar questions about Laird's rather cryptic references in his budget presentation to a similar deferral of "about $160 million" in the Minuteman ICBM program. The most important part of that "saving" is due, as Laird told House Armed Services on March 27, to "a slowdown in the deployment of Minuteman III." This is the Minuteman which will carry MIRV—"multiple independently targeted re-entry vehicles," i.e., additional warheads independently targeted. It was tested for the first time last August 16 with three warheads.[12] "While we are confident," Laird said, "that the Minuteman III will perform as intended, we believe it would be prudent to reduce somewhat the previously planned deployment rate, at least through the FY 1970 procurement lead-time." Why only "somewhat," and what does "somewhat" mean for the whole program? "This delay," Laird went on, "would serve to reduce the amount of overlapping of R and D and production and provide more time for production." Why risk overlapping altogether until testing has been completed? Laird himself said he was planning to accelerate operational testing "to help ensure that the missile is working well before we return to the originally planned rate in fiscal 1971." "Mr. Chairman," Laird said, patting himself warmly on the back, "this reflects our determination to minimize cost overruns resulting from R and D modifications after production has commenced." But perhaps more serious cost overruns could be avoided if Minuteman III, like SRAM, were subjected to further deferrals.

A franker if ironic account of the Minuteman III cuts appeared May 5 in *Aviation Week*. It says, "The reason for the reduction is fear of reliability problems with the new missile." It said the Air Force had "decided 'to reduce the concurrency of development and production' of the missile in order to insure reliability of all components." Even the Foreign Service could not have hit upon a smoother phrase to equal that "concurrency of development and production." *Aviation Week* added, "The cutback was publicized by some Defense Dept. sources as evidence of U.S.

12 "On August 16," said a special survey in *Space/Aeronautics*, page 88, last January, "Poseidon and Minuteman III were launched with ten and three warheads respectively."

willingness to reduce strategic offensive armaments prior to arms reduction talks with the Soviets, but that was not the reason."

This effort to make the Minuteman cuts look like evidence of Pentagon enthusiasm for arms talks originated in Laird's own presentation on April 1. In a super-slick conclusion he told the committee, "Our decision to slow the Minuteman III deployment—though necessitated for other reasons—provides a period of time in which arms limitation agreements could become effective at a lower level of armaments. . . . It remains to be seen, of course, whether our potential adversaries will similarly indicate with actions that they, too, are serious about desiring meaningful arms limitation talks." These are the moments when Laird sounds as if he were dreamed up by Molière.

June 5, 1969
New York Review

HEADING FOR A BIGGER ARMS RACE IN THE SEVENTIES

Despite euphoric reports about the SALT talks and the $5.9 billion cut in the final defense budget this fiscal year, the military monster is far from being subdued. It takes a long time before cuts in congressional authorization and appropriation bills actually lead to cuts in expenditure. The best guide to actual expenditures is the daily U.S. Treasury statement. Its January 2 statement covering all but the last two days of the first half of the 1970 fiscal year is not encouraging. The cash deficit for the six months was $12.4 billion as against $7.8 billion in the same period last year. To this deficit the military establishment was a prime contributor, despite the first withdrawals from Vietnam and talk of

reduced commitments. In the first half of the fiscal year the
military drew more than half a billion ($685 million) *more*
from the Treasury than in the corresponding period a year
ago. The *rate* of increase seemed to be going up. In December alone military spending was more than $1 billion higher
than in December a year ago. The tempo of military spending is still feeding the fires of inflation.

The Tax Foundation estimates that in 1970 the average
tax burden per American family for defense will be $1,250.
For those families lucky enough to be on the gravy train
of the military-industrial complex, this tax is easily out-
weighed by their earnings. Indeed from an economic point
of view the arms race is a device for taxing the poor to the
profit of the well-to-do. The prospect for a change in the
seventies is dim. The Arms Control and Disarmament
Agency estimates that the world has spent $4,000 billion on
arms since 1900, and at the current rate of increase will
spend that much again in the coming decade alone. That,
too, will not help our chronic inflationary fevers.

There is little reason to believe that the Strategic Arms
Limitation Talks (SALT) will change the picture much, if
at all. The two biggest escalations which lie ahead are those
to be sparked by MIRV and the ABM. There is no sign that
Washington or Moscow is prepared to halt either. The constant and pleased assurances from the State Department and
the Pentagon that the Russians at Helsinki were behaving
splendidly and avoiding "propaganda" are—in our opinion
—cause for depression, not optimism. If Moscow were mili-
tantly for disarmament or arms control, we may be sure this
would be stigmatized as "propaganda."

Disarmament buffs had naïvely assumed that a main purpose of the SALT talks was to block MIRV, for once the
missiles on both sides are outfitted with the multiple warheads, it will be impossible for either side to know by aerial
surveillance how many warheads there are atop each missile
on the other. The fog and the fear will come down again,
and it will be hard to keep the arms race within any bounds
at all. But the Pentagon is now leaking the revelation that

there has never been much if any intention on our side to
curb MIRV. William Beecher, who covers the Pentagon
for the *New York Times*, reported in a dispatch to that
paper December 31 that while the Johnson Administration
in the summer of 1968 was prepared to propose a freeze on
strategic weapons, there was to be no limitation on "improvement of systems within the limited numbers," including MIRV's. This was the first public disclosure of the Johnson negotiating position. George C. Wilson, who covers the
Pentagon for the *Washington Post*, reported (January 1)
from a similar briefing with unnamed officials that "the
Nixon Administration view is that multiple-warhead submarines are a fact of life already," so MIRV discussion
would focus on the land-based missiles "but, according to
informed sources, the Soviets showed little interest at the
SALT talks in calling off the flight tests of MIRV missiles."
Clearly the Nixon Administration shares this lack of interest.

The second biggest item of future arms spending is the
ABM. The Pentagon is beginning to leak stories designed to
build up support for its escalation. Beecher reported in the
New York Times January 2, "Administration Expected to
Back ABM Expansion." The AP was given a similar backgrounder, "Soviet Buildup Spurs New Anti-Missile Plans"
(Washington *Star*, January 3). This was an effort to revive
the first-strike scare of last spring. The AP was told that if
the Russians continue building SS-9's at the current rate
they will have 420 by 1974–75, and that these 420 would
then be able to wipe out 95 percent of our 1,000 Minutemen in a surprise attack. The arithmetic sounds like pure
Pentagon Munchhausen. Unanswered is the question of
why anyone would risk a first strike at our Minutemen
when this would expose the Soviet Union to destruction
from our submarine missile fleet. Another question no one
raised at the backgrounder was, if land-based missiles are
now so vulnerable to first attack, are they not obsolete? Indeed the House Appropriations Committee report on the
new defense budget (December 3, page 78) suggests that

instead of spending millions to bury the missiles in "very costly" hard-rock silos and in defending them with more ABM's, it would be better to replace them altogether with submarine or mobile land missiles. "The final argument for expansion," the AP account said, with unintended irony, "is that it would cost less now than later in the face of rising prices and inflation."

The House report noted that the fiscal 1969 military budget was 7 times the military budget of 1948, just two decades ago. It may easily double and redouble within the next ten years. The reductions in the 1970 budget were mostly cuts in fat and waste. Old ships were mothballed, headquarter staffs—military and civilian—were cut down. Development contracts were stretched out. The budget cuts were a tactical retreat. In that retreat the Pentagon saved the major new weapons systems, whose costs will proliferate into billions during the next decade. Senator Hatfield (R. Ore.) spelled out a few of them in his speech on final passage December 15. There was $100 million for AMSA, the new strategic bomber; it will eventually cost from $8 to $23 billion. The $450 million for the new F-14 plane launches a program that will cost from $15 to $30 billion. The $425 million for a new nuclear attack aircraft carrier will give us 15 such task forces eventually; each costs $1 billion. The $5 million for the new Navy underwater missile system (ULMS) is another item which will escalate into billions. These are but a few samples of the spiraling expenditures ahead.

Most important of all, despite talk of cutbacks the new troop level strength next June will still be 3.2 million men, down only 260,000 from the previous June, and three quarters of a million men higher than in the first Kennedy year, when the military buildup began. This huge force is the embodiment of a continued Pax Americana, "a projection of threats and contingencies," Hatfield said, "that are far overdrawn and bear little relation to the contemporary realities of international affairs." This year's appropriation, though reduced somewhat, still "allows us to station troops on foreign soil throughout the globe, where their mere presence often contributes more to the undermining of our relations with foreign nations than to our own security."

January 12, 1970

PART VI

Disarmament: A Century of Futility

HOW EARTH DAY
WAS POLLUTED

The week the devoted band of youngsters who ran the Vietnam Moratorium gave up in despair was the week in which other youngsters all over the country, with the full support of the Establishment and its press, celebrated Earth Day. On the grassy slopes of the Sylvan Theatre in the shadow of the Washington Monument, where so many anti-war teach-ins have been held, a predominantly youthful audience jumped with joy as the rock bands played. Looking out at that tumultuous sea of sweet faces, in their long hair and bizarre costumes, I felt that just as the Caesars once used bread and circuses so ours were at last learning to use rock-and-roll, idealism and non-inflammatory social issues to turn the youth off from more urgent concerns which might really threaten the power structure. And I said so in my speech.

The pollution issue is real enough, though a little exaggerated, but it cannot be solved in isolation. From one viewpoint, the Earth Day affair was a gigantic snow job. Here was the country slipping into a wider war in Southeast Asia. Even as we spoke the news was leaking that U.S. officers in civilian clothes, either CIA or military, were directing a South Vietnamese offensive into Cambodia, and that six days earlier the U.S. had already promised the new Cambodian regime a few thousand rifles but had asked them (*New York Times*, April 23, 1970) to keep the shipment secret. Two days before the Earth Day rally, Secretary of Defense Laird had made a speech to the AP which can only be read as a deliberate effort to sabotage the SALT talks, but here we were talking as if we had nothing to worry about but our drains.

The anti-pollution campaign was saved providentially

from a Nixon message, but half the Cabinet were on the day's soap-boxes. The only bright note was provided by the oldest section of the American revolutionary movement, the DAR. Their convention denounced anti-pollution as a subversive movement. The clear proof: it was being entertained by Pete Seeger, "a documented Communist." "It's strange, isn't it," one DAR speaker noted astutely (ah, if only the CIA and the FBI were as sharp as these old dowagers!), "that today is Lenin Day and Earth Day." If it was anybody else in the White House but Richard Nixon they'd have been calling him Vladimir Ilyich.

The Nixon budget should clear him of suspicion. He called air and water pollution a "now-or-never" task, but turned in a budget which allocates 52 cents of every general revenue dollar to the military and space, but only four-tenths of one cent per dollar to air and water pollution. New weaponry alone gets $5.4 billion while air and water pollution get $569 million. Senator Tydings at the University of Maryland Earth Day said we ought to be spending on pollution what we are spending on the Vietnam war. But nobody knows what that is. Laird said months ago it would be $17 billion, but this year for the first time in history part of the military budget is blacked out, and no figures are given for certain items, Vietnam among them.

Unless there is a sharp change of course we are already in the first stages of a wider and more costly Second Indochinese War. Our secret services brought it on, upsetting the status quo in Cambodia by encouraging the anti-Sihanouk coup, as they upset the Laotian status quo with their Plain of Jars offensive last year. The enemy took up the challenge, and now Nixon's latest Vietnam message has raised the stakes by putting Cambodia and Laos squarely into the area of our concern. We must either get out altogether or plunge in further, for the military consequences otherwise would leave South Vietnam outflanked. You can kiss good-bye to any hope of controlling inflation if Nixon takes the plunge.

What a time to talk about pollution! What a time to fill the campuses, the press, the radio and TV with Earth Day talk when such momentous secret decisions are being made. Education on the complex tasks of air and water control are all to the good, and should be sharpened to a fundamental discussion of governmental and corporate policy the Establishment doesn't want. But how much more urgent and important to educate the public, while there is still time, to the more critical issues of the widening war in Southeast Asia and the SALT talks in Vienna. On both Nixon is waging a con game, and Earth Day distracted from it. In the former he remains a prisoner of the terrible power of inertia. He still wants to avoid humiliation. How to avoid some humiliation for so many disastrous mistakes? He still wants victory of some sort; indeed he speaks as if it were possible and imminent. And what is the meaning of the message leaked through James Reston (*New York Times*, April 22, 1970) that he will use "any" weapon to prevent a major military defeat as and when more troops are withdrawn? Are we back in desperation to the lunatic nonsense of threatening to use nuclear weapons?

The campuses and the communications media should be full of these questions, as they should be full of discussion about SALT. There the battle to curb the arms race is being lost even as it begins. The day the SALT talks opened, Nixon had leading Senators in for a snow job. What Nixon is really trying to pull off was indicated four days earlier when Nixon won the support of Mendel Rivers and the House Armed Services Committee for a $1.4 billion expansion of the ABM in return for $300 million more for the Navy. The ABM expansion was cleared publicly the day the SALT talks reopened. Seen from the other side this signals a U.S. drive for an area defense and an area defense is a necessity for a first-strike strategy. The night before the SALT talks opened, Secretary Rogers chose the significant vehicle of an interview with Radio Free Berlin to declare again our intention to go ahead with MIRV. Add MIRV to

ABM and there is nothing for SALT to do but ratify a new spiral in the arms race. That has been Nixon's intention from the beginning.

Senator Jackson, whom Nixon wanted as Secretary of Defense, is working hard on the Hill, and Laird, whom Nixon took as second choice, is working hard out of the Pentagon to make sure that SALT does not succeed. The Laird speech to the AP April 20 is the most mendacious performance by a U.S. official since the days of John Foster Dulles. The Soviets are several years behind us in nuclear proficiency. They have just begun to deploy a solid-fuel equivalent of Minuteman. They have just begun to develop MRV (multiple warheads). We had it several years ago and are already developing MIRV. The latest report of the London Institute of Strategic Studies, released April 11, showed that thanks to MIRV our present total of 4,200 deliverable warheads (as against the Soviet's just under 1,900) would become 11,000 by 1975—a stupendous imbalance, clearly raising the threat of a first strike. Yet Laird told the AP editors we had been standing still for five years while the Russians have been forging ahead!

Laird achieved this bit of trickery by ignoring the enormous qualitative advances we have made in those five years and focusing on the Soviet's effort to make up in numbers and in megatonnage (which is wasteful) for their lag in accuracy, multiple independently targeted warheads *and* numbers. He continued to impute to the Russians a desire to achieve what our Air Force has long sought—first-strike capacity. If the roles were reversed and a Soviet official were to present so false and inflammatory a picture of the power balance we would decide that it was time to pack our bags and head for home. Let pollution buffs notice Dr. Panofsky's testimony that we already have enough weapons between us to make the entire Northern Hemisphere unlivable in one swift nuclear exchange. If SALT fails and we up the firepower, we may wake up one morning and find there is nothing left of Earth to pollute.

May 4, 1970

WHY SALT SPELLS FRAUD

The folly of competition in arms was recognized by philosophers in the eighteenth century and statesmen in the nineteenth. The first disarmament conference was held at The Hague in 1899. Except for the period of the two world wars, there has hardly been a year in which disarmament negotiations of some kind have not been going on. These have become a ritual, and almost a comedy, punctuating the pauses and fresh starts of the arms race. The military machines and their allies have learned to turn them into an elaborate kind of game, designed to befuddle public opinion into believing that something was being done about the ever-growing expense and danger.

Not only the State Department but the Pentagon and the Joint Chiefs of Staff have developed subdivisions skilled in "arms control," that is, talk about arms control. This gamesmanship has been perfected to the point where it may actually be used to cover up a new spiral in the arms race, or indeed even to sell the public on the need for new weapons and higher expenditures. This is the only safe, if cynical, perspective from which to view the Nixon Administration's preparations for new talks on strategic weapons. The men named to direct these talks and the negotiating positions being mapped out in advance are not calculated to restrain or reduce the arms race but to move it forward into the higher and more dangerous levels represented by the ABM and the MIRV. SALT—Strategic Arms Limitation Talks—will prove a fraud.

Some apparent motion toward arms talks was essential to the Nixon Administration on the eve of the Senate battle over ABM. This was a political necessity to convince wavering Senators that the ABM is just a bargaining card to use in negotiations, and to keep alive the hope that this dangerous and expensive new development will be made unnecessary by joint agreement. But if you look closely you will see that nowhere has the Nixon Administration explicitly said it would forgo an ABM if the Russians did likewise. On the contrary, you will see that the Nixon Administration is not prepared to negotiate *whether* there will be an ABM but only *how much* of one.

This was implicit in a hint dropped by the President March 14 at the original press conference announcing the ABM, when he was asked whether he would "be willing to consider abandoning the ABM program altogether if the Soviets showed a similar willingness or, indeed, if they showed a readiness to place limitations on offensive weapons?" Nixon replied that "the arms talks that at least preliminarily have been discussed, *do not involve limitation or reduction*. They involve only freezing where we are" (my italics). Then Nixon went on to say that he "would imagine that the Soviet Union would be just as reluctant as we would be to leave their country naked against a potential Chinese Communist threat," and added, "So the abandoning of the entire system, particularly as the Chinese threat is there, I think neither country would look upon with much favor." Moscow must have been startled to hear Nixon speaking for it.

The full meaning of Nixon's remarks begins to be spelled out by a pamphlet, *Safeguard: What Are the True Answers?*, sent out recently to editors all over the country by Nixon's Director of Communications, Herbert G. Klein. The answer to the question, "How would Safeguard affect prospects for arms control?," after spelling out various possibilities, concludes by saying—

However, those parts of the Safeguard program designed for defense against China, small countries with a strategic delivery capability or accidental or unauthorized attacks from any source would not be affected by arms control agreements with the Soviet Union, nor do we expect the Soviet Union to forgo deployments designed for similar purposes.

This means the only part of the Safeguard system open in negotiation is that small part designed specifically to protect our Minuteman bases. This leaves out the major part of the system, the Spartans and the computer-radars which go with them and the Sprints to protect the computer-radars.

Indeed, from the rest of the reply to this question it is not even clear just how much of our Minuteman defenses would be negotiable. It says, "If the Soviet Union slows down or stops its deployment of the large payload SS-9 missile or if the likelihood that these missiles will be armed with accurate multiple warheads is materially reduced, we can readily *limit* that part of the Safeguard program which is designed to defend our land-based missiles." The italics are ours, to emphasize what is here offered is limitation of planned deployment and not reduction.

But what if the development of the Soviet SS-9 is an answer to our MIRV, as it seems to be? This does not say that we would give up our MIRV if they did not develop theirs. It says we would limit our ABM missiles if they slow down or stop the deployment of the SS-9 and "materially reduce" the "likelihood"—whatever these terms mean—that they will be armed with "accurate multiple warheads." So we are proposing to bargain our ABM's against their MRV's instead of negotiating ABM's against ABM's and MIRV's against MIRV's to put a stop to both monstrous developments. (MRV's are multiple warheads; MIRV's are multiple *and* independently targeted.)

This slick stance becomes clearer in the next sentence— "Even more favorable reductions in the Soviet offensive and defensive threat could be matched by further restraints in our ABM deployment." There is no indication of any readiness to put our own MRV's and MIRV's on the table, nor even to go beyond "further restraints" in our ABM deployment.

The Administration's negotiating position on MRV's and MIRV's is less clear. But there are clues in an article Harold Brown, former Secretary of the Air Force, wrote in *Foreign Affairs* last April. Brown is one of six men picked for the negotiating team in the SALT talks. Brown is regarded as the most dovish of the six, and Brown is not much of a

dove, as we shall see. The others are Major General Royal B.
Allison, former arms control specialist for the Joint Chiefs
of Staff; Paul H. Nitze, a Dean Acheson hard-liner from
way back, Deputy Secretary of Defense under Johnson,
more recently picked by the new Pentagon team as "con-
sultant" to prepare for the new talks; Llewellyn Thompson, former Ambassador to Moscow; and two standard-
model State Department types who were once assistants to
John Foster Dulles—Gerard C. Smith, now head of the
Arms Control and Disarmament Agency and Philip J. Far-
ley, deputy assistant Secretary of State for political-military
affairs.

At first glance Brown's article seems to be in favor of
arms control, but reading it closely one can see that it is for
arms control *after* and not before the construction of anti-
ballistic missiles and the deployment of multiple warheads
on each side. If this is to be the position of the Nixon Administration, then the effect of new arms talks—even if successful—would be *to initiate rather than prevent a new
spiral in the arms race.*

Insofar as ABM is concerned, Brown says a limit of 100
would be enough protection against "small accidental
strikes" but 1,000 would be "much more satisfactory . . .
against third-country attacks." He admits that 1,000 "might
begin to threaten the stability of the U.S.-Soviet deterrence, since it might give the attacker the capacity to
eliminate most of the retaliatory weapons that would survive a first strike employing improved MIRV technology."
Brown then suggests a limit of several hundred launchers
for city defense "as opposed to missile site defense," for
which he gives no concrete number. So this envisages city
defense *as well as* missile site ABM's, though not as many as
1,000 altogether. An agreement on these lines would thus
open and vastly enlarge this new ABM sector of the arms
race.

Insofar as MIRV is concerned, Brown at first seems to be
against its deployment. "Clearly," he writes, "an agreement
to ban the deployment of MIRV's would be desirable to

forestall erosion of the capability to deter." But this soon
begins to blur. For Brown goes on to say, "But the agreement *should* allow multiple re-entry vehicles that are *not*
capable of being individually guided." The italics are
Brown's. But then Brown admits by implication that once
we move into multiple warheads it is difficult if not impossible to tell by aerial surveillance how many there are atop
each missile and whether they are independently guided or
not. As Brown says, "Unfortunately a check on deployment of different types of payload clearly requires on-site
inspection of a very obtrusive kind." A "very obtrusive
kind" is presumably the kind we, as well as the Russians,
would object to.

The one clear answer to this problem is to negotiate an
agreement banning both MRV's and MIRV's while there is
still time to prevent this new and destabilizing development.
Brown suggests instead a murky compromise. "It is possible," he suggests, "that even without on-site inspection we
can tell enough about each other's missiles to obtain reasonable assurance." He says, "This is so because the probable
number of warheads per missile is proportionate to the payload of the missile, and payload, in turn, is directly related
to the gross volume, which we may be able to determine
unilaterally," i.e., by aerial reconnaissance.[1]

"Thus," Brown goes on, "a ceiling on numbers and sizes
of missiles could also limit MIRV's to a number less than
that needed for an effective first strike, *and yet permit
enough re-entry vehicles to penetrate missile defenses—as*
required for deterrence" (my italics). If we need multiple warheads to overcome ABM, why not negotiate an
agreement to deploy neither?

Brown's further suggestions admit that once ABM's and
MRV's are allowed, policing such an agreement would be
difficult. He says we would not only need an agreement to
limit the number of ABM's and missiles but "to ban com-

[1] For a startling revelation of how much we can now learn by aerial
reconnaissance see Jeremy J. Stone's chapter, "Can The Communists Deceive Us?," in the symposium on the ABM edited by Abram Chayes and
Jerome B. Weisner.

pletely any mobile land-based missiles, since they would make it easier to conceal illicit increases in a missile force." Once the horse was stolen, any number of locks would be needed for the stable door. "A subsequent agreement," Brown continues, "should then be worked out to limit the size of missiles and thus prevent the *unlimited growth* of the MIRV threat through development of larger and larger missiles" (my italics). But even this is not enough because, as Brown writes—

All deterrence systems tend to obsolesce. Thus, the increasing accuracy and miniaturization of missile warheads reduce the survivability of missiles in silos; improved antisubmarine warfare techniques have the same effect upon Polaris; improved FOBS or submarine-launched missiles lessen the effectiveness of the bomber; and new ABM or anti-aircraft techniques might seriously affect weapons penetration—all without an increase in the quantity of weapons.

This opens the prospect of an endless arms race in quality if not quantity once ABM and MIRV are accepted. To meet the menace of perpetual improvement, Brown adds another rickety device to his Rube Goldbergian arms control structure. "In order to attain a lasting treaty," he writes, "we might need an understanding on exactly what sort of improvements would or would not be allowed." This in turn would "also require some form of relatively simple on-site inspection to ensure compliance." The inspectors would have no easy time of it. For Brown would design the treaty limits "to control the first-strike threat," but he says they "should not inhibit the countermeasures which must be taken against gradual improvements in the other side's forces or against illicit improvements." Finally Brown admits that "the problem is complicated by the fine line between first-strike and second-strike capabilities." No wonder we are already being told cheerfully in backgrounders from the Pentagon that the negotiations might take years! How achieve stability once you embark—as Brown would have us embark—on two such destabilizing developments as ABM and MIRV?

There is a hidden ploy in the recesses of this negotiating position. An agreement to limit the number and size of missiles would freeze U.S. superiority. We are ahead of the Russians in miniaturization and accuracy of warheads as well as in the development of MRV and MIRV. The MRV's in clusters of three are already deployed in Polaris A3 missiles, possibly even in Minuteman III, though the latter is not certain. We have already budgeted $2 billion for the coming fiscal year to deploy Poseidon and Minuteman III, both MIRVed. The Russians have only tested cluster MRV's. We began to deploy MRV's in Polaris as far back as 1966. Thus the Russians, in accepting an agreement of this kind, would have to settle for a position of inferiority in which the U.S. might achieve a first-strike capacity without violating any of the various agreements set forth by Brown. After all, we are putting 10 or more warheads in each Polaris submarine with Poseidon and three or more in each Minuteman without any significant increase in the size of the missile and no increase in their numbers. These MIRV's will soon increase our capacity to the point where the Soviets would have reason to fear a first strike.

Such corkscrew negotiating positions, almost certain to ensure failure and thus excuse a further surge in the arms race, suits the solidly Goldwaterite chain of command which will oversee the talks for the Pentagon. The new Deputy Secretary of Defense for Policy Planning and Arms Control is Dr. Yuan-li Wu, originally a refugee from Communist China, more recently a scholar at that cold war citadel, the Hoover Institute of War and Revolution at Stanford. Goldwater welcomed the appointment in a Senate speech June 5 and attended Dr. Wu's swearing in, where the Senator found himself among old friends. Dr. Wu's superior is Dr. G. Warren Nutter, the new Assistant Secretary of State for International Security Affairs. The ISA is the Pentagon's own little State Department and Dr. Nutter has been described (by Karl Hess, Goldwater's famous ghost writer) as "the anchor man" of Goldwater's "think tank team" in 1964. And Nutter's superior, of course, is

Secretary of Defense Laird, who presided over the writing
of Goldwater's platform in 1964, and whose inflammatory
campaign for the ABM is hardly calculated to make the
Russians feel they are dealing with an Administration soberly and sincerely anxious for arms talks and détente.

This sour impression will not be corrected by the political complexion of the General Advisory Committee Nixon
has just appointed to the Arms Control and Disarmament
Agency. The most prominent appointee is Dean Rusk,
whom Nixon greatly admires; no Secretary of State ever
cared less about disarmament. The most disquieting appointee is that same William J. Casey, the lawyer-public relations man who is chairman of the Citizens Committee for
Peace with Security which was organized out of the White
House basement and has already distinguished itself by a
highly dubious poll showing 84 percent—why not 99 percent?—of the American people in favor of the ABM. There
is not one strong voice for disarmament on the advisory
committee; the doves are weak, the hawks are strong. This
should be no surprise. A President who wanted Senator
Jackson as Secretary of Defense and settled for Laird, and
whose most influential mentor seems to be Major General
Strom Thurmond, is not likely to negotiate an end to the
arms race.

July 14, 1969

A CENTURY OF FUTILITY

For almost a century and a half there has been agitation for
disarmament. For almost a century there have been few
years in which disarmament of one kind or another has not
been under negotiation. During those tumultuous years
every other movement for social reform has made striking
progress. It has been a century of futility for the struggle

against the arms race. As the strategic arms limitation talks (SALT) open in Vienna, it is time to cast up this account and ask why.

It was not for lack of understanding or of leadership. The principal arguments we make against the arms race today are the same as those that thoughtful men have used for more than a century. That it raises tension, but it does not change the balance of power but only the level of destructiveness and cost, that it wastes resources needed for social reconstruction—these arguments were as familiar in the nineteenth as in the twentieth century, and proved as futile.

The guns of Waterloo had hardly fallen silent before the first peace societies began to urge disarmament in Britain and America. The Napoleonic Wars, like the two world wars, had a sobering effect, but then as later this soon wore off. "What is the advantage of one power greatly increasing its army and navy?" the British Prime Minister, Sir Robert Peel, asked in a once-famous speech against the arms race in 1841. "Does it not see that if it proposes such increases for self-protection and defense, the other powers would follow its example?" The consequence, he went on, is "no increase of relative strength" but only "a universal consumption of the resources of every country in military preparations." One hundred and twenty-eight years later, Secretary of State Rogers made exactly the same appeal in his speech last November as the preparatory SALT talks were about to begin in Helsinki:

Competitive accumulation of more sophisticated weapons would not add to the basic security of either side. Militarily it probably would produce little or no net advantage. Economically it would divert resources needed elsewhere. Politically it woud perpetuate the tensions and fears that are the social fallout of the nuclear arms race.

In the intervening years, only the level of danger and of cost has changed. But these have grown enormously.

The United States, the most powerful nation of the twentieth century, is repeating the experience of Britain, the most powerful nation of the nineteenth. Despite the H-bomb and the ICBM, a British Victorian statesman would find himself quite at home in our current debate over arms policy. The industrialization of war and the growing militarization of industry, which we now call the military-industrial complex, began in England in the middle of the last century. To dip back into the history of armament agitation before World War I is to experience a strong feeling of *déjà vu*.[1] Then as now we see the defeat of reason over and over again by the same alliance of primitive instinct, private interest, and technological momentum, in a world without law.

The most powerful and the most respected political leaders of the time were unable to prevail over this still irresistible combination. The most extraordinary manifesto against the arms race was issued in 1857, when the two great rivals of nineteenth-century British politics, Disraeli and Gladstone, joined Lord John Russell and Richard Cobden, the century's foremost advocate of disarmament, in an appeal for a reduction in military expenditures. These had soared in the just-ended Crimean War. All their popularity and influence, however, could not keep Parliament that very year from raising naval appropriations 50 percent above prewar levels. On two occasions statesmen of the first rank —one Tory, one Liberal—resigned from high office in equally impotent protest against rising arms expenditures: Lord Randolph Churchill (Sir Winston's father) as Chancellor of the Exchequer in 1886, and Gladstone as Prime Minister in 1892, after a false war alarm led Parliament to more than double the Admiralty budget.

Such heroic resignations have yet to occur in our time. In all else armament politics remain substantially the same: the hopes and fears, the contending principles in which they are

[1] For the period to 1907 the best account I have come across, and to which I am indebted, is Merze Tate's *The Disarmament Illusion*, published by Macmillan and Harvard in 1942, long out of print but soon to be reissued by Russell & Russell, which has just republished her later book, *The US and Armaments* (Harvard, 1948), on which I have also relied. Miss Tate is a professor of history at Howard University.

rationalized, even the tactics and the cast of characters. Nineteenth-century Britain had its "gaps" and its Joe Alsops, too. Recurrent appeals to lift the burden of armament and divert the funds to eradicate slums and other social evils were countered with recurrent panics about enemy buildups. In these the British Admiralty, the shipbuilders, and the gunpowder manufacturers played a hidden part, making use of frenetic newspapermen in their orbit of influence, as the Air Force lobby with the aviation, electronics, and shipbuilding industries do today. Antiwar political leaders and journalists exposed these scares then as now, but with no permanent effect.

The strongest and safest country in the world, and the one with the largest navy, was a victim of the worst invasion nightmares, just as today the strongest nation on earth seems to spend more time than any other worrying about its security. There were six "panics" between 1847 and 1892, all fomented for their beneficial effect in boosting military and naval expenditures. The earliest exposé of these hobgoblins was Richard Cobden's *Three Panics* (third ed., 1862). The last, on the eve of World War I, was *The Six Panics* (1913), by F. W. Hirst, then editor of *The Economist*. They still make instructive reading.

These panics illustrate the tactic, still in use today, of projecting some fantastic possibility and treating it as if it were a reality. The earliest precursor of our latest equivalent, the Nixon-Laird scare about the Soviet SS-9, was the panic created by Lord Palmerston and the Duke of Wellington in 1847 when they seized on some dockyard expansion in France to picture England in danger of what we would now call a "first strike." Palmerston insisted that the shift to steam navigation had "thrown a bridge across the Channel," suddenly filling the ancient moat which had so long protected England from invasion. The seventy-seven-year-old Duke of Wellington, then doddering, said 50,000 men could be moved across this bridge undetected in a single night from Cherbourg and make a surprise attack on London the next morning! This "bridge of steam" was the first of many graphic but wholly fallacious metaphors which have supplied the melodrama for armament scares ever since.

Experts were mobilized by the peace forces to explain away and to ridicule these fears, as patiently as a psychiatrist trying to deal with a paranoid patient, or a present-day anti-ABM scientist from MIT disentangling fact from fancy in one of Laird's latest. Of the six synthetic panics between 1847 and 1892, the first five were aimed at France, the last at Germany, which after 1870 replaced France as The Enemy. Sir William Harcourt, who tried unsuccessfully to stem the panic of 1892 as Chancellor of the Exchequer, summed up the techniques still in use today. "The principle of the alarmists," he said, "is to pile up every conceivable contingency, probable or improbable, on one side and to admit no possible contingency on the other."

Then as now no level of preparation was enough to satisfy the military. "If you believe the doctors," Lord Salisbury said of these ever-more-costly apprehensions, "nothing is wholesome; if you believe the theologians, nothing is innocent; if you believe the soldiers, nothing is safe." So it is now, when weapons systems like Minuteman are sold to us as marvels of invulnerability one day and declared the next to be so weak as to be in peril of instant destruction. However egregiously mistaken the generals and admirals have proven in a century of warfare, they have never failed to earn their medals for salesmanship.

Alfred Vagts, to whose solid and passionate *History of Militarism* I owe these quotations from Lord Salisbury and Sir William Harcourt,[2] tells us how these tactics spread to the parliamentary politics of the Continent. What he says of Western Europe in the half-century before World War I applies as well to our presidential campaigns since World War II. "Either allied with the bureaucracy or on its own motion," he writes, "the party in opposition often produced

[2] Lord Salisbury is quoted on p. 362 and Sir William on p. 364 of Vagts, *A History of Militarism, Civilian and Military* (Meridian, rev. ed., 1959), which deserves a better fate than the remainder counter on which I found it.

an alarm by accusing the party in power of neglecting the country's defenses." These were the tactics of the Democratic party's alarms about a Bomber Gap in 1956 and a Missile Gap in 1960, and of Nixon's about a Security Gap in 1968. Their precursors were the Battleship Gaps fomented by Navy leagues in Britain and Germany before 1914. Their assiduity in exaggerating the other side's naval strength and in publicizing every aggressive statement on the other side, however obscure or unrepresentative its source, played a major role in bringing on World War I. Their counterparts today could push us down the slope to World War III.

In an effort to reverse the tide before World War I, the first international disarmament conference was held at The Hague in 1899 and a second in 1907. The military and their allies quickly developed the expertise to frustrate them. Both conferences were called on the initiative of the Czar, and this gave hostile propaganda an opportunity along lines which have a quite contemporary ring. The Russian proposal was portrayed as a plot to undermine the security of Western Europe, or alternatively as an effort to halt arms competition in the West in order to free Russian energies for further expansion in Asia at the expense of China.

When the Russian Foreign Ministry proposed to forbid the development of more powerful explosives, Secretary of State John Hay objected that this would restrain "the inventive genius of our people." [3] As a brake on pacifist enthusiasm, Captain Alfred T. Mahan, whose *Influence of Seapower Upon History* was the Bible of American imperialism, was named to the U.S. delegation. When the Czar proposed an agreement to abstain from the use of "asphyxiating or deleterious gases," Captain Mahan argued as a cheerful old salt that it was no more cruel to asphyxiate

[3] Similarly a French admiral at the Washington Naval Conference in 1921 defended the continued use of submarines by saying, "You could not stop the progress of humanity" (Vagts, p. 403).

one's enemies than to drown them by torpedoing a vessel.[4] Present-day advocates of chemical and bacteriological weapons speak with the same tender impartiality.

Though the first Hague Conference succeeded in setting up the International Court of Arbitration, and the second reached an agreement against the use of poison gas in time to be broken in World War I, both managed to avoid even a weapons freeze, much less arms reduction. "All the great powers," Miss Merze Tate wrote in her authoritative *US and Armaments*, "considered the Czar's proposals troublesome, but felt that they had to express their attitudes cautiously in view of the pacific tenor of public opinion." [5] In the private sessions Captain Mahan said "his government will on no account even discuss the creation of any limitation of naval armaments" since the U.S. needed a larger navy "in the struggle for Chinese markets." [6]

Loftier considerations were invoked publicly against the popular cry for arms reduction. Teddy Roosevelt, a skeptical and unwilling participant in the 1907 conference, cautioned that venerable liberal, Carl Schurz, a leader of the disarmament movement, that peace must be "second to righteousness"—quite in the manner a half-century later of that secular parson of the cold war, John Foster Dulles. At the second conference the delegates managed, by tacit agreement, a triumph of diplomacy. They succeeded in limiting discussion of disarmament to twenty-five minutes and their only action to passage of a resolution declaring that because arms expenditures had risen considerably since the first Hague conference, it was "eminently desirable that the governments should resume the serious examination of this question." This was adopted by unanimous acclamation.[7]

After these arduous efforts the conference, before adjourning, resolved to meet again in seven years. The out-

[4] Tate, *US and Armaments*, p. 43.
[5] *Ibid.*, p. 44.
[6] Tate, *Disarmament Illusion*, p. 292.
[7] Tate, *US and Armaments*, p. 58.

break of war in 1914 made a repetition of the comedy unnecessary. Yet the war itself, the long stalemate in the
muddy trenches, and the unprecedented butchery seemed
at last to promise the triumph of disarmament when the war
was over. As early as 1915 a consensus began to appear,
ranging from the Socialist movement to men in power like
Sir Edward Grey, that the arms race had been a major cause
of the war, and that disarmament was necessary if a new
war were to be avoided.

In January 1917, Woodrow Wilson in a special message
to the Senate termed this "the most immediately and intensely practical question" facing mankind, and said there
could be "no sense of safety" among nations if the arms
race continued. The fourth of his famous Fourteen Points
for peace specified "that national armaments will be reduced to the lowest point consistent with domestic safety,"
i.e., to what was needed for internal order. A League of
Nations was to create a framework of enforceable world
law for the settlement of international disputes. To prevent
the machinations of the munitions makers, which played so
malevolent a role in the prewar arms race, Wilson's first
draft for the Convenant of the League also provided "that
munitions and implements of war shall not be manufactured
by private enterprise."

But as the war drew to a close, these brave beginnings
soon turned into another comedy on a grander scale. In the
Paris peace negotiations the phrase about reducing armament
to the lowest point consistent with "domestic safety" was
changed to "national safety," which made it meaningless
and opened the door to a new arms race. The British Admiralty—loyal to the shipbuilding and armorplate industries—
led the objections to abolishing private manufacture of arms.
Article 8 of the Covenant was diluted to read that members of the League agreed "that manufacture by private
enterprise of munitions and implements of war is open to
grave objection." Therefore the Council of the League was
to "advise how the evil effect attendant upon such manufacture can be prevented," but with "due regard" for "the

necessities of those members of the League which are not able to manufacture" the war materials "necessary for their safety." It would take a Swift or a Voltaire to match such splendid satire.

The price was the resurgence of a militaristic Germany and World War II. The disarmament of Germany was predicated on general disarmament by the victors. "In order to render possible the initiation of a general limitation of the armaments of all nations," the Treaty of Versailles said, "Germany undertakes strictly to observe the military, naval and air clauses which follow." While German power was sharply cut back, negotiations for general disarmament proceeded at a pace which exasperatingly recalled one of the Eleatic paradoxes that deny the reality of motion. Negotiations seemed to be moving—for one could see the experts rustling papers and watch the documentation piling up in the League archives—but when one looked again, the crowded train seemed still to be in the station.

In 1920 the League set up a Permanent Advisory Commission to which each member of the Council named an Army, Navy, and Air officer. These soon created a technical thicket calculated to keep exploratory discussions running around in circles. It took six more years before the Conference for the Reduction and Limitation of Armaments finally convened in Geneva in February, 1932. The day it met the Japanese bombardment of Shanghai was already signaling the breakdown of the postwar order. To this conference, President Herbert Hoover—for once sublimely quixotic—proposed the abolition of tanks, chemical warfare, and aerial bombardment. But though the smaller countries applauded, England and France would not support what now appears as a last wan hope. Within a few months Hitler had come to power and begun the rearmament of Germany in preparation for World War II.

German rancor and cynicism over the failure of the other great powers to keep their promises to disarm were ingredients in the witch's brew of National Socialism. In justice to the German people, it must not be forgotten that despite the terrible inflation of 1923, the rankling inequality imposed by Versailles, and the world depression, they never gave Hitler a majority in a free election. Had there been general disarmament in the early twenties, had the Powers then proceeded to set up the machinery of military and economic sanctions the League Covenant envisaged for the punishment of any international lawbreaker, the Weimar Republic might have survived and World War II been avoided. Who has imagination enough to grasp the magnitude of the suffering which might never have happened *if . . . ?*

Will the same heartbreaking question some day be asked about the pledges made by the two nuclear superpowers in the Nuclear Non-Proliferation Pact? Will the fanfare with which it has just been ratified in Washington, London, and Moscow some day appear to have been another bit of sour "theater"? Will a parallel some day be drawn with the disarmament pledges of the Versailles Treaty? Will it be said that some new monster like Hitler might never have arisen, that World War III might never have occurred, if the United States and the Soviet Union had fulfilled the pledge they gave *unwillingly* in Article VI of the Non-Proliferation Pact? Article VI says—and every word should be read carefully—

Each of the parties to the Treaty undertakes to pursue negotiations in good faith on effective measures relating to cessation of the nuclear-arms race at an early date and to nuclear disarmament, and on a Treaty on general and complete disarmament under strict and effective international control.

This Article VI was put into the treaty at the insistence of the non-nuclear powers. It was not in the drafts submitted by the two nuclear superpowers. Those contained similar pledges but only in the preamble. Perhaps the non-nuclear powers recalled that the pledge of general disarmament in the Versailles Pact was also in a preamble, and the jurists held that preambles did not embody specific obligations. "One of the most attractive features of this much maligned class of experts," Salvador de Madariaga once wrote of this quibbling over the 1919 disarmament pledges, was "their natural tendency to put a minimum value on their own words."[8] The non-nuclear powers are as cynical about the NNPP as the Germans were about Versailles. When the U.S. and Soviet drafts were first presented to the eighteen-nation disarmament conference in Geneva in 1965, the UAR delegate commented caustically that a non-proliferation treaty should do more than "bless and perpetuate the nuclear monopoly and supremacy of the five Powers which possess the bomb." M. Messmer, the French Defense Minister, said with cruel but precise wit that it was aimed merely to castrate the impotent.[9]

While most of the nations of the earth have signed the pact (the count was 97 as this went to press) and half of them (49 at last count) had ratified it, the half-dozen non-nuclear powers within reach of achieving the bomb on their own are delaying signature or ratification until they see in the SALT talks whether Article VI is to be—in a once-famous phrase of sinister history—another scrap of paper. Their cynicism is not allayed by the recollection that almost nine years ago the U.S. and the USSR in a joint report to the United Nations General Assembly on the result of the McCloy-Zorin negotiations had already pledged themselves to general and complete disarmament down to only enough non-nuclear forces sufficient "to maintain internal order" and "provide agreed manpower for a UN peace force," words which recall Wilson's original proposals. The McCloy-Zorin agreement today is as vaguely remembered as the law tablets of Hammurabi.

[8] Quoted in Tate, *US and Armaments*, p. 70.
[9] Quoted in Elizabeth Young's Adelphi Paper, *The Control of Proliferation* (London: Institute for Strategic Studies, April 1969), pp. 6 and 11, respectively.

The amnesia of the superpowers is only matched by the prodigality of their pledges. Among other goodies the Mc-Cloy-Zorin agreement promised to bring down the nuclear chimney for Christmas were "disbanding of armed forces . . . [and] bases," cessation of arms production, "elimination of all stockpiles of nuclear, chemical, bacteriological and other weapons of mass destruction," and cessation of their production, "elimination of all means of delivery of weapons of mass destruction," abolition of military organizations and training, and "discontinuance of military expenditures." [10] One can only wonder how many bottles of vodka were consumed before these top-level negotiators signed on the dotted line for the millennium. The morning after, it was all forgotten! Obviously disarmament talks take place in a realm of discourse in which no words, however solemn and specific, can be taken seriously. Article 26 of the UN Charter adopted a quarter-century ago is as monumental a dead-letter. It provided that—

In order to promote the establishment and maintenance of international security with the least diversion for armaments of the world's human and economic resources, the Security Council shall be responsible for formulating, with the assistance of the Military Staff Committee referred to in Article 47, plans to be submitted to the Members of the United Nations for the establishment of the regulation of armaments.

This, too, has for all practical purposes vanished from memory.

The SALT talks will be the fourth, and possibly the last, real opportunity since World War II to bring the nuclear arms race under control.

April 9, 1970
New York Review

[10] *Facts on File,* 1961, p. 407.

THEATER OF DELUSION

The Strategic Arms Limitation Talks (SALT) now re-opening in Vienna may best be seen as the latest in a series of fumbling attempts by mankind to pick up the pieces in the wake of Hiroshima. A month after that first atomic bomb dropped, Einstein said what is still the last word of wisdom on the subject, though we are as far as ever from applying it. To a UPI reporter who tracked him down in a forest cabin near Lake Saranac, Einstein said "the only salvation for civilization and the human race" now lay in "the creation of a world government. As long as sovereign states continue to have separate armaments and armament secrets," he warned, "new world wars will be inevitable." [1]

This idea, like so much else in the repetitive and frustrating history of the struggle against the arms race in the last hundred years, was not new. It appeared at least as early as 1913, in a novel by H. G. Wells, *The World Set Free*. Wells predicted the splitting of the atom—by some stroke of luck or intuitive genius placing the event in 1933, when it actually occurred. He also forecast the use of nuclear energy in a world war so catastrophic it shook men and nations out of their accustomed habits and led them to form a world government as their only assurance henceforth of survival. [2]

[1] Otto Nathan and Heinz Norden, eds., *Einstein on Peace* (New York: Schocken, 1968), p. 336.

[2] In a recently published fragment of autobiography, the late Leo Szilard, discussing the origins of the atomic bomb, wrote of the impression made on him by the Wells novel. It is to the Szilard memoir in *The Intellectual Migration: Europe and America, 1930–1960* (edited by Donald Fleming and Bernard Bailyn, Belknap Press of Harvard University Press, 1969) that I owe my knowledge of Wells's prophetic book. Szilard first read the novel in Berlin in 1932 and thought of it again in London in September of the following year after hearing Lord Rutherford tell the British Association for the Advancement of Science it was "the merest moonshine" to look for sources of power on a commercial scale from nuclear fission!

For a fleeting moment, since forgotten, the dropping of the first bomb did push the American government in the direction of world government. The horrors of Hiroshima and then Nagasaki, the realization of what a third and nuclear world war would do to mankind, shocked American political leaders and scientists into a project whose novelty and magnitude began to be commensurate with the peril they foresaw. But the Baruch-Lilienthal-Acheson plan for the international control of atomic energy they then presented to the United Nations proved to be the first of four lost opportunities since the war to bring the nuclear monster under control; the SALT talks represent another chance, and I fear it too will be lost.

The Baruch plan, as put forward in 1946, would have set up a kind of world superstate for the nuclear age. Unfortunately the plan seems to have passed through three stages, in which the original idealistic impulse was successively revised to make it more "practical" politically. In the process it also grew less magnanimous. It ended up looking—from Moscow's point of view—like a plan for domination of the world and the economy of the Soviet Union by the United States, as Acheson now admits in a section of his newly published memoirs which has escaped attention.[3]

Dean Acheson, then Under Secretary of State, was chairman of a committee appointed by President Truman after the war to draw up a plan for the international control of atomic energy. This committee in turn set up a consultative group of scientists and big-business executives[4] under David E. Lilienthal and including J. Robert Oppenheimer. The

[3] I was struck by it because I made a similar criticism of the plan when it was first presented a quarter century ago with no knowledge of the intramural misgivings and differences of which Acheson now provides a glimpse. I was then Washington editor of *The Nation*. See my three Washington letters in that publication: "Atomic Pie in The Sky" (April 6, 1946), "Atomic Report: Second Reading" (April 13, 1946), and "The McMahon Bill" (April 20, 1946). Lilienthal, because of his association with the TVA, was then a hero of the liberals and the left, and my colleagues were shocked that I should criticize a plan which bore his magic name.

[4] From New Jersey Bell Telephone, General Electric, and Monsanto Chemical, companies which had played key roles in the making of the bomb.

original sketch for a world authority to take over all sources of uranium and to control all nuclear production facilities came from the Lilienthal group.

This was at least twice revised before publication by the Acheson committee. The others on his comittee were General Leslie R. Groves, who headed the Manhattan Project which built the bomb; Dr. Vannevar Bush, who organized science for war in World War II; Dr. James B. Conant, then president of Harvard; and John J. McCloy, Assistant Secretary of War under Henry L. Stimson. Stimson recognized very early that the secret of the bomb would soon vanish and had best be shared while it might still be used to build a more stable world.

The main drawback in the original Acheson-Lilienthal plan was that it asked the Soviet Union and all other countries to hand over control of their uranium deposits and open themselves to geological survey at once in return for a promise at some unspecified future date to cease our own production of bombs and hand over their secret to an international authority—if Congress did not change its mind when the time came.

The hedges not only became more onerous but began to seem deliberate pitfalls by the time the plan was revised again by Bernard Baruch, whom Truman named in March, 1946, as U.S. representative on the United Nations Atomic Energy Commission. The group Baruch chose to work with him in revising the Acheson-Lilienthal plan for presentation to the UN contained neither liberals, idealists, nor scientists. It was the earliest official postwar collection of cold warriors: John Hancock of Lehman Brothers; Ferdinand Eberstadt, another Wall Street banker with strong military ties; Fred Searls of Newmont Mining, a concern of imperial dimensions and worldwide cartel connections; and Herbert Bayard Swope, the journalist who had become Baruch's personal public relations man.

The Baruch plan, as it became known when it was submitted to the UN, must have seemed to Moscow the blueprint for a world capitalist superstate in which the U.S.

would retain its atomic monopoly behind the façade of an international organization under U.S. control. In *Present at the Creation* (Norton, 1969), Acheson discloses publicly for the first time that he felt the plan as transformed by Baruch contained provisions "almost certain to wreck any possibility of Russian acceptance" because Moscow would see them "as an attempt to turn the United Nations into an alliance to support a U.S. threat of war against the USSR unless it ceased its efforts" to develop an atom bomb, too.[5]

Even the earlier pre-Baruch version would have been hard to sell a ruler of Stalin's ferocious suspicions and primitive Marxist views. The Baruch plan was enough to have frightened off even a gentle Menshevik. It would have eliminated the veto in the UN Security Council to assure, in Baruch's words, "swift and certain punishment" of any violator. It would have thrown the war-torn and terribly weakened Soviet Union open to Western inspection, and at the mercy of a U.S.-led majority in the Security Council. Baruch was no fool and he knew the Russians well. His rhetoric in presenting the plan matched the occasion. The choice, he told the UN, is "world peace or world destruction." But his draftsmanship ensured a Russian *nyet*. So the first opportunity was lost.

In retrospect the failure transcends the personalities who took part. Mankind just was not ready. The U.S. was not generous enough. The Soviet Union was not trusting enough. If the roles had been reversed, it is hard to believe that the Russian regime, self-righteously Communist and deeply nationalistic, would even have made the gesture. If the view from the Kremlin had been of a war-wrecked U.S.A., their hard-liners would have dismissed such idealism as weakness and seized the opportunity (as our hard-liners did) for an attempt at world domination. Even if the U.S. had been more generous, the Soviets would have been too mistrustful. Even if Russia had not been Communist, even if it had been a capitalist ally, the realities of domestic politics would still have kept the American government from being

[5] p. 155.

magnanimous enough to relinquish the atomic secret without attaching strings intended to maintain its control.

The proof of this lies in our nuclear relations with our
closest ally, Britain. The production of the world's first
atomic weapons was a joint Anglo-American achievement.
But by 1945 Britain found itself excluded from information
and control despite specific Roosevelt-Churchill agreements
for sharing them. Britain was forced to go it alone at Har-
well and produce its nuclear weapons on its own. In April,
1946 (two months before the Baruch plan was presented to
the UN) Congress went a step further and in the McMahon Act forbade the sharing of atomic secrets with Britain
or any other nation.[6] Nations and men as the last war ended
just had not reached the necessary stage of understanding.
Wells, if he were still alive, might have said that the shock
of atom bombs falling on two cities was not enough. In his
novel, men came to their senses only after an all-out nuclear
war had destroyed every city on earth.

After each lost opportunity for nuclear disarmament
since the war, a new monster of destruction has been born.
When the Baruch plan failed, there was only the A-bomb.
It had been dwarfed by the H-bomb when the second lost
opportunity arrived almost a decade later. This was what
Philip Noel-Baker, the grand old man of the world disarmament movement, still active in his eighties, called "The Moment of Hope: May 10, 1955."[7] On that date Moscow
made a dramatic about-face at the UN disarmament subcommittee meeting in London and substantially accepted

[6] This was most recently recalled in The Adelphi Paper, *The Control
of Proliferation*, by Elizabeth Young (*op. cit.*).

[7] In his indispensable book, *The Arms Race* (New York: Oceana
Publications, 1959). As a Labour MP and British delegate Noel-Baker has
been a figure at most of the disarmament conferences since World War
I. Among his earlier books, which deserve the attention of a new generation, the most important is *The Private Manufacture of Armaments*
(1937), the most complete account of the intrigues of what we now term
the military-industrial complex before and after World War I. It has
long been out of print, and should be made available again.

Western proposals for general and nuclear disarmament it had long derided. It offered to lift the Iron Curtain and permit international inspection on a wide scale as part of that scheme, only to have the West suddenly lose interest.

The proposals of May 10, 1955, were part of a larger reversal in Russian policy which followed the accession of Khrushchev to power in February of that year and the confidence generated by successful detonation of a Soviet H-bomb. The Soviet disarmament proposals in London were the second of three dramatic about-faces in Soviet foreign policy in the space of little more than one month. The first was the announcement on April 15 that the Russians, after nine years of fruitless negotiation by the West, had agreed to withdraw their troops from Austria and to sign a four-power pact guaranteeing its independence. The third was the arrival of Khrushchev and Bulganin at Belgrade airport on May 26, where Tito impassively heard them declare that they "sincerely regret" Stalin's efforts to overthrow him. This Canossa was the most dramatic manifestation of the new regime's eagerness for a fresh start in foreign policy.

The May 10 disarmament statement was as big a surprise. For years the West had complained that the Soviet Union's disarmament proposals would "ban the bomb" but deny inspection and maintain its superiority in conventional arms. The Western powers were for "total prohibition" of nuclear arms but insisted that it had to be accompanied (1) by reduction of the conventional armies of the U.S., the USSR, and China to a figure between one and one-and-one-half million men and those of Britain and France to about 650,000, and (2) by "the establishment of a control organ" with powers "adequate to guarantee the effective observance of the agreed prohibitions and reductions." [8]

On May 10, 1955, the Russians tabled a draft treaty accepting the West's ceilings on the size of conventional armies, its proposed cut-off by stages in the production and stocks of all "weapons of mass destruction," and the estab-

[8] From the Anglo-French memorandums of June 11, 1954 and March 29, 1955, quoted on pages 15 and 18 of Noel-Baker's *The Arms Race*.

lishment of an international control organ. This organ, in
the Soviet draft treaty, would have had a staff of internationally recruited inspectors residing permanently in all sig-
natory states. The inspectors would have had "within the
bounds of the control functions they exercise, unimpeded
access at all times to all objects of control." They would
also have had "unimpeded access to records relating to the
budgetary appropriations of States for military needs," and
the "rights and powers to exercise control, including inspection on a continuing basis, to the extent necessary to
ensure implementation of the above-mentioned Convention." [9] The Russians added a new proposal of their own:
the establishment of "Control Posts" at large ports, at railway junctions, on main motor highways, and at air fields to
guard against the danger of surprise attack.

The Western delegates in London were startled. M. Jules
Moch for France said, "The whole thing looks too good to
be true." The U.S. delegate to the disarmament talks declared himself "gratified to find that the concepts which we
have put forward over a considerable length of time, and

[9] Conventional Western writers on disarmament and standard Western
news compilations like *Keesing's* in London, our own *Facts on File,* and
even the new *Yearbook of World Armaments and Disarmament* issued by
the Stockholm International Peace Research Institute (compare its feeble
account on p. 152 with Noel-Baker's and the new material presented in
this article) have all joined in brushing this draft treaty and the moment
of hope it represented under the rug as if not in accordance with the
Western "party-line" on disarmament, much as historians do in the Soviet
Union with matters which run counter to theirs.

The text is hard to come by. Noel-Baker quotes it from Cmd. [British
parliamentary "command papers"] 9639, pp. 33–42. For those who do
not have access (as I didn't) to this British document in the famous series
issued by HMS Stationery Office, the full text is also available as Document 89, p. 382, of *Disarmament and Security: A Collection of Documents, 1919–1955* published sixteen years ago by the Senate Foreign Relations Committee subcommittee on disarmament "pursuant to Sen. Res.
93, and Continued by Sen. Res. 185, 84th Congress," U.S. Government
Printing Office, 1956, now very rare but invaluable.

If I may be pardoned a personal note, I had the joy of finding it while
working on this article after a frantic search through a small mountain
of documents in my garage. A new generation of revisionist historians
may also be interested in an immediate contemporary reaction to the
May 10, 1955, draft treaty, "Russia Offers to Lift Its Iron Curtain for
Peace," in the May 16, 1955, issue of my weekly newsletter.

which we have repeated many times during the past two months, have been accepted in a large measure by the Soviet Union." The British delegate said he was glad the Western "policy of patience" had "now achieved this welcome dividend" and that the Western proposals "have now been largely, and in some cases entirely, adopted by the Soviet Union." [10] Even John Robinson Beal's official biography of John Foster Dulles, which is as slick and corkscrew as its subject was, admitted that "the new Soviet proposals actually were plagiarized from the French and British and *were by no means acceptable,* but for the first time there were signs of Russian movement"! [11] (The exclamation point and the italics are added.)

But Washington was curiously unmoved. The State Department, which knows how to orchestrate the press, played the news down, and so did the news media. The day after the news from London the President was asked about it at a press conference by Walter Kerr of the New York *Herald Tribune.* The colloquy was less than jubilant:

Q: Mr. President, I wonder if you have had an opportunity to see a report on the latest Soviet disarmament plan.

THE PRESIDENT: On what?

Q: On what has been described as the recent Soviet disarmament plan submitted to the summit.

THE PRESIDENT: You mean the one submitted through the Disarmament Commission in London?

Q: Yes, sir.

THE PRESIDENT: Well, I have just had a chance to glance at it.

Q: Do you care to comment on it, sir?

THE PRESIDENT: No, not at the moment. The whole question is so confused. It has still some of the elements they have always had in it. They want to get rid of one kind; we would like to get rid of everything. It is something that has to be studied before you can really comment on it.[12]

---

[10] *The Arms Race,* pp..21–22. Citing Cmd. 9650, pp. 607 *et seq.,* where the subcommittee's discussion of the Russian proposal may be found.

[11] John Robinson Beal, *John Foster Dulles* (New York: Harper & Row, 1957), p. 298.

[12] *Public Papers of the Presidents, Eisenhower 1955,* pp. 497–8.

Not until his press conference of July 6 did Eisenhower give any indication of his thinking and then both the question and answer indicated that the American government was cooling off on its own proposals now that they were in danger—that seems to be the only word for it—of being turned into reality by the unexpected Soviet acceptance of them. This was the implication when Edward P. Morgan asked the President that day if he could give the press the benefit of his "personal thoughts" on the subject of disarmament. "For instance," Mr. Morgan prompted, "do you feel that we, the American people, are going to have to move away somewhat from the concept of total drastic disarmament toward a sort of standoff?" The question, I suspect, knowing how the State Department operates, reflected "backgrounders" downgrading the significance of the breakthrough in London.

Total "drastic" disarmament had been the declared goal of U.S. policy since the "Essential Principles for a Disarmament Program" had been tabled by the U.S. at the UN in April of 1952. Inspection, the U.S. had then and has since stressed, was the heart of the problem. But now Eisenhower wondered aloud whether we really wanted inspection. This was Eisenhower's answer to Mr. Morgan in that rambling but revealing way Eisenhower had of talking to the press:

I wouldn't want to have anything I now say taken as authoritative, for the simple reason that the more one studies intensively this problem of disarmament, the more he finds himself in a kind of squirrel's cage. . . . Everything comes back, as I see it, to acceptable methods of enforcement. How do you enforce such things? This brings us instantly to the question of examinations, of inspections. Now, one way to approach this problem is what would we, in the United States, [sic] suppose took a vote of this body today or we started as a committee of the whole to study it, what kind of inspection are we ready to accept? Are we ready to open up every one of our factories, every place where something might be going on that could be inimical to the interests of somebody else?[13]

13 Ibid., pp. 676–7.

Eisenhower did not complain—as he could have—that the Soviet proposals on inspection did not go far enough, that they did not define "objects of control" or more fully spell out the powers of the inspectors, or that they left enforcement unclear since the control organ presumably would operate under the UN Security Council where the Soviet Union had a veto. Instead, now that a workable system of inspection seemed within reach of negotiation, he was worrying about how much inspection *we* would stand for. It was now we who were suspicious of intrusion, fearful for our secrets, hesitating to lift our own "curtain." [14]

In London, where the Soviet delegation wanted to go on with the negotiations, the Western governments insisted on a recess. The debates were not resumed until August 29. After one week, the U.S. delegate Harold Stassen made a surprising announcement. He wiped the slate clean of all past U.S. proposals and freed his government from commitment to them:

The United States does now place a reservation upon all of its pre-Geneva substantive positions taken in this sub-committee on Disarmament or in the Disarmament Commission or in the UN on these questions in relationship to levels of armament.

In other words, as Noel-Baker points out, the manpower ceilings, the cut-off arrangements on nuclear stocks, "the detailed plan for inspection and control, all the other proposals urged with such vigor and persistence only three months before—all were withdrawn."

In the meantime, at the summit conference in Geneva on July 21, Eisenhower had come up with a wholly new plan that Nelson Rockefeller, always a cold warrior and never a

---

[14] Noel-Baker writes (*The Arms Race*, p. 545) that the mutual inspection safeguards later established by the West European Union treaty and Euratom, the West European Nuclear Energy agency, show that Western "General Staffs are still reluctant to accept the 'sacrifices' of sovereignty such inspection must involve" and cites as an example in a footnote a London *Times* report (Oct. 12, 1956) that "under the WEU system five days' notice must be given of any inspection, and that component parts of armament were excluded" from inspection. "These restrictions," Noel-Baker comments, "would make inspection a farce."

friend of disarmament, had helped to draw up, the so-called "open skies" proposal.[15] Rockefeller was then Eisenhower's Special Assistant for Cold War Strategy.[16] "I have been searching my mind and heart," Eisenhower said as he unveiled the new plan at Geneva with more than a touch of *schmaltz*, "for something that I could say here that could convince everyone of the great sincerity of the U.S. in approaching this problem of disarmament." [17]

It is indicative that he felt it necessary at that point to prove U.S. sincerity. He then proposed to Bulganin and Khrushchev that the U.S. and the USSR "give each other a complete blueprint of our military establishments, from beginning to end" and "provide within our countries facilities for aerial reconnaissance to the other country . . . where you can make all the pictures you choose."

It is hard to believe that the same man who was so hesitant on July 6 about the lesser measures of inspection proposed by the Russians was now sincerely ready two weeks later to exchange "a complete blueprint" of all military establishments with them. The plan looked more like public relations razzle-dazzle to cover a U.S. retreat on disarmament. It must have been put forward only because Washington was sure that Moscow would reject it. For years we had accused the Russians of proposing disarmament without inspection. Now it looked as if we were proposing inspection without disarmament. Though it was presented as a way to prevent surprise attack, it would obviously have provided the Strategic Air Command with exactly the maps its bombers needed. The response could not have been a surprise. In his memoirs Eisenhower writes that Khrushchev rejected the "open skies" plan as "nothing more than a bald espionage plot against the USSR." [18]

Though negotiations went on interminably, hope of an agreement had disappeared. The U.S. line had so far reversed

[15] Dwight D. Eisenhower, *Mandate for Change* (New York: Doubleday, 1963), p. 519.
[16] *Ibid.*, p. 511.
[17] *Facts on File*, 1955, p. 245.
[18] *Mandate for Change*, p. 521.

itself that by May 4 of the following year (1956) Stassen was telling the UN disarmament subcommittee, "It is the U.S. view that low force levels and drastic reduction in armaments—even though carried out under an armaments agreement—would not, if they were not accompanied by progress in the settlement of the major political issues, be in the interest of any country represented at this subcommittee table. These reductions would increase the danger of the outbreak of war. . . ." [19] Arms reduction had become a menace to peace! The major political issue which is one key to the 1955 failure was the future of Germany. Washington wanted a reunified and rearmed Germany free to join the Western camp. The May 10 disarmament proposals would have ended the hope of this by liquidating both the NATO and Warsaw pacts with their forward bases and paving the way for a Germany that would be reunited but neutral ("the Austrian solution") and with limited military forces.

One crucial date must not be forgotten. Five days before the dramatic Soviet about-face on disarmament, West Germany had joined NATO. Today the Bonn Federal Republic has 460,000 men under arms, NATO's largest European contingent. If the Western proposals for ceilings on conventional armies had been put into effect after their acceptance by the Soviet Union, West Germany would not have been allowed to mobilize anywhere near that number of men.

It is May 5 that explains May 10. Germany was to be our main military bulwark in Europe, as we now hope to make Japan our main military bulwark in Asia. German rearmament was the stumbling block to general disarmament. But it is hard to avoid the conclusion that even if there had been no German problem, some other excuse would have been found to keep the arms race going. Not until Kennedy took office was there another real chance to bring it under control, and by that time a new monster had made its appearance, the Intercontinental Ballistic Missile,

[19] *The Arms Race*, p. 23.

able to carry an H-bomb warhead in thirty minutes in either direction between the U.S. and the USSR.

The opportunity at the beginning of the Kennedy Administration for a fresh start in curbing the nuclear arms race was not so dramatic as the Baruch plan or the May 10, 1955 Soviet draft treaty, but was nevertheless substantial. It was lost, and while it was lost two new monsters were secretly being gestated, the ABM and the MIRV, the latter a new ICBM with multiple heads like some terrifying Hindu god of destruction.

Basically the opportunity was missed because Kennedy as president, like Kennedy as senator and as candidate, tried to ride two horses at once in two opposite directions, rearmament *and* disarmament. I can recall an occasion in the Senate when in the short space of one week he made two speeches, one idealistic and eloquent on the need to end the arms race, the other alarmist on the need to fill that nonexistent missile gap. This might have been fallacious logic but it was—as they say—practical politics. It served to keep his lines open to two antagonistic constituencies, the powerful armament makers with their allies in the military bureaucracy, and a public increasingly anxious about the mounting cost and danger.

In justice to John F. Kennedy it must be said that the effort to please both at once was characteristic of all the great powers before World War I, as it has been of every U.S. administration since World War II. This was the trap that private interest, the sheer inertial mass of the military bureaucracy, and the ancient instincts of mankind had set, and in which we are still caught. The result has been to make disarmament negotiations nothing more than an exercise to disarm the public, while the arms race spirals ever upward.

A lovely sample of the Pied Piper rationalizations supplied by intellectuals in every generation for this ultimately suicidal political strategy may be found in the little book which Arthur Schlesinger, Jr., wrote for the 1960 campaign, *Kennedy or Nixon: Does It Make Any Difference?* [20] Schlesinger wrote that Kennedy promised "creative idealism," but Schlesinger's formulation of it in the sphere of disarmament only offered the same old glamorous but opportunistic rhetoric. "A new spirit arising within our nation," he wrote—

will lead to a reconstruction of our approach to foreign affairs. Instead of responding interminably to the initiatives of others, we will begin to take the initiative ourselves in the fight for a decent peace. Disarmament, instead of being an occupation for clerks, will receive the top priority it deserves in the conduct of our foreign affairs.

But, Schlesinger goes on, as if the Kennedy of the two faces were looking over his shoulder as he wrote—

Pending the establishment of a reliable disarmament system, of course we have no choice but to remove the existing gaps in our own defenses; *indeed, only by showing that we can stay in the arms race as long as they*, can we convince the Russians of the imperative need for arms control. But we will arm in order to disarm (my italics).

This was the same old Kennedy tactic. What greater nonsense than this idea that the richest nation on earth had to prove to a contender with less than half its resources that we could stay in the arms race as long as the Russians could? Every sophisticated observer knew that the insiders in Washington had long rationalized the arms race as a form of economic warfare, which—in wondrous asymmetry— kept them poor while it kept us rich, or at least that portion of us who drew benefits from arms production and research. To this day it has been a cardinal axiom of U.S. policy that by forcing the diversion of the Soviet's more limited natural resources, productive capacity, and skilled manpower from its enormous backlog of consumer needs to armament we were imposing burdens so heavy we could exact a political price for lifting them in arms negotiations.

[20] New York: Macmillan, 1960, p. 42.

It is enlightening to test Schlesinger's final proposition "we will arm to disarm"—the dialectic in the service of the arms race!—against his own later account, in *A Thousand Days*, of what happened behind the scenes in the new Administration. He writes[21] that "the Soviet Union watched the arrival of the new Administration with marked interest." Khrushchev "had given up on Eisenhower after the U-2 incident and the collapse of the Paris summit" in 1960 and had "seized several opportunities to semaphore his hopes for Kennedy." Khrushchev's "messages to Harriman and others after the election were followed by a Pugwash meeting on disarmament in Moscow in December." Walt Rostow and Jerome Wiesner were among the Americans who took part, and they saw V. V. Kuznetsov of the Soviet Foreign Office to urge the release of two American RB-47 fliers shot down over the Arctic. "In the course of their talk," Schlesinger's account reveals—

Kuznetsov mentioned the campaign furor about a "missile gap" and suggested that, if the new Administration went in for massive rearmament, it could not expect the Russians to sit still.

Both sides knew by then that what Schlesinger calls "the campaign furor" about a missile gap was a fake; this is indeed implicit in the disparaging phrase he chooses for it. What follows shows what spurious rationalizations intellectuals will indulge in when they take service with political leaders—

Rostow replied that any Kennedy rearmament would be designed to improve the stability of the deterrent, and that the Soviet Union should recognize this as in the interests of peace . . .

Kuznetsov must have felt that he was being taken, that he was dealing with a con man. Now let us return to Schlesinger's narrative—

. . . but Kuznetsov, *innocent of the higher calculus of deterrence as recently developed in the United States*, brusquely dismissed the explanation.

21 Houghton Mifflin, 1965, p. 301.

The italics are mine. They make the reader realize what a great humorist was lost when Schlesinger turned to history.

Here was the genesis of the stepped-up arms race in the sixties, from which the SALT talks are now supposed to deliver us. Here was the test of the proposition that we were only arming in order to disarm. When Schlesinger 200 pages later in his narrative comes to explain why the new Administration embarked on a huge missile buildup even though it knew there was no missile gap, he forgets this slick poppycock about "the higher calculus of deterrence." He gives us instead an intramural picture of decision-making which, despite its subtle court-historian apologetics, is immensely valuable. For it begins to uncover the real motivations and the real difficulties which have hampered every attempt to curb the arms race during the past century.

"There remained for a moment," Schlesinger begins his account of how Kennedy formulated his first budget, "the question of the 'missile gap.' Though disowned by McNamara in February, the gap had persisted as a center of intra-service argument, with the Air Force continuing to claim that the Russians had 600 to 800 ballistic missiles while the CIA estimated 450 and the Navy 200." [22] Schlesinger does not say so, but each service was, as usual, tailoring its intelligence estimates to support its own budgetary demands. The Air Force overestimated because it wanted more planes and missiles. The Navy set a low figure because it wanted more money for ships.

It is curious that Schlesinger does not give us the estimate Army intelligence put forward. General Maxwell Taylor, just retired as U.S. Army Chief of Staff, had been recalled to active service by Kennedy in July 1961 as "Presidential Military Adviser for foreign and military policy and intelligence operations." [23] Taylor was an advocate of a "minimum deterrent" of from 100 to 200 ballistic missiles as a sufficient umbrella against general war while allowing the Army to carry on "limited" and brush-fire war. The point

[22] *Ibid.*, pp. 499–500.
[23] *Facts on File*, 1961, 237E2.

of his book *The Uncertain Trumpet* (Harper, 1960) was a plea to spend more money on the Army's general purposes forces and less on strategic nuclear weapons. The Kennedy decision to build 1,000 missiles went directly contrary to the views of the man he had chosen as his military adviser. I wonder if Schlesinger would now explain why he left the Army point of view out.

Let us return to his narrative at the point where we broke off. "But on Thanksgiving week-end," Schlesinger continues, "when the President convened his defense experts for a meeting at Hyannis Port, the weight of evidence was plainly against the Air Force, and the issue finally withered away." Withered away? That is a strange phrase to use in view of what follows immediately after. "The budget nevertheless," Schlesinger goes on, "contemplated a sizeable increase in missiles; *and the White House staff, while favoring a larger Minuteman force than the original Eisenhower proposal, wondered whether the new budget was not providing for more missiles than national security required*" (my italics).

How did Kennedy react to that? "The President," Schlesinger continues, "though intimating a certain sympathy with this view [perhaps a vestige of that creative idealism Schlesinger had promised?], was not prepared to overrule McNamara's recommendation." But was it just McNamara's recommendation? I showed in an earlier article for *The New York Review* (November 7, 1968) that the White House slapped McNamara down when he, an innocent to armament politics, let slip the truth about the missile gap to the press as soon as he caught up with the facts in his new office as Secretary of Defense. The White House next day insisted that there *was* a gap. It would seem more reasonable to assume from this incident alone that it was Kennedy, not McNamara, who insisted on building more missiles.

To see how far Schlesinger distorts history in the service of Kennedy one need only check the contemporary public accounts. Unless Rostow and Wiesner were incredibly ill-informed, they must have known that U.S. nuclear power was overwhelmingly superior to the Soviet Union's. Five days before Kennedy's Inaugural, the well-informed Pentagon correspondent of the conservative Washington *Star* reported (January 15), "New national intelligence estimates of Soviet missile production indicate the 'missile gap' may have disappeared." Two years before, at the height of the missile gap scare, it was estimated that by 1961 the Soviet Union would have 50 to 100 missiles operational "but intelligence officers," said the *Star*, reflecting what we later learned were actual counts by aerial reconnaissance, "cannot find nearly that number."

A report reaching Washington before Kennedy's Inaugural (by the British Institute of Strategic Studies, which depends ultimately on U.S. intelligence) credited the Soviets with about thirty-five operational ICBM's and about 200 long-range bombers. The Russians then, as now, did have more intercontinental land-based missiles than the U.S. But the imbalance of total power was stupefying. It turned out that we had ten times their total nuclear delivery capacity.

This was made public in the House of Representatives five days after the inaugural, by the Republicans. They were smarting under Kennedy's implication that eight years of their rule had somehow left the U.S. with inadequate defenses. The main presentation that day was made for the Republicans by—of all people—Representative Melvin Laird, now Nixon's Secretary of Defense. Two years later, he was himself to join the alarmists with his book *America's Strategy Gap*. But here are the figures he gave that day, without rebuttal from the Democrats or the new Administration. These declared that we had:

—about 16 Atlas ICBM's.
—two Polaris submarines with a total of 32 missiles capable of reaching Russia.
—"over 600 long-range B-52 jet bombers, each carrying more destructive, explosive power than that used by all the combatants in World War II."
—nearly 1,400 B-47 medium-range jet bombers based abroad

and at home with a 4,500-mile range "and distances beyond
with air-to-air refueling."
—the first of SAC's B-58 Hustlers, supersonic medium-range
bombers.
—"14 aircraft carriers able to launch more aircraft than the
entire Soviet heavy bomber force."
—"18 wings of tactical aircraft, each wing with a substantial nuclear attack capability deployed globally."
—64 IRBM's [intermediate-range ballistic missiles] in England,
capable of reaching Russia, and 30 Jupiter IRBM's being deployed in Italy, "from which Russia can be hit."
(Or "well over 2,000 nuclear carrying vehicles capable of
reaching Russia.")

In addition, the Republicans pointed out that under the
final Eisenhower budgets, there would be 600 Minuteman
missiles by the end of 1964; 129 Atlas and 126 Titan ICBM's
by the end of 1962; 4 more Polarises in service by the end
of 1961, with 64 more missiles; and that 15 Jupiter IRBM's
were being erected in Turkey.[24]
Dr. Ralph Lapp, the outspoken atomic physicist, estimated on the basis of the figures disclosed in the House that
we were in a position to dump more than 30,000 megatons
on the Soviet Union. The USSR, he further computed, has
about three million square miles of inhabited territory. It
takes about one megaton, he said, to render 1,000 square
miles uninhabitable. At that rate it would take 3,000 megatons, evenly spread, literally to wipe out the Soviet Union.
We could deliver more than ten times that much!
In the light of those figures, the contrast of tone between
Eisenhower's farewell and Kennedy's debut was hardly
creative idealism. Eisenhower finished with a series of warnings against the forces making for a stepped-up arms race.
His final State of the Union message, January 12, said the
bomber gap "had always been a fiction, and the 'missile gap'
shows every sign of being the same." He said U.S. power
was sufficient to deter "and if need be to destroy predatory

24 *Congressional Record,* Jan. 25, 1961, pp. 1227–37.

forces." In his TV farewell of January 17 he sought to put the country on guard against the growing influence of "an immense military establishment and a large arms industry" which he termed the military-industrial complex.

Kennedy, instead of joining in that warning, demonstrated the political power that the complex could exert. The inaugural invoked Isaiah—as Johnson did, too, four years later, before taking us into a new war. Kennedy called on the Russians to negotiate disarmament since both nations were "overburdened by the cost of modern weapons and both rightly alarmed by the steady spread of the deadly atom." But his first State of the Union message, January 30, stepped up the arms race immediately. He spoke of "an hour of national peril," implied that the country was in danger because of inadequate defenses and, though he did not mention the missile gap, he said he was giving orders to accelerate the missile program, to step up the construction of Polaris submarines, and to increase our airlift capacity so our conventional forces would be better able "to respond with discrimination and speed to any problem at any spot on the globe at a moment's notice." These were the trumpets of Pax Americana and imperialism, premonitions—if the country had but known—of Vietnam and the Bay of Pigs.

How gullible does Schlesinger expect his readers to be? Against this background, his account of the discussion later that year about the first Kennedy budget is incredible: that Kennedy showed "a certain sympathy" for the White House staff view that we were building more missiles than we needed but that he was "not prepared to overrule McNamara's recommendation."

Implicit in Schlesinger's opaque account is a damning revelation. This can be seen if one looks closely enough at his explanation of why McNamara recommended more missiles than he thought we needed. "As for the Secretary," Schlesinger writes, "he did not believe that doubling or even tripling our striking power would enable us to destroy the hardened missile sites or missile-launching submarines of our adversary." To any knowledgeable readers this means that Kennedy and his advisers were not discussing deterrent but *first-strike* capacity.

The targets of deterrence are Russian cities and industry; the purpose is to let the enemy know that if he hits us, we can destroy him. But the targets of first strike are the missiles and the missile-carrying submarines of the enemy. A first strike, to be successful, must first destroy these lest they destroy our cities and industry in retaliation. Apparently the Air Force, in asking for more missiles, wanted a first-strike capability, and McNamara was arguing that we couldn't hope to achieve a first-strike capability even if we doubled or tripled our striking force. This is Schlesinger's unwitting revelation.

Eisenhower, we have seen, had ordered a build-up of Minutemen to 600 missiles. The Air Force wanted 3,000, according to a recent revelation by Dr. Jerome Wiesner, who was a Kennedy science adviser.[25] McNamara settled for 1,000 Minutemen and eventually for forty-one Polaris submarines with sixteen missiles each or a total of 256 seaborne missiles, 160 more than Eisenhower had projected.

Schlesinger implies that McNamara and Kennedy upped the Minuteman program from 600 to 1,000 and the Polaris program from six to an eventual forty-one even though McNamara knew this increase was not needed for deterrence and was not—*could never be*—big enough for a first strike. Why? Schlesinger says McNamara "was already engaged in a bitter fight with the Air Force over his effort to disengage from the B-70, a costly high-altitude manned bomber rendered obsolescent by the improvement in Soviet ground-to-air missiles. After cutting down the original Air Force missile demands considerably, he perhaps felt that he could not do more without risking public conflict with the Joint Chiefs and the vociferous B-70 lobby in Congress. As a result," Schlesinger concludes, "the President went along with

[25] Dr. Wiesner revealed the figure on a national educational television show, *The Advocates*, Sunday, March 1, 1970.

the policy of multiplying Polaris and Minuteman missiles." [26]

Schlesinger expects us to believe that Kennedy merely "went along with the policy of multiplying Polaris and Minutemen" in order to let McNamara appease an Air Force angry over the loss of the B-70! This, even if true, was not "the higher calculus of deterrence," much less the dialectic of "arming to disarm." But I find it impossible to believe decisions which cost so many billions—and were so profitable to the arms industry—were merely the result of intramural bureaucratic bargaining and appeasement.

There may be a better clue in a cryptic passage of Kennedy's first State of the Union message. "We are moving into a period of uncertain risks and great commitment," he said, "in which both the military *and diplomatic* possibilities require a Free World force so powerful as to make any aggression clearly futile" (my italics). The bomber generals and their friends in Congress had long argued that the best card in military *and diplomatic* confrontations was the existence of a first-strike capability. This too was Laird's theme in *America's Strategy Gap*, two years after Kennedy's inaugural. Kennedy may well have agreed. He may indeed have felt, after the Cuban missile crisis, that fear of an American first strike was the card with which he had won.

The final touch of bitter irony is that 1961, the year Kennedy stepped up the arms race even though there was no missile gap, was also the year in which Kennedy joined Khrushchev in pledging general and complete disarmament. Their special representatives, McCloy and Zorin respectively, even submitted a signed joint agreement to the UN General Assembly on September 20 of that year in which the two superpowers agreed to the total abolition of all weapons of mass destruction, the reduction of conventional forces to the minimum necessary for internal order, and the establishment of an international control agency under the UN but free of the veto, so that inspectors could have "unrestricted access" for "effective verification." What more

[26] *A Thousand Days*, p. 500.

does one need than this gap—an abyss wide—between word and deed to see that disarmament negotiations had become a form of political theater, a theater of delusion?

April 23, 1970
New York Review

THE TEST BAN COMEDY

Our last installment ended by calling disarmament negotiations a theater of delusion. The outstanding example is the Limited Nuclear Test Ban Treaty. In appearance it was one of the few successes in the history of armament negotiations and the great achievement of the Kennedy Administration. It seemed to promise that we were at last to bring the nuclear monster under control. Logically, the SALT talks could—and should—have begun seven years ago in 1963 after that treaty was signed, with so much mutual congratulation, in Moscow. It was the first time the two superpowers had reached a major formal agreement. It signaled a thaw in the cold war. In the manic-depressive cycle of the sick relationship between Washington and Moscow, it was the "up" phase after the terrifying "down" of the Cuban missile crisis the year before. It seemed a most propitious moment for the kind of strategic arms limitation talks now belatedly beginning in Vienna.

In a television address the night after the treaty was signed, the youthful President addressed the country and the world with jubilation and hope. He put the moment in a perspective of grandeur. "Since the beginning of history," Kennedy said, "war has been mankind's constant companion." Now, when war "would not be like any in history," when it could kill 300 million people in America, Europe, and Russia in "less than 60 minutes," there was a chance "to turn the world away from war."

Let us, the President said, "make the most of this opportunity . . . to slow down the perilous nuclear arms race, and to check the world's slide toward final annihilation." Yet this was, as a Hindu philosopher would say, all delusion, a dream which bore little resemblance, as we shall see, to the Kennedy Administration's waking and working plans for the aftermath of the treaty.

When one goes back into the records to try to understand how and why the opportunity was lost, one comes upon a deeper mystery and falls into a worse despair. Though the treaty contained no concrete measure of disarmament, and though it banned nuclear testing in the atmosphere, underwater, and in outer space, but not underground, it did seem a first limit at least on testing and on the nuclear arms race. The real question is how and why it proved to be a curtain-raiser instead on a new and more intense period of competition and expenditure in atomic weaponry.

The arms race merely moved underground. What seemed a minor loophole opened, metaphorically and literally, into an enormous cavern. The total volume of testing *increased* instead of decreasing. The magnitude reached the point where two years ago we began to test underground in the megaton range. By miracles of ingenuity, we learned to do underground almost everything which scientists once thought could only be done in the atmosphere: the development and testing, for example, of those "penetration aids" designed to let loose a fusillade of deception in combat between whole fleets of missile and anti-missile. In this intensified testing the two new monsters, MIRV and ABM, were perfected and are still being improved. What looked like the peace movement's greatest triumph in 1963 proved to be a bonanza for the military and its industrial allies.

The signing of the limited test ban, the fourth major lost opportunity since World War II to curb the nuclear arms race, differed in one vital respect from the others. The treaty was the culmination of a worldwide campaign against atmospheric testing. It mobilized overwhelming majority support in the United States, Japan, and every other

country aware of the danger from the radioactivity those
atmospheric tests released.

For the first time the opponents of the nuclear arms race
had an issue more effective than a generalized, albeit cata-
clysmic, danger. Suddenly, in the shape of strontium 90, the
menace turned up in the baby's milk bottle and in cancer
statistics. Hypochondria was mobilized in the service of
idealism and the combination worked. Adlai Stevenson put
the issue on the political map in the 1956 campaign by calling for an end to H-bomb tests, while Nixon, in a Republican chorus of derision, called any restriction on testing "a
fearful risk." In Kennedy's 1960 campaign the issue was
muted, but it was there.[1]

The hypochondria which made the campaign against atmospheric testing so effective proved a weakness in victory.
Support evaporated rapidly when the treaty was signed and
atmospheric testing stopped. It proved impossible to keep a
full head of steam in the boiler of the disarmament campaign when all one had left was the more familiar issue of
the danger in continuing the nuclear arms race, even if it no
longer threatened baby's milk. Somehow talk of universal
holocaust proved not half so effective as being able to tell
the individual he or his child might get cancer because of
testing. Death, even, perhaps especially, on a mass scale, is
really beyond the imagination of mankind. Constant pre-
dictions of cosmic disaster produce a yawn. No one really
believes in the possibility of his own death.

Fear of death has rarely stopped a common brawl, much
less a war. But everybody is nervous about having to go to
the doctor. Peace propaganda rested—and this is a lesson
we have yet to learn—on a vastly oversimplified psychology. Just as the vivid portrayal of hellfire in old-fashioned

[1] It was not a gut issue with Kennedy, as it was with Stevenson. "In the
early stages of his public career," Theodore C. Sorensen, his other official
biographer, says in his Kennedy (Harper & Row, 1965), "His foreign
policy speeches had a militant ring. Defense, in his view, was the bulk of
diplomacy and disarmament was only a dream. But with increased perspective and responsibility came a renewed commitment to peace. Nothing gave him greater satisfaction in the White House than signing the
Nuclear Test Ban treaty."

gospel evangelism only gave sin an extra dimension of zest, so subconsciously the doomsday theme had an appeal to man's love of excitement and horror. It was like turning on another TV thriller, and it was as unreal.

Despite worldwide fear of fallout, the limited nuclear test ban might never have been signed were it not for some extraordinary circumstances. It is doubtful whether the force of public opinion alone would have brought it about. One was the shock of the Cuban missile crisis, which only a few months earlier had brought the two superpowers and the world for the first time to the brink of nuclear war. The second I believe was the political desperation of Khrushchev, soon to be deposed, and striving desperately for a way out of the arms race and its heavy cost for Russia; his destalinization campaign could only survive if international tension could be lightened and the standard of living in the Soviet Union dramatically raised. Roger Hilsman summed it up neatly in his memoirs of the Kennedy Administration[2] when he wrote:

The Soviets put missiles into Cuba in an attempt to solve a set of problems—a strategic imbalance, the exigencies of the Sino-Soviet dispute, and the impossible combination of demands on their limited resources made by defense, their space program, their peoples' appetite for consumers' goods, and the drain of foreign aid needed to support their foreign policy. When the crisis was over, the missiles withdrawn, the same set of problems remained. The irony is that these same problems, which brought the world so close to nuclear war, later brought about the so-called *détente*—a relaxation of Cold War tensions. For it was the same pressure that led the Soviets to put missiles in Cuba that later led them to take up Kennedy's proposal for a treaty banning nuclear testing.

For five years, ever since the formal nuclear test ban negotiations began in 1958, the Soviets had insisted that they would never accept an accord which did not ban all nuclear testing, in all environments, underground included.

[2] *To Move A Nation: The Politics of Foreign Policy in the Administration of John F. Kennedy* (New York: Doubleday, 1967), p. 228.

Khrushchev backed down on this, as he backed down on the Cuban missiles and as he had backed down in 1955 on the Austrian treaty, which was the admission price to a summit on Germany and disarmament. For these backdowns he got nothing, nothing but a temporary change of international atmosphere.

Potentially, this was worthwhile, for in the changed atmosphere agreement on substantive issues became possible. But they were never forthcoming. The West took what Khrushchev had to offer but gave nothing in return. This I believe is the key to his downfall, and perhaps part of the explanation for the more rigid, cautious, and unimaginative policies of his successors. Khrushchev all too soon after the signing ceremonies in Moscow must have begun to look like an easy mark and a dupe. For when the treaty had to be sold to the U.S. military bureaucracy and the U.S. Senate, it was sold not as a victory against the arms race but as a victory in it, *an acknowledgement by Moscow of American superiority and a new way to maintain it.* This is why no substantive disarmament agreement followed, though many the world over hoped for it in the détente the treaty created.

There was another reason Khrushchev accepted the treaty on Western terms. That lay in the growing tension between Moscow and Peking. Moscow was at a crossroads of policy in 1963. This was dramatized by two negotiations in Moscow, which overlapped in time but faced in totally different directions. Talks with the Chinese began there July 5. Talks with the U.S. and Britain on a test ban agreement opened July 15, while the negotiations with Peking's representatives were still under way. In an open letter to Peking released the day before the talks with the West began, the Central Committee of the Soviet Communist party declared it[3]

[3] Senator George McGovern, *A Time of War, A Time of Peace* (New York: Random House, 1968), p. 44. A first-rate summary of the Sino-Soviet factor in the achievement of the treaty from his memorable speech in the Senate, Sept. 16, during the ratification debate.

. . . a necessary duty to tell the party and the people with all frankness that in questions of war and peace the Chinese Communist party leadership is based on principle differences with us. . . . The essence of these differences lies in the diametrically opposite approach to such vital problems as the possibility of averting a world thermonuclear war, peaceful coexistence of states with different social systems, and interconnection between the struggle for peace and the development of the world revolutionary movement.

In the overlapping negotiations "the Soviets clearly gave more attention to the test ban group, and no doubt intended this as a deliberate slap at the Chinese and a deliberate effort to emphasize that they were opting for a policy of détente with the West, even if it would be at the expense of a further disintegration in Sino-Soviet relations." [4] A study at the cold-warrish Hoover Institute found that the test ban treaty was "perhaps the final straw that brought the schism into the open." For Peking, "symbolically" it represented "Moscow's joining what Peking deemed an imperialist conspiracy, not only to try to block China's nuclear program, but to oppose her political advance in the third world." [5] For Washington the treaty was a political coup, solidifying the split in the world communist movement. Even so Khrushchev had to pay a high price for it.

The American University speech, in which Kennedy announced the three-power agreement to hold the Moscow test ban talks, was one of Kennedy's best. It was published in full next day in *Izvestia*. Khrushchev later told Harriman it was "the best speech by any President since Roosevelt." [6] But the Administrations' psychological warriors could hardly have been unaware that its new tone of friendliness to Moscow would whet the suspicions of Peking and nourish the growing split. According to Sorensen, who drafted the speech,[7] Kennedy was skeptical about the possibility

[4] Morton H. Halperin and Dwight H. Perkins (East Asian Research Center), *Communist China and Arms Control* (Harvard, 1965), p. 169.

[5] Walter C. Clemens, Jr., *The Arms Race and Sino-Soviet Relations* (Stanford, Calif.: Hoover Institute, 1968), p. 50.

[6] Sorensen, *Kennedy*, p. 733.

[7] *Ibid.*, p. 730.

that the talks would succeed. Moscow was still insisting on an agreement banning tests in all environments. Kennedy seemed to regard the speech in part at least as an exercise in political propaganda. In preparing for it, he "valued in particular," Sorensen relates,[8] "a letter from Norman Cousins" suggesting that "the exposition of a peaceful posture prior to the May meeting of the Soviet Communist Party Central Committee, even if it could not deter a new rash of attacks on U.S. policy, might at least make those attacks sound hollow and hypocritical outside the Communist world."

Kennedy's first move after the speech was to visit and reassure the ever-nervous Germans. Sorensen's account of Kennedy's feelings on the eve of the Moscow talks is revealing:[9]

The Adenauer government still took an alarmist attitude about the whole matter. But the trip to West Germany had improved popular as well as official feeling in that country about our intentions, the President told his negotiators [i.e., before they left for Moscow], "and I am willing to draw on that as much as necessary, if it's worthwhile. I don't, however, want to do what we did in the Berlin talks, getting the Germans suspicious if the Russians aren't going to agree to anything anyway." *Inasmuch as even a limited test ban treaty required a Soviet acceptance of permanent American superiority in nuclear weapons*, he refused to count too heavily on the success of the Moscow meetings (my italics).

But on July 2, three days before the talks with China were to open and thirteen days before the test ban talks with the West began, Khrushchev reversed the Soviet's past position and agreed to accept the West's proposal for a ban on tests in the atmosphere, outer space, and underwater, but not underground. This was not only to accept "permanent inferiority" but to leave the door open to a form of testing in which the U.S. was far more proficient and for which it could more easily bear the expense. He asked in return only that it be linked with a non-aggression pact between NATO

8 *Ibid.*, p. 730.
9 *Ibid.*, p. 734.

and the Warsaw powers. This would have made the Chinese feel that he was thereby protecting his rear in the West in the event of a conflict with them in the East.

But Kennedy was in no mood to pay this price even though Sorensen says there was "apprehension that Khrushchev would insist on both or neither." [10] The negotiators were instructed, before leaving for Moscow, to stall on the request for a non-aggression pact. Such a pact was always a bugaboo with Adenauer, who still dreamed that the cold war, the arms race, and the rearmament of Germany would some day force the Russians to accept its reunification on Western terms. The negotiators finally threw Khrushchev a very slim bone. He had to be satisfied with a noncommittal paragraph at the end of the Agreed Communiqué on the treaty which mentioned his proposal only to bury it in diplomatic double-talk: [11]

The heads of the three delegations discussed the Soviet proposal relating to a pact of non-aggression between the participants in the North Atlantic Treaty Organization and the participants in the Warsaw Treaty. The three governments have agreed *fully* [My italics. A delicate touch of humor in that adverb, since they had agreed to nothing!] to inform their respective allies in the two organizations concerning these talks and to consult with them about continuing discussions on this question with the purpose of achieving agreement satisfactory to all participants.

That was the last anybody heard of any such discussions. In any case, if the reader will look at the skillful wording again, the communiqué did not promise discussions but only consultations (i.e., with the Germans) on *whether* to discuss the Pact. This was exquisite conmanship.

The final sentence of the communiqué, cryptic and inconsequential as it appeared to be at the time, marked the burial of Khrushchev's other hopes. "A brief exchange of

[10] *Ibid.,* p. 736.
[11] Text on p. 8 of the Senate Foreign Relations Committee hearings on the Nuclear Test Ban Treaty, August 12–27, 1963.

views also took place," the communiqué ended, "with regard to other measures directed at a relaxation of tension."
The "other measures" Khrushchev had in mind were indicated in a speech he made July 20, five days before the
treaty was finally initialed, and in an interview with *Pravda*
and *Izvestia* as soon as the final agreement was reached.[12] It
was the year before Khrushchev's ouster, and these two
declarations show the central role of disarmament in his
domestic and international program. He quoted Lenin in
support of the policy of coexistence and to attack those
who saw in war the final victory of socialism. He defended
destalinization by citing Hungary as an example of what
happens when "the cult of personality" alienates the masses.
He said people would judge socialism "by what it gives
them" in the way of better living standards. He hoped the
limited test ban would make it possible to freeze or reduce
military budgets and he suggested among ways to lessen
tension that each side reduce its troops in Germany and that
the Western powers post inspectors in the East and the
Warsaw powers in the West at airfields, railway junctions,
and airports as assurance against surprise attack. "After all,"
he added in the July 26 interview after the treaty had been
initialed, "it is necessary to keep clearly in mind that the ban
on nuclear weapons tests does not mean the end of the arms
race . . . does not do away with the burden of armaments.
. . . Let us now advance further . . . toward liquidating
the 'cold war.' " But all this was exactly what the Adenauer
regime and our military feared.

I see no reason to believe that Kennedy did not feel the
same way. Sorensen's account reveals how tightly Kennedy
held the reins of the negotiations in his own hands: "All
communications to the delegation were cleared through
Kennedy. Frequently he altered or rewrote completely the
daily cable of instructions prepared in the State Department." [13] Sorensen provides no clue to the differences this

[12] For the former see the *Current Digest of the Soviet Press*, Vol. XV,
No. 29. The latter is in Vol. XV, No. 30.
[13] *Op. Cit.*, p. 735.

implies between the departmental drafts and the final White House orders. The former could hardly have been more hard-line than Kennedy's proved to be. The delegation was instructed sharply to limit the agreement in Moscow to a limited ban on testing. If Kennedy had wanted progress on further and broader issues, if he had wanted to lay the groundwork for a more general armament agreement or political settlement, Khrushchev seemed more than ready for it. At a bare minimum, Kennedy could have had a final communiqué promising wider arms talks in the future. Instead he got a hard and narrow bargain, and it must be assumed that this is all he wanted.

Khrushchev got nothing concrete in return for accepting his terms for a limited test ban treaty. Seen from within the Kremlin, where opposition was brewing, Khrushchev's failure to win some relaxation of the arms race must have made the treaty seem another humiliating defeat for his policy of wooing Kennedy, as the U-2 was for his policy of wooing Eisenhower. I believe these sealed his political fate.

Both leaders had two constituencies, the universal two-party system of mankind, whether it lives under freely chosen representatives or imposed regimes: the hard-liners and the soft, the tough and the conciliatory. In Moscow the advocates of heavy (military) industry and a return to the heavy hand this entailed were waiting in the wings to take over. In Washington the hard-liners were preparing to use a minority veto—the constitutional requirement of a two-thirds vote in the Senate for treaty ratification—to block Kennedy unless he met their terms. In both capitals there was a military-industrial complex, buttressed by the same paranoia and cave-man instinct. In both there were factions which saw the only hope for peace in the extermination of the other side.

The Neanderthals on both sides, with touching faith in science, still hoped that in the arms race they could acquire (but they alone) a new magic weapon which would keep nuclear extermination from being mutual. In both countries there was also a public concerned with the costs and dangers of the arms race, but its strength never matched its numbers.

The difference is that Khrushchev, as leader of the weaker nation, returned from the signing of the treaty with nothing but atmospherics as his trophy. Kennedy could offer the opposition the assurance of another period of American military predominance, and the maintenance for a longer period of the American position as the senior firm in the world atomic oligopoly.

For the treaty was also the first non-proliferation pact. The other nations, in signing it, were pledging themselves never to test except underground, which was very difficult and expensive. Some of them might be close to building a bomb of their own, but adherence to the treaty put up another barrier to their becoming nuclear powers. The treaty also gave both superpowers an excuse not to share the secrets of the new weaponry with importunate allies. As Kennedy said in his TV address the night after it was signed, "This treaty can be a step toward preventing the spread of nuclear weapons to nations not now possessing them." [14]

Kennedy had a right to feel that he had brought quite a prize package home from Moscow. Trouble was nevertheless building up in the Senate. "Congressional Republicans," Sorensen relates, "had consistently bombarded the President with attacks on his 'fuzzy-minded disarmament advisers.'" Predictably, leading members of the Joint Committee on Atomic Energy, a watchdog that had become a Pentagon poodle, were saying that anything other than "a reasonably sound-proof test ban agreement . . . could be a greater risk to the national security than an arms race."

Senator Jackson, the Democratic party's leading liberal advocate of perpetual arms race, was "skeptical" even after Khrushchev accepted Kennedy's terms. Senator Russell, chairman of the Armed Services Committee and the military's most prestigious ally in the Senate, opposed the treaty from the beginning and (unlike Jackson) was one of the nineteen who voted against it. Conservative congress-

[14] *Public Papers of the Presidents: John F. Kennedy, 1963*, p. 604.

men and newspapermen charged that Kennedy had made a
"secret deal" with Khrushchev in Moscow.[15] Whatever the
"gaps" between America and Russia, the two nations were
obviously neck-and-neck when it came to paranoid politicians.

The biggest obstacle was the Joint Chiefs of Staff. Sorensen tells us that the President had been careful to obtain
their approval in advance of the negotiations. "But their
agreement," he adds, "had assumed that a test ban, *like all
other disarmament proposals*, was only a diplomatic pose
unlikely to achieve reality" (my italics). When they found
themselves confronted with an actual agreement, "they
hedged." [16] Phil G. Goulding, in his newly published memoirs of his years as the Pentagon's top press officer,[17] gives us
a description of how McNamara went over the treaty point
by point with the Joint Chiefs in sessions that lasted several
days and took many hours each day. "When they were finally finished," Goulding reports, "the Joint Chiefs agreed
with McNamara's own basic position—that the treaty carried with it certain risks, but that the alternative risks of continued atmospheric testing were far more grave, both from
the moral standpoint of the health of unborn generations
*and from the hard military standpoint that unlimited testing
on both sides was allowing the Soviet Union to narrow the
gap*" (my italics). That obviously was the clincher.

Part of the price which had to be paid, nevertheless, for
the support of the Joint Chiefs, was that we would use the
advantage given us by the treaty to widen that gap by intensified underground testing. This was imperfectly understood at the time. When Kennedy, the day after the treaty
was initialed, made his eloquent TV address for public support,[18] he said the treaty would not "prevent this nation
from testing underground" but he also added that "unlim-

[15] Sorensen, pp. 736–37.
[16] *Ibid.*, p. 738.
[17] P. G. Goulding, *Confirm or Deny: Informing the People on National Security* (New York: Harper & Row, 1970). See pp. 173–74.
[18] *Public Papers of the Presidents: John F. Kennedy, 1963*. Text begins at p. 601.

ited competition in the testing and development of new
types of destructive nuclear weapons will not make the
world safer for either side." No one could have guessed
from this that we were on the verge of an intensified period
of underground testing designed to enable us to pull far
ahead technologically of the Russians.

This was one of the main selling points in the Senate hearings on the treaty. "By limiting Soviet testing to the underground environment, where testing is more difficult and
more expensive and where the United States has substantially more experience," McNamara said in his opening
presentation,[19] "we can at least retard Soviet progress and
thereby prolong the duration of our technological superiority." He added—but to this the senators seem to have paid
little attention—"A properly inspected comprehensive test
ban would, of course, serve this purpose still better."

It was not our intention merely to retard Soviet progress
while maintaining our margin of superiority. This would
have been a freeze, stabilizing the level of destructive capacity and putting a ceiling on the arms race. To reread McNamara's presentation on the treaty August 13, 1963, to the
Senate Foreign Relations Committee (along with senators
from Armed Services and the Joint Committee on Atomic
Energy) is to see why the better atmosphere created by the
signing of the limited nuclear test ban treaty was never used
for substantive negotiations to stabilize or reduce the burden
of armaments. For what McNamara outlined that day was
a program for a sharp step-up in the arms race, both qualita-
tively and quantitatively.

First, the quantitative. McNamara said the U.S. then
had "more than 500 missiles—Atlas, Titan, Minuteman, Polaris" and planned to more than triple the number in the
next two years "to over 1,700 by 1966." Though McNamara did not say so, this was the goal originally set by the
Kennedy Administration in its first budget preparations in
the fall of 1961. Obviously he and Kennedy saw no reason
to change it because of the nuclear test ban treaty.

[19] Senate hearings already cited, p. 105.

McNamara estimated that the Soviets had "only a fraction as many ICBM missiles." Perhaps he did not give a concrete figure because it would have shown a missile gap so lopsidedly in our favor as to make the planned step-up look fantastic. The 1962–63 edition of the annual Military Balance issued by the Institute for Strategic Studies in London credited the Soviet Union with "75+" as of early 1963. If this figure is correct then we had more than six times as many ICBM's as the Soviet Union at the time that McNamara announced that we would more than triple the number by 1966. As for submarine-launched missiles, McNamara said those of the Soviets were "short range, require surface launch, and generally are not comparable to our Polaris force." McNamara said that by 1966 "our ballistic missile numerical superiority will increase both absolutely and relatively." [20] When that testimony was read in the Kremlin, the gathering opposition must have felt that Khrushchev had lost his mind in believing that the treaty was a step toward lightening the burden and danger of the arms race.

McNamara dealt next with plans to improve the quality of our nuclear weapons. In four pages of testimony,[21] some of it opaque to protect classified information, McNamara indicated the wide variety of improvements we could and would make by underground testing. The only field in which the Soviets were ahead was in large-yield weapons. They had tested a 60-megaton "device" (he did not say bomb) and he thought it could be turned into a weapon of 100 megatons. But they had no missile that could carry such a monster and it would be "suitable only for vulnerable high altitude or suicide low level delivery," i.e., against our air defenses.

The U.S., McNamara said, could "without any further testing" develop a warhead of 50 to 60 megatons for B-52 delivery. But the U.S. believed that smaller bombs, with greater accuracy, were far more efficient. The key improvement, as admitted throughout the hearings, was in

[20] Senate hearings, p. 100.
[21] Senate hearings, pp. 100–105.

weight-to-yield ratios, i.e., packing more punch into smaller warheads.

We know now in retrospect that this was essential for the next great breakthrough, which was to put more warheads on each missile (MRV) and then target them separately (MIRV). With these we are now on the verge of multiplying the number of warheads on these 1,700 missiles by three in the case of Minuteman, and by ten in the case of Poseidon, the most stupendous expansion yet in nuclear delivery power.

It is even more extraordinary to reread those pages which concern the ABM. McNamara outlined what we could and would do in developing "penetration aids" to confuse any enemy ABM, and techniques to make it difficult for the enemy to counter any ABM of our own. "The ABM warhead designs we now have," McNamara said that day, "or can develop through underground testing will provide a high probability of killing Soviet warheads *even if they incorporate advanced technology far beyond what now exists*" (my italics).[22]

Against this background one can now better understand the full significance of the "safeguards" on which the Joint Chiefs of Staff insisted and to which Kennedy and McNamara agreed before the Chairman of the Joint Chiefs, General Taylor, would tell the Senate that "while there are military disadvantages to the treaty, they are not so serious as to render it unacceptable."[23] They ensured an intensified arms race. The safeguards, as given by General Taylor in the Senate hearings, read like a meticulously spelled-out treaty between the military and the Kennedy Administration, an agreement between two bureaucratic superpowers. It proved more significant than the treaty itself. The terms are worth looking at in full text as a warning for the future, since the peace movement tended euphorically to skip over them as a kind of bone thrown the military. The bone

[22] Senate hearings, p. 103.
[23] Senate hearings, p. 275.

proved to be the giant skeleton for a new stage in the arms race. Here are the safeguards Kennedy promised the Joint Chiefs:

(a) The conduct of comprehensive, aggressive, and continuing underground nuclear test programs designed to add to our knowledge and improve our weapons in all areas of significance to our military posture for the future.

(b) The maintenance of modern nuclear laboratory facilities and programs in theoretical and exploratory nuclear technology which will attract, retain, and insure the continued application of our human scientific resources to these programs on which continued progress in nuclear technology depends.

(c) The maintenance of the facilities and resources necessary to institute promptly nuclear tests in the atmosphere *should they be deemed essential to our national security* or should the treaty or any of its terms be abrogated by the Soviet Union. [The italics are added. In other words, the military was promised that we would abrogate the treaty—and resume atmospheric tests if we felt that necessary to national security— even if the Soviets were abiding by it.]

(d) The improvement of our capability, within feasible and practical limits, to monitor the terms of the treaty, to detect violations, and to maintain our knowledge of Sino-Soviet activity, capability and achievements.[24]

This has the precise and wary wording of a treaty between two powers in which one at least, in this case the military, wholly distrusts the other, in this case the civilian—ostensibly and constitutionally the superior power. The military might well have mustered that one vote more than one-third which is all that the Constitution requires to block a treaty. They had the power and they exacted their price. Even so there were nineteen negative votes to eighty yeas in the Senate when the treaty was ratified September 24, 1963. During the debate Senator McGovern emphasized to the doubters "the repeated assurance of our President and our military leaders that underground testing will be energetically pushed and that we will be prepared to re-

[24] Senate hearings, pp. 274–75.

sume atmospheric tests if that becomes necessary." Then he added, in an exasperation events have justified beyond even his apprehensions at the time:

Indeed, Mr. President, the Administration has been called upon to give so many assurances of our continued nuclear efforts after treaty ratification that a casual observer might assume that we are approving this treaty so that we can accelerate the arms race and beef up the war-making facilities of our country! [25]

In retrospect this proved to be exactly what the treaty did. A month earlier, in the first flush of enthusiasm over negotiation of the treaty, Senator McGovern made a memorable address in the Senate (August 2) proposing that $5 billion be diverted from strategic weapons to social needs at home. He asked that plans be drawn up for the conversion of war industry to peacetime needs. McGovern said our nuclear stockpiles already represented a huge overkill capacity. "How many times," he asked the Senate, "is it necessary to kill a man or a nation?" He quoted from a story leaked to the New York Times June 30 of that year which said the Kennedy Administration was considering (this was before the treaty talks) a substantial cutback in the production of nuclear weapons. A "policy-making official" was quoted as saying, "We have tens or hundreds of times more weapons than we would ever drop even in an all-out war, and we have had more than we needed for at least two years."

If that was a Kennedy Administration viewpoint, it was not shared by McNamara. I believe the story represents the surfacing in the news of conclusions reached by certain arms-study groups Kennedy had appointed early in his Administration. The closely guarded secret of their existence has slowly become known over the years to some reporters, including myself, but only on an off-the-record basis, so we still are unable to reveal or independently confirm the participants or the conclusions.

They were kept under wraps because they upset the Pen-

[25] From p. 40 of his speech of Sept. 16, 1963, as reprinted in his book *A Time of War, A Time of Peace* already cited above.

tagon and because, if they had become known at the time, they would have cut the ground from under the 1,700-missile expansion which emerged from the first Kennedy-McNamara military budget in late 1961. Maybe some of the participants will some day tell us more in their memoirs, for they were men of weight in both the scientific and general community.

McGovern seems to have touched a tender nerve with his speech, particularly since it was caustic about McNamara's latest rationalization for so many missiles—the "controlled counterforce" or "no cities" doctrine unveiled in the Ann Arbor speech of June, 1962. The idea was that we needed so many missiles because, if the Russians spared our cities in a first strike, hitting only our missile bases, we would not hit their cities in retaliation but only *their* missile sites. This required an enormous amount of missiles. It also required a lot of addlepated computerism. McGovern blew this nonsense sky-high with two questions in his August 2 speech:

If the United States were aiming at the effective destruction of Russia's nuclear forces, how could we apply such a strategy unless we knocked out the Soviet missiles before they were launched from their silos? What military objective could we achieve by knocking out missile launchers after their rockets had hit American targets?

The silly doctrine was custom-made for missile salesmanship. It is significant that when McNamara compiled his principle speeches and reports on leaving the Pentagon in 1968 in his book, *The Essence of Security*, the Ann Arbor speech was omitted. There isn't even a reference to it in the index.

But when McNamara appeared before the Senate hearings to ask ratification of the test ban treaty, eleven days after that plea by McGovern to reduce spending on missiles, he was in no mood for second thoughts. When Senator Symington asked him about McGovern's speech, McNamara insisted that he was holding the defense budget "to an absolute minimum." McNamara submitted a formal memorandum declaring that any such cuts as McGovern proposed would represent "a substantial risk to our national security." [26] As for McGovern's charge of overkill capacity in our nuclear weapons inventories, McNamara replied cryptically, "I think it is possible to say that we have more weapons than would be utilized in a particular war situation, without concluding that our inventories are excessive." Such was the evasive nonsense McNamara was still uttering after the treaty offered an opportunity to freeze or reduce the inventories on both sides. I believe he would agree today with the unnamed officials the *New York Times* quoted in that news story of June 30, 1968, as fearing that the production of atomic weapons was "coming to be based more on the capabilities of the Atomic Energy Commission to manufacture them than on the actual requirements of the military." Yet this mindless momentum continued despite the treaty, and McNamara was its prisoner and tool.

When Senator Aiken asked McNamara what effect approval of the treaty might have on the military budget during the next few years, McNamara was discouraging:

MCNAMARA: I believe the treaty *per se* should not lead to a reduction in the budget. As I mentioned, I think we should all be concerned lest we be lulled into a false sense of security and act to reduce the budget for our military forces.

AIKEN (*still trying to be hopeful*): Do you think it might have some tendency perhaps to stabilize the budget at about the present level?

MCNAMARA: No, sir; I really don't believe that the treaty by itself will have any, should have any, important influence on the budget.

AIKEN: It would have no effect whatsoever?

MCNAMARA: No, sir.[27]

When the Joint Chiefs appeared before the senators a few days later they were blunter:

---

[26] See pp. 146–50 of the Senate hearings.
[27] Senate hearings, p. 128.

SENATOR CURTIS: If the safeguards that you favor are adequately carried out, is this test ban, would this test ban, then be a money-saver?

GENERAL WHEELER: On the contrary I would say, Senator, if I may offer my opinion first. As I look at it, the military threat to our security from the Soviet Union specifically and from the Communist bloc in general is not lessened in one degree by this treaty. The safeguards, also, in my opinion, are going to cost sums of money over and above the sizable military budget that the chairman pointed out this morning.

GENERAL LEMAY: I would agree that the military budget will probably go up as a result of the treaty, not down.

SENATOR CURTIS: I see.[28]

Earlier that same day Senator Morse had asked the Joint Chiefs an untactful question. In the Pentagon it must have seemed downright indecent, almost pornographic.

MORSE: Now, you gentlemen have close contact with the large defense contractors of this country. What has been their view generally of this treaty?

GENERAL LEMAY: I certainly have no idea. I have not discussed it with any of them.

MORSE: Any of you know of any opposition by the defense contractors?

GENERAL LEMAY: I don't know of any.

GENERAL WHEELER: I would like to speak for myself, Senator, I have no contact with the large defense contractors of the country and I, too, have not discussed it with any of them.

ADMIRAL McDONALD: I haven't discussed it, nor have they discussed it with me.

GENERAL SHOUP: I have no contacts with them.[29]

How reassuring that after so many years in the services every member of the Joint Chiefs of Staff would turn out—so to speak—to be a virgin! But what need was there for seduction by industry, when the insiders so obviously planned to permit no letup in the arms race in the wake of the treaty?

It is startling now to check back and see how our testing has increased since it was "limited" by treaty. I phoned the

[28] Senate hearings, pp. 404–5.
[29] Senate hearings, p. 369.

Atomic Energy Commission April 3, 1970, as this was being written and asked for the figures on testing as of that day. Its press officer told me there had been ninety-eight U.S. tests from 1945 until the treaty went into force on August 5, 1963. Since then there were 210 U.S. tests, or more than twice as many in the seven years since the treaty as in the eighteen years before it. When I asked for the costs, I was given year-by-year figures including those for the next fiscal year in the new budget. The total cost of testing for those eight years will be $1,834 million, an average of more than $200 million a year. It was some $206 million in fiscal 1964, the year the treaty went into effect. It will be $226 million in fiscal 1971. I have never seen these figures published before.

On the other hand the AEC's figures on Soviet testing show a sharp decline. It credits the Soviet Union with 126 tests in the years before the treaty, including one underground. It lists only three Soviet tests since. But these figures, like so much else the AEC does, are tricky, indeed doubly so. For the AEC also lists what it calls thirty-five "seismic signals" from known Soviet proving grounds. These are announced in this form: "The U.S. has today recorded seismic signals which originated from the Soviet nuclear test area in the Semiplatinsk region. The signals are equivalent to those of a nuclear test in the low-intermediate range."

When I asked the AEC why these were not listed as Soviet tests, the answer was that we could not be sure they *were* tests without actually digging a hole on the site where it took place. When I asked how they could be sure of the three Soviet underground tests they do list as such, the answer was that these "vented" and threw radioactivity into the air which we detected in the same way as we detect atmospheric tests.

All this is part of a phony charade in which the AEC has been engaged ever since talk of a nuclear test ban began in the fifties. It is designed to support the AEC's view that we could never be absolutely sure an underground test had taken place without on-site inspection. In a sense, of course, this is true. But the standard of absolute assurance on which the AEC and the other opponents of a comprehensive test ban have always insisted goes beyond normal experience and scientific necessity. If bridegrooms sought the same degree of assurance in marriage, every bride would be put into an iron chastity belt immediately after the ceremony and followed for the rest of her life by two detectives, both eunuchs.

There have always been two ways to approach the statistics on the probability of test detection. The probability has always been high and has grown higher. Today they are probably 98 chances in 100. One can then shake one's head sadly as the AEC does and say there *is* a 2 percent chance of evasion. The other, the normal and sensible way, is to say that any power which set out to evade the treaty would have to do so knowing that there were 98 chances in 100 that it would be caught out. This is more assurance than one gets in the normal transactions of life.

The seismic signal nonsense is only one of the ways in which the AEC's statistics are tricky and understate the volume of testing on both sides since the treaty. The other way is that its figures—the Soviets give out none—are only for what it calls "announced" tests. We do not announce all our tests, in order to confuse the other side's monitors, and we do not announce all the tests or "seismic signals" we detect on the other side, in order to hide from them just how sensitive *our* monitoring facilities are. All this has another dividend, of course, in hiding from the public the full extent of testing since the treaty.

Fortunately there are independent sources which also monitor tests, and these indicate that the number of "unannounced" tests is very large indeed. The Swedes have a very sensitive seismic recording station at Upsala. "The Swedish Research Institute for National Defense," the new *Yearbook on World Armaments* for 1968–69, issued by the Stockholm International Peace Research Institute[30] notes,

[30] New York: Humanities Press, pp. 245–46.

"has for each year since the Moscow treaty reported about twice as many Soviet tests as the U.S. Atomic Energy Commission," i.e., twice as many as the three radioactively monitored tests plus the thirty-five "seismic signals." The Swedish station also reports that there were at least thirty more Soviet atmospheric tests in the years before the treaty than the AEC announced.

The compilers of the Yearbook believe that U.S. testing has been similarly understated by the AEC. "A search was made," it says, "in the Bulletin of the International Seismological Centre, Edinburgh, Scotland, for the period 16 January to 14 April 1964. This indicated thirteen [seismic] events whose location in the Nevada test site indicates that they were U.S. tests. During this period the AEC announced only five tests." The Yearbook concludes that "the true figure" on the number of tests by the two superpowers "could be anything up to twice as large" as those the AEC has announced.

One final touch on this bitter comedy: The day before the limited nuclear test ban treaty was ratified, Richard Nixon gave it his qualified endorsement, but warned against any further agreements with the Soviet Union. He said the treaty signaled the beginning of "the most dangerous period in the cold war." [31] Perhaps it would have been more precise to say arms race rather than cold war. But he could hardly have realized how true that was, though not in the sense he intended. For in this underground testing we were to develop the multiple independently targeted warheads and the anti-ballistic missiles, the extensive penetration aids and improved missile accuracy, that now threaten to destabilize the precarious balance of terror.

May 7, 1970
New York Review

[31] *Facts on File, 1963*, p. 335 A2.

PART VII

That Barroom Brawl with the Lights Out Revisited

ALL WE REALLY KNOW
IS THAT WE FIRED
THE FIRST SHOTS

A major, if inadvertent, revelation in McNamara's new testimony on the Tonkin Gulf affair has been overlooked. If there was indeed an attack involving two U.S. destroyers on the night of August 4, 1964, we began the attack, we opened fire first. Indeed the only shots we are completely sure of beyond any shadow of doubt even at this late date are those which came from our own vessels. McNamara's new version of the attack contradicts the melodramatic account he gave four years ago, two days after the incident, behind the closed doors of a joint executive session of the Senate's Foreign Relations and Armed Services Committees. It was this graphic, but (as it now appears) untrue version which helped stampede the Senate into voting the Tonkin Gulf resolution.

That earlier testimony was given August 6, 1964. When the transcript of that hearing is now compared with the new one held by the Senate Foreign Relations Committee, one can begin to get some idea of the full dimensions of the mendacity by which the Johnson Administration obtained that resolution which was its blank check for war in Southeast Asia. "The attack," McNamara told the Senate committees four years ago, "occurred at night. It appeared to be a deliberate attack in the nature of an ambush. Torpedoes were launched, automatic weapons fire was directed against the vessels [the *Maddox* and the *Turner Joy*]. *They returned the fire*" (my italics).

The Secretary put it even more vividly when Senator Lausche asked him, "Do you know how many of the torpedoes were set in motion and what small arms were used?"

SECRETARY McNAMARA: It is difficult to estimate. This was a very dark night. The attack was carried out during the night, the hours of darkness. It was a premeditated attack, a pre-planned attack. It was described as an ambush in the reports from the commanders, but because it was night it is very difficult to estimate the total amount of fire.

SENATOR LAUSCHE: The shots were again initiated by the North Vietnamese?

SECRETARY McNAMARA: Yes.

GENERAL WHEELER: That is correct.

Thus was drawn a picture of "unprovoked aggression." It was magnified and emotionalized by President Johnson when he went on TV after the attack and declared "This new act of aggression, aimed directly at our own forces, again brings home to all of us in the United States the importance of the struggle for peace and security in Southeast Asia." This was echoed in the same high dramatic vein by Adlai Stevenson at the UN Security Council next day: "Without any shadow of doubt . . . planned deliberate military aggression against vessels lawfully present in international waters" was Stevenson's description. The rhetoric made it sound like a new Pearl Harbor.

But when McNamara appeared before the Senate Foreign Relations Committee on February 20 he knew that the Committee had in its possession documents from Defense Department files which cast doubt on every aspect of that earlier version. He had to tone down his own presentation to fit. So in his prepared statement, as given out to the press that day, he gave a very different picture from that drawn four years ago:

At about 9:39 P.M., both *Maddox* and *Turner* opened fire on the approaching craft *when it was evident from their maneuvers* [my italics—not from any shots but from their maneuvers] that they were pressing in for attack positions. At about this time, the boats were at a range of 6,000 yards from *Maddox* when the radar tracking indicated *that the contact had turned away and begun to open in range* [my italics]. Torpedo noises were then heard by the *Maddox*'s sonar. A report of the torpedo noise was immediately passed to the *Turner Joy* by inter-ship radio and both ships took evasive action to avoid the torpedo. A torpedo wake was then sighted passing abeam *Turner Joy* from after to forward.

Even this scaled-down version was still a deceptive picture of what actually had transpired. McNamara released his statement during the noon recess of the February 20 hearing, which was held behind closed doors. He thus jumped the gun on the Committee by getting his version out first, perhaps hoping that it might be some time before the Committee could publish the full transcript.[1] Fortunately Senator Morse, to whom the country owes so much in this whole affair, courageously defied security regulations and in a Senate speech next day made public much of the intramural Pentagon messages obtained by the Committee. This and the Committee's anger over McNamara's tricky action in releasing his own testimony brought about the swift publication of the whole record, with some security deletions.

If the transcript of the two hearings and the text of McNamara's prepared statement are now placed side by side, it is quite clear that he and Secretary Rusk and General Wheeler lied—there is no other word for it—to the Senate committees four years ago, and that McNamara is still trying hard to lie about it now. His whole performance is the shameful climax of what many had believed to be an honorable record as Secretary of Defense. He withheld from the committees then—and in his prepared statement tried to withhold from the public now—many crucial facts which cast doubt on the whole story of the August 4 attack. You have to go from his tricky language to the Morse speech and to the hearing transcript to learn that three or four hours after the supposed attack, the task force commander on the *Maddox* cabled a warning that "freak weather," an "overeager sonarman" and the absence of any "visual sightings" cast doubt on the attack stories and called for "com-

---

[1] Pentagon and State managed to tie up the transcript of the August 6, 1964 hearing in so many security snafus that it was not finally released, until more than two years later, on Nov. 24, 1966—Thanksgiving Day, when it was calculated to attract as little attention as possible.

plete evaluation before any further action." No one would know from his accounts then or now that no debris had been found, though we claimed to have sunk two and possibly three enemy vessels, and that we ordered our retaliatory attack without waiting to learn the outcome of a belated order to search for debris.

You have to go back to that master of shyster lawyer language, John Foster Dulles, to match McNamara's performance. If an attack occurred, how is it that every single captured North Vietnamese naval man, including one who was very cooperative, denied knowledge of any such attack? How is it that Hanoi, which boasted of the August 2 attack, has always denied the August 4 attack? If Hanoi attacked on August 4, in the face of Johnson's warning after August 2, how is it that its entire tiny fleet was caught by surprise in our retaliatory attack the next day? "Why," as North Vietnam asked in its own White Paper, which has been kept from the U.S. public, "does this small country with its negligible naval forces embark on a systematic provocation of the U.S. Seventh Fleet with its 125 vessels and 650 airplanes?" And then take no precautions against a counter-attack?

Fake incidents are hardly new in the history of military bureaucracies. The Japanese military staged one near Mukden in 1931 to begin its seizure of Manchuria despite parliamentary disapproval. The *Pueblo* incident illustrates another notorious military tactic: they play incidents up or down like an organist depending on whether they want to make or avoid war. Faked or exaggerated, the Tonkin incidents were used for a war buildup the White House and Pentagon wanted. The full truth is still hidden and we applaud Senator Gruening's demand that the staff study prepared by the Fulbright Committee be released. We are told that McNamara urged "a decisive commitment" in Vietnam on Johnson a few days after the Kennedy assassination. If the Foreign Relations Committee digs further, it will find that both the bombing of the North and the commitment of combat troops to Vietnam were planned at the Pentagon several months before the Tonkin Gulf incidents, that the Tonkin Gulf resolution was prepared beforehand, and that the course pursued beginning in July, 1964, was calculated to create some kind of incident sooner or later, *to justify the expansion of the conflict already decided upon.* A Rostow Plan No. 6 for "PT-boat raids on North Vietnamese coastal installations and then by strategic bombing raids flown by U.S. pilots under either the U.S. or South Vietnamese flags" was disclosed in *Newsweek* as early as March 9, 1964. The coastal raids began in July, 1964, by vessels we supplied the South Vietnamese, with crews we trained, backstopped by intelligence our planes and ships provided. The collection of such information was the business of those "routine patrols" on which we sent our destroyers.

We cannot claim freedom of the seas for such missions. If Russian vessels backstopped Cuban naval attacks on Florida, we would take counter-action even if they stayed outside our three-mile limit. There are no territorial limits in war, and this would be war. We merely compounded the offense and assured an "incident" by instructing our destroyers to ignore North Vietnam's 12-mile limit. McNamara in his prepared statement fell back on the disingenuous argument that we had no "official documentary" evidence of this 12-mile limit. Even the Geographer's Office at the State Department admitted to us in a telephone inquiry that it had always been assumed that North Vietnam's limit, like China's and North Korea's, was 12 miles. What was McNamara waiting for—an affidavit from Ho Chi Minh? Men who can so twist the truth are a menace to national security.

March 4, 1968

McNAMARA AND TONKIN BAY: THE UNANSWERED QUESTIONS

The big surprise at the Tonkin Gulf hearing held by the Senate Foreign Relations Committee was the attitude of Secretary McNamara. Chairman Fulbright greeted him with affection and respect. "I for one," Fulbright said, "regret to see you leave the Government at this very perilous time in our history." The Committee's mood was nostalgic. Even Morse, McNamara's sharpest interrogator, called him "one of the most dedicated public servants I have experienced in my twenty-eight years in the Senate." Fulbright assured the Secretary that in seeking to establish the truth about the Tonkin Gulf incidents of August 2 and 4, 1964 "the purpose is not to assess blame on anyone, certainly not upon you." It was "simply to review the decision-making processes of our Government in time of crisis."

At the beginning of the hearing Fulbright was characteristically gentle and philosophical. He expected McNamara, in this last appearance before a Senate committee after seven years as Secretary of Defense, to enter into the investigation in the same spirit. Fulbright was encouraged in this expectation by McNamara's manner the previous Sunday on *Meet The Press*, when the Secretary referred sadly if cryptically to the many mistakes made in Vietnam and volunteered a confession of personal responsibility for those committed at the Bay of Pigs. Fulbright said he had long since admitted his own shortcomings in connection with the Tonkin Gulf affair. "I am a firm believer," Fulbright said, "in the idea that to acknowledge my mistakes of yesterday is but another way of saying I am a wiser man today." He expressed the view that it might be helpful to future Senators and Secretaries "and even future Presidents" if the way decisions were reached in the Tonkin Gulf affair was reviewed. "Mr. Secretary," Fulbright said, "I believe all of us here share your own desire that the United States profit from its mistakes—not repeat them."

But McNamara came on not as a fellow philosopher, ready to reminisce on the common errors of the past, but—as one staff member later phrased it—"like a 10-ton tank." At no point was he prepared to admit that *any* mistake had been made in the Tonkin Gulf affair. He showed no readiness for reflection, much less contrition. The Pentagon's own internal communications on the Tonkin Gulf incidents, as obtained by the Committee, were confused and murky. The full truth about the incidents, which triggered the first American bombing raids upon North Vietnam, is unlikely ever to be uncovered. But in McNamara's version they were evaluated with accuracy, beyond a shadow of a doubt, and responded to with precision. This was neither dove nor hawk but a fighting cock, insisting that he had had everything at all times completely under control. It was as if the Committee had touched the most sensitive depths of his pride, and perhaps also threatened to open up aspects of the story McNamara preferred to remain untold. In retrospect his belligerence may prove as significant as it was unexpected.

Very early in the hearing McNamara indicated that he was going to play rough. He was examined in executive session, and at the very beginning Fulbright expressed the wish that McNamara withhold his prepared statement from the press "until after the Committee has gone through the hearings" and decided what to do about its own staff report on the Tonkin Gulf incidents. "I thought it would be much fairer," Fulbright said, "if we could arrange to release them simultaneously." McNamara seemed to agree, but added, "I doubt very much that we will be able to withstand the pressures of the press today without releasing it." The Pentagon is not exactly inexperienced in the ways of withholding information it does not wish to release. Sure enough, during the luncheon recess it seized upon a remark by Senator McCarthy to the UPI as an excuse to release McNamara's prepared statement to the press, jumping the gun on the Committee and getting McNamara's version into the papers first. McNamara told Fulbright when the executive session resumed after lunch that McCarthy told the UPI McNamara had admitted that one of our destroyers had penetrated North Vietnam's twelve-mile limit. "That is just contrary to what I said this morning," McNamara said. "I cannot stand by without having what I said in my statement issued." McNamara could not have hung his release on a more finely split hair. Indeed the difference between what McNamara said and what McCarthy said he said does not speak well for McNamara's candor.[1]

The real purpose served by the release of the statement even before the executive session was over was not to correct McCarthy but to make the headlines with the counter-attack with which McNamara ended his prepared statement. "As a final point," McNamara said,

I must address the insinuation that, in some way, the Government of the United States induced the incident on 4 August with the intent of providing an excuse to take the retaliatory action which we in fact took. I can only characterize such insinuations as monstrous . . . I find it inconceivable that any-

[1] McCarthy said McNamara had admitted that the *Maddox* had invaded North Vietnam's twelve-mile territorial limits. What McNamara said (page 13 of the hearing) was that "at no time . . . did the *Maddox* depart from international waters. It had been instructed to approach the North Vietnamese coastline no closer than eight nautical miles and any offshore island no closer than four nautical miles." This invasion of the twelve-mile limit was defended by the Secretary on the grounds (1) that the U.S. "recognizes no claim of a territorial sea in excess of three miles" and (2) that there is "no official documentary confirmation" of North Vietnam's claim to twelve miles. Presumably, even if there were such a claim, we would not recognize it. Four years ago McNamara simply deleted from the first Senate hearing (pages 32–33) the fact that our destroyers were instructed to penetrate North Vietnam's twelve-mile limit in order to keep this provocative action from public knowledge. Morse's Senate speech of February 29 (at the bottom of col. 1 p. S1948 of the *Congressional Record*) disclosed a portion of the orders to the *Maddox* which McNamara did not mention. The destroyers were instructed *not* to approach the Communist Chinese coast any closer than 15 miles. Why did we honor Peking's twelve-mile claim and not Hanoi's? Obviously we were willing to risk provoking the North Vietnamese but not the Chinese Communists.

one even remotely familiar with our society and system of Government could suspect the existence of a conspiracy which would include almost, if not all, the entire chain of military command in the Pacific, the Chairman of the Joint Chiefs of Staff, the Joint Chiefs, the Secretary of Defense, and his chief Civilian Assistants, the Secretary of State, and the President of the United States.

Put in this question-begging form, of course it was monstrous. Nobody had implied any such widespread conspiracy to bring about the incident—real or alleged—of August 4. But the more one studies the evidence so far available the more one does begin to see the outlines of a conspiracy, not to fabricate the incident of August 4, but to plan and to put into motion a sharp escalation of the Vietnamese war in the very year Johnson was campaigning for election as a man of peace. The aerial deployments necessary, not for the one retaliatory strike which followed the Tonkin Gulf affair, but for the continuous bombing of North Vietnam which began in February, 1965, were ordered and accomplished— as was the alerting of combat troops—in the very year Johnson was promising *not* to widen the war. This was the conspiracy and this *was* monstrous and this is what will fully appear if the Senate Foreign Relations Committee finishes its job. One major and one minor aspect of this conspiracy are left tantalizingly unexplored in the record of the new hearing at which McNamara testified.

The major aspect involves the steps taken to widen the war *before* the Tonkin Gulf incidents which provided the public excuse for them. As these steps began to figure in Fulbright's examination of McNamara, it was curious to see how McNamara—who remembered so much and so exactly at other points in the hearing—suddenly suffered from lapses of memory. Fulbright cited an article by Hanson Baldwin in the *New York Times* in July of 1964—a month before the Tonkin Gulf incidents—saying that Pentagon sources were then arguing for extension of the war into the North. "Were there in fact," Fulbright asked, "recommendations by the U.S. military at any time from late 1963 until July of 1964 to extend the war into the North by bombing or any other means?" This was hardly a minor question, especially for an executive like McNamara who prided himself on a detailed knowledge of what was going on at the Pentagon. Suddenly the super whiz kid went blank. "Mr. Chairman," McNamara said, "I would have to check the record on that." He couldn't recall any such recommendations but he would be happy to check his records and supply an answer. The answer as supplied and inserted in the printed record at page 22 was amazingly cryptic and inconclusive. It consisted of two short sentences saying, "We have identified no such recommendation. A check of the records of the Joint Chiefs of Staff is continuing." Will the Committee drop the matter, or will it insist on an answer?

Fulbright turned at this point from McNamara to General Wheeler, Chairman of the Joint Chiefs of Staff, and asked, "I wonder if General Wheeler knows at this time?" The General's answer will repay careful study. "I don't believe so, Mr. Chairman," General Wheeler began. This was a curious reply. A witness asked if he knows something will usually reply (1) yes, or (2) no, or (3) that he can't recall. The General came up with a new one. Asked if he "knows at this time," he replied "I don't believe so." What does it mean when a witness says he doesn't believe he knows something? That he is waiting to go home and interrogate himself more closely? The rest of his reply, in its odd qualifications, indicates that the General was not being frank with the Committee. "I think that the proper answer would be," General Wheeler continued, "that there were certain intelligence activities [deleted] but to the best of my knowledge and belief during that period there was no thought of extending the war into the North *in the sense of our participating in such actions, activities*" (my italics). He too promised to check for the record.

Now, in one of the three speeches Morse made on the

Senate floor after the hearing (on February 21, 28, and 29) one may find the key to what Wheeler meant by saying "there was no thought of extending the war into the North in the sense of our participating in such actions." In those three speeches Morse courageously "declassified" most of the hitherto secret material the Foreign Relations Committee obtained from Pentagon files in its investigation. In his speech on February 29 Morse threw new light on the program for commando raids on the North, known as OPLAN 34A, which figured in the background of the Tonkin Gulf incidents. He revealed for the first time that this was initiated as early as February, 1964 jointly by the South Vietnamese forces and the U.S. military advisory group in Saigon. Under this program Morse told the Senate,

U.S. personnel were assigned to provide advice, training and assistance for South Vietnam maritime operations against North Vietnam. A U.S. Navy detachment was assigned to train and advise the South Vietnamese. For the first few months in 1964, the operations consisted of intelligence and interdiction missions. In July of 1964—the same month the *Maddox* began its patrol—the U.S. made available eight fast patrol craft to the Government of South Vietnam. The new craft permitted an extension northward of the attacks on North Vietnam.

From this account it appears that General Wheeler was being disingenuous when he said "there was no thought of extending the war into the North in the sense of our participating in such actions." If General Wheeler interrogates himself more closely he may come to believe that he knows more than he believed he knew when he was before the Committee.

While this secret extension of the war northward was going on, the State Department was not idle. It was drawing up that blank check resolution for a wider war in Southeast Asia which has come to be known as the Tonkin Gulf resolution. This was drawn up well in advance of the Tonkin Gulf incidents. Here again McNamara suffered a lapse of memory. When Fulbright asked him whether he had ever seen the draft resolution before the Tonkin Gulf incidents,

McNamara said, "I don't believe I ever saw it." McNamara
added that he called William P. Bundy, Assistant Secretary
of State for Far Eastern and Pacific Affairs, "to ask him if
he had any recollection that I ever saw it. He states that he
has no recollection that I did, and he believes that I did not.
But I can't testify absolutely on that. My memory is not
that clear." What followed in the interrogation shows how
even the best of our human IBM machines can on occasion
falter:

THE CHAIRMAN: Mr. Bundy told this committee that this
draft was prepared some months before the Tonkin incidents
in the hearing. You know that.
SECRETARY MCNAMARA: I know that, but I don't think he
said I saw it.
THE CHAIRMAN: No, I was asking you, you don't think you
saw it?
SECRETARY MCNAMARA: I don't believe I saw it, and he
doesn't believe I saw it.
THE CHAIRMAN: Isn't it customary for the State Department
to consult you on a matter of this kind?
SECRETARY MCNAMARA: Well, if it were a working paper
and that is apparently what it was, no. It hadn't advanced to a
point of decision within the Government.

Presumably "the point of decision" was the August 4 incident. It is hard to believe that a Secretary of Defense as
famous for his memory as McNamara would recall so little.
The war was being extended northward through these new
South Vietnamese activities under American auspices, and a
resolution was being readied to authorize the President to
widen the war any way he saw fit. Yet McNamara cannot
recall that he ever heard of it.

The same kind of amnesia appeared when Fulbright went
on to open up the most important question of all. This was
whether the aerial and troop deployments announced under
cover of the Tonkin Gulf incidents were actually made *before* those incidents occurred. This is where the body is
buried and this is where the Senate Foreign Relations Committee owes the country an obligation to complete its job.

To understand the tricky story of these deployments one must go back to Secretary McNamara's appearance before the Senate Foreign Relations and Armed Services Committees on August 6, 1964—the original hearing on the Tonkin Gulf resolutions. In his formal statement at the joint hearings, the Secretary said "the President and his principal advisers" had decided "that additional precautionary measures were required in Southeast Asia" and that "certain military deployments to the area are therefore now underway." Six measures were announced, including "movement of fighter-bomber aircraft into Thailand" and "the alerting and readying for movement of certain Army and Marine forces." In retrospect this was the signal that the Johnson Administration was getting ready for the bombing of the North (which could only be done on a heavy and continuous scale by using Thai bases) and for the dispatch of combat troops to South Vietnam. But this was not discussed with the Senators at the joint session nor did it figure in the Senate debate on the Tonkin Gulf resolution. If known, it would have alerted the Senate and the public to what was being cooked up under cover of the incidents and the resolution. It would also have ruined Johnson's image as a peace candidate against Goldwater. So this information was withheld. It was included in McNamara's prepared statement and inserted later in the hearing record, but this record was so tied up in security snafus by the Pentagon and the State Department, and by other forms of delay, that it was not finally released until more than two years later, on November 24, 1966. Even the date was skillfully chosen, for that was Thanksgiving Day, when it was likely to attract little public attention.

By that time the hearing record looked like ancient history to the press anyway, and nobody noticed the significance of the military deployments disclosed in McNamara's prepared statement. I myself never read it until several weeks later when I began to do the research for the three-part series on Senator Fulbright which I wrote for *The New York Review*. It was in the second installment of that series, published in *The New York Review* January 12, 1967,[2] that public attention was first called to the significance of those carefully buried revelations. I later learned that although the prepared statement was passed around at the hearing, no member of either committee seems to have had time to read it and ask questions while McNamara was on the stand. Later, other Senators could only have noticed it if they had taken the trouble to come to the committee hearing rooms and read the record there, for as a classified document it was not—until November 24, 1966—available elsewhere *and it was not available to the staff assistants on whom Senators depend*. This was perhaps the most ingenious devise ever hit upon to make a record which could effectively be kept secret while allowing the Administration afterward to claim that they had disclosed it.

The transcript of the new hearing of last February 20 shows that McNamara and his military aides are still unwilling to be wholly frank about these deployments. The McNamara statement of four years ago said that because of "the unprovoked and deliberate attacks in international waters . . . certain military deployments are now underway." This gives the impression that the deployments were a result of the Tonkin Gulf incidents, even though—as any sharp reader will notice now—they were taken *before* the passage of the Tonkin Gulf resolution, which was Johnson's authority for widening the war. But now the Senate committee found neither McNamara nor Wheeler ready to assure it that the deployments did in fact follow the incidents.

When Fulbright could get only a fuzzy reply from McNamara on the deployments, he turned to General Wheeler and said, "Maybe you are more familiar with military equipment. Is it not true that fighter-bombers were moved into Vietnam and Thailand immediately after this [the incident of August 4] took place?" General Wheeler replied,

[2] The series may be found reprinted in my book *In a Time of Torment* (Random House). See pp. 343-4.

"We moved some bombers in 1964, but I don't have the exact dates." But Wheeler had not been asked for exact dates, but only whether the deployments followed the second incident. So now Fulbright asked him, "Were these units alerted to impending movement prior to the Tonkin Gulf incidents?" The question, prepared by staff, reflected the fact that the Senate committee had collected considerable evidence that certain units *had* been alerted for movement before the incidents. Wheeler's reply was wary:

GENERAL WHEELER: To the best of my knowledge, not, Mr. Chairman, but I will check that also, and make sure.

THE CHAIRMAN: Would you check whether or not you considered sending these units to South Vietnam and Thailand prior to the Tonkin incidents?

GENERAL WHEELER: I will check that particular point.

At this point in the printed record there is a notation, "The following information was later supplied: We have not identified any air unit which had been alerted for movement into South Vietnam or Thailand prior to the Tonkin Gulf incidents. A check of the records is continuing." This is not a very responsive reply. It does not answer the question of whether such movements were "considered" before the incidents. The phrasing is odd and in one respect revealing. It does not say that *no* units were alerted. It says only that it has not "identified" any "*air* unit" so alerted. The reply is confined to air units. The key to this may lie in a fact to which John McDermott first called attention in his penetrating review of Roger Hilsman's *To Move a Nation*.[3] McDermott noted a series of steps taken in the first half of 1964 to escalate the Vietnamese conflict, including the announcement on July 27, just six days before the first Tonkin Gulf incident, that we were sending another 5,000 troops to South Vietnam. Oddly enough no discussion of this appears in the Committee hearing. Were the "selected Army and Marine forces" to which McNamara referred in his statement of August 6, 1964 in addition to this 5,000? If so, were

[3] *The New York Review,* Sept. 14, 1967.

the new combat troops alerted before the incidents? Why this nonsense about "a check of the records is continuing," as if we were dealing here with some obscure disappearance of a recruit or a mislaid shipment of rifles? Could men as able as McNamara and Wheeler really be so ignorant of so important a matter? Why were they unable by unequivocal answer to scotch a suspicion most damaging to them and the Administration?

Morse interrupted at this point in order, as he said, to "help" the Secretary refresh his memory, and read McNamara his own description of these deployments in his prepared statement of four years ago. McNamara replied:

I will be very happy to determine when those movements were first initiated, when the units were put on alert, and whether it occurred before the Tonkin Gulf incidents. I don't recall that information.

This was followed by a veritable cascade of non-recalls by a Secretary who is otherwise famous for his phenomenal memory:

THE CHAIRMAN: Mr. Secretary, if there had not been a Tonkin Gulf resolution would you have recommended to the President and Congress that the U.S. step up its military assistance to South Vietnam . . . ?

SECRETARY MCNAMARA: Mr. Chairman, I think it is a speculative question. . . .

CHAIRMAN FULBRIGHT: But to be more specific, was there any plan for such an intensification of the U.S. involvement?

SECRETARY MCNAMARA: No, not that I can recall.

CHAIRMAN FULBRIGHT: Did it then include the bombing of North Vietnam?

SECRETARY MCNAMARA: Not that I know of, Mr. Chairman.

The Secretary seemed a little nervous about that last non-recall, for he hastened to add, "I don't mean to say that contingencies and targets hadn't been examined, because they had been, prior to that time, but there was no plan for further buildup that I can remember, and no plan for the bombing of the North." So he did remember that "contingencies and targets" had been "examined." In that case in what special sense did he mean that there was "no plan for the bombing of the North"? Any lawyer will agree this was not a very frank witness. The information he offered to supply was not forthcoming in time for the published record. Nine days later McNamara stepped down as Secretary of Defense. Will the committee insist on the full answer promised it?

I now want to bring up a matter I cannot prove, though I am willing to give the Committee the name of the witness who will confirm it. This is that a few days after the assassination of Kennedy, Secretary McNamara, with the support of McGeorge Bundy and Secretary Rusk, urged on the new President the need for "a decisive commitment" in Vietnam, and insisted—over Johnson's reluctance to be rushed quite that fast into so important a decision—that it had to be made quickly. This is known to quite a few insiders, and it is perhaps one reason why in an earlier period Senator Morse—who is, I might say in passing, not the source of this information—used to call it "McNamara's war." The Committee ought to recall McNamara and insist that he clear up the whole question of just when this major step-up in the war was initiated. For all this goes back to the question not just of decision-making in a crisis *but of crisis-making to support a secretly pre-arranged decision.* Here the war-making power of Congress was clearly usurped by a private cabal in the executive department, which was soon to confront Congress and the country with a *fait accompli,* and to do so within a few months after Johnson was elected on the pledge not to do what this inner circle had already decided he would do.

Now we come to a related matter which the Committee has left unexplored, though it goes to the very heart of how the incident came about that was used to cover and to authorize the deployments for a wider war, for the bombing of the North and for the commitment of combat troops in the South. This other "buried body" may be found in Mc-

Namara's prepared statement for the February 20 hearing. Its significance has escaped attention, perhaps because it could not be fully understood except against the background of the new revelations made by Morse in his Senate speeches of February 2, 28, and 29. The country and future historians owe Morse an enormous debt for those speeches, as for those four years ago on August 5 and 6, 1964, in which he first began to lift the bureaucratic curtain of secrecy surrounding the Tonkin Gulf incidents.

In his prepared statement McNamara made an admission which must have cost his pride a good deal. It shows that he was not in full control of his own Department at a crucial moment. The fact that he disclosed it himself would lead a trained lawyer to believe that he knew or feared that documents in the hands of the Committee's staff had already disclosed this, and that he thought it best to slip the fact into his statement to protect himself under interrogation. This is what the Secretary said: "I learned subsequent to my testimony of August 6, 1964, that another South Vietnamese bombardment took place on the night of August 3–4." And at page 90 of the printed record, under interrogation by Senator Cooper, McNamara added a supplementary revelation. "At the time of the specific incidents of August 4," he admitted to Cooper, "I did not know of the attack by the South Vietnamese, but we knew of the operations, and some senior commanders above the level of the commanders of the task force did know the specific dates of the operations." This seems to mean that certain senior commanders knew something McNamara still did not know three days later when he appeared before the Senate committees on the Tonkin Gulf resolution four years ago.

To appreciate the import of this revelation one must turn to the Morse speeches, and to the classified messages and information he courageously made public in them. If we look at Morse's speech of February 29 we will see that the patrols on which the *Maddox* was engaged were far from "routine," not only in the sense that they were electronic espionage missions, but that, when the first attack occurred on the *Maddox* August 2, 1964, it was only the third occasion since 1962—or within two and a half years—on which an American naval ship had approached the North Vietnamese coast. "The appearance of an American destroyer along the Vietnam coast," Morse disclosed on the basis of the Pentagon documents obtained by the committee but still classified, "was highly unusual." The next point to be noted is that the first attack on the *Maddox* followed by 40 hours the first coastal bombardment of North Vietnam by the raiding vessels we had supplied the South Vietnamese.

Now we can understand the significance of McNamara's revelation. On August 2 the *Maddox* was attacked for the first time. On August 3 the President warned of serious consequences if that attack were repeated and announced that we were not only sending the *Maddox* back into those waters but a second destroyer, the *Turner Joy*, with it. That night, the night of August 3–4, there was a second coastal bombardment, the knowledge of which—so McNamara says—was kept from him though it was known to certain higher naval commanders and presumably arranged by the joint South Vietnamese and MACV headquarters in Saigon, which we now know from this new hearing directed these naval attacks. It was the night after this second bombardment—the night of August 4–5—that the alleged second attack on the *Maddox* and the new destroyer accompanying it took place. Whether the second attack actually took place or not—and this is still unclear—that new coastal bombardment was a provocation likely to make a second clash more probable, and therefore to trigger the retaliation Johnson had already threatened.

The Committee cannot close its books on its investigation without determining who was responsible for so provocative a move at so tense a moment, why it was not disclosed to the Secretary of Defense, and whether it was known to the White House. This is the kind of provocation military bureaucracies have often committed in the past to set off a war against the wishes of civilian authorities; a well-known example was the Mukden incident in which the Japanese military themselves blew up one of their own troop and supply trains to give them the excuse they wanted in 1931 for war on China and the annexation of Manchuria. If Chairman Fulbright really wants to explore decision-making in a crisis, he cannot leave these questions hanging.

One final but intensely important point ought also to be explored. *The Politics of Escalation*[4] shows that the Tonkin Gulf incidents occurred just when,

within a two-week period, proposals for a Geneva-type conference on Vietnam and, more largely, Southeast Asia had emanated from three important sources—U Thant, France and the USSR—and had been favorably received in Hanoi and Peking. None of these proposals, it should be noted, specified conditions or "preconditions" in urging that a solution be sought for the Indo-Chinese crises.

On July 24, the day after De Gaulle urged reconvening the Geneva conference, Johnson rejected it as a conference "to ratify terror," and declared "our policy is unchanged." But pressure for negotiations was rising. A bright chance for peace was torpedoed in the Tonkin Gulf that August night four years ago, and the Senate Foreign Relations Committee has a duty to find out how and why.

March 28, 1968
New York Review

━━━━━━━━━━

THE SUPINENESS
OF THE SENATE

"It was on the dignity of the Senate that Augustus and his successors founded their new empire. . . . In the adminis-

---

[4] By Franz Schurmann, Peter Dale Scott, and Reginald Zelnik; Foreword by Arthur Schlesinger, Jr. (Fawcett, 1966).

tration of their own powers, they frequently consulted the great national council, and *seemed* to refer to its decision the most important concerns of peace and war. . . . The masters of the Roman world surrounded their throne with darkness, concealed their irresistible strength, and humbly professed themselves the accountable ministers of the Senate, whose supreme decrees they dictated and obeyed. . . . Augustus was sensible that mankind is governed by names; nor was he deceived in his expectation, that the Senate and the people would submit to slavery, provided they were respectfully assured that they still enjoyed their ancient freedom" (italics in original).

—Gibbon's *Decline and Fall*
of the Roman Empire

A major item of business for the Senate in the session now beginning is finally to act upon Resolution 187. More than any other single piece of proposed legislation, it reflects the widespread revulsion in Congress against foreign adventures created by the Vietnamese war. It would express "the sense of the Senate" that in the future no President should commit the United States to use its armed forces abroad without "affirmative action" by Congress. The intent is to prevent future Vietnams.

The resolution was introduced by Senator Fulbright in 1967. Nothing he has done in years won such instant and wide support. It was unanimously approved, within his Senate Foreign Relations Committee, by Republicans and Democrats, doves and hawks. It was also endorsed outside the Committee by Democrats as conservative and influential as Russell of Georgia and McClellan of Arkansas, and by Republicans as far to the right as Allott of Colorado and Young of North Dakota. Its passage, overwhelmingly, by the Senate seemed assured. Yet it was somehow kept off the floor all through the 1968 session.

The Johnson Administration opposed the resolution, as did the military bureaucracy, and managed without protest from Fulbright or any other Senator to keep it from a vote. Mansfield, who had voted for the resolution in committee, turned around and put it on the shelf as majority leader, but promised to let it come to a vote this year. The resolution takes on added importance as a possible restraint on the new Administration. Nixon showed his interventionist tendencies as early as 1954 in Vietnam, and his Secretary of Defense, Melvin R. Laird, in his book *America's Strategy Gap: A House Divided*, thought Eisenhower was too weak in the Hungarian revolt and Kennedy at the Bay of Pigs. The excuse for putting off a vote at the last session was that it might upset the peace talks on Vietnam, though the resolution clearly applies only to future commitments. The Paris talks, dragging on, may provide a similar excuse this year. So easily is the Senate deflected from its purposes.

The terms of the resolution were intended to shore up the fast disappearing Constitutional right of Congress to decide when the United States shall go to war. When the Foreign Relations Committee after extensive hearings[1] sent the resolution to the Senate in 1967, it did so with a report[2] which spelled out the reasons why the framers of the Constitution gave the power to declare war exclusively to Congress. It also spelled out step by step the steady usurpation of that power by the Presidency since 1900 and particularly since the Korean war in 1950, the first full-scale war in which the United States ever engaged without a declaration of war by Congress.

The essence of the story is that in the case of America, as of Rome, imperial adventures abroad weakened constitutional controls at home. "The use of the armed forces against sovereign nations without authorization by Congress," the committee reported, "became common practice

[1] "US Commitments to Foreign Powers," Senate Foreign Relations Committee Hearings on Senate Resolution 151, August 16–23 and September 19, 1967. [This later became Senate Resolution 187.]

[2] "National Commitments: Report No. 797," 90th Congress, First Session, November 20, 1967, Senate Foreign Relations Committee.

in the twentieth century." It began with Teddy Roosevelt's
use of the Navy against Colombia in the Panama affair, and
continued with the military interventions of Taft and Wilson in the Caribbean and Central America. The trend, the
report said, was "accelerated by Franklin Roosevelt" and
"continued at a rapid rate" under Truman, Eisenhower,
Kennedy, and Johnson, "bringing the country to the point
at which the real power to commit the country to war is
now in the hands of the President."

When the committee contrasted this practice with American constitutional principles, its stately old-fashioned language seemed to be invoking a past as irretrievable as Rome
before the Caesars:

There is no uncertainty or ambiguity about the intent of the
framers of the Constitution with respect to the war power.
Greatly dismayed by the power of the British Crown to commit Great Britain—and with it the American colonies—to war,
fearful of the possible development of monarchical tendencies
in their new republic, and fearful as well of the dangers of large
standing armies and military defiance of civilian authority, they
vested the power to commit the United States to war exclusively in Congress. This power was not, like certain others,
divided between the executive and the legislature; it was conferred upon Congress and Congress alone.

"The dangers of large standing armies and military defiance
of civilian authority" are not antiquarianisms. To put the
war power in the hands of the President is to put decision-
making behind the closed doors of the White House and
the Pentagon where the sheer inertial power of our huge
standing armed forces may count for more than public
opinion, and secrecy fosters "military defiance of civilian
authority." This is how Presidents, though elected, can become Caesars, and like them the masters and the pawns of
the imperial legions.

Nuclear weapons invest the process with terrifying dimensions. "The executive, by acquiring the authority to
commit the country to war," the committee said in a grave
and eloquent conclusion, "now exercises something ap-

proaching absolute power over the life and death of every
living American—to say nothing of millions of other people
all over the world." It warned that unless the constitutional
checks on the war-making power were restored, "the
American people will be threatened with tyranny or disaster." It is not often that so sedate a committee speaks so
strongly.

The incident which occurred, or is supposed to have occurred, in the Gulf of Tonkin three years earlier, and unleashed our first bombings of North Vietnam, weighed
heavily in the making of that Committee report. It called
Lyndon Johnson's Tonkin Gulf resolution of August,
1964 "the extreme point in the process of constitutional
erosion [of the Congressional war-making power] that
began in the first years of this century." Yet, as often
happens, the judicious gravity of the words bears little relationship to the Senate Committee's haphazard, grasshopper-
minded tendency to leave the most serious matters hanging, forever unfinished, in mid-air. Its chairman, Fulbright,
and its staff—whether with or without the concurrence of
its members, we are not told—have just brushed its five-
year-old off-and-on-again investigation of the Tonkin Gulf
affair under the rug, uncompleted. This is the one story
which, fully disclosed, might have dramatized for the country the dangers on which that "no more Vietnams" resolution dwelt and thus mobilized the popular support required
to push it through the Senate this year.

For some unexplained reason this inquiry has instead
been brought to a sudden end with a twenty-page document so obscurely put together that its wider significance
went unnoticed and few newspapers paid it any attention at
all.[3] The timing of the release, just five days before Christmas, with Congress out of session and most Committee

[3] For three that did, see Walter Pincus in the *Washington Post*, Joseph
R. L. Sterne in the *Baltimore Sun*, and a shorter, less comprehensible dispatch in the *New York Times*, all on December 20.

members home for the holiday, and the form—an exchange of letters between Fulbright and the Pentagon with the scantiest explanation—were alike calculated to attract as little attention as possible.

This hasty burial is of special interest to readers of *The New York Review of Books*. When this writer, in the issue dated March 28, 1968, called attention to the questions left skillfully unanswered by Secretary of Defense McNamara and by General Wheeler, chairman of the Joint Chiefs of Staff, in the hearing held by the Committee on the Tonkin Gulf affair in February, 1968, Senator Fulbright put the article into the *Congressional Record* (March 22, 1968), with a compliment to the writer ("one of the most industrious and perceptive journalists I know") and a pledge to get the answers. "I can assure Senators," Fulbright told the Senate that day, "that the Committee intends to continue to press the Department of Defense for the information we have thus far not received."

The only result, however, is the flimsy little "Part II" released by Fulbright in December. The Committee in this document fails to explain what it did get and to pursue what it didn't. The military bureaucracy, with adeptness and effrontery, has left the Committee's main questions and requests as unanswered as they were in the hearing a year ago. How can Congress, and particularly the Senate, pick up the reins given it in the Constitution over war-making when the Senate Foreign Relations Committee, its main reliance in foreign policy, proves so slack?

The Tonkin Gulf episode provides a model of how *not* to run an investigation. The first hearing was little more than a rigged affair, held jointly by the Foreign Relations and Armed Services Committees of the Senate. It was designed to help the White House stampede the Senate into voting a blank check for wider war in Southeast Asia, as it did next day, with only two negative votes, those of Morse and Gruening, both tragically lost in the last election. Fulbright in that hearing, as in the Senate debate, ran interference for the Administration.

A second hearing was held secretly in May, 1966, after Fulbright became disillusioned, but the record has never been released; indeed its very existence is little known. I verified the fact that it had taken place after noting some scattered references to it by Senators in later years. A third, and it now appears the final, hearing was held last February 20, and a censored text released shortly afterward. So the only hearing made public which can really be called investigatory was limited to a single day and heard only the two official witnesses, Secretary McNamara and General Wheeler. At the close of that hearing Senator Gore was so exasperated by the evasions and contradictions that he told Fulbright, "I think we must plow forth and get to the full truth and make a report to the public." [4] But the plowing has ended in mid-furrow. Fulbright and the Committee have written finis to the investigation without making *any* report.

A considerable number of participants in the Tonkin Gulf affair were so antagonized by what they considered the falsities in the official accounts that they volunteered, at considerable risk to their careers, to tell what they saw. Some that night were on board our destroyers in the Tonkin Gulf. Others were in the command and control center at the Pentagon through which a series of frantic messages passed before the President went on the air and ordered our reprisal raids on North Vietnam.[5] But none of them was ever put on the stand to testify before the Foreign Relations Committee, and Fulbright has never explained why.

In his brief Preface to Part II, released in December, Ful-

[4] February 20, 1968 Hearing, p. 109.
[5] The AP had a special team digging out and interrogating these witnesses and sent out an extensive story on what they had to say. But few papers published it. The fullest version we have seen appeared in the Arkansas *Gazette*, July 16, 1967, and may be found at Page S1888 of the *Congressional Record* last February 28. See also the interviews with participants by David Wise in his penetrating account for *Esquire* in April of last year.

bright acknowledges that "several participants in the Tonkin incidents—or individuals in some way associated with the incidents—have voluntarily offered information." But he says, without giving the reasons for it, that the Committee "decided early during our reexamination of this incident to limit published material to that related directly to official documents or communications." To do so was to limit the public record to the documents the Pentagon could be prevailed upon to supply, and to the testimony and examination of the two official witnesses. So one-sided a procedure gave the advantage to the Administration. Fulbright says defensively in the closing sentence of his Preface to Part II that "nothing of an unofficial nature which came to the Committee's attention would, in my opinion, alter in any significant way any conclusion which might be reached by a careful examination of the printed record." What conclusion? That the August 4 incident never happened? That it was a fraud? Fulbright owes the Senate and the country something better than this coy and cryptic teaser.

The first stage in smothering the Tonkin Gulf affair appears in retrospect to have been Fulbright's decision not to publish his staff study even of the documents supplied by the Pentagon. This was circumvented in part by Morse, who put most of them into the *Congressional Record* as part of the speeches he made on February 21, 28, and 29. These courageous analyses will stand as the closest thing to a final report. But his disclosures were no substitute for the staff study itself. Few people will know that Morse's source was the staff study. We are left without the benefit of the staff's own conclusions and of the Committee's considered judgment.

The second and final step in blanketing the investigation is embodied in the so-called Part II released in December. This acquiesces in the Pentagon's refusal to deal with the questions left unanswered by McNamara and Wheeler in February. Fulbright could have taken his fight for the an-

swers to the Senate floor this session. He could, as a minimum, have drawn public attention strongly to the Pentagon's unwillingness to give the Senate anywhere near the
full truth. He has done neither.

By far the most important document the Committee
wanted last February was the "command and control report" which covered the flow of messages through the Pentagon and the White House the night the decision was
made to attack North Vietnam. That such a report existed
was kept from the Committee's staff investigators when
they asked the Pentagon for relevant reports and documents. Its existence became known only through an anonymous letter dated December 26, 1967, which Morse put
into the record of last February's hearing (pages 84–5).
"I doubt that all the power of the United States Senate,"
the anonymous letter said, "could ever penetrate far enough
into the super-secret world to learn much about what goes
on." The letter said the situation was so bad that "right now
the JCS [Joint Chiefs of Staff] is refusing materials in their
field wanted by people working on Vietnam for the Secretary of Defense, most obviously because they are fearful it
would serve the Secretary of Defense's purposes, not
theirs."

Such are the Byzantine labyrinths created by the size and
secrecy of the military establishment. The anonymous
letter gave the full title of the command and control study
so the Committee could ask for it. The anonymous letter
said the document would show that "after the first report
of the attack there was a report there probably had not
been an attack at all. But the President was to go on the air
to address the nation about the retaliatory attacks *that had
already been planned* . . ." (my italics). The President
would have missed out on prime television time if the decision had been held up for confirmation. The attacks already
planned would have had to be called off if further investigation had shown that no attack occurred.

This is where the body is buried. The Joint Chiefs of Staff, according to an article published by Hanson Baldwin in the *New York Times* a month before the Tonkin Gulf incidents, had been arguing for an extension of the war into North Vietnam. All was ready for the bombings. This was a case study in instant crisis. It shows how easily Congress can be stampeded and how readily the truth may be hidden. The Senate Committee had some powerful levers at its disposal to obtain that report or to learn its contents. A colloquy on page 77 of the February hearing disclosed that there were forty copies extant and Senator Gore said, "You will find some at the Rand Corporation." If the Pentagon refused to supply a copy, one could have been subpoenaed from Rand. The same page disclosed the name of the man who wrote the report, a man identified only as Ponturo. It took only a telephone call on our part to locate a John Ponturo at the Institute for Defense Analysis, and to learn from him (1) that he was employed by IDA in 1964 at the time it made this report for the Joint Chiefs of Staff, (2) that the report was still classified, and (3) that no one from the Foreign Relations Committee ever contacted, much less questioned, him.

The same page of the hearing last February contains a similarly vague reference to a man identified only as "Fubini." The context indicates that he was a Pentagon official who was dubious about the August 4th incident. Fulbright even got McNamara to say that he had no objection to Fubini's being called as a witness. McNamara said that Fubini, at the time of the Tonkin Gulf incident, was Deputy Director of Research and Engineering. There is reason to believe Fubini saw the excited exchange of messages that night. He too was never called as a witness, though his background would have made his appearance before the Committee impressive. Instead he is left buried in this shadowy reference in last February's hearing.

When we checked the *New York Times* index, we found that Dr. Eugene G. Fubini, a brilliant Italian-born physicist who served as an electronics expert with our

armed forces in World War II, became Deputy Director of
Research and Engineering at the Pentagon in March, 1961,
and was made an Assistant Secretary of Defense by Kennedy in June, 1963. He resigned in June, 1965, to become a
vice-president in charge of research for International Business Machines Corporation, but stipulated that he would
not work on any military business for IBM.[6] A *New York
Times* story of July 4, 1965 said he had become an abomi-
nated " 'no' man" at the Pentagon because he had so often
vetoed proposed military research projects. Fubini also was
never questioned by the Foreign Relations Committee or its
staff. What a way to run an investigation!

The tactics used by Fulbright in dealing with the Pentagon in the wake of last February's hearing—as newly disclosed in Part II—were extraordinarily weak. It turns out
from the first document, Fulbright's letter of request to
Secretary Clifford, dated last March 1, that he did not
really ask for the command and control report. He merely
asked about "*the status* of the command and control report
evaluating the Tonkin Gulf incidents" (my italics). So
flaccid an approach invited the rejection it evoked. Acting
Secretary of Defense Paul C. Warnke replied last April 4
that "the study is not considered appropriate for dissemina-
tion outside the Department." The excuses given were that
it was "an internal study," that it "was not intended to be
. . . a comprehensive evaluation of the incidents themselves," and that it "was not prepared for review by the
Chairman of the Joint Chiefs of Staff." One wonders how
much would have been left of the report if the Chairman
had "reviewed" it.

Fulbright not only took this lying down but did not even
refer to the command and control report and the Pentagon's refusal to release it in the brief Preface, little more
than a page in length, with which he introduced Part II.
There is much in these few extra documents released last
December which was worthy of explanation. They provide

[6] In January 1966, he was appointed to a four-year term on the Defense Science Board.

further evidence that we knew North Vietnam claimed a twelve-mile limit when we ordered our destroyers to penetrate it before the "incidents." There is a page which shows that the destroyer *Maddox* carried sixteen electronics experts, four from Taiwan, in addition to its regular crew, convincing evidence of its espionage mission.

From the tortured and disingenuous language of the Pentagon's replies to Fulbright, an expert—but only an expert —can learn just how spurious was that ultra top-secret information which McNamara several times showed the Committee—after clearing the hearing room of its staff, on the excuse that staff members had no security clearances higher than top secret! [7]

This was supposed to be an intercepted message which proved that the enemy attack of August 4 did take place. Now it turns out, from an assertion which Fulbright made in a letter of May 29, and which the Pentagon reply did not deny, that this "source never said that there had been an attack on August 4," and that all this source did was give the Defense Department "the name of a man already known."

It is a pity this revelation of official mendacity is buried so deeply and obscurely that few will ever be aware of it. One can also learn for the first time from Part II that a cooperative captured North Vietnamese naval officer who earlier told U.S. naval interrogators that there *was* an attack on our

---

[7] We call attention, for its amusement and enlightenment value, to the colloquy which occurred at this point in the hearing last February. The hearing was held behind closed doors, with press and public barred. But that was not enough for McNamara. He wanted the committee staff barred also:

THE CHAIRMAN [Fulbright]: The staff . . . are cleared for top secret information. . . .

MR. [CARL] MARCY [Committee Chief of Staff]: All of the members of the staff who are here submitted renewal requests for top secret clearance recently and, so far as I know, all of these requests have been granted.

SECRETARY MCNAMARA: But that is not the issue. Clearance is above top secret for the particular information involved in this situation. [February Hearings, p. 36]

Apparently the bigger the whopper the higher the classification.

destroyers August 2 but *not* August 4 was able to speak
with authority. He was second in command of the enemy
squadron which was supposed to have made the second attack!

There are also vital lessons to be learned from the exquisite samples in Part II of the rich double-talk the military
bureaucracy can fabricate to hide the facts from civilian authority. These merit attention in future crises and deserved
comment and explanation by Fulbright and his Committee.
One of the unanswered questions—and hardly a minor one
—was whether any air units had been alerted for the bombing of the North even before the alleged attack on August 4
occurred. The answer supplied was brief, crisp, and
opaque:

The Joint Chiefs of Staff have not identified any air unit which
had been alerted for movement into South Vietnam or Thailand
prior to the Tonkin Gulf incidents.

One answer might have been that no air units *were* alerted
before the bombing; another answer might have been that
they were. If the Joint Chiefs of Staff cannot answer yes or
no to that simple question, there is something seriously
wrong with their control of the armed forces. To reply instead that they have not "identified" any units alerted before the incidents is an obvious evasion. The Joint Chiefs of
Staff doesn't even say they *cannot* identify such units.

Fulbright let them get away with a similar bit of bureaucratic obfuscation in reply to another key question. This, as
Fulbright put it in his letter of last March 1, was "whether
recommendations were made by the Joint Chiefs of Staff
[before the Tonkin Gulf incidents occurred] to extend the
war to North Vietnam." This also could have been answered "yes" or "no." Instead the Joint Chiefs of Staff reply
was that (1) while the Joint Chiefs of Staff during "the first
part of 1964" before the August incidents had "examined
several possible types of military action against North Viet-

nam in order to deter that country from continuing its aggression against South Vietnam" and (2) "contingency planning for these actions was taken," "no *definitive* recommendations for extending the war to the North had in fact been made by the Joint Chiefs of Staff" (my italics). What does "definitive" mean? Why "definitive" instead of "definite"? Could it be that there was a definite recommendation but the "definitive" orders to attack were waiting for the incident?

Fulbright not only accepts these evasions but fails to comment upon them in his dry and equivocal Preface. He says the new documents have been made public "because of the possible historical interest"! And he adds that his purpose was not "to revive the controversy over the incidents in the Gulf of Tonkin but to complete, to the best of the committee's ability, the public record."

What a sham!

February 13, 1969
New York Review

PART VIII

Endless War

WHY NOT TIMBUKTU
OR EASTER ISLAND?

Lyndon Johnson does not give the impression of a man eager to reach the peace table. He seems, on the contrary, sorry that he ever brought the matter up. Little more than a year ago in his letter of February 6, 1967, to Ho Chi Minh, Johnson suggested that peace talks might be held in Moscow. Now he balks even at Pnom Penh or Warsaw. He seems to have Walt Rostow feverishly thumbing through the geography books for places Hanoi would be most likely to turn down. The presence of an embassy and adequate communications are among the conditions sprouting up all around Mr. Johnson's often repeated "anywhere, any time." But the latest batch of 10 suggestions are all countries in which Hanoi has no embassy. And in two of them the only places remotely describable as cities—Kabul in Afghanistan and Katmandu in Nepal—may not even have a telegraph office. Only Timbuktu or Easter Island could be more exotic. Lyndon Johnson is willing to show up anywhere Ho Chi Minh won't go.

In that earlier letter to Ho, Johnson suggested "bilateral discussions." Now he is beginning to give out invitations wholesale. Each invitation adds another obstacle to the choice of a site, and if talks ever do get under way the more kibitzers the less the danger of reaching an agreement. One of the newer conditions is adequate press facilities. Johnson normally is not so tender of the press. He is no goldfish-bowl operator. When he really wants to make a deal, he gets his prospect alone and pulls down the blinds. In his letter to Ho last year suggesting peace talks in Moscow, Johnson felt sure of rejection because Hanoi had insisted all along on complete and unconditional cessation of bombings as a precondition. He must have felt equally secure on

March 31 when he asked Hanoi to talk while bombing
went on between the 17th and 20th parallels. It must have
been a harrowing experience when this time Ho tricked him
by accepting. The White House may be piling up conditions to protect it from a similar surprise in the future.
Johnson would like to go on getting credit for making
peace offers so long as he can be sure nothing will come of
them.

"Everything is unclear," U Thant told the AP as he left
New York for Paris April 20. This succinctly summarizes
the situation. I see several significant strands as I try to un-
ravel what Johnson has been weaving. One is that anti-
aircraft defenses around Hanoi and Haiphong had made
bombing in that area prohibitively expensive. Roger Hilsman, Assistant Secretary of State for Far Eastern Affairs in
1963–64, reported in the April issue of *Foreign Affairs*
quarterly that "as of several months ago" the bombing of
the North was estimated to have cost the U.S. $6 billion
"while the dollar value of the facilities destroyed in the
North is estimated to be $340 million." On this basis, Hils-
man said, "Some experts argue that an end to the bombing
might actually result in a military gain rather than a loss."

Hilsman said the targets are few and most of them easily
repaired. He quotes one discouraged pilot as saying, "The
hell of it is that we fly through all that flak for what? To
attack a two-bit bridge that we've already knocked down
five or six times. The damned center spans are now made of
wood, and they put them up again in hours." In any case
the weather above the 20th parallel has been bad; the monsoon in that area won't lift until May. So in the haggling
within Administration councils, it was decided to limit the
bombing to the Panhandle, where there has been little anti-
aircraft. As an extra dividend to the hawks, it was decided
to try and do as much bombing in that narrow coastal strip
as had previously been done in all of North Vietnam.

The second strand in the policy shift was to borrow a
favorite cliché of the Kennedy brothers and propose to
shift more of the war to the South Vietnamese. Johnson

always likes to steal the opposition's thunder, and this was the easiest way out when confronted with Westmoreland's demand for 200,000 troops. This made General Creighton Abrams the logical candidate to succeed Westmoreland, since he has been working with the ARVN forces, and has been their advocate in asking for more and better weapons.[1] As Secretary Clifford explained at his press conference April 11, the ARVN forces are to be given "a degree of preference" in the supply of "our most modern weapons" because we want to "work ourselves into a posture where the South Vietnamese will take over the war."

This is *really* clutching at a straw. There wouldn't be a half million U.S. troops in South Vietnam if the Saigon ruling clique over the past decade hadn't demonstrated its utter political and military incapacity. They themselves know it. "We are not going to press for real all-out mobilization," one Senator blurted out during the new draft law debate in the Saigon legislature (*Washington Post*, April 18), "we have to appease American public opinion by showing we are trying to do something." A day after Robert Kennedy said that if elected President he "would try to bring American troops home and substitute South Vietnamese soldiers," Peter Braestrup reported from Saigon (*Washington Post*, April 15), "Few U.S. or South Vietnamese military men see this as a practical proposition." He reported that if the U.S. troops pulled out, the ARVN forces would have to abandon the five northern provinces including Hué and Danang "just to hold their own farther South." This realistic if gloomy estimate illustrates the continued and wondrous capacity of the U.S. government to adopt policies which a substantial portion of its own military and diplomatic bureaucracy privately think make no sense.

Nevertheless this decision to shift the burden of the war to the South Vietnamese must have decisive impact on the

[1] From a different point of view we can't see much sense in putting a World War II tank general into command of a war that calls for political finesse.

third strand of policy—to make another try at winning by peace talks what the U.S. has been unable to win by military means, and that is an "independent," non-Communist South Vietnam.

Johnson's new "peace" offer and his "abdication" served to disarm the opposition and throw the peace movement off balance. (McCarthy has proven much smarter and abler than Kennedy in seeing through it.) The best guess is that he did not expect Hanoi to accept his offer, which would give him a chance to have both credit for a peace move and later an excuse (when the monsoon ends) to resume full bombing of the North if he wants to. Hanoi by its qualified acceptance put the ball back into his court. But how can Johnson pursue the policy of handing over the war to the South Vietnamese, how can he get Thieu to mobilize more men, if at the same time he agrees with Hanoi's demand that all bombing end before peace talks begin?

As I reconstruct the scenario of events, Thieu must ask Washington for two or three years leeway to prove that he can take over the war. To stop the bombing and enter on talks now would pull the rug from under the Saigon military regime and Mr. Johnson's hopes. A coalition or a neutralist regime would seem to Johnson that "fake solution" he says he will never accept. So Johnson must stall as long as he can before going to the conference table, and seize on every possible way to delay a conclusion when he gets there. If there are no talks or the prospect of talks breaks down too early, his popularity will go down again and his credibility gap widen as never before. This is the bind in which Hanoi has put him.

But Johnson is no Joshua to bid time stand still. The shadows of three crises lie ahead. One is military. The U.S. military is doing splendidly again—in the field of public relations. Khesanh is advertised as a victory for airpower and "Operation Complete Victory" (What will they call the next one? Operation *Even More* Complete Victory?) is sweeping the enemy victoriously away from Saigon. But the steady resumption of shelling day after day at Khesanh indicates the enemy didn't withdraw very far in that area. And on the night of April 16, for the first time since Têt, the Viet Cong bombarded a South Vietnamese Reserve Officers School on the outskirts of Saigon, killing four and wounding 30 of the Saigon military; there were also heavy civilian casualties in the adjoining quarters for officers' families. This attack took place not far from the powerful U.S. air base at Bien Hoa and in the very heart of the area supposedly cleaned up by "Operation Complete Victory."

One of the most experienced war correspondents in South Vietnam, François Nivolon, in reporting this attack (*Le Figaro*, April 18) said, "It has proved anew, and this will surprise no one here, that it is almost impossible to assure the security of the capital of South Vietnam and its environs." M. Nivolon recalled that after the Têt offensive representatives of the U.S. military command estimated that it would take ten divisions to guarantee absolutely the security of Saigon. That is roughly half the strength of the U.S. Army. It is clear that the enemy can still strike almost anywhere he chooses and that surprises may lie ahead. One cannot exclude a new offensive strong enough to unseat the Saigon regime, and replace it with Buddhist and other non-Communist elements willing to negotiate peace.

April 29, 1968

PLAYING FOR TIME
TO CONTINUE THE WAR

A high (and hawkish) Pentagon official told a friend of mine recently, "The purpose of the partial bombing pause and the talks in Paris is to reduce the fighting to a level the American people will tolerate for a long time without giv-

ing up our basic aim," i.e., an "independent" South Vietnam. This remark I believe is the best key to the confused
and tangled talks in Paris. A similar clue may be found in
Max Frankel's dispatch from Austin in the *New York
Times* June 2. "It was primarily," he wrote, "to buy time at
home to keep waging the war's military and diplomatic battles abroad that Johnson accepted the dovish counsel of at
least a partial halt in the bombing on March 31 and threw in
his retirement for good measure." Frankel added, "So far
the tactic has worked better than he dared to hope. The
bitter controversy has abated and the political candidates
have been muted." The purpose is to defuse the peace issue
during the election campaign, to tread water until after it is
over.

I thought at one time that Johnson would make peace as
the best way to undercut Bobby Kennedy, whom he hates,
and elect Humphrey, or perhaps even run for reelection
himself as the man who made peace. But I think I underestimated Johnson's craftiness. His strategy is to undercut Mc-
Carthy and Kennedy by *appearing* to seek peace. This political strategy fits his immediate and urgent economic
needs. The U.S. cannot escalate the war, adding another
200,000 men to those already in Vietnam, without imposing
the kind of wartime taxes and economic controls which
would be dangerously unpopular in an election year. *The
campaign dictated a pause.* But there is no sign that Johnson
has given up his ultimate aims nor changed his deep emo-
tional attachment to this imperialist crusade in Southeast
Asia. He was speaking from the heart when at the Korean
Consulate in Honolulu April 17 he forecast a continued
American protectorate over "the New Asia"—what a euphemism for Chiang Kai-shek and the corrupt oligarchies
under our wing! "I deeply believe," Johnson said, "that my
successor—whoever he may be—will act in ways that will
reflect America's abiding interest in Asia's freedom and in
Asia's security." This will certainly prove true if his successor is Humphrey or Nixon, Rockefeller or Reagan.

Much that may seem puzzling falls into place if the peace

talks and the limited bombing pause are viewed as a tactic for a breathing spell. There are, for example, beginning to percolate through Washington bits and pieces of off-the-record talks which preceded the Paris conference. The U.S. negotiators seem to have done very little thinking or planning for any kind of a compromise political settlement. The U.S. is ready for mutual de-escalation, but mutual de-escalation in the absence of a political settlement merely means that the other side give up the revolt and the war and leave the military junta in power in Saigon. This seems to be the shape of that "satisfactory solution" for which, as Humphrey told students at St. Paul May 27, we should be willing to stay at the conference table "for months and if necessary for years." This is what Senator McCarthy sensed in his interview with Frank McGee of NBC June 2, when he said the government wasn't saying or doing anything different from what it had been saying or doing "before the negotiations supposedly began"—

We're still saying no coalition government—Dean Rusk is—no recognition of the National Liberation Front, accelerate the war, call up more troops. There is no pullback, there is no limitation on the search and destroy missions.

There is no change because no real change has taken place.

Jeremy Campbell from Washington in the London *Evening Standard* May 8, and Stuart H. Loory from Washington in the *Los Angeles Times* May 31, both reported that Johnson's March 31 "abdication" address was preceded two weeks earlier by a dramatic reversal of opinion on the part of Johnson's non-official advisers on the war. A panel which includes retired generals Bradley, Taylor and Ridgway, Douglas Dillon, McGeorge Bundy and George Ball, had always before been for vigorous prosecution of the war, the only dissenter being Ball. After their meeting March 18—so goes this story—they startled the President by reporting that continued escalation, intensified bombing and increased American troop strength "would," so Loory writes, "do no good." But there is no indication that these somber military conclusions had any firm political impact. Far from preparing the public mind for compromise, the Administration has shut the door firmly on talk of a coalition. Westmoreland was allowed to use the forum of a Presidential press conference at the LBJ ranch May 30 for another of those silly performances that build up the illusion that a military victory is possible. And now we learn that on May 6 a secret directive was issued by Westmoreland to U.S. commanders in Vietnam calling for "a major breakthrough to a military victory." You don't waste more lives if you're really serious about peace.

June 10, 1968

THE WILLFUL BLINDNESS OF McGEORGE BUNDY

McGeorge Bundy's speech at De Pauw University is a victory for the peace movement and a justification for those of us who will vote for neither Nixon nor Humphrey. It is a victory in that one of the chief architects of our Vietnamese policy now says that we must end the bombing of the North and deescalate the American military effort, irrespective of what Hanoi does. The speech is also a justification for the election cop-out because this Republican, who was in charge of foreign policy at the White House for Kennedy and Johnson, this symbol of the bi-partisan prowar Establishment, sketches out a new consensus for a new Administration which would neither get us out of the Southeast Asian quagmire nor forestall more Vietnams elsewhere.

The logic of Bundy's position is withdrawal. The man who advised Johnson three years ago to bomb the North now says the bombing is futile and that the war cannot be won no matter how much we escalate it. He says an annual cost of $30 billion, a yearly toll of 10,000 American lives, "the increasing bitterness and polarization of our people," and "the growing alienation of a generation which is the best we have had" are "now plainly unacceptable. So we must not go on as we are going."

But then he turns around and says that "we should cut back—but we need not and should not give up." This man who was so arrogant and smug three years ago in rejecting the anti-war protests of his old academic colleagues is still unprepared to change our basic course or to admit any mistakes. But until those mistakes are clearly faced we are bound to repeat them. He even reminds those who favor the bombing and escalation that his own shift of position does not spring from "moral outrage or political hostility to the objective." This is a confession of moral callousness and willful political blindness.

This is a preview of the best we can expect from either candidate. It is not good enough. Bundy wants us to cut back but to get ready to keep troops indefinitely in Vietnam. He proposes the withdrawal of 100,000 to 150,000 troops in 1969 with a saving of $5 to $8 billion, and a comparable reduction in 1970. These puny half-measures will not free the funds or moral energies we need to meet our racial and urban crises. The Pentagon can swallow up those few billions saved and grab for more on the excuse that we must give our fighting men, especially since their numbers have been reduced, the very best and newest equipment. Bundy would have us dig in for a long war by military reforms which would make it possible to keep combat troops there for longer than the present 12-month rotation. Yet he seriously offers this mishmash as a means by which a new Administration can "reknit the essential relation of confidence between itself and the nation."

To hang around in Southeast Asia is to invite trouble. Without a fundamental revision of policy, we will continue to bleed away our youth and substance in this trap of our own making. Bundy still wants an American protectorate over Southeast Asia. The climax of his folly lies in his assertion that "in a policy of cutback there is still ample room for steadfast support of our friends, and ample guarantee against defeat imposed by the external aggressors . . . ample demonstration for all who live in the area not only that we keep our commitments but that we know how to change our course with care and clarity." Those conceited words will be read with derision in Saigon, Bangkok and Taipei. What if the withdrawal leads to a series of Dienbienphus as the guerrillas overwhelm our shrunken enclaves? What if the Saigon regime collapses as "our friends" head for Switzerland with the money our troops have spent in their bars and bordellos? What if Thailand erupts into a second Vietnam? Bundy's mini-imperialism is a recipe for new disasters.

All this springs from Bundy's unwillingness to reassess a past for which he bears so much responsibility. That is why we find him saying that though "the burden of this war must now be lifted" that does not mean "it should never have been fought" nor that "we are required now, by our new necessities, to lose what has been gained in the strategic sense." What have we gained? We have made a mess of Vietnam and Vietnam has made a mess of the United States. Yet Bundy is still pursuing that line of policy to which we have several times called attention as the key to Johnson's abdication. *This is to reduce the level of conflict to a point the American people will tolerate for a long pull without giving up the basic aim of restoring a South Vietnam under American control.* This is Macchiavellianism parading as a search for peace. It will not work politically and it will not work militarily. Yet this is the best the Establishment offers for the next four years.

Bundy says that a nation ready "to keep at least 100,000 troops in place for years" cannot be accused of "faithless withdrawal." To whom would we be faithless? Three years ago just before the bombing of the North began he was in Saigon trying to bring peace amid the warring factions on our side. The situation there is worse than ever. The recent rumors of a new coup reflect the fears of the die-hards that Big Minh's return may foreshadow a broader government and peace negotiations. Bundy will not admit publicly that the Saigon regime today, with a military junta and a rigged Constitution, has the same unrepresentative social base as Diem's dictatorship. It is heavily weighted on the side of the 10 percent pro-war Catholic minority against the pro-peace Buddhist majority. It is heavily weighted on the side of the landlords against the peasants. It is heavily weighted on the side of North Vietnamese refugee generals who want to reconquer the North against a South and Central Vietnamese majority *of every class* which is for some kind of compromise with the Viet Cong for the sake of peace.

In the name of "self-determination" we are allowing a minority to prevent the majority from determining its own future. This is the sham Bundy would continue, and this is much the same sham bolstered by our Special Forces and Green Berets and electronic anti-guerrilla sniffers and snoopers and all the vast panoply of our military power in the Third World. The only way to free our resources, financial and spiritual, for that "greater America" Bundy calls for is, to free us from militarist delusions, to cut the Pentagon down to size, to try and build a better world through the United Nations, and not by putting navies on every sea and armies on every continent in the effort at a Pax Americana which can only bring our country's ruin. Only such a New Charter can win the best of this generation back to normal politics.

October 21, 1968

WHY THE CASUALTIES RISE AS THE PEACE TALKS GO ON

President Nixon's dismissal of a cease-fire in Vietnam calls for close examination. It was sophistry to say that a cease-fire "may be meaningless" in a guerrilla war because of the difficulty in controlling it. Whatever element of truth this may contain as a general proposition, the history of past truces in the nine-year-old Vietnam war shows that the other side has had little difficulty in enforcing a cease-fire on its own troops. Cease-fires have been broken by the other side on any meaningful scale only when they wanted to break it, as in the Têt offensive last year, or in defensive response to the aggressive patrolling which has been our military's own way of getting around cease-fire orders in holiday truces. Until the bombing pause the U.S. official line was to call for a cease-fire as the price of a bombing halt. The line has changed because we hope to exploit the present situation by "clean-up" operations against the guerrillas in the South. That is why casualties still rise as the peace talks go on.

A neat bit of censorship is helping to hide the truth. The Pentagon gives out figures on attacks initiated from our side but the figures on enemy-initiated attacks are "classified," an antiseptic word for censored. One of these censored figures came to light last December 14 when the *New York Times* in an editorial, "Endangering the Peace Talks," said "Since the bombing halt, the enemy has initiated only one battalion-sized assault. By comparison last month American troops mounted 63 battalion operations and South Vietnam staged 664 such campaigns." It said the purpose was "to extend South Vietnamese Government control over disputed areas and territory long controlled by the Vietcong" and warned that such an effort "to upset the balance in Vietnam in advance of a settlement in Paris is bound to produce a reaction sooner or later" and risk a flareup "that could wreck the chance for a negotiated peace."

In the wake of the Nixon press conference, we went over to the Pentagon to check the *Times* figures and bring them up to date. We found the tempo of offensive operations from our side had gone up about 25 percent in December over November. The figures on battalion-sized operations from our side in December were 824 South Vietnamese, 84 U.S. and 48 combined, or a total of 956 as against the 727 figure the *Times* gave for November. But when we asked for the figures on enemy-initiated actions of battalion size, we were told that all the figures on enemy-initiated actions were in classified tables. We went to two different sources and finally put in a formal question on why such figures were classified, but we're still waiting for an answer. The *New York Times* assertion was not challenged.

One officer explained that any paper with a man in Saigon who kept a sharp eye on the daily communiqués could get figures on enemy-initiated attacks. Obviously the totals on enemy attacks do not keep any information from the enemy he does not already know. This is political not military censorship, designed not to confuse the enemy but to hide what is going on from the American public. We hope some members of Congress will insist that these figures be released.

The course in Vietnam becomes clearer if one compares it with U Thant's original three-point plan for peace. At his press conference January 28, the Secretary General noted that two of the points had been put into effect—the bombing of the North had ended and talks among all the parties involved had begun. U Thant's third point was a gradual de-escalation of the fighting. Instead of de-escalating in response to the considerable de-escalation on the other side, we have been stepping up both ground and aerial action in the South, as we have the bombings over Laos.

Tacitly or explicitly, it is now becoming clearer, Johnson exacted a sharp price when he ended the bombing of the

North. He imposed severe restrictions on enemy activity while making it possible for us to increase ours. The Nixon Administration is carrying on the strategy of Johnson's. This strategy has two elements. The first is to threaten resumption of the bombing in the North if the other side should resume substantial forays or shellings from the DMZ or should attack the larger cities. The second is to take advantage of these military limitations on the other side to move considerable forces from the northern part of South Vietnam where they had been on guard against a possible invasion from the DMZ. These forces have been moved south, for "pacification" operations in the Mekong Delta. This has been a guerrilla stronghold since the earliest days of the uprising against the French. The aim is to reconquer the Delta for the Saigon regime.

The bombing of the North ended November 1. The escalation from our side began at the same time. In the three months since, more than 2,000 Americans have lost their lives. White House orders explain the rising .casualty lists. Clark Clifford lifted the curtain on them last November 24 when he said, "General Abrams has specific instructions to maintain constant and intensive pressure on the enemy." The fight-and-talk strategy was ours. Our Madison Avenue-minded military invented a new soap ad phrase to sell this accelerated warfare. They renamed it "accelerated pacification." Clifford added loyally that this was "the right psychology and the right strategy to follow now," but he expressed the hope that when "we begin to make progress in Paris" and agreement "in certain areas" was reached, "then instruction could be given by Hanoi to their battlefield commanders, and instruction could be given here by President Johnson to General Abrams to withdraw from contacts with enemy forces." The enemy began withdrawing from contact and trying to evade battle months ago. But there has been no de-escalation on our side. Three weeks later on *Face the Nation*, Clifford declared himself "inordinately impatient with the continued deaths of American boys in Vietnam" and urged a cease-fire. Neither Johnson nor Nixon seem to share this impatience. Nixon can cut the casualties any time he orders de-escalation and a defensive strategy, as proposed by Senator McGovern in a speech February 3 to Clergy and Laymen Concerned About Vietnam.

The premise of negotiations is that neither side can win a military victory. If we are negotiating, why go on killing? If we hope to achieve our aims in South Vietnam by a step-up in the killing, why negotiate? The cynical answer is that the negotiations serve as a smokescreen. Neither the U.S. military nor the Saigon regime ever wanted to negotiate. The Paris talks for them only make it easier to continue the war. There is a steady flow of optimistic stories from Saigon on how well the war is now going. One by Charles Mohr in the *New York Times* January 3 put its finger on a crucial, though nonmilitary factor. "One important factor on which present optimism is based," Mohr wrote, "is the hope that a decision to continue to prosecute the war can be reconciled with the domestic American desire 'to ease the pain.'"

Few noticed the realities reflected in the last AP weekly casualty report from Saigon (*Washington Post*, January 31). The report covered the week ended January 18 (196 U.S. dead and 1,277 wounded) and the week ended January 25 (190 U.S. dead and 1,224 wounded). Why are casualties still so heavy? The AP explained that while "there has been no sustained large-scale fighting since last fall . . . thousands of U.S. and government troops carry out daily operations in search of the elusive enemy." It added that "pushes are also being made into areas long held by the Vietcong, and in these, even when no opposition is encountered, there are casualties from mines and booby traps." How long can these offensive operations go on without a counter-offensive from the other side? As we write, for the first time in three months, there have been three battalion-sized enemy attacks in the past few days. It is time to make the U.S. public aware of all this before fighting flares up again in full fury.

It is nonsense to say that you cannot have a cease-fire in
Vietnam. Fighting ended in the first Vietnamese war when
a cease-fire was negotiated at Geneva in 1954. Then it was
part of the general settlement. The question is one of policy, not feasibility. The Viet Cong and Hanoi oppose a cease-
fire until there has been a political settlement. The U.S. and
Saigon don't want a cease-fire until there has been a military
"settlement." They cling to the old hope that the war will
end with the enemy "fading away," a favorite phrase of
Henry Cabot Lodge, whom Nixon resuscitated to be his
chief negotiator at Paris. The U.S. military seem to be making their plans on the assumption that there will be no settlement in Paris. They plan a prolonged American occupation, though on a reduced scale. "From those most deeply
involved in overall strategy" in Saigon and Washington,
U.S. News & World Report January 27 reported that our
military foresee a slow reduction of U.S. forces in Vietnam
to 200,000 men by the end of 1971. They set that level as
"the basis for a long-haul, low-cost effort in Vietnam that
could continue indefinitely." On such a scale "low cost"
could still mean $5 or $6 billion. The military men *U.S. News*
interviewed regard Korea as a precedent. There we still
have 50,000 men 15 years after the shooting stopped. We
also have no peace treaty, a continued trickle of casualties
and the ever-present danger that the war may break out
again at any time. That is not a comforting precedent.

For the Vietnamese people the end of bombing in the
North has meant an intensified terror from the skies in the
South. B-52's are employed like buckshot, spreading destruction over wide areas, often on the edge of the cities,
wherever we think a few guerrillas may be hiding. Nobody
but the victims has any conception of what this horror
means. It is not strange that in Saigon, despite press control
and the thousands imprisoned for peace agitation, the cry
for a cease-fire has been rising, though little reported in the
U.S. press. Both *Le Monde* (January 28–29) and *Le Figaro*
(January 29) report that elements which have hitherto
strongly supported Thieu have joined the militant Buddhists

in demanding a cease-fire. They quote Father Ca Van Lau, head of the Dan-Tien bloc in the Saigon Chamber of Deputies, as calling for a cease-fire now, as have two leaders of the Don Xa and the Grand Union Forces, organs respectively of the Hoa Hao sect and one faction of the Catholics. Both parties demonstrated last November in favor of Thieu. Now both parties have swung over to the Buddhist demand for an immediate cease-fire. In this, as in so much else, we are very poorly informed as to what ordinary Vietnamese think. To call for peace is still to risk jail in Saigon. The ungagged voice of popular sentiment may be better expressed in a manifesto issued in Paris (*Le Monde*, January 30) of a Movement of the Free Forces of Vietnam, representing both civilian exiles and former Vietnamese officers who fought in the army organized by the French. It terms the present regime "nothing but a prolongation of the Fascist regime of Ngo Dinh Diem," which "governs by terror." It calls for its replacement by a provisional government which can negotiate in Paris with the Viet Cong and Hanoi.

This parallels the position taken by Hanoi and the NLF in the Paris peace talks. The NLF spokesman called for the formation of a broadly representative provisional government in Saigon which would organize "free general elections in South Vietnam" and be prepared to deal with the NLF in the Paris talks as an independent and equal party (see texts in *Le Monde*, January 28). "Although they speak of negotiations for peace," the NLF delegate to the Paris talks said, "the United States continues to intensify the war," and "still does not wish to renounce their aggressive aims in South Vietnam." We are paying heavily in American lives in an effort to impose the Saigon regime by force on the South Vietnamese. That is why the casualties rise as the peace talks go on.

February 10, 1969

THE BEST-KEPT SECRET
OF THE VIETNAM WAR

It is hard to imagine a document less candid and more opaque than General Westmoreland's report on the Vietnamese war. He was in command in the years of its greatest escalation, and his account is about on a par with a complacent author reviewing his own book. It was—in his own considered opinion—a continuous triumph, a military marvel, in which any shortcomings and the singular lack of a final victory were all due to other factors—the limitations imposed on him by his political superiors and the impatience of the U.S. public. His account nevertheless contains an inadvertent revelation, and this in turn shows how effectively the U.S. military can close the shutters on an "open society" and keep the American people from knowing what is really going on. The revelation concerns the year 1965, when Westmoreland took over and made Vietnam an American war. This was the year we began to bomb the North and to put combat troops into the South.

It has always been assumed that we committed our troops again to an Asian ground war at the request of the Saigon government to save it from defeat. It now appears from Westmoreland's narrative that the commitment of U.S. combat troops was a unilateral decision by our military, that the South Vietnamese were not only reluctant to see our combat troops enter the country but when they did arrive tried to restrict their deployment and keep them as far as possible from Saigon and other populated areas. It is easy to imagine the uproar in Congress and the country if this had not been kept hidden at the time. If it had been known that the Saigon regime itself feared "Americanization" of the war, this would have strengthened the demand that we negotiate instead of escalate—that we do then what we are finally doing now after four years of futile bloodshed. It is heartbreaking to look back and notice that on February 1, 1965, just before we took over the war, only 258 Americans had been killed in Vietnam.

It is strange how, with all the correspondents there were in Vietnam, Saigon's misgivings were kept from public knowledge. This, the best-kept secret of the Vietnamese war, can now be pieced together from three passing references in Westmoreland's account. The first is on pages 98–99 in his chapter on 1965 as "The Year of Commitment." There he says that by the late spring of 1965 he was convinced that the Saigon government could not survive for more than six months unless the U.S. put in "substantial numbers" of combat troops. He nowhere says Saigon asked for them, only that *he* became convinced of their need. The troops began to arrive in July and the first combat commitment put the 1st Cavalry Division (Airmobile) into the Central Highlands. Saigon "concurred" in the decision to deploy the 1st Cavalry in the Highlands. "In fact," Westmoreland discloses, "they suggested that all deploying U.S. combat forces be concentrated in this comparatively remote area *in order to minimize the impact upon the South Vietnamese economy and populace*" (My italics). That sounds as if Saigon were less fearful of defeat than of American "invasion."

Westmoreland reveals that he decided to override Saigon's objections. He says he felt it "essential" that U.S. combat units "be available to reinforce and stiffen South Vietnamese forces in the critical areas of high population density." He adds, "Consequently, I planned to build up U.S. forces in an arc around Saigon and in the populous coastal areas *and not to restrict U.S. troops to the Central Highlands*" (My italics). To ignore Saigon's wishes was, clearly, to treat South Vietnam as a colonial possession, where we made the final decisions, just as the French had. This does not keep Westmoreland, eight pages later, from referring blandly to "the enemy's absurd claim that the U.S. was no more than a colonial power"!

When one checks back ón what was happening in Saigon at the time, one begins to wonder whether Westmoreland may not have had other contingencies in mind when he insisted on deploying U.S. troops around Saigon. In 1965, peace sentiment surfaced strongly in South Vietnam. In February the Buddhists launched a campaign for a negotiated settlement, demanding the withdrawal of both U.S. and Communist forces. In March the Saigon police broke up an attempt by the smaller but powerful Cao Dai sect to begin a similar campaign. In May, Catholic die-hards accused Saigon's last civilian government, that of Phan Huy Quat, of secretly conspiring with the Buddhists to purge the military and negotiate peace. In June they forced the civilian regime to resign and brought in the Thieu-Ky military dictatorship. The military made its debut by ordering all of Saigon's thirty-six Vietnamese-language papers suspended for "purification," no doubt of peace sentiment. Was Westmoreland anxious to put U.S. troops around Saigon so they would be ready to intervene if a government committed to negotiating peace had come to power?

Even after the military takeover in Saigon, the South Vietnamese regime still wanted to confine U.S. combat troops to areas remote from population centers. This is indicated on page 114 in Westmoreland's chapter on 1966 as "The Year of Development." [1] There he tells how he positioned U.S. combat troops around Saigon. "This again affirmed my conviction," he writes, "that the combined U.S.–South Vietnamese military effort must begin in the critical areas in which the population was concentrated." Apparently the South Vietnamese government still disagreed with him, even though Ky was now Premier. For Westmoreland adds, "Secretary McNamara, on a visit to Saigon, supported me in my opposition *to yet another South Vietnamese suggestion* that U.S. forces be deployed only to remote areas such as the Central Highlands" (My italics). In this carefully sanitized narrative, we are not told *why* Saigon persisted in its "suggestion." One reason may appear

[1] I.e., military development.

on page 132. There, in discussing 1967 as "The Year of the Offensive," Westmoreland says that while half of our combat troops continued to be deployed "in close proximity to the heavily populated areas of the country," the other half were used as highly mobile "fire brigade" forces. Westmoreland says "their tremendous fire power made it vastly more desirable that they fight in remote, unpopulated areas if the enemy would give battle there. *This would enable the full U.S. fire potential to be employed without the danger of civilian casualties*" (My italics).

This is what Saigon feared. In discussing Psychological Operations/Civic Action, Westmoreland says on page 239, "Even though reports indicated that civilian losses ran well behind those experienced in World Wars I and II and Korea, I continued to emphasize the efforts to keep losses at a minimum." But the world wars were *total* wars, and the Korean war after the first few months was waged largely in North Korea, which was enemy territory and where we leveled just about everything. South Vietnam was not supposed to be an enemy country. Jonathan Schell, the *New Yorker* correspondent, spent several weeks flying over Quang Ngai Province in South Vietnam in the spring of 1967 in the two-seater FAC (Forward Air Control) planes which helped to find targets for air strikes. He found that 70 percent of the villages in the province had been destroyed, that about 40 percent of the population lived in "refugee camps" and that another 40 percent lived underground beneath their destroyed homes in areas that were shelled regularly by artillery fire. In his book *The Military Half*, Schell reported "the overriding fantastic fact that we are destroying, simply by inadvertence, the very country we are supposedly protecting."

Saigon also feared the effect of U.S. combat troops—as Westmoreland writes—"upon the . . . populace." Foreign troops always stir resentment, not only as an occupying power but even as an ally, largely because in an immemorial fashion they turn so many of the women into whores. But there was a special reason why Saigon had to fear the impact on its people. The "Americanization" of the war meant that a decade after the French had left, here was another, white man's army, taking over in South Vietnam. For so nationalistic a people as the Vietnamese, this was bound to impair the "face" of the Saigon regime, to make it seem a puppet again, and to drive more of the youth into disaffection or the rebellion.

Westmoreland writes (page 71) that on his arrival in South Vietnam the "strong and direct connection between military and political problems was quickly impressed upon me." In an appendix on "Psychological Operations/Civic Action" (on page 239) he speaks of Vietnam as "a politically sophisticated war." But there is very little evidence that he understands the politics of the war. Politics at bottom are people, and people are not Westmoreland's specialty. There is no sign in him of humor or humanity, even in dealing with our own troops—much less the enemy. I do not mean to imply that the general is an inhumane man; the best word to describe him is "wooden"—I first heard it from someone who knew him well in Vietnam. For him as for Admiral Sharp, who was in charge of the air and naval bombardment of the North, the war was an Operation Bulldozer, the application of overwhelming power to punish and to terrorize into submission, what the Germans in World War I called *Schrecklichkeit*.

The two main political problems were the fierce nationalism of the Vietnamese and the land hunger of the peasantry. You will find no light on either in the 350 double-columned pages of the Westmoreland-Sharp report on the war and the bombing. The nationalistic factor is what General Giap had in mind when he said that when the U.S. had a million men in Vietnam, the National Liberation Front would have won the war. We would have been well on the way to that million now if Johnson had given Westmoreland the 200,-000 more men he wanted instead of kicking him upstairs to Army Chief of Staff. The land question was summed up in a captured Viet Cong document first published in Saigon in

1966.[2] "The essence of the national problem," it said, "is the farmer's problem. The basic problem of the farmers is land. This is a strategic problem we can never neglect."

Land Reform is the No. 1 unmentionable in the Westmoreland report. His appendix on pacification talks of the "revolutionary development" teams, but he never explains what, if anything, was revolutionary about them. We are told they help the peasants improve "hygiene, sanitation, education and medical facilities." They ask for land and we give them latrines! The Army's Area Handbook for South Vietnam (1967 edition, page 319) says 2.5 percent of the landowners held half the cultivated land "and more than 80 percent of the land was cultivated by peasants owning no land at all" whom the landlords could dispossess "without cause." The peasant helped the Viet Cong because their defeat would mean the return of the landlords. This is the key to the war, and Westmoreland talks (page 242) of the "wealth of counterinsurgency experience" we have amassed in the war. But this, the basic lesson, he has never learned. Indeed a story probably lies buried behind his silence on this issue. Former Secretary of Agriculture Orville Freeman told a reporter recently (Richard Critchfield in the Washington *Star*, March 16) that in 1966 the U.S. Embassy in Saigon "informed Washington it opposed land reform on the grounds it would create political instability"!

Westmoreland no more understands the politics of the war at home than he did the politics of the war in Vietnam. In his first posture statement as Army Chief of Staff to the Senate Armed Services Committee on March 25 he said, "There are disturbing indications that deliberate efforts are being made to introduce the divisiveness found in our society into the Army." "Divisiveness" is what a free society is all about. If we are divided about Vietnam it is because the

[2] Page 28 of the report on Land Reform in Vietnam by the Stanford Research Institute for AID. It appeared originally in an August 1966 JUSPAO report on "The South Vietnamese Communists and Rural Vietnam."

country is waking up to the lack of candor and the lack
of competence in the way he and the military have been
running the war. The draftees reflect this same disillusion
and dismay, and the same fear that our military are endangering the American economy and the stability of our
society.

Even in his final report on the war Westmoreland is still
relying on the body count as his primary index of military
progress. He wages war by computer. "Since January 1,
1961," he reported to the Senate Armed Services Committee, "the NVA and VC have lost almost four times as many
men killed in battle as have the South Vietnamese and Free
World forces." This ratio, he added, "includes the figures
for 1968, when the enemy lost 5.67 men killed for each
allied soldier killed." The precision verges on caricature.
Body-count statistics have long been a bitter joke among
the troops, but Westmoreland takes them as seriously as a
baseball box-score. Asia is no place for body-count warfare.
Even with a 4-to-1 ratio in our favor, we could easily run
out of American bodies long before we had made a dent in
the teeming millions of Asia.

April 21, 1969

IMMEDIATE WITHDRAWAL
BECOMING A BANDWAGON

Whom the gods would destroy, they first drive inane. At the
press conference last week it was hard to distinguish Nixon
from Agnew. He implied that to criticize his slowdown in
Southern school desegregation—15 years after the Brown
decision—was to ask for "instant integration"! He could
see no ethical problem in replacing Fortas, the judicial
moonlighter, with Haynsworth, the judiciary's most ab-

sent-minded stock speculator. He said there were no American combat troops in Laos, except maybe in certain activities he did not care to discuss. He denied there was any numbers game in picturing the cancellation of 50,000 draft calls for November and December as a sign of approaching peace in Vietnam, although from June to October he had drafted 56,000 *more* men than last year and four days earlier the Pentagon had announced as an economy move that it would be taking 70,300 *fewer* men into the armed services. He rejoiced that at the UN he had found "no significant criticism" of U.S. policy in Vietnam; the Secret Service must have rushed him through the delegates' lounge pretty fast. He is against the Goodell bill to remove all U.S. troops from Vietnam by December 1, 1970 because he wants to get them out sooner, but it is better not to let the enemy know because that would destroy his incentive to negotiate. All we need to bring peace, he said, is a "united front" at home. The united front hasn't been advocated so openly since the 1937 convention of the Communist party. As for the student moratorium of October 15 and the other antiwar demonstrations planned for this fall, Nixon said "under no circumstances" would he "be affected whatever." Before making that remark, he should have phoned that man down on the ranch.

Either the wiretaps at 1029 Vermont Avenue have broken down or Nixon hasn't caught up with the transcripts. That has suddenly become the busiest place in Washington. On the tumultuous eighth floor, with 17 telephones and 11 outside lines, veterans of the McCarthy movement, led by David Hawk and Sam Brown, are swamped by the response to the Vietnam moratorium, a campus study-stoppage for peace on October 15. On the floor above, the more politically unkempt but equally vigorous New Mobilization Committee to End the War in Vietnam is having trouble coping with public response to its November 15 "March Against Death" to Washington and its "No Peace for Nixon" drive, aimed to make his public appearances uncomfortable until all U.S. troops are out of

Vietnam. The best index of the response is that even the bucolic state college in South Dakota where Nixon last June 3 could safely attack student dissent has defected; the names of the Vietnam dead will be read there on October 15 and a "tree of life" planted.

When Howard Zinn in *The Nation* a few years ago first proposed immediate and unconditional withdrawal, he was a political leper. Now this is becoming a bandwagon. When Congressman Allard K. Lowenstein, the founding father of the dump-Johnson movement, called a press conference last week to demand immediate withdrawal, he was flanked by spokesmen for organizations as sedately respectable as ADA and SANE. The next day Senator Goodell, once solidly right-of-center, called a press conference to launch S3000, to cut off all funds for U.S. military personnel of any kind in Vietnam after Dec. 1, 1970. Goodell named it "the Vietnam Disengagement Act." It is his bold move to build a peace and left-of-center constituency for re-election in the face of Republican New York Old Guard unwillingness even to renominate him. The bill brought an anguished cry from Rockefeller, who appointed Goodell to the Senate last year and wishes he hadn't. The Goodell bill gives the peace movement a focus and a target date. It also raises the ante for former Justice Goldberg, Goodell's most probable opponent, who will have to be explicit to match S3000.

Morse and Gruening would hardly recognize the Senate these days. Four Senators, Goodell, Hatfield, McCarthy and McGovern, have already endorsed the October 15 Moratorium. Senator Harris, the chairman of the Democratic National Committee, met with eleven other Senators and twelve Congressmen to extend the moratorium into the halls of Congress. There is talk of a movement to stay away that day and deny both houses a quorum. Senator Fulbright has promised hearings on the Goodell bill; these should provide a continuous antiwar forum. The most striking evidence of the rising rebellion came when Senator Cooper offered an amendment to the $20 billion military authorization bill to forbid any funds for U.S. combat troops in Laos or Thailand. This threw the Pentagon into a dither. Normally the bill would easily have been voted down, but Stennis was so afraid of a vote he decided to sweet-talk it instead. He said he approved its purpose, but sought to de-fang the bill by interpreting it as applicable only to funds available in the $2.5 billion military aid bill. He then voted for it, precipitating unanimous approval, eighty-six to zero. This was the first time in history that the leadership could only block a measure by marshaling a unanimous vote *for* it, albeit trickily reinterpreted. But the maneuver, even if effective, leaves the door wide open to a less ambiguous amendment when the military appropriation bill reaches the Senate.

October 6, 1969

LESSONS FOR NIXON

The United States may have yet to lose a war, but it is an illusion to believe that it has never suffered defeat. Vietnam is our third in Asia, as Castro's Cuba is our second in Latin America. In his book *The Limits of Intervention*, Townsend Hoopes tells us that Johnson, after campaigning as a peace candidate in 1964, ordered combat troops into Vietnam in 1965 because he did not wish to become "the first American President to lose a war." Nixon nine months after his election said the same thing to Steward Alsop of *Newsweek*, to the joy of Brother Joe.

But Vietnam is not the first example of the limits on our power to intervene. The Chinese Nationalists were driven off the mainland despite a small army of American military advisers, arsenals stocked with American arms and several billion dollars in aid. In the Korean war, primitively armed Chinese Communist "volunteers" pushed us back from the Yalu to the thirty-eighth parallel and reoccupied North

Korea even after we had completely crushed the North
Korean armies and leveled just about everything above
ground. In the perspective of Asia, these were victorious
stages in the ebb tide of white imperialism, which began
with Japan's defeat of Russia in 1905. In the perspective of
American policy, China, Korea, and Vietnam are warnings
that we cannot add Asia to Latin America as our imperial
sphere of influence.

Even in the contiguous areas of Latin America, we have
not had everything our own way. Long before the Green
Berets and the CIA, U.S. Marines and operatives, whether
governmental or from U.S. business, dominated the political life of Central America and the Caribbean. Yet Mexico
was a series of defeats for the military-economic warfare an
earlier generation of American anti-imperialists called gun-
boat and dollar diplomacy. From the bombardment of Vera
Cruz in 1913 under Wilson to the world-wide blockade we
imposed on Mexican oil under FDR, we were unable to
stem the successive stages of a nationalist and peasant revolt
that seized—and kept—millions of dollars in U.S. land
and oil properties. Fidel was not the first to defy Yanqui
imperialism and get away with it. Wilson, Roosevelt, Truman, Eisenhower, and Kennedy—at the Bay of Pigs—had
to swallow the bitter pill of political-military defeat, and
did so rather than gamble on a longer and wider war. Nixon
will be in good company if he has to do likewise in Vietnam.

The adjustment to reality is always painful, the recovery
from illusion is never smooth, and relapses are normal.
Hoopes spells out the process brilliantly in his account-
from-within of how Johnson was finally led to de-escalate
the war, and then began to regret it, as Nixon seems to be
doing now. His memoir is given added value because
Hoopes is a defector who had two decades of intimate association with the buildup of the military juggernaut which
has come a cropper in Vietnam. "I too," he writes, "was a

child of the cold war." In 1947–48 he was assistant to the Chairman of the House Armed Services Committee, the military's chief outpost on Capitol Hill. He went from there to the Pentagon, as an assistant to James Forrestal, the first Secretary of Defense, a fanatical cold warrior. He stayed on in the Pentagon as young man of all work for his three successors, Louis Johnson, General Marshall, and Robert Lovett. In 1957 he became secretary to the Military Panel of the Rockefeller Brothers Special Study Project and, with Henry Kissinger, he was a principal draftsman of its report on military policy. He calls this "the pioneering effort" to replace massive retaliation with "the concept of graduated deterrence and flexible response."

This was also, though he does not say so, a blueprint for the military requirements needed to police the world and protect American business and other interests against a wide range of threats, in a time of revolutionary turmoil. Symbolically and practically it came naturally from a study project set up by the Rockefeller Brothers, for it was tailored to the needs of the private empire Standard Oil and Chase Manhattan administer. For them it made no sense to have a muscle-bound military machine which could only threaten a universal nuclear Doomsday when somebody made a pass at their oil wells in Peru.

They finally got from the Democrats what the economy-minded Eisenhower Administration denied them. Under Kennedy and McNamara the armed forces were reshaped to meet the varying levels of violence required for a Pax Americana, and it was under McNamara that Hoopes returned to the Pentagon in 1965 as Deputy Assistant Secretary of Defense for International Security Affairs, i.e., No. 2 man in the Pentagon's own little State Department. This gradually, and his story shows how and why, became infested with doves while the State Department under Rusk remained a nest of hawks. He then moved up to Under Secretary of the Air Force during 1967–69. Thus his return to the Pentagon coincided with Johnson's decision to Americanize the Vietnam war, and he stayed on under Clark

Clifford and helped to turn that policy around. It is quite a
conversion when a man of this background describes the
Vietnamese war as the beginning of the end for the Pax
Americana, though he phrases it less bluntly—

as the probable high watermark of America's tidal impulse to
political military intervention in the period following the
Second World War.

He sees the war also as marking the end of "a doctrinaire
anti-Communism, a social evangelism forming around the
idea of American-financed economic development in the
Third World and an unquestioning faith in the ultimate
efficacy of military alliances and of U.S. military power."
Vietnam was our biggest war of intervention. It cost
easily $100 billion. It tied down close to 800,000 men in
and around Southeast Asia. It cost more casualties than any
war except the Civil War and the two world wars. It is
not strange that the disillusion should also have momentous
dimensions, though this has only begun to dawn on the
principal actors and even on some of the dissenters, who
still regard Vietnam as no more than a blunder.

Perhaps the most important lesson to be drawn from the
experience is that the bigger and more diverse a nation's military establishment the bigger and more diverse the troubles
it will get that nation into. Iceland may be indignant over
what is happening in Southeast Asia but it is fortunately
helpless to do anything about it. Johnson got into Vietnam when and because we were ready to get in. "By
1965," Hoopes writes, "McNamara's prodigious labors to
strengthen and broaden the U.S. military posture were
about completed . . . U.S. 'general purpose' forces were
now organized to intervene swiftly and with modern equipment in conflicts of limited scope, well below the nuclear
threshold."
The Rockefeller Brothers report on military policy had

recommended the reorganization of the armed services into functional commands, which combined naval, air, and army contingents. One such was to be a strike command, framed for swift and distant interventions. Accordingly STRIKE-COM—another of those Pentagon acronymic monsters— had been set up, directly under the Joint Chiefs of Staff, and ready at the President's hand, like the thunderbolts of a new Jove.

This new military capability, Hoopes writes,

had been designed precisely to arrest or restore those deteriorating situations in the world where important or vital U.S. interests were judged to be engaged, to deal with ambiguous subversion-aggressions characterized by little warning and a low silhouette, to blunt national liberation wars.

(How antiseptic it all sounds in the vocabulary of the Pentagon!) Hoopes continues, "To a rational activist like McNamara, with a very thin background in foreign affairs, it seemed entirely logical to employ a portion of this immense U.S. power if that could arrest the spreading erosion in South Vietnam." In retrospect, what McNamara lacked was not a firmer background in foreign affairs, but in human and political understanding. To McNamara the outcome seemed certain. "Surely," as Hoopes explains, "the use of limited U.S. power, applied with care and precision, but with the threat of more to come, would bring a realistic Ho Chi Minh to early negotiations." How do you quantify for a computer the irreducible logic and power of men willing to die?

So the means lay at hand for Johnson's natural pugnacity, and we plunged into the quagmire. What I want to suggest here is that one may deduce from the experience some fundamental axioms of statecraft and history. One is that a large military establishment must justify its existence by finding work to do. The other is that nations which have spent huge sums on a large military establishment will react to complex economic, social, and political problems by trying to solve them with force. What's the good of all those

billions spent on such highly perfected military instruments
if you don't use them? So if you have a STRIKECOM, you
are bound sooner or later to have a Vietnam.

Hoopes's disillusion began early. At the end of 1965 he
sent a memorandum to the late John T. McNaughton, then
his superior as Assistant Secretary of State for International
Security Affairs, which showed an insidious skepticism. He
expressed his doubts about the view held "by Lodge, pro-
ably Westmoreland and maybe McNamara" that the Viet
Cong would just "fade away" when they realized they
could not win, making negotiation unnecessary. This is still
Secretary Rogers's favorite bedtime story, as it was Rusk's.
Hoopes thought the USSR and China too deeply committed to allow the U.S. any such clear-cut victory. He had
the temerity to suggest that were the situation reversed and
150,000 Chinese Communists in Mexico, "it seems reasonable to believe the U.S. would be determined to fight for
decades and even generations to expel them."

Such objectivity was downright subversive, but it began
to spread. By the spring of 1967 McNaughton came back
from a White House conference on the war to tell him
acidly, "We seem to be proceeding on the assumption that
the way to eradicate the Viet Cong is to destroy all the village structures, defoliate all the jungles, and then cover the
entire surface of South Vietnam with asphalt."

Hoopes recorded a similar satiric comment in late 1967
from the famous Major Be, a South Vietnamese officer who
got himself fired because he really tried to win "hearts and
minds" to the detriment of province chiefs more interested
in getting their rake-off from "pacification." "Everyone is a
Communist," Major Be said of the methods used to "pacify" the villages. "Using the police way, every Vietnamese
[in the countryside] would have to be killed and our villages repopulated with Americans." There was nothing
wrong in Southeast Asia which could not be cured by removing Vietnam and the Vietnamese.

Later that year, in his testimony before the Senate Armed Services Committee on the futility of bombing the North, McNamara jolted Johnson into complaining, "That military genius, McNamara, has gone dovish on me." He found himself promoted to head of the World Bank, although its directors had just voted to keep George Wood in office for another year until the end of 1968. "The most Byzantine of American Presidents," Hoopes comments, "had given McNamara a fast shuffle, and had gauged his man's character, inner ambivalence and fatigue well enough to be confident that he would go quietly and suffer the indignity in silence." Thus do men put their loyalty to their bureaucratic team over their loyalty to their country.

It was not safe in the Pentagon to speak one's doubts aloud until the Têt offensive in February, 1968. It showed the idiocy of Westmoreland's view that war was neither strategy nor art but simply extermination, as in termite control. "The doctrine of search-and-destroy," Hoopes writes, "had resulted in scattering U.S. forces all over uninhabited border lands; the Têt offensive had made blindingly clear the fatuousness of Westmoreland's ground strategy."

Têt led to a miniature rising in the halls of the Pentagon. The offensive, Hoopes reports, "performed the curious service of fully revealing the doubters and dissenters to each other, in a lightning flash." Even that veteran "Prussian" cold warrior, Paul Nitze, who had succeeded Cyrus Vance as No. 2 man in the Pentagon, suddenly spoke out— i.e., within the Pentagon—on "the unsoundness of reinforcing weakness" and the need to review Vietnam in the light of American commitments elsewhere. Paul Warnke thought Têt showed our military strategy was "foolish to the point of insanity." Alain Enthoven of the Systems Analysis office used to explain to reporters how a certain quantity of military input would produce an equally certain quantity of guerrilla "output" until the computer curve happily reduced them to zero. Now he began to say, "I fell off the boat when the troop level reached 170,000." The revolt had spread from the Mekong to the Potomac.

The man who precipitated the turnaround on Vietnam was General Westmoreland, with his request in February, 1968, for 206,000 more troops, 100,000 of them in sixty days. This had the full support of the Joint Chiefs of Staff. At a Pentagon conference called by McNamara—his last— to discuss this request, the body count nonsense finally boomeranged in a big way. Secretary of the Navy Paul Ignatius wanted to know why Westmoreland needed so many men in a hurry when we were supposed to have killed 30,000 enemy troops since Têt.

The cost estimates were shocking. McNamara figured that to meet Westmoreland's request would require calling up 400,000 more men for military service and adding $10 billion a year to the $30 billion already being spent on the Vietnam war. Worst of all, there was little reason to believe even these sharp increases would bring victory any closer. In a memorandum to McNamara's successor, Clark Clifford, Hoopes pointed out that based on the manpower ratios in three years of war, the enemy could neutralize an increase of 206,000 in our forces by adding a mere 50,000 to his own.

The final blow was delivered by Dean Acheson, whom Johnson trusted as a veteran cold warrior and hardliner. "With all due respect, Mr. President," Acheson told him in a remark which should serve as a warning to all future incumbents of the White House, "the Joint Chiefs of Staff don't know what they're talking about." This salutary discovery had by then cost $100 billion and some 30,000 lives.

By now the story of how hawks like McGeorge Bundy, Cyrus Vance, and Douglas Dillon among Johnson's senior advisers lost faith in the war has been sufficiently told, though the task of distilling its lessons has hardly begun and not only Acheson but even Clifford has been drawn to some extent into Nixon's camp.[1] The debacle and the

[1] In a disturbing speech (Washington *Star*, October 15), Clifford attacked the Goodell resolution for withdrawal of all troops, combat and

belated awakening were only the latest variant in the old fairy tale about the Emperor's clothes. Is it inevitable in any bureaucracy that few men will be found willing to risk advancement or influence by speaking the truth until the disaster has reached such proportions it can no longer be ignored even by the cowardly and self-serving? How do you design a system for courage? What levers can be substituted for the pull of careerism?

Even now the more important part of the story, because it continues under the Nixon Administration, is that "these prodigious efforts," as Hoopes writes, "did not really change President Johnson's mind about the Vietnam war." In retrospect the period between March 31, 1968, when Johnson de-escalated the bombing of the North, to November 3, 1969, when Nixon threatened to re-escalate the war, appears as a rearguard action to appease antiwar sentiment at home while hoping for victory, military or political, abroad.

The Joint Chiefs may not know what they're talking about, but virtually the same Chiefs remained at Johnson's elbow and at Nixon's. General Wheeler, who also wanted 206,000 troops sent to South Vietnam, is still Chairman, and the only change is hardly for the better—Westmoreland is now Army Chief of Staff, a post to which he was promoted by Johnson. There is no sign that the quality or the tenor of their advice has changed. The civilian rebels have left the government, their job half-done, but the same military bureaucrats are in power, still hoping to snatch a political victory from a military stalemate, or even to escalate the conflict again if they cannot get it. The prestige and future of our huge military establishment is at stake, and its managers

---

support, by the end of 1970 as "unrealistic and impractical," said it would lead to a "bloodbath" in South Vietnam, and declared the country had "a moral obligation" to support Vietnamization of the war. The speech, in a local Washington school, was meant to be off the record but was reported by a Washington *Star* reporter who happened to be present. One result of the speech seems to have been that it torpedoed Fulbright's plan for hearings on the Goodell resolution with Clifford, Harriman, and Cyrus Vance as the first witnesses. The hearings were called off after it became clear that Clifford would oppose the resolution.

may prefer to gamble on a wider war rather than admit that the biggest military machine in human history couldn't win a third-rate war against ill-armed guerrillas with no air force or napalm.

The whole story of Johnson's limited bombing halt has yet to be told. In retrospect, Hoopes notes, it appears that the hardliners "assumed that Hanoi would give a negative response" since it had always insisted on a total halt as a condition for talks. Hoopes does not say so, but a rejection of the Johnson offer could have been made a new excuse for wider bombing. Hanoi surprised Washington by agreeing to talk on the basis of the limited bombing halt, though insisting the talks could only be to arrange a full cessation.

Maxwell Taylor, with the support of Rostow and the Joint Chiefs, began to bombard the President with memoranda on how serious were the military consequences of the limited bombing halt, while Clifford, Harriman, and Vance pressed for a total halt in the bombing of the North since the other side refused to negotiate until it ended. The controversy was bedeviled by the fiction that the bombing halt increased casualties, though as Hoopes wrote in a letter to Clifford, "Present U.S. casualty levels are a function of the U.S. ground strategy in the South; they are only distantly related to the bombing."

Johnson delayed the start of negotiations more than a month by a ludicrous squabble over where to meet, though he had often said he was ready to "meet anywhere, at any time." By autumn, Hoopes reveals, Johnson was telling Clifford "that his primary purpose was now to leave his successor with 'the best possible military posture in Vietnam' "! This was not the remark of a President who took negotiations seriously or had stopped listening to the Joint Chiefs of Staff.

"Clifford argued," Hoopes discloses, "that, for the sake of the President's ultimate standing before the bar of history, he ought to want something much broader and more positive, namely, to leave his successor, 'an ongoing, substantial negotiation, firmly committed to ending the war

and reducing the American involvement in Vietnam.'"
Though Johnson finally ordered a total halt in bombing the
North in October, it was followed by a sharp step-up in the
bombing of Laos and the South, and in offensive operations
on the ground to extend the areas under Saigon's control.

Hoopes says that as the Johnson Administration left
office, ambivalence was at the heart of its Vietnam policy.
"Were we in Paris," he asks, "to negotiate a political compromise on the clearly accepted premise that military
victory was infeasible? Or were we there to stone-wall
Hanoi in the belief that, given enough time, we could grind
out something resembling a military victory in South Vietnam and thus avoid the dangers, and the further affronts to
our prestige, that would attend a compromise political
settlement?" The ambivalence has developed into something worse with Nixon's November 3 speech. Clearly the
second alternative is his aim. He still seeks a political victory, and says he is willing to re-escalate if necessary to get
it.

The strategy of victory through de-escalation began to be
formulated many months before the Têt debacle. As far
back as November, 1966, Westmoreland in Saigon told
Tom Braden, then editor of the Oceanside, California,
Blade-Tribune, that war weariness at home might be dealt
with by reducing U.S. combat operations to 100 a week, or
about the level—the general added charmingly—of the annual toll from auto accidents. An unnamed general I now
believe to have been Westmoreland said in an off-the-record
briefing of correspondents here in Washington more than a
year ago that the fighting would be reduced to a level the
American public would tolerate for a long pull.

A secret scenario by Herman Kahn for appeasing the
peaceniks while holding out for victory began to circulate
in the capital last year. Its main outlines were indicated by
his article "If Negotiations Fail" in *Foreign Affairs* for
July, 1968. There he proposed to "reduce U.S. forces in the

next two or three years to between two and three hundred thousand men," while building up the capacity of the ARVN forces to counter hostilities "with air, artillery and logistic support" by the United States. "To deter a resumption of major hostilities," Kahn also proposed, "the U.S. stations one or two divisions in South Vietnam for a considerable period." That sounds like a preview of Laird's "residual force" and Nixon's "Vietnamization."

In retrospect there appears to be a clear continuity between the Johnson and Nixon Administrations. The theme of "Vietnamization" appeared in Johnson's "abdication" address of March 31, 1968, though little noticed at the time. "We shall accelerate the re-equipment of South Vietnam's armed forces," Johnson said, "in order to meet the enemy's increased firepower. This will enable them progressively to undertake a larger share of combat operations against the Communist invaders." Johnson's warning that we would not accept "a fake solution" foreshadowed Nixon's insistence that a political settlement must include acceptance of the Thieu-Ky regime.

Even the new Agnew-Nixon campaign against dissenters can be traced back to Johnson. It recalls his ferocious attack before the National Farmers Union in Minneapolis on March 18, 1968, on those who would "cut and run" and "tuck our tail and violate our commitments." In that speech, like Agnew and Nixon more recently, Johnson pictured a plot to divide America and obtain by treachery here what the enemy could not win on the battlefield. So long as the enemy, Johnson said, "feels that he can win something by propaganda in the country—that he can undermine the leadership—that he can bring down the government—that he can get something in the Capital that he can't get from our men out there—he is going to keep on trying. But I point out to you that the time has come when we ought to unite, when we ought to stand up and be counted. . . ." This is the same nonsense Nixon elaborated when he said, "Let us be united for peace. Let us be united against defeat. Because let us understand: North Vietnam cannot defeat or humiliate the United States. Only Americans can do that."

This is a new stab-in-the-back myth to absolve the Joint Chiefs and the military bureaucracy for their military and political incompetence. From this common Johnson-Nixon premise, it is a step to Agnew's call at Harrisburg, Pa., October 30, for the polarization of the country and for separating these insidious traitors "from our society—with no more regret than we should feel over discarding rotten apples in a barrel." Even the so-called Guam Doctrine may be traced to Johnson. Less than a month after his "abdication," he was telling General Park of South Korea at their meeting in Honolulu (April 17, 1968), "We wish to see Asia—like Europe—take an increasing responsibility for shaping its own destiny. And we intend and we mean to help it do so."

The Hoopes book shows how isolated Johnson had become, and how hard it was for contrary opinion to get past the Rostow barrier. Nixon is similarly situated, and the hawks are at his ear and elbow, too. William S. White is a credible witness on this point, for he is himself a hawk. In a recent column (*Washington Post*, October 4) he said word had passed to Senate hawks like Tower and Goldwater "that if remorselessly driven to it by final enemy refusal to talk reason and by unbroken dove assault upon the present American posture of marked conciliation, the President has a clear option." This, White went on, "would be not only a halt the process of troop withdrawal but also to order American offensive action on a scale far heavier than is currently seen." A month later just such a threat appeared in the November 3 speech when Nixon said, "If the level of infiltration or our own casualties increase . . . I shall not hesitate to take strong and effective measures to deal with that situation." If this means anything at all, it is a threat to re-escalate.[2]

[2] A glimpse of what the Nixon Administration may be planning can be read in a curious recent Gallup poll (*Washington Post*, October 19). This tested public reaction to a proposal which had not hitherto been broached publicly: "The U.S. would keep aircraft carriers off the coast of Vietnam, to help insure that North Vietnam does not send troops or

White was skeptical about re-escalation but felt there were "certain objective and undeniable realities that point in this direction." The first and greatest of these, White wrote, is the fact that "those members of the White House palace guard who are openly hawkish are far closer to his [Nixon's] elbow every time the hard outlines of this dilemma are put down on the table for discussion than are those more or less dovish members of his entourage." "To be specific," White said, "the big men on foreign crisis" are never Secretary of State Rogers or Under Secretary Richardson. "Always they are, instead, such as Henry Kissinger . . . and a man not much connected with foreign affairs, Attorney General John Mitchell." If the Nixon policy creates more dissent, Mitchell is the man to deal with it and the men he has gathered around him in the Justice Department do not seem likely to let the First Amendment stand in his way.

While Rostow kept telling Johnson he was just like Lincoln, somebody—probably Kissinger—has been suggesting to Nixon that he is Woodrow Wilson. The November 3 speech escalated the rhetoric of the war. It is now another war to end war, with Ho Chi Minh cast as the Kaiser. The Nixon dramaturgy recalls Marx's famous remark in the *18th Brumaire* that history repeats itself, first as tragedy and then as farce. But it may be a costly farce, if Nixon is not forced to cool it.

His November 3 speech began by distorting the origins of the Vietnamese war and ended by distorting the significance of Ho Chi Minh's final private letter to him. Any un-

---

war material into South Vietnam." Where did Gallup get this ominous idea? It was presented as part three of a new three-part peace plan (internationally supervised elections and withdrawal of "troops"—combat only? —within twelve months, were the other two provisions). The plan won 54 percent approval. Equally tantalizing and perhaps related are certain brief items in the news recently about U.S. aircraft carriers steaming out of various ports here and abroad so rapidly that part of their crews were left ashore.

wary listener would be led to believe that the Vietnamese war began fifteen years ago with a Communist aggression to which Eisenhower replied with the first U.S. commitment of aid. The fact is that fifteen years ago Nixon was doing his best to keep peace from breaking out in Indochina. This has been Nixon's pet war for a long time. In the fall of 1953 he went to Indochina and tried to persuade the French not to negotiate. Fifteen years ago, just before the Geneva Conference opened, Nixon told the American Society of Newspaper Editors—in a famous "not for attribution" speech that leaked—that we ought to "put our boys" into Indochina if necessary to prevent a peace settlement from being made.

The interventionist plans of Nixon, Admiral Radford, and John Foster Dulles were vetoed by Eisenhower, after an astringent report from General Ridgway. "Having avoided one total war with Red China the year before in Korea when he had United Nations support," Sherman Adams comments in his memoirs, "he [Eisenhower] was in no mood to provoke another one in Indochina." It was a measure of Nixon's fanaticism, or cynicism, or both that he was asking Eisenhower to plunge into a second Asian land war only a year after Ike had been elected—and kept his pledge—to end another. Nixon showed himself no man to wait for majorities, silent or otherwise. An Indochina war on the heels of Korea would have torn this country apart.

Nixon's speech was as deceitful in discussing the letter he sent to Ho Chi Minh last summer and the letter with which Ho replied a few days before his death. Nixon read his letter but not Ho's on TV, saying that Ho "flatly rejected my initiative." But there was no initiative in Nixon's letter and no flat rejection in Ho's.

The latter, as Muskie pointed out in a little-noticed Senate speech November 7, was couched in conciliatory language and embodied distinct negotiating concessions. It referred to the ten points of the NLF as a "logical and reasonable basis" for settlement rather than as the "only correct basis" as many earlier statements from Hanoi had done. It

referred to "the right of the population *of the South* and of
the Vietnamese nation to dispose of themselves without
foreign influence" (my italics). This was not too different, Muskie pointed out, from Nixon's insistence that "the
people of South Vietnam" have "an opportunity to choose
their own future." Ho's concluding sentence—"with good
will on both sides, we might arrive at common efforts in
view of finding a correct solution to the Vietnam problem"
—was as Muskie said "probably as forthcoming a generality
as the old revolutionary had ever addressed to a Western
leader at any time in his long lifetime."

Muskie also gave Nixon low marks for discretion. "I cannot see how the goal of a negotiated peace," he told an
almost empty Senate chamber, "is promoted by the publication of private diplomatic exchanges. I cannot see how Ambassador Lodge's task of getting meaningful private discussions under way is served by revealing the eleven times he
has been able to meet with the Communist representatives to
date."

One can only conclude that Nixon does not want successful negotiations, for these would involve political compromise. Hoopes spelled out the course Nixon is trying to
avoid. In a memorandum to Clifford shortly after the latter
took office, Hoopes proposed "a cessation of the bombing
to get talks started, as soon as we have regained our military
poise [i.e., after Têt]; a shift of our forces to the primary
task of protecting the population centers; willingness to talk
to the NLF and to accept a coalition government; organization of the international community, including especially
the Soviet Union, to guarantee the military neutralization
of Vietnam, Laos and Cambodia; and ultimately the phased
withdrawal of U.S. forces."

To focus solely on a peacemeal and suspiciously indefinite withdrawal, as Nixon does, is to dodge the hard issues
of negotiation and lull the U.S. public into believing that

peace is on the way. "Vietnamization" means handing over the future of South Vietnam not to its people but to a discredited military junta, one that jails or brushes aside those very elements that are ready to negotiate with the NLF.[3] It is not a new policy, a thoughtful reaction to America's military and political defeat, but an effort to retreat to earlier policies, though these have already proved a failure. It was because a decade of "Vietnamization" under Diem and his successors failed to work that we finally took over the combat operations from which we would now like to disengage.

It is to Hoopes's credit that unlike Clifford he argues that there is no real alternative to complete withdrawal, not only of combat troops but also of the 200,000 or more support and air forces Clifford would leave in indefinitely. Hoopes sees partial withdrawal as "a prescription for an interminable war, partially disguised by the declining level of U.S. participation." He concludes by warning that it would "in fact require our country to sustain a continuing burden of war casualties and heavy dollar costs that would become explicitly open-ended as we leveled off our forces at 100,000 men or thereabouts."

Sooner or later, he says,

the American people would reawaken to the fact that they were still committed to the endless support of a group of men in Saigon who represented nobody but themselves, preferred war to the risks of a political settlement, and could not remain

[3] A substantial non-Communist pro-peace grouping seems to have made its appearance in Saigon and among the exiles in Paris under the leadership of General "Big" Minh and Senator Tran Van Don, the general who led the overthrow of Diem and won a larger vote than any other candidate in the Senate elections. He is head of a Front of National Preservation which could form the basis of an alternative government. In Paris, where the peace forces can speak more freely, its tenor was indicated by a manifesto issued on November 1, South Vietnam's National Day, which celebrates the overthrow of Diem. "It is only by a broad union of forces," the manifesto said, "that we can clearly show the government of the United States that for patriotic Vietnamese the card of anti-Communism has long lost its power in the face of the suffering of the South Vietnamese population under American bombardment" (*Le Monde*, November 1).

in power more than a few months without our large-scale presence.

These are lessons Nixon still refuses to learn.

December 4, 1969
New York Review

THE ATROCITIES NIXON
CONDONES AND CONTINUES

The Pinkville massacre falls into perspective if we remember that from the first days of the struggle against the French, General Giap's strategy has been to fight a "People's War." Without our ever fully realizing it, ours has become an "Anti-People's" war. Some years ago an American colonel, who was never identified, put it very plainly. Mao Tse-Tung, the foremost theoretician of the People's War, said that the guerrilla swims among the people as a fish does in the sea. The U.S. colonel said we would "dry up the sea." Our strategy has been to destroy the villages and the crops, to drive out or kill the people, wherever we suspect Viet Cong. We set out to create a desert where no "fish" could live. The soldiers at Pinkville may not have been ordered to kill women and children but they were certainly ordered to burn down the village and kill the livestock, to destroy their homes and their food supply. If the main target of a "People's War" is to win the confidence and support of the peasantry, the main target of an Anti-People's War is to uproot or destroy the peasantry the guerrillas may have won over. From such a strategy Pinkvilles come naturally.

In the rules of war, soldiers and civilians used to be separate categories. The strategy of the Anti-People's War has given us that legal monstrosity we now read about—the "innocent civilian." This implies that some civilians are innocent and some are guilty. The latter are not only fair game, but the safe rule when in doubt is to shoot first and investigate later, or just add them to the body count. Horrible as this may sound, it has its logic and the logic grows stronger as the spiral of hate mounts on both sides. The guerrillas use civilians in their area—like the home population in any war—for many auxiliary tasks. The civilians—including women and children—take up those tasks ever more willingly as they see their homes and livestock, their menfolk and ancestral graves, destroyed by indiscriminate bombing and artillery fire and by "search and destroy" missions like the one in Pinkville. Relations are not improved by calling them "gooks" or—more politely, as in Lieutenant Calley's indictment—"Oriental human beings." They retaliate with home-made mines and booby traps, including the "ponji," the sharpened stick coated with excrement. The biggest and dirtiest booby trap of all is the filthy pit of this war itself, from which we emerge stinking in the nostrils of mankind.

There is a flurry of stories from Saigon about "reindoctrinating" troops on the humane treatment of civilians. But we are dealing here not with an occasional atrocity but with a deliberate policy. What a fear-crazed and hate-filled GI may do in occupying a hostile village can be put down to the brutalization of war. The real crime is higher up. When the President announced that he was revising our chemical and bacteriological warfare program and sending the Geneva Protocol to the Senate for ratification, it looked like a gesture of contrition. It turned out to be the most hypocritical kind of public relations. For it excepted from these restrictions the two weapons of gas and chemical warfare from which the civilian population of Vietnam suffer most. These are the tear and lung gases which drive them out of their home-made bomb shelters into the open where our B-52's and fragmentation "anti-personnel" bombs can destroy them, and the herbicides which kill their crops and threaten—like Thalidomide—their unborn children.

How can we convince the world that we have not turned barbarian when a White House announcement, designed to take the curse off Pinkville and demonstrate our concern for international law, perpetuates a gross violation of it? We refer to the use of crop-killers. It is said that the Geneva Protocol banning chemical warfare does not mention herbicides. True. But earlier treaties to which we are a party do. The Army Field Manual (FM27–10) in paragraph 37 cites that provision of the Hague Convention of 1907 which says, "It is especially forbidden . . . to employ poison or poison weapons." The Army interpretation which follows says this "does not prohibit measures . . . to destroy, through chemical or bacteriological agents, harmless to man, crops intended *solely* [my emphasis] for consumption by the armed forces (if that fact can be determined)." But even this tortuous sophistry admits we may not destroy crops just because we believe *some* of the supplies may feed guerrillas, and that we may not employ chemical or bacteriological agents which *are* harmful to humans.

Two years ago the Japan Science Council[1] released a report on anticrop warfare in Vietnam which said nearly 1,000 peasants and more than 13,000 livestock had been killed by it. Han Swyter, a former aide to Secretary McNamara, told the House Foreign Affairs Committee December 2 that since 1962 we have sprayed about 100 million pounds of herbicides over four million acres, an area the size of Massachusetts. He said that since late 1967 there have been increasing reports and pictures in the Saigon press of a new kind of abormality in newly born children. These reports have found confirmation in a still secret report for the National Cancer Institute (see *Scientific Research*, November 10) which found that one herbicide, 2,4,5-T was "probably dangerous" and 2,4-D "potentially dangerous" as teratogenic agents, i.e., capable, like Thalidomide, of producing gross birth defects if ingested by pregnant women. As a result the Pentagon has "restricted" the use of the first,

[1] P. 153 of Seymour M. Hersh's indispensable recent book *Chemical and Bacteriological Warfare* (New York: Bobbs-Merrill).

but not the second, substance to areas remote from human population. But how much reliance can be placed on this restriction remains to be seen and the crop-killing itself goes on. So will the civilian-killing, via the tear-gas route. The government's position is that the Geneva Protocol does not cover tear gas. The Protocol itself speaks of "asphyxiating, poisonous or *other* gases" (my italics). The British government ever since 1930, like many other signatories of the Protocol, has held that tear gases, too, are outlawed. Congressman McCarthy (D. N.Y.) told a Montreal audience December 1 that when in London he heard the U.S. government was pressuring the British government to change its position on tear gas. This is not academic in Britain. Imagine the massacre during the blitz if the Nazis had been able to flush people out of the subways and other shelters with tear gases before the bombing, as we do in Vietnam.

The enormous quantities of tear and lung gas we use in Vietnam—almost 14 million pounds since 1964, or more than half the total weight of the mustard gases used by both sides in World War I—testify how far we have gone from exceptional use in "riot-like" circumstances to routine application before bombardment. These are the atrocities Nixon condones and continues.

December 15, 1969

NIXON, INFLATION AND THE WAR

Like Lyndon Johnson, Nixon plays the numbers game. In his TV address on the Health, Education and Welfare veto, he said the new budget for fiscal 1971 would call for "a smaller percentage of federal spending for defense than in

any year since 1950." This tricky wording is deceptive. In
fiscal 1950 total federal spending was $76.7 billion and the
military took $13 billion, or about 16 percent. The fiscal
1971 budget on the other hand will be in the neighborhood
of $198 billion. The best information available (*Aviation
Week*, January 26, 1970) as this is written, almost a week
before the new budget is to be published, places the military's portion at $71.1 billion. That is about 35 percent of
total federal outlays, or twice the percentage in 1950, and
the total is five and a half times as great. It is $20 billion—
or 40 percent—larger than military spending in the most
costly year of the Korean war, and less than $20 billion be-
low the peak year of the Second World War. That is
not much to boast about when Vietnam is supposed to be
tapering off.

Despite a flood of figures about cuts, military spending is
tapering off very slowly. So is the Vietnam war. Although Defense Department appropriations for the current
fiscal year are $5.3 billion below last year, this has yet to be
reflected in actual spending. The latest Treasury cash dis-
bursal figures show that on January 22, after almost seven
months of this fiscal year, total Department of Defense
spending was almost $400 million *greater* than in the corre-
sponding period of fiscal 1969. If the current rate is projected for the rest of the fiscal year, actual spending would
be almost $78 billion, or $6 billion more than has been budgeted. This is possible because (as the House appropriations
report on fiscal 1970 noted) the military has almost $40 bil-
lion in unexpended balances from past years. From an inflationary point of view, it is the spending that counts. This
spending record makes the disputed extra $1 billion on the
Health, Education and Welfare bill look like a minor matter.
It is indeed about one-half of one percent of the total
budget and one-tenth of one percent of Gross National
Product. In stressing it, Nixon was straining at a gnat while
swallowing a camel.

The main source of the inflation is military spending, and
the biggest single item is still the Vietnam war. If Nixon

were seriously preparing to get out of it as soon as possible, he would be emphasizing this. Instead the veto broadcast, like the State of the Union message, distracts attention from the role of the war in inflation, and seeks instead to blame the inflation on general Democratic spending policies. This is the impression created when he said the inflation was caused by a cumulative $57 billion deficit in the decade of the sixties. This again gives a false picture. Deficits have been the rule during the past two decades. The Republicans under Eisenhower and Nixon only balanced the budget in three of their eight years in office, and their biggest deficit, $12 billion in fiscal 1959, and 50 percent greater than any Democratic deficit until Johnson plunged into the Vietnam war in 1965.

Truman, by raising taxes and imposing excess profits taxes, kept deficit financing within bounds during the Korean war. Johnson used deficit financing for three years without objection from the Republicans either to the war or to his failure to prevent inflation by raising taxes to meet the cost. The result was a cumulative deficit of almost $38 billion for the first three years of the war, from fiscal 1966 (which began July 1, 1965) through fiscal 1968. This was the biggest inflationary shot in the arm for the economy since World War II. By the Pentagon's own latest figures, the Vietnamese war by next June 30 will have cost us $104.5 billions in 5 years, or an average of $25 billion a year. It is this stupendous and wasteful expenditure which provided a stock market boom for the well-to-do and set off the inflation eating into the average family's budget. This is why we are paying now with a business contraction and an unemployment rise to get the inflation under control. The poor pay the most, but every family pays some of these hidden "taxes" which inflation and deflation impose. The cause is the Vietnam war.

The latest Pentagon projection for the cost of the war in the fiscal year beginning July 1 is $17 billion. This is $6.2 billion less than the projected cost this fiscal year. If this "peace dividend" were made available to civilian needs,

then the new Department of Defense budget ought to be
$6.2 billion below the $71.6 billion budget for fiscal 1970.
The figure which leaked from the Pentagon to industry
sources for fiscal 1971, however, is $71.1 billion. If this is
correct then the Pentagon gets all but half a billion of that
"peace dividend." So while Nixon is picking a major political fight over $1 billion more for education, and represent-
ing this as somehow crucial in the battle against inflation,
the military is quietly adding to its expenditures $5 billion
or more in expected savings on the Vietnam war.

*Nixon is playing down the significance of the Vietnam
war in the inflationary picture because he is in no hurry to
bring it to a close.* He has been encouraged in this by public
apathy, and the comfortable belief that the war is practically over. In this connection I want to call attention to pas-
sages in the State of the Union message which are most disturbing. These repeatedly emphasized a "just peace." Just
what Nixon means by a just peace was nowhere made clear.
He wants "our generation" to be remembered "not so much
as the generation that suffered in war" but for "the courage
and character" to win "the kind of a just peace that the next
generation was able to keep." Courage and character are
only necessary if the struggle is to be long drawn out. This
is an echo of the Johnson-Rusk rhetoric which portrayed
the leader of a tiny Southeast Asian country as if he were
Der Feuhrer of a major Western military power which
threatened world conquest. Any compromise in this perspective was "Munich" all over again, a case of appeasement, buying peace now at the expense of war later. If
Vietnam is of that importance, it is our duty to stick until
we have won victory. That's how Johnson and Rusk saw it.
Is that how Nixon sees it too?

What is a "just peace" in Vietnam? Is it "just" to keep
this divided country plunged into bloodshed until we have
shown that the Pax Americana dare not be challenged?
Does a just peace mean continuing the fighting, whether we
carry the main military burden or the South Vietnamese
army does, until South Vietnam is firmly established like

South Korea in the American sphere of influence? Is it a just peace to impose a military dictatorship on the South Vietnamese people in the process? Is it just to support a regime which denies them freedom of press and political activity? Is it just to avoid any compromise which would bring the terrible bloodshed to an end? What does Nixon mean by "justice" in this context? What is he asking us to show "courage and character" for? Was he afraid to use the plainer term "patience" to a country impatient for an end of the fighting? Is it "just" to ask the American people to go on tightening their belts, eschewing urgent reforms, postponing necessary social expenditures to pursue the same Johnson-Rusk dream of a final political (and therefore military) victory in a far-off Asian country?

There are other indications that Nixon is settling down for a long pull in Vietnam. Stuart H. Loory in the *Los Angeles Times*, January 20, called attention to one. In his December 8 press conference, Nixon said "We have a plan for the reduction of American forces in Vietnam, for removing all combat forces from Vietnam, regardless of what happens in the negotiations." But on January 19, three days before the State of the Union message, his press secretary, Ron Ziegler, told the press the goal was "to remove American troops from a combat role in Vietnam." As Mr. Loory pointed out, "There is a big difference between removing troops from a combat role, while possibly leaving them in Vietnam, and removing combat troops from the country altogether." But in response to questions Mr. Ziegler three times repeated the same formula. It fits with earlier indications that the plan is to leave sufficient combat troops in Vietnam to protect the installations from which our air, artillery and other auxiliary forces would operate in support of the South Vietnamese army. Obviously we don't have enough faith in "Vietnamization" to trust these installations to the protection of the ARVN troops.

To "remove American troops from a combat role" is to move them into enclaves, not enclaves in preparation for a cease-fire, as in the Gavin plan, but into enclaves which would be fortresses from which our support troops would help ARVN continue the war until they get what Nixon and Thieu consider a just peace. Since our half-million troops were about equally divided between combat and support forces, this new formula could easily mean a minimum of 300,000 troops in South Vietnam for a protracted stay. The peak year of Vietnam expenditures was fiscal 1969, Johnson's last, ending June 30, 1969. The Pentagon, which doesn't overestimate these things, figures the cost that year at $28.8 billion. Half that would be $14 billion. A force of 300,000, or 50,000 more than half, could easily cost $17 billion, which is what the Pentagon figures for the next fiscal year. That's a lot of money when we're pinching everything else.

Nixon's State of the Union message reminded me of so many mediocre sermons I covered years ago as a cub reporter. It had the same innocuous "inspirational" rhetoric, firmly against sin—in this case pollution—but not so specifically as to alarm any rich parishioners. It is appalling that all this self-congratulatory purple prose is taken so seriously by our communication media. It served only to hide a reality the country must face. Until the Vietnam war is over, the fight against inflation cannot be won. Until that fight is won, every effort at ending pollution and our other social ills is doomed by high interest rates, constricted credit and a business slowdown. Peace in Vietnam is the first priority. Withdrawal is the first necessity. "It is time," Nixon said of the litter in the cities, "for those who make massive demands on our society to make some minimal demands on themselves." This a dirty dig at the blacks and the poor in the ghettoes. It will be much appreciated in white Southern country clubs.

We would like to turn the dig around. Who makes the most massive demands on our society? The Pentagon. It is time the military was forced to make the minimal acknowledgment that the Vietnam war is not worth its enormous cost from any point of view, and that we cannot face the problems crowding in on us until we get our troops out. Until then, talk of ending the pollution of our air and water, the erosion of our resources, the decay of our cities and the racial polarization of our country is just the kind of Billy Graham hot air in which Richard Nixon loves to indulge.

February 9, 1970

━━━━━━━━

NIXON'S IRON CURTAIN ON THE COST OF THE WAR

Nixon's new budget takes secrecy in government two steps beyond LBJ. Nixon has blacked out the cost of the war in Vietnam and he has also blacked out military spending from his budgetary projections for the next four years. "A budget," Nixon said in his message, "must be a blueprint for the future." In his blueprint these two main parts are missing. "In the past," Nixon said about his new four-year projections, "the federal government has been unwilling to pull all the pieces together and present the results of projecting Government finances into the future." He said this was essential for "an enlightened discussion of public policies even though precise figures are, of course, impossible." Why then omit expenditures which eat up more than half the general revenues of the government?

Contradictory explanations have been given for blacking out the cost of the war. In the press briefings which preceded the release of the budget, the Pentagon briefers disagreed with the Budget Bureau briefers. The Pentagon briefers said the figures had been left out deliberately, so as not to tip off the President's plans. Budget Director Robert P. Mayo, on the other hand, implied that no such figure had been calculated. A Pentagon official put it bluntly to a persistent newsman, "I didn't say there wasn't a dollar figure. I am saying I am not going to tell you what it is." The clearest statement on the record is hidden away on page 81 of the main budget volume. "We expect," it says—

that further troop withdrawals can be made in the future. However, U.S. actions depend upon the actions of the other side in Paris and on the battlefield, as well as progress in Vietnamization. Consequently estimates are not shown for either the size or the timing of our future actions. Because of the need to maintain the security of the plan, certain information included in recent budgets does not appear this year.

The first part of this statement implies that there is no timetable because this depends on Hanoi and Saigon. The final sentence implies that Nixon does have one but is keeping it secret so as not to tip his hand. We expect this will confuse the enemy as much as it will the Congress.

Until now the only items known to be kept secret in the U.S. budget have been the expenditures of the CIA and the various military intelligence agencies. Now the Vietnam war has been added. This should be an issue for the Democrats. Yet the statement on national priorities just issued by the Democratic Policy Council, their more militant or less pusillanimous wing, does no more than say weakly that while it welcomes the cuts announced in the Pentagon budget, "the Administration's figures on expenditures make it difficult to assess the nature and extent of the military reductions which have been proposed." Protest could hardly be worded more feebly. This is what happens when certain lobbyist-lawyers double in brass as Nixon advisers and liberal Democrats.

The blackout hides the size of the peace dividend. The Administration would like to expunge even the phrase. Budget Director Mayo referred to it scornfully as a "rather oddball concept." The decision to keep it secret must have been taken at the last moment. About ten days before the budget was released the Pentagon information office was still telling reporters that the cost of the war during the next fiscal year would be about $17 billion. When Secretary Laird first gave out this figure in October, 1969, he said this would mean a $13 billion saving over the $30 billion the war cost in fiscal 1969, its peak. Total military costs in 1969 ("defense by function") were $81.2 billion. But total military costs budgeted for fiscal 1971, instead of being $13 billion less than that (or $68.2 billion) are $73.5 billion, or only $7.7 billion less. This means that non-Vietnam military spending is *up* by $5.3 billion. This *increase* in non-Vietnam military spending is itself more than twice as large as total outlays budgeted for natural resources ($2.5 billion) including air and water despite all Nixon's "now or never" rhetoric on pollution.

This may understate the realities. Proxmire in a Senate speech February 10 estimated that the Pentagon "has heisted $10 billion of the peace dividend." He takes into account not only Laird's predicted cut in Vietnam war costs but his announcement last October 16 that henceforth the Pentagon would plan its level of forces for one major and one minor war instead of two major and one minor wars, as it has since the Kennedy-McNamara period. Proxmire said the money thus saved is going to strategic hardware, including the second phase of the ABM, conversion of Polaris into the MIRVed Poseidon, on which the overruns are now $3 billion; into MIRVed Minuteman III, where the overruns are also about $3 billion; into the Navy, which is getting $2.6 billion to modernize the fleet, an increase of $1 billion over 1967–69 expenditures; and into a huge AWACS, over-the-horizon warning system. "Some $18 billion has already been spent for SAGE and AWACS," Proxmire said of these two anti-bomber systems, "even though the Russians have no modern intercontinental bomber. These huge funds were expended to meet a non-existent threat." This is hardly austere military budgeting.

This brings me to the related blackout the Nixon Administration is imposing on military spending and planning. "We have learned," Nixon said in the economic report, "that 1-year planning leads to almost as much confusion as no planning at all." He said that was why he was opening up the books, and making long-range projections "that will enable the people to discuss their choices more effectively."

He published a four-year projection which shows, among other things, that Nixon's new civilian initiatives including welfare and pollution will go up from $3 billion in the first year to $18 billion in the fourth. Yet there are no similar projections on the military side.

When Budget Director Mayo was on *Meet The Press* February 8, Edwin L. Dale, Jr., of the *New York Times* said, "Your four-year projection of the grand total of government spending under current programs of something like $240 billion is hard to make sense of unless you have an idea of what the defense assumptions are." Mr. Dale asked whether the grand totals assumed "the current force levels, the pre-Vietnam force levels, the levels at the end of the new fiscal year? What?" The Budget Director replied, "We preferred not to be too specific." Mr. Mayo would disclose no more than that the overall four-year projections assumed "a considerable lessening of the expenditures for Vietnam" and also "the effect of higher prices on all weapons systems" though at a lower rate of inflation. "We have also worked in," he added as a final concession, "what we think is a reasonable projection on the military side." But both the details and the totals on the military side were blacked out.

There is an interesting revelation in this connection at page 77 of the annual report of the President's Council of Economic Advisers. It shows that elaborate studies and projections *have* been made on the military as well as the civilian side. It says—

Among the most important steps in this direction have been the interrelated studies conducted through the National Security Council and the Cabinet Committee on Economic Policy. These studies examined alternative defense strategies with their associated costs and alternative nondefense programs. Various defense strategies were translated with rough accuracy into a large number of possible forces and budgets. Similarly alternative nondefense federal programs were developed.

How can Nixon say that he is making long-range four-year projections available to "enable the people to discuss their choices more effectively" when the military side of these projections—by far the biggest single share—is hidden from them? "We must become increasingly aware," Nixon also said in the Budget Message, "that small decisions today often lead to large cash outlays in the future." Of no part of the budget is this more resoundingly true than the military sector. A speech by Congressman Reuss in Milwaukee February 10 provided a swift glimpse of such "small decisions" and the large cash outlays they entail. "There is a $1.5 billion item for the ABM," Reuss said of the new budget, "expected ultimately to cost anywhere from $10 to $50 billion. There is $87 million for AWACS, a new airborne radar system with an ultimate $15-billion price tag. There is almost a billion dollars for continued deployment of the Navy's new F-14 fighter plane, with an expected total program cost of up to $36 billion. There is $370 million in the budget for a start on the F-15, the Air Force's new superiority jet fighter. Costs of this program are expected to exceed $25 billion." These programs impose a heavy mortgage on future budgets, but these are among the military commitments blacked out.

If the budget were candid, the public would see that all the projected spending on welfare and pollution are peanuts compared to the military outlays. Of the grand four-year total of $240 billion, the military portion must be somewhere between a third and a half, or between $80 and $120 billion. These colosssal sums imply a continuation of the arms race, indeed a new spiral in it, for that is what the go-ahead decisions on ABM and MIRV mean. The military only has to drag its heels a few months longer and it will be too late for the SALT talks to be anything more than futile palaver.

The budget presentation is shot through with deceit. "For the first time in two full decades," Nixon boasted in the message, "the federal government will spend more money on human resource programs than on national defense." This was illustrated with a pie chart showing 41 cents of the budget dollar going to human resources and only 36 cents to national defense. But if the government's huge social security and other trust fund receipts are deducted, we can see that the military spends 53 cents of every dollar of the general revenues.

If the huge social security payments and other trust funds are deducted from the "human resources" account, then we see that these get only seven cents of every dollar of general revenues. Even so, "human resources" are padded by including in them $8.5 billion of veterans benefits, although up to now these have been on the national defense side of the budget as part of the cost of fighting past wars. As for the fight against pollution, this is buried in "natural resources," which altogether get one and two-tenths cents of every dollar in the consolidated budget, *one-tenth of a cent less than last year*. The total appropriations asked to fight pollution of the air ($106 million) and water ($465 million) next year total $571 million. In a budget in which 53 cents of every general revenue dollar goes to the military, only four-tenths of a cent will go to save the air we breathe and the water we drink though it may soon be too late to save them. Nixon's anti-pollution rhetoric is miles from his budgetary realities.

February 23, 1970

ONLY THE BUMS CAN
SAVE THE COUNTRY NOW

The race is on between protest and disaster. Despite the first four martyr "bums" of Nixon-Agnewism at Kent State, the college shutdown their deaths precipitated, the outpouring of student and other protesters here last weekend, the campus lobbyists beginning to flood the halls of Congress, the Senate resolutions to limit or end Indochinese military operations, and the smoldering near-revolt within the Nixon Administration itself, we are still on the brink. We are in the first stages of a new and wider war from which withdrawal will be difficult. The military holds the reins and can precipitate new provocations and stage new alarms. The only hope is that the students can create such a Plague for Peace, swarming like locusts into the halls of Congress, that they stop all other business and make an end to the war the No. 1 concern it ought to be. Washington must no longer be the privileged sanctuary of the warmakers. The slogan of the striking students ought to be "Suspend Classes and Educate the Country." I see no other visible and adequate means to stop the slide into a conflict that may sweep very suddenly beyond the confines of Indochina if the man who gambled on Cambodia ends by gambling on the use of nuclear weapons.

In a dispatch from a landing zone in Cambodia, Jack Foisie of the *Washington Post* (May 8) described GIs jumping from helicopters under enemy fire with derisive denunciations of the war scrawled on their helmets. One of those he copied down sums up the situation of the whole country in this war. "We are the unwilling," it said, "led by the unqualified, doing the unnecessary, for the ungrateful." As usual the country is not being told the truth about why we went into Cambodia. In his war address of April 30 Nixon pictured the attack across the border as a pre-emptive exercise to hit an "enemy building up to launch massive attacks on our forces and those of South Vietnam." It was described as a swift preventive action from which we would soon withdraw and which was not part of any broader intervention in Cambodian affairs.

But thanks to the indiscretion of one Congressman, we now have the private—and more candid—version given members of Congress at special State Department briefings. This puts the origins and purpose of the Cambodian action in a very different light. The Congressman is Representative Hamilton Fish (R. N.Y.), a right-winger who has long questioned the logic of our heavy commitment in so peripheral an area as Southeast Asia. In a letter to constituents

released May 13, Mr. Fish summarizes a private briefing by
Under Secretary of State Richardson for selected members
of Congress. Nixon said we moved across the border to nip
enemy plans for an imminent attack. But from Richardson's
briefing, Mr. Fish reports, "It was clear that the present
military thrust into Cambodia hinged largely on the report-
edly surprise overthrow of Prince Sihanouk." Nixon said in
his April 30 speech that for five years "neither the U.S. nor
South Vietnam moved against those enemy sanctuaries because we did not wish to violate the territory of a neutral
nation." But Richardson gave the Congressmen a different
story. He told them, "U.S. intelligence had known for years
of those enclaves from which attacks on South Vietnam
have been launched" but we had never attacked them before "because it was feared that Sihanouk would counter
any invasion by allowing NVA [North Vietnamese
Army] forces to enlarge their occupied areas."

Sihanouk was trying to maintain a precarious neutrality
by playing one side against the other. Nixon was deceitful
when he said in the April 30 speech that our policy since the
Geneva Conference of 1954 "has been to scrupulously respect the neutrality of the Cambodian people" and added
—as proof of our virtue—that since last August we have
had a diplomatic mission in Pnom Penh "of fewer than 15"
and that for the previous four years "we did not have any
diplomatic mission whatever." The truth is that Sihanouk
ousted our mission and broke relations in 1965 because he
claimed the CIA had been plotting against him for years
and even tried twice to kill him. Sihanouk was especially
resentful of the Khmer Serei (Free Khmer) mercenaries the
CIA and our Special Forces had enlisted from among Cambodians living in South Vietnam and Thailand to act as an
anti-Sihanouk commando force. The CIA gave it facilities to
broadcast anti-Sihanouk propaganda from Saigon.

"For the past five years," Nixon said with bland hypocrisy, "we have provided no military assistance and no economic assistance whatever to Cambodia." He did not explain that Sihanouk threw out our military mission because

he said it had been trying to turn his armed forces against him, and gave up economic aid, too, rather than have it used as a cover for U.S. agents trying to overthrow him. This was not a figment of Sihanouk's imagination. As far back as 1958, in a police raid on the villa of one of his generals, Sihanouk found a letter from President Eisenhower pledging full support to a projected coup and to a reversal of Cambodian neutrality. This was part of a "Bangkok plan" worked out between the dictators of South Vietnam and Thailand (Diem and Marshal Sarit Thanarit) to dismember Cambodia and instigate civil war (see William Worthy's account in the York, Pa., *Gazette & Daily* of April 30). When Sihanouk resumed relations last August, in his desperate see-saw between the two sides, his condition was that the U.S. mission be kept small. He didn't want too many CIA agents roaming around.

That was poor Sihanouk's mistake. Cambodia neutrality was ended when the military we had long wooed finally overthrew Sihanouk on March 18. The most complete account yet published of the events leading up to the coup is to be found in *Le Monde Diplomatique* for April. It is by Daniel Roy, a Frenchman with 15 years' experience in Indochina who was for a time press attaché to Prince Sihanouk. He claims that funds for the coup were provided by a Cambodian adventurer turned banker in Bangkok who was associated in the enterprise with the notorious Son Ngoc Thanh, puppet President of Cambodia under the Japanese occupation. The latter fled to Thailand after the war and according to M. Roy is "today in the service of the CIA." M. Roy also charges that the coup was prepared by Khmer Serei forces who went over the border with their arms and wives and pretended that they were defecting to Sihanouk. They infiltrated the army and the police as a Trojan Horse for the CIA.

Let us now return to Congressman Fish's account of the private State Department briefing. "Following the fall of Sihanouk," the Congressmen were told, "the new anti-Communist government cut all supply lines [of the NVA and Viet Cong] except the Ho Chi Minh trail" which, of course, lies largely outside Cambodian territory. "*To resecure their severed supply routes,*" the account in the private briefing continued, "*VC and NVA began moving out of the enclaves, thereby threatening the overthrow of the Cambodian government*" (my italics). It is "against this background," Representative Fish's account of the briefing concludes, "that the American-South Vietnamese strikes into Cambodia were ordered."

The sequence is quite different from that given publicly by Mr. Nixon. Instead of preparing an attack on our forces in South Vietnam, the enemy was reacting to an attack on its supply lines. This upset the status quo, and risked a complete take-over of Cambodia by the other side. We intervened to save it from the consequences. Did our government give the new Lon Nol government of Cambodia assurances that we would defend it if its action in cutting all the supply routes precipitated an attack upon it?

It is true that at the State Department briefing "it was stressed that the present attacks were not aimed at either the confrontation of the estimated 40,000 to 50,000 VC and NVA believed operating in Cambodia or the defense of the present government of Cambodia. The raids were described as strictly 'spoiling actions,' aimed at supply, bunker and communication network destruction" and to give the South Vietnamese army additional time while the enemy rebuilds its supplies. But you have to be pretty feeble-minded to accept this at face value. What if Sihanouk, with NVA and Peking support, is restored to power, this time not as a precarious neutral but as an ally of the other side? What if we are then faced with the prospect, not just of restoring the old supply lines and bases but of Cambodia turning into one big enemy base? Who can believe that the Nixon Administration will stand by and let this happen?

This is the wider war which lies ahead. The overthrow of Sihanouk was a grave political mistake. It gave the other side a new ally with legitimacy and mass support, basic necessities for the Indochinese People's War which has already been proclaimed against us. The situation inside Cambodia was succinctly summed up in an interview which the pro-Nixon and pro-war *U.S. News & World Report* for May 18 held by cable with its correspondent, James N. Wallace, in Pnom Penh:

Q. Have the allied attacks in eastern Cambodia saved the rest of the country from a Communist take-over?

A. No. Unless the allied drive completely overwhelms the Communists, Cambodia's position remains about the same . . . the short-run result is even more chaos and confusion . . .

Q. Did the Cambodians welcome the Allied move?

A. Again, no. Cambodians do not like . . . the idea of South Vietnamese troops' rolling across Cambodia . . .

Q. What kind of reception would Sihanouk get?

A. Almost certainly he would receive more popular support than the Lon Nol government cares to admit. Sihanouk still is popular among a great many of Cambodia's 5.5 million peasants, who respected his traditional status as a god-king and liked his earthly personal relations with villagers.

The French journalist Max Clos, who has been covering Indochina for years during both the French and U.S. wars, foresees (*Le Figaro*, May 2–3) a Cambodian resistance based on peasant support, doing in their country what the Viet Cong have done in Vietnam and creating a "liberated zone" from which in time they will be able to take over Pnom Penh. "Mr. Nixon," M. Clos wrote, "hopes to withdraw his troops from Cambodia in a month and a half. Even if he succeeds, it is safe to predict he will have to send them back again."

The political folly of our latest move is not limited to Cambodia. The newly enlarged war must add to the shaky character of the Thieu regime, which has had to close down all the South Vietnamese schools in a rising student revolt much like our own. The idea of South Vietnamese troops being used to bolster a government which has been massacring Cambodian citizens of Vietnamese origin must add to Thieu's unpopularity. The bitterness between the Viets and the Khmers of Cambodia is incomparably older and more bitter than the recent animosities of the Russo-American cold war. It is only two centuries since the Viets seized the Mekong delta from the Khmers. Sihanouk, unlike his successors, never stirred up the mob against the Vietnamese and the VC and NVA intruders, unlike our forces, did not bomb and devastate Cambodian villages. This new shift strengthens the forces opposing our puppets on both sides.

This has been a political war from its very beginning against the French. We go on believing as they did that a political problem can be solved by military means. The annals of their war, like ours, is full of sensationally billed search-and-destroy operations which were finally going to cripple the rebels, like this latest "Operation Total Victory" across the Cambodian border. The Communists under Ho Chi Minh seized national leadership in the war against the French, as the adroit Sihanouk did in Cambodia. Now they both are allied against us. Sihanouk will now make it possible for the other side to implement the basic strategy of a People's War on a wider scale. The strategy is to force maximum dispersion upon the hated foreign invader to make him widen the area of his activity and stretch his lines of communication so that the guerrillas can pick and choose the most advantageous weak points for their concentrated attacks. We have picked up their treacherous gambit by invading Cambodia and sooner or later unless we get out of Indochina altogether, we must send ground troops into Laos and Cambodia, perhaps even into North Vietnam where a fresh army of 250,000 or more awaits our landing. Nowhere has airpower, however overwhelming and unchallenged, been able to win a war.

What will happen when the country wakes up to find that instead of withdrawing troops we are going to send in fresh divisions? What happens to inflation, the budget and the stock market? To student and racial unrest? Nixon, in a mood of self-pity, complained in his April 30 address that past war Presidents did not have to face a nation "assailed by counsels of doubt and defeat from some of the most widely known opinion leaders of the nation." He seems to

attribute this to some perversity. He takes it as personal. He
does not stop to consider why this war has aroused so much
more opposition than any past war, and done so in every
class and every region and every age-group, from Wall
Street financiers to campus radicals. Even National Guardsmen give the V-sign to students, and soldiers go into battle
with peace amulets around their necks. He seems to think
there is something wrong with the critics. He will not face
up to the possibility that there is something wrong with the
war. Certainly this generation of Americans would prove
no less patriotic and brave than any other if our country
were really in danger.

It is a measure of our stupid leadership that the Cambodian war was started on the phoney pretext that just across
the border was a kind of enemy Pentagon and that we
could cripple the enemy by smashing it. One measure of the
mendacity may be found in an intelligence briefing the
New York Times reported April 4, two weeks after Sihanouk's overthrow. It said COSVN, the enemy HQ, had
been moved from Cambodian to South Vietnamese territory. The story even carried a map showing the old location at Mimot—which figures in recent accounts of the
Cambodian operation—in the "fishhook" and the new location in a thick jungle area described as "virtually inacces-
sible to ground troops" and "probably not seriously vulnerable to air attacks." It is difficult to believe that Nixon and
his aides are such idiots as not to be aware of this intelligence
information.

The Eichmann trial taught the world the banality of evil.
Nixon is teaching the world the evil of banality. The man
so foolish as to talk to protesting students about football
and surfing is the same man who (like Johnson) sees war in
the puerile terms of "humiliation" and a challenge to his
virility. He doesn't want us to be a "helpless giant" (which
we are in Indochina) so he is plunging us into a wider quagmire where we will end up more helpless than ever.

The past week is the week in which the Nixon Administration began to come apart. Letters like Hickel's showed

how isolated he is even from members of his own Cabinet, where there seems to be a silent majority against him. The antiwar round robin signed by more than 200 employes of the State Department shows how deeply the Cambodian affair has stirred even the most timid, conformist and conventional section of the bureaucracy. Nothing Nixon says can be taken at face value. Even when he said on April 20, in his troop withdrawal announcement, that a "just peace" was at last in sight, he must have been planning this expansion of the war. Indeed, General Westmoreland as Army Chief of Staff had already begun to lobby for a Cambodian invasion in off-the-record briefings.

There were two remarks of the deepest significance in the Nixon press conference of May 8. One was that if we withdraw from Vietnam "America is finished insofar as the peace-keeper in the Asian world is concerned." This revealed that he is still committed, despite that vague "low posture" talk on Guam, to a Pax Americana in Asia. If we are to police Asia we are in for many years of war and internal disruption. The folly is as great as if China were to try and become the "peace-keeper" of Latin America. The other remark was that unlike Johnson he would not escalate step by step but "move decisively." This is the Goldwater-LeMay thesis that we could have won the Vietnam war if we had smashed Hanoi and Haiphong in one great blow, perhaps with nuclear weapons. Hanoi, especially after the recent big bombing raids, expects something of the kind. Moscow and Peking are already trying to patch up their differences in expectation of it. If Nixon goes to nuclear weapons, the end result may well be World War III. Unless an army of students can fan out to the grass roots and make the country aware of these dangerous possibilities, terrible days may lie ahead.

May 18, 1970

PART IX

The Mideast

HOLY WAR

Stripped of propaganda and sentiment, the Palestine problem is, simply, the struggle of two different peoples for the same strip of land. For the Jews, the establishment of Israel was a Return, with all the mystical significance the capital R implies. For the Arabs it was another invasion. This has led to three wars between them in twenty years. Each has been a victory for the Jews. With each victory the size of Israel has grown. So has the number of Arab homeless.

Now to find a solution which will satisfy both peoples is like trying to square a circle. In the language of mathematics, the aspirations of the Jews and the Arabs are incommensurable. Their conflicting ambitions cannot be fitted into the confines of any ethical system which transcends the tribalistic. This is what frustrates the benevolent outsider, anxious to satisfy both peoples. For two years Jean-Paul Sartre has been trying to draw Israelis and Arabs into a confrontation in a special number of his review, *Les Temps Modernes*. The third war between them broke out while it was on the press.

This long-awaited special issue on *Le conflit israélo-arabe* is the first confrontation in print of Arab and Israeli intellectuals. But it turns out to be 991 pages not so much of dialogue as of dual monologue. The two sets of contributors sit not just in separate rooms, like employers and strikers in a bitter labor dispute, but in separate universes where the simplest fact often turns out to have diametrically opposite meanings. Physics has begun to uncover a new conundrum in the worlds of matter and anti-matter, occupying the same space and time but locked off from each other by their obverse natures, forever twin yet forever sundered. The Israeli-Arab quarrel is the closest analogue in the realm of international politics.

The conditions exacted for the joint appearance of Israe-

lis and Arabs in the same issue of *Les Temps Modernes*
excluded not only collaboration but normal editorial medi-
ation or midwifery. Claude Lanzmann, who edited this special issue, explains in his Introduction that the choice of authors and of subjects had to be left "in full sovereignty" (*en
toute souveraineté*) to each of the two parties. The Arabs
threatened to withdraw if an article was included by A. Ra-
zak Abdel-Kader, an Algerian who is an advocate of Israeli-
Arab reconciliation. When the Israelis objected that *Les
Temps Modernes* at least allow Abdel-Kader to express
himself as an individual, the Arabs insisted on an absolute
veto: there would be no issue if Abdel-Kader were in it.

In his Preface Jean-Paul Sartre lays bare the conflicting
emotions which led him to embark on so difficult a task as
to attempt the role—in some degree—of peacemaker between Arab and Israeli. They awaken the memories of his
finest hours. One was that of the Resistance. "For all those
who went through this experience," M. Sartre writes, "it is
unbearable to imagine that another Jewish community,
wherever it may be, whatever it may be, should endure this
Calvary anew and furnish martyrs to a new massacre." The
other was Sartre's aid to the Arabs in their struggle for Algerian independence. These memories bind him to both
peoples, and give him the respect of both, as the welcome
he received in both Egypt and Israel last year attests. His
aim in presenting their views is, he says wistfully, merely to
inform. His hope is that information in itself will prove pac-
ifying "because it tends more or less slowly to replace passion by knowledge." But the roots of this struggle lie
deeper than reason. It is not at all certain that information
will replace passion with knowledge.

The experiences from which M. Sartre draws his emo-
tional ties are irrelevant to this new struggle. Both sides
draw from them conclusions which must horrify the man
of rationalist tradition and universalist ideals. The bulk of

the Jews and the Israelis draw from the Hitler period the conviction that, in this world, when threatened one must be prepared to kill or be killed. The Arabs draw from the Algerian conflict the conviction that, even in dealing with so rational and civilized a people as the French, liberation was made possible only by resorting to the gun and the knife. Both Israeli and Arabs in other words feel that only force can assure justice. In this they agree, and this sets them on a collision course. For the Jews believe justice requires the recognition of Israel as a fact; for the Arabs, to recognize the fact is to acquiesce in the wrong done them by the conquest of Palestine. If God as some now say is dead, He no doubt died of trying to find an equitable solution to the Arab-Jewish problem.

The argument between them begins with the Bible. "I give this country to your posterity," God said to Abraham (Gen. XV:18) "from the river of Egypt up to the great river, Euphrates." Among the Jews, whether religious or secular mystics, this is the origin of their right to the Promised Land. The opening article in the Arab section of *Les Temps Modernes* retorts that the "posterity" referred to in Genesis includes the descendants of Ishmael since he was the son of Abraham by his concubine Ketirah, and the ancestor of all the Arabs, Christian or Muslim.

All this may seem anachronistic nonsense, but this is an anachronistic quarrel. The Bible is still the best guide to it. Nowhere else can one find a parallel for its enthnocentric fury. Nowhere that I know of is there a word of pity in the Bible for the Canaanites whom the Hebrews slaughtered in taking possession. Of all the nonsense which marks the Jewish-Arab quarrel none is more nonsensical than the talk from both sides about the Holy Land as a symbol of peace. No bit of territory on earth has been soaked in the blood of more battles. Nowhere has religion been so zestful an excuse for fratricidal strife. The Hebrew *shalom* and the Arabic *salaam* are equally shams, relics of a common past as Bedouins. To this day inter-tribal war is the favorite sport

of the Bedouins; to announce "peace" in the very first word
is a necessity if any chance encounter is not to precipitate
bloodshed.

In Biblical perspective the Jews have been going in and
out of Palestine for 3,000 years. They came down from the
Euphrates under Abraham; returned from Egypt under
Moses and Joshua; came back again from the Babylonian
captivity and were dispersed again after Jerusalem fell to
the Romans in 70 A.D. This is the third return. The Arabs
feel they have a superior claim because they stayed put.
This appearance side by side in *Les Temps Modernes* provides less than the full and undiluted flavor of an ancient
sibling rivalry. Both sides have put their better foot forward. The Arab section includes no sample of the blood-
curdling broadcasts in which the Arab radios indulge; the
Israeli, no contribution from the right-wing Zionists who
dream of a greater Israel from the Nile to the Euphrates (as
promised in Genesis) with complete indifference to the fate
of the Arab inhabitants. On neither side is there a frank exposition of the *Realpolitik* which led Arab nationalists like
Nasser to see war on Israel as the one way to achieve Arab
unity, and leads Jewish nationalists like Ben Gurion and
Dayan to see Arab disunity and backwardness as essential
elements for Israeli security and growth. No voice on the
Arab side preaches a Holy War in which all Israel would be
massacred, while no voice on the Israeli side expresses the
cheerfully cynical view one may hear in private that Israel
has no realistic alternative but to hand the Arabs a bloody
nose every five or ten years until they accept the loss of
Palestine as irreversible.

The picture, however, is not wholly symmetrical. There
is first of all the asymmetry of the victorious and the defeated. The victor is ready to talk with the defeated if the
latter will acquiesce in defeat. The defeated, naturally, is
less inclined to this kind of objectivity. The editor, Claude
Lanzmann, speaks of an "asymmetry between the two col-

lections of articles which derives at one and the same time
from a radical difference in their way of looking at the conflict and from the difference in the nature of the political
regimes in the countries involved." Even if not expressly
authorized by their governments or organizations to participate, M. Lanzmann explains, all the Arabs except the
North Africans wrote only after consultation and defend a
common position, while the Israelis, "as is normal in a West-
ern-style democracy," speak either for themselves or for one
of their numerous parties. But this diversity may be exaggerated. On the fundamental issue which divides the two
sides, no Arab contributor is prepared to advocate recognition of the state of Israel, while only one Israeli contributor
is prepared to advocate its transformation into something
other than a basically Jewish state.

The depth of this nationalistic difference may be measured by what happened to Israel's Communist party. Elsewhere national centrifugal tendencies have made their appearance in the once monolithic world of communism. In
Israel the same nationalist tendencies split the Communist
party into two, one Jewish the other Arab. The days when
Arab Communists faithfully followed Moscow's line
straight into the jails of Egypt, Iraq, Syria, and Jordan by
supporting the 1947 partition plan have long passed away.
Today Arab and Jewish Communists no longer find common ground.[1] It would be hard to find an Arab who would
agree with Moshe Sneh, head of the Jewish Communist
party (Maki) in Israel, when he told *L'Express* (June 19–
25), "Our war is just and legitimate. What united the 13
Arab States against us, irrespective of their regime, was not
anti-imperialism but pan-Arabism and anti-Jewish chauvin-
ism." He added boldly that Moscow in supporting the
Arabs had "turned its back on the politics of the international left and on the spirit of Tashkent." But even Sneh's
bitter rival, Meir Vilner, the Jewish leader of, and one of

[1] The relative strength of the two since the split may be seen from the
fact that the Jewish branch was able to elect only one deputy while the
Arab branch, which draws the largest vote among the Arab minority,
elected three, two Arabs and one Jew.

the few Jews left in, the Arab Communist party (Rakka) expresses himself in *Les Temps Modernes* in terms with which no Arab contributor to it agrees. M. Vilner is for the return of all the refugees who wish it, for full equality to Arabs in Israel and for a neutralist policy, but he defends the existence of Israel as a legitimate fact and denies that "one can in any way compare the people (of Israel) to Algerian colons or the Crusaders." The comparisons rejected by the leader of the Arab Communist party in Israel are the favorite comparisons of the Arabs outside Israel. The diversity of viewpoint on the Israeli side thus ends with the basic agreement on its right to exist, and to exist as a Jewish state. This is precisely where the Arab disagreement begins.

The gulf between Arab and Jewish views becomes even clearer when one reads two supplementary pieces contributed by two French Jews, Maxime Rodinson, a distinguished sociologist and Orientalist, and Robert Misrahi, a well-known writer of the left. The former takes the Arab and the latter the Zionist side. But while M. Misrahi's article appears with the Israelis, M. Rodinson's contribution—by far the most brilliant in the whole volume—appears alone. He refused, for reasons of principle, to appear in the Arab ensemble. It is not hard to see why. For while M. Rodinson gives strong support to every basic Arab historical contention, he is too much the humanist (and in the last analysis no doubt the Jew) to welcome an apocalyptic solution at the expense of Israel's existence. There is still a gulf between M. Rodinson's pro-Arab position and the most moderate view any Arab statesman has yet dared express, that of Tunisia's President Bourguiba. Bourguiba's famous speech in Jericho, March 3, 1965, is reprinted in an appendix by *Les Temps Modernes*, along with an interview he gave *Le Nouvel Observateur* (April 15) a month later. But Bourguiba's speech, though it created a sensation by its relative moderation, merely suggested that the Arabs proceed to regain Palestine as they did Tunisia, by a series of more or less peaceful compromises. When *Le Nouvel Observateur* asked him whether this did not imply the progressive disappearance of the State of Israel, he would not go beyond the cryptic reply, "That is not certain."

The Arab section of the symposium is nevertheless far from being uniform. A Moroccan, Abdallah Larouia, professor of literature in Rabat, not only ends by saying that the possibilities of peaceful settlement must be kept open because a war would settle nothing, but even goes so far as to express the hope that the time may come when a settlement is possible without making a new exile, i.e., of the Israelis, pay for the end of another exile, i.e. of the Arabs from Palestine. He even suggests that under certain conditions, a Jewish community "with or without political authority"—a most daring remark—may prove compatible with Arab progress and development.

When we examine these conditions, we come to the heart of the fears expressed by the Arabs in this symposium. The Palestinian Arabs, from the first beginnings of Zionism, foresaw the danger of being swamped and dislodged by Jewish immigration. Neighboring Arab states feared that this immigration would stimulate a continuous territorial expansion at their expense and create a Jewish state powerful enough to dominate the area. The relative size and population of Israel when compared to its Arab neighbors are deceptive and may make these fears seem foolish, but historically the Middle East has often been conquered and dominated by relatively small bands of determined intruders. Even now, as the recent fighting showed, tiny Israel could without difficulty have occupied Damascus, Amman, and Cairo, and—were it not for the big powers and the UN—dictated terms to its Arab neighbors.

It was the attempt of the British to allay Arab apprehension by setting limits on Jewish immigration that precipitated the struggle between the British and the Jews. The 1917 Balfour Declaration, when it promised a "Jewish National Home" in Palestine, also said—in a passage Zionists have always preferred to forget—"that nothing shall be

done which may prejudice the civil and religious rights of
the existing non-Jewish communities in Palestine." British
White Papers in 1922, in 1930, and again in 1939 tried to
fulfill this companion pledge by steps which would have
kept the Jews a permanent minority. It is this persistent and
—as events have shown—justifiable Arab fear which is reflected in M. Laroui's article. In calling the Palestine problem "A Problem of the Occident" his basic point is that if
the Occident wipes out anti-Semitism, or keeps it within
harmless proportions, making refuge in Israel unnecessary
for the bulk of Jewry, and Israel divorces its politics from
the Zionist dream of gathering in all the Jews from Exile,
this will end the danger of an inexorable expansion in search
of *"lebensraum"* at the expense of the Palestinian Arabs,
and finally make peace possible between the two peoples.
Since immigration into Israel has dwindled in recent years,
this Arab fear seems at the moment less a matter of reality
than of Zionist theory and of a past experience which leads
them to take it seriously.

The suggestion that Israel abandon its supra-nationalist
dream finds its only echo on the other side of this collection
of essays in Israel's No. 1 maverick and champion of Arab
rights, Uri Avnery. Avnery was born in Germany in 1923
and went to Palestine at the age of ten, the year Hitler took
power. He began his political career on the far nationalist
right, as a member of the Irgun terrorist group in the struggle against the British, but has since swung over to the far
left of Israeli opinion, to the point where he is considered
anti-nationalist. In the wake of the first Suez war, he supported the Egyptian demand for evacuation of the Canal
Zone and in 1959 he formed an Israeli committee to aid the
Algerian rebels. At one time he organized a movement
which asserted that the Israelis were no longer Jews but
"Canaanites" and therefore one with the Arabs, forcibly
converted remnants of the same indigenous stock. When
this far-out conception attracted few Jews and even fewer
Canaanites, he formed a "Semitic Action" movement which
has now become "the Movement of New Forces." This

polled 1.2 percent of the vote in the 1965 elections and by virtue of proportional representation put Avnery into Parliament. Avnery has been more successful as a publisher. He has made his weekly *Haolam Hazeh* ("This World") the largest in Israel by combining non-conformist politics with what the rather puritanical Israelis call pornography, though that weekly's girlie pictures would seem as old-fashioned as the *Police Gazette* in America.

Avnery writes in *Les Temps Modernes* that he would turn Israel into a secular, pluralist, and multi-national state. He would abolish the Law of Return which gives every Jew the right to enter Israel and automatically become a citizen. Avnery says this pan-Judaism of Zionism feeds the anti-Zionism of pan-Arabism by keeping alive "the myth of an Israel submerged by millions of immigrants who, finding no place to settle, would oblige the government to expand the country by force of arms."

Yet Avnery, who asks Israel to give up its Zionist essence, turns out to be a Jewish nationalist, too. After sketching out a plan for an Arab Palestinian state west of the Jordan, Avnery writes, "The Arabic reader will justly ask at this point, 'And the return of Israel to the limits of the UN plan of 1947?' " Since Israel in the 1947–48 fighting seized about 23 percent more territory than was allotted to it in the 1947 partition plan, this implies a modification of frontiers in favor of the Arab state which was supposed to be linked with it in an economically united Palestine. But to this natural Arab question Avnery replies,[2] "Frankly we see no possibility of this kind. The Arab armies are already 15 kilometers from Israel's most populous city (Tel Aviv) and at Nathanya are even closer to the sea." The Arabs may feel that Avnery is as unwilling to give up the fruits of conquest as any non-"Canaanite." Avnery is as reluctant as any conventional Zionist to see his fellow Canaanite too close to Tel Aviv.

It is easy to understand why neither side trusts the other.

[2] Avnery was writing, of course, before the new outbreak of warfare had again changed these borders to Israel's advantage.

In any case M. Sartre's symposium is a confrontation largely of moderates and leftists, and on neither side do these elements command majority support. Another complexity is that while in settled societies the left tends to be less nationalistic than the right, in colonial societies the revolutionary left is often more nationalistic than the native conservative and propertied classes.

The overwhelming majority opinion on both sides, even as expressed in a symposium as skewed leftward as this one, shows little tendency to compromise. The Arabs argue that Israel is a colonialist implantation in the Middle East, supported from the beginning by imperialist powers; that it is an enemy of Arab union and progress; that the sufferings of the Jews in the West were the consequence of an anti-Semitism the Arabs have never shared; and that there is no reason why the Arabs of Palestine should be displaced from their homes in recompense for wrongs committed by Hitler Germany. M. Laroui alone is sympathetic enough to say that if the Jewish National Home had been established in Uganda, the Arabs who felt compassion for the sufferings of the Jews of Europe would have shown themselves as uncomprehending of the rights of the Ugandans as the West has been in Palestine. At the other end of the Arab spectrum a fellow Moroccan, a journalist, Tahar Benziane, ends up in classic anti-Semitism, blaming the Jews themselves, their separatism and their sense of superiority, for the prejudice against them. Benziane sees the only solution not just in the liquidation of Israel but in the disappearance of world Jewry through assimilation. His would indeed be a Final Solution. This bitter and hateful opinion, widespread in the Arab world, explains why Nazism found so ready an echo before the war in the Middle East and Nazi criminals so welcome a refuge in Egypt. It also disposes of the semantic nonsense that Arabs being Semite cannot be anti-Semitic!

The Zionist argument is that the Jewish immigration was a return to the Jewish homeland. Robert Misrahi even goes so far as to argue that the Jews had an older claim to Palestine than the Arabs since the Jews had lived there in the ancient kingdom of the Hebrews long before the Hegira of Mohammed! Misrahi argues the familiar Zionist thesis that their struggle against Britain proves them to be anti-imperialist, that their colonies are socialist, that their enemies are the feudal elements in the Arab world, and that the Arab refugees are the moral responsibility of the Arab leaders since it was on their urging that the Arabs ran away.

There is a good deal of simplistic sophistry in the Zionist case. The whole earth would have to be reshuffled if claims 2,000 years old to *irredenta* were suddenly to be allowed. Zionism from its beginning tried to gain its aims by offering to serve as outpost in the Arab world for one of the great empires. Herzl sought to win first the Sultan and then the Kaiser by such arguments. Considerations of imperial strategy finally won the Balfour Declaration from Britain. The fact that the Jewish community in Palestine afterward fought the British is no more evidence of its not being a colonial implantation than similar wars of British colonists against the mother country, from the American Revolution to Rhodesia. In the case of Palestine, as of other such struggles, the Mother Country was assailed because it showed more concern for the native majority than was palatable to the colonist minority. The argument that the refugees ran away "voluntarily" or because their leaders urged them to do so until after the fighting was over not only rests on a myth but is irrelevant. Have refugees no right to return? Have German Jews no right to recover their properties because they too fled?

The myth that the Arab refugees fled because the Arab radios urged them to do so was analyzed by Erskine B. Childers in the London *Spectator* May 12, 1961. An examination of British and U.S. radio monitoring records turned up no such appeals; on the contrary there were appeals and "even orders to the civilians of Palestine, *to stay put*." The most balanced and humane discussion of the question may be found in Christopher Sykes's book *Crossroads to Israel:*

1917–48 (at pages 350–5). "It can be said with a high degree of certainty," Mr. Sykes wrote, "that most of the time
in the first half of 1948 the mass exodus was the natural,
thoughtless, pitiful movement of ignorant people who had
been badly led and who in the day of trial found themselves
forsaken by their leaders. . . . But if the exodus was by
and large an accident of war in the first stage, in the later
stages it was consciously and mercilessly helped on by Jewish threats and aggression toward Arab populations. . . .
It is to be noted, however, that where the Arabs had leaders who refused to be stampeded into panic flight, the
people came to no harm." Jewish terrorism, not only by the
Irgun, in such savage massacres as Deir Yassin, but in milder
form by the Haganah, itself "encouraged" Arabs to leave
areas the Jews wished to take over for strategic or demo-
graphic reasons. They tried to make as much of Israel as
free of Arabs as possible.

The effort to equate the expulsion of the Arabs from Palestine with the new Jewish immigration out of the Arab
countries is not so simple nor so equitable as it is made to
appear in Zionist propaganda. The Palestinian Arabs feel
about this "swap" as German Jews would if denied restitution on the grounds that they had been "swapped" for German refugees from the Sudetenland. In a sanely conceived
settlement, some allowance should equitably be made for
Jewish properties left behind in Arab countries. What is ob-
jectionable in the simplified version of this question is the
idea that Palestinian Arabs whom Israel didn't want should
have no objection to being "exchanged" for Arabic Jews it
did want. One uprooting cannot morally be equated with
the other.

A certain moral imbecility marks all ethnocentric movements. The Others are always either less than human, and
thus their interests may be ignored, or more than human,
and therefore so dangerous that it is right to destroy them.
The latter is the underlying pan-Arab attitude toward the
Jews; the former is Zionism's basic attitude toward the
Arabs. M. Avnery notes that Herzl in his book *The Jewish*

State, which launched the modern Zionist movement, dealt
with working hours, housing for workers, and even the national flag but had not one word to say about the Arabs!
For the Zionists the Arab was the Invisible Man. Psycholog-
ically he was not there. Achad Ha-Am, the Russian Jew
who became a great Hebrew philosopher, tried to draw attention as early as 1891 to the fact that Palestine was not an
empty territory and that this posed problems. But as little
attention was paid to him as was later accorded his successors in "spiritual Zionism," men like Buber and Judah
Magnes, who tried to preach *Ichud,* "unity," i.e., with the
Arabs. Of all the formulas with which Zionism comforted
itself none was more false and more enduring than Israel
Zangwill's phrase about "a land without people for a people
without a land." Buber related that Max Nordau, hearing
for the first time that there was an Arab population in Palestine, ran to Herzl crying, "I didn't know that—but then we
are committing an injustice." R. J. Zwi Werblowsky, dean
of the faculty of letters at the Hebrew University, in the
first article of this anthology's Israeli section, writes with
admirable objectivity, "There can be no doubt that if Nordau's reaction had been more general, it would seriously
have paralyzed the *élan* of the Zionist movement." It took
refuge, he writes, in "a moral myopia."

This moral myopia makes it possible for Zionists to dwell
on the 1,900 years of Exile in which Jews have longed
for Palestine but dismiss as nugatory the nineteen years in
which Arab refugees have also longed for it. "Homelessness" is the major theme of Zionism, but this pathetic passion
is denied to Arab refugees. Even Meir Yaari, the head of
Mapam, the leader of the "Marxist" Zionists of Hashomer
Hatzair, who long preached bi-nationalism, says Israel can
only accept a minority of the Arab refugees because the
essential reason for the creation of Israel was to "welcome
the mass of immigrant Jews returning to their historic father-
land!" If there is not room enough for both, the Jews must
have precedence. This is what leads Gabran Majdalany, a
Baath Socialist, to write that Israel is "a racist state founded

from its start on discrimination between Jew and non-Jew."
He compares the Zionists to the Muslim Brotherhood who
"dream of a Muslim Israel in which the non-Muslims will be
the gentiles, second-class citizens sometimes tolerated but
more often repressed." It is painful to hear his bitter re-
proach—

Some people admit the inevitably racist character of Israel but
justify it by the continual persecutions to which the Jews have
been subjected during the history of Europe and by the massacres of the Second World War. We consider that, far from
serving as justification, these facts constitute an aggravating circumstance; for those who have known the effects of racism and
of discrimination in their own flesh and human dignity, are less
excusably racist than those who can only imagine the negative
effects of prejudice.

When Israel's Defense Minister, Moshe Dayan, was on
Face the Nation June 11, after Israel's latest victories, this
colloquy occurred:

SYDNEY GRUSON (*New York Times*): Is there any possible
way that Israel could absorb the huge number of Arabs whose
territory it has gained control of now?
GEN. DAYAN: Economically we can; but I think that is not
in accord with our aims in the future. It would turn Israel into
either a bi-national or poly-Arab-Jewish state instead of the
Jewish state, and we want to have a Jewish state. We can
absorb them, but then it won't be the same country.
MR. GRUSON: And it is necessary in your opinion to maintain this as a Jewish state and purely a Jewish state?
GEN. DAYAN: Absolutely—absolutely. We want a Jewish
state like the French have a French state.

This must deeply disturb the thoughtful Jewish reader.
Ferdinand and Isabella in expelling the Jews and Moors
from Spain were in the same way saying they wanted a
Spain as "Spanish," (i.e., Christian) as France was French. It
is not hard to recall more recent parallels.

It is a pity the editors of *Les Temps Modernes* didn't
widen their symposium to include a Jewish as distinct from
an Israeli point of view. For Israel is creating a kind of
moral schizophrenia in world Jewry. In the outside world

the welfare of Jewry depends on the maintenance of secular, non-racial, pluralistic societies. In Israel, Jewry finds itself defending a society in which mixed marriages cannot be legalized, in which non-Jews have a lesser status than Jews, and in which the ideal is racial and exclusionist. Jews must fight elsewhere for their very security and existence—against principles and practices they find themselves defending in Israel. Those from the outside world, even in their moments of greatest enthusiasm amid Israel's accomplishments, feel twinges of claustrophobia, not just geographical but spiritual. Those caught up in Prophetic fervor soon begin to feel that the light they hoped to see out of Zion is only that of another narrow nationalism.

Such moments lead to a reexamination of Zionist ideology. That longing for Zion on which it is predicated may be exaggerated. Its reality is indisputable but its strength can easily be overestimated. Not until after World War II was it ever strong enough to attract more than a trickle of Jews to the Holy Land. By the tragic dialectic of history, Israel would not have been born without Hitler. It took the murder of six million in his human ovens to awaken sufficient nationalist zeal in Jewry and sufficient humanitarian compassion in the West to bring a Jewish state to birth in Palestine. Even then humanitarian compassion was not strong enough to open the gates of the West to Jewish immigration in contrition. The capitalist West and the Communist East preferred to displace Arabs rather than to welcome the Jewish "displaced persons" in Europe's postwar refugee camps.

It must also be recognized, despite Zionist ideology, that the periods of greatest Jewish creative accomplishment have been associated with pluralistic civilizations in their time of expansion and tolerance: in the Hellenistic period, in the Arab civilization of North Africa and Spain, and in Western Europe and America. Universal values can only be the fruit of a universal vision; the greatness of the Prophets lay in their overcoming of ethnocentricity. A Lilliputian nationalism cannot distill truths for all mankind. Here lie the roots of a growing divergence between Jew and Israeli; the former with a sense of mission as a Witness in the human wilderness, the latter concerned only with his own tribe's welfare.

But Jewry can no more turn its back on Israel than Israel on Jewry. The ideal solution would allow the Jews to make their contributions as citizens in the diverse societies and nations which are their homes while Israel finds acceptance as a Jewish State in a renascent Arab civilization. This would end Arab fears of a huge inflow to Israel. The Jews have as much reason to be apprehensive about that prospect as the Arabs.

It can only come as the result of a sharp recrudescence in persecution elsewhere in the world. Zionism grows on Jewish catastrophe. Even now it casts longing eyes on Russian Jewry. But would it not be better, more humanizing, and more just, were the Soviet Union to wipe out anti-Semitism and to accord its Jews the same rights of cultural autonomy and expression it gives all its other nationalities? The Russian Jews have fought for Russia, bled for the Revolution, made no small contribution to Russian literature and thought; why should they be cast out? This would be a spiritual catastrophe for Russia as well as Jewry even though it would supply another flow of desperate refugees to an Israel already short of Jews if it is to expand as the Zionist militants hope to expand it.

Israel has deprived anti-Semitism of its mystique. For the visitor to Israel, anti-Semitism no longer seems a mysterious anomaly but only another variant of minority-majority friction. *Es is schwer zu sein eid Yid* ("It's hard to be a Jew") was the title of Sholom Aleichem's most famous story. Now we see that it's hard to be a goy in Tel Aviv, especially an Arab goy. Mohammad Watad, a Muslim Israeli, one of the five Arabic contributors to the Israeli side of this symposium, begins his essay with words which startlingly resemble the hostile dialogue Jews encounter elsewhere. "I

am often asked," he writes, "about my 'double' life which is
at one and the same time that of an Arab and that of an
Israeli citizen." Another Arab contributor from Israel, Ibrahim Shabath, a Christian who teaches Hebrew in Arabic
schools and is editor-in-chief of *Al Mirsad,* the Mapam
paper in Arabic, deplores the fact that nineteen years after
the creation of Israel "the Arabs are still considered strangers by the Jews." He relates a recent conversation with
Ben Gurion. "You must know," Ben Gurion told him, "that
Israel is the country of the Jews and only of the Jews.
Every Arab who lives here has the same rights as any minority citizen in any country of the world, but he must admit the fact that he lives in a Jewish country." The implications must chill Jews in the outside world.

The Arab citizen of Israel, Shabath complains, "is the
victim today of the same prejudices and the same generali-
zations as the Jewish people elsewhere." The bitterest account of what they undergo may be found in an anonymous report sent to the United Nations in 1964 by a group
of Arabs who tried unsuccessfully to found an independent
Socialist Arab movement and publication. Military authorities, despite a Supreme Court order, refused to permit this,
and the courts declined to overrule the military. Their petition is reprinted in the Israeli section of this symposium.
Though the military rule complained of was abolished last
year, and police regulations substituted, it is too soon—especially because of the new outbeak of warfare—to determine what the effect will be on Arab civil liberties. Israelis
admit with pleasure that neither in the Christian villages of
Central Galilee nor in the Muslim villages of the so-called
"Triangle" was there the slightest evidence of any Fifth
Column activity. Those Israelis who have fought for an end
of all discrimination against the Arabs argue that they have
demonstrated their loyalty and deserve fully to be trusted.

It is to Israel's credit that the Arab minority is given place
in its section to voice these complaints while no similar place

is opened for ethnic minority opinion in the Arabic section.
Indeed except for Lebanon and to some degree Tunisia
there is no place in the Arab world where the dissident of
any kind enjoys freedom of the press. There is no frank
discussion of this in the Arab section. One of the most vigorous and acute expositions of the Arab point of view, for
example, is an article by an Egyptian writer, Lotfallah Soliman, who has played a distinguished role in bringing modern ideas to the young intellectuals of his country since
World War II. His autobiographical sketch says cryptically, if discreetly, "He lives presently in Paris." I stumbled
on a more candid explanation. In preparing for this review,
I read an earlier article in *Les Temps Modernes* (August–
September 1960) by Adel Montasser on *La répression anti-
démocratique en Egypte*. Appended to it was a list of intellectuals imprisoned by Nasser. Among them was Lotfallah
Soliman. Obviously it's hard to be a free Egyptian intellectual in Nasser's Egypt. Many of those then imprisoned have
since been freed, but it is significant that a writer as trench-
ant and devoted as Soliman has to work in exile.

It is true that the full roster of Arab minority complaints
in Israel had to be presented anonymously for fear of the
authorities. But in the Arab section of this book no place
was allowed even anonymously for the Jewish and the various Christian minorities to voice their complaints. As a result the Arab contributors were able to write as if their
countries, unlike Europe, were models of tolerance. They
hark back to the great days of Arabic Spain where (except
for certain interludes not mentioned) Christian and Jew enjoyed full equality, religious, cultural, and political, with
the Muslim: Spain did not become synonymous with
intolerance, Inquisition, and obscurantism until the Christian Reconquest. But today no Arab country except, pre-
cariously, Lebanon, dimly resembles Moorish Spain. As a
result the Jews from the Arabic countries tend to hate the
Arab far more than Jews from Europe who have never
lived under his rule, which often recalls medieval Christian-
dom. A glimpse of these realities may be found in the most

moving article in this whole symposium. This is by Attalah Mansour, a young Christian Arabic Israeli novelist of peasant origin who has published two novels, one in Arabic and the other in Hebrew, and worked as a journalist on Avnery's paper *Haolam Hazeh* and on the staff of *Haaretz*, Israel's best and most objective daily paper. M. Mansour knows doubly what it is to be a "Jew." He is as an Arab a "Jew" to the Israelis and as a Christian a "Jew" to the Muslims. He tells a touching story of an accidental encounter in (of all places) the Paris Metro with a young man who turned out like him to be Greek-rite Christian though from Egypt. They exchanged stories of their troubles, like two Jews in the Diaspora. "We in Egypt," the young stranger told him, "have the same feelings as you. There is no law discriminating between us and the Muslims. But the governmental administration, at least on the everyday level, prefers Mahmoud to Boulos and Achmed to Samaan"—i.e. the man with the Muslim name to the man with the Christian. "Omar Sharif, the well-known movie actor," the Egyptian Christian added, "is Christian in origin. But he had to change his Christian name for a Muslim to please the public." In Israel, similarly, Ibrahim often becomes Abraham to pass as a Jew and to avoid widespread housing discrimination.

If in this account I have given more space to the Arab than the Israeli side it is because as a Jew, closely bound emotionally with the birth of Israel,[3] I feel honor bound to report the Arab side, especially since the U.S. press is so overwhelmingly pro-Zionist. For me, the Arab-Jewish struggle is a tragedy. The essence of tragedy is a struggle of right against right. Its catharsis is the cleansing pity of seeing how good men do evil despite themselves out of un-

[3] I first arrived in Palestine on Balfour Day Nov. 2, 1945, the day the Haganah blew up bridges and watch towers to begin its struggle against the British and immigration restrictions. The following spring I was the first newspaperman to travel with illegal Jewish immigrants from the Polish-Czech border through the British blockade. In 1947 I celebrated Passover in the British detention camps in Cyprus and in 1948 I covered the Arab-Jewish war. See my *Underground to Palestine* (1946) and *This is Israel* (1948). I was back in 1949, 1950, 1951, 1956, and 1964.

avoidable circumstance and irresistible compulsion. When
evil men do evil, their deeds belong to the realm of pathol-
ogy. But when good men do evil, we confront the essence
of human tragedy. In a tragic struggle, the victors become
the guilty and must make amends to the defeated. For me
the Arab problem is also the No. 1 Jewish problem. How
we act toward the Arabs will determine what kind of
people we become: either oppressors and racists in our turn
like those from whom we have suffered, or a nobler race
able to transcend the tribal xenophobias that afflict mankind.[4]

Israel's swift and extraordinary victories have suddenly
transmuted this ideal from the realm of impractical sentiment to urgent necessity. The new frontiers of military
conquest have gathered in most of the Arab refugees. Zionism's dream, the "ingathering of the exiles," has been
achieved, though in an ironic form; it is the Arab exiles who
are back. They cannot be gotten rid of as easily as in 1948.
Something in the order of 100,000 have again been "encouraged" to leave, but the impact on public opinion
abroad and in Israel has forced the state to declare that it
will allow them to return. While the UN proves impotent
to settle the conflict and the Arab powers are unwilling to
negotiate from a situation of weakness, Israel can to some
degree determine its future by the way in which it treats its
new Arab subjects or citizens. The wrangles of the powers
will go on for months, but these people must be fed, clothed,
and housed. How they are treated will change the world's
picture of Israel and of Jewry, soften or intensify Arab

[4] In September [1967], Black Star will publish a vigorous little book
The Aryanization of the Jewish State, by Michael Selzer, a young Paki-
stani Jew who lived in Israel. It may help Jewry and Israel to understand
that the way to a fraternal life with the Arabs inside and outside Israel
must begin with the eradication of the prejudices that greet the Oriental
and Arabic-speaking Jews in Israel who now make up over half the population of the country. The bias against the Arab extends to a bias against
the Jews from the Arab countries. In this, as in so many other respects,
Israel presents in miniature all the problems of the outside world. Were
the rest of the planet to disappear, Israel could regenerate from itself—as
from a new Ark—all the bigotries, follies, and feuds of a vanished mankind (as well as some of its most splended accomplishments).

anger, build a bridge to peace or make new war certain. To establish an Arab state on the West Bank and to link it with Israel, perhaps also with Jordan, in a Confederation would turn these Arab neighbors, if fraternally treated, from enemies into a buffer, and give Israel the protection of strategic frontiers. But it would be better to give the West Bank back to Jordan than to try to create a puppet state—a kind of Arab Bantustan—consigning the Arabs to second-class status under Israel's control. This would only foster Arab resentment. To avoid giving the Arabs first-class citizenship by putting them in the reservation of a second-class state is too transparently clever.

What is required in the treatment of the Arab refugees Israel has gathered in is the conquest both of Jewish exclusivism and the resentful hostility of the Arabs. Even the malarial marshes of the Emek and the sandy wastes of the Negev could not have looked more bleakly forbidding to earlier generations of Zionist pioneers than these steep and arid mountains of prejudice. But I for one have a glimmer of hope. Every year I have gone to Palestine and later Israel I have found situations which seemed impossible. Yet Zionist zeal and intelligence overcame them. Perhaps this extraordinarily dynamic, progressive, and devoted community can even if need be transcend its essential self.

I was encouraged to find in this volume that the most objective view of the Arab question on the Israeli side was written by Yehudah Harkabi, a Haifa-born professional soldier, a brigadier general, but a general who holds a diploma in philosophy and Arabic studies from the Hebrew University and from Harvard. He has written a book on *Nuclear War and Nuclear Peace*. His article "Hawks or Doves" is extraordinary in its ability to rise above prejudice and sentiment. He does not shut his eyes at all to the Arab case. He feels peace can come only if we have the strength to confront its full human reality. "Marx affirms," he concludes, "that knowledge of the truth frees man from the determinism of history." It is only, General Harkabi says, when Israel is prepared "to accept the truth in its entirety that it will find the new strength necessary to maintain and consolidate its existence." The path to safety and the path to greatness lies in reconciliation. The other route, now that the West Bank and Gaza are under Israeli jurisdiction, leads to two new perils. The Arab populations now in the conquered territories make guerrilla war possible within Israel's own boundaries. And externally, if enmity deepens and tension rises between Israel and the Arab states, both sides will by one means or another obtain nuclear weapons for the next round.

This will change the whole situation. No longer will Israeli and Arab be able to play the game of war in anachronistic fashion as an extension of politics by other means. Neither will they be able to depend on a mutual balance of terror like the great powers with their "second-strike" capacity. In this pygmy struggle the first strike will determine the outcome and leave nothing behind. Nor will the great powers be able to stand aside and let their satellites play out their little war, as in 1948, 1956, and 1967. I have not dwelt here on the responsibility of the great powers, because if they did not exist the essential differences in the Arab-Israeli quarrel would still remain, and because both sides use the great power question as an excuse to ignore their own responsibilities. The problem for the new generation of Arabs is the social reconstruction of their decayed societies; the problem will not go away if Israel disappears. Indeed their task is made more difficult by the failure to recognize Israel, since that means a continued emphasis on militarization, diversion of resources, and domination by military men. For Israel, the problem is reconciliation with the Arabs; the problem will not go away even if Moscow and Washington lie down together like the lion and the lamb or blow each other to bits. But the great powers for their part cannot continue the cynical game of arming both sides in a struggle for influence when the nuclear stage is reached. It is significant that the one place where the Israeli and Arab contributors to this symposium tend to common conclusions is in the essays discussing the common nuclear danger. To denuclearize the Middle East, to defuse it, will require some kind of neutralization. Otherwise the Arab-Israeli conflict may some day set off a wider final solution. That irascible Old Testament God of Vengeance is fully capable, if provoked, of turning the whole planet into a crematorium.

August 3, 1967
New York Review

THE NEED FOR DOUBLE VISION IN THE MIDDLE EAST

One way to approach the Middle Eastern crisis is to recognize that Israel is an island in a hostile sea. Its only swift and sure access to the rest of the world is by air. You cannot go by train from Cairo to Tel Aviv's neighboring city, Jaffa, as you still could in 1945 when I first visited Palestine, nor can you take a taxi from Jerusalem to Amman or from Haifa to Beirut, or to Damascus, as I still could in three memorable trips in 1947. There is no exit by land from Israel today; the sea route is slow, and in time of war rendered insecure by Soviet-supplied naval vessels in the hands of the Egyptians and by the new presence of the Soviet navy itself in the Mediterranean.

Only the air is Israel's open door to the rest of the world. More than any other nation today it is the child of the air age. Its swift victory in the Six-Day War last year was a lightning victory by airpower. A major element in its balance of payments, the tourist trade, depends on the air. By air it is only a few hours from New York, London

and Paris. In the days of the Romans and centuries later of
the great Arab empires in North Africa and Spain, it took
slow and arduous months for Jewish pilgrims and poets to
reach the Holy Land. Today only a few hours separates
Israel from its Jewish supporters in the outside world. Perhaps most fundamentally of all, the air alone saves Israel
from the claustrophobia and despair of a nation besieged
ever since its birth 20 years ago.

The new target of the Arab guerrillas is that lifeline. It is
as vulnerable as a man's jugular vein. Israel's national airline,
El Al, owns seven jets. When one was hijacked in Rome
early last year and another attacked in Athens a few weeks
ago, the Arab guerrillas hit Israel's most sensitive point.
This was no sporadic shelling of a border settlement or even
the bombing of a crowded Jerusalem market. The threat,
the repercussions and the possibilities were of a far graver
order. El Al is one of the few national airlines which is in
the black. It would only take a few unsuccessful attacks to
frighten away much of its business; what the Arab guerrillas could not do at Israel's well-guarded main airport in
Lydda, they might do abroad. The next step would be attacks on other airlines which fly into Israel. I can still remember my own desperate feelings in Paris, on my way to
Palestine on the eve of the 1948 war, when the airlines
stopped flying into Lydda and getting there depended on a
chance lift on a special Haganah plane from Geneva. To
cut the air link would be to close an iron ring around Israel.

It is foolish in this perspective to ask why Israel retaliated
against Lebanon, its one moderate Arab neighbor and the
only one which has done little or no fighting against it, the
only neighboring Arab state which has protected its own
Jewish minority from persecution in the blind furies unleashed by three Arab-Israeli wars. The reprisal was not
against the Lebanon. It was against the Arab air lines, and—
to speak frankly—the British companies which insure them
and the American companies which finance them. It was
struck at the nerve center and main air gateway of the Arab
world, the Beirut airport. It sought by damaging the Arab

airlines and their financial links in London and New York to warn the aviation world that airports had best be kept safe for all nations, Israel included. These are the blunt truths of the Beirut affair, and this is a message which had best get a full debate in the air age. For airports can easily become a new and critical nerve point in all the various short-of-war struggles which afflict a cantankerous and quarrelsome mankind.

The price paid by Israel was a political victory for the Arab guerrilla movements. Israel has never been as isolated as it is today in the wake of its unanimous condemnation by the Security Council. The Israeli cabinet, according to reports in Israel's most respected newspaper, *Haaretz*, was deeply split on the eve of the reprisal raid. Its magnitude, despite the sensational success in carrying it off without any loss of life, was bound to seem so disproportionate as to evoke condemnation. To strike at Lebanon, half Christian in population, still substantially French in culture, was bound to arouse traditional protective sympathies in the Vatican and in Paris. It would be just as well for Jewish spokesmen to keep their cool about the reactions of Pope Paul and de Gaulle, and not make more enemies. The feeling of Rome for the ancient Christian communities of the Lebanon is as natural as those of the Jews for Israel. The first point of repair should be with Lebanon, for its success in welding Christian and Moslem communities into a stable nation is a model for what must sooner or later develop in some form between Israel and the Palestinian Arabs if there is to be peace in the Middle East.

Indeed at a time when Ulster's bloody battles between Catholic and Protestant in Ireland show that even the embers of Cromwell's cruel time still smolder, Lebanon seems to be about the only place in the world (look at Belgium torn between Fleming and Walloon, and at French Canada!) where bi-national and multi-national solutions are working smoothly. Something of the sort must come in a reconstructed Palestine of Jewish and Arab states in peaceful coexistence. To bring it about Israel and the Jewish

communities of the world must be willing to look some unpleasant truths squarely in the face, and to rise to heights of
magnanimity which could write the finest chapter in the history of a great people.

One is to recognize that the Arab guerrillas are doing to
us what our terrorists and saboteurs of the Irgun, Stern and
Haganah did to the British. Another is to be willing to
admit that their motives are as honorable as were ours. As a
Jew, even as I felt revulsion against the terrorism, I felt it
justified by the homelessness of the surviving Jews from the
Nazi camps and the bitter scenes when refugee ships sank,
or sank themselves, when refused admission to Palestine.
The best of Arab youth feels the same way; they cannot
forget the atrocities committed by us against villages like
Deir Yassin, nor the uprooting of the Palestinian Arabs
from their ancient homeland, for which they feel the same
deep ties of sentiment as do so many Jews, however assimi-
lated elsewhere.

We made the Palestinian Arabs homeless to make a home
for our own people. That is the simple truth as history will
see it, and until we make amends and resettle the refugees
and create a new political framework in which Jew and
Arab can live together in a new and greater Palestine there
will be no peace. This is a tragic quarrel of brothers, requiring for its resolution that healing double vision which may
at last enable each to see with pity the all-too-human fears
and features of the Other, who is only the mirror image of
ourselves, tightly embraced in hate, where love alone can
free.

Self-pity and self-righteousness, the psychic counterparts
of the siege, can only block a solution. Just as the lofty sky
is Israel's physical way out, so its political and spiritual way
out must be to rise to a higher plane of understanding. To
do so is to clear the way for the political initiatives which
can alone free it from isolation. If Israel wishes to avoid an
imposed solution, then it must come forward with alternative constructive proposals of its own. These should be seen
not as giving away bargaining cards in advance but as a

means of preventing that polarization of sentiment in both the Jewish and Arab communities the die-hards on both sides seek, whether Arab guerrillas or military-minded Israelis. In some form or another this must involve a federated coexistence among Israel, the Palestinian Arabs and the Jordanians, with access to the sea for Jordan and the West Bank. The foundation for such a political settlement must be a major effort to end the Arab refugee problem once and for all time. To this the world Jewish community must show the same generosity we have shown our own uprooted people. So long as more than a million Palestinians live in homeless misery there will be no peace for Israel, and there should be no peace of mind for world Jewry. This is the wrong we must right.

I believe that Charles W. Yost, the American diplomat Nixon has recalled from retirement to act as the U.S. representative at the United Nations, is well suited by experience, insight and humanity to further this cause of reconciliation. I recommend his article on the 1967 war, "How It Began," in the January, 1968, issue of *Foreign Affairs*, and the article he wrote just before his appointment for the January, 1969, issue of *The Atlantic Monthly*, "Israel and The Arabs: The Myths That Block Peace." I agree with the broad outlines of a solution as he has outlined them. A certain hopeful convergence of forces toward a solution is visible in the November, 1967, resolution of the Security Council, the Jarring mission and in the drawing closer of the four big powers toward unified action. "Neither Israel nor the Arabs," *The Times* of London was quite right in warning January 2, "can act as if they were conducting a private vendetta in a vacuum." The Middle East is not Southeast Asia. The Middle East is still the crossroads of the world. Only Berlin could be a more dangerous place for a confrontation of the nuclear superpowers.

Both Washington and Moscow, for all their rivalry, are soberly aware of the dangers. If Israel and the Arabs cannot agree, some solution will have to be imposed which can allow both to live in peace. The die-hards on both sides feel this settlement approaching, and would like to upset it with desperate action. The Beirut affair must be seen in this perspective, too. The fanatical agree only in stalling for time. But it is a myth, as Yost wrote in *The Atlantic Monthly*, to believe that time works in anyone's favor in the Middle East. "A settlement during coming months on the basis of the November resolution may still be feasible," Yost wrote. "Later it may not be. Provocation and counter-provocation may become so shocking and intolerable that compromise will be politically out of the question. If the parties cannot themselves come to a settlement, it will be high time for the UN, with great power backing, to take the initiative. . . . After twenty years, so many dead, so much waste and suffering, world peace more and more threatened, there is no time to lose." To this we can only say Amen.

January 13, 1969

PART X

Pax Americana

HOW THE U.S. PLAYS OUT
A BANANA REPUBLIC
COMEDY IN GREECE

A capsule history would say that German capitalism gambled on Hitler and fell back in defeat on Adenauer. It succeeded (with the help of its opposite numbers in U.S. finance and industry) in regaining power behind the façade of a republic as far to the right as was feasible. To head it West Germany's masters found in Adenauer as authoritarian a figure as ever presided over a parliamentary system. John Foster Dulles, lifelong counsel for German big business interests and an apologist for Nazi expansion, turned up to mold U.S. policy in their favor after the war. He and Adenauer became the Siamese twins of the cold war, a continuation in new guise of Hitler's holy war against Communism. Two major decisions set West Germany's course. In 1949 Adenauer turned to the right, including the far right, rather than to the Social Democrats for the votes he needed to become Chancellor. In 1952 he rejected Soviet proposals for a unified but neutral Reich with an army of its own and chose instead the road of division and NATO. Perhaps the best that can be said of Adenauer was that he was slightly less unlovely than his equally rigid and humorless old antagonist, Ulbricht.

Greece, the first "frontier of freedom" in the cold war and its starting point, is, like West Germany, another example of the U.S. tendency to restore the old order, or as close a simulacrum as possible, under cover of fighting Communism. There the U.S., the world's oldest republic, has been doing its best to maintain Europe's last *un*constitutional monarchy. U.S. propaganda pictures the Greek monarchy as a unifying force between the politically turbulent

Greeks, but its record is one of rightist intrigue. When the monarchy was restored in 1935 after years of republicanism, the King, the present one's uncle, proceeded within a few months to impose a military-Fascist dictatorship on the country which lasted until the Axis invaded in World War II. The pattern seems now to be repeating itself. The monarchist oligarchy ruled Greece with U.S. help until the elections of 1963–64 gave Papandreou's new middle-class liberal Center Union an absolute majority. But the King soon forced him out of office when Papandreou tried to end the system which made the Army officer class the tool of the throne and the preserve of a rightist upper class. Months of intrigue and tension were to have ended with new elections May 28, but the Army has seized power for fear that Papandreou would win them.

One has to be pretty credulous to believe that this coup was pulled off without consulting the King, the U.S. military mission and the CIA. Our guess is that they decided to preserve the appearance of royal detachment. It is reported here that the U.S. Ambassador, in this well-planned charade, even warned the military the U.S. would break off relations if they dethroned the King! There are no reports that we threatened U.S. action unless the Constitution were restored.

May 1, 1967

THE FIRST MILITARY DICTATORSHIP WITH A FREE (BUT SUSPENDED) CONSTITUTION

It is easy to imagine what the U.S. would be saying if the military had seized power in Czechoslovakia, written a Constitution allowing the military junta to suspend indefinitely all basic freedoms, asked the Czechs to vote on that Constitution in an election campaign which allowed no opposition voice, held the plebiscite under martial law, and announced that 99.2 percent of the people had voted approval.

How the Kremlin must envy U.S. technological superiority in arranging such affairs! How clumsy the Kremlin's maneuvers in Czechoslovakia appear beside the smooth operations of the colonels in Greece! The Pentagon's excuse for this extinction of liberty in Greece with U.S. arms is strategic—the need to prevent the rise of a possibly neutralist government on NATO's southern flank. The Kremlin's excuse for the Czech operation is strategic—to prevent the rise of a possibly neutralist regime, outflanking Poland to the north and Hungary to the south. But how few Americans will compare them. The remains of our Old Left is as ready to justify the extinction of liberty in Czechoslovakia as the military and the cold warriors are to justify it in Greece.

The Greek colonels must be given high marks for virtuosity. The new Constitution contains all kinds of democratic guaranties—but leaves it up to the colonels to decide when, if ever, they are to become effective. In the voting, "yes" slips were blue, "no" slips black; there was psychological conditioning in the choice of colors. The voter by dropping or refusing the black ballots could ingratiate himself with the police and military. The two correspondents of *Le Figaro* reported (September 30) they found piles of "no" ballots strewn all over the floor of the balloting places they visited. Many feared reprisals if suspected of voting wrongly.

The early returns were too good. The London *Times* (September 30) carried an *Agence France Presse* dispatch saying the first returns from the north of the country "showed 100 percent in favor." Alfred Friendly in the *Washington Post* (October 1) indicated that the government was embarrassed and holding back early returns which "smacked too much of those traditional to dictatorships." The results from Athens were finally given as 75 percent in favor "compared with 99.8 percent in most rural areas" (*New York Times*, October 1). This reduced the national average to 92.2 percent. It is hard to know how to assess these final figures since the regime did the counting.

The colonels must be spending a fortune on propaganda. "Thirty-five foreign writers, of which five were American," the *Washington Post* reported from Athens (September 29), "have been brought here as guests of the regime with transportation expenses and hotel bills of them and their wives fully paid." Kingsbury Smith of the Hearst press, William F. Buckley and Erwin D. Canham, editor-in-chief of the *Christian Science Monitor*, were among the five. "So confident was the government in the purity of its electoral process," was the way Mr. Canham admitted this in an October 1 dispatch, "that it invited half a hundred news observers, myself included, to be their guests at the voting." With guest-like politeness, Mr. Canham went on to say that he had talked with leading members of the government. "They give the impression," he wrote, "of being dedicated, zealous men."

Similar VIP tours have produced similar compliments from West European parliamentarians. Two British Conservatives issued a statement on their return (London *Times*, September 9) calling the military "dedicated and able" and the people, "in spite of what had been written by hostile writers, happy and relaxed." Six French deputies returned equally euphoric, according to this same story, and declared the Greek economy "wide open to foreign investments."

These happy tidings were interrupted September 21 when a British public relations man, Maurice Fraser, obtained an injunction forbidding the London *Sunday Times* to print a document which had come into its possession. This was a report by Fraser to his employers in the military junta boasting that a British member of Parliament was on his payroll "with the object of influencing other British MP's." A week later, while the injunction was still on appeal, the *Sunday Times* said another British MP was ready to raise the issue in the House of Commons as a breach of parliamentary privilege. The *Sunday Telegraph* the same day named 10 MP's Fraser had flown to Athens with their wives on VIP tours. "During the year," the *Telegraph* added, "six German and six French MP's have also been flown to Athens, as well as numerous journalists, bankers and businessmen."

Freedom's frontier in the Balkans is now the world's first military dictatorship with a free constitution, and the first free constitution which provides indefinite suspension by the military dictators. To the creation of this paradox the U.S. has made no small contribution. Richard J. Barnet has just published a new book, *Intervention and Revolution*. In a chapter on "The Subversion of Undesirable Governments," he quotes a lovely remark by Hubert Humphrey in a happier day during a Senate investigation of the Iranian aid program in 1957. "Do you know what the head of the Iranian army told one of our people?" Humphrey asked. "He said the army was in good shape, thanks to U.S. aid—it was now capable of coping with the civilian population." The same prowess, due to the same aid, is now on display in Greece.

October 7, 1968

PART XI

'It Wasn't for
Lack of Spies . . .'

IT WASN'T FOR
LACK OF SPIES THAT
THE CZARS FELL

Our public controversy over the CIA coincides with the fiftieth anniversary of the Czar's overthrow. There couldn't be a better time to remember that it wasn't for lack of spies that the Russian monarchy fell. No government—except Stalin's—had a more widespread network of secret intelligence operatives at home and abroad than the Romanoffs. The Czars felt, as do American apologists for our own network, that they were up against a sinister, Godless and crafty foe, against whom any tactics were justified to save Holy Russia. Those who exposed police practices were regarded as disloyal.

In my library is a book published in 1930 in London on *The Ochrana, The Russian Secret Police*, by its last chief, A. T. Vassilyev, who died in exile. When I read the apologetics being offered for the CIA, I pulled Vassilyev's memoirs off my shelf. I thought the vigorous going-over that press, radio and TV have given the CIA a wonderful manifestation of health in our own body politic. I was appalled to see even so good a liberal as John Kenneth Galbraith turn out a subtle defense of "the Agency" and speak of "the ravening wolves which in Washington pounce on any individual or agency which has problems" (*Washington Post*, March 12). Vassilyev, like Katzenbach whitewashing the CIA, defends the Ochrana's activities as "always strictly legal." Vassilyev attributes its bad reputation to its adversaries. "It is to be ascribed to the propaganda of these scoundrels," Vassilyev wrote, "that the Secret Political Police acquired such an evil reputation, for the revolutionaries naturally did their utmost to bring discredit upon their bitterest enemy." This is the line today of the CIA, the FBI and the ten other assorted if less glamorized spy organizations—a dozen, no less—represented on the U.S. Intelligence Board. We have but scratched the surface of their pervasive and corrupting influence in eroding the foundations of American freedom. These professional hunters of subversion are our No. 1 subversives.

Just as Central Intelligence was established under Truman in 1947 (when the cold war began) to keep the President posted, so the Ochrana was the Czar's eyes and ears. Twice a month the Ochrana provided the Czar with a publication of which only a single copy was ever printed—for his august eyes alone. "His Majesty was always very desirous," Vassilyev recalled, "of being minutely posted on all the details of the revolutionary movement and of the fight being waged against it. He attached great value to complete accounts of the discovery of secret printing presses, of plots, forbidden libraries." The Czar was even supplied with copies of private letters in which Tolstoy "had given expression to his anti-militarist views." For just as the U.S. has "mail-covers" (as Senator Long of Missouri discovered) so the Ochrana had an elaborate system for reading private correspondence, including invisible ink and codes. This practice, Vassilyev assured his readers, "was never directed against orderly subjects of the Czar but only "seditious elements." The "real honest Russians" (like the real honest Americans?) "were really proud of their Police." Critics, whether Russian or American, are *un*.

The Ochrana carried on not only intelligence but cloak-and-dagger activities. It had so thoroughly penetrated subversive and terrorist organizations that in some cases, as in that of the double agent Azef and the murder of the Prime Minister Stolypin, no one knows to this day whether it was the secret police using the terrorists or the terrorists using the secret police. Those who naively marvel at the CIA's use of liberal and left organizations will find that the Czar's operatives were way ahead of it. In nineteenth-century Europe the ranks of the anarchists were so full of Czarist agents that anarchism was regarded as a kind of Czarist

Comintern to subvert Western Europe. Kerensky in his own memoirs, *Russia and History's Turning Point*, complains that the secret police in 1917 were "almost openly supporting the propaganda of Bolshevik defeatist organizations." Vassilyev in turn (like our own J. Edgar Hoover sneering at "pseudo-liberals") scornfully attacks the Russian "liberals" (his quotation marks) for an "intellectualism" which "was absolutely opposed to the national spirit." For him, Kerensky was only a more subtle menace than Lenin.

Vassilyev could boast that his network had informers everywhere, including members of the Russian Duma or Parliament. It could be said of the Ochrana, as it has been said of the CIA, that it knew everything and understood nothing. The cops never see the underlying grievances. For them, their *nigras* are always happy and contented until secret agitators upset them. It is said in our present controversy that CIA should be limited to intelligence and its cloak-and-dagger operations curtailed or ended. But its clearest successes have been its assassinations. There hasn't been a critical situation, from Cuba to Vietnam, in which the President couldn't get a clearer view of the real situation by carefully reading the newspapers (inadequate as they often are) than by reading his CIA reports. The CIA has been consistently wrong. Clarity of insight is not to be expected from the weird collection of renegades, scholar-mercenaries, Ivy League adventurers, superannuated military men, glorified hotel dicks and just plain corkscrew types that bulk so large in all our intelligence services.

If an omnipresent and well-heeled secret police makes for safety, the Czars should still be on their throne. If what the secret police call "naïveté" and others call the democratic or libertarian tradition is the real danger, then the Revolution when it came should have burst out not in Moscow but in London, where the British were "naïve" enough to allow the arch revolutionaries of our time to work, study, write and agitate unmolested. By all the rules of CIA and FBI, Britain could not have made a greater mistake than

to give Marx and Engels asylum. The lesson that revolutions are not made by conspiracies, nor stopped by assassins,
that you cannot suppress revolutionary agitation without
crippling the debate so necessary to healthy change, is one
that every generation has to learn afresh. We are back again
to fundamentals. The CIA, the FBI and the other networks
would exchange those traditions of which the First Amendment is the symbol for the practices that have sickened the
younger generation in Soviet society and alienated it, as we
are in danger of alienating the best of our own.

March 20, 1967

THE MUJIK AS THE NEGRO
OF THE RUSSIAN REVOLUTION

The historic task which faces the best of the new youth in
the Soviet Union is how to establish free institutions under
socialism. This will require a double revolution, first in
thought and then in action. The first must scrap all the evasive banalities of Communist party talk since the Twentieth
Congress about "cult of personality"—and embark instead
on a reexamination of the Soviet system and its past which
spares neither Lenin nor Marx. All idols must be overthrown, all sacred dogmas exposed to criticism, the windows
thrown open, the cobwebs swept away. This task will have
the value of separating Soviet accomplishments from those
cancerous malformations which, 50 years after the Great
October Revolution, still keep the Soviet system a dictatorship in which neither worker nor peasant dares speak freely.

For American youth our current racial crisis offers a
fresh perspective from which to understand the real roots
of what the Twentieth Congress called the "cult of person-

ality." We are learning from bitter experience what a terrible price can be imposed on a society by slavery and its aftermath. Perhaps the most important single fact in understanding Soviet realities is that a century ago most of the people in Russia were little better than slaves. The *mujik*, the peasant, was Russia's Negro. Their emancipations occurred at the same time: Alexander II's edict freeing Russia's slaves was issued two years before Lincoln's. Both left the intended beneficiaries in a limbo somewhere between bondage and real freedom. Russia, like America, though in a different way, failed to provide 40 acres and a mule. The freed *mujik*, like the freed Negro, remained at the mercy of the master class. All the worst traits attributed to the Negro were attributed to the *mujik*. In America little more than a tenth of our people bear the marks of that crippling past. In Russia it is the overwhelming majority that is of peasant or recent peasant origin.

I once described the American Negro as a case of internal colonialism, a submerged people exploited like those of distant colonies for their cheap labor power, an idea which Stokely Carmichael has developed in his book *Black Power*. This is also true of the *mujik*. For the Russian peasant, the Revolution was indeed a dictatorship of the proletariat. The capital the Soviet Union needed for its industrialization was sweated out of the peasantry—by the huge expropriations which accompanied the liquidation of the *kulaks* and the middle peasantry, by the work extracted from them in the huge labor camps to which they were driven in Siberia and the North, and by the low prices at which the poorer peasants were forced to deliver their products from the collectives and state farms into which they were forced. The *mujik* was Bolshevism's internal empire.

The Revolution was consolidated first by letting the peasant keep the lands he had seized and then by taking back the land in order to get the capital for industrialization. The basic fault of the new peasant proprietors was that they were eating well for the first time in their lives and selling less. By 1927 Russia's global production of wheat had recovered to the prewar level, but it produced only half as much for the market and exported only five percent as much as before the war. The problem was how to get more out of the peasant. The right opposition, led by Bukharin, suggested the carrot. He was impressed by American agriculture. He wanted to stimulate greater farm production by offering the peasant more consumer goods and expanding industry on the basis of a prosperous agriculture. The left opposition, led by the Trotskyists, suggested the stick. Stalin adopted the program of the left, but in practice it took on a ferocity not even he had foreseen; it became a new civil war against the majority of the peasants and it was carried out with the clumsy and wasteful brutality characteristic of Russia's past.

The worker as well as the peasant suffered. The war against the peasant brought on a famine. The Russian worker as well as the peasant had to be subjected to Draconian discipline to keep the economy going. The symbol of the change was the internal passport. This was established by Peter the Great to keep the serf tied down on the farm and in the state factories. It had been abolished by the Revolution as "a police instrument of oppression of the masses." At the end of 1932 internal passports were reestablished to keep workers from changing their jobs and peasants from fleeing to the cities. Soviet citizens must still carry them. In America the passport was used—until the Supreme Court ended the practice—to restrict the movement of suspected citizens abroad; in the Soviet Union it is used to keep police control of everybody's movements at home.

This relic of the past is a reflection, like so much else, of the fundamental if disagreeable fact that the collectivization campaign, like the Bolshevik Revolution from the very beginning, was impressed by a minority of the revolutionaries themselves from above and by terror. All those terrible crimes, "distortions of socialist legality" and "departures from Leninist norms" which the Twentieth Congress attributed to Stalin and the cult of personality flow from this

fundamental fact. Until it is recognized no fundamental reform can be achieved. The backwardness of the country led
the Bolsheviks to deal with it by the backward methods to
which it was habituated—reform from above, an omnipresent secret police system, suppression of dissent, denial of the
freedoms of press and speech.

In the view of Marx and Engels socialism was to be the
natural outgrowth of capitalism, the end result of that evo-
lution by which capitalism collectivizes the processes of industry and the sources of capital while clinging to concep-
tions of private property it was itself rendering obsolete.
The propertyless working class created by capitalism was
to be the natural inheritor and administrator of the new society. This was the Grand Design the Communist Revolution was to fulfill. But Lenin at least as early as 1905 said
that the working class left to itself would only develop a
trade union—and not a socialist—consciousness. The Socialist revolution was to be imposed from above by an elite
of professional revolutionaries who knew better than the
workers what they really wanted. This grandiose vision, itself the product of Russian realities and the Russian past,
implied not a dictatorship *of* the proletariat, but *over* the
proletariat. This is where the so-called evils of the "cult of
personality" began, not in Stalin's personal character.

It is true that Lenin and Trotsky, before they took
power, sometimes spoke in terms very similar to that "par-
ticipatory democracy" which our own New Left cherishes.
In *The State and Revolution*, in August, 1917, Lenin
sketched the outlines of a society in which every official,
whether of the factory or the state, would be subject not
only to election but "to instant recall." "Having conquered
political power," he wrote, "the workers will break up the
old bureaucratic apparatus" and move immediately "to a
state of things when *all* fulfill the functions of control and
superintendence so that *all* become 'bureaucrats for a time,
and *no one* therefore can become a bureaucrat.' " But once
Lenin took power, the new state—as Martov, the greatest
of the Menshevik leaders, noted in 1919—showed a "tend-

ency toward the utmost possible strengthening of the principles of hierarchy and compulsion . . . toward the development of a more specialized apparatus of repression . . . toward the greater independence of the usually elective functions and the annihilation of the control of these functions by the elector masses."

A year earlier the great Polish Jewish revolutionary, Rosa Luxembourg, from her prison cell in Breslau also saw what was coming. Trotsky, she pointed out, had written that in "the open and direct struggle for governmental power, the laboring masses accumulate in the shortest time a considerable amount of political experience and advance quickly from one stage to another of their development." Rosa Luxembourg wrote that "the very giant tasks which the Bolsheviks have undertaken with courage and determination" required the fullest possible development and participation of the masses for their accomplishment. "The public life of countries with limited freedom," she wrote with an insight rare among those supporting the Communists, "is so poverty-stricken, so miserable, so rigid, so unfruitful, precisely because, through the exclusion of democracy, it cuts off the living sources of all spiritual riches and progress." She said no one knew this better and repeated it more often than Lenin, yet "the means he employs: decree, dictatorial force of the factory overseer, draconic penalties, rule by terror" were depriving the masses of all voice in the process. "Without general elections," she declared, "without unrestricted freedom of press and assembly, without a free struggle of opinion, life dies out in every public institution . . . . only the bureaucracy remains as the active element." And in words which link the Revolution with Jefferson and point the way to a free socialism she sketched a reality the Soviet leadership still refuses to recognize—

Freedom only for the supporters of the government, only for the members of one party—however numerous they may be— is no freedom at all. Freedom is always and exclusively freedom for the one who thinks differently. Not because of any fanatical concept of "justice" but because all that is instructive, wholesome and purifying in political freedom depends on this essential characteristic, and its effectiveness vanishes when "freedom" becomes a special privilege.

Two years later Bertrand Russell after a visit to Russia described in his *The Practice and Theory of Bolshevism* the consequences of the course which Rosa Luxembourg had deplored. "The necessity of inculcating Communism," he wrote, "produces a hot-house condition, where every breath of fresh air must be excluded: people are to be taught to think in a certain way, and all free intelligence becomes taboo. The country comes to resemble an immensely magnified Jesuit College."

Every regime must take a choice of risks—the risk of freedom with the danger of popular rejection, even misunderstanding, or the risks of a dictatorship which must increasingly, however well-meaning its founders, become rigid, despotic and encrusted with careerist barnacles. The Bolsheviks chose the latter, and so it is that 50 years after the Revolution, there is still neither free discussion nor free press in the Soviet Union. It has become a gigantic caricature of what socialism was meant to be.

The work of the Twentieth Congress has been aborted because the Party and its leaders fear that full discussion of the "cult of personality" must become a menace to their own monopoly of power and to their habits of ruling by coercion rather than persuasion. The bourgeois state borrowed from feudal experience Magna Charta principles which were developed into a means of protecting the individual from oppressive state action. There is no reason why the proletarian state should not borrow from bourgeois experience. There is no reason why habeas corpus should not exist under socialism as under capitalism, why a man's lawyer may not get him out of jail and force the state to explain why he is being held and subject its accusations to public trial. Had this right existed in the Stalin period some of the best Communists might have been saved—for it was the lickspittles who survived, the brave and the concerned who were liquidated. The only reason for denying so fundamental a right is to retain over the heads of the masses and the intellectuals the shadow of the old terror, the fear that arbitrary arrest is still possible.

The most important change of all, if the Soviet Union is to evolve toward a good society, is freedom of the press. I well remember thirty years ago how the Communists boasted that freedom of the press in Russia under the Constitution newly promulgated by Stalin was broader than in the United States because it not only guaranteed freedom of press and assembly but also ensured these rights "by placing at the disposal of the working people and their organizations printing shops, supplies of paper, public buildings, the streets, means of communication and other material requisites for the exercise of these rights." Thirty years later this is still a bitter hoax.

The Soviet regime's vast apparatus for propaganda serves today as in Stalin's time to hide these realities from the outside world and from many of its own people. All that is worst in the practice of the "bourgeois" states exists in magnified form within the Soviet Union. Despite all the promises of law reform since Stalin died, the law of counterrevolutionary crimes—many times worse in its sweep and vagueness than our Smith Act—is still on the statute books and can still be used to stifle any real discussion. It is only in the worst of the "bourgeois" states—in those of a Fascist character like Spain, Greece, South Vietnam, Brazil and Portugal—that writers are exiled, silenced or imprisoned as Sinyavsky and Daniel are in the Soviet Union. Eleven years after the Twentieth Congress, fourteen years after the death of Stalin, "corrective labor" camps are back in operation and two gifted writers are serving savage sentences of seven and five years respectively in them. Characteristically, no one can find out from the bureaucracy whether or not these sentences have been shortened by the limited amnesty declared in commemoration of the Revolution.

It is for a new generation in the Soviet Union to change these realities. Hegel declared the dialectic had ended in the creation of the despotic Prussian state; the Communists say it ended with the creation of the despotic Soviet state. But truly understood the dialectic goes on forever, and the synthesis of the contradiction between socialism and freedom must be a new state which combines the advantages of both. The great Western tradition which comes down from Spinoza and Milton and Jefferson is fully applicable to socialist society and must be combined with it if Soviet man is to be free and if the socialist ideal is to regain its attraction for youth. The Soviet people who have suffered so much and created so much, who in 50 years have made such giant strides, owe it to themselves and the world to strike out boldly on this new road to the freedom which has so long been denied them.

November 13, 1967

THE REBIRTH OF FREEDOM—
OR OF FASCISM?

In the middle of the next decade, in 1976, we will celebrate the 200th anniversary of independence. There has never been so much doubt whether on that birthday the United States will still be free. The next decade may see a resurgence of fascism in many countries, as the pendulum swings from the permissive to the repressive. A healthy society requires a balance of freedom with order, and of social change with stability. Everywhere in the world this balance has become more difficult to achieve, as population explodes and life becomes more complex. This breeds violence and frustration, as it does when too many animals are pushed into one cage. Hence the snarling and the quarreling. In our country, on top of the universal problems of pollution, urban sprawl and youthful alienation, we are beginning to harvest in a spreading black revolt the bitter fruit of a century of slavery and another century of humiliation. We cannot cope with these interlocking problems unless in the next few years we can raise sharply the level of political understanding and social sympathy and convince the well-to-do majority of the need to forego private luxury in order to wipe out public squalor.

Over the past few years a series of high-level commissions of inquiry has tried to further this task of public education. The latest is the commission on violence appointed 18 months ago after the assassinations of Robert Kennedy and Martin Luther King, Jr. Its final report says again what so many earlier reports have said—that the way to eradicate crime and violence is to eradicate poverty and racial discrimination. The Commission included men as conservative as Senator Hruska, Congressman Hale Boggs of Louisiana and Cardinal Cooke of New York, military vicar of the U.S. Armed Forces. "As a first step" they called for a reversal of the priorities which have given the military establishment first call on the national resources. Yet even as the report was issued the tides were moving in the opposite direction.

Not a single direct word of comment or even thanks came from Mr. Nixon when the report was presented to him. The chairman, Dr. Milton Eisenhower, could announce only that the President had "authorized" him to say he was "gravely concerned" and would "study it with care." The *Weekly Compilation of Presidential Documents* contains four separate speeches and interviews given by Mr. Nixon that week on football, but not one word about the violence report! The Commission proposed that the government increase welfare expenditures by about $20 billion, partly from a "peace dividend" of reduced military expenditure after Vietnam, partly from increased tax revenues as the Gross National Product grows. But Mr. Nixon had already shown at a press conference a few days earlier how foreign such calculations are to his basic thinking.

A reporter asked the President's comment on the statement that there didn't seem much prospect of a peace dividend after Vietnam, but that this rich country could provide all the funds necessary "for the very big problems at home" any time it was prepared to make the necessary sacrifices so "we might very well do it now and get on with the job." Mr. Nixon did not dispute the statement that the end of the Vietnam war would not release substantial funds for domestic needs—a significant key to his own planning. Nor did he deny that we had ample wealth to meet domestic problems. He took a very different tack, one that seemed to foreclose hope. He said federal, state and local taxes already take 25 to 37 percent of the nation's total income (30 percent is the usual estimate), and that to take more would mean that the nation would lose "its character of a free enterprise economy." This was saying that the maintenance of the "free enterprise system" takes precedence even over social problems that may tear the country apart. He implied that if necessary poverty must go on so that profit can thrive. This is vintage Republicanism. It is also the somber diagnosis of Marxist-Leninist fatalism. No radical has said anything more subversive than Mr. Nixon's few unfeeling words.

All this runs directly contrary to the best advice of the violence commission and its predecessors. The so-called Southern strategy, which has led wags here to call the Nixon White House, Uncle Strom's Cabin, is more than Southern. It aims to mobilize the smug against the concerned, the unthinking wealthy against the despairing poor, bewildered middle age against idealistic youth, and bigoted whites against desperate blacks. This strategy may indeed put Wallace out of the running in 1972, as it is intended to do, and let Nixon ride triumphantly back into power on an undivided Know Nothing vote. But the cost in social turmoil will be high, and the price may make the U.S. in 1976 a police state like South Africa. Here as there the price of racial repression must prove to be everybody's freedom.

Seen through the eyes of the blacks, the events of the year end are sinister. The effort to get rid of the 1965 Vot-

ing Act and to slow down school desegregation looks like a
second post-Reconstruction era, an attempt to solidify
white supremacy again in the South. Law-and-order seems
to translate itself in this Administration only into black repression. In New York City a U.S. Attorney who has been
vigorously prosecuting white-collar crime is under White
House pressure to get out just as his investigations touch
financial interests involved in Saigon black marketing and
the Mafia's Swiss bank operations. Crime in the banks
arouse no such passion as crime in the streets. Worst of all is
the trigger-happy lawlessness of the police themselves as
demonstrated in the Black Panther killings in Chicago and
the shoot-out in Los Angeles. These have stirred terrible
fears.

The Black Panther raids have sent seismic tremors
through a black community which has hitherto had little
sympathy with this revolutionary fringe. It is amazing how
many blacks are obsessed with what happened to the Jews
in Germany. They fear—however horrible this may sound
to decent whites—a similar fate. They see the Black Panther affair in a long perspective. For two centuries, under
slavery and after, the militant has been the special target of
harassment and killing. In the ghettoes today too many policemen treat suspected militants with a hatred they rarely
show drug peddlers or pimps. The Chicago killings look like
the climax in a series of "search and destroy" operations designed to wipe out the Panthers, and as a first step—however wildly exaggerated that may sound—toward genocide
should blacks insist on their rights. If this fear of a bloody
confrontation and a Nazi-style "final solution" be paranoia,
it is up to the white community to dispel it. For these fears
are a menace to our common future.

Normal politics will no longer do. Normal politics is the
Southern strategy. Normal politics is the new tax bill, in
which both parties compete to give tax relief when we require a sharp increase in taxing and spending. We need a
campaign of public education, reaching into every town
and village, carrying to town meetings across the country

the findings and the recommendations of the Kerner commission and the Eisenhower violence commission and all the other sober counsels of recent years. We need to convert a benighted into an enlightened majority. We need a small army of youthful Thomas Jeffersons to bring home again the lessons of freedom and of social change as the framer of the Declaration so well understood them. We need a mobilization to make us realize that whatever our differences we are trapped together, breathing the same air, drinking the same water, walking the same streets. The rich could buy no finer luxury than to pay the cost of keeping them clean and safe. To wipe out poverty and racism would be to make America really secure. But to get the kind of planning and spending required we need a revolution in public understanding. No other revolution will work, for it is the comfortable majority itself which must be converted. To bring that about is the truest challenge of the seventies, a task worthy of our finest youth.

December 29, 1969

WHO ARE THE REAL KOOKS IN OUR SOCIETY?

It's hard to judge which is worse—the vulgarity or the stupidity of government officials in dealing with the Chicago conspiracy trial. The U.S. Attorney, Foran, attacks the defendants as "fags," sneaks and scum. The Cook County sheriff has them sheared of their long hair in jail and exhibits the photos at a political rally as an example of "how Republicans get things done." Vice President Agnew calls them "kooks." If the Administration wants to provoke more student rioting, this is the course to pursue. Nothing could make a sizeable portion of our youth more sympathetic to the defendants than forcible hair-cuts, for their hair is the symbol of their revulsion against a society they see as morally bankrupt. The name-calling will sound all too reminiscent of parents too dense to understand the anguish of youth.

Agnew asked that these "kooks . . . demagogues . . . social misfits" be kept off the front pages and the TV screens. If the Administration wanted to keep them off, it should have had more sense than to bring them to trial. An AP dispatch[1] reveals that there were lawyers in the Justice Department who warned that the statute making it a crime to cross state lines to incite a riot was of doubtful constitutionality, that the trial would inevitably become political and that the accused might turn it into a circus which would embarrass the government. Attorney General Mitchell overruled them and now the Vice President seems to want more of the same. He told the Governors Conference in Washington, "Let us react automatically, briskly and effectively to the threat of violent revolution and recognize it for the clear and present danger it constitutes." To call it "a clear and present danger" is to invoke the Supreme Court's rationale for justifying the restriction of fundamental liberties in a time of imminent danger. Only the far-out Weatherman faction of the SDS is kooky enough to join Agnew in imagining that a rash of window-breaking by students puts the government of the United States in imminent danger of overthrow. And nothing would do more to foster blind revolutionary rage on the campuses and in the ghettoes than to start filling the jails with more student and radical leaders.

An Agnew at large poses more danger to social stability than the Chicago defendants. One passage in his appeal to the Governors was the authentic voice of repressionist ideology. He called on the Governors "to withstand the criticism of the liberal community, who are presently so blinded by total dedication to individual freedom that they cannot

1 Jean Heller, AP, in the *Washington Post*, February 27.

see the steady erosion of collective freedom . . ." To speak of being "blinded by total dedication to individual freedom" is strange language from an American Vice President in the capital of the so-called free world. This is not Jeffersonianism. It is a compote of decayed Leninism and leftovers from the Fascist era. The only meaningful freedom is individual. "Collective freedom" is the jailhouse liberty the Communist bureaucracy imposes on dissidents in Moscow, Warsaw and Prague, and the military junta of Papadapoulos on Athens. There are a few wacky Maoists on the fringes of the youth movement who sound in this respect just like Agnew. The Vice President has taken a great leap forward. . . .

March 9, 1970

WHERE THE FUSE
ON THAT DYNAMITE LEADS

> The search of the youth today is for ways and means to make the machine—and the vast bureaucracy of the corporation state and of government that runs that machine—the servant of man. That is the revolution that is coming. That revolution . . . need not be a repetition of 1776. It could be a revolution in the nature of an explosive political regeneration. It depends on how wise the Establishment is. If, with its stockpile of arms, it resolves to suppress the dissenters, America will face, I fear, an awful ordeal.
>
> *Points of Rebellion:* Justice Douglas.

The *New York Times* editorial Friday March 13 on the rash of bombings and bomb scares in New York City was called "Not Idealists: Criminals." This was the standard reaction of a liberal publication, the easy way to clear its

skirts of any suspicion of the slightest sympathy with revolutionary radicalism. But it is a dangerous cliché. Falsely to
diagnose the trouble is to move toward the wrong remedies,
and the wrong remedies will worsen the disease. Statistics
on bombings from cities around the country suggest that
we may be entering the first stages of an urban guerrilla
movement. A guerrilla movement is a political, not a criminal
phenomenon, however many crimes it may commit. Experience has shown over and over again that a guerrilla movement can only be defeated by political means. The effort to
treat it simply as a criminal matter, without resolving its
political causes, ends by increasing the number of the guerrillas and widening their support in the larger community.

Whether the New York bombings prove to be a spasm in
the wake of the Greenwich Village explosion, when a radical arsenal blew up, or the beginning of a serious terrorist
movement will now depend on the authorities, and their
ability to keep their cool. The first requisite—*and* the second, *and* the third—is understanding.

The Weatherman kids can be seen in various ways, and it
is necessary to see them in as many as possible. The Weatherman faction of SDS, whence several different "direct action" splinter groups seem to derive, can be looked at like a
distraught child. They can be viewed as spoiled brats, in a
tantrum with a world which will not change overnight to
suit them. But they are also the most sensitive of a generation
which feels in its bones what we older people only grasp as
an unreal abstraction, that the world is headed for nuclear
annihilation and something must be done to stop it. The
Weatherman manifesto from which they take their name is
from one point of view a mishmash of ill-digested pseudo-
Marxist rubbish, an effort to compete with their bitterest
rivals, the "square" sectarian ideologists of that other far-out
splinter group, Progressive Labor. The manifesto spurns
every normal base of revolutionary support and ends up
squarely in the clouds: the middle class is, of course, no
good; the working class is corrupted; the college generation
will soon sell out; their only hope is in the juvenile Robes-

pierres of the high schools. It sounded like the Children's Crusade come back to life, a St. Vitus dance of hysterical politics.

It is from just such despair that terrorist movements have grown. This recalls the Russian pre-revolutionary *Narodnya Volya* (People's Will) through which a handful of disaffected middle class and noble youths sought by bomb and pistol to overthrow the mighty Czarist order, with roots so deep in the religious reverence of the peasant masses as to seem impregnable. How to overturn their Little Father? A movement which has no faith in the masses seeks out the desperate few idealists willing to sacrifice their lives in gestures they realize may be futile. Some of our young revolutionaries are chillingly sober and disconcertingly sensible. Their criticism of conventional dissenters like myself and our futility, as the war goes on, is hard to rebut. Others in recent months have displayed a morbid development, a tendency to glorify violence for its own sake, as when they make Manson a hero for killing "bourgeois pigs," i.e., people exactly like their fathers and mothers. The ultimate menace they fear is their own secret selves in their own parents. This is what they are acting out on the stage of national politics.

But these psychological aspects are only a part of the whole complex picture. These wild and wonderful—yes, wonderful!—kids also serve quite rational political ends. I became strongly aware of this when I ran into an old friend on an early morning Washington street corner the other day who is working hard in a respectable do-good reformist organization, the very kind the youthful radicals despise. I told him that in talks on various campuses I had tried to talk the young people out of the typically American idea that revolution could be "instant" like coffee or iced tea. "Don't discourage them," was his unexpected plea. "If they stop acting up, we'll never get the Establishment to budge."

From a longer range political point of view, the New Left and the hippies and the Yippies may, in however weird a form, also forecast the future. They see Soviet Communism merely as a further stage of capitalism, a mass production bureaucratic society concentrated on the production of goods rather than the liberation of the spirit. They see the working class becoming "middle class" under it, and the need for a newer revolution against making the individual a *thing* in a mindless industrial process rather than the loving center of a universe meant to be joyous in our brief moment of passage through it. To study their irrationality is to become aware of ours.

The immediate lesson is this: If the police authorities are high-handed and arbitrary in their hunt for the bombers—as some already are—they will turn more moderates into activists. The answer to the revolutionaries is to behave with justice, to demonstrate that the system can operate under pressure in accordance with its own best ideals. *And first and above all to end the war.* Again and again, the overreaction and panic of an established order has turned a handful of conspirators into a revolutionary movement. This is, of course, exactly what the Chicago trial has done in radicalizing youth and destroying its faith in the courts. What happens on appeal may represent the last chance of winning them back to rational discourse and faith in peaceful change. In these, rather than a blind and volcanic upheaval, I see mankind's only chance. For the problems which confront us lie deep in the conditioning of man and in the power of technology to enslave him. No one is yet wise enough to chart the way out, as the most perceptive of the kids themselves admit. They merely hope something better will turn up out of the ruins. But I do not believe in salvation by holocaust. Hate and hysteria certainly will not create a new man or build a better world. Political suicide is not revolution.

But I must confess that I almost feel like throwing rocks through windows myself when I see Judge Julius Hoffman turn up as an honored guest at the White House and when I see Billy Graham like a smoother Rasputin dishing out saccharine religiosity there: If all Americans would only repeat the Lord's Prayer together, he said, "He could lead us out of our dilemma"—and at no increase in taxes either! I sense in Nixon and his entourage no anguish, no awareness, no real comprehension. When has there been a more inane leadership as storm clouds gather? Not since Marie Antoinette has there been a remark to match Moynihan's "benign neglect."

Between the disaffected white youth and the growing anger of the blacks, we could be on the verge of a wild upheaval. I hold my breath as I go to press waiting to see whether Rap Brown is dead or alive. In the black community here in Washington those who knew Ralph Featherstone best, and remember his efforts only two weeks ago to advise the ghetto youth against violence, do not believe he was transporting explosives. They think he was murdered. They see the police and the FBI engaged in an effort to throw the blame upon the dead men themselves. Hoover's name at the bottom of that cryptic FBI report on the bombing is a provocation to the blacks. For them Hoover is an old ally of the Southern racists in Congress. In the black community, too, the established order is recruiting the forces which threaten it. Until the war in Southeast Asia is ended, until the Pentagon is cut down drastically, until priorities are revised to make racial reconciliation and social reconstruction our No. 1 concerns, the dynamite that threatens us sizzles on a fuse that leads straight back to the White House.

March 23, 1970

PART XII

The Streets

THE RICH MARCH ON
WASHINGTON ALL THE TIME

> No other Western country permits such a large propor-
> tion of its people to endure the lives we press on our
> poor. To make four-fifths of a nation more affluent than
> any people in history, we have degraded one-fifth
> mercilessly.
>
> *Report of the Citizens Inquiry into Hunger*

To see the Poor People's March on Washington in perspective, remember that the rich have been marching on Washington ever since the beginning of the Republic. They came
in carriages and they come on jets. They don't have to put
up in shanties. Their object is the same, but few respectable
people are untactful enough to call it handouts. Washington owes its very existence as the capital to a deal for the
benefit of wealthy speculators. They had bought up the de-
faulted bonds issued to finance the revolution, paying as
little as 15 cents on the dollar to the needy original investors. The speculators wanted repayment at full face value.
It was only by promising to move the capital from Philadelphia to a new city to be built on the Potomac that Alexander Hamilton could get enough Southern votes to swing
the deal.

The fiscal and banking system of the new republic was
thus solidly established on the basis of a $20 million handout
to the rich and on the Hamiltonian theory that if the new
government would channel enough of the national wealth
to the top some of it would eventually trickle down. In the
meantime the farmer and the consumer would pay the taxes
and the tariffs to keep the investor fat and happy. Ever
since then the public treasury and the public lands have
been a major source of the great American fortunes, down

to our own day of never-ending oil depletion allowances. The tax structure and the laws bear the imprint of countless marches on Washington; these have produced billions in hidden grants for those who least need them. Across the facade of the U.S. Treasury should be engraved, "To him who hath shall be given."

One easy and equitable way to finance an end to abject poverty in this country would be to end the many tax privileges the wealthy have acquired. A 12-man committee of industrialists and financiers has just recommended to Governor Rockefeller of New York a form of that guaranteed income the marching poor will demand. The committee proposes a negative income tax to raise 30 million of our neediest above the poverty level. Instead of paying income taxes they would receive enough from the Treasury to bring their incomes up to a minimum of $3300 a year for a family of four. The additional cost would be about $11 billion a year. That is what the more obvious tax loopholes for the rich now drain from the U.S. Treasury.[1]

Few people realize that our present tax and welfare structure is such as to encourage the wealthy to speculate and the poor to vegetate. If a rich man wants to speculate, he is encouraged by preferential capital gains and loss provisions which give him a 25 percent cushion against losses and take less than half as much on his speculative gains as on his normal earnings. But if a poor man on relief took a part-time job, he had until very recently to pay a 100 percent tax on his earnings in the shape of a dollar-for-dollar reduction in his relief allowance. Even now after a belated reform in the welfare system, a poor man on relief, after his first $30 a month in extra earnings, must turn back to the Treasury 70 cents on the dollar while the rich man need pay the Treasury only 25 cents of every dollar he wins on the market even when his normal income tax rate is more than 50 percent. Such is the topsy-turvy morality of the Internal Revenue laws.

[1] The figure is from a staff study made for Senator Proxmire as chairman of the Joint Economic Committee of Congress.

A heart-breaking report on hunger by a Citizens Board of Inquiry has just lifted the curtain on why the poor are marching. In the richest country in the world people eat clay to still the pains of an empty belly, children come to school too hungry to learn, and the infants of the poor suffer irreversible brain damage from protein deprivation. Much of the crime in the streets springs from hunger in the home. Much of this hunger is also linked to hand-outs for those who do not need them. Some of its roots may be found in subsidy programs designed to encourage farmers to make more money by producing less food. The effect has been to push the poor off the land and into the ghettoes. A program designed 30 years ago ostensibly to help the desperate family farmer has become a source of huge handouts to big farmers and farm corporations.

In 1967 the 42.7 percent of our farmers with incomes of less than $2,500 a year received only 4.5 percent of total farm subsidies paid by the government while the top 10 percent, many of them farm corporations or vertical trusts in food processing, received 64.5 percent of these subsidies. The contrast between these handouts for rich farming interests and the stingy surplus food allotments for the poor is dramatically displayed in the statistical appendices of the Citizens Report on Hunger. In the calendar year 1966 a quarter billion dollars in farm subsidies was paid to a lucky landowning two one-hundredths of one percent of the population of Texas while the 28.8 percent of its population below the poverty line received less than $8 million in all forms of food assistance. Such grotesque maldistribution of federal aid is not limited to the South. That same year the U.S. Treasury paid almost $36 million in farm subsidies to one-third of one percent of the population of Nebraska while only $957,000 in surplus food allotments went to the 26.1 percent of its population which is in poverty. One farm company in California, J. G. Boswell, was given $2,807,633 in handouts by the Treasury that year and the Hawaiian Commercial and Sugar Company got $1,236,355 in federal sweetening.

Such are the huge hogs that crowd the public trough. Other even bigger corporations live on the gravy that drips from the military and space programs. We may never reach the moon—or know what to do with it when we get there —but the race for it has already created a new generation of Texas millionaires. The arms race and the space race guarantee the annual incomes of many in the country club set.

Even before the marchers began arriving, the President at his latest press conference was already inviting them to leave. Their demands would be "seriously" considered, he said, "and then we expect to get on with running the government as it should be." For years, "running the government as it should be" has meant financing and planning these programs which are the welfare systems of the American upper classes. Three-quarters of the poor get no help. Two-thirds of our hungry schoolchildren are not reached by the school lunch program. But finding the money to help them is not part of "running the government as it should be," i.e., with a budget allocated 80 percent to the Pentagon and 10 percent to health, education and welfare.

Ours is a warfare, not a welfare, state. And unless the better conscience of the country can be mobilized, it will wage war upon the poor, too. Only twice before in our history have the poor marched on Washington—Coxey's Army of the jobless in 1894 and the bonus marchers in 1932. Both times they were easily dispersed by force. The last heartless chapter of the flinty Hoover Administration was the attack of General MacArthur's troops upon the encampment of the bonus marchers on the Anacostia flats. This time the shanties will not be burned down nor the poor scattered so easily. A clash could set off the hottest summer yet of our nascent civil war. The poor may prove an irresistible force. The Congress is certainly an immovable óbject.

At this dangerous juncture we need a crusade of the progressive well-to-do to supplement the efforts of the Poor People's March. We are glad to see that SANE and a group of other organizations is calling for demonstrations of support throughout the country for Saturday, May 25. We need volunteers to stand on street corners and collect money to feed the encampment of the poor in Washington. And we need an army of young white idealists to ring doorbells in the suburbs and awaken the middle class to the crisis the poor may precipitate. What lies ahead may be far more important than the election.

We wish the unaware millions of the suburbs could have heard the extraordinary collection of spokesmen for the poor whom the Reverend Ralph David Abernathy brought to Wesley A.M.E. Church for a preliminary rally here last week. The volcanic despair of our Negroes, Puerto Ricans, Indians, Spanish Americans and poor whites has thrown up new and unknown leaders able to present their case with an untaught and unmatchable eloquence. The descenders of the enslaved, the conquered and the dispossessed have found voices which makes one realize what human resources lie untapped among them. It was also thrilling in a time of rising separation to join hands again with blacks in singing "We Shall Overcome" and to feel how truly this movement stems from Martin Luther King's teaching. If this fails, multi-racialism and non-violence will fail with it. Yet fail it must unless the middle class and the suburb can be aroused to pressure Congress for the steps required to wipe out poverty. "There is nothing," Martin Luther King said, "except a tragic death wish, to prevent us from reordering our priorities, so that the pursuit of peace will take precedence over the pursuit of war." Now is the time for the white and the fortunate to organize themselves for this work of solidarity. This—it cannot be said too often—may be our last chance.

May 13, 1968

THEY PLEADED GUILTY
OF BURNING PAPER
INSTEAD OF CHILDREN

In the days of the New Deal the WPA had something called Living Theatre. Living theatre is what radicals have begun to produce. One example is the black comedy a wild horde of hippies and yippies wove around the House Un-American Activities Committee, driving it to suspend its hearings into the Chicago peace demonstrations. Those shopworn inquisitors did not know what to do with witnesses who acted out the procedure's essential irrationality.

Another example is the morality play the Catonsville Nine have been enacting. They staged their first act on May 17 when they entered a local draft board in Catonsville, Md., and burned up its files, with napalm they manufactured themselves from a recipe in the U.S. Special Forces Handbook. "Our apologies, good friends," said Father Daniel Berrigan, the poet-priest who was one of their leaders, "for the fracture of good order, the burning of paper instead of children."

The second act was in a federal court in Baltimore last week before Chief Judge Roszel C. Thomsen. The Nine are all Catholic, clergy and lay. Their types are recognizable through history: the stuff of which saints are made, moved by a deeper sensitivity to human suffering. They joyfully admitted their guilt, like early brethren preparing for the lions. No legalisms spoiled the second act curtain.

The government, in its own dramaturgy, picked a black man to prosecute them. First Assistant U.S. Attorney Arthur G. Murphy said the morality of the war was not at issue, though he admitted in passing that a reasonable man might think it illegal. The issue, he said, was simply destroying property and obstructing the law. The chief defense attorney, William Kunstler, insisted "The trial is not simple, any more than those of Jesus and Socrates were simple."

Judge Thomsen, like a certain forerunner, kept washing his hands of the affair by allowing the defendants extraordinary latitude in explaining why they did it. The two most wondrous characters among the Nine, the ex-priest Thomas Melville and his wife, the ex-nun, were even allowed to touch on the sufferings they saw in Guatemala which ended by driving them into the arms of the guerrillas and out of the Church. Their quiet sobriety is in strange contrast to the traumas that so transformed their lives.

The trial drew some 2,000 zealots from all over the country. The deepest appeal of the spectacle for them was in Father Daniel Berrigan's testimony when he said, "I was in danger of verbalizing my moral impulses out of existence. I sought a way to defy the state even if I was too old to defy the draft." Of course they were found guilty. Not to acquiesce in murder, the chief and most ancient business of the State, is clearly subversive. On November 8 they will be sentenced. The third and longest act will be when they and their supporters use the appeals to put the show on the road. We cannot think of a finer way to stir the sluggish conscience of the nation.

October 21, 1968

IN DEFENSE OF
THE CAMPUS REBELS

I hate to write on subjects about which I know no more than the conventional wisdom of the moment. One of these

subjects is the campus revolt. My credentials as an expert
are slim. I always loved learning and hated school. I wanted
to go to Harvard, but I couldn't get in because I had graduated forty-ninth in a class of fifty-two from a small-town
high school. I went to college at the University of Pennsylvania, which was obligated—this sounds like an echo of a
familiar black demand today—to take graduates of high
schools in neighboring communities no matter how ill-fitted.
My boyhood idol was the saintly Anarchist Kropotkin. I
looked down on college degrees and felt that a man should
do only what was sincere and true and without thought of
mundane advancement. This provided lofty reasons for not
doing homework. I majored in philosophy with the vague
thought of teaching it but though I revered two of my pro-
fessors I disliked the smell of a college faculty. I dropped
out in my third year to go back to newspaper work. Those
were the twenties and I was a pre-depression radical. So I
might be described I suppose as a premature New Leftist,
though I never had the urge to burn anything down.

In microcosm, the *Weekly* and I have become typical of
our society. The war and the military have taken up so
much of our energies that we have neglected the blacks, the
poor and students. Seen from afar, the turmoil and the
deepening division appear to be a familiar tragedy, like
watching a friend drink himself to death. Everybody
knows what needs to be done, but the will is lacking. We
have to break the habit. There is no excuse for poverty in a
society which can spend $80 billion a year on its war ma-
chine. If national security comes first, as the spokesmen for
the Pentagon tell us, then we can only reply that the clearest danger to the national security lies in the rising revolt of
our black population. Our own country is becoming a
Vietnam. As if in retribution for the suffering we have imposed, we are confronted by the same choices: either to satisfy the aspirations of the oppressed or to try and crush them
by force. The former would be costly, but the latter will be
disastrous.

This is what the campus rebels are trying to tell us, in the only way which seems to get attention. I do not like much of what they are saying and doing. I do not like to hear opponents shouted down, much less beaten up. I do not like to hear any one group or class, including policemen, called pigs. I do not think four-letter words are arguments. I hate *hate*, intolerance and violence. I see them as man's most ancient and enduring enemies and I hate to see them welling up on my side. But I feel about the rebels as Erasmus did about Luther. Erasmus helped inspire the Reformation but was repelled by the man who brought it to fruition. He saw that Luther was as intolerant and as dogmatic as the Church. "From argument," as Erasmus saw it, "there would be a quick resort to the sword, and the whole world would be full of fury and madness." Two centuries of religious wars without parallel for blood-lust were soon to prove how right were his misgivings. But while Erasmus "could not join Luther, he dared not oppose him, lest haply, as he confessed 'he might be fighting against the spirit of God.' " [1] I feel that the New Left and the black revolutionists, like Luther, are doing God's work, too, in refusing any longer to submit to evil, and challenging society to reform or crush them.

Lifelong dissent has more than acclimated me cheerfully to defeat. It has made me suspicious of victory. I feel uneasy at the very idea of a Movement. I see every insight degenerating into a dogma, and fresh thoughts freezing into lifeless party line. Those who set out nobly to be their brother's keeper sometimes end up by becoming his jailer. Every emancipation has in it the seeds of a new slavery, and every truth easily becomes a lie. But these perspectives, which seem so irrefutably clear from a pillar in the desert, are worthless to those enmeshed in the crowded struggle. They are no better than mystical nonsense to the humane student who has to face his draft board, the dissident soldier who is determined not to fight, the black who sees his people doomed by shackles stronger than slavery to racial humiliation and decay. The business of the moment is to end the

[1] Froude's Life and Letters of Erasmus.

war, to break the growing dominance of the military in our
society, to liberate the blacks, the Mexican-American, the
Puerto Rican and the Indian from injustice. This is the business of our best youth. However confused and chaotic, their
unwillingness to submit any longer is our one hope.

There is a wonderful story of a delegation which came
here to see Franklin D. Roosevelt on some reform or other.
When they were finished the President said, "Okay, you've
convinced me. Now go on out and bring pressure on me."
Every thoughtful official knows how hard it is to get anything done if someone isn't making it uncomfortable *not to*.
Just imagine how helpless the better people in government
would be if the rebels, black and white, suddenly fell silent.
The war might smolder on forever, the ghettoes attract as
little attention as a refuse dump. It is a painful business ex-
tricating ourselves from the stupidity of the Vietnamese
war; we will only do so if it becomes more painful *not to*. It
will be costly rebuilding the ghettoes, but if the black revolt
goes on, it will be costlier *not to*. In the workings of a free
society, the revolutionist provides the moderate with the
clinching argument. And a little *un*-reason does wonders,
like a condiment, in reinvigorating a discussion which has
grown pointless and flat.

We ought to welcome the revolt as the one way to prod
us into a better America. To meet it with cries of "law and
order" and "conspiracy" would be to relapse into the sterile
monologue which precedes all revolutions. Rather than
change old habits, those in power always prefer to fall back
on the theory that all would be well but for a few
malevolent conspirators. It is painful to see academia dis-
rupted, but under the surface were shams and horrors that
needed cleansing. The disruption is worth the price of
awakening us. The student rebels are proving right in the
daring idea that they could revolutionize American society
by attacking the universities as its soft underbelly. But I
would also remind the students that the three evils they
fight—war, racism and bureaucracy—are universal. The
Marxism-Leninism some of the rebels cling to has brought

into power a bureaucracy more suffocating than any under capitalism; the students demonstrate everywhere on our side but are stifled on the other. War and imperialism have not been eliminated in the relations between Communist states. Black Africa, at least half-freed from the white man, is hardly a model of fraternity or freedom. Man's one real enemy is within himself. Burning America down is no way to Utopia. If battle is joined and our country polarized, as both the revolutionists and the repressionists wish, it is the better and not the worse side of America which will be destroyed. Someone said a man's character was his fate, and tragedy may be implicit in the character of our society *and* of its rebels. How make a whisper for patience heard amid the rising fury?

May 19, 1969

BITTER BATTLES LIE AHEAD

From my days as an editorial writer on one of the few pro-New Deal papers in the country, I remember how bitterly the Democrats complained about the hostility of the press and radio; they portrayed Roosevelt as a dangerous revolutionary. When he won his landslide victory in 1936 it was over their overwhelming opposition. We felt as the Nixon crowd does now that the news media were one-sided, but there are crucial differences between the two periods. Poor people don't own newspapers. The news media now as then are in wealthy, mostly conservative and largely Republican hands. It takes a lot of steam in the boiler before they turn against a Republican President. Their growing opposition testifies to the unpopularity of the war and the spreading suspicion that Nixon wants to hang on, whatever the cost, until he can get a political victory. Nixon might as well complain about the unfairness of the stock market. It has been going down steadily since it sized up the November 3 speech as the signal for a prolonged war. Nothing Huntley ever said to Brinkley is as subversive as the Dow-Jones ticker. Wall Street—the citadel of the GOP—has lost confidence in Nixon and in Nixon's war.

Nixon's real complaint is that the news media don't agree with him. Since the First Amendment doesn't require the press to agree with the President, he doesn't dare say this openly and instead charges unfairness. It is remarkable how little evidence of this the Administration is able to cite, after gathering transcripts from every TV station on what they said about the November 3 speech. When Agnew—Nixon's Papadapoulos and official cleanser of the U.S. media—went on TV ten days later, all he could offer was a scurrilous attack on Averell Harriman and a colorful but curiously vague bill of particulars. He complained about "a raised eyebrow, an inflection of the voice, a caustic remark dropped in the middle of a broadcast." What caustic remark? What insidious inflection? Whose raised eyebrow? Couldn't Klein find anything more specific? Is this Athens where the cops even watch eyebrows?

Equally feeble in its vagueness was Agnew's attack a week later on the *New York Times* and the *Washington Post*. You'd think Agnew could do better than complaining about one story which missed the early edition and that the Pope's support for Nixon made page 11 instead of page 1. Is that all the White House researchers could find? Agnew was so desperate he made like a liberal at one point and attacked "monopolization of the news." We welcome him to the fold. But neither New York nor Washington are one-newspaper towns. In New York the pro-Nixon *Daily News* circulation is far bigger than the *Times* and the *Post* combined. In Washington, both the *Daily News* and the *Star* are conservative and pro-Nixon (as is the *Washington Post* quite often, most recently on Haynsworth and, alternate days, on Nixon's war policy). It is true that just three days after Agnew spoke a Washington paper had the impudence to write—

From the first announcement of the Mobilization plans, the Administration reacted by building a wall of indifference and hostility between itself and the demonstrators. The opposition was generally classified as the product of either stupidity or subversion. There was little attempt to reason, and a massive effort at rejection.

But that was an editorial in the conservative *Star* (November 23).

We are seeing a marriage of paranoias. Nixon has always felt (remember his outburst after he lost the Governorship in California) that the media were against him. The military and its supporters in the State Department and the White House have been grumbling about press coverage ever since the Vietnam intervention began. The animosity deepened every time the reporters were proven right and the generals wrong. The baldest and most recent expression of the bureaucracy's delusions came when General Walt of the Marines told a press conference in Danang (*Washington Post*, November 23) that the war would have been over a year ago if the American people had supported Lyndon Johnson! He criticized the news media for failing to present a "positive" picture of the conflict and said how long the war lasts would "depend in lots of respects on how good treatment it gets from our news media." So the main obstacle to victory is the First Amendment, and Jeffersonianism will soon be un-American again.

In Saigon the regime is cracking down on the press as dissatisfaction rises. Here the Administration is trying to make independent reporting seem unpatriotic. In the events of the tumultuous last two weeks, the Administration has been demonstrating its incompetence on many levels; to give it freedom from criticism would be an invitation to mismanagement. The Haynsworth affair was one example. We cheer the outcome but note that it was a self-inflicted defeat. The Attorney General was slipshod in his preliminary inquiry; the White House was crude in its pressure tactics. The low point was the crass attempt at political blackmail—the threat to impeach Mr. Justice Douglas if the nomination were rejected. The revolt in the Northern Republican leadership showed the bankruptcy of the Southern strategy and its corollary, the attempt to compete with Wallace in Know Nothingism. Such hands at the wheel of state are a safety hazard.

The handling of the Mobilization missed disaster by a hair's breadth. Until the intervention of Mayor Washington, the Administration was on the verge of denying a parade permit and doing a Daley. At the Pentagon, on the eve of the Mobilization, a Mass in the south concourse, where it blocked no traffic, was broken up by the police (all black for the occasion) and an Episcopal Bishop and the peaceful celebrants arrested just as it drew to its close. It was an ugly scene a modicum of good sense would have avoided. Before the Mobilization, the Administration ostentatiously moved troops into the capital, as if for an uprising, and filled the press with alarms. It reminded me of the days when Hoover called out the troops under MacArthur and drove the Bonus Marchers out of town in a glorious military victory. It sealed Hoover's defeat in 1932. The Republicans are trigger-happy again.

Despite the incendiary forecasts, the Mobilization proved as pacific as the Moratorium. The March of Death was a masterpiece of dramaturgy. Thanks to an army of marshals, and logistic preparations few armies could match, Saturday's parade went off without incident, the greatest outpouring of its kind in U.S. history. It was quite a contrast to the sparse turnout and screwball tone of the pro-Nixon demonstration four days earlier. Even so, when the Mobilization drew to its close, the police roughed up departing citizens on the Monument grounds and outside churches where buses were being loaded, as if someone higher up regretted the absence of violence. In the same spirit the Attorney General over-reacted to the Justice Department demonstration against the Conspiracy Trial by drenching the downtown areas with tear gas and locking up passersby and two reporters with imbecile impartiality.

Nothing is more dangerous than weak men who think they are tough guys. The resignations of Lodge and Walsh at the Paris peace talks, coming after the threat to re-escalate in the November 3 speech, indicate that the Administration is getting ready to be "tough" in Vietnam as at home. There is no sign that it is heeding the repeated warnings of the Gallup organization that its good showing in the public opinion polls is predicated on the expectation that Nixon "will remove U.S. troops from Vietnam within a reasonable time" (*New York Times*, November 23). That "silent majority," if any, will evaporate if this expectation is disappointed. This is where Nixon is most vulnerable. It is the job of the peace movement to fan out into the country with a campaign of education while it can. This Administration is capable of suicidal folly. It may resume the bombing of the North. It may try another witch hunt at home. We believe that if it tries either it will be swept away in a landslide in 1972, as Hoover was 40 years ago. But there are bitter battles ahead. We had better get ready for them.

December 1, 1969

INDEX

ABOUT THE AUTHOR

Born in 1907, I. F. Stone, who died in 1989, was a working newspaperman from the age of fourteen when, during his sophomore year at a small-town high school, he launched a monthly, *The Progress*, which supported — among other causes — the League of Nations and Gandhi's first efforts at freedom for India.

While at school and college, he worked for daily newspapers in Camden, New Jersey, Philadelphia, and New York.

Since 1940 he served in succession as a Washington correspondent and commentator for *The Nation*, the newspaper *PM*, the *New York Post*, and the *Daily Compass*. In 1953 he launched *I. F. Stone's Weekly*, a legendary venture in independent, one-man journalism, which he edited and published for nineteen years. He wrote extensively for the *New York Review of Books* and long served as a contributing editor.

In semiretirement Mr. Stone returned to the philosophy and classical history he had studied in college. He taught himself ancient Greek and wrote *The Trial of Socrates*, a controversial probe of the most famous free-speech case of all time, widely acclaimed on publication in 1988.

THE STORY

THE STORY

THE BIBLE AS ONE CONTINUING STORY OF GOD AND HIS PEOPLE

SELECTIONS FROM THE NEW INTERNATIONAL VERSION

ZONDERVAN.com/
AUTHORTRACKER
follow your favorite authors

Published by Zondervan
3900 Sparks Drive SE, Grand Rapids, Michigan 49546, USA

www.zondervan.com

Biblica provides God's Word to people through translation, publishing and Bible engagement in Africa, Asia Pacific, Europe, Latin America, Middle East, and North America. Through its worldwide reach, Biblica engages people with God's Word so that their lives are transformed through a relationship with Jesus Christ.

Contents

Welcome to *The Story*— God's Story

THIS BOOK TELLS THE GRANDEST, most compelling story of all time: the story of a true God who loves his children, who established for them a way of salvation and provided a route to eternity. Each story in these 31 chapters reveals the God of grace — the God who speaks; the God who acts; the God who listens; the God whose love for his people culminated in his sacrifice of Jesus, his only Son, to atone for the sins of humanity.

What's more: this same God is alive and active today — still listening, still acting, still pouring out his grace on us. His grace extends to our daily foibles; our ups, downs, and in-betweens; our moments of questions and fears; and most important, our response to his call on our lives. He's the same God who forgave David's failures and rescued Jonah from the dark belly of a fish. This same heavenly Father who shepherded the Israelites through the wilderness desires to shepherd us through our wanderings, to help us get past our failures and rescue us for eternity.

It's our prayer that these stories will encourage you to listen for God's call on your life, as he helps write your own story.

MAX LUCADO and RANDY FRAZEE

Preface

THE STORY, THROUGH ITS UNIQUE and easy-to-read format, opens a door to God's truth. It's a door that every person is consciously or unconsciously searching for. A door that leads to freedom, hope and God himself! The Bible is filled with exciting and intense stories of love, war, birth, death and miracles. There's poetry, culture, history and theology. It's a suspense novel, a book of sociology, a history lesson — all woven around one eternal conflict: good versus evil. This story offers a glimpse of people in a different time and place who are yet very much like us today.

As you read *The Story* you will encounter not only the story of humankind but also the story of who God is and what he has done for us — for *you*. This story makes the insistent claim that a loving God has sought you and provided a way of redemption — a way for you to enter a relationship with him.

The Story includes the actual, God-breathed words of the Bible. The 31 chapters that comprise *The Story* contain portions of Scripture that were thoughtfully and carefully excerpted and then placed in chronological order. Transitions, which appear in *Italic*, were written to summarize omitted Scripture text in order to help the storyline read smoothly. The texts were chosen to retain the overall flow of the narrative, so that when you read this story, you will get a sense of the "big picture" of the Bible. Line spaces were added when text was omitted, and a chart at the back of this book will let you know what portions of Scripture were included.

Other helpful material placed at the end of *The Story* include an epilogue that gives you an idea of the global impact this story has had on the world, a discussion guide with questions for you to reflect on personally or with a group and a cast of characters with brief descriptions so that you can tell who's who at a glance.

The Scripture text used in *The Story* is taken from the New International Version (NIV). Our goal was to make the Bible read smoothly and easily, so that you can read it just like you'd read a novel. But *The Story* you're reading isn't any ordinary story. You are reading a story that has the power to change who you are, what you think and how you view life. You are exposing yourself to deep, transforming truth.

So sit back and enjoy the truest, greatest story ever written.

Timeline of *The Story**

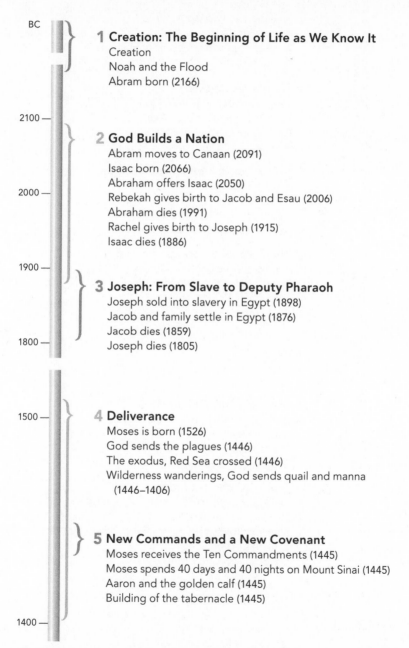

BC

1 Creation: The Beginning of Life as We Know It
Creation
Noah and the Flood
Abram born (2166)

2100

2 God Builds a Nation
Abram moves to Canaan (2091)
Isaac born (2066)
Abraham offers Isaac (2050)
Rebekah gives birth to Jacob and Esau (2006)
Abraham dies (1991)
Rachel gives birth to Joseph (1915)
Isaac dies (1886)

2000

1900

3 Joseph: From Slave to Deputy Pharaoh
Joseph sold into slavery in Egypt (1898)
Jacob and family settle in Egypt (1876)
Jacob dies (1859)
Joseph dies (1805)

1800

4 Deliverance
Moses is born (1526)
God sends the plagues (1446)
The exodus, Red Sea crossed (1446)
Wilderness wanderings, God sends quail and manna
    (1446–1406)

1500

5 New Commands and a New Covenant
Moses receives the Ten Commandments (1445)
Moses spends 40 days and 40 nights on Mount Sinai (1445)
Aaron and the golden calf (1445)
Building of the tabernacle (1445)

1400

*Dates are approximate and dependent on the interpretative theories of various scholars.

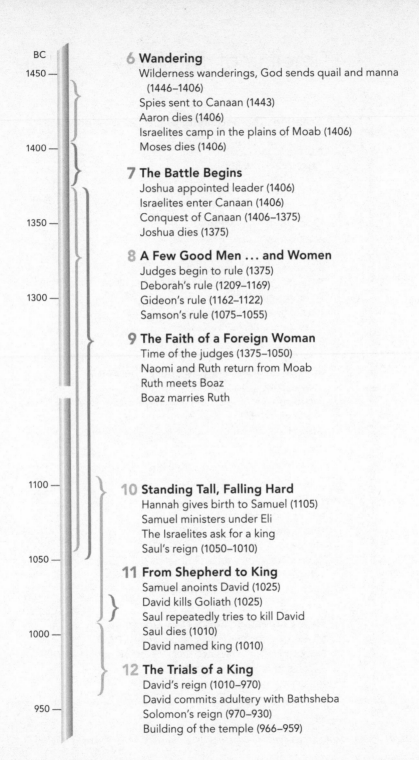

BC

1450 —

6 Wandering
Wilderness wanderings, God sends quail and manna
   (1446–1406)
Spies sent to Canaan (1443)
Aaron dies (1406)
Israelites camp in the plains of Moab (1406)
Moses dies (1406)

1400 —

7 The Battle Begins
Joshua appointed leader (1406)
Israelites enter Canaan (1406)
Conquest of Canaan (1406–1375)
Joshua dies (1375)

1350 —

8 A Few Good Men ... and Women
Judges begin to rule (1375)
Deborah's rule (1209–1169)
Gideon's rule (1162–1122)
Samson's rule (1075–1055)

1300 —

9 The Faith of a Foreign Woman
Time of the judges (1375–1050)
Naomi and Ruth return from Moab
Ruth meets Boaz
Boaz marries Ruth

1100 —

10 Standing Tall, Falling Hard
Hannah gives birth to Samuel (1105)
Samuel ministers under Eli
The Israelites ask for a king
Saul's reign (1050–1010)

1050 —

11 From Shepherd to King
Samuel anoints David (1025)
David kills Goliath (1025)
Saul repeatedly tries to kill David
Saul dies (1010)
David named king (1010)

1000 —

12 The Trials of a King
David's reign (1010–970)
David commits adultery with Bathsheba
Solomon's reign (970–930)
Building of the temple (966–959)

950 —

1000—

13 The King Who Had It All
David dies (970)

950—
Solomon's reign (970–930)
Solomon displays great wisdom
Building of the temple (966–959)
Solomon marries foreign wives and betrays God

900—
14 A Kingdom Torn in Two
Division of the kingdom (930)
King Jeroboam I of Israel reigns (930–909)
King Rehoboam of Judah reigns (930–913)

850—
King Ahab of Israel reigns (874–853)
King Jehoshaphat of Judah (872–848)

15 God's Messengers
Elijah's ministry in Israel (875–848)

800—
Elisha's ministry in Israel (c. 848–797)
Amos's ministry in Israel (760–750)
Hosea's ministry in Israel (750–715)

750—

16 The Beginning of the End (of the Kingdom of Israel)
Fall of Israel (722)

700—
Exile of Israel to Assyria (722)
Isaiah's ministry in Judah (740–681)
Hezekiah's reign (715–686)

17 The Kingdoms' Fall
650—
Manasseh's reign (697–642)
Amon's reign (642–640)
Josiah's reign (640–609)
Jeremiah's ministry in Judah (626–585)
Jehoiakim's reign (609–598)

600—
Zedekiah's reign (597–586)
Ezekiel's ministry (593–571)
Fall of Jerusalem (586)

18 Daniel in Exile
550—
Daniel exiled to Babylon (605)
Daniel's ministry (605–536)
Nebuchadnezzar's reign (605–562)
Daniel and the lions' den (539)

500—
Fall of Babylon (539)

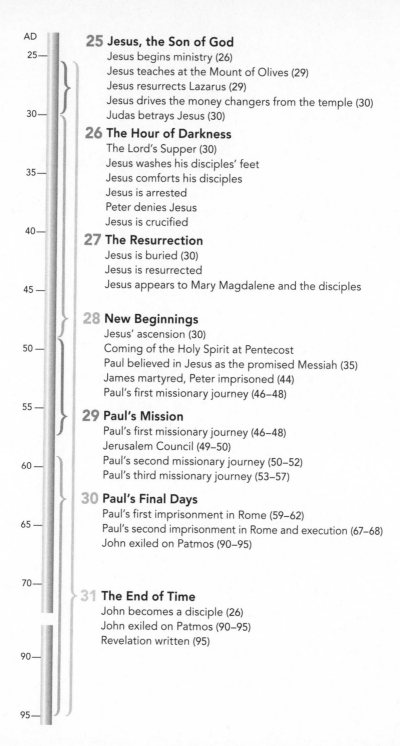

1

Creation:
The Beginning of Life as We Know It

IN THE BEGINNING God created the heavens and the earth. Now the earth was formless and empty, darkness was over the surface of the deep, and the Spirit of God was hovering over the waters.

And God said, "Let there be light," and there was light. God saw that the light was good, and he separated the light from the darkness. God called the light "day," and the darkness he called "night." And there was evening, and there was morning — the first day.

And God said, "Let there be a vault between the waters to separate water from water." So God made the vault and separated the water under the vault from the water above it. And it was so. God called the vault "sky." And there was evening, and there was morning — the second day.

And God said, "Let the water under the sky be gathered to one place, and let dry ground appear." And it was so. God called the dry ground "land," and the gathered waters he called "seas." And God saw that it was good.

Then God said, "Let the land produce vegetation: seed-bearing

Creation   Noah and the Flood   Abram born

BC   2166

Full timeline information starts on page xi.

plants and trees on the land that bear fruit with seed in it, according to their various kinds." And it was so. The land produced vegetation: plants bearing seed according to their kinds and trees bearing fruit with seed in it according to their kinds. And God saw that it was good. And there was evening, and there was morning — the third day.

And God said, "Let there be lights in the vault of the sky to separate the day from the night, and let them serve as signs to mark sacred times, and days and years, and let them be lights in the vault of the sky to give light on the earth." And it was so. God made two great lights — the greater light to govern the day and the lesser light to govern the night. He also made the stars. God set them in the vault of the sky to give light on the earth, to govern the day and the night, and to separate light from darkness. And God saw that it was good. And there was evening, and there was morning — the fourth day.

And God said, "Let the water teem with living creatures, and let birds fly above the earth across the vault of the sky." So God created the great creatures of the sea and every living thing with which the water teems and that moves about in it, according to their kinds, and every winged bird according to its kind. And God saw that it was good. God blessed them and said, "Be fruitful and increase in number and fill the water in the seas, and let the birds increase on the earth." And there was evening, and there was morning — the fifth day.

And God said, "Let the land produce living creatures according to their kinds: the livestock, the creatures that move along the ground, and the wild animals, each according to its kind." And it was so. God made the wild animals according to their kinds, the livestock according to their kinds, and all the creatures that move along the ground according to their kinds. And God saw that it was good.

Then God said, "Let us make mankind in our image, in our likeness, so that they may rule over the fish in the sea and the birds in the sky, over the livestock and all the wild animals, and over all the creatures that move along the ground."

So God created mankind in his own image,
in the image of God he created them;
male and female he created them.

God blessed them and said to them, "Be fruitful and increase in number; fill the earth and subdue it. Rule over the fish in the sea and the birds in the sky and over every living creature that moves on the ground."

Then God said, "I give you every seed-bearing plant on the face of the whole earth and every tree that has fruit with seed in it. They will be yours for food. And to all the beasts of the earth and all the birds in the sky and all the creatures that move along the ground — everything that has the breath of life in it — I give every green plant for food." And it was so.

God saw all that he had made, and it was very good. And there was evening, and there was morning — the sixth day.

Thus the heavens and the earth were completed in all their vast array.

By the seventh day God had finished the work he had been doing; so on the seventh day he rested from all his work. Then God blessed the seventh day and made it holy, because on it he rested from all the work of creating that he had done.

This is the account of the heavens and the earth when they were created, when the LORD God made the earth and the heavens.

Now no shrub had yet appeared on the earth and no plant had yet sprung up, for the LORD God had not sent rain on the earth and there was no one to work the ground, but streams came up from the earth and watered the whole surface of the ground. Then the LORD God formed a man from the dust of the ground and breathed into his nostrils the breath of life, and the man became a living being.

Now the LORD God had planted a garden in the east, in Eden; and there he put the man he had formed. The LORD God made all kinds of trees grow out of the ground — trees that were pleasing to the eye and good for food. In the middle of the garden were the tree of life and the tree of the knowledge of good and evil.

The LORD God took the man and put him in the Garden of Eden to work it and take care of it. And the LORD God commanded the man, "You are free to eat from any tree in the garden; but you must not eat from the tree of the knowledge of good and evil, for when you eat from it you will certainly die."

The LORD God said, "It is not good for the man to be alone. I will make a helper suitable for him."

Now the LORD God had formed out of the ground all the wild animals and all the birds in the sky. He brought them to the man to see what he would name them; and whatever the man called each living creature, that was its name. So the man gave names to all the livestock, the birds in the sky and all the wild animals.

But for Adam no suitable helper was found. So the LORD God caused the man to fall into a deep sleep; and while he was sleeping, he took one of the man's ribs and then closed up the place with flesh. Then the LORD God made a woman from the rib he had taken out of the man, and he brought her to the man.

The man said,

> "This is now bone of my bones
> and flesh of my flesh;
> she shall be called 'woman,'
> for she was taken out of man."

That is why a man leaves his father and mother and is united to his wife, and they become one flesh.

Adam and his wife were both naked, and they felt no shame.

God had created a beautiful world and filled it with glorious, diverse creatures. Of all his creation, he singled out two humans to build a relationship with — Adam and Eve. These two people were blessed to share their paradise with each other and God, so why would they want anything else?

Now the serpent was more crafty than any of the wild animals the LORD God had made. He said to the woman, "Did God really say, 'You must not eat from any tree in the garden'?"

The woman said to the serpent, "We may eat fruit from the trees in the garden, but God did say, 'You must not eat fruit from the tree that is in the middle of the garden, and you must not touch it, or you will die.'"

"You will not certainly die," the serpent said to the woman. "For God knows that when you eat from it your eyes will be opened, and you will be like God, knowing good and evil."

When the woman saw that the fruit of the tree was good for food and pleasing to the eye, and also desirable for gaining wisdom, she took some and ate it. She also gave some to her husband, who was with her, and he ate it. Then the eyes of both of them were opened, and they realized they were naked; so they sewed fig leaves together and made coverings for themselves.

Then the man and his wife heard the sound of the LORD God as he was walking in the garden in the cool of the day, and they hid from the LORD God among the trees of the garden. But the LORD God called to the man, "Where are you?"

He answered, "I heard you in the garden, and I was afraid because I was naked; so I hid."

And he said, "Who told you that you were naked? Have you eaten from the tree that I commanded you not to eat from?"

The man said, "The woman you put here with me — she gave me some fruit from the tree, and I ate it."

Then the LORD God said to the woman, "What is this you have done?"

The woman said, "The serpent deceived me, and I ate."

So the LORD God said to the serpent, "Because you have done this,

> "Cursed are you above all livestock
>   and all wild animals!
> You will crawl on your belly

and you will eat dust
 all the days of your life.
And I will put enmity
 between you and the woman,
 and between your offspring and hers;
he will crush your head,
 and you will strike his heel."

To the woman he said,

"I will make your pains in childbearing very severe;
 with painful labor you will give birth to children.
Your desire will be for your husband,
 and he will rule over you."

To Adam he said, "Because you listened to your wife and ate fruit from the tree about which I commanded you, 'You must not eat from it,'

"Cursed is the ground because of you;
 through painful toil you will eat food from it
 all the days of your life.
It will produce thorns and thistles for you,
 and you will eat the plants of the field.
By the sweat of your brow
 you will eat your food
until you return to the ground,
 since from it you were taken;
for dust you are
 and to dust you will return."

Adam named his wife Eve, because she would become the mother of all the living.

The LORD God made garments of skin for Adam and his wife and clothed them. And the LORD God said, "The man has now become like one of us, knowing good and evil. He must not be allowed to reach out his hand and take also from the tree of life and eat, and live forever." So the LORD God banished him from the Garden of Eden to work the ground from which he had been taken. After he drove the man out, he placed on the east side of the Garden of Eden cherubim and a flaming sword flashing back and forth to guard the way to the tree of life.

Adam made love to his wife Eve, and she became pregnant and gave birth to Cain. She said, "With the help of the LORD I have brought forth a man." Later she gave birth to his brother Abel.

Now Abel kept flocks, and Cain worked the soil. In the course of time Cain brought some of the fruits of the soil as an offering[1] to the LORD. And Abel also brought an offering — fat portions from some of the firstborn of his flock. The LORD looked with favor on Abel and his offering, but on Cain and his offering he did not look with favor. So Cain was very angry, and his face was downcast.

Then the LORD said to Cain, "Why are you angry? Why is your face downcast? If you do what is right, will you not be accepted? But if you do not do what is right, sin[2] is crouching at your door; it desires to have you, but you must rule over it."

Now Cain said to his brother Abel, "Let's go out to the field." While they were in the field, Cain attacked his brother Abel and killed him.

The tragic accounts of the mistakes and poor choices of Adam and Eve, and their firstborn son Cain, are echoed in the later stories of hardship and tragedy for their children and their children's children. As people began to populate the globe, leaving the area of Eden and traveling as far as feet and beast could carry them, humanity's legacy of hate, anger, murder and deception play out as people continue to neglect their relationship with God. Eventually, nearly everyone just plain forgets their Creator and the whole point of being alive. For most

---

[1]**Offering:** Something given to God in an act of thankfulness, worship or payment for disobedience. In the Old Testament, there were five kinds of offerings: burnt, grain, fellowship, sin and guilt. The death of Jesus in the New Testament is the ultimate offering that paid the full price of sin. This word is synonymous with *sacrifice.*
[2]**Sin:** Evil, moral shortcoming, wrongdoing or disobedience. This term refers to any action, thought or attitude that does not meet the standards set by God.

people, life becomes one big party with no thought of conse-
quences ... except for one man.

The LORD saw how great the wickedness of the human race had
become on the earth, and that every inclination of the thoughts of
the human heart was only evil all the time. The LORD regretted
that he had made human beings on the earth, and his heart was
deeply troubled. So the LORD said, "I will wipe from the face of the
earth the human race I have created — and with them the animals,
the birds and the creatures that move along the ground — for I
regret that I have made them." But Noah found favor in the eyes
of the LORD.

This is the account of Noah and his family.

Noah was a righteous[3] man, blameless among the people of
his time, and he walked faithfully with God. Noah had three sons:
Shem, Ham and Japheth.

Now the earth was corrupt in God's sight and was full of violence. God saw how corrupt the earth had become, for all the
people on earth had corrupted their ways. So God said to Noah, "I
am going to put an end to all people, for the earth is filled with violence because of them. I am surely going to destroy both them and
the earth. So make yourself an ark of cypress wood; make rooms
in it and coat it with pitch inside and out. This is how you are to
build it: The ark is to be three hundred cubits long, fifty cubits
wide and thirty cubits high. Make a roof for it, leaving below the
roof an opening one cubit high all around. Put a door in the side
of the ark and make lower, middle and upper decks. I am going to
bring floodwaters on the earth to destroy all life under the heavens, every creature that has the breath of life in it. Everything on
earth will perish. But I will establish my covenant[4] with you, and
you will enter the ark — you and your sons and your wife and your
sons' wives with you. You are to bring into the ark two of all liv-

---

[3]**Righteous:** Living according to the standards set by God. *God's righteousness* refers to his
justice and perfection.
[4]**Covenant:** An agreement or promise between two parties. A covenant was intended to be
unbreakable.

ing creatures, male and female, to keep them alive with you. Two of every kind of bird, of every kind of animal and of every kind of creature that moves along the ground will come to you to be kept alive. You are to take every kind of food that is to be eaten and store it away as food for you and for them."

Noah did everything just as God commanded him.

The LORD then said to Noah, "Go into the ark, you and your whole family, because I have found you righteous in this generation.

Seven days from now I will send rain on the earth for forty days and forty nights, and I will wipe from the face of the earth every living creature I have made."

Noah was six hundred years old when the floodwaters came on the earth. And Noah and his sons and his wife and his sons' wives entered the ark to escape the waters of the flood. Pairs of clean and unclean animals, of birds and of all creatures that move along the ground, male and female, came to Noah and entered the ark, as God had commanded Noah. And after the seven days the floodwaters came on the earth.

On that very day Noah and his sons, Shem, Ham and Japheth, together with his wife and the wives of his three sons, entered the ark. They had with them every wild animal according to its kind, all livestock according to their kinds, every creature that moves along the ground according to its kind and every bird according to its kind, everything with wings. Pairs of all creatures that have the breath of life in them came to Noah and entered the ark. The animals going in were male and female of every living thing, as God had commanded Noah. Then the LORD shut him in.

For forty days the flood kept coming on the earth, and as the waters increased they lifted the ark high above the earth. The waters rose and increased greatly on the earth, and the ark floated on the surface of the water. They rose greatly on the earth, and all the high mountains under the entire heavens were covered. The waters rose and covered the mountains to a depth of more than fifteen cubits. Every living thing that moved on land perished — birds, livestock, wild animals, all the creatures that swarm over the earth, and all mankind. Everything on dry land that had the breath of life in its nostrils died. Every living thing on the face of the earth was wiped out; people and animals and the creatures that move along the ground and the birds were wiped from the earth. Only Noah was left, and those with him in the ark.

The waters flooded the earth for a hundred and fifty days.

But God remembered Noah and all the wild animals and the livestock that were with him in the ark, and he sent a wind over the earth, and the waters receded. Now the springs of the deep and the floodgates of the heavens had been closed, and the rain had stopped falling from the sky. The water receded steadily from the earth. At the end of the hundred and fifty days the water had gone down, and on the seventeenth day of the seventh month the ark came to rest on the mountains of Ararat. The waters continued to recede until the tenth month, and on the first day of the tenth month the tops of the mountains became visible.

By the first day of the first month of Noah's six hundred and first year, the water had dried up from the earth. Noah then removed the covering from the ark and saw that the surface of the ground was dry. By the twenty-seventh day of the second month the earth was completely dry.

Then God said to Noah, "Come out of the ark, you and your wife and your sons and their wives. Bring out every kind of living creature that is with you — the birds, the animals, and all the creatures that move along the ground — so they can multiply on the earth and be fruitful and increase in number on it."

So Noah came out, together with his sons and his wife and his sons' wives. All the animals and all the creatures that move along the ground and all the birds — everything that moves on land — came out of the ark, one kind after another.

Then Noah built an altar to the LORD and, taking some of all the clean animals and clean birds, he sacrificed burnt offerings on it. The LORD smelled the pleasing aroma and said in his heart: "Never again will I curse the ground because of humans, even though every inclination of the human heart is evil from childhood. And never again will I destroy all living creatures, as I have done."

Then God blessed Noah and his sons, saying to them, "Be fruitful and increase in number and fill the earth. The fear and dread of you will fall on all the beasts of the earth, and on all the birds in the sky, on every creature that moves along the ground, and on all the fish in the sea; they are given into your hands."

Then God said to Noah and to his sons with him: "I now establish my covenant with you and with your descendants after you and with every living creature that was with you — the birds, the livestock and all the wild animals, all those that came out of the ark with you — every living creature on earth. I establish my covenant with you: Never again will all life be destroyed by the waters of a flood; never again will there be a flood to destroy the earth."

And God said, "This is the sign of the covenant I am making between me and you and every living creature with you, a covenant for all generations to come: I have set my rainbow in the clouds, and it will be the sign of the covenant between me and the earth.

"Whenever the rainbow appears in the clouds, I will see it and remember the everlasting covenant between God and all living creatures of every kind on the earth."

The earth recovered from this great flood. Animal and plant life flourished. Noah's family repopulated the earth. The cycle of life continued, and people remembered God. Ancient businesses grew, homesteads and farms developed, and trade routes brought wealth and opportunity for travel. It was time for God's next move, time to build a nation in a land that would become the cultural and ethnic home to … well, that part of the story is yet to come.

Abram (whose name God later changed to Abraham) had all the wrong qualifications for being a founder of God's nation: His relatives worshiped other gods in a country far from what would become the promised land; Abram and his wife, Sarai (whose name God later changed to Sarah), were way beyond childbearing years and Sarai couldn't get pregnant—no children meant no people to populate God's nation. No problem. God promised the impossible to Abram, and Abram watched as the impossible occurred. Here's how it happened.

2

God Builds a Nation

THE LORD HAD SAID TO ABRAM, "Go from your country, your people and your father's household to the land I will show you.

> "I will make you into a great nation,
>   and I will bless you;
> I will make your name great,
>   and you will be a blessing.
> I will bless those who bless you,
>   and whoever curses you I will curse;
> and all peoples on earth
>   will be blessed through you."

So Abram went, as the LORD had told him; and Lot went with him. Abram was seventy-five years old when he set out from Harran. He took his wife Sarai, his nephew Lot, all the possessions they had accumulated and the people they had acquired in Harran, and they set out for the land of Canaan, and they arrived there.

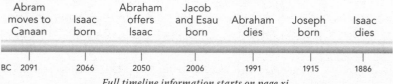

Abram moves to Canaan	Isaac born	Abraham offers Isaac	Jacob and Esau born	Abraham dies	Joseph born	Isaac dies
BC 2091	2066	2050	2006	1991	1915	1886

Full timeline information starts on page xi.

By faith[1] Abraham, when called to go to a place he would later receive as his inheritance, obeyed and went, even though he did not know where he was going.

Abram traveled through the land as far as the site of the great tree of Moreh at Shechem. At that time the Canaanites were in the land. The LORD appeared to Abram and said, "To your offspring I will give this land." So he built an altar there to the LORD, who had appeared to him.

Now Lot, who was moving about with Abram, also had flocks and herds and tents. But the land could not support them while they stayed together, for their possessions were so great that they were not able to stay together.

The LORD said to Abram after Lot had parted from him, "Look around from where you are, to the north and south, to the east and west. All the land that you see I will give to you and your offspring forever. I will make your offspring like the dust of the earth, so that if anyone could count the dust, then your offspring could be counted. Go, walk through the length and breadth of the land, for I am giving it to you."

So Abram went to live near the great trees of Mamre at Hebron, where he pitched his tents. There he built an altar to the LORD.

By faith he made his home in the promised land like a stranger in a foreign country; he lived in tents, as did Isaac and Jacob, who were heirs with him of the same promise. For he was looking forward to the city with foundations, whose architect and builder is God.

Lot made some bad decisions and found himself in deep trouble. He took up residence near Sodom. In retrospect, it was a poor choice of real estate. Soon the kings of Sodom, Gomorrah

---

[1]**Faith:** Complete trust. True faith is much deeper than mere intellectual agreement with certain facts — it affects the desires of one's heart.

and three other kings squared off in battle against an enemy army. The kings of Sodom and Gomorrah lost, and the cities were looted. Lot and his family were among the captives.

When this news reached Abram, he pulled together 318 trusted men and without hesitation set out to rescue his nephew. Their night attack caught the looters by surprise. Abram freed the captives and recovered the spoil. Meeting a priest by the name of Melchizedek, he gave him a tenth of the spoils and delivered to the king what rightfully belonged to him.

Despite Abram's growing sense of God's power, one problem remained that even the Almighty seemed unable to solve. It was Abram's greatest worry and the main topic of his dialogues with God.

After this, the word of the LORD came to Abram in a vision:

> "Do not be afraid, Abram.
>   I am your shield,
>   your very great reward."

But Abram said, "Sovereign[2] LORD, what can you give me since I remain childless and the one who will inherit my estate is Eliezer of Damascus?" And Abram said, "You have given me no children; so a servant in my household will be my heir."

Then the word of the LORD came to him: "This man will not be your heir, but a son who is your own flesh and blood will be your heir." He took him outside and said, "Look up at the sky and count the stars — if indeed you can count them." Then he said to him, "So shall your offspring be."

Abram believed the LORD, and he credited it to him as righteousness.

Against all hope, Abraham in hope believed and so became the father of many nations, just as it had been said to him, "So shall your offspring be." Without weakening in his faith, he faced the fact that his body was as good as dead — since he was about a

---

[2]**Sovereign:** This term describes the fact that God has complete control over all things.

hundred years old — and that Sarah's womb was also dead. Yet he did not waver through unbelief regarding the promise of God, but was strengthened in his faith and gave glory to God, being fully persuaded that God had power to do what he had promised. This is why "it was credited to him as righteousness."

Abram believed that the promised child would come from his own body, but as far as he and Sarai knew, God didn't specify that Sarai would be the mother. In a move common during this time, they decided that Sarai's slave, Hagar, would be a surrogate mother for the promised child. However, after Hagar conceived, she and Sarai quarreled, and Hagar was sent away, helpless and pregnant to wander in the wilderness. Just as she despaired of her life, God spoke to her.

Then the angel of the LORD told her, "Go back to your mistress and submit to her." The angel added, "I will increase your descendants so much that they will be too numerous to count."

The angel of the LORD also said to her:

> "You are now pregnant
> and you will give birth to a son.
> You shall name him Ishmael,
> for the LORD has heard of your misery.
> He will be a wild donkey of a man;
> his hand will be against everyone
> and everyone's hand against him,
> and he will live in hostility
> toward all his brothers."

She gave this name to the LORD who spoke to her: "You are the God who sees me," for she said, "I have now seen the One who sees me." That is why the well was called Beer Lahai Roi; it is still there, between Kadesh and Bered.

So Hagar bore Abram a son, and Abram gave the name Ishmael to the son she had borne. Abram was eighty-six years old when Hagar bore him Ishmael.

When Abram was ninety-nine years old, the LORD appeared to him and said, "I am God Almighty; walk before me faithfully and be blameless. Then I will make my covenant between me and you and will greatly increase your numbers."

Abram fell facedown, and God said to him, "As for me, this is my covenant with you: You will be the father of many nations. No longer will you be called Abram; your name will be Abraham, for I have made you a father of many nations. I will make you very fruitful; I will make nations of you, and kings will come from you. I will establish my covenant as an everlasting covenant between me and you and your descendants after you for the generations to come, to be your God and the God of your descendants after you. The whole land of Canaan, where you now reside as a foreigner, I will give as an everlasting possession to you and your descendants after you; and I will be their God."

Then God said to Abraham, "As for you, you must keep my covenant, you and your descendants after you for the generations to come. This is my covenant with you and your descendants after you, the covenant you are to keep: Every male among you shall be circumcised.[3] You are to undergo circumcision, and it will be the sign of the covenant between me and you.

"Any uncircumcised male, who has not been circumcised in the flesh, will be cut off from his people; he has broken my covenant."

God also said to Abraham, "As for Sarai your wife, you are no longer to call her Sarai; her name will be Sarah. I will bless her and will surely give you a son by her. I will bless her so that she will be the mother of nations; kings of peoples will come from her."

Now the LORD was gracious to Sarah as he had said, and the LORD did for Sarah what he had promised. Sarah became pregnant

---

[3]**Circumcised, circumcision:** A surgical removal of the foreskin of the male genitals, performed on the eighth day following birth. In the Old Testament this ritual symbolized the baby's entrance into the Hebrew community. Biblical uses of the term are often metaphorical, referring to the obedience of the heart represented by the outward symbol of circumcision.

and bore a son to Abraham in his old age, at the very time God had promised him.

And by faith even Sarah, who was past childbearing age, was enabled to bear children because she considered him faithful who had made the promise. And so from this one man, and he as good as dead, came descendants as numerous as the stars in the sky and as countless as the sand on the seashore.

Abraham gave the name Isaac[4] to the son Sarah bore him. When his son Isaac was eight days old, Abraham circumcised him, as God commanded him. Abraham was a hundred years old when his son Isaac was born to him.

Sarah said, "God has brought me laughter, and everyone who hears about this will laugh with me." And she added, "Who would have said to Abraham that Sarah would nurse children? Yet I have borne him a son in his old age."

God gave Abraham a child of promise. But Abraham had a child already through Hagar—Ishmael. What would become of him?

The child grew and was weaned, and on the day Isaac was weaned Abraham held a great feast. But Sarah saw that the son whom Hagar the Egyptian had borne to Abraham was mocking, and she said to Abraham, "Get rid of that slave woman and her son, for that woman's son will never share in the inheritance with my son Isaac."

The matter distressed Abraham greatly because it concerned his son. But God said to him, "Do not be so distressed about the boy and your slave woman. Listen to whatever Sarah tells you, because it is through Isaac that your offspring will be reckoned. I will make the son of the slave into a nation also, because he is your offspring."

Early the next morning Abraham took some food and a skin of

---

[4]**Isaac:** *Isaac* means "he laughs."

water and gave them to Hagar. He set them on her shoulders and then sent her off with the boy. She went on her way and wandered in the Desert of Beersheba.

When the water in the skin was gone, she put the boy under one of the bushes. Then she went off and sat down about a bow-shot away, for she thought, "I cannot watch the boy die." And as she sat there, she began to sob.

God heard the boy crying, and the angel of God called to Hagar from heaven and said to her, "What is the matter, Hagar? Do not be afraid; God has heard the boy crying as he lies there. Lift the boy up and take him by the hand, for I will make him into a great nation."

Then God opened her eyes and she saw a well of water. So she went and filled the skin with water and gave the boy a drink.

God was with the boy as he grew up. He lived in the desert and became an archer.

Some time later God tested Abraham. He said to him, "Abraham!"

"Here I am," he replied.

Then God said, "Take your son, your only son, whom you love — Isaac — and go to the region of Moriah. Sacrifice him there as a burnt offering on a mountain I will show you."

Early the next morning Abraham got up and loaded his donkey. He took with him two of his servants and his son Isaac. When he had cut enough wood for the burnt offering, he set out for the place God had told him about. On the third day Abraham looked up and saw the place in the distance. He said to his servants, "Stay here with the donkey while I and the boy go over there. We will worship and then we will come back to you."

Abraham took the wood for the burnt offering and placed it on his son Isaac, and he himself carried the fire and the knife. As the two of them went on together, Isaac spoke up and said to his father Abraham, "Father?"

"Yes, my son?" Abraham replied.

"The fire and wood are here," Isaac said, "but where is the lamb for the burnt offering?"

Abraham answered, "God himself will provide the lamb for the burnt offering, my son." And the two of them went on together.

When they reached the place God had told him about, Abraham built an altar there and arranged the wood on it. He bound his son Isaac and laid him on the altar, on top of the wood. Then he reached out his hand and took the knife to slay his son. But the angel of the LORD called out to him from heaven, "Abraham! Abraham!"

"Here I am," he replied.

"Do not lay a hand on the boy," he said. "Do not do anything to him. Now I know that you fear God, because you have not withheld from me your son, your only son."

Abraham looked up and there in a thicket he saw a ram caught by its horns. He went over and took the ram and sacrificed it as a burnt offering instead of his son.

By faith Abraham, when God tested him, offered Isaac as a sacrifice. He who had embraced the promises was about to sacrifice his one and only son, even though God had said to him, "It is through Isaac that your offspring will be reckoned." Abraham reasoned that God could even raise the dead, and so in a manner of speaking he did receive Isaac back from death.

So Abraham called that place The LORD Will Provide. And to this day it is said, "On the mountain of the LORD it will be provided."

The angel of the LORD called to Abraham from heaven a second time and said, "I swear by myself, declares the LORD, that because you have done this and have not withheld your son, your only son, I will surely bless you and make your descendants as numerous as the stars in the sky and as the sand on the seashore. Your descendants will take possession of the cities of their enemies, and through your offspring all nations on earth will be blessed, because you have obeyed me."

Eventually Sarah died, and Abraham bought a field and buried her, wondering all the while what would become of him and Isaac and God's promise. Abraham had taken another wife, a woman named Keturah, and had more children. Yet his entire estate went to the special son of promise, Isaac. Abraham died when he was 175 years old and was laid to rest next to Sarah. But the story is far from over.

Isaac married Rebekah. As was the custom, she was chosen for him, but he truly loved her. Twenty years after the wedding, the couple was still childless; but in response to many prayers, Rebekah gave birth to twins. Esau, the elder brother, grew up to love the outdoors and hunting; he was his dad's favorite. Jacob, the younger brother, was quiet and stayed at home; he was clearly his mother's favorite. The two boys vied for the inheritance rights, and Jacob proved to be a master manipulator and schemer.

One day Esau came home famished, demanding some of the stew Jacob was cooking. Seeing an opportunity, Jacob "sold" a meal to his brother in exchange for Esau's birthright—the double share of inheritance due to Esau (because he was the older brother).

Sometime later, as Isaac lay in bed, weak and blind, he asked his hunter son for a tasty meal of char-grilled wild meat. After the meal, Isaac would officially pass on his blessing—and God's favor—to Esau. This was to be Esau's long-awaited big day.

Rebekah overheard Isaac's plan and came up with a plan of her own. She dressed her favorite son, Jacob, in Esau's clothes and covered his hands and neck with goatskins to resemble Esau's hairy skin. She quickly cooked up some meat and sent Jacob, posing as Esau, into Isaac's bedroom. Isaac, squinting his eyes and touching Jacob, wondered if this was really his hunter son. Twice deceitful Jacob lied to his aged dad. Isaac ate. After kissing his son and smelling his scent, Isaac was convinced he was talking to Esau. Then Isaac gave the blessing, also confirming the double share of the material inheritance, to Jacob, irrevocably and completely.

Soon after, Esau arrived with his own platter of grilled meat,

*only to discover that mom and brother had robbed him of his
entire future. Angry to the point of fury, he planned to kill Jacob.
Rebekah intervened once more and sent Jacob to live with relatives until Esau's anger abated.*

*Forced vacations may sometimes result in pleasant surprises.
In this case, Jacob fell in love with his boss's (and uncle's) daughter, Rachel, and worked for her family until she could become
his wife. As part of the deal to marry Rachel, Jacob first had
to marry her older sister, Leah. For twenty years Jacob tended
flocks and farmland, and finally he took his large family home to
meet Esau once again. But Jacob was careful to approach Esau
with respect and humility. The wounds between them were
deep and long, and he wasn't sure if Esau was friend or foe.*

Jacob sent messengers ahead of him to his brother Esau in the
land of Seir, the country of Edom. He instructed them: "This is
what you are to say to my lord Esau: 'Your servant Jacob says, I
have been staying with Laban and have remained there till now.
I have cattle and donkeys, sheep and goats, male and female servants. Now I am sending this message to my lord, that I may find
favor in your eyes.'"

When the messengers returned to Jacob, they said, "We went
to your brother Esau, and now he is coming to meet you, and four
hundred men are with him."

In great fear and distress Jacob divided the people who were
with him into two groups, and the flocks and herds and camels as
well. He thought, "If Esau comes and attacks one group, the group
that is left may escape."

Then Jacob prayed, "O God of my father Abraham, God of my
father Isaac, LORD, you who said to me, 'Go back to your country
and your relatives, and I will make you prosper,' I am unworthy
of all the kindness and faithfulness you have shown your servant.
I had only my staff when I crossed this Jordan, but now I have
become two camps. Save me, I pray, from the hand of my brother
Esau, for I am afraid he will come and attack me, and also the

mothers with their children. But you have said, 'I will surely make you prosper and will make your descendants like the sand of the sea, which cannot be counted.'"

He spent the night there, and from what he had with him he selected a gift for his brother Esau: two hundred female goats and twenty male goats, two hundred ewes and twenty rams, thirty female camels with their young, forty cows and ten bulls, and twenty female donkeys and ten male donkeys. He put them in the care of his servants, each herd by itself, and said to his servants, "Go ahead of me, and keep some space between the herds."

He instructed the one in the lead: "When my brother Esau meets you and asks, 'Who do you belong to, and where are you going, and who owns all these animals in front of you?' then you are to say, 'They belong to your servant Jacob. They are a gift sent to my lord Esau, and he is coming behind us.'"

He also instructed the second, the third and all the others who followed the herds: "You are to say the same thing to Esau when you meet him. And be sure to say, 'Your servant Jacob is coming behind us.'" For he thought, "I will pacify him with these gifts I am sending on ahead; later, when I see him, perhaps he will receive me." So Jacob's gifts went on ahead of him, but he himself spent the night in the camp.

That night Jacob got up and took his two wives, his two female servants and his eleven sons and crossed the ford of the Jabbok. After he had sent them across the stream, he sent over all his possessions. So Jacob was left alone, and a man wrestled with him till daybreak. When the man saw that he could not overpower him, he touched the socket of Jacob's hip so that his hip was wrenched as he wrestled with the man. Then the man said, "Let me go, for it is daybreak."

But Jacob replied, "I will not let you go unless you bless me."

The man asked him, "What is your name?"

"Jacob," he answered.

Then the man said, "Your name will no longer be Jacob, but

Israel, because you have struggled with God and with humans and have overcome."

Jacob said, "Please tell me your name."

But he replied, "Why do you ask my name?" Then he blessed him there.

So Jacob called the place Peniel, saying, "It is because I saw God face to face, and yet my life was spared."

Jacob looked up and there was Esau, coming with his four hundred men; so he divided the children among Leah, Rachel and the two female servants. He put the female servants and their children in front, Leah and her children next, and Rachel and Joseph in the rear. He himself went on ahead and bowed down to the ground seven times as he approached his brother.

But Esau ran to meet Jacob and embraced him; he threw his arms around his neck and kissed him. And they wept. Then Esau looked up and saw the women and children. "Who are these with you?" he asked.

Jacob answered, "They are the children God has graciously given your servant."

Then the female servants and their children approached and bowed down. Next, Leah and her children came and bowed down. Last of all came Joseph and Rachel, and they too bowed down.

Esau asked, "What's the meaning of all these flocks and herds I met?"

"To find favor in your eyes, my lord," he said.

But Esau said, "I already have plenty, my brother. Keep what you have for yourself."

"No, please!" said Jacob. "If I have found favor in your eyes, accept this gift from me. For to see your face is like seeing the face of God, now that you have received me favorably. Please accept the present that was brought to you, for God has been gracious to me and I have all I need." And because Jacob insisted, Esau accepted it.

Then Esau said, "Let us be on our way; I'll accompany you."

Then God said to Jacob, "Go up to Bethel and settle there, and build an altar there to God, who appeared to you when you were fleeing from your brother Esau."

So Jacob said to his household and to all who were with him, "Get rid of the foreign gods you have with you, and purify yourselves and change your clothes. Then come, let us go up to Bethel, where I will build an altar to God, who answered me in the day of my distress and who has been with me wherever I have gone." So they gave Jacob all the foreign gods they had and the rings in their ears, and Jacob buried them under the oak at Shechem. Then they set out, and the terror of God fell on the towns all around them so that no one pursued them.

Jacob and all the people with him came to Luz (that is, Bethel) in the land of Canaan. There he built an altar, and he called the place El Bethel, because it was there that God revealed himself to him when he was fleeing from his brother.

After Jacob returned from Paddan Aram, God appeared to him again and blessed him. God said to him, "Your name is Jacob, but you will no longer be called Jacob; your name will be Israel." So he named him Israel.

And God said to him, "I am God Almighty; be fruitful and increase in number. A nation and a community of nations will come from you, and kings will be among your descendants. The land I gave to Abraham and Isaac I also give to you, and I will give this land to your descendants after you."

Then they moved on from Bethel. While they were still some distance from Ephrath, Rachel began to give birth and had great difficulty. And as she was having great difficulty in childbirth, the midwife said to her, "Don't despair, for you have another son." As she breathed her last — for she was dying — she named her son Ben-Oni. But his father named him Benjamin.

So Rachel died and was buried on the way to Ephrath (that is, Bethlehem).

While Israel was living in that region, Reuben went in and slept with his father's concubine Bilhah, and Israel heard of it.

Jacob came home to his father Isaac in Mamre, near Kiriath Arba (that is, Hebron), where Abraham and Isaac had stayed. Isaac lived a hundred and eighty years. Then he breathed his last and died and was gathered to his people, old and full of years. And his sons Esau and Jacob buried him.

God's story of promise and prosperity moves from Jacob to his son Joseph. Of Jacob's 12 sons, Joseph was clearly Jacob's favorite, leading the rest of Jacob's boys to resent their younger brother. Jacob only heightened the family stress when he gave a beautiful coat to Joseph. And Joseph didn't help matters when he twice told his older brothers that he had a dream that

Jacob

*These were the sons of Jacob,
who were born to him in Paddan Aram.*

*The sons of Rachel:
Joseph and Benjamin.*

*The sons of Leah:
Issachar and Zebulun.*

*The sons of Leah's servant Zilpah:
Gad and Asher.*

*The sons of Rachel's servant Bilhah:
Dan and Naphtali.*

*The sons of Leah:
Simeon, Levi, Judah.
Reuben the firstborn.*

they would someday bow to him. Finally, the brothers had heard enough from their arrogant little brother. They hatched a conspiracy. For seventeen-year-old Joseph, it would be a very bad day indeed.

3

Joseph:
From Slave to Deputy Pharaoh

Now his brothers had gone to graze their father's flocks near Shechem, and Israel said to Joseph, "As you know, your brothers are grazing the flocks near Shechem. Come, I am going to send you to them."

"Very well," he replied.

So he said to him, "Go and see if all is well with your brothers and with the flocks, and bring word back to me." Then he sent him off from the Valley of Hebron.

When Joseph arrived at Shechem, a man found him wandering around in the fields and asked him, "What are you looking for?"

He replied, "I'm looking for my brothers. Can you tell me where they are grazing their flocks?"

"They have moved on from here," the man answered. "I heard them say, 'Let's go to Dothan.'"

So Joseph went after his brothers and found them near Dothan. But they saw him in the distance, and before he reached them, they plotted to kill him.

"Here comes that dreamer!" they said to each other. "Come

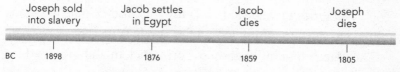

Joseph sold into slavery	Jacob settles in Egypt	Jacob dies	Joseph dies
1898	1876	1859	1805

BC

Full timeline information starts on page xi.

now, let's kill him and throw him into one of these cisterns and say that a ferocious animal devoured him. Then we'll see what comes of his dreams."

When Reuben heard this, he tried to rescue him from their hands. "Let's not take his life," he said. "Don't shed any blood. Throw him into this cistern here in the wilderness, but don't lay a hand on him." Reuben said this to rescue him from them and take him back to his father.

So when Joseph came to his brothers, they stripped him of his robe — the ornate robe he was wearing — and they took him and threw him into the cistern. The cistern was empty; there was no water in it.

As they sat down to eat their meal, they looked up and saw a caravan of Ishmaelites coming from Gilead. Their camels were loaded with spices, balm and myrrh, and they were on their way to take them down to Egypt.

Judah said to his brothers, "What will we gain if we kill our brother and cover up his blood? Come, let's sell him to the Ishmaelites and not lay our hands on him; after all, he is our brother, our own flesh and blood." His brothers agreed.

So when the Midianite merchants came by, his brothers pulled Joseph up out of the cistern and sold him for twenty shekels of silver to the Ishmaelites, who took him to Egypt.

When Reuben returned to the cistern and saw that Joseph was not there, he tore his clothes. He went back to his brothers and said, "The boy isn't there! Where can I turn now?"

Then they got Joseph's robe, slaughtered a goat and dipped the robe in the blood. They took the ornate robe back to their father and said, "We found this. Examine it to see whether it is your son's robe."

He recognized it and said, "It is my son's robe! Some ferocious animal has devoured him. Joseph has surely been torn to pieces."

Then Jacob tore his clothes, put on sackcloth and mourned for his son many days. All his sons and daughters came to comfort him, but he refused to be comforted. "No," he said, "I will continue to mourn until I join my son in the grave." So his father wept for him.

Meanwhile, the Midianites sold Joseph in Egypt to Potiphar, one of Pharaoh's officials, the captain of the guard.

Now Joseph had been taken down to Egypt. Potiphar, an Egyptian who was one of Pharaoh's officials, the captain of the guard, bought him from the Ishmaelites who had taken him there.

The LORD was with Joseph so that he prospered, and he lived in the house of his Egyptian master. When his master saw that the LORD was with him and that the LORD gave him success in everything he did, Joseph found favor in his eyes and became his attendant. Potiphar put him in charge of his household, and he entrusted to his care everything he owned. From the time he put him in charge of his household and of all that he owned, the LORD blessed the household of the Egyptian because of Joseph. The blessing of the LORD was on everything Potiphar had, both in the house and in the field. So Potiphar left everything he had in Joseph's care; with Joseph in charge, he did not concern himself with anything except the food he ate.

Now Joseph was well-built and handsome, and after a while his master's wife took notice of Joseph and said, "Come to bed with me!"

But he refused. "With me in charge," he told her, "my master does not concern himself with anything in the house; everything he owns he has entrusted to my care. No one is greater in this house than I am. My master has withheld nothing from me except you, because you are his wife. How then could I do such a wicked thing and sin against God?" And though she spoke to Joseph day after day, he refused to go to bed with her or even be with her.

One day he went into the house to attend to his duties, and none of the household servants was inside. She caught him by his cloak and said, "Come to bed with me!" But he left his cloak in her hand and ran out of the house.

When she saw that he had left his cloak in her hand and had run out of the house, she called her household servants. "Look," she said to them, "this Hebrew has been brought to us to make sport of us! He came in here to sleep with me, but I screamed. When he heard me scream for help, he left his cloak beside me and ran out of the house."

She kept his cloak beside her until his master came home. Then she told him this story: "That Hebrew slave you brought us came to me to make sport of me. But as soon as I screamed for help, he left his cloak beside me and ran out of the house."

When his master heard the story his wife told him, saying, "This is how your slave treated me," he burned with anger. Joseph's master took him and put him in prison, the place where the king's prisoners were confined.

But while Joseph was there in the prison, the LORD was with him; he showed him kindness and granted him favor in the eyes of the prison warden. So the warden put Joseph in charge of all those held in the prison, and he was made responsible for all that was done there. The warden paid no attention to anything under Joseph's care, because the LORD was with Joseph and gave him success in whatever he did.

Joseph's administrative skills surfaced both in the house of his Egyptian master and in jail. Joseph also cultivated another talent while confined to Pharaoh's stinking prison: God gifted him with the unusual ability to discern the meaning of dreams. Once during his confinement, Joseph helped two of Pharaoh's civil servants interpret their dreams. When Pharaoh's dream life took a bizarre turn, Joseph was summoned to the royal court.

When two full years had passed, Pharaoh had a dream.

In the morning his mind was troubled, so he sent for all the magicians and wise men of Egypt. Pharaoh told them his dreams, but no one could interpret them for him.

So Pharaoh sent for Joseph, and he was quickly brought from

the dungeon. When he had shaved and changed his clothes, he came before Pharaoh.

Pharaoh said to Joseph, "I had a dream, and no one can interpret it. But I have heard it said of you that when you hear a dream you can interpret it."

"I cannot do it," Joseph replied to Pharaoh, "but God will give Pharaoh the answer he desires."

Pharaoh explained his two dreams this way: Seven beautiful, fat cows emerge from the Nile only to be eaten by seven ugly, skinny cows; then seven savory heads of grain on a single stalk are swallowed up by seven dried up, worthless heads. "What do you make of that?" Pharaoh asked Joseph.

Giving credit to God for this gift of interpretation, Joseph told Pharaoh that the twin dreams foretold seven years of bumper crops to be followed by seven years of dried up fields and famine. God planned it this way, Joseph said, so there could be no doubt it would happen.

Joseph's recommendation to Pharaoh was to put a wise man in charge of storing food and preparing for the coming famine.

The plan seemed good to Pharaoh and to all his officials.

Then Pharaoh said to Joseph, "Since God has made all this known to you, there is no one so discerning and wise as you. You shall be in charge of my palace, and all my people are to submit to your orders. Only with respect to the throne will I be greater than you."

So Pharaoh said to Joseph, "I hereby put you in charge of the whole land of Egypt." Then Pharaoh took his signet ring from his finger and put it on Joseph's finger. He dressed him in robes of fine linen and put a gold chain around his neck. He had him ride in a chariot as his second-in-command, and people shouted before him, "Make way!" Thus he put him in charge of the whole land of Egypt.

Then Pharaoh said to Joseph, "I am Pharaoh, but without your word no one will lift hand or foot in all Egypt."

Sure enough, for seven wonderful years Egyptian farmers could hardly believe how full their harvests were. Farms yielded enough for the people to eat well and still store up for the coming bad times. Joseph knew another kind of fruitfulness during this time: his wife had two sons. He gave them the names Manasseh[1] and Ephraim.[2] Then, as Joseph had predicted, the blue skies over Egypt became hot and parched; the crops withered. But Joseph had already planned ahead and stored a sufficient supply of food to keep the Egyptians healthy and Pharaoh's foreign trade business even healthier.

Even the weather patterns fit into God's bigger plan. Because the drought was so severe, neighboring nations began to approach Egypt for help just to stay alive. And just look who shows up.

When Jacob learned that there was grain in Egypt, he said to his sons, "Why do you just keep looking at each other?" He continued, "I have heard that there is grain in Egypt. Go down there and buy some for us, so that we may live and not die."

Then ten of Joseph's brothers went down to buy grain from Egypt. But Jacob did not send Benjamin, Joseph's brother, with the others, because he was afraid that harm might come to him.

Now Joseph was the governor of the land, the person who sold grain to all its people. So when Joseph's brothers arrived, they bowed down to him with their faces to the ground. As soon as Joseph saw his brothers, he recognized them, but he pretended to be a stranger and spoke harshly to them. "Where do you come from?" he asked.

"From the land of Canaan," they replied, "to buy food."

Although Joseph recognized his brothers, they did not recognize him. Then he remembered his dreams about them and said to them, "You are spies! You have come to see where our land is unprotected."

---

[1]**Manasseh:** *Manasseh* sounds like and may be derived from the Hebrew for "forget."
[2]**Ephraim:** *Ephraim* sounds like the Hebrew for "twice fruitful."

"No, my lord," they answered. "Your servants have come to buy food. We are all the sons of one man. Your servants are honest men, not spies."

"No!" he said to them. "You have come to see where our land is unprotected."

But they replied, "Your servants were twelve brothers, the sons of one man, who lives in the land of Canaan. The youngest is now with our father, and one is no more."

Joseph said to them, "It is just as I told you: You are spies! And this is how you will be tested: As surely as Pharaoh lives, you will not leave this place unless your youngest brother comes here. Send one of your number to get your brother; the rest of you will be kept in prison, so that your words may be tested to see if you are telling the truth. If you are not, then as surely as Pharaoh lives, you are spies!" And he put them all in custody for three days.

On the third day, Joseph said to them, "Do this and you will live, for I fear God: If you are honest men, let one of your brothers stay here in prison, while the rest of you go and take grain back for your starving households. But you must bring your youngest brother to me, so that your words may be verified and that you may not die." This they proceeded to do.

They said to one another, "Surely we are being punished because of our brother. We saw how distressed he was when he pleaded with us for his life, but we would not listen; that's why this distress has come on us."

Reuben replied, "Didn't I tell you not to sin against the boy? But you wouldn't listen! Now we must give an accounting for his blood." They did not realize that Joseph could understand them, since he was using an interpreter.

He turned away from them and began to weep, but then came back and spoke to them again. He had Simeon taken from them and bound before their eyes.

Joseph developed a deceitful plan: He imprisoned one of his brothers, Simeon, as a supposed "hostage" until his absent

*younger brother Benjamin could appear in Egypt; he secretly
returned the money used to purchase their grain to the brothers' bags; he kept his own identity from them by using his second language, all the while hearing perfectly well their own
expressed fears.*

These ten brothers were desperately confused.

*But father Jacob wasn't confused at all. When the ten sons
told him the terms of sale, Jacob wouldn't budge. No way
would he surrender the young Benjamin to this Egyptian leader's examination, or even to the sorry band of sons who had
allegedly lost Joseph to a wild beast so many years before.*

*It looked like a stalemate—stubborn souls refusing to con-
front their secret fears—until hunger, that great persuader,
drove them toward compromise and compliance.*

Now the famine was still severe in the land. So when they had
eaten all the grain they had brought from Egypt, their father said
to them, "Go back and buy us a little more food."

But Judah said to him, "The man warned us solemnly, 'You will
not see my face again unless your brother is with you.'"

Then their father Israel said to them, "If it must be, then do
this: Put some of the best products of the land in your bags and
take them down to the man as a gift—a little balm and a little
honey, some spices and myrrh, some pistachio nuts and almonds.

"Take your brother also and go back to the man at once. And
may God Almighty grant you mercy before the man so that he will
let your other brother and Benjamin come back with you. As for
me, if I am bereaved, I am bereaved."

So the men took the gifts and double the amount of silver, and
Benjamin also. They hurried down to Egypt and presented themselves to Joseph.

When Joseph came home, they presented to him the gifts they

had brought into the house, and they bowed down before him to the ground. He asked them how they were, and then he said, "How is your aged father you told me about? Is he still living?"

They replied, "Your servant our father is still alive and well." And they bowed down, prostrating themselves before him.

As he looked about and saw his brother Benjamin, his own mother's son, he asked, "Is this your youngest brother, the one you told me about?" And he said, "God be gracious to you, my son." Deeply moved at the sight of his brother, Joseph hurried out and looked for a place to weep. He went into his private room and wept there.

After he had washed his face, he came out and, controlling himself, said, "Serve the food."

The men had been seated before him in the order of their ages, from the firstborn to the youngest; and they looked at each other in astonishment. When portions were served to them from Joseph's table, Benjamin's portion was five times as much as anyone else's. So they feasted and drank freely with him.

Now Joseph gave these instructions to the steward of his house: "Fill the men's sacks with as much food as they can carry, and put each man's silver in the mouth of his sack. Then put my cup, the silver one, in the mouth of the youngest one's sack, along with the silver for his grain." And he did as Joseph said.

As morning dawned, the men were sent on their way with their donkeys. They had not gone far from the city when Joseph said to his steward, "Go after those men at once, and when you catch up with them, say to them, 'Why have you repaid good with evil? Isn't this the cup my master drinks from and also uses for divination? This is a wicked thing you have done.'"

When he caught up with them, he repeated these words to them. But they said to him, "Why does my lord say such things? Far be it from your servants to do anything like that! We even brought back to you from the land of Canaan the silver we found inside the mouths of our sacks. So why would we steal silver or gold from your master's house? If any of your servants is found to have it, he will die; and the rest of us will become my lord's slaves."

"Very well, then," he said, "let it be as you say. Whoever is found to have it will become my slave; the rest of you will be free from blame."

Each of them quickly lowered his sack to the ground and opened it. Then the steward proceeded to search, beginning with the oldest and ending with the youngest. And the cup was found in Benjamin's sack. At this, they tore their clothes. Then they all loaded their donkeys and returned to the city.

Joseph was still in the house when Judah and his brothers came in, and they threw themselves to the ground before him. Joseph said to them, "What is this you have done? Don't you know that a man like me can find things out by divination?"

"What can we say to my lord?" Judah replied. "What can we say? How can we prove our innocence? God has uncovered your servants' guilt. We are now my lord's slaves — we ourselves and the one who was found to have the cup."

But Joseph said, "Far be it from me to do such a thing! Only the man who was found to have the cup will become my slave. The rest of you, go back to your father in peace."

Then Judah went up to him and said: "Pardon your servant, my lord, let me speak a word to my lord. Do not be angry with your servant, though you are equal to Pharaoh himself.

"Your servant my father said to us, 'You know that my wife bore me two sons. One of them went away from me, and I said, "He has surely been torn to pieces." And I have not seen him since. If you take this one from me too and harm comes to him, you will bring my gray head down to the grave in misery.'

"So now, if the boy is not with us when I go back to your servant my father, and if my father, whose life is closely bound up with the boy's life, sees that the boy isn't there, he will die. Your servants will bring the gray head of our father down to the grave in sorrow. Your servant guaranteed the boy's safety to my father. I said, 'If I do not bring him back to you, I will bear the blame before you, my father, all my life!'

"Now then, please let your servant remain here as my lord's slave in place of the boy, and let the boy return with his brothers. How can I go back to my father if the boy is not with me? No! Do not let me see the misery that would come on my father."

Then Joseph could no longer control himself before all his attendants, and he cried out, "Have everyone leave my presence!" So there was no one with Joseph when he made himself known to his brothers. And he wept so loudly that the Egyptians heard him, and Pharaoh's household heard about it.

Joseph said to his brothers, "I am Joseph! Is my father still living?" But his brothers were not able to answer him, because they were terrified at his presence.

Then Joseph said to his brothers, "Come close to me." When they had done so, he said, "I am your brother Joseph, the one you sold into Egypt! And now, do not be distressed and do not be angry with yourselves for selling me here, because it was to save lives that God sent me ahead of you. For two years now there has been famine in the land, and for the next five years there will be no plowing and reaping. But God sent me ahead of you to preserve for you a remnant on earth and to save your lives by a great deliverance.

"So then, it was not you who sent me here, but God. He made me father to Pharaoh, lord of his entire household and ruler of all Egypt. Now hurry back to my father and say to him, 'This is what your son Joseph says: God has made me lord of all Egypt. Come down to me; don't delay. You shall live in the region of Goshen and be near me — you, your children and grandchildren, your flocks and herds, and all you have. I will provide for you there, because five years of famine are still to come. Otherwise you and your household and all who belong to you will become destitute.'

"You can see for yourselves, and so can my brother Benjamin, that it is really I who am speaking to you. Tell my father about all the honor accorded me in Egypt and about everything you have seen. And bring my father down here quickly."

Then he threw his arms around his brother Benjamin and wept, and Benjamin embraced him, weeping. And he kissed all his brothers and wept over them. Afterward his brothers talked with him.

So they went up out of Egypt and came to their father Jacob in the land of Canaan. They told him, "Joseph is still alive! In fact, he is ruler of all Egypt." Jacob was stunned; he did not believe them. But when they told him everything Joseph had said to them, and when he saw the carts Joseph had sent to carry him back, the spirit of their father Jacob revived. And Israel said, "I'm convinced! My son Joseph is still alive. I will go and see him before I die."

So Israel set out with all that was his, and when he reached Beersheba, he offered sacrifices to the God of his father Isaac.

And God spoke to Israel in a vision at night and said, "Jacob! Jacob!"

"Here I am," he replied.

"I am God, the God of your father," he said. "Do not be afraid to go down to Egypt, for I will make you into a great nation there. I will go down to Egypt with you, and I will surely bring you back again. And Joseph's own hand will close your eyes."

Then Jacob left Beersheba, and Israel's sons took their father Jacob and their children and their wives in the carts that Pharaoh had sent to transport him.

Now Jacob sent Judah ahead of him to Joseph to get directions to Goshen. When they arrived in the region of Goshen, Joseph had his chariot made ready and went to Goshen to meet his father Israel. As soon as Joseph appeared before him, he threw his arms around his father and wept for a long time.

Israel said to Joseph, "Now I am ready to die, since I have seen for myself that you are still alive."

So Joseph settled his father and his brothers in Egypt and gave them property in the best part of the land, the district of Rameses, as Pharaoh directed.

Jacob lived in Egypt seventeen years, and the years of his life were a hundred and forty-seven. When the time drew near for Israel to die, he called for his son Joseph and said to him, "If I have found favor in your eyes, put your hand under my thigh and promise that you will show me kindness and faithfulness. Do not bury me in Egypt, but when I rest with my fathers, carry me out of Egypt and bury me where they are buried."

"I will do as you say," he said.

"Swear to me," he said. Then Joseph swore to him, and Israel worshiped as he leaned on the top of his staff.

Then Israel said to Joseph, "I am about to die, but God will be with you and take you back to the land of your fathers."

Jacob died at the ripe age of 147 years. Before that last day, he gathered his sons to bless them, pronounce their future and give them ongoing responsibilities. Not all the sons got what they wanted. Reuben, for example, was chastised for an earlier sexual sin that no doubt he had hoped his father would not remember. Jacob's last words foretold that some of his sons and their descendants would experience success, others hard times. Jacob adopted Joseph's two sons, Manasseh and Ephraim, as his own; this allowed Jacob to give Joseph a double inheritance as one whose character had earned his trust and confidence.

When Joseph's brothers saw that their father was dead, they said, "What if Joseph holds a grudge against us and pays us back for all the wrongs we did to him?" So they sent word to Joseph, saying, "Your father left these instructions before he died: 'This is what you are to say to Joseph: I ask you to forgive your brothers the sins and the wrongs they committed in treating you so badly.' Now please forgive the sins of the servants of the God of your father." When their message came to him, Joseph wept.

His brothers then came and threw themselves down before him. "We are your slaves," they said.

But Joseph said to them, "Don't be afraid. Am I in the place of God? You intended to harm me, but God intended it for good to accomplish what is now being done, the saving of many lives. So then, don't be afraid. I will provide for you and your children." And he reassured them and spoke kindly to them.

Joseph stayed in Egypt, along with all his father's family. He lived a hundred and ten years and saw the third generation of Ephraim's children. Also the children of Makir son of Manasseh were placed at birth on Joseph's knees.

Then Joseph said to his brothers, "I am about to die. But God will surely come to your aid and take you up out of this land to the land he promised on oath to Abraham, Isaac and Jacob." And Joseph made the Israelites swear an oath and said, "God will surely come to your aid, and then you must carry my bones up from this place."

So Joseph died at the age of a hundred and ten. And after they embalmed him, he was placed in a coffin in Egypt.

4

Deliverance

Now Joseph and all his brothers and all that generation died, but the Israelites were exceedingly fruitful; they multiplied greatly, increased in numbers and became so numerous that the land was filled with them.

Then a new king, to whom Joseph meant nothing, came to power in Egypt. "Look," he said to his people, "the Israelites have become far too numerous for us. Come, we must deal shrewdly with them or they will become even more numerous and, if war breaks out, will join our enemies, fight against us and leave the country."

So they put slave masters over them to oppress them with forced labor, and they built Pithom and Rameses as store cities for Pharaoh. But the more they were oppressed, the more they multiplied and spread; so the Egyptians came to dread the Israelites and worked them ruthlessly. They made their lives bitter with harsh labor in brick and mortar and with all kinds of work in the fields; in all their harsh labor the Egyptians worked them ruthlessly.

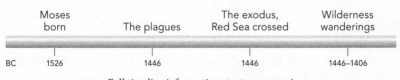

	Moses born	The plagues	The exodus, Red Sea crossed	Wilderness wanderings
BC	1526	1446	1446	1446–1406

Full timeline information starts on page xi.

Then Pharaoh gave this order to all his people: "Every Hebrew boy that is born you must throw into the Nile, but let every girl live."

Now a man of the tribe of Levi married a Levite woman, and she became pregnant and gave birth to a son. When she saw that he was a fine child, she hid him for three months. But when she could hide him no longer, she got a papyrus basket for him and coated it with tar and pitch. Then she placed the child in it and put it among the reeds along the bank of the Nile. His sister stood at a distance to see what would happen to him.

Then Pharaoh's daughter went down to the Nile to bathe, and her attendants were walking along the riverbank. She saw the basket among the reeds and sent her female slave to get it. She opened it and saw the baby. He was crying, and she felt sorry for him. "This is one of the Hebrew babies," she said.

Then his sister asked Pharaoh's daughter, "Shall I go and get one of the Hebrew women to nurse the baby for you?"

"Yes, go," she answered. So the girl went and got the baby's mother. Pharaoh's daughter said to her, "Take this baby and nurse him for me, and I will pay you." So the woman took the baby and nursed him. When the child grew older, she took him to Pharaoh's daughter and he became her son. She named him Moses, saying, "I drew him out of the water."

One day, after Moses had grown up, he went out to where his own people were and watched them at their hard labor. He saw an Egyptian beating a Hebrew, one of his own people. Looking this way and that and seeing no one, he killed the Egyptian and hid him in the sand. The next day he went out and saw two Hebrews fighting. He asked the one in the wrong, "Why are you hitting your fellow Hebrew?"

The man said, "Who made you ruler and judge over us? Are you thinking of killing me as you killed the Egyptian?" Then Moses was afraid and thought, "What I did must have become known."

When Pharaoh heard of this, he tried to kill Moses, but Moses fled from Pharaoh and went to live in Midian, where he sat down by a well. Now a priest of Midian had seven daughters, and they came to draw water and fill the troughs to water their father's flock. Some shepherds came along and drove them away, but Moses got up and came to their rescue and watered their flock.

When the girls returned to Reuel their father, he asked them, "Why have you returned so early today?"

They answered, "An Egyptian rescued us from the shepherds. He even drew water for us and watered the flock."

"And where is he?" Reuel asked his daughters. "Why did you leave him? Invite him to have something to eat."

Moses agreed to stay with the man, who gave his daughter Zipporah to Moses in marriage. Zipporah gave birth to a son, and Moses named him Gershom, saying, "I have become a foreigner in a foreign land."

During that long period, the king of Egypt died. The Israelites groaned in their slavery and cried out, and their cry for help because of their slavery went up to God. God heard their groaning and he remembered his covenant with Abraham, with Isaac and with Jacob. So God looked on the Israelites and was concerned about them.

Now Moses was tending the flock of Jethro his father-in-law, the priest of Midian, and he led the flock to the far side of the wilderness and came to Horeb, the mountain of God. There the angel of the LORD appeared to him in flames of fire from within a bush. Moses saw that though the bush was on fire it did not burn up. So Moses thought, "I will go over and see this strange sight — why the bush does not burn up."

When the LORD saw that he had gone over to look, God called to him from within the bush, "Moses! Moses!"

And Moses said, "Here I am."

"Do not come any closer," God said. "Take off your sandals, for the place where you are standing is holy[1] ground." Then he said, "I

---

[1]**Holy, holiness:** The common literal meaning of this word is *set apart*. God is holy and fundamentally different from humans because of his purity and perfection; however, God invites people to be holy and live in a way that is set apart to serve him.

am the God of your father, the God of Abraham, the God of Isaac and the God of Jacob." At this, Moses hid his face, because he was afraid to look at God.

The LORD said, "I have indeed seen the misery of my people in Egypt. I have heard them crying out because of their slave drivers, and I am concerned about their suffering. So I have come down to rescue them from the hand of the Egyptians and to bring them up out of that land into a good and spacious land, a land flowing with milk and honey—the home of the Canaanites, Hittites, Amorites, Perizzites, Hivites and Jebusites. And now the cry of the Israelites has reached me, and I have seen the way the Egyptians are oppressing them. So now, go. I am sending you to Pharaoh to bring my people the Israelites out of Egypt."

But Moses said to God, "Who am I that I should go to Pharaoh and bring the Israelites out of Egypt?"

And God said, "I will be with you. And this will be the sign to you that it is I who have sent you: When you have brought the people out of Egypt, you will worship God on this mountain."

Moses said to God, "Suppose I go to the Israelites and say to them, 'The God of your fathers has sent me to you,' and they ask me, 'What is his name?' Then what shall I tell them?"

God said to Moses, "I AM WHO I AM. This is what you are to say to the Israelites: 'I AM has sent me to you.'"

God also said to Moses, "Say to the Israelites, 'The LORD, the God of your fathers—the God of Abraham, the God of Isaac and the God of Jacob—has sent me to you.'

> "This is my name forever,
>> the name you shall call me
>> from generation to generation."

Moses said to the LORD, "Pardon your servant, Lord. I have never been eloquent, neither in the past nor since you have spoken to your servant. I am slow of speech and tongue."

The LORD said to him, "Who gave human beings their mouths?

Who makes them deaf or mute? Who gives them sight or makes them blind? Is it not I, the LORD? Now go; I will help you speak and will teach you what to say."

But Moses said, "Pardon your servant, Lord. Please send someone else."

Then the LORD's anger burned against Moses and he said, "What about your brother, Aaron the Levite? I know he can speak well. He is already on his way to meet you, and he will be glad to see you. You shall speak to him and put words in his mouth; I will help both of you speak and will teach you what to do. He will speak to the people for you, and it will be as if he were your mouth and as if you were God to him. But take this staff in your hand so you can perform the signs with it."

The LORD said to Aaron, "Go into the wilderness to meet Moses." So he met Moses at the mountain of God and kissed him. Then Moses told Aaron everything the LORD had sent him to say, and also about all the signs he had commanded him to perform.

Moses and Aaron brought together all the elders of the Israelites, and Aaron told them everything the LORD had said to Moses. He also performed the signs before the people, and they believed. And when they heard that the LORD was concerned about them and had seen their misery, they bowed down and worshiped.

Unfortunately, things didn't go so well with Moses and Aaron's first audience with Pharaoh. He not only refused their request to let the people of Israel hold a festival to the Lord in the wilderness, but he also made their slave labor even more difficult. Without reducing their production of bricks, they would have to find their own straw to mix in with the clay.

The Israelite overseers realized they were in trouble when they were told, "You are not to reduce the number of bricks required of you for each day." When they left Pharaoh, they found Moses and Aaron waiting to meet them, and they said, "May the LORD look on you and judge you! You have made us obnoxious to Pharaoh and his officials and have put a sword in their hand to kill us."

Moses returned to the LORD and said, "Why, Lord, why have you brought trouble on this people? Is this why you sent me? Ever since I went to Pharaoh to speak in your name, he has brought trouble on this people, and you have not rescued your people at all."

Then the LORD said to Moses, "Now you will see what I will do to Pharaoh: Because of my mighty hand he will let them go; because of my mighty hand he will drive them out of his country."

God also said to Moses, "I am the LORD. I appeared to Abraham, to Isaac and to Jacob as God Almighty, but by my name the LORD I did not make myself fully known to them. I also established my covenant with them to give them the land of Canaan, where they resided as foreigners. Moreover, I have heard the groaning of the Israelites, whom the Egyptians are enslaving, and I have remembered my covenant.

"Therefore, say to the Israelites: 'I am the LORD, and I will bring you out from under the yoke of the Egyptians. I will free you from being slaves to them, and I will redeem² you with an outstretched arm and with mighty acts of judgment. I will take you as my own people, and I will be your God. Then you will know that I am the LORD your God, who brought you out from under the yoke of the Egyptians. And I will bring you to the land I swore with uplifted hand to give to Abraham, to Isaac and to Jacob. I will give it to you as a possession. I am the LORD.'"

The LORD said to Moses and Aaron, "When Pharaoh says to you, 'Perform a miracle,' then say to Aaron, 'Take your staff and throw it down before Pharaoh,' and it will become a snake."

So Moses and Aaron went to Pharaoh and did just as the LORD commanded. Aaron threw his staff down in front of Pharaoh and his officials, and it became a snake. Pharaoh then summoned wise men and sorcerers, and the Egyptian magicians also did the same

---

²**Redeem:** In this instance, *redeem* refers to rescue from captivity. It can also refer to the payment of the price required to release a guilty person from an obligation.

things by their secret arts: Each one threw down his staff and it became a snake. But Aaron's staff swallowed up their staffs. Yet Pharaoh's heart became hard and he would not listen to them, just as the LORD had said.

Then the LORD said to Moses, "Pharaoh's heart is unyielding; he refuses to let the people go. Go to Pharaoh in the morning as he goes out to the river. Confront him on the bank of the Nile, and take in your hand the staff that was changed into a snake. Then say to him, 'The LORD, the God of the Hebrews, has sent me to say to you: Let my people go, so that they may worship me in the wilderness. But until now you have not listened. This is what the LORD says: By this you will know that I am the LORD: With the staff that is in my hand I will strike the water of the Nile, and it will be changed into blood. The fish in the Nile will die, and the river will stink; the Egyptians will not be able to drink its water.'"

The LORD said to Moses, "Tell Aaron, 'Take your staff and stretch out your hand over the waters of Egypt — over the streams and canals, over the ponds and all the reservoirs — and they will turn to blood.' Blood will be everywhere in Egypt, even in vessels of wood and stone."

Moses and Aaron did just as the LORD had commanded. He raised his staff in the presence of Pharaoh and his officials and struck the water of the Nile, and all the water was changed into blood. The fish in the Nile died, and the river smelled so bad that the Egyptians could not drink its water. Blood was everywhere in Egypt.

But the Egyptian magicians did the same things by their secret arts, and Pharaoh's heart became hard; he would not listen to Moses and Aaron, just as the LORD had said. Instead, he turned and went into his palace, and did not take even this to heart. And all the Egyptians dug along the Nile to get drinking water, because they could not drink the water of the river.

The next plague included millions of frogs, hopping into every kitchen, every street and every field in Egypt. Pharaoh's court magicians again were able to conjure their own similar plague, and then even more frogs were leaping about. Unable to take one more amphibian, Pharaoh agreed to let the Hebrews go if Moses would get rid of the frogs. Moses prayed and the frogs died. With the immediate crisis resolved, Pharaoh again stubbornly refused to make good on his part of the deal.

So Moses hit the dust with his staff, and gnats swarmed the land. Pharaoh's magicians could not replicate this plague, and they expressed respect for the Hebrews' God. Still Pharaoh would not budge. God continued to show his power as he prepared to rescue his people.

The cycle continued through plagues that included swarms of flies, a disease that killed livestock, terrible boils that afflicted people and animals, thunderstorms with destructive hail, devouring locusts and a frightening time of darkness. After each devastating plague, Pharaoh assured Moses that he could leave with the people. But later he would change his mind.

But the LORD hardened Pharaoh's heart, and he was not willing to let them go. Pharaoh said to Moses, "Get out of my sight! Make sure you do not appear before me again! The day you see my face you will die."

"Just as you say," Moses replied. "I will never appear before you again."

Now the LORD had said to Moses, "I will bring one more plague on Pharaoh and on Egypt. After that, he will let you go from here, and when he does, he will drive you out completely."

So Moses said, "This is what the LORD says: 'About midnight I will go throughout Egypt. Every firstborn son in Egypt will die, from the firstborn son of Pharaoh, who sits on the throne, to the firstborn son of the female slave, who is at her hand mill, and all the firstborn of the cattle as well. There will be loud wailing throughout Egypt — worse than there has ever been or ever will be again. But among the Israelites not a dog will bark at any person or animal.' Then you will know that the LORD makes a distinction between Egypt and Israel. All these officials of yours will come to me, bowing down before me and saying, 'Go, you and all the people who follow you!' After that I will leave." Then Moses, hot with anger, left Pharaoh.

The LORD said to Moses and Aaron in Egypt, "This month is to be for you the first month, the first month of your year. Tell the whole community of Israel that on the tenth day of this month each man is to take a lamb for his family, one for each household.

"The animals you choose must be year-old males without defect, and you may take them from the sheep or the goats. Take care of them until the fourteenth day of the month, when all the members of the community of Israel must slaughter them at twilight. Then they are to take some of the blood and put it on the sides and tops of the doorframes of the houses where they eat the lambs. That same night they are to eat the meat roasted over the fire, along with bitter herbs, and bread made without yeast.

"This is how you are to eat it: with your cloak tucked into your belt, your sandals on your feet and your staff in your hand. Eat it in haste; it is the LORD's Passover.[3]

"On that same night I will pass through Egypt and strike down every firstborn of both people and animals, and I will bring judgment on all the gods of Egypt. I am the LORD. The blood will be a sign for you on the houses where you are, and when I see the blood, I will pass over you. No destructive plague will touch you when I strike Egypt."

Then Moses summoned all the elders of Israel and said to them, "Go at once and select the animals for your families and slaughter the Passover lamb. Take a bunch of hyssop, dip it into the blood in

---

[3]**Passover:** The feast that celebrates the deliverance of the Israelites from slavery in Egypt. The *Passover Lamb* refers to the animal sacrificed prior to the feast. This parallels the sacrifice of Jesus in the New Testament, which released humanity from the debt of sin.

the basin and put some of the blood on the top and on both sides of the doorframe. None of you shall go out of the door of your house until morning. When the LORD goes through the land to strike down the Egyptians, he will see the blood on the top and sides of the doorframe and will pass over that doorway, and he will not permit the destroyer to enter your houses and strike you down.

"Obey these instructions as a lasting ordinance for you and your descendants."

The Israelites did just what the LORD commanded Moses and Aaron.

At midnight the LORD struck down all the firstborn in Egypt, from the firstborn of Pharaoh, who sat on the throne, to the firstborn of the prisoner, who was in the dungeon, and the firstborn of all the livestock as well. Pharaoh and all his officials and all the Egyptians got up during the night, and there was loud wailing in Egypt, for there was not a house without someone dead.

During the night Pharaoh summoned Moses and Aaron and said, "Up! Leave my people, you and the Israelites! Go, worship the LORD as you have requested. Take your flocks and herds, as you have said, and go. And also bless me."

The Egyptians urged the people to hurry and leave the country. "For otherwise," they said, "we will all die!"

Now the length of time the Israelite people lived in Egypt was 430 years. At the end of the 430 years, to the very day, all the LORD's divisions left Egypt.

God had remembered his enslaved people and rescued them. They packed their carts with supplies and spoils freely given to them by the Egyptians and prepared for a long, dusty journey. God provided a sure-fire way for them to stay on course, day and night. But their deliverance from Egypt wasn't complete yet...

By day the LORD went ahead of them in a pillar of cloud to guide them on their way and by night in a pillar of fire to give them light, so that they could travel by day or night. Neither the pillar of cloud by day nor the pillar of fire by night left its place in front of the people.

Then the LORD said to Moses, "Tell the Israelites to turn back and encamp near Pi Hahiroth, between Migdol and the sea. They are to encamp by the sea, directly opposite Baal Zephon. Pharaoh will think, 'The Israelites are wandering around the land in confusion, hemmed in by the desert.' And I will harden Pharaoh's heart, and he will pursue them. But I will gain glory for myself through Pharaoh and all his army, and the Egyptians will know that I am the LORD." So the Israelites did this.

When the king of Egypt was told that the people had fled, Pharaoh and his officials changed their minds about them and said, "What have we done? We have let the Israelites go and have lost their services!" So he had his chariot made ready and took his army with him. He took six hundred of the best chariots, along with all the other chariots of Egypt, with officers over all of them. The LORD hardened the heart of Pharaoh king of Egypt, so that he pursued the Israelites, who were marching out boldly. The Egyptians — all Pharaoh's horses and chariots, horsemen and troops — pursued the Israelites and overtook them as they camped by the sea near Pi Hahiroth, opposite Baal Zephon.

As Pharaoh approached, the Israelites looked up, and there were the Egyptians, marching after them. They were terrified and cried out to the LORD. They said to Moses, "Was it because there were no graves in Egypt that you brought us to the desert to die? What have you done to us by bringing us out of Egypt? Didn't we say to you in Egypt, 'Leave us alone; let us serve the Egyptians'? It would have been better for us to serve the Egyptians than to die in the desert!"

Moses answered the people, "Do not be afraid. Stand firm and you will see the deliverance the LORD will bring you today. The

Egyptians you see today you will never see again. The LORD will fight for you; you need only to be still."

Then the LORD said to Moses, "Why are you crying out to me? Tell the Israelites to move on. Raise your staff and stretch out your hand over the sea to divide the water so that the Israelites can go through the sea on dry ground. I will harden the hearts of the Egyptians so that they will go in after them. And I will gain glory through Pharaoh and all his army, through his chariots and his horsemen. The Egyptians will know that I am the LORD when I gain glory through Pharaoh, his chariots and his horsemen."

Then the angel of God, who had been traveling in front of Israel's army, withdrew and went behind them. The pillar of cloud also moved from in front and stood behind them, coming between the armies of Egypt and Israel. Throughout the night the cloud brought darkness to the one side and light to the other side; so neither went near the other all night long.

Then Moses stretched out his hand over the sea, and all that night the LORD drove the sea back with a strong east wind and turned it into dry land. The waters were divided, and the Israelites went through the sea on dry ground, with a wall of water on their right and on their left.

The Egyptians pursued them, and all Pharaoh's horses and chariots and horsemen followed them into the sea. During the last watch of the night the LORD looked down from the pillar of fire and cloud at the Egyptian army and threw it into confusion. He jammed the wheels of their chariots so that they had difficulty driving. And the Egyptians said, "Let's get away from the Israelites! The LORD is fighting for them against Egypt."

Then the LORD said to Moses, "Stretch out your hand over the sea so that the waters may flow back over the Egyptians and their chariots and horsemen." Moses stretched out his hand over the sea, and at daybreak the sea went back to its place. The Egyptians were fleeing toward it, and the LORD swept them into the sea. The water flowed back and covered the chariots and horsemen — the entire army of Pharaoh that had followed the Israelites into the sea. Not one of them survived.

But the Israelites went through the sea on dry ground, with a wall of water on their right and on their left.

This unforgettable escape impressed upon the Israelites that God was indeed taking care of them. Enemy horses and chariot drivers were thrown into the sea! The people celebrated and sang for joy.

Then Moses led Israel from the Red Sea and they went into the Desert of Shur. For three days they traveled in the desert without finding water. When they came to Marah, they could not drink its water because it was bitter. (That is why the place is called Marah.) So the people grumbled against Moses, saying, "What are we to drink?"

Then Moses cried out to the LORD, and the LORD showed him a piece of wood. He threw it into the water, and the water became fit to drink.

There the LORD issued a ruling and instruction for them and put them to the test. He said, "If you listen carefully to the LORD your God and do what is right in his eyes, if you pay attention to his commands and keep all his decrees, I will not bring on you any of the diseases I brought on the Egyptians, for I am the LORD, who heals you."

Then they came to Elim, where there were twelve springs and seventy palm trees, and they camped there near the water.

The whole Israelite community set out from Elim and came to the Desert of Sin, which is between Elim and Sinai, on the fifteenth day of the second month after they had come out of Egypt. In the desert the whole community grumbled against Moses and Aaron. The Israelites said to them, "If only we had died by the LORD's hand in Egypt! There we sat around pots of meat and ate all the food we wanted, but you have brought us out into this desert to starve this entire assembly to death."

So Moses and Aaron said to all the Israelites, "In the evening you will know that it was the LORD who brought you out of Egypt, and in the morning you will see the glory of the LORD, because he has heard your grumbling against him. Who are we, that you should grumble against us?" Moses also said, "You will know that it was the LORD when he gives you meat to eat in the evening and all the bread you want in the morning, because he has heard your grumbling against him. Who are we? You are not grumbling against us, but against the LORD."

Then Moses told Aaron, "Say to the entire Israelite community, 'Come before the LORD, for he has heard your grumbling.'"

While Aaron was speaking to the whole Israelite community, they looked toward the desert, and there was the glory of the LORD appearing in the cloud.

The LORD said to Moses, "I have heard the grumbling of the Israelites. Tell them, 'At twilight you will eat meat, and in the morning you will be filled with bread. Then you will know that I am the LORD your God.'"

That evening quail came and covered the camp, and in the morning there was a layer of dew around the camp. When the dew was gone, thin flakes like frost on the ground appeared on the desert floor. When the Israelites saw it, they said to each other, "What is it?" For they did not know what it was.

Moses said to them, "It is the bread the LORD has given you to eat."

The people called these honey-tasting crackers manna, which sounds like "What is it?" They all received exactly as much as they needed for each day. On the sixth day of the week they gathered a double portion, for no manna fell on the seventh day, the holy day set apart for rest and worship. And so the people learned to trust God to provide for them and lead them to a new land ... well, not quite.

The whole Israelite community set out from the Desert of Sin, traveling from place to place as the LORD commanded. They camped at Rephidim, but there was no water for the people to drink. So they quarreled with Moses and said, "Give us water to drink."

Moses replied, "Why do you quarrel with me? Why do you put the LORD to the test?"

But the people were thirsty for water there, and they grumbled against Moses. They said, "Why did you bring us up out of Egypt to make us and our children and livestock die of thirst?"

Then Moses cried out to the LORD, "What am I to do with these people? They are almost ready to stone me."

The LORD answered Moses, "Go out in front of the people. Take with you some of the elders of Israel and take in your hand the staff with which you struck the Nile, and go. I will stand there before you by the rock at Horeb. Strike the rock, and water will come out of it for the people to drink." So Moses did this in the sight of the elders of Israel. And he called the place Massah and Meribah because the Israelites quarreled and because they tested the LORD saying, "Is the LORD among us or not?"

5

New Commands
and a New Covenant

ON THE FIRST DAY of the third month after the Israelites left
Egypt — on that very day — they came to the Desert of Sinai. After
they set out from Rephidim, they entered the Desert of Sinai, and
Israel camped there in the desert in front of the mountain.

Then Moses went up to God, and the LORD called to him from
the mountain and said, "This is what you are to say to the descendants of Jacob and what you are to tell the people of Israel: 'You
yourselves have seen what I did to Egypt, and how I carried you
on eagles' wings and brought you to myself. Now if you obey me
fully and keep my covenant, then out of all nations you will be my
treasured possession. Although the whole earth is mine, you will
be for me a kingdom of priests and a holy nation.' These are the
words you are to speak to the Israelites."

The LORD said to Moses, "I am going to come to you in a dense
cloud, so that the people will hear me speaking with you and will
always put their trust in you." Then Moses told the LORD what the
people had said.

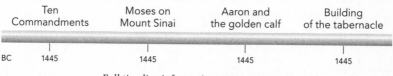

Ten Commandments	Moses on Mount Sinai	Aaron and the golden calf	Building of the tabernacle
BC 1445	1445	1445	1445

Full timeline information starts on page xi.

And the LORD said to Moses, "Go to the people and consecrate[1] them today and tomorrow. Have them wash their clothes
and be ready by the third day, because on that day the LORD will
come down on Mount Sinai in the sight of all the people. Put limits
for the people around the mountain and tell them, 'Be careful that
you do not approach the mountain or touch the foot of it. Whoever touches the mountain is to be put to death. They are to be
stoned or shot with arrows; not a hand is to be laid on them. No
person or animal shall be permitted to live.' Only when the ram's
horn sounds a long blast may they approach the mountain."

After Moses had gone down the mountain to the people, he
consecrated them, and they washed their clothes. Then he said
to the people, "Prepare yourselves for the third day. Abstain from
sexual relations."

On the morning of the third day there was thunder and lightning, with a thick cloud over the mountain, and a very loud
trumpet blast. Everyone in the camp trembled. Then Moses led
the people out of the camp to meet with God, and they stood at
the foot of the mountain. Mount Sinai was covered with smoke,
because the Lord descended on it in fire. The smoke billowed up
from it like smoke from a furnace, and the whole mountain trembled violently. As the sound of the trumpet grew louder and louder,
Moses spoke and the voice of God answered him.

The LORD descended to the top of Mount Sinai and called
Moses to the top of the mountain. So Moses went up and the
LORD said to him, "Go down and warn the people so they do not
force their way through to see the LORD and many of them perish.
Even the priests, who approach the LORD, must consecrate them-
selves, or the LORD will break out against them."

Moses said to the LORD, "The people cannot come up Mount
Sinai, because you yourself warned us, 'Put limits around the
mountain and set it apart as holy.'"

The LORD replied, "Go down and bring Aaron up with you.

---

[1]**Consecrate:** To dedicate a person or thing to God's service.

But the priests and the people must not force their way through to come up to the LORD, or he will break out against them."

So Moses went down to the people and told them.

When the people saw the thunder and lightning and heard the trumpet and saw the mountain in smoke, they trembled with fear. They stayed at a distance and said to Moses, "Speak to us yourself and we will listen. But do not have God speak to us or we will die."

Moses said to the people, "Do not be afraid. God has come to test you, so that the fear of God will be with you to keep you from sinning."

The people remained at a distance, while Moses approached the thick darkness where God was.

On the cloud-covered summit of Mount Sinai, God handed down the ten most-quoted, best-known rules humankind has ever heard—straightforward, no-nonsense rules for how the Israelites were to relate to God (commands 1–4) and to each other (commands 5–10).

"I am the LORD your God, who brought you out of Egypt, out of the land of slavery.

"You shall have no other gods before me.

"You shall not make for yourself an image in the form of anything in heaven above or on the earth beneath or in the waters below. You shall not bow down to them or worship them; for I, the LORD your God, am a jealous God, punishing the children for the sin of the parents to the third and fourth generation of those who hate me, but showing love to a thousand generations of those who love me and keep my commandments.

"You shall not misuse the name of the LORD your God, for the LORD will not hold anyone guiltless who misuses his name.

"Remember the Sabbath day by keeping it holy. Six days you shall labor and do all your work, but the seventh day is a sabbath to the LORD your God. On it you shall not do any work, neither you, nor your son or daughter, nor your male or female servant, nor your animals, nor any foreigner residing in your towns. For in six days the LORD made the heavens and the earth, the sea, and all that is in them, but he rested on the seventh day. Therefore the LORD blessed the Sabbath day and made it holy.

"Honor your father and your mother, so that you may live long in the land the LORD your God is giving you.

"You shall not murder.

"You shall not commit adultery.

"You shall not steal.

"You shall not give false testimony against your neighbor.

"You shall not covet your neighbor's house. You shall not covet your neighbor's wife, or his male or female servant, his ox or donkey, or anything that belongs to your neighbor."

Moses was clearly the intermediary between God and the Hebrew people. After Moses received the Ten Commandments, he was given the laws of the Book of the Covenant — consisting largely of expansions of the Ten Commandments. Now he would lead the Israelites in establishing their covenant with the Lord.

When Moses went and told the people all the LORD's words and laws, they responded with one voice, "Everything the LORD has said we will do." Moses then wrote down everything the LORD had said.

He got up early the next morning and built an altar at the foot of the mountain and set up twelve stone pillars representing the twelve tribes of Israel.[2] Then he sent young Israelite men, and they offered burnt offerings and sacrificed young bulls as fellowship offerings to the LORD. Moses took half of the blood and put it in bowls, and the other half he splashed against the altar. Then he took the Book of the Covenant and read it to the people. They

---

[2]**Twelve tribes of Israel:** The twelve groups that inhabited Israel after leaving Egypt. Each group was descended from one of Jacob's twelve sons.

responded, "We will do everything the LORD has said; we will obey."

Moses then took the blood, sprinkled it on the people and said, "This is the blood of the covenant that the LORD has made with you in accordance with all these words."

The LORD said to Moses, "Come up to me on the mountain and stay here, and I will give you the tablets of stone with the law and commandments I have written for their instruction."

When Moses went up on the mountain, the cloud covered it, and the glory of the LORD settled on Mount Sinai. For six days the cloud covered the mountain, and on the seventh day the LORD called to Moses from within the cloud. To the Israelites the glory of the LORD looked like a consuming fire on top of the mountain. Then Moses entered the cloud as he went on up the mountain. And he stayed on the mountain forty days and forty nights.

The LORD said to Moses, "Tell the Israelites to bring me an offering. You are to receive the offering for me from everyone whose heart prompts them to give.

"Then have them make a sanctuary for me, and I will dwell among them. Make this tabernacle[3] and all its furnishings exactly like the pattern I will show you."

Along with giving Moses the Ten Commandments and other laws, God instructed him as to how to organize worship for the Israelites. From that time on, God's presence would reside in the tabernacle, a portable tent of worship. Inside the tabernacle sat the lavishly designed ark of the covenant,[4] containing the stone tablets of the Ten Commandments.

---

[3]**Tabernacle:** A portable structure, also referred to as the *tent of meeting,* in which the presence of God dwelled with his people. A permanent temple replacing the tabernacle was later built by King Solomon.

[4]**Ark of the covenant:** A portable wooden chest covered with gold, about four feet by two-and-a-half feet wide, which contained the Ten Commandments. The Israelites considered it the most important symbol of God's continual presence with them.

God set apart priests for service, who conducted ritual sacrifices and other important worship activities. One day every week—the Sabbath—was set apart to worship God and to rest from chores and business.

Moses was away on the mountain for nearly six weeks. Meanwhile in the valley below, the people's impatience would lead to Moses facing a bitter homecoming.

When the people saw that Moses was so long in coming down from the mountain, they gathered around Aaron and said, "Come, make us gods who will go before us. As for this fellow Moses who brought us up out of Egypt, we don't know what has happened to him."

Aaron answered them, "Take off the gold earrings that your wives, your sons and your daughters are wearing, and bring them to me." So all the people took off their earrings and brought them to Aaron. He took what they handed him and made it into an idol[5] cast in the shape of a calf, fashioning it with a tool. Then they said, "These are your gods, Israel, who brought you up out of Egypt."

When Aaron saw this, he built an altar in front of the calf and announced, "Tomorrow there will be a festival to the LORD." So the next day the people rose early and sacrificed burnt offerings and presented fellowship offerings. Afterward they sat down to eat and drink and got up to indulge in revelry.

Then the LORD said to Moses, "Go down, because your people, whom you brought up out of Egypt, have become corrupt. They have been quick to turn away from what I commanded them and have made themselves an idol cast in the shape of a calf. They have bowed down to it and sacrificed to it and have said, 'These are your gods, Israel, who brought you up out of Egypt.'

"I have seen these people," the LORD said to Moses, "and they are a stiff-necked people. Now leave me alone so that my anger may burn against them and that I may destroy them. Then I will make you into a great nation."

---

[5]**Idol:** Any object, person or idea that someone worships other than the one true God.

But Moses sought the favor of the LORD his God. "LORD," he said, "why should your anger burn against your people, whom you brought out of Egypt with great power and a mighty hand? Why should the Egyptians say, 'It was with evil intent that he brought them out, to kill them in the mountains and to wipe them off the face of the earth'? Turn from your fierce anger; relent and do not bring disaster on your people. Remember your servants Abraham, Isaac and Israel, to whom you swore by your own self: 'I will make your descendants as numerous as the stars in the sky and I will give your descendants all this land I promised them, and it will be their inheritance forever.'" Then the LORD relented and did not bring on his people the disaster he had threatened.

Moses turned and went down the mountain with the two tablets of the covenant law in his hands. They were inscribed on both sides, front and back. The tablets were the work of God; the writing was the writing of God, engraved on the tablets.

When Joshua heard the noise of the people shouting, he said to Moses, "There is the sound of war in the camp."

Moses replied:

> "It is not the sound of victory,
>   it is not the sound of defeat;
>   it is the sound of singing that I hear."

When Moses approached the camp and saw the calf and the dancing, his anger burned and he threw the tablets out of his hands, breaking them to pieces at the foot of the mountain. And he took the calf the people had made and burned it in the fire; then he ground it to powder, scattered it on the water and made the Israelites drink it.

He said to Aaron, "What did these people do to you, that you led them into such great sin?"

"Do not be angry, my lord," Aaron answered. "You know how prone these people are to evil. They said to me, 'Make us gods who will go before us. As for this fellow Moses who brought us up out of Egypt, we don't know what has happened to him.' So I told them, 'Whoever has any gold jewelry, take it off.' Then they gave me the gold, and I threw it into the fire, and out came this calf!"

Moses saw that the people were running wild and that Aaron had let them get out of control and so become a laughingstock to their enemies. So he stood at the entrance to the camp and said, "Whoever is for the LORD, come to me." And all the Levites rallied to him.

Then he said to them, "This is what the LORD, the God of Israel, says: 'Each man strap a sword to his side. Go back and forth through the camp from one end to the other, each killing his brother and friend and neighbor.'" The Levites did as Moses commanded, and that day about three thousand of the people died. Then Moses said, "You have been set apart to the LORD today, for you were against your own sons and brothers, and he has blessed you this day."

The next day Moses said to the people, "You have committed a great sin. But now I will go up to the LORD; perhaps I can make atonement for your sin."

So Moses went back to the LORD and said, "Oh, what a great sin these people have committed! They have made themselves gods of gold. But now, please forgive their sin — but if not, then blot me out of the book you have written."

The LORD replied to Moses, "Whoever has sinned against me I will blot out of my book. Now go, lead the people to the place I spoke of, and my angel will go before you. However, when the time comes for me to punish, I will punish them for their sin."

And the LORD struck the people with a plague because of what they did with the calf Aaron had made.

Then the LORD said to Moses, "Leave this place, you and the people you brought up out of Egypt, and go up to the land I promised on oath to Abraham, Isaac and Jacob, saying, 'I will give it to your descendants.' I will send an angel before you and drive out the Canaanites, Amorites, Hittites, Perizzites, Hivites and Jebusites. Go up to the land flowing with milk and honey. But I will not go with you, because you are a stiff-necked people and I might destroy you on the way."

Now Moses used to take a tent and pitch it outside the camp some distance away, calling it the "tent of meeting." Anyone inquiring of the LORD would go to the tent of meeting outside the camp. And whenever Moses went out to the tent, all the people rose and stood at the entrances to their tents, watching Moses until he entered the tent. As Moses went into the tent, the pillar of cloud would come down and stay at the entrance, while the LORD spoke with Moses. Whenever the people saw the pillar of cloud standing at the entrance to the tent, they all stood and worshiped, each at the entrance to their tent. The LORD would speak to Moses face to face, as one speaks to a friend. Then Moses would return to the camp, but his young aide Joshua son of Nun did not leave the tent.

Moses said to the LORD, "You have been telling me, 'Lead these people,' but you have not let me know whom you will send with me. You have said, 'I know you by name and you have found favor with me.' If you are pleased with me, teach me your ways so I may know you and continue to find favor with you. Remember that this nation is your people."

The LORD replied, "My Presence will go with you, and I will give you rest."

Then Moses said to him, "If your Presence does not go with us, do not send us up from here. How will anyone know that you are pleased with me and with your people unless you go with us? What else will distinguish me and your people from all the other people on the face of the earth?"

And the LORD said to Moses, "I will do the very thing you have asked, because I am pleased with you and I know you by name."

Then Moses said, "Now show me your glory."

And the LORD said, "I will cause all my goodness to pass in front of you, and I will proclaim my name, the LORD, in your presence. I will have mercy on whom I will have mercy, and I will have compassion on whom I will have compassion. But," he said, "you cannot see my face, for no one may see me and live."

Then the LORD said, "There is a place near me where you may stand on a rock. When my glory passes by, I will put you in a cleft in the rock and cover you with my hand until I have passed by. Then I will remove my hand and you will see my back; but my face must not be seen."

The LORD said to Moses, "Chisel out two stone tablets like the first ones, and I will write on them the words that were on the first tablets, which you broke. Be ready in the morning, and then come up on Mount Sinai. Present yourself to me there on top of the mountain. No one is to come with you or be seen anywhere on the mountain; not even the flocks and herds may graze in front of the mountain."

So Moses chiseled out two stone tablets like the first ones and went up Mount Sinai early in the morning, as the LORD had commanded him; and he carried the two stone tablets in his hands. Then the LORD came down in the cloud and stood there with him and proclaimed his name, the LORD. And he passed in front of Moses, proclaiming, "The LORD, the LORD, the compassionate and gracious God, slow to anger, abounding in love and faithfulness, maintaining love to thousands, and forgiving wickedness, rebellion and sin. Yet he does not leave the guilty unpunished; he punishes the children and their children for the sin of the parents to the third and fourth generation."

Moses bowed to the ground at once and worshiped. "Lord," he said, "if I have found favor in your eyes, then let the Lord go with us. Although this is a stiff-necked people, forgive our wickedness and our sin, and take us as your inheritance."

Then the LORD said: "I am making a covenant with you. Before all your people I will do wonders never before done in any nation in all the world. The people you live among will see how awesome is the work that I, the LORD, will do for you.

"Do not worship any other god, for the LORD, whose name is Jealous, is a jealous God."

Then the LORD said to Moses, "Write down these words, for in accordance with these words I have made a covenant with you and with Israel." Moses was there with the LORD forty days and forty nights without eating bread or drinking water. And he wrote on the tablets the words of the covenant — the Ten Commandments.

When Moses came down from Mount Sinai with the two tablets of the covenant law in his hands, he was not aware that his face was radiant because he had spoken with the LORD. When Aaron and all the Israelites saw Moses, his face was radiant, and they were afraid to come near him. But Moses called to them; so Aaron and all the leaders of the community came back to him, and he spoke to them. Afterward all the Israelites came near him, and he gave them all the commands the LORD had given him on Mount Sinai.

When Moses finished speaking to them, he put a veil over his face. But whenever he entered the LORD's presence to speak with him, he removed the veil until he came out. And when he came out and told the Israelites what he had been commanded, they saw that his face was radiant. Then Moses would put the veil back over his face until he went in to speak with the LORD.

Moses had experienced God's awesome presence, and it showed. Now God would come down and reside among his people — in the tabernacle. This holy tent provided space for the rituals of sacrifice and cleansing from sin that God required. The best Hebrew artisans used their skills in woodworking, metalworking, weaving and embroidering to craft the materials for the tabernacle, including the lampstand, the table for sacred bread and the ark of the covenant. The ark was gold-covered, with poles of acacia wood, also covered with gold, for transport. The specifications for all these materials were quite detailed, and the results must have been beautiful indeed. Yet the most awesome and important feature of this portable temple was not the furniture that filled it, but the Person who filled it.

Then the cloud covered the tent of meeting, and the glory of the LORD filled the tabernacle. Moses could not enter the tent of meeting because the cloud had settled on it, and the glory of the LORD filled the tabernacle.

In all the travels of the Israelites, whenever the cloud lifted from above the tabernacle, they would set out; but if the cloud did not lift, they did not set out — until the day it lifted. So the cloud of the LORD was over the tabernacle by day, and fire was in the cloud by night, in the sight of all the Israelites during all their travels.

During the year that the Israelites were camped near Mount Sinai, God taught them who he was and what he required of them: "I am holy, so you are to be holy." God instructed his people to bring specific offerings to the tabernacle—burnt offerings, grain offerings, fellowship offerings, sin offerings and guilt offerings. The line of priests was anointed[6] and an intricate system of animal sacrifices was instituted for the atonement of the people's sins.

The Hebrews learned God's laws about marriage and divorce, appropriate sexual relations, punishment for murder and robbery and how to make restitution for wrongs. God desired that his people become compassionate, merciful and just.

The promise to Abraham, Isaac and Jacob was now a reality. And this new nation was to be different, so that the entire world would know and worship the one true God, the very source of life and hope.

---

[6]**Anoint, anointed:** To pour oil on a person (usually on their head) as a ceremonial symbol, setting him or her apart for blessings or special service to God. An object can also be anointed to show its sacredness or significance in worship. The term *anointed* can sometimes be interchanged with *choose*, as in the phrase, "God's anointed."

6

Wandering

ON THE TWENTIETH DAY of the second month of the second year, the cloud lifted from above the tabernacle of the covenant law. Then the Israelites set out from the Desert of Sinai and traveled from place to place until the cloud came to rest in the Desert of Paran. They set out, this first time, at the LORD's command through Moses.

> *The people marched out from their yearlong campout near Mount Sinai in organized units, grouped according to the 12 tribes (named after the 12 sons of Jacob). God continued to guide them with the cloud by day and the pillar of fire by night. He had rescued his people from slavery, showed them his power, guided their steps, given them his law and gifted them with his presence. By now, perhaps the people would trust God and his leading. But the Israelites continued to blame God for their hardships.*

Now the people complained about their hardships in the hearing of the LORD, and when he heard them his anger was aroused. Then fire from the LORD burned among them and consumed

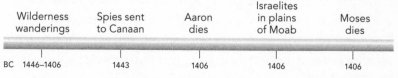

Wilderness wanderings	Spies sent to Canaan	Aaron dies	Israelites in plains of Moab	Moses dies
BC 1446–1406	1443	1406	1406	1406

Full timeline information starts on page xi.

some of the outskirts of the camp. When the people cried out to Moses, he prayed to the LORD and the fire died down. So that place was called Taberah,[1] because fire from the LORD had burned among them.

The rabble with them began to crave other food, and again the Israelites started wailing and said, "If only we had meat to eat! We remember the fish we ate in Egypt at no cost — also the cucumbers, melons, leeks, onions and garlic. But now we have lost our appetite; we never see anything but this manna!"

The manna was like coriander seed and looked like resin. The people went around gathering it, and then ground it in a hand mill or crushed it in a mortar. They cooked it in a pot or made it into loaves. And it tasted like something made with olive oil. When the dew settled on the camp at night, the manna also came down.

Moses heard the people of every family wailing at the entrance to their tents. The LORD became exceedingly angry, and Moses was troubled. He asked the LORD, "Why have you brought this trouble on your servant? What have I done to displease you that you put the burden of all these people on me? Did I conceive all these people? Did I give them birth? Why do you tell me to carry them in my arms, as a nurse carries an infant, to the land you promised on oath to their ancestors? Where can I get meat for all these people? They keep wailing to me, 'Give us meat to eat!' I cannot carry all these people by myself; the burden is too heavy for me. If this is how you are going to treat me, please go ahead and kill me — if I have found favor in your eyes — and do not let me face my own ruin."

The LORD said to Moses:

"Tell the people: 'Consecrate yourselves in preparation for tomorrow, when you will eat meat. The LORD heard you when you wailed, "If only we had meat to eat! We were better off in Egypt!" Now the LORD will give you meat, and you will eat it. You will not eat it for just one day, or two days, or five, ten or twenty days, but for

---

[1]**Taberah:** *Taberah* means "burning."

a whole month — until it comes out of your nostrils and you loathe it — because you have rejected the LORD, who is among you, and have wailed before him, saying, "Why did we ever leave Egypt?"'"

But Moses said, "Here I am among six hundred thousand men on foot, and you say, 'I will give them meat to eat for a whole month!' Would they have enough if flocks and herds were slaughtered for them? Would they have enough if all the fish in the sea were caught for them?"

The LORD answered Moses, "Is the LORD's arm too short? Now you will see whether or not what I say will come true for you."

Now a wind went out from the LORD and drove quail in from the sea. It scattered them up to two cubits deep all around the camp, as far as a day's walk in any direction. All that day and night and all the next day the people went out and gathered quail. No one gathered less than ten homers. Then they spread them out all around the camp. But while the meat was still between their teeth and before it could be consumed, the anger of the LORD burned against the people, and he struck them with a severe plague. Therefore the place was named Kibroth Hattaavah,[2] because there they buried the people who had craved other food.

> *Though God had dealt harshly with the people's lack of faith, soon there was more trouble in the ranks, this time from Moses' own sister and brother.*

Miriam and Aaron began to talk against Moses because of his Cushite wife, for he had married a Cushite. "Has the LORD spoken only through Moses?" they asked. "Hasn't he also spoken through us?" And the LORD heard this.

(Now Moses was a very humble man, more humble than anyone else on the face of the earth.)

At once the LORD said to Moses, Aaron and Miriam, "Come out to the tent of meeting, all three of you." So the three of them

---

[2]**Kibroth Hattaavah:** *Kibroth Hattaavah* means "graves of craving."

went out. Then the LORD came down in a pillar of cloud; he stood at the entrance to the tent and summoned Aaron and Miriam. When the two of them stepped forward, he said, "Listen to my words:

> "When there is a prophet[3] among you,
>> I, the LORD, reveal myself to them in visions,
>> I speak to them in dreams.
> But this is not true of my servant Moses;
>> he is faithful in all my house.
> With him I speak face to face,
>> clearly and not in riddles;
>> he sees the form of the LORD.
> Why then were you not afraid
>> to speak against my servant Moses?"

The anger of the LORD burned against them, and he left them.

When the cloud lifted from above the tent, Miriam's skin was leprous — it became as white as snow. Aaron turned toward her and saw that she had a defiling skin disease, and he said to Moses, "Please, my lord, I ask you not to hold against us the sin we have so foolishly committed. Do not let her be like a stillborn infant coming from its mother's womb with its flesh half eaten away."

So Moses cried out to the LORD, "Please, God, heal her!"

The LORD replied to Moses, "If her father had spit in her face, would she not have been in disgrace for seven days? Confine her outside the camp for seven days; after that she can be brought back." So Miriam was confined outside the camp for seven days, and the people did not move on till she was brought back.

After that, the people left Hazeroth and encamped in the Desert of Paran.

The LORD said to Moses, "Send some men to explore the land of Canaan, which I am giving to the Israelites. From each ancestral tribe send one of its leaders."

---

[3]**Prophet:** A person selected by God to deliver divinely-inspired messages to his people.

When Moses sent them to explore Canaan, he said, "Go up through the Negev and on into the hill country. See what the land is like and whether the people who live there are strong or weak, few or many. What kind of land do they live in? Is it good or bad? What kind of towns do they live in? Are they unwalled or fortified? How is the soil? Is it fertile or poor? Are there trees in it or not? Do your best to bring back some of the fruit of the land." (It was the season for the first ripe grapes.)

So they went up and explored the land from the Desert of Zin as far as Rehob, toward Lebo Hamath.

When they reached the Valley of Eshkol, they cut off a branch bearing a single cluster of grapes. Two of them carried it on a pole between them, along with some pomegranates and figs.

At the end of forty days they returned from exploring the land.

They came back to Moses and Aaron and the whole Israelite community at Kadesh in the Desert of Paran. There they reported to them and to the whole assembly and showed them the fruit of the land. They gave Moses this account: "We went into the land to which you sent us, and it does flow with milk and honey! Here is its fruit. But the people who live there are powerful, and the cities are fortified and very large. We even saw descendants of Anak there."

Then Caleb silenced the people before Moses and said, "We should go up and take possession of the land, for we can certainly do it."

But the men who had gone up with him said, "We can't attack those people; they are stronger than we are." And they spread among the Israelites a bad report about the land they had explored. They said, "The land we explored devours those living in it. All the people we saw there are of great size. We saw the Nephilim there (the descendants of Anak come from the Nephilim). We seemed like grasshoppers in our own eyes, and we looked the same to them."

That night all the members of the community raised their voices and wept aloud. All the Israelites grumbled against Moses and Aaron, and the whole assembly said to them, "If only we had died in Egypt! Or in this wilderness! Why is the LORD bringing us to this land only to let us fall by the sword? Our wives and children will be taken as plunder. Wouldn't it be better for us to go back to Egypt?" And they said to each other, "We should choose a leader and go back to Egypt."

Then Moses and Aaron fell facedown in front of the whole Israelite assembly gathered there. Joshua son of Nun and Caleb son of Jephunneh, who were among those who had explored the land, tore their clothes and said to the entire Israelite assembly, "The land we passed through and explored is exceedingly good. If the LORD is pleased with us, he will lead us into that land, a land flowing with milk and honey, and will give it to us. Only do not rebel against the LORD. And do not be afraid of the people of the land, because we will devour them. Their protection is gone, but the LORD is with us. Do not be afraid of them."

But the whole assembly talked about stoning them. Then the glory of the LORD appeared at the tent of meeting to all the Israelites. The LORD said to Moses, "How long will these people treat me with contempt? How long will they refuse to believe in me, in spite of all the signs I have performed among them? I will strike them down with a plague and destroy them, but I will make you into a nation greater and stronger than they."

Moses said to the LORD, "Then the Egyptians will hear about it! By your power you brought these people up from among them. And they will tell the inhabitants of this land about it. They have already heard that you, LORD, are with these people and that you, LORD, have been seen face to face, that your cloud stays over them, and that you go before them in a pillar of cloud by day and a pillar of fire by night. If you put all these people to death, leaving none alive, the nations who have heard this report about you will say, 'The LORD was not able to bring these people into the land he promised them on oath, so he slaughtered them in the wilderness.'

"Now may the Lord's strength be displayed, just as you have declared: 'The LORD is slow to anger, abounding in love and forgiving sin and rebellion. Yet he does not leave the guilty unpunished; he punishes the children for the sin of the parents to the third and fourth generation.' In accordance with your great love, forgive the sin of these people, just as you have pardoned them from the time they left Egypt until now."

The LORD replied, "I have forgiven them, as you asked. Nevertheless, as surely as I live and as surely as the glory of the LORD fills the whole earth, not one of those who saw my glory and the signs I performed in Egypt and in the wilderness but who disobeyed me and tested me ten times — not one of them will ever see the land I promised on oath to their ancestors. No one who has treated me with contempt will ever see it. But because my servant Caleb has a different spirit and follows me wholeheartedly, I will bring him into the land he went to, and his descendants will inherit it. Since the Amalekites and the Canaanites are living in the valleys, turn back tomorrow and set out toward the desert along the route to the Red Sea."

The LORD said to Moses and Aaron: "How long will this wicked community grumble against me? I have heard the complaints of these grumbling Israelites. So tell them, 'As surely as I live, declares the LORD, I will do to you the very thing I heard you say: In this wilderness your bodies will fall — every one of you twenty years old or more who was counted in the census and who has grumbled against me. Not one of you will enter the land I swore with uplifted hand to make your home, except Caleb son of Jephunneh and Joshua son of Nun. As for your children that you said would be taken as plunder, I will bring them in to enjoy the land you have rejected. But as for you, your bodies will fall in this wilderness. Your children will be shepherds here for forty years, suffering for your unfaithfulness, until the last of your bodies lies in the wilderness. For forty years — one year for each of the forty days you explored the land — you will suffer for your sins and know what it is like to have me against you.' I, the LORD, have spoken, and I will surely do these things to this whole wicked community, which has banded together against me. They will meet their end in this wilderness; here they will die."

Grumbling, complaining, plotting, unbelieving—the Hebrews were slow learners. As God declared, the Israelites wandered in the wilderness until the people 20 years old or more at the time died.

The story picks up again nearly 40 years later. The Israelites return to Kadesh, site of the rebellion that occurred when the spies returned from Canaan. The promised land lies before them again. By now, most of the people 20 years old or more at the time of that tragic rebellion had died. Sadly, however, the attitude of this generation clearly resembles that of the previous one.

In the first month the whole Israelite community arrived at the Desert of Zin, and they stayed at Kadesh. There Miriam died and was buried.

Now there was no water for the community, and the people gathered in opposition to Moses and Aaron. They quarreled with Moses and said, "If only we had died when our brothers fell dead before the LORD! Why did you bring the LORD's community into this wilderness, that we and our livestock should die here? Why did you bring us up out of Egypt to this terrible place? It has no grain or figs, grapevines or pomegranates. And there is no water to drink!"

Moses and Aaron went from the assembly to the entrance to the tent of meeting and fell facedown, and the glory of the LORD appeared to them. The LORD said to Moses, "Take the staff, and you and your brother Aaron gather the assembly together. Speak to that rock before their eyes and it will pour out its water. You will bring water out of the rock for the community so they and their livestock can drink."

So Moses took the staff from the LORD's presence, just as he commanded him. He and Aaron gathered the assembly together in front of the rock and Moses said to them, "Listen, you rebels, must we bring you water out of this rock?" Then Moses raised his arm and struck the rock twice with his staff. Water gushed out, and the community and their livestock drank.

But the LORD said to Moses and Aaron, "Because you did not trust in me enough to honor me as holy in the sight of the Israelites, you will not bring this community into the land I give them."

These were the waters of Meribah, where the Israelites quarreled with the LORD and where he was proved holy among them.

The frustration and anger that had built up in Moses over the last 40 years came to expression. In his rage, Moses struck the rock rather than obeying God's instructions to speak to it. Moses (and evidently Aaron) demonstrated a lack of trust in God and respect for his presence among his people. The consequences were clear: neither Moses nor Aaron would enter the promised land.

As the Israelites continued their march to Canaan, they came to the edge of territory controlled by their distant cousins, the Edomites (descended from Esau, Jacob's brother). But their foreign policy negotiations proved to be difficult. They requested permission for passage, a shortcut, across that land. "No way, not without a fight," replied the king of Edom, who promptly sent a large and powerful army to ensure they didn't enter his territory. Thwarted, the Israelites soon had other sad events to attend to.

The whole Israelite community set out from Kadesh and came to Mount Hor. At Mount Hor, near the border of Edom, the LORD said to Moses and Aaron, "Aaron will be gathered to his people. He will not enter the land I give the Israelites, because both of you rebelled against my command at the waters of Meribah. Get Aaron and his son Eleazar and take them up Mount Hor. Remove Aaron's garments and put them on his son Eleazar, for Aaron will be gathered to his people; he will die there."

Moses did as the LORD commanded: They went up Mount Hor in the sight of the whole community. Moses removed Aaron's garments and put them on his son Eleazar. And Aaron died there on top of the mountain. Then Moses and Eleazar came down from the mountain, and when the whole community learned that Aaron had died, all the Israelites mourned for him thirty days.

When the Canaanite king of Arad, who lived in the Negev, heard that Israel was coming along the road to Atharim, he attacked the Israelites and captured some of them. Then Israel made this vow to the LORD: "If you will deliver these people into our hands, we will totally destroy their cities." The LORD listened to Israel's plea and gave the Canaanites over to them. They completely destroyed them and their towns; so the place was named Hormah.[4]

They traveled from Mount Hor along the route to the Red Sea, to go around Edom. But the people grew impatient on the way; they spoke against God and against Moses, and said, "Why have you brought us up out of Egypt to die in the wilderness? There is no bread! There is no water! And we detest this miserable food!"

Then the LORD sent venomous snakes among them; they bit the people and many Israelites died. The people came to Moses and said, "We sinned when we spoke against the LORD and against you. Pray that the LORD will take the snakes away from us." So Moses prayed for the people.

The LORD said to Moses, "Make a snake and put it up on a pole; anyone who is bitten can look at it and live." So Moses made a bronze snake and put it up on a pole. Then when anyone was bitten by a snake and looked at the bronze snake, they lived.

The Israelites traveled on through the dusty wilderness. As they had done with the nation of Edom, they requested cooperation from the king of the Amorites to pass through their land. And as with the Edomites, God's people found that the Amorites were less than helpful.

---

[4]**Hormah:** *Hormah* means "destruction."

Israel sent messengers to say to Sihon king of the Amorites:

"Let us pass through your country. We will not turn aside into any field or vineyard, or drink water from any well. We will travel along the King's Highway until we have passed through your territory."

But Sihon would not let Israel pass through his territory. He mustered his entire army and marched out into the wilderness against Israel. When he reached Jahaz, he fought with Israel. Israel, however, put him to the sword and took over his land from the Arnon to the Jabbok, but only as far as the Ammonites, because their border was fortified. Israel captured all the cities of the Amorites and occupied them, including Heshbon and all its surrounding settlements. Heshbon was the city of Sihon king of the Amorites, who had fought against the former king of Moab and had taken from him all his land as far as the Arnon.

So Israel settled in the land of the Amorites.

After Moses had sent spies to Jazer, the Israelites captured its surrounding settlements and drove out the Amorites who were there. Then they turned and went up along the road toward Bashan, and Og king of Bashan and his whole army marched out to meet them in battle at Edrei.

The LORD said to Moses, "Do not be afraid of him, for I have delivered him into your hands, along with his whole army and his land. Do to him what you did to Sihon king of the Amorites, who reigned in Heshbon."

So they struck him down, together with his sons and his whole army, leaving them no survivors. And they took possession of his land.

With results such as this, local kings were intimidated by Israel's forces. One king, Balak, ruler of Moab, called on a pagan diviner, Balaam, to curse the Israelites. Caught between assurances of wealth from Balak and God's command not to curse them, Balaam was in a dilemma. He finally mounted his donkey to head out to Moab, but the donkey refused to move. Balaam tried his whip, and the donkey suddenly talked, objecting to unfair treatment.

Donkey: "Did I ever hurt you?"

Balaam: "No."

Donkey: "So why are you whipping me?"

Balaam: "Because you're not moving, you stupid animal."

Donkey: "Open your eyes and see why!"

Then Balaam saw the angel of the Lord in the road, opposing him. As a result of this strange occurrence, Balaam gained the courage he needed to tell Balak what God wanted him to hear: Israel would be blessed; Moab would be cursed.

In the meantime, Moabite women were doing more damage to Hebrew solidarity than Balak's army ever could.

While Israel was staying in Shittim, the men began to indulge in sexual immorality with Moabite women, who invited them to the sacrifices to their gods. The people ate the sacrificial meal and bowed down before these gods. So Israel yoked themselves to the Baal of Peor. And the LORD's anger burned against them.

The LORD said to Moses, "Take all the leaders of these people, kill them and expose them in broad daylight before the LORD, so that the LORD's fierce anger may turn away from Israel."

So Moses said to Israel's judges,[5] "Each of you must put to death those of your people who have yoked themselves to the Baal of Peor."

Then an Israelite man brought into the camp a Midianite woman right before the eyes of Moses and the whole assembly of Israel while they were weeping at the entrance to the tent of meeting. When Phinehas son of Eleazar, the son of Aaron, the priest, saw this, he left the assembly, took a spear in his hand and followed the Israelite into the tent. He drove the spear into both of them, right through the Israelite man and into the woman's stomach. Then the plague against the Israelites was stopped; but those who died in the plague numbered 24,000.

---

[5]**Judges:** National leaders and deliverers of Israel.

The LORD said to Moses, "Phinehas son of Eleazar, the son of Aaron, the priest, has turned my anger away from the Israelites. Since he was as zealous for my honor among them as I am, I did not put an end to them in my zeal. Therefore tell him I am making my covenant of peace with him. He and his descendants will have a covenant of a lasting priesthood, because he was zealous for the honor of his God and made atonement for the Israelites."

As the battle for the promised land approached, Moses took a census and discovered that all the Israelites who had rebelled against God's instruction to enter Canaan nearly 40 years earlier had passed away. After all these years, the next generation was finally poised to enter the land. But Moses himself had to face the sad reality of some tough consequences.

Then the LORD said to Moses, "Go up this mountain in the Abarim Range and see the land I have given the Israelites. After you have seen it, you too will be gathered to your people, as your brother Aaron was, for when the community rebelled at the waters in the Desert of Zin, both of you disobeyed my command to honor me as holy before their eyes." (These were the waters of Meribah Kadesh, in the Desert of Zin.)

Moses said to the LORD, "May the LORD, the God who gives breath to all living things, appoint someone over this community to go out and come in before them, one who will lead them out and bring them in, so the LORD's people will not be like sheep without a shepherd."

So the LORD said to Moses, "Take Joshua son of Nun, a man in whom is the spirit of leadership, and lay your hand on him. Have him stand before Eleazar the priest and the entire assembly and commission him in their presence. Give him some of your authority so the whole Israelite community will obey him."

Moses did as the LORD commanded him. He took Joshua and had him stand before Eleazar the priest and the whole assembly.

Then he laid his hands on him and commissioned him, as the LORD instructed through Moses.

> Many administrative details required Moses' attention before he died and the people crossed the Jordan River. How to arrange worship, how to handle captives and spoils from battle, how to deal with crime and vengeance inside the Hebrew nation, how to set up inheritance rights—God, through Moses, was preparing a basic governmental system for life in the promised land. Moses' final task regarding the anxious and excited people was a grand valedictory speech. "Remember who you are," he told them, "and to Whom you belong."

These are the words Moses spoke to all Israel in the wilderness east of the Jordan:

The LORD your God has blessed you in all the work of your hands. He has watched over your journey through this vast wilderness. These forty years the LORD your God has been with you, and you have not lacked anything.

Ask now about the former days, long before your time, from the day God created human beings on the earth; ask from one end of the heavens to the other. Has anything so great as this ever happened, or has anything like it ever been heard of? Has any other people heard the voice of God speaking out of fire, as you have, and lived? Has any god ever tried to take for himself one nation out of another nation, by testings, by signs and wonders, by war, by a mighty hand and an outstretched arm, or by great and awesome deeds, like all the things the LORD your God did for you in Egypt before your very eyes?

You were shown these things so that you might know that the LORD is God; besides him there is no other. From heaven he made you hear his voice to discipline you. On earth he showed you his great fire, and you heard his words from out of the fire. Because he loved your ancestors and chose their descendants after them, he brought you out of Egypt by his Presence and his great strength, to drive out before you nations greater and stronger than you and to bring you into their land to give it to you for your inheritance, as it is today.

Acknowledge and take to heart this day that the LORD is God in heaven above and on the earth below. There is no other. Keep his decrees and commands, which I am giving you today, so that it may go well with you and your children after you and that you may live long in the land the LORD your God gives you for all time.

Hear, O Israel: The LORD our God, the LORD is one. Love the LORD your God with all your heart and with all your soul and with all your strength. These commandments that I give you today are to be on your hearts. Impress them on your children. Talk about them when you sit at home and when you walk along the road, when you lie down and when you get up.

Be careful to follow every command I am giving you today, so that you may live and increase and may enter and possess the land the LORD promised on oath to your ancestors. Remember how the LORD your God led you all the way in the wilderness these forty years, to humble and test you in order to know what was in your heart, whether or not you would keep his commands. He humbled you, causing you to hunger and then feeding you with manna, which neither you nor your ancestors had known, to teach you that man does not live on bread alone but on every word that comes from the mouth of the LORD. Your clothes did not wear out and your feet did not swell during these forty years. Know then in your heart that as a man disciplines his son, so the LORD your God disciplines you.

Hear, Israel: You are now about to cross the Jordan to go in and dispossess nations greater and stronger than you, with large cities

that have walls up to the sky. The people are strong and tall—
Anakites! You know about them and have heard it said: "Who
can stand up against the Anakites?" But be assured today that the
LORD your God is the one who goes across ahead of you like a
devouring fire. He will destroy them; he will subdue them before
you. And you will drive them out and annihilate them quickly, as
the LORD has promised you.

After the LORD your God has driven them out before you, do
not say to yourself, "The LORD has brought me here to take possession of this land because of my righteousness." No, it is on account
of the wickedness of these nations that the LORD is going to drive
them out before you. It is not because of your righteousness or
your integrity that you are going in to take possession of their
land; but on account of the wickedness of these nations, the LORD
your God will drive them out before you, to accomplish what he
swore to your fathers, to Abraham, Isaac and Jacob. Understand,
then, that it is not because of your righteousness that the LORD
your God is giving you this good land to possess, for you are a
stiff-necked people.

Moses summoned all the Israelites and said to them:

Your eyes have seen all that the LORD did in Egypt to Pharaoh,
to all his officials and to all his land. With your own eyes you saw
those great trials, those signs and great wonders. But to this day
the LORD has not given you a mind that understands or eyes that
see or ears that hear. Yet the LORD says, "During the forty years
that I led you through the wilderness, your clothes did not wear
out, nor did the sandals on your feet. You ate no bread and drank
no wine or other fermented drink. I did this so that you might
know that I am the LORD your God."

Now what I am commanding you today is not too difficult for
you or beyond your reach. It is not up in heaven, so that you have
to ask, "Who will ascend into heaven to get it and proclaim it to

us so we may obey it?" Nor is it beyond the sea, so that you have to ask, "Who will cross the sea to get it and proclaim it to us so we may obey it?" No, the word is very near you; it is in your mouth and in your heart so you may obey it.

See, I set before you today life and prosperity, death and destruction. For I command you today to love the LORD your God, to walk in obedience to him, and to keep his commands, decrees and laws; then you will live and increase, and the LORD your God will bless you in the land you are entering to possess.

But if your heart turns away and you are not obedient, and if you are drawn away to bow down to other gods and worship them, I declare to you this day that you will certainly be destroyed. You will not live long in the land you are crossing the Jordan to enter and possess.

This day I call the heavens and the earth as witnesses against you that I have set before you life and death, blessings and curses. Now choose life, so that you and your children may live and that you may love the LORD your God, listen to his voice, and hold fast to him. For the LORD is your life, and he will give you many years in the land he swore to give to your fathers, Abraham, Isaac and Jacob.

Though Moses often complained that he was not a public speaker, his strong words of encouragement kept the people faithful, focused and hopeful for many years. Moses knew God well, and he loved the people. That knowledge and love were often expressed in poetic prayers full of lament, joy, passion and devotion.

Then Moses summoned Joshua and said to him in the presence of all Israel, "Be strong and courageous, for you must go with this people into the land that the LORD swore to their ancestors to give them, and you must divide it among them as their inheritance. The LORD himself goes before you and will be with you; he will never leave you nor forsake you. Do not be afraid; do not be discouraged."

On that same day the LORD told Moses, "Go up into the Abarim Range to Mount Nebo in Moab, across from Jericho, and view Canaan, the land I am giving the Israelites as their own possession. There on the mountain that you have climbed you will die and be gathered to your people, just as your brother Aaron died on Mount Hor and was gathered to his people. This is because both of you broke faith with me in the presence of the Israelites at the waters of Meribah Kadesh in the Desert of Zin and because you did not uphold my holiness among the Israelites. Therefore, you will see the land only from a distance; you will not enter the land I am giving to the people of Israel."

Then Moses climbed Mount Nebo from the plains of Moab to the top of Pisgah, across from Jericho. There the LORD showed him the whole land — from Gilead to Dan, all of Naphtali, the territory of Ephraim and Manasseh, all the land of Judah as far as the Mediterranean Sea, the Negev and the whole region from the Valley of Jericho, the City of Palms, as far as Zoar. Then the LORD said to him, "This is the land I promised on oath to Abraham, Isaac and Jacob when I said, 'I will give it to your descendants.' I have let you see it with your eyes, but you will not cross over into it."

And Moses the servant of the LORD died there in Moab, as the LORD had said. He buried him in Moab, in the valley opposite Beth Peor, but to this day no one knows where his grave is. Moses was a hundred and twenty years old when he died, yet his eyes were not weak nor his strength gone. The Israelites grieved for Moses in the plains of Moab thirty days, until the time of weeping and mourning was over.

Since then, no prophet has risen in Israel like Moses, whom the LORD knew face to face, who did all those signs and wonders the LORD sent him to do in Egypt — to Pharaoh and to all his officials and to his whole land. For no one has ever shown the mighty power or performed the awesome deeds that Moses did in the sight of all Israel.

7

The Battle Begins

AFTER THE DEATH OF MOSES the servant of the LORD, the LORD said to Joshua son of Nun, Moses' aide: "Moses my servant is dead. Now then, you and all these people, get ready to cross the Jordan River into the land I am about to give to them — to the Israelites. I will give you every place where you set your foot, as I promised Moses. Your territory will extend from the desert to Lebanon, and from the great river, the Euphrates — all the Hittite country — to the Mediterranean Sea in the west. No one will be able to stand against you all the days of your life. As I was with Moses, so I will be with you; I will never leave you nor forsake you. Be strong and courageous, because you will lead these people to inherit the land I swore to their ancestors to give them.

"Be strong and very courageous. Be careful to obey all the law my servant Moses gave you; do not turn from it to the right or to the left, that you may be successful wherever you go. Keep this Book of the Law always on your lips; meditate on it day and night, so that you may be careful to do everything written in it. Then you will be prosperous and successful. Have I not commanded you? Be

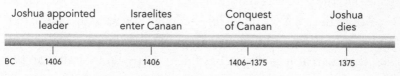

Joshua appointed leader	Israelites enter Canaan	Conquest of Canaan	Joshua dies
1406	1406	1406–1375	1375

BC

Full timeline information starts on page xi.

strong and courageous. Do not be afraid; do not be discouraged, for the LORD your God will be with you wherever you go."

So Joshua ordered the officers of the people: "Go through the camp and tell the people, 'Get your provisions ready. Three days from now you will cross the Jordan here to go in and take possession of the land the LORD your God is giving you for your own.'"

Then they answered Joshua, "Whatever you have commanded us we will do, and wherever you send us we will go. Just as we fully obeyed Moses, so we will obey you. Only may the LORD your God be with you as he was with Moses. Whoever rebels against your word and does not obey it, whatever you may command them, will be put to death. Only be strong and courageous!"

Then Joshua son of Nun secretly sent two spies from Shittim. "Go, look over the land," he said, "especially Jericho." So they went and entered the house of a prostitute named Rahab and stayed there.

The king of Jericho was told, "Look, some of the Israelites have come here tonight to spy out the land." So the king of Jericho sent this message to Rahab: "Bring out the men who came to you and entered your house, because they have come to spy out the whole land."

But the woman had taken the two men and hidden them. She said, "Yes, the men came to me, but I did not know where they had come from. At dusk, when it was time to close the city gate, they left. I don't know which way they went. Go after them quickly. You may catch up with them." (But she had taken them up to the roof and hidden them under the stalks of flax she had laid out on the roof.) So the men set out in pursuit of the spies on the road that leads to the fords of the Jordan, and as soon as the pursuers had gone out, the gate was shut.

Before the spies lay down for the night, she went up on the roof and said to them, "I know that the LORD has given you this land and that a great fear of you has fallen on us, so that all who live in this country are melting in fear because of you. We have heard how the LORD dried up the water of the Red Sea for you when you came out of Egypt, and what you did to Sihon and Og, the two kings of the Amorites east of the Jordan, whom you completely destroyed. When we heard of it, our hearts melted in fear and everyone's courage failed because of you, for the LORD your God is God in heaven above and on the earth below.

"Now then, please swear to me by the LORD that you will show kindness to my family, because I have shown kindness to you. Give me a sure sign that you will spare the lives of my father and mother, my brothers and sisters, and all who belong to them — and that you will save us from death."

"Our lives for your lives!" the men assured her. "If you don't tell what we are doing, we will treat you kindly and faithfully when the LORD gives us the land."

So she let them down by a rope through the window, for the house she lived in was part of the city wall. She said to them, "Go to the hills so the pursuers will not find you. Hide yourselves there three days until they return, and then go on your way."

When they left, they went into the hills and stayed there three days, until the pursuers had searched all along the road and returned without finding them. Then the two men started back. They went down out of the hills, forded the river and came to Joshua son of Nun and told him everything that had happened to them. They said to Joshua, "The LORD has surely given the whole land into our hands; all the people are melting in fear because of us."

Two things separated the Israelites from their promise of a homeland. First, the Jordan River, a formidable barrier in an era before span bridges. Second, the rite of circumcision, the sign of God's covenant with his people. (None of this generation had been circumcised.)

Joshua organized the march to the land, with the ark of the covenant leading the way. When the priests carrying the sacred ark touched the river bank, the Jordan's brisk flow ceased. All

*the people crossed on dry ground. Once camped on the other
side, the circumcisions were performed. For a few painful days,
the only able-bodied people in the camp were females.*

*Then came the first battle—a test of faith and courage after
40 years of training.*

Now the gates of Jericho were securely barred because of the
Israelites. No one went out and no one came in.

Then the LORD said to Joshua, "See, I have delivered Jericho
into your hands, along with its king and its fighting men. March
around the city once with all the armed men. Do this for six days.
Have seven priests carry trumpets of rams' horns in front of the
ark. On the seventh day, march around the city seven times, with
the priests blowing the trumpets. When you hear them sound a
long blast on the trumpets, have the whole army give a loud shout;
then the wall of the city will collapse and the army will go up,
everyone straight in."

So Joshua son of Nun called the priests and said to them, "Take
up the ark of the covenant of the LORD and have seven priests
carry trumpets in front of it." And he ordered the army, "Advance!
March around the city, with an armed guard going ahead of the
ark of the LORD."

When Joshua had spoken to the people, the seven priests carrying the seven trumpets before the LORD went forward, blowing
their trumpets, and the ark of the LORD's covenant followed them.
The armed guard marched ahead of the priests who blew the
trumpets, and the rear guard followed the ark. All this time the
trumpets were sounding. But Joshua had commanded the army,
"Do not give a war cry, do not raise your voices, do not say a word
until the day I tell you to shout. Then shout!" So he had the ark of
the LORD carried around the city, circling it once. Then the army
returned to camp and spent the night there.

Joshua got up early the next morning and the priests took up
the ark of the LORD. The seven priests carrying the seven trumpets
went forward, marching before the ark of the LORD and blow-

ing the trumpets. The armed men went ahead of them and the rear guard followed the ark of the LORD, while the trumpets kept sounding. So on the second day they marched around the city once and returned to the camp. They did this for six days.

On the seventh day, they got up at daybreak and marched around the city seven times in the same manner, except that on that day they circled the city seven times. The seventh time around, when the priests sounded the trumpet blast, Joshua commanded the army, "Shout! For the LORD has given you the city! The city and all that is in it are to be devoted to the LORD. Only Rahab the prostitute and all who are with her in her house shall be spared, because she hid the spies we sent."

When the trumpets sounded, the army shouted, and at the sound of the trumpet, when the men gave a loud shout, the wall collapsed; so everyone charged straight in, and they took the city. They devoted the city to the LORD and destroyed with the sword every living thing in it — men and women, young and old, cattle, sheep and donkeys.

Joshua said to the two men who had spied out the land, "Go into the prostitute's house and bring her out and all who belong to her, in accordance with your oath to her." So the young men who had done the spying went in and brought out Rahab, her father and mother, her brothers and sisters and all who belonged to her. They brought out her entire family and put them in a place outside the camp of Israel.

Then they burned the whole city and everything in it, but they put the silver and gold and the articles of bronze and iron into the treasury of the LORD's house. But Joshua spared Rahab the prostitute, with her family and all who belonged to her, because she hid the men Joshua had sent as spies to Jericho — and she lives among the Israelites to this day.

At that time Joshua pronounced this solemn oath: "Cursed before the LORD is the one who undertakes to rebuild this city, Jericho."

So the LORD was with Joshua, and his fame spread throughout the land.

God had told Joshua and the Israelites that the spoil of war was his alone. And everyone obeyed—except for one man, Achan. As a result of Achan's sin, God was not with the Israelite army when they attacked Ai. Joshua and the other leaders were humiliated and confused. When God revealed that the defeat was because Achan had sinned, the people repented, and Achan was killed for his actions.

Then the LORD said to Joshua, "Do not be afraid; do not be discouraged. Take the whole army with you, and go up and attack Ai. For I have delivered into your hands the king of Ai, his people, his city and his land. You shall do to Ai and its king as you did to Jericho and its king, except that you may carry off their plunder and livestock for yourselves. Set an ambush behind the city."

Early the next morning Joshua mustered his army, and he and the leaders of Israel marched before them to Ai. The entire force that was with him marched up and approached the city and arrived in front of it. They set up camp north of Ai, with the valley between them and the city. Joshua had taken about five thousand men and set them in ambush between Bethel and Ai, to the west of the city. So the soldiers took up their positions—with the main camp to the north of the city and the ambush to the west of it. That night Joshua went into the valley.

When the king of Ai saw this, he and all the men of the city hurried out early in the morning to meet Israel in battle at a certain place overlooking the Arabah. But he did not know that an ambush had been set against him behind the city. Joshua and all Israel let themselves be driven back before them, and they fled toward the wilderness. All the men of Ai were called to pursue them, and they pursued Joshua and were lured away from the city. Not a man remained in Ai or Bethel who did not go after Israel. They left the city open and went in pursuit of Israel.

Then the LORD said to Joshua, "Hold out toward Ai the javelin that is in your hand, for into your hand I will deliver the city." So Joshua held out toward the city the javelin that was in his hand. As soon as he did this, the men in the ambush rose quickly from their position and rushed forward. They entered the city and captured it and quickly set it on fire.

The men of Ai looked back and saw the smoke of the city rising up into the sky, but they had no chance to escape in any direction; the Israelites who had been fleeing toward the wilderness had turned back against their pursuers. For when Joshua and all Israel saw that the ambush had taken the city and that smoke was going up from it, they turned around and attacked the men of Ai. Those in the ambush also came out of the city against them, so that they were caught in the middle, with Israelites on both sides. Israel cut them down, leaving them neither survivors nor fugitives.

Twelve thousand men and women fell that day — all the people of Ai.

Then Joshua built on Mount Ebal an altar to the LORD, the God of Israel, as Moses the servant of the LORD had commanded the Israelites.

Afterward, Joshua read all the words of the law — the blessings and the curses — just as it is written in the Book of the Law. There was not a word of all that Moses had commanded that Joshua did not read to the whole assembly of Israel, including the women and children, and the foreigners who lived among them.

God helped the Israelites to be victorious over the army of Ai. Yet Joshua made a mistake in not turning to God to guide him when some deceptive people from Gibeon arrived. They pretended to be from a far-off land, and they sought a treaty with the Israelites. Joshua made the treaty without consulting the wisdom of the Lord. Then he found out that the delegation was really from Gibeon, a neighboring tribe. He was constrained by his treaty, so he could not conquer the people and take their land. Word got out about Joshua's peace treaty, and other kings took up arms.

Now Adoni-Zedek king of Jerusalem heard that Joshua had taken Ai and totally destroyed it, doing to Ai and its king as he had done to Jericho and its king, and that the people of Gibeon had made a treaty of peace with Israel and had become their allies. He and his people were very much alarmed at this, because Gibeon was an important city, like one of the royal cities; it was larger than Ai, and all its men were good fighters. So Adoni-Zedek king of Jerusalem appealed to Hoham king of Hebron, Piram king of Jarmuth, Japhia king of Lachish and Debir king of Eglon. "Come up and help me attack Gibeon," he said, "because it has made peace with Joshua and the Israelites."

Then the five kings of the Amorites — the kings of Jerusalem, Hebron, Jarmuth, Lachish and Eglon — joined forces. They moved up with all their troops and took up positions against Gibeon and attacked it.

The Gibeonites then sent word to Joshua in the camp at Gilgal: "Do not abandon your servants. Come up to us quickly and save us! Help us, because all the Amorite kings from the hill country have joined forces against us."

So Joshua marched up from Gilgal with his entire army, including all the best fighting men. The LORD said to Joshua, "Do not be afraid of them; I have given them into your hand. Not one of them will be able to withstand you."

After an all-night march from Gilgal, Joshua took them by surprise. The LORD threw them into confusion before Israel, so Joshua and the Israelites defeated them completely at Gibeon. Israel pursued them along the road going up to Beth Horon and cut them down all the way to Azekah and Makkedah. As they fled before Israel on the road down from Beth Horon to Azekah, the

LORD hurled large hailstones down on them, and more of them died from the hail than were killed by the swords of the Israelites.

On the day the LORD gave the Amorites over to Israel, Joshua said to the LORD in the presence of Israel:

> "Sun, stand still over Gibeon,
>   and you, moon, over the Valley of Aijalon."
> So the sun stood still,
>   and the moon stopped,
>   till the nation avenged itself on its enemies,

as it is written in the Book of Jashar.

The sun stopped in the middle of the sky and delayed going down about a full day. There has never been a day like it before or since, a day when the LORD listened to a human being. Surely the LORD was fighting for Israel!

Then Joshua returned with all Israel to the camp at Gilgal.

Now the five kings had fled and hidden in the cave at Makkedah. When Joshua was told that the five kings had been found hiding in the cave at Makkedah, he said, "Roll large rocks up to the mouth of the cave, and post some men there to guard it. But don't stop; pursue your enemies! Attack them from the rear and don't let them reach their cities, for the LORD your God has given them into your hand."

So Joshua and the Israelites defeated them completely, but a few survivors managed to reach their fortified cities. The whole army then returned safely to Joshua in the camp at Makkedah, and no one uttered a word against the Israelites.

Joshua said, "Open the mouth of the cave and bring those five kings out to me." So they brought the five kings out of the cave — the kings of Jerusalem, Hebron, Jarmuth, Lachish and Eglon. When they had brought these kings to Joshua, he summoned all the men of Israel and said to the army commanders who had come with him, "Come here and put your feet on the necks of these kings." So they came forward and placed their feet on their necks.

Joshua said to them, "Do not be afraid; do not be discouraged. Be strong and courageous. This is what the LORD will do to all the enemies you are going to fight." Then Joshua put the kings to death and exposed their bodies on five poles, and they were left hanging on the poles until evening.

At sunset Joshua gave the order and they took them down from the poles and threw them into the cave where they had been hiding. At the mouth of the cave they placed large rocks, which are there to this day.

That day Joshua took Makkedah. He put the city and its king to the sword and totally destroyed everyone in it. He left no survivors. And he did to the king of Makkedah as he had done to the king of Jericho.

So Joshua subdued the whole region, including the hill country, the Negev, the western foothills and the mountain slopes, together with all their kings. He left no survivors. He totally destroyed all who breathed, just as the LORD, the God of Israel, had commanded. Joshua subdued them from Kadesh Barnea to Gaza and from the whole region of Goshen to Gibeon. All these kings and their lands Joshua conquered in one campaign, because the LORD, the God of Israel, fought for Israel.

Then Joshua returned with all Israel to the camp at Gilgal.

When Jabin king of Hazor heard of this, he sent word to Jobab king of Madon, to the kings of Shimron and Akshaph, and to the northern kings who were in the mountains, in the Arabah south of Kinnereth, in the western foothills and in Naphoth Dor on the west; to the Canaanites in the east and west; to the Amorites, Hittites, Perizzites and Jebusites in the hill country; and to the Hivites below Hermon in the region of Mizpah. They came out with all their troops and a large number of horses and chariots — a huge army, as numerous as the sand on the seashore. All these kings joined forces and made camp together at the Waters of Merom to fight against Israel.

The LORD said to Joshua, "Do not be afraid of them, because

by this time tomorrow I will hand all of them, slain, over to Israel. You are to hamstring their horses and burn their chariots."

So Joshua and his whole army came against them suddenly at the Waters of Merom and attacked them, and the LORD gave them into the hand of Israel. They defeated them and pursued them all the way to Greater Sidon, to Misrephoth Maim, and to the Valley of Mizpah on the east, until no survivors were left. Joshua did to them as the LORD had directed: He hamstrung their horses and burned their chariots.

At that time Joshua turned back and captured Hazor and put its king to the sword. (Hazor had been the head of all these kingdoms.) Everyone in it they put to the sword. They totally destroyed them, not sparing anyone that breathed, and he burned Hazor itself.

Joshua took all these royal cities and their kings and put them to the sword. He totally destroyed them, as Moses the servant of the LORD had commanded. Yet Israel did not burn any of the cities built on their mounds — except Hazor, which Joshua burned. The Israelites carried off for themselves all the plunder and livestock of these cities, but all the people they put to the sword until they completely destroyed them, not sparing anyone that breathed. As the LORD commanded his servant Moses, so Moses commanded Joshua, and Joshua did it; he left nothing undone of all that the LORD commanded Moses.

So Joshua took the entire land, just as the LORD had directed Moses, and he gave it as an inheritance to Israel according to their tribal divisions. Then the land had rest from war.

These ancient cities defeated by Joshua and the Israelites have been forgotten by history. Yet, for the Israelites, each name listed represented risk, loss, hardship and struggle. God's promise to Abraham centuries earlier was coming to pass. A new nation was being formed. Much of the promised land was theirs; much still remained to be taken. In the meantime, their leader had some final words of encouragement and challenge.

After a long time had passed and the LORD had given Israel rest from all their enemies around them, Joshua, by then a very old man, summoned all Israel—their elders, leaders, judges and officials—and said to them: "I am very old. You yourselves have seen everything the LORD your God has done to all these nations for your sake; it was the LORD your God who fought for you. Remember how I have allotted as an inheritance for your tribes all the land of the nations that remain—the nations I conquered—between the Jordan and the Mediterranean Sea in the west. The LORD your God himself will push them out for your sake. He will drive them out before you, and you will take possession of their land, as the LORD your God promised you.

"Now I am about to go the way of all the earth. You know with all your heart and soul that not one of all the good promises the LORD your God gave you has failed. Every promise has been fulfilled; not one has failed. But just as all the good things the LORD your God has promised you have come to you, so he will bring on you all the evil things he has threatened, until the LORD your God has destroyed you from this good land he has given you. If you violate the covenant of the LORD your God, which he commanded you, and go and serve other gods and bow down to them, the LORD's anger will burn against you, and you will quickly perish from the good land he has given you."

Then Joshua assembled all the tribes of Israel at Shechem. He summoned the elders, leaders, judges and officials of Israel, and they presented themselves before God.

Joshua said to all the people, "This is what the LORD, the God of Israel, says: 'Long ago your ancestors, including Terah the father of Abraham and Nahor, lived beyond the Euphrates River and worshiped other gods. But I took your father Abraham from the land beyond the Euphrates and led him throughout Canaan and gave him many descendants. I gave him Isaac, and to Isaac I gave Jacob and Esau. I assigned the hill country of Seir to Esau, but Jacob and his family went down to Egypt.

"'Then I sent Moses and Aaron, and I afflicted the Egyptians by what I did there, and I brought you out. When I brought your people out of Egypt, you came to the sea, and the Egyptians pursued them with chariots and horsemen as far as the Red Sea. But they cried to the LORD for help, and he put darkness between you and the Egyptians; he brought the sea over them and covered them. You saw with your own eyes what I did to the Egyptians. Then you lived in the wilderness for a long time.

"'I brought you to the land of the Amorites who lived east of the Jordan. They fought against you, but I gave them into your hands. I destroyed them from before you, and you took possession of their land. When Balak son of Zippor, the king of Moab, prepared to fight against Israel, he sent for Balaam son of Beor to put a curse on you. But I would not listen to Balaam, so he blessed you again and again, and I delivered you out of his hand.

"'Then you crossed the Jordan and came to Jericho. The citizens of Jericho fought against you, as did also the Amorites, Perizzites, Canaanites, Hittites, Girgashites, Hivites and Jebusites, but I gave them into your hands. I sent the hornet ahead of you, which drove them out before you — also the two Amorite kings. You did not do it with your own sword and bow. So I gave you a land on which you did not toil and cities you did not build; and you live in them and eat from vineyards and olive groves that you did not plant.'

"Now fear the LORD and serve him with all faithfulness. Throw away the gods your ancestors worshiped beyond the Euphrates River and in Egypt, and serve the LORD. But if serving the LORD seems undesirable to you, then choose for yourselves this day whom you will serve, whether the gods your ancestors served beyond the Euphrates, or the gods of the Amorites, in whose land you are living. But as for me and my household, we will serve the LORD."

And the people said to Joshua, "We will serve the LORD our God and obey him."

On that day Joshua made a covenant for the people, and there at Shechem he reaffirmed for them decrees and laws. And Joshua recorded these things in the Book of the Law of God. Then he took a large stone and set it up there under the oak near the holy place of the LORD.

"See!" he said to all the people. "This stone will be a witness against us. It has heard all the words the LORD has said to us. It will be a witness against you if you are untrue to your God."

Then Joshua dismissed the people, each to their own inheritance.

After these things, Joshua son of Nun, the servant of the LORD, died at the age of a hundred and ten. And they buried him in the land of his inheritance, at Timnath Serah in the hill country of Ephraim, north of Mount Gaash.

Israel served the LORD throughout the lifetime of Joshua and of the elders who outlived him and who had experienced everything the LORD had done for Israel.

8

A Few Good Men
... and Women

THE PEOPLE SERVED THE LORD throughout the lifetime of Joshua and of the elders who outlived him and who had seen all the great things the LORD had done for Israel.

Joshua son of Nun, the servant of the LORD, died at the age of a hundred and ten. And they buried him in the land of his inheritance, at Timnath Heres in the hill country of Ephraim, north of Mount Gaash.

After that whole generation had been gathered to their ancestors, another generation grew up who knew neither the LORD nor what he had done for Israel. Then the Israelites did evil in the eyes of the LORD and served the Baals.[1] They forsook the LORD, the God of their ancestors, who had brought them out of Egypt. They followed and worshiped various gods of the peoples around them. They aroused the LORD's anger because they forsook him and served Baal and the Ashtoreths. In his anger against Israel the LORD gave them into the hands of raiders who plundered them. He

---

[1]**Baal(s), Ashtoreth, Asherah:** False gods of ancient pagan cultures.

Judges begin to rule	Deborah's rule	Gideon's rule	Samson's rule
BC 1375	1209–1169	1162–1122	1075–1055

Full timeline information starts on page xi.

sold them into the hands of their enemies all around, whom they were no longer able to resist. Whenever Israel went out to fight, the hand of the LORD was against them to defeat them, just as he had sworn to them. They were in great distress.

Then the LORD raised up judges, who saved them out of the hands of these raiders. Yet they would not listen to their judges but prostituted themselves to other gods and worshiped them. They quickly turned from the ways of their ancestors, who had been obedient to the LORD's commands. Whenever the LORD raised up a judge for them, he was with the judge and saved them out of the hands of their enemies as long as the judge lived; for the LORD relented because of their groaning under those who oppressed and afflicted them. But when the judge died, the people returned to ways even more corrupt than those of their ancestors, following other gods and serving and worshiping them. They refused to give up their evil practices and stubborn ways.

Therefore the LORD was very angry with Israel and said, "Because this nation has violated the covenant I ordained for their ancestors and has not listened to me, I will no longer drive out before them any of the nations Joshua left when he died. I will use them to test Israel and see whether they will keep the way of the LORD and walk in it as their ancestors did."

The Israelites did evil in the eyes of the LORD; they forgot the LORD their God and served the Baals and the Asherahs. The anger of the LORD burned against Israel so that he sold them into the hands of Cushan-Rishathaim king of Aram Naharaim, to whom the Israelites were subject for eight years. But when they cried out to the LORD, he raised up for them a deliverer, Othniel son of Kenaz, Caleb's younger brother, who saved them. The Spirit of the LORD[2] came on him, so that he became Israel's judge and went to war. The LORD gave Cushan-Rishathaim king of Aram into the

---

[2]**The Spirit of the LORD:** In the Old Testament, this term referred to the intangible presence of God and all of his attributes. The phrase is used to show how God empowered certain individuals to carry out specific callings.

hands of Othniel, who overpowered him. So the land had peace for forty years, until Othniel son of Kenaz died.

Eventually the people of Israel turned away from God again, and the cycle of social chaos began anew. The Moabite leader, Eglon, forged a coalition and for 18 years oppressed Israel. The people cried out to God, who faithfully gave them another judge/leader, Ehud, to deliver them. Ehud tricked Eglon into a private meeting and killed the king with his sword in a surprise attack. The king was so overweight that the sword handle was covered by his fat girth. With Eglon dead, Moab fell easily to Ehud's raiders. Then the Israelites had peace for 80 years.

Again the Israelites did evil in the eyes of the LORD, now that Ehud was dead. So the LORD sold them into the hands of Jabin king of Canaan, who reigned in Hazor. Sisera, the commander of his army, was based in Harosheth Haggoyim. Because he had nine hundred chariots fitted with iron and had cruelly oppressed the Israelites for twenty years, they cried to the LORD for help.

Now Deborah, a prophet, the wife of Lappidoth, was leading Israel at that time. She held court under the Palm of Deborah between Ramah and Bethel in the hill country of Ephraim, and the Israelites went up to her to have their disputes decided. She sent for Barak son of Abinoam from Kedesh in Naphtali and said to him, "The LORD, the God of Israel, commands you: 'Go, take with you ten thousand men of Naphtali and Zebulun and lead them up to Mount Tabor. I will lead Sisera, the commander of Jabin's army, with his chariots and his troops to the Kishon River and give him into your hands.'"

Barak said to her, "If you go with me, I will go; but if you don't go with me, I won't go."

"Certainly I will go with you," said Deborah. "But because of the course you are taking, the honor will not be yours, for the LORD will deliver Sisera into the hands of a woman." So Deborah went with Barak to Kedesh. There Barak summoned Zebulun and

Naphtali, and ten thousand men went up under his command. Deborah also went up with him.

Now Heber the Kenite had left the other Kenites, the descendants of Hobab, Moses' brother-in-law, and pitched his tent by the great tree in Zaanannim near Kedesh.

When they told Sisera that Barak son of Abinoam had gone up to Mount Tabor, Sisera summoned from Harosheth Haggoyim to the Kishon River all his men and his nine hundred chariots fitted with iron.

Then Deborah said to Barak, "Go! This is the day the LORD has given Sisera into your hands. Has not the LORD gone ahead of you?" So Barak went down Mount Tabor, with ten thousand men following him. At Barak's advance, the LORD routed Sisera and all his chariots and army by the sword, and Sisera got down from his chariot and fled on foot.

Barak pursued the chariots and army as far as Harosheth Haggoyim, and all Sisera's troops fell by the sword; not a man was left. Sisera, meanwhile, fled on foot to the tent of Jael, the wife of Heber the Kenite, because there was an alliance between Jabin king of Hazor and the family of Heber the Kenite.

Jael went out to meet Sisera and said to him, "Come, my lord, come right in. Don't be afraid." So he entered her tent, and she covered him with a blanket.

"I'm thirsty," he said. "Please give me some water." She opened a skin of milk, gave him a drink, and covered him up.

"Stand in the doorway of the tent," he told her. "If someone comes by and asks you, 'Is anyone in there?' say 'No.'"

But Jael, Heber's wife, picked up a tent peg and a hammer and went quietly to him while he lay fast asleep, exhausted. She drove the peg through his temple into the ground, and he died.

Just then Barak came by in pursuit of Sisera, and Jael went out to meet him. "Come," she said, "I will show you the man you're looking for." So he went in with her, and there lay Sisera with the tent peg through his temple — dead.

On that day God subdued Jabin king of Canaan before the Israelites. And the hand of the Israelites pressed harder and harder against Jabin king of Canaan until they destroyed him.

Following this victory, the land experienced 40 years of peace. After that, another strong leader was needed, but at this point in Israel's history, the roster seemed empty. A splintered, tribal coalition could not sustain its national identity. The people, forgetting their special relationship to God, began to adapt to the surrounding cultures, eventually joining their unconquered neighbors in pagan worship. As a result, God no longer aided the Israelite army, which began losing battles. Once again the people discovered the tragic cycle of the consequences of their disobedience.

The Israelites did evil in the eyes of the LORD, and for seven years he gave them into the hands of the Midianites. Because the power of Midian was so oppressive, the Israelites prepared shelters for themselves in mountain clefts, caves and strongholds. Whenever the Israelites planted their crops, the Midianites, Amalekites and other eastern peoples invaded the country. They camped on the land and ruined the crops all the way to Gaza and did not spare a living thing for Israel, neither sheep nor cattle nor donkeys. They came up with their livestock and their tents like swarms of locusts. It was impossible to count them or their camels; they invaded the land to ravage it. Midian so impoverished the Israelites that they cried out to the LORD for help.

When the Israelites cried out to the LORD because of Midian, he sent them a prophet, who said, "This is what the LORD, the God of Israel, says: I brought you up out of Egypt, out of the land of slavery. I rescued you from the hand of the Egyptians. And I delivered you from the hand of all your oppressors; I drove them out before you and gave you their land. I said to you, 'I am the LORD your God; do not worship the gods of the Amorites, in whose land you live.' But you have not listened to me."

In their hunger and weakness, the Israelites appealed to God, who informed them that their big problem was not agricultural or military, but spiritual. To illustrate, God picked for service a farmer from the weakest clan in his tribe. Like most new leaders, Gideon was uncertain if he could measure up. But God was looking for a faithful follower, not a decorated soldier.

The angel of the LORD came and sat down under the oak in Ophrah that belonged to Joash the Abiezrite, where his son Gideon was threshing wheat in a winepress to keep it from the Midianites. When the angel of the LORD appeared to Gideon, he said, "The LORD is with you, mighty warrior."

"Pardon me, my lord," Gideon replied, "but if the LORD is with us, why has all this happened to us? Where are all his wonders that our ancestors told us about when they said, 'Did not the LORD bring us up out of Egypt?' But now the LORD has abandoned us and given us into the hand of Midian."

The LORD turned to him and said, "Go in the strength you have and save Israel out of Midian's hand. Am I not sending you?"

"Pardon me, my lord," Gideon replied, "but how can I save Israel? My clan is the weakest in Manasseh, and I am the least in my family."

The LORD answered, "I will be with you, and you will strike down all the Midianites, leaving none alive."

Gideon replied, "If now I have found favor in your eyes, give me a sign that it is really you talking to me. Please do not go away until I come back and bring my offering and set it before you."

And the LORD said, "I will wait until you return."

Gideon went inside, prepared a young goat, and from an ephah of flour he made bread without yeast. Putting the meat in a basket and its broth in a pot, he brought them out and offered them to him under the oak.

The angel of God said to him, "Take the meat and the unleavened bread, place them on this rock, and pour out the broth." And Gideon did so. Then the angel of the LORD touched the meat and the unleavened bread with the tip of the staff that was in his hand. Fire flared from the rock, consuming the meat and the bread. And the angel of the LORD disappeared. When Gideon realized that it was the angel of the LORD, he exclaimed, "Alas, Sovereign LORD! I have seen the angel of the LORD face to face!"

But the LORD said to him, "Peace! Do not be afraid. You are not going to die."

So Gideon built an altar to the LORD there and called it The LORD Is Peace. To this day it stands in Ophrah of the Abiezrites.

Now all the Midianites, Amalekites and other eastern peoples joined forces and crossed over the Jordan and camped in the Valley of Jezreel. Then the Spirit of the LORD came on Gideon, and he blew a trumpet, summoning the Abiezrites to follow him. He sent messengers throughout Manasseh, calling them to arms, and also into Asher, Zebulun and Naphtali, so that they too went up to meet them.

Gideon said to God, "If you will save Israel by my hand as you have promised — look, I will place a wool fleece on the threshing floor. If there is dew only on the fleece and all the ground is dry, then I will know that you will save Israel by my hand, as you said." And that is what happened. Gideon rose early the next day; he squeezed the fleece and wrung out the dew — a bowlful of water.

Then Gideon said to God, "Do not be angry with me. Let me make just one more request. Allow me one more test with the fleece, but this time make the fleece dry and let the ground be covered with dew." That night God did so. Only the fleece was dry; all the ground was covered with dew.

Early in the morning, Jerub-Baal (that is, Gideon) and all his men camped at the spring of Harod. The camp of Midian was north of them in the valley near the hill of Moreh. The LORD said to Gideon, "You have too many men. I cannot deliver Midian into their hands, or Israel would boast against me, 'My own strength has saved me.' Now announce to the army, 'Anyone who trembles with fear may turn back and leave Mount Gilead.'" So twenty-two thousand men left, while ten thousand remained.

But the LORD said to Gideon, "There are still too many men. Take them down to the water, and I will thin them out for you there. If I say, 'This one shall go with you,' he shall go; but if I say, 'This one shall not go with you,' he shall not go."

So Gideon took the men down to the water. There the LORD told him, "Separate those who lap the water with their tongues as a dog laps from those who kneel down to drink." Three hundred of them drank from cupped hands, lapping like dogs. All the rest got down on their knees to drink.

The LORD said to Gideon, "With the three hundred men that lapped I will save you and give the Midianites into your hands. Let all the others go home." So Gideon sent the rest of the Israelites home but kept the three hundred, who took over the provisions and trumpets of the others.

Now the camp of Midian lay below him in the valley. During that night the LORD said to Gideon, "Get up, go down against the camp, because I am going to give it into your hands. If you are afraid to attack, go down to the camp with your servant Purah and listen to what they are saying. Afterward, you will be encouraged to attack the camp." So he and Purah his servant went down to the outposts of the camp. The Midianites, the Amalekites and all the other eastern peoples had settled in the valley, thick as locusts. Their camels could no more be counted than the sand on the seashore.

Gideon arrived just as a man was telling a friend his dream. "I had a dream," he was saying. "A round loaf of barley bread came tumbling into the Midianite camp. It struck the tent with such force that the tent overturned and collapsed."

His friend responded, "This can be nothing other than the sword of Gideon son of Joash, the Israelite. God has given the Midianites and the whole camp into his hands."

When Gideon heard the dream and its interpretation, he bowed down and worshiped. He returned to the camp of Israel and called out, "Get up! The LORD has given the Midianite camp into your hands." Dividing the three hundred men into three companies, he placed trumpets and empty jars in the hands of all of them, with torches inside.

"Watch me," he told them. "Follow my lead. When I get to the edge of the camp, do exactly as I do. When I and all who are with me blow our trumpets, then from all around the camp blow yours and shout, 'For the LORD and for Gideon.'"

Gideon and the hundred men with him reached the edge of the camp at the beginning of the middle watch, just after they had changed the guard. They blew their trumpets and broke the jars that were in their hands. The three companies blew the trumpets and smashed the jars. Grasping the torches in their left hands and holding in their right hands the trumpets they were to blow, they shouted, "A sword for the LORD and for Gideon!" While each man held his position around the camp, all the Midianites ran, crying out as they fled.

When the three hundred trumpets sounded, the LORD caused the men throughout the camp to turn on each other with their swords. The army fled to Beth Shittah toward Zererah as far as the border of Abel Meholah near Tabbath. Israelites from Naphtali, Asher and all Manasseh were called out, and they pursued the Midianites. Gideon sent messengers throughout the hill country of Ephraim, saying, "Come down against the Midianites and seize the waters of the Jordan ahead of them as far as Beth Barah."

So all the men of Ephraim were called out and they seized the waters of the Jordan as far as Beth Barah. They also captured two of the Midianite leaders, Oreb and Zeeb. They killed Oreb at the rock of Oreb, and Zeeb at the winepress of Zeeb. They pursued the Midianites and brought the heads of Oreb and Zeeb to Gideon, who was by the Jordan.

Thus Midian was subdued before the Israelites and did not raise its head again. During Gideon's lifetime, the land had peace forty years.

No sooner had Gideon died than the Israelites again prostituted themselves to the Baals. They set up Baal-Berith as their god and did not remember the LORD their God, who had rescued them from the hands of all their enemies on every side.

Once again the Israelites forgot their faithful, holy God—and once again they suffered the consequences of their unbelief. Several Israelite leaders tried to keep enemies at bay, with mixed results. No one had Gideon's daring or success. But God was still working, and he sent an angel to make an extraordinary announcement.

Again the Israelites did evil in the eyes of the LORD, so the LORD delivered them into the hands of the Philistines for forty years.

A certain man of Zorah, named Manoah, from the clan of the Danites, had a wife who was childless, unable to give birth. The angel of the LORD appeared to her and said, "You are barren and childless, but you are going to become pregnant and give birth to a son. Now see to it that you drink no wine or other fermented drink and that you do not eat anything unclean. You will become pregnant and have a son whose head is never to be touched by a razor because the boy is to be a Nazirite, dedicated to God from the womb. He will take the lead in delivering Israel from the hands of the Philistines."

The birth happened just as the angel had said, and the parents raised the child as God had directed. Young Samson, wild and unusually strong, became a man with a secret.

The woman gave birth to a boy and named him Samson. He grew and the LORD blessed him, and the Spirit of the LORD began to stir him while he was in Mahaneh Dan, between Zorah and Eshtaol.

Samson went down to Timnah and saw there a young Philistine woman. When he returned, he said to his father and mother,

"I have seen a Philistine woman in Timnah; now get her for me as my wife."

His father and mother replied, "Isn't there an acceptable woman among your relatives or among all our people? Must you go to the uncircumcised Philistines to get a wife?"

But Samson said to his father, "Get her for me. She's the right one for me." (His parents did not know that this was from the LORD, who was seeking an occasion to confront the Philistines; for at that time they were ruling over Israel.)

Samson went down to Timnah together with his father and mother. As they approached the vineyards of Timnah, suddenly a young lion came roaring toward him. The Spirit of the LORD came powerfully upon him so that he tore the lion apart with his bare hands as he might have torn a young goat. But he told neither his father nor his mother what he had done. Then he went down and talked with the woman, and he liked her.

Some time later, when he went back to marry her, he turned aside to look at the lion's carcass, and in it he saw a swarm of bees and some honey. He scooped out the honey with his hands and ate as he went along. When he rejoined his parents, he gave them some, and they too ate it. But he did not tell them that he had taken the honey from the lion's carcass.

Now his father went down to see the woman. And there Samson held a feast, as was customary for young men. When the people saw him, they chose thirty men to be his companions.

"Let me tell you a riddle," Samson said to them. "If you can give me the answer within the seven days of the feast, I will give you thirty linen garments and thirty sets of clothes. If you can't tell me the answer, you must give me thirty linen garments and thirty sets of clothes."

"Tell us your riddle," they said. "Let's hear it."

He replied,

> "Out of the eater, something to eat;
>   out of the strong, something sweet."

For three days they could not give the answer.

On the fourth day, they said to Samson's wife, "Coax your husband into explaining the riddle for us, or we will burn you and your father's household to death. Did you invite us here to steal our property?"

Then Samson's wife threw herself on him, sobbing, "You hate me! You don't really love me. You've given my people a riddle, but you haven't told me the answer."

"I haven't even explained it to my father or mother," he replied, "so why should I explain it to you?" She cried the whole seven days of the feast. So on the seventh day he finally told her, because she continued to press him. She in turn explained the riddle to her people.

Before sunset on the seventh day the men of the town said to him,

> "What is sweeter than honey?
>   What is stronger than a lion?"

Samson said to them,

> "If you had not plowed with my heifer,
>   you would not have solved my riddle."

Then the Spirit of the LORD came powerfully upon him. He went down to Ashkelon, struck down thirty of their men, stripped them of everything and gave their clothes to those who had explained the riddle. Burning with anger, he returned to his father's home. And Samson's wife was given to one of his companions who had attended him at the feast.

Later on, at the time of wheat harvest, Samson took a young goat and went to visit his wife. He said, "I'm going to my wife's room." But her father would not let him go in.

"I was so sure you hated her," he said, "that I gave her to your companion. Isn't her younger sister more attractive? Take her instead."

Samson said to them, "This time I have a right to get even with the Philistines; I will really harm them." So he went out and caught three hundred foxes and tied them tail to tail in pairs. He then fastened a torch to every pair of tails, lit the torches and let the foxes loose in the standing grain of the Philistines. He burned up the shocks and standing grain, together with the vineyards and olive groves.

When the Philistines asked, "Who did this?" they were told, "Samson, the Timnite's son-in-law, because his wife was given to his companion."

So the Philistines went up and burned her and her father to death. Samson said to them, "Since you've acted like this, I swear that I won't stop until I get my revenge on you." He attacked them viciously and slaughtered many of them. Then he went down and stayed in a cave in the rock of Etam.

The Philistines went up and camped in Judah, spreading out near Lehi. The people of Judah asked, "Why have you come to fight us?"

"We have come to take Samson prisoner," they answered, "to do to him as he did to us."

Then three thousand men from Judah went down to the cave in the rock of Etam and said to Samson, "Don't you realize that the Philistines are rulers over us? What have you done to us?"

He answered, "I merely did to them what they did to me."

They said to him, "We've come to tie you up and hand you over to the Philistines."

Samson said, "Swear to me that you won't kill me yourselves."

"Agreed," they answered. "We will only tie you up and hand you over to them. We will not kill you." So they bound him with two new ropes and led him up from the rock. As he approached Lehi, the Philistines came toward him shouting. The Spirit of the LORD came powerfully upon him. The ropes on his arms became like charred flax, and the bindings dropped from his hands. Finding a fresh jawbone of a donkey, he grabbed it and struck down a thousand men.

Then Samson said,

> "With a donkey's jawbone
> I have made donkeys of them.
> With a donkey's jawbone
> I have killed a thousand men."

When he finished speaking, he threw away the jawbone; and the place was called Ramath Lehi.

Because he was very thirsty, he cried out to the LORD, "You have given your servant this great victory. Must I now die of thirst and fall into the hands of the uncircumcised?" Then God opened up the hollow place in Lehi, and water came out of it. When Samson drank, his strength returned and he revived. So the spring was called En Hakkore, and it is still there in Lehi.

Samson led Israel for twenty years in the days of the Philistines.

One day Samson went to Gaza, where he saw a prostitute. He went in to spend the night with her. The people of Gaza were told, "Samson is here!" So they surrounded the place and lay in wait for him all night at the city gate. They made no move during the night, saying, "At dawn we'll kill him."

But Samson lay there only until the middle of the night. Then he got up and took hold of the doors of the city gate, together with the two posts, and tore them loose, bar and all. He lifted them to his shoulders and carried them to the top of the hill that faces Hebron.

Some time later, he fell in love with a woman in the Valley of Sorek whose name was Delilah. The rulers of the Philistines went to her and said, "See if you can lure him into showing you the secret of his great strength and how we can overpower him so we may tie him up and subdue him. Each one of us will give you eleven hundred shekels of silver."

So Delilah said to Samson, "Tell me the secret of your great strength and how you can be tied up and subdued."

Samson answered her, "If anyone ties me with seven fresh bowstrings that have not been dried, I'll become as weak as any other man."

Then the rulers of the Philistines brought her seven fresh bowstrings that had not been dried, and she tied him with them. With men hidden in the room, she called to him, "Samson, the Philistines are upon you!" But he snapped the bowstrings as easily as a piece of string snaps when it comes close to a flame. So the secret of his strength was not discovered.

Then Delilah said to Samson, "You have made a fool of me; you lied to me. Come now, tell me how you can be tied."

He said, "If anyone ties me securely with new ropes that have never been used, I'll become as weak as any other man."

So Delilah took new ropes and tied him with them. Then, with men hidden in the room, she called to him, "Samson, the Philistines are upon you!" But he snapped the ropes off his arms as if they were threads.

Delilah then said to Samson, "All this time you have been making a fool of me and lying to me. Tell me how you can be tied."

He replied, "If you weave the seven braids of my head into the fabric on the loom and tighten it with the pin, I'll become as weak as any other man." So while he was sleeping, Delilah took the seven braids of his head, wove them into the fabric and tightened it with the pin.

Again she called to him, "Samson, the Philistines are upon you!" He awoke from his sleep and pulled up the pin and the loom, with the fabric.

Then she said to him, "How can you say, 'I love you,' when you won't confide in me? This is the third time you have made a fool of me and haven't told me the secret of your great strength." With such nagging she prodded him day after day until he was sick to death of it.

So he told her everything. "No razor has ever been used on my head," he said, "because I have been a Nazirite dedicated to God from my mother's womb. If my head were shaved, my strength would leave me, and I would become as weak as any other man."

When Delilah saw that he had told her everything, she sent word to the rulers of the Philistines, "Come back once more; he has told me everything." So the rulers of the Philistines returned with the silver in their hands. After putting him to sleep on her lap, she called for someone to shave off the seven braids of his hair, and so began to subdue him. And his strength left him.

Then she called, "Samson, the Philistines are upon you!"

He awoke from his sleep and thought, "I'll go out as before and shake myself free." But he did not know that the LORD had left him.

Then the Philistines seized him, gouged out his eyes and took him down to Gaza. Binding him with bronze shackles, they set him to grinding grain in the prison. But the hair on his head began to grow again after it had been shaved.

Now the rulers of the Philistines assembled to offer a great sacrifice to Dagon their god and to celebrate, saying, "Our god has delivered Samson, our enemy, into our hands."

When the people saw him, they praised their god, saying,

> "Our god has delivered our enemy
>   into our hands,
> the one who laid waste our land
>   and multiplied our slain."

While they were in high spirits, they shouted, "Bring out Samson to entertain us." So they called Samson out of the prison, and he performed for them.

When they stood him among the pillars, Samson said to the servant who held his hand, "Put me where I can feel the pillars that support the temple, so that I may lean against them." Now the temple was crowded with men and women; all the rulers of the Philistines were there, and on the roof were about three thousand men and women watching Samson perform. Then Samson prayed to the LORD, "Sovereign LORD, remember me. Please, God, strengthen me just once more, and let me with one blow get revenge on the Philistines for my two eyes." Then Samson reached toward the two central pillars on which the temple stood. Bracing himself against them, his right hand on the one and his left hand on the other, Samson said, "Let me die with the Philistines!" Then he pushed with all his might, and down came the temple on the rulers and all the people in it. Thus he killed many more when he died than while he lived.

Then his brothers and his father's whole family went down to get him. They brought him back and buried him between Zorah and Eshtaol in the tomb of Manoah his father. He had led Israel twenty years.

After Samson, the Israelites continued their pattern of spiritual compromise during this sad period of their history. Enter Ruth, a young Moabite woman, into God's story. If the Hebrew people thought God was their exclusive property, this foreign woman challenged that myth. Ruth was loyal, determined, lovely and clever. She became part of the lineage of King David. More important, she was God's choice to illustrate the worldwide reach of God's special gift of hope and life—his plan of salvation as broad and deep as his divine love.

9

The Faith
of a Foreign Woman

IN THE DAYS when the judges ruled, there was a famine in the land. So a man from Bethlehem in Judah, together with his wife and two sons, went to live for a while in the country of Moab. The man's name was Elimelek, his wife's name was Naomi, and the names of his two sons were Mahlon and Kilion. They were Ephrathites from Bethlehem, Judah. And they went to Moab and lived there.

Now Elimelek, Naomi's husband, died, and she was left with her two sons. They married Moabite women, one named Orpah and the other Ruth. After they had lived there about ten years, both Mahlon and Kilion also died, and Naomi was left without her two sons and her husband.

When Naomi heard in Moab that the LORD had come to the aid of his people by providing food for them, she and her daughters-in-law prepared to return home from there. With her two daughters-in-law she left the place where she had been living and set out on the road that would take them back to the land of Judah.

Time of the judges	Naomi and Ruth return from Moab	Ruth meets Boaz	Boaz marries Ruth

BC   1375–1050

Full timeline information starts on page xi.

Then Naomi said to her two daughters-in-law, "Go back, each of you, to your mother's home. May the LORD show you kindness, as you have shown kindness to your dead husbands and to me. May the LORD grant that each of you will find rest in the home of another husband."

Then she kissed them goodbye and they wept aloud and said to her, "We will go back with you to your people."

But Naomi said, "Return home, my daughters. Why would you come with me? Am I going to have any more sons, who could become your husbands? Return home, my daughters; I am too old to have another husband. Even if I thought there was still hope for me — even if I had a husband tonight and then gave birth to sons — would you wait until they grew up? Would you remain unmarried for them? No, my daughters. It is more bitter for me than for you, because the LORD's hand has turned against me!"

At this they wept aloud again. Then Orpah kissed her mother-in-law goodbye, but Ruth clung to her.

"Look," said Naomi, "your sister-in-law is going back to her people and her gods. Go back with her."

But Ruth replied, "Don't urge me to leave you or to turn back from you. Where you go I will go, and where you stay I will stay. Your people will be my people and your God my God. Where you die I will die, and there I will be buried. May the LORD deal with me, be it ever so severely, if even death separates you and me." When Naomi realized that Ruth was determined to go with her, she stopped urging her.

So the two women went on until they came to Bethlehem. When they arrived in Bethlehem, the whole town was stirred because of them, and the women exclaimed, "Can this be Naomi?"

"Don't call me Naomi," she told them. "Call me Mara, because the Almighty has made my life very bitter. I went away full, but the LORD has brought me back empty. Why call me Naomi? The LORD has afflicted me; the Almighty has brought misfortune upon me."

So Naomi returned from Moab accompanied by Ruth the

Moabite, her daughter-in-law, arriving in Bethlehem as the barley harvest was beginning.

Now Naomi had a relative on her husband's side, a man of standing from the clan of Elimelek, whose name was Boaz.

And Ruth the Moabite said to Naomi, "Let me go to the fields and pick up the leftover grain behind anyone in whose eyes I find favor."

Naomi said to her, "Go ahead, my daughter." So she went out, entered a field and began to glean behind the harvesters. As it turned out, she was working in a field belonging to Boaz, who was from the clan of Elimelek.

Just then Boaz arrived from Bethlehem and greeted the harvesters, "The LORD be with you!"

"The LORD bless you!" they answered.

Boaz asked the overseer of his harvesters, "Who does that young woman belong to?"

The overseer replied, "She is the Moabite who came back from Moab with Naomi. She said, 'Please let me glean and gather among the sheaves behind the harvesters.' She came into the field and has remained here from morning till now, except for a short rest in the shelter."

So Boaz said to Ruth, "My daughter, listen to me. Don't go and glean in another field and don't go away from here. Stay here with the women who work for me. Watch the field where the men are harvesting, and follow along after the women. I have told the men not to lay a hand on you. And whenever you are thirsty, go and get a drink from the water jars the men have filled."

At this, she bowed down with her face to the ground. She asked him, "Why have I found such favor in your eyes that you notice me —a foreigner?"

Boaz replied, "I've been told all about what you have done for your mother-in-law since the death of your husband—how you left your father and mother and your homeland and came to live with a people you did not know before. May the LORD repay you for what you have done. May you be richly rewarded by the LORD, the God of Israel, under whose wings you have come to take refuge."

"May I continue to find favor in your eyes, my lord," she said. "You have put me at ease by speaking kindly to your servant — though I do not have the standing of one of your servants."

At mealtime Boaz said to her, "Come over here. Have some bread and dip it in the wine vinegar."

When she sat down with the harvesters, he offered her some roasted grain. She ate all she wanted and had some left over. As she got up to glean, Boaz gave orders to his men, "Let her gather among the sheaves and don't reprimand her. Even pull out some stalks for her from the bundles and leave them for her to pick up, and don't rebuke her."

So Ruth gleaned in the field until evening. Then she threshed the barley she had gathered, and it amounted to about an ephah. She carried it back to town, and her mother-in-law saw how much she had gathered. Ruth also brought out and gave her what she had left over after she had eaten enough.

Her mother-in-law asked her, "Where did you glean today? Where did you work? Blessed be the man who took notice of you!"

Then Ruth told her mother-in-law about the one at whose place she had been working. "The name of the man I worked with today is Boaz," she said.

"The LORD bless him!" Naomi said to her daughter-in-law. "He has not stopped showing his kindness to the living and the dead." She added, "That man is our close relative; he is one of our guardian-redeemers."

Then Ruth the Moabite said, "He even said to me, 'Stay with my workers until they finish harvesting all my grain.'"

Naomi said to Ruth her daughter-in-law, "It will be good for you, my daughter, to go with the women who work for him, because in someone else's field you might be harmed."

So Ruth stayed close to the women of Boaz to glean until the barley and wheat harvests were finished. And she lived with her mother-in-law.

One day Ruth's mother-in-law Naomi said to her, "My daughter, I must find a home for you, where you will be well provided for. Now Boaz, with whose women you have worked, is a relative of ours. Tonight he will be winnowing barley on the threshing floor. Wash, put on perfume, and get dressed in your best clothes. Then go down to the threshing floor, but don't let him know you are there until he has finished eating and drinking. When he lies down, note the place where he is lying. Then go and uncover his feet and lie down. He will tell you what to do."

"I will do whatever you say," Ruth answered. So she went down to the threshing floor and did everything her mother-in-law told her to do.

When Boaz had finished eating and drinking and was in good spirits, he went over to lie down at the far end of the grain pile. Ruth approached quietly, uncovered his feet and lay down. In the middle of the night something startled the man; he turned — and there was a woman lying at his feet!

"Who are you?" he asked.

"I am your servant Ruth," she said. "Spread the corner of your garment over me, since you are a guardian-redeemer of our family."

"The LORD bless you, my daughter," he replied. "This kindness is greater than that which you showed earlier: You have not run after the younger men, whether rich or poor. And now, my daughter, don't be afraid. I will do for you all you ask. All the people of my town know that you are a woman of noble character. Although it is true that I am a guardian-redeemer of our family, there is another who is more closely related than I. Stay here for the night, and in the morning if he wants to do his duty as your guardian-redeemer, good; let him redeem you. But if he is not willing, as surely as the LORD lives I will do it. Lie here until morning."

So she lay at his feet until morning, but got up before anyone could be recognized; and he said, "No one must know that a woman came to the threshing floor."

He also said, "Bring me the shawl you are wearing and hold it out." When she did so, he poured into it six measures of barley and placed the bundle on her. Then he went back to town.

When Ruth came to her mother-in-law, Naomi asked, "How did it go, my daughter?"

Then she told her everything Boaz had done for her and added, "He gave me these six measures of barley, saying, 'Don't go back to your mother-in-law empty-handed.'"

Then Naomi said, "Wait, my daughter, until you find out what happens. For the man will not rest until the matter is settled today."

Meanwhile Boaz went up to the town gate and sat down there just as the guardian-redeemer he had mentioned came along. Boaz said, "Come over here, my friend, and sit down." So he went over and sat down.

Boaz took ten of the elders of the town and said, "Sit here," and they did so. Then he said to the guardian-redeemer, "Naomi, who has come back from Moab, is selling the piece of land that belonged to our relative Elimelek. I thought I should bring the matter to your attention and suggest that you buy it in the presence of these seated here and in the presence of the elders of my people. If you will redeem it, do so. But if you will not, tell me, so I will know. For no one has the right to do it except you, and I am next in line."

"I will redeem it," he said.

Then Boaz said, "On the day you buy the land from Naomi, you also acquire Ruth the Moabite, the dead man's widow, in order to maintain the name of the dead with his property."

At this, the guardian-redeemer said, "Then I cannot redeem it because I might endanger my own estate. You redeem it yourself. I cannot do it."

(Now in earlier times in Israel, for the redemption and transfer of property to become final, one party took off his sandal and gave it to the other. This was the method of legalizing transactions in Israel.)

So the guardian-redeemer said to Boaz, "Buy it yourself." And he removed his sandal.

Then Boaz announced to the elders and all the people, "Today you are witnesses that I have bought from Naomi all the property of Elimelek, Kilion and Mahlon. I have also acquired Ruth the Moabite, Mahlon's widow, as my wife, in order to maintain the name of the dead with his property, so that his name will not disappear from among his family or from his hometown. Today you are witnesses!"

Then the elders and all the people at the gate said, "We are witnesses. May the LORD make the woman who is coming into your home like Rachel and Leah, who together built up the family of Israel. May you have standing in Ephrathah and be famous in Bethlehem. Through the offspring the LORD gives you by this young woman, may your family be like that of Perez, whom Tamar bore to Judah."

So Boaz took Ruth and she became his wife. When he made love to her, the LORD enabled her to conceive, and she gave birth to a son. The women said to Naomi: "Praise be to the LORD, who this day has not left you without a guardian-redeemer. May he become famous throughout Israel! He will renew your life and sustain you in your old age. For your daughter-in-law, who loves you and who is better to you than seven sons, has given him birth."

Then Naomi took the child in her arms and cared for him. The women living there said, "Naomi has a son!" And they named him Obed. He was the father of Jesse, the father of David.

Within Ruth's story we catch a glimpse of an amazing tale yet to come—the life of her great-grandson David, the renowned shepherd-king. But much will take place before David's golden reign. A godly priest and prophet of Israel will first become an important player in this drama. Samuel was himself a child miraculously born out of struggle and promise. After being recognized by the people as the Lord's prophet, Samuel's first order of business was to call the people back to God and subdue the Philistines. Then he had the unenviable task of finding the nation a king. It seemed that nothing happened easily for God's people, but all that happened was part of God's faithful plan.

10

Standing Tall, Falling Hard

THERE WAS A CERTAIN MAN from Ramathaim, a Zuphite from the hill country of Ephraim, whose name was Elkanah son of Jeroham, the son of Elihu, the son of Tohu, the son of Zuph, an Ephraimite. He had two wives; one was called Hannah and the other Peninnah. Peninnah had children, but Hannah had none.

Year after year this man went up from his town to worship and sacrifice to the LORD Almighty at Shiloh, where Hophni and Phinehas, the two sons of Eli, were priests of the LORD. Whenever the day came for Elkanah to sacrifice, he would give portions of the meat to his wife Peninnah and to all her sons and daughters. But to Hannah he gave a double portion because he loved her, and the LORD had closed her womb. Because the LORD had closed Hannah's womb, her rival kept provoking her in order to irritate her. This went on year after year. Whenever Hannah went up to the house of the LORD, her rival provoked her till she wept and would not eat. Her husband Elkanah would say to her, "Hannah, why are you weeping? Why don't you eat? Why are you down-hearted? Don't I mean more to you than ten sons?"

Samuel born	Samuel ministers under Eli	The Israelites ask for a king	Saul's reign
1105			1050–1010

BC

Full timeline information starts on page xi.

Once when they had finished eating and drinking in Shiloh, Hannah stood up. Now Eli the priest was sitting on his chair by the doorpost of the LORD's house. In her deep anguish Hannah prayed to the LORD, weeping bitterly. And she made a vow, saying, "LORD Almighty, if you will only look on your servant's misery and remember me, and not forget your servant but give her a son, then I will give him to the LORD for all the days of his life, and no razor will ever be used on his head."

As she kept on praying to the LORD, Eli observed her mouth. Hannah was praying in her heart, and her lips were moving but her voice was not heard. Eli thought she was drunk and said to her, "How long are you going to stay drunk? Put away your wine."

"Not so, my lord," Hannah replied, "I am a woman who is deeply troubled. I have not been drinking wine or beer; I was pouring out my soul to the LORD. Do not take your servant for a wicked woman; I have been praying here out of my great anguish and grief."

Eli answered, "Go in peace, and may the God of Israel grant you what you have asked of him."

She said, "May your servant find favor in your eyes." Then she went her way and ate something, and her face was no longer downcast.

Early the next morning they arose and worshiped before the LORD and then went back to their home at Ramah. Elkanah made love to his wife Hannah, and the LORD remembered her. So in the course of time Hannah became pregnant and gave birth to a son. She named him Samuel, saying, "Because I asked the LORD for him."

When her husband Elkanah went up with all his family to offer the annual sacrifice to the LORD and to fulfill his vow, Hannah did not go. She said to her husband, "After the boy is weaned, I will take him and present him before the LORD, and he will live there always."

"Do what seems best to you," her husband Elkanah told her. "Stay here until you have weaned him; only may the LORD make good his word." So the woman stayed at home and nursed her son until she had weaned him.

After he was weaned, she took the boy with her, young as he was, along with a three-year-old bull, an ephah of flour and a skin of wine, and brought him to the house of the LORD at Shiloh. When the bull had been sacrificed, they brought the boy to Eli, and she said to him, "Pardon me, my lord. As surely as you live, I am the woman who stood here beside you praying to the LORD. I prayed for this child, and the LORD has granted me what I asked of him. So now I give him to the LORD. For his whole life he will be given over to the LORD." And he worshiped the LORD there.

Then Hannah prayed and said:

> "My heart rejoices in the LORD;
>   in the LORD my horn is lifted high.
> My mouth boasts over my enemies,
>   for I delight in your deliverance.
>
> "There is no one holy like the LORD;
>   there is no one besides you;
>   there is no Rock like our God."

Each year his mother made him a little robe and took it to him when she went up with her husband to offer the annual sacrifice. Eli would bless Elkanah and his wife, saying, "May the LORD give you children by this woman to take the place of the one she prayed for and gave to the LORD." Then they would go home. And the LORD was gracious to Hannah; she gave birth to three sons and two daughters. Meanwhile, the boy Samuel grew up in the presence of the LORD.

The boy Samuel ministered before the LORD under Eli. In those days the word of the LORD was rare; there were not many visions.

One night Eli, whose eyes were becoming so weak that he could barely see, was lying down in his usual place. The lamp of God had not yet gone out, and Samuel was lying down in the house of the LORD, where the ark of God was. Then the LORD called Samuel.

Samuel answered, "Here I am." And he ran to Eli and said, "Here I am; you called me."

But Eli said, "I did not call; go back and lie down." So he went and lay down.

Again the LORD called, "Samuel!" And Samuel got up and went to Eli and said, "Here I am; you called me."

"My son," Eli said, "I did not call; go back and lie down."

Now Samuel did not yet know the LORD: The word of the LORD had not yet been revealed to him.

A third time the LORD called, "Samuel!" And Samuel got up and went to Eli and said, "Here I am; you called me."

Then Eli realized that the LORD was calling the boy. So Eli told Samuel, "Go and lie down, and if he calls you, say, 'Speak, LORD, for your servant is listening.'" So Samuel went and lay down in his place.

The LORD came and stood there, calling as at the other times, "Samuel! Samuel!"

Then Samuel said, "Speak, for your servant is listening."

And the LORD said to Samuel: "See, I am about to do something in Israel that will make the ears of everyone who hears about it tingle. At that time I will carry out against Eli everything I spoke against his family — from beginning to end. For I told him that I would judge his family forever because of the sin he knew about; his sons blasphemed God, and he failed to restrain them. Therefore I swore to the house of Eli, 'The guilt of Eli's house will never be atoned for by sacrifice or offering.'"

Samuel lay down until morning and then opened the doors of the house of the LORD. He was afraid to tell Eli the vision, but Eli called him and said, "Samuel, my son."

Samuel answered, "Here I am."

"What was it he said to you?" Eli asked. "Do not hide it from me. May God deal with you, be it ever so severely, if you hide from me anything he told you." So Samuel told him everything, hiding nothing from him. Then Eli said, "He is the LORD; let him do what is good in his eyes."

The LORD was with Samuel as he grew up, and he let none of Samuel's words fall to the ground. And all Israel from Dan to Beersheba recognized that Samuel was attested as a prophet of the LORD. The LORD continued to appear at Shiloh, and there he revealed himself to Samuel through his word.

And Samuel's word came to all Israel.

Now the Israelites went out to fight against the Philistines. The Israelites camped at Ebenezer, and the Philistines at Aphek. The Philistines deployed their forces to meet Israel, and as the battle spread, Israel was defeated by the Philistines, who killed about four thousand of them on the battlefield. When the soldiers returned to camp, the elders of Israel asked, "Why did the LORD bring defeat on us today before the Philistines? Let us bring the ark of the LORD's covenant from Shiloh, so that he may go with us and save us from the hand of our enemies."

So the people sent men to Shiloh, and they brought back the ark of the covenant of the LORD Almighty, who is enthroned between the cherubim. And Eli's two sons, Hophni and Phinehas, were there with the ark of the covenant of God.

When the ark of the LORD's covenant came into the camp, all Israel raised such a great shout that the ground shook. Hearing the uproar, the Philistines asked, "What's all this shouting in the Hebrew camp?"

When they learned that the ark of the LORD had come into the camp, the Philistines were afraid. "A god has come into the camp," they said. "Oh no! Nothing like this has happened before. We're doomed! Who will deliver us from the hand of these mighty gods? They are the gods who struck the Egyptians with all kinds of plagues in the wilderness. Be strong, Philistines! Be men, or you will be subject to the Hebrews, as they have been to you. Be men, and fight!"

So the Philistines fought, and the Israelites were defeated and every man fled to his tent. The slaughter was very great; Israel lost thirty thousand foot soldiers. The ark of God was captured, and Eli's two sons, Hophni and Phinehas, died.

That same day a Benjamite ran from the battle line and went to Shiloh with his clothes torn and dust on his head. When he arrived, there was Eli sitting on his chair by the side of the road, watching, because his heart feared for the ark of God. When the man entered the town and told what had happened, the whole town sent up a cry.

Eli heard the outcry and asked, "What is the meaning of this uproar?"

The man hurried over to Eli, who was ninety-eight years old and whose eyes had failed so that he could not see. He told Eli, "I have just come from the battle line; I fled from it this very day."

Eli asked, "What happened, my son?"

The man who brought the news replied, "Israel fled before the Philistines, and the army has suffered heavy losses. Also your two sons, Hophni and Phinehas, are dead, and the ark of God has been captured."

When he mentioned the ark of God, Eli fell backward off his chair by the side of the gate. His neck was broken and he died, for he was an old man, and he was heavy. He had led Israel forty years.

No doubt the loss of his sons staggered Eli, but the loss of the ark of the covenant hit him even harder. The sacred ark in pagan hands? Unthinkable! The very presence of God, now captured by the Philistines? A tragedy!

The Philistines understood what a symbolic victory they had won and promptly placed the ark next to the statue of their god Dagon in the great temple in Ashdod, one of the five fortified Philistine cities. But God would not be mocked by the false gods of the Philistines. Israel had been brought here in the first place for the very purpose of showing the one true God to these people. So the Dagon statue tumbled to pieces on the temple floor.

Next, God afflicted the Philistines with tumors, and after seven months of pure misery, the Philistines put the ark on a cart and sent it back to the Israelites, who kept it in the border town of Kiriath Jearim for 20 years, wondering what to do with it.

Meanwhile, Samuel insisted that the Israelites stop worshiping pagan deities and return to the true God. He led the people in successfully subduing the Philistines. But the people stubbornly thought that having a king like everybody else would solve their leadership problems.

When Samuel grew old, he appointed his sons as Israel's leaders. The name of his firstborn was Joel and the name of his second was Abijah, and they served at Beersheba. But his sons did not follow his ways. They turned aside after dishonest gain and accepted bribes and perverted justice.

So all the elders of Israel gathered together and came to Samuel at Ramah. They said to him, "You are old, and your sons do not follow your ways; now appoint a king to lead us, such as all the other nations have."

But when they said, "Give us a king to lead us," this displeased Samuel; so he prayed to the LORD. And the LORD told him: "Listen to all that the people are saying to you; it is not you they have rejected, but they have rejected me as their king. As they have done from the day I brought them up out of Egypt until this day, forsaking me and serving other gods, so they are doing to you. Now listen to them; but warn them solemnly and let them know what the king who will reign over them will claim as his rights."

Samuel told all the words of the LORD to the people who were asking him for a king. He said, "This is what the king who will reign over you will claim as his rights: He will take your sons and make them serve with his chariots and horses, and they will run in front of his chariots. Some he will assign to be commanders of thousands and commanders of fifties, and others to plow his ground and reap his harvest, and still others to make weapons of war and equipment for his chariots. He will take your daughters to be perfumers and cooks and bakers. He will take the best of your fields and vineyards and olive groves and give them to his attendants. He will take a tenth of your grain and of your vintage and give it to his officials and attendants. Your male and female servants and the best of your cattle and donkeys he will take for his own use. He will take a tenth of your flocks, and you yourselves will become his slaves. When that day comes, you will cry out for relief from the king you have chosen, but the LORD will not answer you in that day."

But the people refused to listen to Samuel. "No!" they said. "We want a king over us. Then we will be like all the other nations, with a king to lead us and to go out before us and fight our battles."

When Samuel heard all that the people said, he repeated it before the LORD. The LORD answered, "Listen to them and give them a king."

Then Samuel said to the Israelites, "Everyone go back to your own town."

There was a Benjamite, a man of standing, whose name was Kish son of Abiel, the son of Zeror, the son of Bekorath, the son of Aphiah of Benjamin. Kish had a son named Saul, as handsome a young man as could be found anywhere in Israel, and he was a head taller than anyone else.

Now the donkeys belonging to Saul's father Kish were lost, and Kish said to his son Saul, "Take one of the servants with you and go and look for the donkeys." So he passed through the hill country of Ephraim and through the area around Shalisha, but they did not find them. They went on into the district of Shaalim, but the donkeys were not there. Then he passed through the territory of Benjamin, but they did not find them.

When they reached the district of Zuph, Saul said to the servant who was with him, "Come, let's go back, or my father will stop thinking about the donkeys and start worrying about us."

But the servant replied, "Look, in this town there is a man of God; he is highly respected, and everything he says comes true. Let's go there now. Perhaps he will tell us what way to take."

"Good," Saul said to his servant. "Come, let's go." So they set out for the town where the man of God was.

They went up to the town, and as they were entering it, there was Samuel, coming toward them on his way up to the high place.

Now the day before Saul came, the LORD had revealed this to Samuel: "About this time tomorrow I will send you a man from the land of Benjamin. Anoint him ruler over my people Israel; he will deliver them from the hand of the Philistines. I have looked on my people, for their cry has reached me."

When Samuel caught sight of Saul, the LORD said to him, "This is the man I spoke to you about; he will govern my people."

Saul approached Samuel in the gateway and asked, "Would you please tell me where the seer's house is?"

"I am the seer," Samuel replied. "Go up ahead of me to the high place, for today you are to eat with me, and in the morning I will send you on your way and will tell you all that is in your heart. As for the donkeys you lost three days ago, do not worry about them; they have been found. And to whom is all the desire of Israel turned, if not to you and your whole family line?"

Saul answered, "But am I not a Benjamite, from the smallest tribe of Israel, and is not my clan the least of all the clans of the tribe of Benjamin? Why do you say such a thing to me?"

Then Samuel took a flask of olive oil and poured it on Saul's head and kissed him, saying, "Has not the LORD anointed you ruler over his inheritance? When you leave me today, you will meet two men near Rachel's tomb, at Zelzah on the border of Benjamin. They will say to you, 'The donkeys you set out to look for have been found. And now your father has stopped thinking about them and is worried about you. He is asking, "What shall I do about my son?"'

"After that you will go to Gibeah of God, where there is a Philistine outpost. As you approach the town, you will meet a procession of prophets coming down from the high place with lyres, timbrels, pipes and harps being played before them, and they will be prophesying. The Spirit of the LORD will come powerfully upon you, and you will prophesy with them; and you will be changed into a different person. Once these signs are fulfilled, do whatever your hand finds to do, for God is with you."

As Saul turned to leave Samuel, God changed Saul's heart, and all these signs were fulfilled that day.

Samuel summoned the people of Israel to the LORD at Mizpah and said to them, "This is what the LORD, the God of Israel, says: 'I brought Israel up out of Egypt, and I delivered you from the power of Egypt and all the kingdoms that oppressed you.' But you have now rejected your God, who saves you out of all your disasters and calamities. And you have said, 'No, appoint a king over us.' So now present yourselves before the LORD by your tribes and clans."

When Samuel had all Israel come forward by tribes, the tribe of Benjamin was taken by lot. Then he brought forward the tribe of Benjamin, clan by clan, and Matri's clan was taken. Finally Saul son of Kish was taken. But when they looked for him, he was not to be found. So they inquired further of the LORD, "Has the man come here yet?"

And the LORD said, "Yes, he has hidden himself among the supplies."

They ran and brought him out, and as he stood among the people he was a head taller than any of the others. Samuel said to all the people, "Do you see the man the LORD has chosen? There is no one like him among all the people."

Then the people shouted, "Long live the king!"

Samuel explained to the people the rights and duties of kingship. He wrote them down on a scroll and deposited it before the LORD. Then Samuel dismissed the people to go to their own homes.

Saul also went to his home in Gibeah, accompanied by valiant men whose hearts God had touched.

The future king found hiding among the supplies may have been history's most inauspicious royal inauguration. The rest of

Saul's story is just as unpredictable. Though he was chosen by God, he was a jealous, impatient and impetuous man. Yet he led the people into battle, and they rallied to support a strong central leader, forging a nation out of local tribes.

Nahash the Ammonite went up and besieged Jabesh Gilead. And all the men of Jabesh said to him, "Make a treaty with us, and we will be subject to you."

But Nahash the Ammonite replied, "I will make a treaty with you only on the condition that I gouge out the right eye of every one of you and so bring disgrace on all Israel."

The elders of Jabesh said to him, "Give us seven days so we can send messengers throughout Israel; if no one comes to rescue us, we will surrender to you."

When the messengers came to Gibeah of Saul and reported these terms to the people, they all wept aloud. Just then Saul was returning from the fields, behind his oxen, and he asked, "What is wrong with everyone? Why are they weeping?" Then they repeated to him what the men of Jabesh had said.

When Saul heard their words, the Spirit of God came powerfully upon him, and he burned with anger. He took a pair of oxen, cut them into pieces, and sent the pieces by messengers throughout Israel, proclaiming, "This is what will be done to the oxen of anyone who does not follow Saul and Samuel." Then the terror of the LORD fell on the people, and they came out together as one. When Saul mustered them at Bezek, the men of Israel numbered three hundred thousand and those of Judah thirty thousand.

They told the messengers who had come, "Say to the men of Jabesh Gilead, 'By the time the sun is hot tomorrow, you will be rescued.'" When the messengers went and reported this to the men of Jabesh, they were elated. They said to the Ammonites, "Tomorrow we will surrender to you, and you can do to us whatever you like."

The next day Saul separated his men into three divisions; during the last watch of the night they broke into the camp of the

Ammonites and slaughtered them until the heat of the day. Those who survived were scattered, so that no two of them were left together.

The people then said to Samuel, "Who was it that asked, 'Shall Saul reign over us?' Turn these men over to us so that we may put them to death."

But Saul said, "No one will be put to death today, for this day the LORD has rescued Israel."

Then Samuel said to the people, "Come, let us go to Gilgal and there renew the kingship." So all the people went to Gilgal and made Saul king in the presence of the LORD. There they sacrificed fellowship offerings before the LORD, and Saul and all the Israelites held a great celebration.

Samuel said to all Israel, "I have listened to everything you said to me and have set a king over you. Now you have a king as your leader.

"When you saw that Nahash king of the Ammonites was moving against you, you said to me, 'No, we want a king to rule over us' —even though the LORD your God was your king. Now here is the king you have chosen, the one you asked for; see, the LORD has set a king over you. If you fear the LORD and serve and obey him and do not rebel against his commands, and if both you and the king who reigns over you follow the LORD your God — good! But if you do not obey the LORD, and if you rebel against his commands, his hand will be against you, as it was against your ancestors.

"Now then, stand still and see this great thing the LORD is about to do before your eyes! Is it not wheat harvest now? I will call on the LORD to send thunder and rain. And you will realize what an evil thing you did in the eyes of the LORD when you asked for a king."

Then Samuel called on the LORD, and that same day the LORD sent thunder and rain. So all the people stood in awe of the LORD and of Samuel.

The people all said to Samuel, "Pray to the LORD your God for your servants so that we will not die, for we have added to all our other sins the evil of asking for a king."

"Do not be afraid," Samuel replied. "You have done all this evil; yet do not turn away from the LORD, but serve the LORD with all your heart. Do not turn away after useless idols. They can do you no good, nor can they rescue you, because they are useless. For the sake of his great name the LORD will not reject his people, because the LORD was pleased to make you his own. As for me, far be it from me that I should sin against the LORD by failing to pray for you. And I will teach you the way that is good and right. But be sure to fear the LORD and serve him faithfully with all your heart; consider what great things he has done for you. Yet if you persist in doing evil, both you and your king will perish."

After Samuel's stern warning, Saul attempted to reign success-fully, but he seemed always to be one step behind common sense. When facing battle, he failed to measure the strength of the enemy, then impulsively took matters into his own hands while waiting for Samuel. What sort of king was this?

Saul was thirty years old when he became king, and he reigned over Israel forty-two years.

Saul chose three thousand men from Israel; two thousand were with him at Mikmash and in the hill country of Bethel, and a thousand were with Jonathan at Gibeah in Benjamin. The rest of the men he sent back to their homes.

Jonathan attacked the Philistine outpost at Geba, and the Philistines heard about it. Then Saul had the trumpet blown throughout the land and said, "Let the Hebrews hear!" So all Israel heard the news: "Saul has attacked the Philistine outpost, and now Israel has become obnoxious to the Philistines." And the people were summoned to join Saul at Gilgal.

The Philistines assembled to fight Israel, with three thousand chariots, six thousand charioteers, and soldiers as numerous as the sand on the seashore. They went up and camped at Mikmash, east of Beth Aven. When the Israelites saw that their situation was critical and that their army was hard pressed, they hid in caves and thickets, among the rocks, and in pits and cisterns. Some Hebrews even crossed the Jordan to the land of Gad and Gilead.

Saul remained at Gilgal, and all the troops with him were quaking with fear. He waited seven days, the time set by Samuel; but Samuel did not come to Gilgal, and Saul's men began to scatter. So he said, "Bring me the burnt offering and the fellowship offerings." And Saul offered up the burnt offering. Just as he finished making the offering, Samuel arrived, and Saul went out to greet him.

"What have you done?" asked Samuel.

Saul replied, "When I saw that the men were scattering, and that you did not come at the set time, and that the Philistines were assembling at Mikmash, I thought, 'Now the Philistines will come down against me at Gilgal, and I have not sought the LORD's favor.' So I felt compelled to offer the burnt offering."

"You have done a foolish thing," Samuel said. "You have not kept the command the LORD your God gave you; if you had, he would have established your kingdom over Israel for all time. But now your kingdom will not endure; the LORD has sought out a man after his own heart and appointed him ruler of his people, because you have not kept the LORD's command."

Samuel said to Saul, "I am the one the LORD sent to anoint you king over his people Israel; so listen now to the message from the LORD. This is what the LORD Almighty says: 'I will punish the Amalekites for what they did to Israel when they waylaid them as they came up from Egypt. Now go, attack the Amalekites and totally destroy all that belongs to them. Do not spare them; put to death men and women, children and infants, cattle and sheep, camels and donkeys.'"

So Saul summoned the men and mustered them at Telaim — two hundred thousand foot soldiers and ten thousand from Judah.

Then Saul attacked the Amalekites all the way from Havilah

to Shur, near the eastern border of Egypt. He took Agag king of the Amalekites alive, and all his people he totally destroyed with the sword. But Saul and the army spared Agag and the best of the sheep and cattle, the fat calves and lambs — everything that was good. These they were unwilling to destroy completely, but everything that was despised and weak they totally destroyed.

Saul sinned against God again. God had instructed him to destroy all of the Amalekite property, but Saul and his men instead kept a good share of it. Sparing the good livestock, Saul claimed he intended to offer them as animal sacrifices to God. It was still disobedience. Samuel, sad that Saul had failed as king, warned Saul that his time was up. It was time to find a successor. But having enjoyed the perks of high office, Saul would not go without resistance.

11

From Shepherd to King

THE LORD SAID TO SAMUEL, "How long will you mourn for Saul, since I have rejected him as king over Israel? Fill your horn with oil and be on your way; I am sending you to Jesse of Bethlehem. I have chosen one of his sons to be king."

Samuel did what the LORD said. When he arrived at Bethlehem, the elders of the town trembled when they met him. They asked, "Do you come in peace?"

Samuel replied, "Yes, in peace; I have come to sacrifice to the LORD. Consecrate yourselves and come to the sacrifice with me." Then he consecrated Jesse and his sons and invited them to the sacrifice.

When they arrived, Samuel saw Eliab and thought, "Surely the LORD's anointed stands here before the LORD."

But the LORD said to Samuel, "Do not consider his appearance or his height, for I have rejected him. The LORD does not look at the things people look at. People look at the outward appearance, but the LORD looks at the heart."

Then Jesse called Abinadab and had him pass in front of

Samuel anoints David	David kills Goliath	Saul tries to kill David	Saul dies	David named king
BC 1025	1025		1010	1010

Full timeline information starts on page xi.

Samuel. But Samuel said, "The LORD has not chosen this one either." Jesse then had Shammah pass by, but Samuel said, "Nor has the LORD chosen this one." Jesse had seven of his sons pass before Samuel, but Samuel said to him, "The LORD has not chosen these." So he asked Jesse, "Are these all the sons you have?"

"There is still the youngest," Jesse answered. "He is tending the sheep."

Samuel said, "Send for him; we will not sit down until he arrives."

So he sent for him and had him brought in. He was glowing with health and had a fine appearance and handsome features.

Then the LORD said, "Rise and anoint him; this is the one."

So Samuel took the horn of oil and anointed him in the presence of his brothers, and from that day on the Spirit of the LORD came powerfully upon David.

Now the Philistines gathered their forces for war and assembled at Sokoh in Judah. They pitched camp at Ephes Dammim,

David

Jesse the father of David,

Obed the father of Jesse,

Boaz the father of Obed,

Salmon the father of Boaz,

Nahshon the father of Salmon,

Amminadab the father of Nahshon,

Ram the father of Amminadab,

Hezron the father of Ram,

Perez the father of Hezron.

between Sokoh and Azekah. Saul and the Israelites assembled and camped in the Valley of Elah and drew up their battle line to meet the Philistines. The Philistines occupied one hill and the Israelites another, with the valley between them.

A champion named Goliath, who was from Gath, came out of the Philistine camp. His height was six cubits and a span. He had a bronze helmet on his head and wore a coat of scale armor of bronze weighing five thousand shekels; on his legs he wore bronze greaves, and a bronze javelin was slung on his back. His spear shaft was like a weaver's rod, and its iron point weighed six hundred shekels. His shield bearer went ahead of him.

Goliath stood and shouted to the ranks of Israel, "Why do you come out and line up for battle? Am I not a Philistine, and are you not the servants of Saul? Choose a man and have him come down to me. If he is able to fight and kill me, we will become your subjects; but if I overcome him and kill him, you will become our subjects and serve us." Then the Philistine said, "This day I defy the armies of Israel! Give me a man and let us fight each other." On hearing the Philistine's words, Saul and all the Israelites were dismayed and terrified.

For forty days the Philistine came forward every morning and evening and took his stand.

Now Jesse said to his son David, "Take this ephah of roasted grain and these ten loaves of bread for your brothers and hurry to their camp. Take along these ten cheeses to the commander of their unit. See how your brothers are and bring back some assurance from them. They are with Saul and all the men of Israel in the Valley of Elah, fighting against the Philistines."

Early in the morning David left the flock in the care of a shepherd, loaded up and set out, as Jesse had directed. He reached the camp as the army was going out to its battle positions, shouting the war cry. Israel and the Philistines were drawing up their lines facing each other. David left his things with the keeper of supplies, ran to the battle lines and asked his brothers how they were. As he was talking with them, Goliath, the Philistine champion from Gath, stepped out from his lines and shouted his usual defiance, and David heard it. Whenever the Israelites saw the man, they all fled from him in great fear.

Now the Israelites had been saying, "Do you see how this man keeps coming out? He comes out to defy Israel. The king will give great wealth to the man who kills him. He will also give him his daughter in marriage and will exempt his family from taxes in Israel."

David asked the men standing near him, "What will be done for the man who kills this Philistine and removes this disgrace from Israel? Who is this uncircumcised Philistine that he should defy the armies of the living God?"

They repeated to him what they had been saying and told him, "This is what will be done for the man who kills him."

When Eliab, David's oldest brother, heard him speaking with the men, he burned with anger at him and asked, "Why have you come down here? And with whom did you leave those few sheep in the wilderness? I know how conceited you are and how wicked your heart is; you came down only to watch the battle."

"Now what have I done?" said David. "Can't I even speak?" He then turned away to someone else and brought up the same matter, and the men answered him as before. What David said was overheard and reported to Saul, and Saul sent for him.

David said to Saul, "Let no one lose heart on account of this Philistine; your servant will go and fight him."

Saul replied, "You are not able to go out against this Philistine and fight him; you are only a young man, and he has been a warrior from his youth."

But David said to Saul, "Your servant has been keeping his father's sheep. When a lion or a bear came and carried off a sheep from the flock, I went after it, struck it and rescued the sheep from its mouth. When it turned on me, I seized it by its hair, struck it and killed it. Your servant has killed both the lion and the bear; this uncircumcised Philistine will be like one of them, because he has defied the armies of the living God. The LORD who rescued me from the paw of the lion and the paw of the bear will rescue me from the hand of this Philistine."

Saul said to David, "Go, and the LORD be with you."

Then Saul dressed David in his own tunic. He put a coat of armor on him and a bronze helmet on his head. David fastened on his sword over the tunic and tried walking around, because he was not used to them.

"I cannot go in these," he said to Saul, "because I am not used to them." So he took them off. Then he took his staff in his hand, chose five smooth stones from the stream, put them in the pouch of his shepherd's bag and, with his sling in his hand, approached the Philistine.

Meanwhile, the Philistine, with his shield bearer in front of him, kept coming closer to David. He looked David over and saw that he was little more than a boy, glowing with health and handsome, and he despised him. He said to David, "Am I a dog, that you come at me with sticks?" And the Philistine cursed David by his gods. "Come here," he said, "and I'll give your flesh to the birds and the wild animals!"

David said to the Philistine, "You come against me with sword and spear and javelin, but I come against you in the name of the LORD Almighty, the God of the armies of Israel, whom you have defied. This day the LORD will deliver you into my hands, and I'll strike you down and cut off your head. This very day I will give the carcasses of the Philistine army to the birds and the wild animals, and the whole world will know that there is a God in Israel. All those gathered here will know that it is not by sword or spear that the LORD saves; for the battle is the LORD's, and he will give all of you into our hands."

As the Philistine moved closer to attack him, David ran quickly toward the battle line to meet him. Reaching into his bag and taking out a stone, he slung it and struck the Philistine on the forehead. The stone sank into his forehead, and he fell facedown on the ground.

So David triumphed over the Philistine with a sling and a stone;

without a sword in his hand he struck down the Philistine and killed him.

David ran and stood over him. He took hold of the Philistine's sword and drew it from the sheath. After he killed him, he cut off his head with the sword.

When the Philistines saw that their hero was dead, they turned and ran. Then the men of Israel and Judah surged forward with a shout and pursued the Philistines to the entrance of Gath and to the gates of Ekron. Their dead were strewn along the Shaaraim road to Gath and Ekron. When the Israelites returned from chasing the Philistines, they plundered their camp.

David took the Philistine's head and brought it to Jerusalem; he put the Philistine's weapons in his own tent.

Saul was impressed with David's victory over Goliath. During their post-battle interview, Saul asked David about his family and then drafted David into service at the king's court. David and Saul's son Jonathan had an instant rapport. The two young men formed a friendship of love and loyalty as strong as any brothers'. But David's popularity did not play well in the final days of Saul's reign.

As soon as David returned from killing the Philistine, Abner took him and brought him before Saul, with David still holding the Philistine's head.

"Whose son are you, young man?" Saul asked him.

David said, "I am the son of your servant Jesse of Bethlehem."

After David had finished talking with Saul, Jonathan became one in spirit with David, and he loved him as himself. From that day Saul kept David with him and did not let him return home to his family. And Jonathan made a covenant with David because he loved him as himself. Jonathan took off the robe he was wearing and gave it to David, along with his tunic, and even his sword, his bow and his belt.

Whatever mission Saul sent him on, David was so successful

that Saul gave him a high rank in the army. This pleased all the troops, and Saul's officers as well.

When the men were returning home after David had killed the Philistine, the women came out from all the towns of Israel to meet King Saul with singing and dancing, with joyful songs and with timbrels and lyres. As they danced, they sang:

> "Saul has slain his thousands,
>   and David his tens of thousands."

Saul was very angry; this refrain displeased him greatly. "They have credited David with tens of thousands," he thought, "but me with only thousands. What more can he get but the kingdom?" And from that time on Saul kept a close eye on David.

The next day an evil spirit from God came forcefully on Saul. He was prophesying in his house, while David was playing the lyre, as he usually did. Saul had a spear in his hand and he hurled it, saying to himself, "I'll pin David to the wall." But David eluded him twice.

Saul was afraid of David, because the LORD was with David but had departed from Saul. So he sent David away from him and gave him command over a thousand men, and David led the troops in their campaigns. In everything he did he had great success, because the LORD was with him. When Saul saw how successful he was, he was afraid of him. But all Israel and Judah loved David, because he led them in their campaigns.

Saul was struggling to make sense of the mess he was in and becoming more paranoid and unstable as the days progressed. Many of Saul's subjects, as well as members of his own family, including Jonathan and Saul's daughter, Michal, seemed to prefer the young shepherd warrior over the unreasonable king. Consumed by anger and jealousy, on numerous occasions Saul tried to kill David, whom he perceived as his greatest internal threat.

Finally, David, in fear for his life, fled from Saul. But Saul was driven to hunt down David. He even ordered the slaughter of 85 priests who had given David shelter.

About 600 loyal men gathered around David, a militia too small to challenge Israel's army but large enough to provide an offensive force. Inside Saul's palace, Jonathan became a double agent. While Saul groomed Jonathan for kingship, Jonathan passed information to David. Jonathan recognized that David would be Israel's next leader. But this prospect seemed increasingly unlikely as Saul's army approached David's battalion in the Desert of En Gedi. In danger, David did what he always did: he poured out his fears to God and prayed for help.

Deliver me from my enemies, O God;
be my fortress against those who are attacking me.
Deliver me from evildoers
and save me from those who are after my blood.

See how they lie in wait for me!
Fierce men conspire against me
for no offense or sin of mine, LORD.
I have done no wrong, yet they are ready to attack me.
Arise to help me; look on my plight!
You, LORD God Almighty,
you who are the God of Israel,
rouse yourself to punish all the nations;
show no mercy to wicked traitors.

You are my strength, I watch for you;
you, God, are my fortress,
my God on whom I can rely.

But I will sing of your strength,
in the morning I will sing of your love;
for you are my fortress,
my refuge in times of trouble.

You are my strength, I sing praise to you;
you, God, are my fortress,
my God on whom I can rely.

No matter how close Saul got, David consistently outmaneu-

vered him. David was quite accustomed to commando-type raids, but none was so daring as his encounter with Saul in a darkened cave.

After Saul returned from pursuing the Philistines, he was told, "David is in the Desert of En Gedi." So Saul took three thousand able young men from all Israel and set out to look for David and his men near the Crags of the Wild Goats.

He came to the sheep pens along the way; a cave was there, and Saul went in to relieve himself. David and his men were far back in the cave. The men said, "This is the day the LORD spoke of when he said to you, 'I will give your enemy into your hands for you to deal with as you wish.'" Then David crept up unnoticed and cut off a corner of Saul's robe.

Afterward, David was conscience-stricken for having cut off a corner of his robe. He said to his men, "The LORD forbid that I should do such a thing to my master, the LORD's anointed, or lay my hand on him; for he is the anointed of the LORD." With these words David sharply rebuked his men and did not allow them to attack Saul. And Saul left the cave and went his way.

Then David went out of the cave and called out to Saul, "My lord the king!" When Saul looked behind him, David bowed down and prostrated himself with his face to the ground. He said to Saul, "Why do you listen when men say, 'David is bent on harming you'? This day you have seen with your own eyes how the LORD delivered you into my hands in the cave. Some urged me to kill you, but I spared you; I said, 'I will not lay my hand on my lord, because he is the LORD's anointed.' See, my father, look at this piece of your robe in my hand! I cut off the corner of your robe but did not kill you. See that there is nothing in my hand to indicate that I am guilty of wrongdoing or rebellion. I have not wronged you, but you are hunting me down to take my life. May the LORD judge between you and me. And may the LORD avenge the wrongs you have done to me, but my hand will not touch you. As the old saying goes, 'From evildoers come evil deeds,' so my hand will not touch you.

"Against whom has the king of Israel come out? Who are you

pursuing? A dead dog? A flea? May the LORD be our judge and decide between us. May he consider my cause and uphold it; may he vindicate me by delivering me from your hand."

When David finished saying this, Saul asked, "Is that your voice, David my son?" And he wept aloud. "You are more righteous than I," he said. "You have treated me well, but I have treated you badly. You have just now told me about the good you did to me; the LORD delivered me into your hands, but you did not kill me. When a man finds his enemy, does he let him get away unharmed? May the LORD reward you well for the way you treated me today. I know that you will surely be king and that the kingdom of Israel will be established in your hands. Now swear to me by the LORD that you will not kill off my descendants or wipe out my name from my father's family."

So David gave his oath to Saul. Then Saul returned home, but David and his men went up to the stronghold.

David sang to the LORD the words of this song when the LORD delivered him from the hand of all his enemies and from the hand of Saul. He said:

> "The LORD is my rock, my fortress and my deliverer;
>   my God is my rock, in whom I take refuge,
>   my shield and the horn of my salvation.
> He is my stronghold, my refuge and my savior —
>   from violent people you save me.
>
> "I called to the LORD, who is worthy of praise,
>   and have been saved from my enemies.
> The waves of death swirled about me;
>   the torrents of destruction overwhelmed me.
> The cords of the grave coiled around me;
>   the snares of death confronted me.
>
> "In my distress I called to the LORD;
>   I called out to my God.
> From his temple he heard my voice;
>   my cry came to his ears.

"The LORD lives! Praise be to my Rock!
Exalted be my God, the Rock, my Savior!"

*The peace treaty between David and Saul (basically an agree-
ment to not kill each other) should have settled the matter. But
Saul, always unpredictable, turned on David and pursued him
once again. Wisely, David retreated with his band of loyalists to
Philistine territory, out of Saul's reach. How ironic that David,
Israel's king-to-be, pitched his tent with the very people who
waged war against his own nation and eventually took the life
of his closest friend.*

Now the Philistines fought against Israel; the Israelites fled
before them, and many fell dead on Mount Gilboa. The Philistines were in hot pursuit of Saul and his sons, and they killed his
sons Jonathan, Abinadab and Malki-Shua. The fighting grew fierce
around Saul, and when the archers overtook him, they wounded
him critically.

Saul said to his armor-bearer, "Draw your sword and run me
through, or these uncircumcised fellows will come and run me
through and abuse me."

But his armor-bearer was terrified and would not do it; so Saul
took his own sword and fell on it. When the armor-bearer saw
that Saul was dead, he too fell on his sword and died with him. So
Saul and his three sons and his armor-bearer and all his men died
together that same day.

When the Israelites along the valley and those across the Jordan saw that the Israelite army had fled and that Saul and his sons
had died, they abandoned their towns and fled. And the Philistines
came and occupied them.

The next day, when the Philistines came to strip the dead, they
found Saul and his three sons fallen on Mount Gilboa. They cut
off his head and stripped off his armor, and they sent messengers
throughout the land of the Philistines to proclaim the news in the
temple of their idols and among their people. They put his armor

in the temple of the Ashtoreths and fastened his body to the wall of Beth Shan.

When the people of Jabesh Gilead heard what the Philistines had done to Saul, all their valiant men marched through the night to Beth Shan. They took down the bodies of Saul and his sons from the wall of Beth Shan and went to Jabesh, where they burned them.

David grieved deeply over not only Jonathan's death but also Saul's. But over the course of time, God directed David to assert his calling as king. His own tribe of Judah came to Hebron to anoint him king over the house of Judah. But it wasn't until after a seven-year struggle between David and those loyal to Saul's son Ish-Bosheth that David was made king over all of Israel.

Soon afterward, David twice led the Israelites in decisive victories over the troublesome Philistines. This period also saw one of David's most important accomplishments: he defeated the Jebusites who lived in Jerusalem — making it Israel's national and spiritual capital.

David was concerned about more than just military success. He loved God deeply and wanted his nation to love God too. David's passion for God led him to retrieve the ark of the covenant stored at the house of Abinadab. It was a joyous parade of people that set out to bring the ark to its new home in Jerusalem, the City of David.

David again brought together all the able young men of Israel — thirty thousand. He and all his men went to Baalah in Judah to bring up from there the ark of God, which is called by the Name, the name of the LORD Almighty, who is enthroned between the cherubim on the ark. They set the ark of God on a new cart and brought it from the house of Abinadab, which was on the hill. Uzzah and Ahio, sons of Abinadab, were guiding the new cart with the ark of God on it, and Ahio was walking in front of it. David and all Israel were celebrating with all their might before the LORD, with castanets, harps, lyres, timbrels, sistrums and cymbals.

When they came to the threshing floor of Nakon, Uzzah reached out and took hold of the ark of God, because the oxen stumbled. The LORD's anger burned against Uzzah because of his irreverent act; therefore God struck him down, and he died there beside the ark of God.

Then David was angry because the LORD's wrath had broken out against Uzzah, and to this day that place is called Perez Uzzah.

David was afraid of the LORD that day and said, "How can the ark of the LORD ever come to me?" He was not willing to take the ark of the LORD to be with him in the City of David. Instead, he took it to the house of Obed-Edom the Gittite. The ark of the LORD remained in the house of Obed-Edom the Gittite for three months, and the LORD blessed him and his entire household.

Now King David was told, "The LORD has blessed the household of Obed-Edom and everything he has, because of the ark of God." So David went to bring up the ark of God from the house of Obed-Edom to the City of David with rejoicing. When those who were carrying the ark of the LORD had taken six steps, he sacrificed a bull and a fattened calf. Wearing a linen ephod, David was dancing before the LORD with all his might, while he and all Israel were bringing up the ark of the LORD with shouts and the sound of trumpets.

David's infectious delight led him to put on quite a public display of exuberance and worship when the ark was brought into Jerusalem. Most onlookers shared David's enthusiasm. But David's wife Michal was none too happy with her uninhibited husband.

As the ark of the LORD was entering the City of David, Michal daughter of Saul watched from a window. And when she saw King David leaping and dancing before the LORD, she despised him in her heart.

They brought the ark of the LORD and set it in its place inside the tent that David had pitched for it, and David sacrificed burnt offerings and fellowship offerings before the LORD. After he had finished sacrificing the burnt offerings and fellowship offerings, he blessed the people in the name of the LORD Almighty. Then he gave a loaf of bread, a cake of dates and a cake of raisins to each person in the whole crowd of Israelites, both men and women. And all the people went to their homes.

When David returned home to bless his household, Michal daughter of Saul came out to meet him and said, "How the king of Israel has distinguished himself today, going around half-naked in full view of the slave girls of his servants as any vulgar fellow would!"

David said to Michal, "It was before the LORD, who chose me rather than your father or anyone from his house when he appointed me ruler over the LORD's people Israel — I will celebrate before the LORD. I will become even more undignified than this, and I will be humiliated in my own eyes. But by these slave girls you spoke of, I will be held in honor."

And Michal daughter of Saul had no children to the day of her death.

Aware that the treasured ark deserved a majestic home, David began to conceive of a permanent temple so awesome that people all over the world would say, "The God of the Israelites is great indeed!" David consulted with Nathan, a trusted prophet of God, about his plans. And the prophet's reply, reflecting God's mind on the matter, must have stunned David.

After David was settled in his palace, he said to Nathan the prophet, "Here I am, living in a house of cedar, while the ark of the covenant of the LORD is under a tent."

Nathan replied to David, "Whatever you have in mind, do it, for God is with you."

But that night the word of God came to Nathan, saying:

"Go and tell my servant David, 'This is what the LORD says: You are not the one to build me a house to dwell in. I have not dwelt in a house from the day I brought Israel up out of Egypt to this day. I have moved from one tent site to another, from one dwelling place to another. Wherever I have moved with all the Israelites, did I ever say to any of their leaders whom I commanded to shepherd my people, "Why have you not built me a house of cedar?"'

"Now then, tell my servant David, 'This is what the LORD Almighty says: I took you from the pasture, from tending the flock, and appointed you ruler over my people Israel. I have been with you wherever you have gone, and I have cut off all your enemies from before you. Now I will make your name like the names of the greatest men on earth. And I will provide a place for my people Israel and will plant them so that they can have a home of their own and no longer be disturbed. Wicked people will not oppress them anymore, as they did at the beginning and have done ever since the time I appointed leaders over my people Israel. I will also subdue all your enemies.

"'I declare to you that the LORD will build a house for you: When your days are over and you go to be with your ancestors, I will raise up your offspring to succeed you, one of your own sons, and I will establish his kingdom. He is the one who will build a house for me, and I will establish his throne forever. I will be his father, and he will be my son. I will never take my love away from him, as I took it away from your predecessor. I will set him over my house and my kingdom forever; his throne will be established forever.'"

Nathan reported to David all the words of this entire revelation. Then King David went in and sat before the LORD, and he said:

"Who am I, LORD God, and what is my family, that you have brought me this far? And as if this were not enough in your sight, my God, you have spoken about the future of the house of your servant. You, LORD God, have looked on me as though I were the most exalted of men.

"What more can David say to you for honoring your servant? For you know your servant, LORD. For the sake of your servant and according to your will, you have done this great thing and made known all these great promises.

"There is no one like you, LORD, and there is no God but you, as we have heard with our own ears. And who is like your people Israel—the one nation on earth whose God went out to redeem a people for himself, and to make a name for yourself, and to perform great and awesome wonders by driving out nations from before your people, whom you redeemed from Egypt? You made your people Israel your very own forever, and you, LORD, have become their God.

"And now, LORD, let the promise you have made concerning your servant and his house be established forever. Do as you promised, so that it will be established and that your name will be great forever. Then people will say, 'The LORD Almighty, the God over Israel, is Israel's God!' And the house of your servant David will be established before you.

"You, my God, have revealed to your servant that you will build a house for him. So your servant has found courage to pray to you. You, LORD, are God! You have promised these good things to your servant. Now you have been pleased to bless the house of your servant, that it may continue forever in your sight; for you, LORD, have blessed it, and it will be blessed forever."

A king without an army is not a king for long. David organized an effective army with trusted leadership and used it strategically to stabilize his borders and eliminate regional opposition. Mercenaries could not defeat him, and two-front battles still ended in decisive victories for him. David was a warrior, a poet and a man after God's heart. He was a leader who put God first, who loved and followed God. Everywhere the record showed that God blessed this shepherd-king.

But David was not a perfect man. One day, with his generals gone to war, the king was confronted by an internal foe as intense as any enemy he faced on the battlefield.

12

The Trials of a King

IN THE SPRING, at the time when kings go off to war, David sent Joab out with the king's men and the whole Israelite army. They destroyed the Ammonites and besieged Rabbah. But David remained in Jerusalem.

One evening David got up from his bed and walked around on the roof of the palace. From the roof he saw a woman bathing. The woman was very beautiful, and David sent someone to find out about her. The man said, "She is Bathsheba, the daughter of Eliam and the wife of Uriah the Hittite." Then David sent messengers to get her. She came to him, and he slept with her. (Now she was purifying herself from her monthly uncleanness.) Then she went back home. The woman conceived and sent word to David, saying, "I am pregnant."

So David sent this word to Joab: "Send me Uriah the Hittite." And Joab sent him to David. When Uriah came to him, David asked him how Joab was, how the soldiers were and how the war was going. Then David said to Uriah, "Go down to your house and wash your feet." So Uriah left the palace, and a gift from the king was sent after him. But Uriah slept at the entrance to the palace with all his master's servants and did not go down to his house.

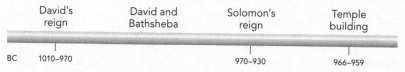

David's reign	David and Bathsheba	Solomon's reign	Temple building

BC   1010–970   970–930   966–959

Full timeline information starts on page xi.

David was told, "Uriah did not go home." So he asked Uriah, "Haven't you just come from a military campaign? Why didn't you go home?"

Uriah said to David, "The ark and Israel and Judah are staying in tents, and my commander Joab and my lord's men are camped in the open country. How could I go to my house to eat and drink and make love to my wife? As surely as you live, I will not do such a thing!"

Then David said to him, "Stay here one more day, and tomorrow I will send you back." So Uriah remained in Jerusalem that day and the next. At David's invitation, he ate and drank with him, and David made him drunk. But in the evening Uriah went out to sleep on his mat among his master's servants; he did not go home.

In the morning David wrote a letter to Joab and sent it with Uriah. In it he wrote, "Put Uriah out in front where the fighting is fiercest. Then withdraw from him so he will be struck down and die."

So while Joab had the city under siege, he put Uriah at a place where he knew the strongest defenders were. When the men of the city came out and fought against Joab, some of the men in David's army fell; moreover, Uriah the Hittite died.

When Uriah's wife heard that her husband was dead, she mourned for him. After the time of mourning was over, David had her brought to his house, and she became his wife and bore him a son. But the thing David had done displeased the LORD.

The LORD sent Nathan to David. When he came to him, he said, "There were two men in a certain town, one rich and the other poor. The rich man had a very large number of sheep and cattle, but the poor man had nothing except one little ewe lamb he had bought. He raised it, and it grew up with him and his children. It shared his food, drank from his cup and even slept in his arms. It was like a daughter to him.

"Now a traveler came to the rich man, but the rich man

refrained from taking one of his own sheep or cattle to prepare a meal for the traveler who had come to him. Instead, he took the ewe lamb that belonged to the poor man and prepared it for the one who had come to him."

David burned with anger against the man and said to Nathan, "As surely as the LORD lives, the man who did this must die! He must pay for that lamb four times over, because he did such a thing and had no pity."

Then Nathan said to David, "You are the man! This is what the LORD, the God of Israel, says: 'I anointed you king over Israel, and I delivered you from the hand of Saul. I gave your master's house to you, and your master's wives into your arms. I gave you all Israel and Judah. And if all this had been too little, I would have given you even more. Why did you despise the word of the LORD by doing what is evil in his eyes? You struck down Uriah the Hittite with the sword and took his wife to be your own. You killed him with the sword of the Ammonites. Now, therefore, the sword will never depart from your house, because you despised me and took the wife of Uriah the Hittite to be your own.'

"This is what the LORD says: 'Out of your own household I am going to bring calamity on you. Before your very eyes I will take your wives and give them to one who is close to you, and he will sleep with your wives in broad daylight. You did it in secret, but I will do this thing in broad daylight before all Israel.'"

Then David said to Nathan, "I have sinned against the LORD."

Unlike Saul, David didn't make excuses for his sin. Humbled and broken in heart, David acknowledged his sin and poured out his feelings in this prayer.

> Have mercy on me, O God,
>   according to your unfailing love;
> according to your great compassion
>   blot out my transgressions.[1]

---

[1]**Transgression(s):** Offense against God; synonymous with *sin*.

Wash away all my iniquity
    and cleanse me from my sin.

For I know my transgressions,
    and my sin is always before me.
Against you, you only, have I sinned
    and done what is evil in your sight;
so you are right in your verdict
    and justified when you judge.
Surely I was sinful at birth,
    sinful from the time my mother conceived me.
Yet you desired faithfulness even in the womb;
    you taught me wisdom in that secret place.

Cleanse me with hyssop, and I will be clean;
    wash me, and I will be whiter than snow.
Let me hear joy and gladness;
    let the bones you have crushed rejoice.
Hide your face from my sins
    and blot out all my iniquity.

Create in me a pure heart, O God,
    and renew a steadfast spirit within me.
Do not cast me from your presence
    or take your Holy Spirit[2] from me.
Restore to me the joy of your salvation
    and grant me a willing spirit, to sustain me.

The king was humbled by the same sexual weakness known to many men. But unlike many men, David understood that his sin had broken a relationship with God. He had disappointed God by his greed, lust and murder. David's sin was a breach in a divine friendship that needed repairing. His repentance was real, but there were still consequences for his actions.

---

[2]**Holy Spirit:** The manifestation of God who dwells within those who believe in Jesus Christ and empowers them to follow God's way. God is one God but acts in three "persons" of God the Father, Jesus the Son and the Holy Spirit.

Nathan replied, "The LORD has taken away your sin. You are not going to die. But because by doing this you have shown utter contempt for the LORD, the son born to you will die."

After Nathan had gone home, the LORD struck the child that Uriah's wife had borne to David, and he became ill. David pleaded with God for the child. He fasted and spent the nights lying in sackcloth on the ground. The elders of his household stood beside him to get him up from the ground, but he refused, and he would not eat any food with them.

On the seventh day the child died. David's attendants were afraid to tell him that the child was dead, for they thought, "While the child was still living, he wouldn't listen to us when we spoke to him. How can we now tell him the child is dead? He may do something desperate."

David noticed that his attendants were whispering among themselves, and he realized the child was dead. "Is the child dead?" he asked.

"Yes," they replied, "he is dead."

Then David got up from the ground. After he had washed, put on lotions and changed his clothes, he went into the house of the LORD and worshiped.

Forgiveness cleanses the wounds of sin. David, filled with remorse, asked God to forgive him, and God said yes. God values the person who respects his holiness and treasures his friendship. David expressed his gratitude for God's gift of forgiveness in one of his psalms.

Blessed is the one
    whose transgressions are forgiven,
    whose sins are covered.
Blessed is the one
    whose sin the LORD does not count against them
    and in whose spirit is no deceit.

When I kept silent,
    my bones wasted away

through my groaning all day long.
For day and night
    your hand was heavy on me;
my strength was sapped
    as in the heat of summer.

Then I acknowledged my sin to you
    and did not cover up my iniquity.
I said, "I will confess
    my transgressions to the LORD."
And you forgave
    the guilt of my sin.

Therefore let all the faithful pray to you
    while you may be found;
surely the rising of the mighty waters
    will not reach them.
You are my hiding place;
    you will protect me from trouble
    and surround me with songs of deliverance.

Many are the woes of the wicked,
    but the LORD's unfailing love
    surrounds the one who trusts in him.

Rejoice in the LORD and be glad, you righteous;
    sing, all you who are upright in heart!

Then David comforted his wife Bathsheba, and he went to her and made love to her. She gave birth to a son, and they named him Solomon. The LORD loved him; and because the LORD loved him, he sent word through Nathan the prophet to name him Jedidiah.[3]

His sin forgiven, David again praised God with a full heart and continued to lead the army with great success. This brilliant strategist knew how to motivate men. Among his own sons, however, a struggle was brewing that David did not see coming.

---

[3]**Jedidiah:** *Jedidiah* means "loved by the LORD."

With respect to his son Absalom especially, David's normally deep insight into human behavior failed him. David failed to act as Absalom subtly undermined his father's administration and courted the populace. Finally, Absalom challenged David's political position. This beautiful man, with an untamed spark that David must have recognized, became a traitor.

David now faced uncharted territory—a rebellion from within his own family, an enemy who was also a beloved son. How do you march against a foe you love? How do you throw a spear into the heart of another, when the thrust crushes your own heart as well?

David mustered the men who were with him and appointed over them commanders of thousands and commanders of hundreds. David sent out his troops, a third under the command of Joab, a third under Joab's brother Abishai son of Zeruiah, and a third under Ittai the Gittite. The king told the troops, "I myself will surely march out with you."

But the men said, "You must not go out; if we are forced to flee, they won't care about us. Even if half of us die, they won't care; but you are worth ten thousand of us. It would be better now for you to give us support from the city."

The king answered, "I will do whatever seems best to you."

So the king stood beside the gate while all his men marched out in units of hundreds and of thousands. The king commanded Joab, Abishai and Ittai, "Be gentle with the young man Absalom for my sake." And all the troops heard the king giving orders concerning Absalom to each of the commanders.

David's army marched out of the city to fight Israel, and the battle took place in the forest of Ephraim. There Israel's troops were routed by David's men, and the casualties that day were great — twenty thousand men. The battle spread out over the whole countryside, and the forest swallowed up more men that day than the sword.

Now Absalom happened to meet David's men. He was riding

his mule, and as the mule went under the thick branches of a large oak, Absalom's hair got caught in the tree. He was left hanging in midair, while the mule he was riding kept on going.

When one of the men saw what had happened, he told Joab, "I just saw Absalom hanging in an oak tree."

Joab said to the man who had told him this, "What! You saw him? Why didn't you strike him to the ground right there? Then I would have had to give you ten shekels of silver and a warrior's belt."

But the man replied, "Even if a thousand shekels were weighed out into my hands, I would not lay a hand on the king's son. In our hearing the king commanded you and Abishai and Ittai, 'Protect the young man Absalom for my sake.' And if I had put my life in jeopardy — and nothing is hidden from the king — you would have kept your distance from me."

Joab said, "I'm not going to wait like this for you." So he took three javelins in his hand and plunged them into Absalom's heart while Absalom was still alive in the oak tree. And ten of Joab's armor-bearers surrounded Absalom, struck him and killed him.

Then Joab sounded the trumpet, and the troops stopped pursuing Israel, for Joab halted them. They took Absalom, threw him into a big pit in the forest and piled up a large heap of rocks over him. Meanwhile, all the Israelites fled to their homes.

During his lifetime Absalom had taken a pillar and erected it in the King's Valley as a monument to himself, for he thought, "I have no son to carry on the memory of my name." He named the pillar after himself, and it is called Absalom's Monument to this day.

Then Joab said to a Cushite, "Go, tell the king what you have seen." The Cushite bowed down before Joab and ran off.

Then the Cushite arrived and said, "My lord the king, hear the good news! The LORD has vindicated you today by delivering you from the hand of all who rose up against you."

The king asked the Cushite, "Is the young man Absalom safe?"

The Cushite replied, "May the enemies of my lord the king and all who rise up to harm you be like that young man."

The king was shaken. He went up to the room over the gateway and wept. As he went, he said: "O my son Absalom! My son, my son Absalom! If only I had died instead of you — O Absalom, my son, my son!"

The king covered his face and cried aloud, "O my son Absalom! O Absalom, my son, my son!"

Absalom's rebellion was suppressed and the political damage repaired. Now David turned his attention to more pleasant concerns. The word of the Lord had come to David that the temple project would fall to his successor, Solomon. David planned big and gathered lavish materials, but Solomon would later manage the construction itself. David's work was nearly done. A time of transition was coming. Would the future be as God-blessed as the past?

Then David said, "The house of the LORD God is to be here, and also the altar of burnt offering for Israel."

So David gave orders to assemble the foreigners residing in Israel, and from among them he appointed stonecutters to prepare dressed stone for building the house of God. He provided a large amount of iron to make nails for the doors of the gateways and for the fittings, and more bronze than could be weighed. He also provided more cedar logs than could be counted, for the Sidonians and Tyrians had brought large numbers of them to David.

David said, "My son Solomon is young and inexperienced, and the house to be built for the LORD should be of great magnificence and fame and splendor in the sight of all the nations. Therefore I will make preparations for it." So David made extensive preparations before his death.

Then he called for his son Solomon and charged him to build a house for the LORD, the God of Israel. David said to Solomon:

"My son, I had it in my heart to build a house for the Name of the Lord my God. But this word of the Lord came to me: 'You have shed much blood and have fought many wars. You are not to build a house for my Name, because you have shed much blood on the earth in my sight. But you will have a son who will be a man of peace and rest, and I will give him rest from all his enemies on every side. His name will be Solomon,[4] and I will grant Israel peace and quiet during his reign. He is the one who will build a house for my Name. He will be my son, and I will be his father. And I will establish the throne of his kingdom over Israel forever.'

"Now, my son, the Lord be with you, and may you have success and build the house of the Lord your God, as he said you would. May the Lord give you discretion and understanding when he puts you in command over Israel, so that you may keep the law of the Lord your God. Then you will have success if you are care-ful to observe the decrees and laws that the Lord gave Moses for Israel. Be strong and courageous. Do not be afraid or discouraged.

"I have taken great pains to provide for the temple of the Lord a hundred thousand talents of gold, a million talents of silver, quantities of bronze and iron too great to be weighed, and wood and stone. And you may add to them. You have many workers: stonecutters, masons and carpenters, as well as those skilled in every kind of work in gold and silver, bronze and iron — craftsmen beyond number. Now begin the work, and the Lord be with you."

Then David ordered all the leaders of Israel to help his son Solomon. He said to them, "Is not the Lord your God with you? And has he not granted you rest on every side? For he has given the inhabitants of the land into my hands, and the land is subject to the Lord and to his people. Now devote your heart and soul to seeking the Lord your God. Begin to build the sanctuary of the Lord God, so that you may bring the ark of the covenant of the Lord and the sacred articles belonging to God into the temple that will be built for the Name of the Lord."

---

[4]**Solomon:** *Solomon* sounds like and may be derived from the Hebrew for "peace."

Then King David said to the whole assembly: "My son Solomon, the one whom God has chosen, is young and inexperienced. The task is great, because this palatial structure is not for man but for the LORD God. With all my resources I have provided for the temple of my God — gold for the gold work, silver for the silver, bronze for the bronze, iron for the iron and wood for the wood, as well as onyx for the settings, turquoise, stones of various colors, and all kinds of fine stone and marble — all of these in large quantities. Besides, in my devotion to the temple of my God I now give my personal treasures of gold and silver for the temple of my God, over and above everything I have provided for this holy temple: three thousand talents of gold (gold of Ophir) and seven thousand talents of refined silver, for the overlaying of the walls of the buildings, for the gold work and the silver work, and for all the work to be done by the craftsmen. Now, who is willing to consecrate themselves to the LORD today?"

Then the leaders of families, the officers of the tribes of Israel, the commanders of thousands and commanders of hundreds, and the officials in charge of the king's work gave willingly. They gave toward the work on the temple of God five thousand talents and ten thousand darics of gold, ten thousand talents of silver, eighteen thousand talents of bronze and a hundred thousand talents of iron. Anyone who had precious stones gave them to the treasury of the temple of the LORD in the custody of Jehiel the Gershonite. The people rejoiced at the willing response of their leaders, for they had given freely and wholeheartedly to the LORD. David the king also rejoiced greatly.

David praised the LORD in the presence of the whole assembly, saying,

> "Praise be to you, LORD,
>   the God of our father Israel,
>   from everlasting to everlasting.
> Yours, LORD, is the greatness and the power
>   and the glory and the majesty and the splendor,

for everything in heaven and earth is yours.
Yours, LORD, is the kingdom;
    you are exalted as head over all.
Wealth and honor come from you;
    you are the ruler of all things.
In your hands are strength and power
    to exalt and give strength to all.
Now, our God, we give you thanks,
    and praise your glorious name.

"But who am I, and who are my people, that we should be able to give as generously as this? Everything comes from you, and we have given you only what comes from your hand. We are foreigners and strangers in your sight, as were all our ancestors. Our days on earth are like a shadow, without hope. LORD our God, all this abundance that we have provided for building you a temple for your Holy Name comes from your hand, and all of it belongs to you. I know, my God, that you test the heart and are pleased with integrity. All these things I have given willingly and with honest intent. And now I have seen with joy how willingly your people who are here have given to you. LORD, the God of our fathers Abraham, Isaac and Israel, keep these desires and thoughts in the hearts of your people forever, and keep their hearts loyal to you. And give my son Solomon the wholehearted devotion to keep your commands, statutes and decrees and to do everything to build the palatial structure for which I have provided."

Then David said to the whole assembly, "Praise the LORD your God." So they all praised the LORD, the God of their fathers; they bowed down, prostrating themselves before the LORD and the king.

What formed the center of this leader's intriguing personality? Was it power and avarice, the normal style of kings? No. It was love of God. David was a man full of drive and passion, his wealth was secure, and his family was as large as a small village. But what ruled his life and consumed his heart was a deep love for God. Take the rest away, and God remained. God was the generous Giver and loving Father who led David from child-hood to old age. David's poetry paints a beautiful picture of his relationship with his God—a protector, Father and Lord.

> The LORD is my shepherd, I lack nothing.
>   He makes me lie down in green pastures,
> he leads me beside quiet waters,
>   he refreshes my soul.
> He guides me along the right paths
>   for his name's sake.
> Even though I walk
>   through the darkest valley,
> I will fear no evil,
>   for you are with me;
> your rod and your staff,
>   they comfort me.
>
> You prepare a table before me
>   in the presence of my enemies.
> You anoint my head with oil;
>   my cup overflows.
> Surely your goodness and love will follow me
>   all the days of my life,
> and I will dwell in the house of the LORD
>   forever.

David knew his days as a warrior were over and his energy to lead a nation was waning. Still he resisted transferring power to his son Solomon. One day his lovely wife Bathsheba whis-pered in his ear: "Now, David, now is the time." And the king complied.

13

The King Who Had It All

WHEN KING DAVID WAS VERY OLD, he could not keep warm even when they put covers over him.

Bathsheba went to see the aged king in his room, where Abishag the Shunammite was attending him. Bathsheba bowed down, prostrating herself before the king.

"What is it you want?" the king asked.

She said to him, "My lord, you yourself swore to me your servant by the LORD your God: 'Solomon your son shall be king after me, and he will sit on my throne.'"

The king then took an oath: "As surely as the LORD lives, who has delivered me out of every trouble, I will surely carry out this very day what I swore to you by the LORD, the God of Israel: Solomon your son shall be king after me, and he will sit on my throne in my place."

Then Bathsheba bowed down with her face to the ground, prostrating herself before the king, and said, "May my lord King David live forever!"

David dies	Solomon's reign	Solomon displays great wisdom	Temple building
BC 970	970–930		966–959

Full timeline information starts on page xi.

When the time drew near for David to die, he gave a charge to Solomon his son.

"I am about to go the way of all the earth," he said. "So be strong, act like a man, and observe what the LORD your God requires: Walk in obedience to him, and keep his decrees and commands, his laws and regulations, as written in the Law of Moses. Do this so that you may prosper in all you do and wherever you go and that the LORD may keep his promise to me: 'If your descendants watch how they live, and if they walk faithfully before me with all their heart and soul, you will never fail to have a successor on the throne of Israel.'"

Then David rested with his ancestors and was buried in the City of David. He had reigned forty years over Israel — seven years in Hebron and thirty-three in Jerusalem. So Solomon sat on the throne of his father David, and his rule was firmly established.

Solomon made an alliance with Pharaoh king of Egypt and married his daughter. He brought her to the City of David until he finished building his palace and the temple of the LORD, and the wall around Jerusalem. The people, however, were still sacrificing at the high places, because a temple had not yet been built for the Name of the LORD. Solomon showed his love for the LORD by walking according to the instructions given him by his father David, except that he offered sacrifices and burned incense on the high places.

The king went to Gibeon to offer sacrifices, for that was the most important high place, and Solomon offered a thousand burnt offerings on that altar. At Gibeon the LORD appeared to Solomon during the night in a dream, and God said, "Ask for whatever you want me to give you."

Solomon answered, "You have shown great kindness to your servant, my father David, because he was faithful to you and righteous and upright in heart. You have continued this great kindness to him and have given him a son to sit on his throne this very day.

"Now, LORD my God, you have made your servant king in place of my father David. But I am only a little child and do not know how to carry out my duties. Your servant is here among the people you have chosen, a great people, too numerous to count or number. So give your servant a discerning heart to govern your people and to distinguish between right and wrong. For who is able to govern this great people of yours?"

The Lord was pleased that Solomon had asked for this. So God said to him, "Since you have asked for this and not for long life or wealth for yourself, nor have asked for the death of your enemies but for discernment in administering justice, I will do what you have asked. I will give you a wise and discerning heart, so that there will never have been anyone like you, nor will there ever be. Moreover, I will give you what you have not asked for — both wealth and honor — so that in your lifetime you will have no equal among kings. And if you walk in obedience to me and keep my decrees and commands as David your father did, I will give you a long life." Then Solomon awoke — and he realized it had been a dream.

He returned to Jerusalem, stood before the ark of the Lord's covenant and sacrificed burnt offerings and fellowship offerings. Then he gave a feast for all his court.

Now two prostitutes came to the king and stood before him. One of them said, "Pardon me, my lord. This woman and I live in the same house, and I had a baby while she was there with me. The third day after my child was born, this woman also had a baby. We were alone; there was no one in the house but the two of us.

"During the night this woman's son died because she lay on him. So she got up in the middle of the night and took my son from my side while I your servant was asleep. She put him by her breast and put her dead son by my breast. The next morning, I got up to nurse my son — and he was dead! But when I looked at him closely in the morning light, I saw that it wasn't the son I had borne."

The other woman said, "No! The living one is my son; the dead one is yours."

But the first one insisted, "No! The dead one is yours; the living one is mine." And so they argued before the king.

The king said, "This one says, 'My son is alive and your son is dead,' while that one says, 'No! Your son is dead and mine is alive.'"

Then the king said, "Bring me a sword." So they brought a sword for the king. He then gave an order: "Cut the living child in two and give half to one and half to the other."

The woman whose son was alive was deeply moved out of love for her son and said to the king, "Please, my lord, give her the living baby! Don't kill him!"

But the other said, "Neither I nor you shall have him. Cut him in two!"

Then the king gave his ruling: "Give the living baby to the first woman. Do not kill him; she is his mother."

When all Israel heard the verdict the king had given, they held the king in awe, because they saw that he had wisdom from God to administer justice.

The people of Judah and Israel were as numerous as the sand on the seashore; they ate, they drank and they were happy. And Solomon ruled over all the kingdoms from the Euphrates River to the land of the Philistines, as far as the border of Egypt. These countries brought tribute and were Solomon's subjects all his life.

God gave Solomon wisdom and very great insight, and a breadth of understanding as measureless as the sand on the seashore. Solomon's wisdom was greater than the wisdom of all the people of the East, and greater than all the wisdom of Egypt. He was wiser than anyone else, including Ethan the Ezrahite — wiser than Heman, Kalkol and Darda, the sons of Mahol. And his fame spread to all the surrounding nations. He spoke three thousand proverbs and his songs numbered a thousand and five. He spoke about plant life,

from the cedar of Lebanon to the hyssop that grows out of walls.
He also spoke about animals and birds, reptiles and fish. From all
nations people came to listen to Solomon's wisdom, sent by all the
kings of the world, who had heard of his wisdom.

*Solomon's name is synonymous with wisdom, in part due to
the collection of his sayings contained in the famous book of
Proverbs. Touching on many life issues, these catchy couplets
offer practical insight into what it means to fear God, to have
God-honoring relationships and how to wisely handle finances,
work and life.*

The proverbs of Solomon son of David, king of Israel:

> for gaining wisdom and instruction;
>   for understanding words of insight;
> for receiving instruction in prudent behavior,
>   doing what is right and just and fair;
> for giving prudence to those who are simple.

> The fear of the LORD is the beginning of knowledge,
>   but fools despise wisdom and instruction.

> My son, if you accept my words
>   and store up my commands within you,
> turning your ear to wisdom
>   and applying your heart to understanding —
> indeed, if you call out for insight
>   and cry aloud for understanding,
> and if you look for it as for silver
>   and search for it as for hidden treasure,
> then you will understand the fear of the LORD
>   and find the knowledge of God.
> For the LORD gives wisdom;
>   from his mouth come knowledge and understanding.

> Wisdom will save you from the ways of wicked men,
>   from men whose words are perverse.

My son, do not forget my teaching,
    but keep my commands in your heart,
for they will prolong your life many years
    and bring you peace and prosperity.

Let love and faithfulness never leave you;
    bind them around your neck,
    write them on the tablet of your heart.
Then you will win favor and a good name
    in the sight of God and man.

Trust in the LORD with all your heart
    and lean not on your own understanding;
in all your ways submit to him,
    and he will make your paths straight.

Do not be wise in your own eyes;
    fear the LORD and shun evil.
This will bring health to your body
    and nourishment to your bones.

Honor the LORD with your wealth,
    with the firstfruits of all your crops;
then your barns will be filled to overflowing,
    and your vats will brim over with new wine.

My son, do not despise the LORD's discipline,
    and do not resent his rebuke,
because the LORD disciplines those he loves,
    as a father the son he delights in.

Can a man walk on hot coals
    without his feet being scorched?
So is he who sleeps with another man's wife;
    no one who touches her will go unpunished.

A king's wrath strikes terror like the roar of a lion;
    those who anger him forfeit their lives.

It is to one's honor to avoid strife,
  but every fool is quick to quarrel.

Sluggards do not plow in season;
  so at harvest time they look but find nothing.

The righteous lead blameless lives;
  blessed are their children after them.

Differing weights and differing measures —
  the LORD detests them both.

Do not love sleep or you will grow poor;
  stay awake and you will have food to spare.

Gold there is, and rubies in abundance,
  but lips that speak knowledge are a rare jewel.

Food gained by fraud tastes sweet,
  but one ends up with a mouth full of gravel.

A gossip betrays a confidence;
  so avoid anyone who talks too much.

If someone curses their father or mother,
  their lamp will be snuffed out in pitch darkness.

An inheritance claimed too soon
  will not be blessed at the end.

Do not say, "I'll pay you back for this wrong!"
  Wait for the LORD, and he will avenge you.

A person's steps are directed by the LORD.
  How then can anyone understand their own way?

The human spirit is the lamp of the LORD
  that sheds light on one's inmost being.

The glory of young men is their strength,
  gray hair the splendor of the old.

In the LORD's hand the king's heart is a stream of water
　　that he channels toward all who please him.

A person may think their own ways are right,
　　but the LORD weighs the heart.

To do what is right and just
　　is more acceptable to the LORD than sacrifice.

Haughty eyes and a proud heart —
　　the unplowed field of the wicked — produce sin.

The plans of the diligent lead to profit
　　as surely as haste leads to poverty.

A fortune made by a lying tongue
　　is a fleeting vapor and a deadly snare.

The violence of the wicked will drag them away,
　　for they refuse to do what is right.

The wicked crave evil;
　　their neighbors get no mercy from them.

Whoever shuts their ears to the cry of the poor
　　will also cry out and not be answered.

A gift given in secret soothes anger,
　　and a bribe concealed in the cloak pacifies great wrath.

When justice is done, it brings joy to the righteous
　　but terror to evildoers.

Whoever loves pleasure will become poor;
　　whoever loves wine and olive oil will never be rich.

Better to live in a desert
　　than with a quarrelsome and nagging wife.

The wise store up choice food and olive oil,
　　but fools gulp theirs down.

Whoever pursues righteousness and love
  finds life, prosperity and honor.

Those who guard their mouths and their tongues
  keep themselves from calamity.

The sacrifice of the wicked is detestable —
  how much more so when brought with evil intent!

A false witness will perish,
  but a careful listener will testify successfully.

There is no wisdom, no insight, no plan
  that can succeed against the LORD.

The horse is made ready for the day of battle,
  but victory rests with the LORD.

Because his father's military success had secured Israel's borders, King Solomon could focus on diplomacy, architecture and temple construction. If David's first approach to neighbors was to brandish a sword, Solomon's was to say a wise word and cut a good deal. David was the warrior king; Solomon was the brilliant general contractor.

When Hiram king of Tyre heard that Solomon had been anointed king to succeed his father David, he sent his envoys to Solomon, because he had always been on friendly terms with David. Solomon sent back this message to Hiram:

"You know that because of the wars waged against my father David from all sides, he could not build a temple for the Name of the LORD his God until the LORD put his enemies under his feet. But now the LORD my God has given me rest on every side, and there is no adversary or disaster. I intend, therefore, to build a temple for the Name of the LORD my God, as the LORD told my father

David, when he said, 'Your son whom I will put on the throne in your place will build the temple for my Name.'

"So give orders that cedars of Lebanon be cut for me. My men will work with yours, and I will pay you for your men whatever wages you set. You know that we have no one so skilled in felling timber as the Sidonians."

When Hiram heard Solomon's message, he was greatly pleased and said, "Praise be to the LORD today, for he has given David a wise son to rule over this great nation."

So Hiram sent word to Solomon:

"I have received the message you sent me and will do all you want in providing the cedar and juniper logs. My men will haul them down from Lebanon to the Mediterranean Sea, and I will float them as rafts by sea to the place you specify. There I will separate them and you can take them away. And you are to grant my wish by providing food for my royal household."

In this way Hiram kept Solomon supplied with all the cedar and juniper logs he wanted, and Solomon gave Hiram twenty thousand cors of wheat as food for his household, in addition to twenty thousand baths of pressed olive oil. Solomon continued to do this for Hiram year after year. The LORD gave Solomon wisdom, just as he had promised him. There were peaceful relations between Hiram and Solomon, and the two of them made a treaty.

In the four hundred and eightieth year after the Israelites came out of Egypt, in the fourth year of Solomon's reign over Israel, in the month of Ziv, the second month, he began to build the temple of the LORD.

Construction details revealed a temple of modest footprint (90 feet by 30 feet) but of spectacular beauty and historic significance. Two bronze pillars led to the portico, which then led to the Holy Place, built with cedar, pine, juniper and olive wood, and then the Most Holy Place, overlaid in gold. The ark of God was placed in the Most Holy Place, where entry was limited to the high priest. The floor plan of Solomon's temple followed the pattern of the tabernacle Moses had built during the Israelites' wilderness journey. Construction took seven years of work by 180,000 conscripted laborers and nearly 4,000 supervisors. The percussion of hammer and chisel rang loud at the quarry. At the building site itself, a quiet solemnity anticipated the inauguration of the house of God.

When all the work King Solomon had done for the temple of the LORD was finished, he brought in the things his father David had dedicated — the silver and gold and the furnishings — and he placed them in the treasuries of the LORD's temple.

Then King Solomon summoned into his presence at Jerusalem the elders of Israel, all the heads of the tribes and the chiefs of the Israelite families, to bring up the ark of the LORD's covenant from Zion, the City of David. All the Israelites came together to King Solomon at the time of the festival in the month of Ethanim, the seventh month.

When all the elders of Israel had arrived, the priests took up the ark, and they brought up the ark of the LORD and the tent of meeting and all the sacred furnishings in it. The priests and Levites carried them up, and King Solomon and the entire assembly of Israel that had gathered about him were before the ark, sacrificing so many sheep and cattle that they could not be recorded or counted.

The priests then brought the ark of the LORD's covenant to its place in the inner sanctuary of the temple, the Most Holy Place, and put it beneath the wings of the cherubim.

The priests then withdrew from the Holy Place. All the priests who were there had consecrated themselves, regardless of their divisions. All the Levites who were musicians — Asaph, Heman, Jeduthun and their sons and relatives — stood on the east side of the altar, dressed in fine linen and playing cymbals, harps and lyres. They were accompanied by 120 priests sounding trumpets. The trumpeters and musicians joined in unison to give praise and thanks to the LORD. Accompanied by trumpets, cymbals and other instruments, the singers raised their voices in praise to the LORD and sang:

> "He is good;
> his love endures forever."

Then the temple of the LORD was filled with the cloud, and the priests could not perform their service because of the cloud, for the glory of the LORD filled the temple of God.

Then Solomon said, "The LORD has said that he would dwell in a dark cloud; I have indeed built a magnificent temple for you, a place for you to dwell forever."

While the whole assembly of Israel was standing there, the king turned around and blessed them.

Then Solomon stood before the altar of the LORD in front of the whole assembly of Israel, spread out his hands toward heaven and said:

"LORD, the God of Israel, there is no God like you in heaven above or on earth below — you who keep your covenant of love with your servants who continue wholeheartedly in your way. You have kept your promise to your servant David my father; with your mouth you have promised and with your hand you have fulfilled it — as it is today.

"But will God really dwell on earth? The heavens, even the highest heaven, cannot contain you. How much less this temple I have built! Yet give attention to your servant's prayer and his plea for mercy, LORD my God. Hear the cry and the prayer that your servant is praying in your presence this day. May your eyes be open toward this temple night and day, this place of which you said, 'My Name shall be there,' so that you will hear the prayer your servant prays toward this place. Hear the supplication of your servant and of your people Israel when they pray toward this place. Hear from heaven, your dwelling place, and when you hear, forgive.

"Now, my God, may your eyes be open and your ears attentive to the prayers offered in this place.

"Now arise, Lord God, and come to your resting place,
  you and the ark of your might.
May your priests, Lord God, be clothed with salvation,
  may your faithful people rejoice in your goodness.
Lord God, do not reject your anointed one.
  Remember the great love promised to David your
    servant."

When Solomon finished praying, fire came down from heaven and consumed the burnt offering and the sacrifices, and the glory of the Lord filled the temple. The priests could not enter the temple of the Lord because the glory of the Lord filled it. When all the Israelites saw the fire coming down and the glory of the Lord above the temple, they knelt on the pavement with their faces to the ground, and they worshiped and gave thanks to the Lord, saying,

"He is good;
  his love endures forever."

When Solomon had finished all these prayers and supplications to the Lord, he rose from before the altar of the Lord, where he had been kneeling with his hands spread out toward heaven. He stood and blessed the whole assembly of Israel in a loud voice, saying:

"Praise be to the Lord, who has given rest to his people Israel just as he promised. Not one word has failed of all the good promises he gave through his servant Moses. May the LORD our God be with us as he was with our ancestors; may he never leave us nor forsake us. May he turn our hearts to him, to walk in obedience to him and keep the commands, decrees and laws he gave our ancestors. And may these words of mine, which I have prayed before the LORD, be near to the LORD our God day and night, that he may uphold the cause of his servant and the cause of his people Israel according to each day's need, so that all the peoples of the earth may know that the LORD is God and that there is no other. And may your hearts be fully committed to the LORD our God, to live by his decrees and obey his commands, as at this time."

Then the king and all the people offered sacrifices before the LORD. And King Solomon offered a sacrifice of twenty-two thousand head of cattle and a hundred and twenty thousand sheep and goats. So the king and all the people dedicated the temple of God.

When Solomon had finished the temple of the LORD and the royal palace, and had succeeded in carrying out all he had in mind to do in the temple of the LORD and in his own palace, the LORD appeared to him at night and said:

"I have heard your prayer and have chosen this place for myself as a temple for sacrifices.

"When I shut up the heavens so that there is no rain, or command locusts to devour the land or send a plague among my people, if my people, who are called by my name, will humble themselves and pray and seek my face and turn from their wicked ways, then I will hear from heaven, and I will forgive their sin and will heal their land. Now my eyes will be open and my ears attentive to the prayers offered in this place. I have chosen and consecrated this temple so that my Name may be there forever. My eyes and my heart will always be there.

"As for you, if you walk before me faithfully as David your father did, and do all I command, and observe my decrees and laws, I will establish your royal throne, as I covenanted with David your father when I said, 'You shall never fail to have a successor to rule over Israel.'

"But if you[1] turn away and forsake the decrees and commands I have given you and go off to serve other gods and worship them, then I will uproot Israel from my land, which I have given them, and will reject this temple I have consecrated for my Name. I will make it a byword and an object of ridicule among all peoples. This temple will become a heap of rubble. All who pass by will be appalled and say, 'Why has the LORD done such a thing to this land and to this temple?' People will answer, 'Because they have forsaken the LORD, the God of their ancestors, who brought them out of Egypt, and have embraced other gods, worshiping and serving them — that is why he brought all this disaster on them.'"

The gold ornamentation and cedar woodwork in the temple brought glory to God and were gifts of beauty to many generations. But God reminded Solomon that faithfulness, integrity of heart, uprightness and obedience were what he desired even more. All this Solomon heard, believed and followed even when faced with the accolades of admirers. Visitors came from everywhere to meet this famous king.

When the queen of Sheba heard about the fame of Solomon and his relationship to the LORD, she came to test Solomon with hard questions. Arriving at Jerusalem with a very great caravan — with camels carrying spices, large quantities of gold, and precious stones — she came to Solomon and talked with him about all that she had on her mind. Solomon answered all her questions; nothing was too hard for the king to explain to her. When the queen of Sheba saw all the wisdom of Solomon and the palace he had built, the food on his table, the seating of his officials, the attending servants in their robes, his cupbearers, and the burnt offerings he made at the temple of the LORD, she was overwhelmed.

---

[1]**You:** The Hebrew is plural for both instances of *you* in this sentence.

She said to the king, "The report I heard in my own country about your achievements and your wisdom is true. But I did
not believe these things until I came and saw with my own eyes.
Indeed, not even half was told me; in wisdom and wealth you have
far exceeded the report I heard. How happy your people must
be! How happy your officials, who continually stand before you
and hear your wisdom! Praise be to the LORD your God, who has
delighted in you and placed you on the throne of Israel. Because of
the LORD's eternal love for Israel, he has made you king to maintain justice and righteousness."

And she gave the king 120 talents of gold, large quantities of
spices, and precious stones. Never again were so many spices
brought in as those the queen of Sheba gave to King Solomon.

King Solomon gave the queen of Sheba all she desired and
asked for, besides what he had given her out of his royal bounty.
Then she left and returned with her retinue to her own country.

The weight of the gold that Solomon received yearly was 666
talents, not including the revenues from merchants and traders
and from all the Arabian kings and the governors of the territories.

King Solomon made two hundred large shields of hammered
gold; six hundred shekels of gold went into each shield. He also
made three hundred small shields of hammered gold, with three
minas of gold in each shield. The king put them in the Palace of
the Forest of Lebanon.

Then the king made a great throne covered with ivory and
overlaid with fine gold. The throne had six steps, and its back had
a rounded top. On both sides of the seat were armrests, with a lion
standing beside each of them. Twelve lions stood on the six steps,
one at either end of each step. Nothing like it had ever been made
for any other kingdom. All King Solomon's goblets were gold, and
all the household articles in the Palace of the Forest of Lebanon
were pure gold. Nothing was made of silver, because silver was
considered of little value in Solomon's days. The king had a fleet

of trading ships at sea along with the ships of Hiram. Once every three years it returned, carrying gold, silver and ivory, and apes and baboons.

King Solomon was greater in riches and wisdom than all the other kings of the earth. The whole world sought audience with Solomon to hear the wisdom God had put in his heart. Year after year, everyone who came brought a gift — articles of silver and gold, robes, weapons and spices, and horses and mules.

Solomon accumulated chariots and horses; he had fourteen hundred chariots and twelve thousand horses, which he kept in the chariot cities and also with him in Jerusalem. The king made silver as common in Jerusalem as stones, and cedar as plentiful as sycamore-fig trees in the foothills. Solomon's horses were imported from Egypt and from Kue — the royal merchants purchased them from Kue at the current price. They imported a chariot from Egypt for six hundred shekels of silver, and a horse for a hundred and fifty. They also exported them to all the kings of the Hittites and of the Arameans.

During Solomon's time, polygamy was considered normal (but was not sanctioned by God). Like other kings, Solomon had a large harem of wives, some of whom were from other nations. For Solomon, unfortunately, the irresistible draw of sweet perfume led to relaxing his guard against pagan worship as well ... a bad decision from a fellow renowned for wisdom. It was the beginning of the end.

King Solomon, however, loved many foreign women besides Pharaoh's daughter — Moabites, Ammonites, Edomites, Sidonians and Hittites. They were from nations about which the LORD had told the Israelites, "You must not intermarry with them, because they will surely turn your hearts after their gods." Nevertheless, Solomon held fast to them in love. He had seven hundred wives of royal birth and three hundred concubines, and his wives led him astray. As Solomon grew old, his wives turned his heart after other gods, and his heart was not fully devoted to the LORD his God, as the heart of David his father had been. He followed Ashtoreth the goddess of the Sidonians, and Molek the detestable god of the Ammonites. So Solomon did evil in the eyes of the LORD; he did not follow the LORD completely, as David his father had done.

The LORD became angry with Solomon because his heart had turned away from the LORD, the God of Israel, who had appeared to him twice. Although he had forbidden Solomon to follow other gods, Solomon did not keep the LORD's command. So the LORD said to Solomon, "Since this is your attitude and you have not kept my covenant and my decrees, which I commanded you, I will most certainly tear the kingdom away from you and give it to one of your subordinates. Nevertheless, for the sake of David your father, I will not do it during your lifetime. I will tear it out of the hand of your son. Yet I will not tear the whole kingdom from him, but will give him one tribe for the sake of David my servant and for the sake of Jerusalem, which I have chosen."

14

A Kingdom Torn in Two

Through the prophet Ahijah, God told a rising young star in Solomon's administration by the name of Jeroboam that he would be the future king. God would give Jeroboam all but one of the tribes of Israel. After possibly making a preemptive bid for the throne, Jeroboam learned to wait on God's timing. Solomon was not ready to relinquish the throne and tried to kill Jeroboam to keep him from becoming king. Jeroboam fled to Egypt and waited there for an opportunity to make his next move.

After Solomon died, his own tribe of Judah automatically accepted his son Rehoboam as the next king. But much of the population, especially from the other tribes, had grown to resent Solomon's heavy taxation and conscripted labor for his grand projects. As representatives from all of Israel gathered to make Rehoboam king, they let their complaints be known.

REHOBOAM WENT TO SHECHEM, for all Israel had gone there to make him king. When Jeroboam son of Nebat heard this (he was still in Egypt, where he had fled from King Solomon), he returned from Egypt. So they sent for Jeroboam, and he and the whole

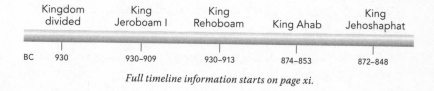

Kingdom divided	King Jeroboam I	King Rehoboam	King Ahab	King Jehoshaphat
BC 930	930–909	930–913	874–853	872–848

Full timeline information starts on page xi.

assembly of Israel went to Rehoboam and said to him: "Your father put a heavy yoke on us, but now lighten the harsh labor and the heavy yoke he put on us, and we will serve you."

Rehoboam answered, "Go away for three days and then come back to me." So the people went away.

Then King Rehoboam consulted the elders who had served his father Solomon during his lifetime. "How would you advise me to answer these people?" he asked.

They replied, "If today you will be a servant to these people and serve them and give them a favorable answer, they will always be your servants."

But Rehoboam rejected the advice the elders gave him and consulted the young men who had grown up with him and were serving him. He asked them, "What is your advice? How should we answer these people who say to me, 'Lighten the yoke your father put on us'?"

The young men who had grown up with him replied, "These people have said to you, 'Your father put a heavy yoke on us, but make our yoke lighter.' Now tell them, 'My little finger is thicker than my father's waist. My father laid on you a heavy yoke; I will make it even heavier. My father scourged you with whips; I will scourge you with scorpions.'"

Three days later Jeroboam and all the people returned to Rehoboam, as the king had said, "Come back to me in three days." The king answered the people harshly. Rejecting the advice given him by the elders, he followed the advice of the young men and said, "My father made your yoke heavy; I will make it even heavier. My father scourged you with whips; I will scourge you with scorpions." So the king did not listen to the people, for this turn of events was from the LORD, to fulfill the word the LORD had spoken to Jeroboam son of Nebat through Ahijah the Shilonite.

When all Israel saw that the king refused to listen to them, they answered the king:

"What share do we have in David,
  what part in Jesse's son?

To your tents, Israel!
Look after your own house, David!"

So the Israelites went home. But as for the Israelites who were living in the towns of Judah, Rehoboam still ruled over them.

*Rehoboam retreated to rule Judah (the smaller, southern
region), while Jeroboam became king over Israel (the larger,
northern region). God had forewarned that the kingdom would
become divided because Solomon failed to keep pagan worship outside the realm. Already divided in worship practices,
the nation now also became divided in politics, in priesthood,
in security and in safety. For two generations, Israel's army had
been the pride of the region, her storerooms filled with precious
metals, her people fed, her cities busy and her temple active.
Now what would happen to Israel and Judah, split by disputes
their leaders could not resolve?*

King Rehoboam sent out Adoniram, who was in charge of forced
labor, but all Israel stoned him to death. King Rehoboam, however,
managed to get into his chariot and escape to Jerusalem. So Israel
has been in rebellion against the house of David to this day.

When all the Israelites heard that Jeroboam had returned,
they sent and called him to the assembly and made him king over
all Israel. Only the tribe of Judah remained loyal to the house of
David.

When Rehoboam arrived in Jerusalem, he mustered all Judah
and the tribe of Benjamin — a hundred and eighty thousand able
young men — to go to war against Israel and to regain the kingdom
for Rehoboam son of Solomon.

But this word of God came to Shemaiah the man of God: "Say
to Rehoboam son of Solomon king of Judah, to all Judah and Benjamin, and to the rest of the people, 'This is what the LORD says:
Do not go up to fight against your brothers, the Israelites. Go
home, every one of you, for this is my doing.'" So they obeyed the
word of the LORD and went home again, as the LORD had ordered.

Then Jeroboam fortified Shechem in the hill country of Ephraim and lived there. From there he went out and built up Peniel.

Jeroboam thought to himself, "The kingdom will now likely revert to the house of David. If these people go up to offer sacrifices at the temple of the LORD in Jerusalem, they will again give their allegiance to their lord, Rehoboam king of Judah. They will kill me and return to King Rehoboam."

After seeking advice, the king made two golden calves. He said to the people, "It is too much for you to go up to Jerusalem. Here are your gods, Israel, who brought you up out of Egypt." One he set up in Bethel, and the other in Dan. And this thing became a sin; the people came to worship the one at Bethel and went as far as Dan to worship the other.

Jeroboam built shrines on high places and appointed priests from all sorts of people, even though they were not Levites. He instituted a festival on the fifteenth day of the eighth month, like the festival held in Judah, and offered sacrifices on the altar. This he did in Bethel, sacrificing to the calves he had made. And at Bethel he also installed priests at the high places he had made. On the fifteenth day of the eighth month, a month of his own choosing, he offered sacrifices on the altar he had built at Bethel. So he instituted the festival for the Israelites and went up to the altar to make offerings.

By the word of the LORD a man of God came from Judah to Bethel, as Jeroboam was standing by the altar to make an offering. By the word of the LORD he cried out against the altar: "Altar, altar! This is what the LORD says: 'A son named Josiah will be born to the house of David. On you he will sacrifice the priests of the high places who make offerings here, and human bones will be burned on you.'" That same day the man of God gave a sign: "This is the sign the LORD has declared: The altar will be split apart and the ashes on it will be poured out."

When King Jeroboam heard what the man of God cried out against the altar at Bethel, he stretched out his hand from the altar and said, "Seize him!" But the hand he stretched out toward the man shriveled up, so that he could not pull it back. Also, the altar was split apart and its ashes poured out according to the sign given by the man of God by the word of the LORD.

Then the king said to the man of God, "Intercede with the LORD your God and pray for me that my hand may be restored." So the man of God interceded with the LORD, and the king's hand was restored and became as it was before.

Even after this, Jeroboam did not change his evil ways, but once more appointed priests for the high places from all sorts of people. Anyone who wanted to become a priest he consecrated for the high places.

At that time, Abijah son of Jeroboam became ill, and Jeroboam said to his wife, "Go, disguise yourself, so you won't be recognized as the wife of Jeroboam. Then go to Shiloh. Ahijah the prophet is there — the one who told me I would be king over this people. Take ten loaves of bread with you, some cakes and a jar of honey, and go to him. He will tell you what will happen to the boy." So Jeroboam's wife did what he said and went to Ahijah's house in Shiloh.

Now Ahijah could not see; his sight was gone because of his age. But the LORD had told Ahijah, "Jeroboam's wife is coming to ask you about her son, for he is ill, and you are to give her such and such an answer. When she arrives, she will pretend to be someone else."

So when Ahijah heard the sound of her footsteps at the door, he said, "Come in, wife of Jeroboam. Why this pretense? I have been sent to you with bad news. Go, tell Jeroboam that this is what the LORD, the God of Israel, says: 'I raised you up from among the people and appointed you ruler over my people Israel. I tore the kingdom away from the house of David and gave it to you, but you have not been like my servant David, who kept my commands and followed me with all his heart, doing only what was right in my eyes. You have done more evil than all who lived before you. You have made for yourself other gods, idols made of metal; you have aroused my anger and turned your back on me.

"'Because of this, I am going to bring disaster on the house of Jeroboam. I will cut off from Jeroboam every last male in Israel— slave or free. I will burn up the house of Jeroboam as one burns dung, until it is all gone. Dogs will eat those belonging to Jeroboam who die in the city, and the birds will feed on those who die in the country. The LORD has spoken!'

"As for you, go back home. When you set foot in your city, the boy will die. All Israel will mourn for him and bury him. He is the only one belonging to Jeroboam who will be buried, because he is the only one in the house of Jeroboam in whom the LORD, the God of Israel, has found anything good.

"The LORD will raise up for himself a king over Israel who will cut off the family of Jeroboam. Even now this is beginning to happen. And the LORD will strike Israel, so that it will be like a reed swaying in the water. He will uproot Israel from this good land that he gave to their ancestors and scatter them beyond the Euphrates River, because they aroused the LORD's anger by making Asherah poles. And he will give Israel up because of the sins Jeroboam has committed and has caused Israel to commit."

Then Jeroboam's wife got up and left and went to Tirzah. As soon as she stepped over the threshold of the house, the boy died. They buried him, and all Israel mourned for him, as the LORD had said through his servant the prophet Ahijah.

Rehoboam son of Solomon was king in Judah. He was forty-one years old when he became king, and he reigned seventeen years in Jerusalem, the city the LORD had chosen out of all the tribes of Israel in which to put his Name.

Judah did evil in the eyes of the LORD. By the sins they committed they stirred up his jealous anger more than those who were before them had done. They also set up for themselves high places, sacred stones and Asherah poles on every high hill and under every spreading tree. There were even male shrine prostitutes in the land; the people engaged in all the detestable practices of the nations the LORD had driven out before the Israelites.

In the fifth year of King Rehoboam, Shishak king of Egypt attacked Jerusalem. He carried off the treasures of the temple of the LORD and the treasures of the royal palace. He took everything, including all the gold shields Solomon had made. So King Rehoboam made bronze shields to replace them and assigned these to the commanders of the guard on duty at the entrance to the royal palace. Whenever the king went to the LORD's temple, the guards bore the shields, and afterward they returned them to the guardroom.

There was continual warfare between Rehoboam and Jeroboam. And Rehoboam rested with his ancestors and was buried with them in the City of David. His mother's name was Naamah; she was an Ammonite. And Abijah his son succeeded him as king.

In the eighteenth year of the reign of Jeroboam son of Nebat, Abijah became king of Judah, and he reigned in Jerusalem three years. His mother's name was Maakah daughter of Abishalom.

He committed all the sins his father had done before him; his heart was not fully devoted to the LORD his God, as the heart of David his forefather had been. Nevertheless, for David's sake the LORD his God gave him a lamp in Jerusalem by raising up a son to succeed him and by making Jerusalem strong. For David had done what was right in the eyes of the LORD and had not failed to keep any of the LORD's commands all the days of his life — except in the case of Uriah the Hittite.

There was war between Abijah and Jeroboam throughout Abijah's lifetime.

And Abijah rested with his ancestors and was buried in the City of David. And Asa his son succeeded him as king.

In the twentieth year of Jeroboam king of Israel, Asa became king of Judah, and he reigned in Jerusalem forty-one years. His grandmother's name was Maakah daughter of Abishalom.

Asa did what was right in the eyes of the LORD, as his father David had done. He expelled the male shrine prostitutes from the land and got rid of all the idols his ancestors had made. He even deposed his grandmother Maakah from her position as queen mother, because she had made a repulsive image for the worship of Asherah. Asa cut it down and burned it in the Kidron Valley. Although he did not remove the high places, Asa's heart was fully committed to the LORD all his life. He brought into the temple of the LORD the silver and gold and the articles that he and his father had dedicated.

There was war between Asa and Baasha king of Israel throughout their reigns. Baasha king of Israel went up against Judah and fortified Ramah to prevent anyone from leaving or entering the territory of Asa king of Judah.

Asa then took all the silver and gold that was left in the treasuries of the LORD's temple and of his own palace. He entrusted it to his officials and sent them to Ben-Hadad son of Tabrimmon, the son of Hezion, the king of Aram, who was ruling in Damascus. "Let there be a treaty between me and you," he said, "as there was between my father and your father. See, I am sending you a gift of silver and gold. Now break your treaty with Baasha king of Israel so he will withdraw from me."

Ben-Hadad agreed with King Asa and sent the commanders of his forces against the towns of Israel. He conquered Ijon, Dan, Abel Beth Maakah and all Kinnereth in addition to Naphtali. When Baasha heard this, he stopped building Ramah and withdrew to Tirzah. Then King Asa issued an order to all Judah — no one was exempt — and they carried away from Ramah the stones and timber Baasha had been using there. With them King Asa built up Geba in Benjamin, and also Mizpah.

As for all the other events of Asa's reign, all his achievements, all he did and the cities he built, are they not written in the book of the annals of the kings of Judah? In his old age, however, his feet became diseased. Then Asa rested with his ancestors and was buried with them in the city of his father David. And Jehoshaphat his son succeeded him as king.

After 22 years as king of Israel, Jeroboam also died. Various kings reigned in Israel and Judah. Most of them did evil. Only a few kings were considered "good," like King Asa of Judah, who "did what was right in the eyes of the LORD." Doing right included ridding the kingdom of idolatry. King Asa went so far as to remove his grandmother, Maakah, from her lofty position of queen mother because of her pagan worship. Asa didn't stop there. He understood that only the Lord God was worthy of worship, and he cleaned the entire land of Judah of its idols.

On the despicable side, Jeroboam's son Nadab "did evil in the eyes of the LORD, following in the ways of his father." A man named Baasha plotted against Nadab and killed the king and Jeroboam's whole family, fulfilling God's prophecy through the prophet Ahijah. But Baasha, "committing the same sin Jeroboam had caused Israel to commit," was no better as a king. Likewise Zimri, who also followed the evil "ways of Jeroboam," killed his predecessor, King Elah, to get onto the throne. But Zimri had failed to calculate his popular support, or lack thereof, and was in power all of seven days before burning himself to death in the palace and leaving the ashes of his discontent to Omri, the people's choice. During his reign Omri made the city of Samaria the capital of the northern kingdom, and "Samaria" also came to signify the entire territory of the northern tribes.

When Omri died, his son Ahab became king of Israel. But the real power in the family was Ahab's infamous wife Jezebel, a powerful woman of iron will and the daughter of a pagan foreign king. Ahab and Jezebel worshiped Baal and hated the prophets of God, of whom Elijah was chief. Elijah became public enemy number one, but God had a fiery confrontation planned to show the people whose side God himself was on.

In the thirty-eighth year of Asa king of Judah, Ahab son of Omri became king of Israel, and he reigned in Samaria over Israel twenty-two years. Ahab son of Omri did more evil in the eyes of the LORD than any of those before him. He not only considered it trivial to commit the sins of Jeroboam son of Nebat, but he also married Jezebel daughter of Ethbaal king of the Sidonians, and began to serve Baal and worship him. He set up an altar for Baal in the temple of Baal that he built in Samaria. Ahab also made an Asherah pole and did more to arouse the anger of the LORD, the God of Israel, than did all the kings of Israel before him.

In Ahab's time, Hiel of Bethel rebuilt Jericho. He laid its foundations at the cost of his firstborn son Abiram, and he set up its gates at the cost of his youngest son Segub, in accordance with the word of the LORD spoken by Joshua son of Nun.

15

God's Messengers

Now Elijah the Tishbite, from Tishbe in Gilead, said to Ahab, "As the Lord, the God of Israel, lives, whom I serve, there will be neither dew nor rain in the next few years except at my word."

Then the word of the Lord came to Elijah: "Leave here, turn eastward and hide in the Kerith Ravine, east of the Jordan. You will drink from the brook, and I have directed the ravens to supply you with food there."

So he did what the Lord had told him. He went to the Kerith Ravine, east of the Jordan, and stayed there. The ravens brought him bread and meat in the morning and bread and meat in the evening, and he drank from the brook.

After a long time, in the third year, the word of the Lord came to Elijah: "Go and present yourself to Ahab, and I will send rain on the land." So Elijah went to present himself to Ahab.

When he saw Elijah, he said to him, "Is that you, you troubler of Israel?"

Elijah's ministry	Elisha's ministry	Amos's ministry	Hosea's ministry
BC 875–848	c. 848–797	760–750	750–715

Full timeline information starts on page xi.

"I have not made trouble for Israel," Elijah replied. "But you and your father's family have. You have abandoned the LORD's commands and have followed the Baals. Now summon the people from all over Israel to meet me on Mount Carmel. And bring the four hundred and fifty prophets of Baal and the four hundred prophets of Asherah, who eat at Jezebel's table."

So Ahab sent word throughout all Israel and assembled the prophets on Mount Carmel. Elijah went before the people and said, "How long will you waver between two opinions? If the LORD is God, follow him; but if Baal is God, follow him."

But the people said nothing.

Then Elijah said to them, "I am the only one of the LORD's prophets left, but Baal has four hundred and fifty prophets. Get two bulls for us. Let Baal's prophets choose one for themselves, and let them cut it into pieces and put it on the wood but not set fire to it. I will prepare the other bull and put it on the wood but not set fire to it. Then you call on the name of your god, and I will call on the name of the LORD. The god who answers by fire — he is God."

Then all the people said, "What you say is good."

Elijah said to the prophets of Baal, "Choose one of the bulls and prepare it first, since there are so many of you. Call on the name of your god, but do not light the fire." So they took the bull given them and prepared it.

Then they called on the name of Baal from morning till noon. "Baal, answer us!" they shouted. But there was no response; no one answered. And they danced around the altar they had made.

At noon Elijah began to taunt them. "Shout louder!" he said. "Surely he is a god! Perhaps he is deep in thought, or busy, or traveling. Maybe he is sleeping and must be awakened." So they shouted louder and slashed themselves with swords and spears, as was their custom, until their blood flowed. Midday passed, and they continued their frantic prophesying until the time for the evening sacrifice. But there was no response, no one answered, no one paid attention.

Then Elijah said to all the people, "Come here to me." They came to him, and he repaired the altar of the LORD, which had been torn down. Elijah took twelve stones, one for each of the tribes descended from Jacob, to whom the word of the LORD had come, saying, "Your name shall be Israel." With the stones he built an altar in the name of the LORD, and he dug a trench around it large enough to hold two seahs[1] of seed. He arranged the wood, cut the bull into pieces and laid it on the wood. Then he said to them, "Fill four large jars with water and pour it on the offering and on the wood."

"Do it again," he said, and they did it again.

"Do it a third time," he ordered, and they did it the third time. The water ran down around the altar and even filled the trench.

At the time of sacrifice, the prophet Elijah stepped forward and prayed: "LORD, the God of Abraham, Isaac and Israel, let it be known today that you are God in Israel and that I am your servant and have done all these things at your command. Answer me, LORD, answer me, so these people will know that you, LORD, are God, and that you are turning their hearts back again."

Then the fire of the LORD fell and burned up the sacrifice, the wood, the stones and the soil, and also licked up the water in the trench.

When all the people saw this, they fell prostrate and cried, "The LORD — he is God! The LORD — he is God!"

Then Elijah commanded them, "Seize the prophets of Baal. Don't let anyone get away!" They seized them, and Elijah had them brought down to the Kishon Valley and slaughtered there.

And Elijah said to Ahab, "Go, eat and drink, for there is the sound of a heavy rain." So Ahab went off to eat and drink, but Elijah climbed to the top of Carmel, bent down to the ground and put his face between his knees.

"Go and look toward the sea," he told his servant. And he went up and looked.

---

[1] **Two seahs:** That is, probably about 24 pounds or about 11 kilograms.

"There is nothing there," he said.

Seven times Elijah said, "Go back."

The seventh time the servant reported, "A cloud as small as a man's hand is rising from the sea."

So Elijah said, "Go and tell Ahab, 'Hitch up your chariot and go down before the rain stops you.'"

Meanwhile, the sky grew black with clouds, the wind rose, a heavy rain started falling and Ahab rode off to Jezreel. The power of the LORD came on Elijah and, tucking his cloak into his belt, he ran ahead of Ahab all the way to Jezreel.

Jezebel was not one to count her losses. When Ahab's own will to fight was exhausted, he could count on Jezebel to keep charging. Her will to win overcame any doubts she might have had about the failure on Mount Carmel.

Now Ahab told Jezebel everything Elijah had done and how he had killed all the prophets with the sword. So Jezebel sent a messenger to Elijah to say, "May the gods deal with me, be it ever so severely, if by this time tomorrow I do not make your life like that of one of them."

Elijah was afraid and ran for his life. When he came to Beersheba in Judah, he left his servant there, while he himself went a day's journey into the wilderness. He came to a broom bush, sat down under it and prayed that he might die. "I have had enough, LORD," he said. "Take my life; I am no better than my ancestors." Then he lay down under the bush and fell asleep.

All at once an angel touched him and said, "Get up and eat." He looked around, and there by his head was some bread baked over hot coals, and a jar of water. He ate and drank and then lay down again.

The angel of the LORD came back a second time and touched him and said, "Get up and eat, for the journey is too much for you." So he got up and ate and drank. Strengthened by that food, he traveled forty days and forty nights until he reached Horeb, the mountain of God. There he went into a cave and spent the night.

And the word of the LORD came to him: "What are you doing here, Elijah?"

He replied, "I have been very zealous for the LORD God Almighty. The Israelites have rejected your covenant, torn down your altars, and put your prophets to death with the sword. I am the only one left, and now they are trying to kill me too."

The LORD said, "Go out and stand on the mountain in the presence of the LORD, for the LORD is about to pass by."

Then a great and powerful wind tore the mountains apart and shattered the rocks before the LORD, but the LORD was not in the wind. After the wind there was an earthquake, but the LORD was not in the earthquake. After the earthquake came a fire, but the LORD was not in the fire. And after the fire came a gentle whisper. When Elijah heard it, he pulled his cloak over his face and went out and stood at the mouth of the cave.

Then a voice said to him, "What are you doing here, Elijah?"

He replied, "I have been very zealous for the LORD God Almighty. The Israelites have rejected your covenant, torn down your altars, and put your prophets to death with the sword. I am the only one left, and now they are trying to kill me too."

The LORD said to him, "Go back the way you came, and go to the Desert of Damascus. When you get there, anoint Hazael king over Aram. Also, anoint Jehu son of Nimshi king over Israel, and anoint Elisha son of Shaphat from Abel Meholah to succeed you as prophet. Jehu will put to death any who escape the sword of Hazael, and Elisha will put to death any who escape the sword of Jehu. Yet I reserve seven thousand in Israel — all whose knees have not bowed down to Baal and whose mouths have not kissed him."

So Elijah went from there and found Elisha son of Shaphat. He was plowing with twelve yoke of oxen, and he himself was driving the twelfth pair. Elijah went up to him and threw his cloak around him. Elisha then left his oxen and ran after Elijah. "Let me kiss my father and mother goodbye," he said, "and then I will come with you."

"Go back," Elijah replied. "What have I done to you?"

So Elisha left him and went back. He took his yoke of oxen and slaughtered them. He burned the plowing equipment to cook the meat and gave it to the people, and they ate. Then he set out to follow Elijah and became his servant.

King Ahab constantly vacillated, appearing kingly one day, then floundering the next. He spared the life of his archenemy Ben-Hadad when God delivered the king of Aram into Ahab's hand in battle. Yet Ahab took the life of his own subject, Naboth, in order to steal Naboth's vineyard. In the end, Ahab died in battle disguised as a foot soldier, hit by a random arrow. His son Ahaziah could not improve on his parents' dismal record, so he also joined the annals of the wicked kings and died without a successor. In Judah, Asa's son Jehoshaphat followed God, survived enemies' threats, and the southern kingdom began to prosper.

Meanwhile, Elijah's time had come to an end. There was never a grander exit than his, or more compelling proof to his successor Elisha that the mantle of divine power had now passed to him.

When the LORD was about to take Elijah up to heaven in a whirlwind, Elijah and Elisha were on their way from Gilgal. Elijah said to Elisha, "Stay here; the LORD has sent me to Bethel."

But Elisha said, "As surely as the LORD lives and as you live, I will not leave you." So they went down to Bethel.

Fifty men from the company of the prophets went and stood at a distance, facing the place where Elijah and Elisha had stopped at the Jordan. Elijah took his cloak, rolled it up and struck the water with it. The water divided to the right and to the left, and the two of them crossed over on dry ground.

When they had crossed, Elijah said to Elisha, "Tell me, what can I do for you before I am taken from you?"

"Let me inherit a double portion of your spirit," Elisha replied.

"You have asked a difficult thing," Elijah said, "yet if you see me when I am taken from you, it will be yours — otherwise, it will not."

As they were walking along and talking together, suddenly a chariot of fire and horses of fire appeared and separated the two of them, and Elijah went up to heaven in a whirlwind. Elisha saw this and cried out, "My father! My father! The chariots and horsemen of Israel!" And Elisha saw him no more. Then he took hold of his garment and tore it in two.

Elisha then picked up Elijah's cloak that had fallen from him and went back and stood on the bank of the Jordan. He took the cloak that had fallen from Elijah and struck the water with it. "Where now is the LORD, the God of Elijah?" he asked. When he struck the water, it divided to the right and to the left, and he crossed over.

The company of the prophets from Jericho, who were watching, said, "The spirit of Elijah is resting on Elisha." And they went to meet him and bowed to the ground before him.

Elijah was gone. Elisha was left to carry on the work, and his dramatic miracles made it clear that his God was one of unspeakable power and glory. In one instance, Elisha purified a spring to provide fresh water to an entire town. Another time, through Elisha's intervention, a poor widow and her sons were saved from financial ruin and slavery by a bottomless jar of oil. Elisha appreciated the small favors that lightened a prophet's stressful load. On one occasion he was offered a meal by a wealthy woman from Shunem, who eventually suggested to her husband that they offer Elisha a place to stay whenever he came to their area. Grateful for her friendship and kindness, Elisha prayed to God for the woman, who had no son.

One day when Elisha came, he went up to his room and lay down there. He said to his servant Gehazi, "Call the Shunammite."

So he called her, and she stood before him. Elisha said to him, "Tell her, 'You have gone to all this trouble for us. Now what can be done for you? Can we speak on your behalf to the king or the commander of the army?'"

She replied, "I have a home among my own people."

"What can be done for her?" Elisha asked.

Gehazi said, "She has no son, and her husband is old."

Then Elisha said, "Call her." So he called her, and she stood in the doorway. "About this time next year," Elisha said, "you will hold a son in your arms."

"No, my lord!" she objected. "Please, man of God, don't mislead your servant!"

But the woman became pregnant, and the next year about that same time she gave birth to a son, just as Elisha had told her.

Later, when the child was older, he grew ill. Imagine his mother's distress when the child died in her arms. Her first move was to travel to see Elisha.

When she reached the man of God at the mountain, she took hold of his feet. Gehazi came over to push her away, but the man of God said, "Leave her alone! She is in bitter distress, but the LORD has hidden it from me and has not told me why."

"Did I ask you for a son, my lord?" she said. "Didn't I tell you, 'Don't raise my hopes'?"

Elisha said to Gehazi, "Tuck your cloak into your belt, take my staff in your hand and run. Don't greet anyone you meet, and if anyone greets you, do not answer. Lay my staff on the boy's face."

But the child's mother said, "As surely as the LORD lives and as you live, I will not leave you." So he got up and followed her.

Gehazi went on ahead and laid the staff on the boy's face, but there was no sound or response. So Gehazi went back to meet Elisha and told him, "The boy has not awakened."

When Elisha reached the house, there was the boy lying dead on his couch. He went in, shut the door on the two of them and prayed to the LORD. Then he got on the bed and lay on the boy, mouth to mouth, eyes to eyes, hands to hands. As he stretched himself out on him, the boy's body grew warm. Elisha turned away and walked back and forth in the room and then got on the bed and stretched out on him once more. The boy sneezed seven times and opened his eyes.

Elisha summoned Gehazi and said, "Call the Shunammite." And he did. When she came, he said, "Take your son." She came in, fell at his feet and bowed to the ground. Then she took her son and went out.

> *Among the many notable deeds of Elisha, one of the most famous began with the testimony of a young girl from Israel. Her name is unknown, but her plight is not uncommon. She was captured by enemy raiders from Aram and then lived as a slave in the household of the commander of their army. This man, Naaman, had leprosy. The Israelite girl compassionately urged him to seek healing from the prophet of her God. In faith born of desperation, Naaman sought out Elisha and received from the prophet surprising instructions: go and wash in the Jordan River. When Naaman complied, he was healed completely. But when Gehazi, Elisha's servant, tried to extract a small fee for this miracle, he became leprous for his greed.*
>
> *Neither the prophet of God nor the words he spoke were to be taken lightly or treated casually. The king of Aram discovered this fact for himself.*

Now the king of Aram was at war with Israel. After conferring with his officers, he said, "I will set up my camp in such and such a place."

The man of God sent word to the king of Israel: "Beware of passing that place, because the Arameans are going down there." So the king of Israel checked on the place indicated by the man of God. Time and again Elisha warned the king, so that he was on his guard in such places.

This enraged the king of Aram. He summoned his officers and

demanded of them, "Tell me! Which of us is on the side of the king of Israel?"

"None of us, my lord the king," said one of his officers, "but Elisha, the prophet who is in Israel, tells the king of Israel the very words you speak in your bedroom."

"Go, find out where he is," the king ordered, "so I can send men and capture him." The report came back: "He is in Dothan." Then he sent horses and chariots and a strong force there. They went by night and surrounded the city.

When the servant of the man of God got up and went out early the next morning, an army with horses and chariots had surrounded the city. "Oh no, my lord! What shall we do?" the servant asked.

"Don't be afraid," the prophet answered. "Those who are with us are more than those who are with them."

And Elisha prayed, "Open his eyes, LORD, so that he may see." Then the LORD opened the servant's eyes, and he looked and saw the hills full of horses and chariots of fire all around Elisha.

As the enemy came down toward him, Elisha prayed to the LORD, "Strike this army with blindness." So he struck them with blindness, as Elisha had asked.

Elisha told them, "This is not the road and this is not the city. Follow me, and I will lead you to the man you are looking for." And he led them to Samaria.

After they entered the city, Elisha said, "LORD, open the eyes of these men so they can see." Then the LORD opened their eyes and they looked, and there they were, inside Samaria.

When the king of Israel saw them, he asked Elisha, "Shall I kill them, my father? Shall I kill them?"

"Do not kill them," he answered. "Would you kill those you have captured with your own sword or bow? Set food and water before them so that they may eat and drink and then go back to their master." So he prepared a great feast for them, and after they had finished eating and drinking, he sent them away, and they returned to their master. So the bands from Aram stopped raiding Israel's territory.

Before Elisha died, he ordered that Jehu be anointed king of Israel. This same Jehu, filled with holy zeal, marched a regiment to the home of Jezebel in the town of Jezreel. Fearlessly Jehu confronted her, calling for her servants to throw her from the window. So the "cursed woman" died that day, and later, all of Ahab's offspring were killed. These events happened in fulfillment of Elijah's prophetic judgment years earlier. Then Jehu turned his sword on ministers of the pagan god Baal, for surely the most subtle and pernicious threats lay in the subversion of worship from the true God. The Baal altars had to be destroyed before Israel could be secure.

Many kings came and went in Israel and Judah. Some achieved godly reforms; others made a mess of what they inherited. Jehoahaz, son of Jehu, lost his army but kept the nation together. Around 797 BC, Elisha made one more pronouncement against the Arameans, responding to the pleas of a desperate King Jehoash. Once the king was assured of victory, Elisha died.

Jeroboam II took the reins and secured Israel's borders, but he never guarded Israel's soul. The worship of false gods and idol-making businesses flourished during his regime. During this prosperous period, a prophet arose with a stirring message of justice and judgment.

The words of Amos, one of the shepherds of Tekoa — the vision he saw concerning Israel two years before the earthquake, when Uzziah was king of Judah and Jeroboam son of Jehoash was king of Israel.

He said:

Hear this word, people of Israel, the word the LORD has spoken against you — against the whole family I brought up out of Egypt:

> "You only have I chosen
> of all the families of the earth;
> therefore I will punish you
> for all your sins."

Proclaim to the fortresses of Ashdod
   and to the fortresses of Egypt:
"Assemble yourselves on the mountains of Samaria;
   see the great unrest within her
   and the oppression among her people."

"They do not know how to do right," declares the LORD,
   "who store up in their fortresses
   what they have plundered and looted."

Therefore this is what the Sovereign LORD says:

"An enemy will overrun your land,
   pull down your strongholds
   and plunder your fortresses."

The Sovereign LORD has sworn by his holiness:
   "The time will surely come
when you will be taken away with hooks,
   the last of you with fishhooks.
You will each go straight out
   through breaches in the wall,
   and you will be cast out toward Harmon,"
                              declares the LORD.

"I gave you empty stomachs in every city
   and lack of bread in every town,
   yet you have not returned to me,"
                              declares the LORD.

"I sent plagues among you
   as I did to Egypt.
I killed your young men with the sword,
   along with your captured horses.
I filled your nostrils with the stench of your camps,
   yet you have not returned to me,"
                              declares the LORD.

"Therefore this is what I will do to you, Israel,

and because I will do this to you, Israel,
   prepare to meet your God."

Seek the LORD and live,
   or he will sweep through the tribes of Joseph like a fire;
it will devour them.

Seek good, not evil,
   that you may live.
Then the LORD God Almighty will be with you,
   just as you say he is.
Hate evil, love good;
   maintain justice in the courts.
Perhaps the LORD God Almighty will have mercy
   on the remnant of Joseph.

"Surely the eyes of the Sovereign LORD
   are on the sinful kingdom.
I will destroy it
   from the face of the earth.
Yet I will not totally destroy
   the descendants of Jacob,"

declares the LORD.

Hosea followed as a prophet in Israel. He poured out his heart, pleading with a nation that refused to love a faithful God. Hosea warned the northern kingdom that if they did not repent and turn back to God, they would face serious consequences.

Hear the word of the LORD, you Israelites,
   because the LORD has a charge to bring
      against you who live in the land:
"There is no faithfulness, no love,
   no acknowledgment of God in the land.
There is only cursing,[2] lying and murder,
   stealing and adultery;

---

[2]**Cursing:** That is, to pronounce a curse on.

they break all bounds,
  and bloodshed follows bloodshed.

"Their deeds do not permit them
  to return to their God.
A spirit of prostitution is in their heart;
  they do not acknowledge the LORD.

"They are unfaithful to the LORD;
  they give birth to illegitimate children.
When they celebrate their New Moon feasts,
  he will devour their fields.

"For I will be like a lion to Ephraim,
  like a great lion to Judah.
I will tear them to pieces and go away;
  I will carry them off, with no one to rescue them.
Then I will return to my lair
  until they have borne their guilt
  and seek my face —
in their misery
  they will earnestly seek me."

"Now he will remember their wickedness
  and punish their sins:
  They will return to Egypt.
Israel has forgotten their Maker
  and built palaces;
  Judah has fortified many towns.
But I will send fire on their cities
  that will consume their fortresses."

The days of punishment are coming,
  the days of reckoning are at hand.
  Let Israel know this.
Because your sins are so many
  and your hostility so great,
the prophet is considered a fool,
  the inspired person a maniac.

Return, Israel, to the LORD your God.
Your sins have been your downfall!
Take words with you
and return to the LORD.
Say to him:
"Forgive all our sins
and receive us graciously,
that we may offer the fruit of our lips."

Though the prophets warned the people, the northern king-dom of Israel didn't listen. They hardened their hearts and continued to ignore God's pleas to return to his ways. The kings of Israel led the people into spiritual and social chaos. Between Jeroboam II and Hoshea came a series of five other kings, noted for doing "evil in the eyes of the LORD." All of them came into power and/or had their reigns ended through assassination.

How long would the people turn their back on God?

16

The Beginning of the End
(of the Kingdom of Israel)

IN THE TWELFTH YEAR of Ahaz king of Judah, Hoshea son of Elah became king of Israel in Samaria, and he reigned nine years. He did evil in the eyes of the LORD, but not like the kings of Israel who preceded him.

Shalmaneser king of Assyria came up to attack Hoshea, who had been Shalmaneser's vassal and had paid him tribute. But the king of Assyria discovered that Hoshea was a traitor, for he had sent envoys to So king of Egypt, and he no longer paid tribute to the king of Assyria, as he had done year by year. Therefore Shalmaneser seized him and put him in prison. The king of Assyria invaded the entire land, marched against Samaria and laid siege to it for three years. In the ninth year of Hoshea, the king of Assyria captured Samaria and deported the Israelites to Assyria. He settled them in Halah, in Gozan on the Habor River and in the towns of the Medes.

All this took place because the Israelites had sinned against the LORD their God, who had brought them up out of Egypt from under the power of Pharaoh king of Egypt. They worshiped other gods.

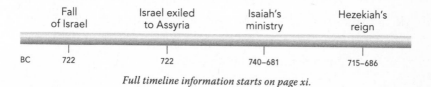

Fall of Israel	Israel exiled to Assyria	Isaiah's ministry	Hezekiah's reign
722	722	740–681	715–686

BC

Full timeline information starts on page xi.

They did wicked things that aroused the LORD's anger. They worshiped idols, though the LORD had said, "You shall not do this." The LORD warned Israel and Judah through all his prophets and seers: "Turn from your evil ways. Observe my commands and decrees, in accordance with the entire Law that I commanded your ancestors to obey and that I delivered to you through my servants the prophets."

But they would not listen and were as stiff-necked as their ancestors, who did not trust in the LORD their God.

So the people of Israel were taken from their homeland into exile in Assyria, and they are still there.

The LORD was very angry with Israel and removed them from his presence. Only the tribe of Judah was left.

Take no prisoners. Terrorize the conquered. Such were the common practices of ancient empires. To ensure against organized rebellion, Sargon II of Assyria deported more than 27,000 people from the northern kingdom of Israel to distant cities after Israel's defenses broke down. Any semblance of a nation—a people with a common cause and heritage—was gone.

In the southern kingdom of Judah, young King Hezekiah watched these developments take place. How do you run a tiny nation when the greatest army in the world is camped on your northern border?

In the third year of Hoshea son of Elah king of Israel, Hezekiah son of Ahaz king of Judah began to reign. He was twenty-five years old when he became king, and he reigned in Jerusalem twenty-nine years. His mother's name was Abijah daughter of Zechariah. He did what was right in the eyes of the LORD, just as his father David had done. He removed the high places, smashed the sacred stones and cut down the Asherah poles.

And the LORD was with him; he was successful in whatever he undertook. He rebelled against the king of Assyria and did not serve him.

The king of Assyria sent his supreme commander, his chief officer and his field commander with a large army, from Lachish to King Hezekiah at Jerusalem. They came up to Jerusalem and stopped at the aqueduct of the Upper Pool, on the road to the Washerman's Field. They called for the king; and Eliakim son of Hilkiah the palace administrator, Shebna the secretary, and Joah son of Asaph the recorder went out to them.

The field commander said to them, "Tell Hezekiah:

"'This is what the great king, the king of Assyria, says: On what are you basing this confidence of yours? You say you have the counsel and the might for war—but you speak only empty words. On whom are you depending, that you rebel against me? Look, I know you are depending on Egypt, that splintered reed of a staff, which pierces the hand of anyone who leans on it! Such is Pharaoh king of Egypt to all who depend on him. But if you say to me, "We are depending on the LORD our God"—isn't he the one whose high places and altars Hezekiah removed, saying to Judah and Jerusalem, "You must worship before this altar in Jerusalem"?

"'Come now, make a bargain with my master, the king of Assyria: I will give you two thousand horses—if you can put riders on them! How can you repulse one officer of the least of my master's officials, even though you are depending on Egypt for chariots and horsemen? Furthermore, have I come to attack and destroy this place without word from the LORD? The LORD himself told me to march against this country and destroy it.'"

Then the commander stood and called out in Hebrew, "Hear the word of the great king, the king of Assyria! This is what the king says: Do not let Hezekiah deceive you. He cannot deliver you from my hand. Do not let Hezekiah persuade you to trust in the LORD when he says, 'The LORD will surely deliver us; this city will not be given into the hand of the king of Assyria.'

"Do not listen to Hezekiah. This is what the king of Assyria says: Make peace with me and come out to me. Then each of you will eat fruit from your own vine and fig tree and drink water from your own cistern, until I come and take you to a land like your own — a land of grain and new wine, a land of bread and vineyards, a land of olive trees and honey. Choose life and not death!

"Do not listen to Hezekiah, for he is misleading you when he says, 'The LORD will deliver us.' Has the god of any nation ever delivered his land from the hand of the king of Assyria?"

Sennacherib, king of Assyria, sent his field commander to intimidate Hezekiah, a king faithful to God. Clearly outnumbered and facing a brutal defeat, Hezekiah appealed to the prophet Isaiah. "Please pray for God's help," the king entreated, tearing his clothes and wearing sackcloth in utter desperation. Isaiah, speaking for God, assured Hezekiah that God would dispose of Sennacherib and his army. With all escape routes cut off, Hezekiah's humble prayer brought dramatic results.

Now Sennacherib received a report that Tirhakah, the king of Cush, was marching out to fight against him. So he again sent messengers to Hezekiah with this word: "Say to Hezekiah king of Judah: Do not let the god you depend on deceive you when he says, 'Jerusalem will not be given into the hands of the king of Assyria.' Surely you have heard what the kings of Assyria have done to all the countries, destroying them completely. And will you be delivered? Did the gods of the nations that were destroyed by my predecessors deliver them — the gods of Gozan, Harran, Rezeph and the people of Eden who were in Tel Assar? Where is the king of Hamath or the king of Arpad? Where are the kings of Lair, Sepharvaim, Hena and Ivvah?"

Hezekiah received the letter from the messengers and read it. Then he went up to the temple of the LORD and spread it out before the LORD. And Hezekiah prayed to the LORD: "LORD, the God of Israel, enthroned between the cherubim, you alone are God over all the kingdoms of the earth. You have made heaven and earth. Give ear, LORD, and hear; open your eyes, LORD, and see; listen to the words Sennacherib has sent to ridicule the living God.

"It is true, LORD, that the Assyrian kings have laid waste these nations and their lands. They have thrown their gods into the fire and destroyed them, for they were not gods but only wood and stone, fashioned by human hands. Now, LORD our God, deliver us from his hand, so that all the kingdoms of the earth may know that you alone, LORD, are God."

Then Isaiah son of Amoz sent a message to Hezekiah: "This is what the LORD, the God of Israel, says: I have heard your prayer concerning Sennacherib king of Assyria. This is the word that the LORD has spoken against him:

"'Who is it you have ridiculed and blasphemed?[1]
　　Against whom have you raised your voice
　and lifted your eyes in pride?
　　Against the Holy One of Israel!
　By your messengers
　　you have ridiculed the Lord.

"'But I know where you are
　　and when you come and go
　　and how you rage against me.
　Because you rage against me
　　and because your insolence has reached my ears,
　I will put my hook in your nose
　　and my bit in your mouth,
　and I will make you return
　　by the way you came.'

"Therefore this is what the LORD says concerning the king of Assyria:

---

[1]**Blasphemed:** Uttered words or actions intended to insult or devalue God.

> " 'He will not enter this city
> or shoot an arrow here.
> He will not come before it with shield
> or build a siege ramp against it.
> By the way that he came he will return;
> he will not enter this city,
>
> declares the LORD.
>
> I will defend this city and save it,
> for my sake and for the sake of David my servant.' "

That night the angel of the LORD went out and put to death a hundred and eighty-five thousand in the Assyrian camp. When the people got up the next morning — there were all the dead bodies! So Sennacherib king of Assyria broke camp and withdrew. He returned to Nineveh and stayed there.

One day, while he was worshiping in the temple of his god Nisrok, his sons Adrammelek and Sharezer killed him with the sword, and they escaped to the land of Ararat. And Esarhaddon his son succeeded him as king.

The greatest of the writing prophets, Isaiah, began his work in Jerusalem (capital of Judah, the southern kingdom) in 740 BC, shortly before King Uzziah died. Isaiah achieved prominence during Hezekiah's reign, helping the king to stand-down the Assyrian threat by relying on God alone. Such a strategy must be founded on rock solid faith, and this kind of faith Isaiah clearly practiced and developed. His call to service came in a powerful vision — an apt start to a prophetic vocation that would span nearly 60 years.

In the year that King Uzziah died, I saw the Lord, high and exalted, seated on a throne; and the train of his robe filled the temple. Above him were seraphim,[2] each with six wings: With two wings they covered their faces, with two they covered their

---

[2]**Seraphim:** Angelic beings occupied constantly in the praise and worship of God.

feet, and with two they were flying. And they were calling to one another:

> "Holy, holy, holy is the LORD Almighty;
>   the whole earth is full of his glory."

At the sound of their voices the doorposts and thresholds shook and the temple was filled with smoke.

"Woe to me!" I cried. "I am ruined! For I am a man of unclean lips, and I live among a people of unclean lips, and my eyes have seen the King, the LORD Almighty."

Then one of the seraphim flew to me with a live coal in his hand, which he had taken with tongs from the altar. With it he touched my mouth and said, "See, this has touched your lips; your guilt is taken away and your sin atoned for."

Then I heard the voice of the Lord saying, "Whom shall I send? And who will go for us?"

And I said, "Here am I. Send me!"

False prophets acted as public relations consultants, measuring their message against audience expectations. But true prophets like Isaiah simply spoke the word of God without bowing to political pressure. This truly literary prophet was no mere stylist. Isaiah's message contained some bad news: Jerusalem would fall. Once announced, that event was sure to happen.

> See now, the Lord,
>   the LORD Almighty,
> is about to take from Jerusalem and Judah
>   both supply and support:
> all supplies of food and all supplies of water,
>   the hero and the warrior,
> the judge and the prophet,
>   the diviner and the elder,
> the captain of fifty and the man of rank,
>   the counselor, skilled craftsman and clever enchanter.

Jerusalem staggers,
    Judah is falling;
their words and deeds are against the LORD,
    defying his glorious presence.
The look on their faces testifies against them;
    they parade their sin like Sodom;
    they do not hide it.
Woe to them!
    They have brought disaster upon themselves.

My people, your guides lead you astray;
    they turn you from the path.

The LORD takes his place in court;
    he rises to judge the people.

Listen, a noise on the mountains,
    like that of a great multitude!
Listen, an uproar among the kingdoms,
    like nations massing together!
The LORD Almighty is mustering
    an army for war.
They come from faraway lands,
    from the ends of the heavens —
the LORD and the weapons of his wrath —
    to destroy the whole country.

The people turned away from God and faced the consequences of exile and oppression. But the story was far from over. God had not forgotten them, and he longed to lavish compassion and grace on them yet again. Isaiah's prophecies also foretold that after God's judgment, the Israelites would return home from Babylon and rebuild their nation, clearly revealing that the Lord God was in control of world events.

The LORD will have compassion on Jacob;
    once again he will choose Israel
    and will settle them in their own land.

Foreigners will join them
    and unite with the descendants of Jacob.
Nations will take them
    and bring them to their own place.
And Israel will take possession of the nations
    and make them male and female servants in the
        LORD's land.
They will make captives of their captors
    and rule over their oppressors.

On the day the LORD gives you relief from your suffering and turmoil and from the harsh labor forced on you, you will take up this taunt against the king of Babylon:

How the oppressor has come to an end!
    How his fury has ended!
The LORD has broken the rod of the wicked,
    the scepter of the rulers.

This is what the LORD says:

"In the time of my favor I will answer you,
    and in the day of salvation I will help you;
I will keep you and will make you
    to be a covenant for the people,
to restore the land
    and to reassign its desolate inheritances,
to say to the captives, 'Come out,'
    and to those in darkness, 'Be free!'"

Shout for joy, you heavens;
    rejoice, you earth;
    burst into song, you mountains!
For the LORD comforts his people
    and will have compassion on his afflicted ones.

But Zion said, "The LORD has forsaken me,
    the Lord has forgotten me."

"Can a mother forget the baby at her breast
    and have no compassion on the child she has borne?
Though she may forget,
    I will not forget you!
See, I have engraved you on the palms of my hands;
    your walls are ever before me.
Your children hasten back,
    and those who laid you waste depart from you.
Lift up your eyes and look around;
    all your children gather and come to you.
As surely as I live," declares the LORD,
    "you will wear them all as ornaments;
    you will put them on, like a bride.

"Then you will know that I am the LORD;
    those who hope in me will not be disappointed.

"Then all mankind will know
    that I, the LORD, am your Savior,
    your Redeemer, the Mighty One of Jacob."

The promised future return of the kingdom of Judah was to be a precursor of something much more glorious that was still to come—God's greater plan for giving his people endless freedom and glory. Isaiah's prophecies ended with promises of a suffering Servant, the Messiah, who would usher in a glorious kingdom without end.

Who has believed our message
    and to whom has the arm of the LORD been revealed?
He grew up before him like a tender shoot,
    and like a root out of dry ground.
He had no beauty or majesty to attract us to him,
    nothing in his appearance that we should desire him.
He was despised and rejected by mankind,
    a man of suffering, and familiar with pain.
Like one from whom people hide their faces
    he was despised, and we held him in low esteem.

Surely he took up our pain
    and bore our suffering,
yet we considered him punished by God,
    stricken by him, and afflicted.
But he was pierced for our transgressions,
    he was crushed for our iniquities;
the punishment that brought us peace was on him,
    and by his wounds we are healed.
We all, like sheep, have gone astray,
    each of us has turned to our own way;
and the LORD has laid on him
    the iniquity of us all.

He was oppressed and afflicted,
    yet he did not open his mouth;
he was led like a lamb to the slaughter,
    and as a sheep before its shearers is silent,
    so he did not open his mouth.
By oppression and judgment he was taken away.
    Yet who of his generation protested?
For he was cut off from the land of the living;
    for the transgression of my people he was punished.
He was assigned a grave with the wicked,
    and with the rich in his death,
though he had done no violence,
    nor was any deceit in his mouth.

Yet it was the LORD's will to crush him and cause him
       to suffer,
    and though the LORD makes his life an offering for sin,
he will see his offspring and prolong his days,
    and the will of the LORD will prosper in his hand.
After he has suffered,
    he will see the light of life and be satisfied;
by his knowledge my righteous servant will justify many,
    and he will bear their iniquities.
Therefore I will give him a portion among the great,

and he will divide the spoils with the strong,
because he poured out his life unto death,
and was numbered with the transgressors.
For he bore the sin of many,
and made intercession for the transgressors.

In the meantime, faithful King Hezekiah died and was buried. Unfortunately, his son, Manasseh, did not follow the faithful example set by his father. Manasseh's reign actively supported detestable religious practices and brutal oppression. The righteous[3] people in the land must have recalled fond memories of the good old days of Hezekiah, while enduring Manasseh's betrayals and compromise.

---

[3]**Righteous:** A righteous person is one who values God above everyone and everything. A righteous person lives a life of obedience to God.

17

The Kingdoms' Fall

MANASSEH WAS TWELVE YEARS OLD when he became king, and he reigned in Jerusalem fifty-five years. His mother's name was Hephzibah.

He did evil in the eyes of the LORD, following the detestable practices of the nations the LORD had driven out before the Israelites. He rebuilt the high places his father Hezekiah had destroyed; he also erected altars to Baal and made an Asherah pole, as Ahab king of Israel had done. He bowed down to all the starry hosts and worshiped them. He built altars in the temple of the LORD, of which the LORD had said, "In Jerusalem I will put my Name." In the two courts of the temple of the LORD, he built altars to all the starry hosts. He sacrificed his own son in the fire, practiced divination, sought omens, and consulted mediums and spiritists. He did much evil in the eyes of the LORD, arousing his anger.

He took the carved Asherah pole he had made and put it in the temple, of which the LORD had said to David and to his son

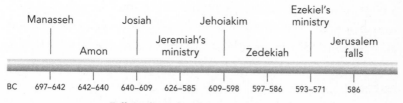

Full timeline information starts on page xi.

Solomon, "In this temple and in Jerusalem, which I have chosen out of all the tribes of Israel, I will put my Name forever. I will not again make the feet of the Israelites wander from the land I gave their ancestors, if only they will be careful to do everything I commanded them and will keep the whole Law that my servant Moses gave them." But the people did not listen. Manasseh led them astray, so that they did more evil than the nations the LORD had destroyed before the Israelites.

The LORD said through his servants the prophets: "Manasseh king of Judah has committed these detestable sins. He has done more evil than the Amorites who preceded him and has led Judah into sin with his idols. Therefore this is what the LORD, the God of Israel, says: I am going to bring such disaster on Jerusalem and Judah that the ears of everyone who hears of it will tingle. I will stretch out over Jerusalem the measuring line used against Samaria and the plumb line used against the house of Ahab. I will wipe out Jerusalem as one wipes a dish, wiping it and turning it upside down. I will forsake the remnant of my inheritance and give them into the hands of enemies. They will be looted and plundered by all their enemies; they have done evil in my eyes and have aroused my anger from the day their ancestors came out of Egypt until this day."

Moreover, Manasseh also shed so much innocent blood that he filled Jerusalem from end to end—besides the sin that he had caused Judah to commit, so that they did evil in the eyes of the LORD.

The LORD spoke to Manasseh and his people, but they paid no attention. So the LORD brought against them the army commanders of the king of Assyria, who took Manasseh prisoner, put a hook in his nose, bound him with bronze shackles and took him to Babylon. In his distress he sought the favor of the LORD his God and humbled himself greatly before the God of his ancestors. And when he prayed to him, the LORD was moved by his entreaty and listened to his plea; so he brought him back to Jerusalem and to his kingdom. Then Manasseh knew that the LORD is God.

Any feelings of new hope and promise aroused by Manasseh's repentance were suppressed when his son Amon became king following Manasseh's death.

Amon was twenty-two years old when he became king, and he reigned in Jerusalem two years. He did evil in the eyes of the LORD, as his father Manasseh had done. Amon worshiped and offered sacrifices to all the idols Manasseh had made. But unlike his father Manasseh, he did not humble himself before the LORD; Amon increased his guilt.

Amon's officials conspired against him and assassinated him in his palace. Then the people of the land killed all who had plotted against King Amon, and they made Josiah his son king in his place.

Amon's son Josiah was only eight years old when he began to reign. Josiah reigned with success, even distinction, for 31 years of spiritual renewal and reform. During his reign the ancient Book of the Law of Moses was discovered after Josiah had ordered the run-down temple to be repaired, and Josiah followed its prescriptions zealously. He put his heart and soul into rediscovering for all the people God's way of living. But as a result of a fateful political decision he died in battle against Pharaoh Necho of Egypt in 609 BC.

The old pattern of father-not-like-son continued, and Josiah's son Jehoahaz was pathetic as king, lasting only three months. Next came Jehoiakim, who was no better.

Jehoiakim was twenty-five years old when he became king, and he reigned in Jerusalem eleven years.

And he did evil in the eyes of the LORD, just as his predecessors had done. During Jehoiakim's reign, Nebuchadnezzar king of Babylon invaded the land, and Jehoiakim became his vassal for three years. But then he turned against Nebuchadnezzar and rebelled. The LORD sent Babylonian, Aramean, Moabite and Ammonite raiders against him to destroy Judah, in accordance with the word of the LORD proclaimed by his servants the prophets.

Jehoiakim rested with his ancestors. And Jehoiachin his son succeeded him as king.

Jehoiachin was eighteen years old when he became king, and he reigned in Jerusalem three months. His mother's name was Nehushta daughter of Elnathan; she was from Jerusalem. He did evil in the eyes of the LORD, just as his father had done.

At that time the officers of Nebuchadnezzar king of Babylon advanced on Jerusalem and laid siege to it, and Nebuchadnezzar himself came up to the city while his officers were besieging it. Jehoiachin king of Judah, his mother, his attendants, his nobles and his officials all surrendered to him.

In the eighth year of the reign of the king of Babylon, he took Jehoiachin prisoner. As the LORD had declared, Nebuchadnezzar removed the treasures from the temple of the LORD and from the royal palace, and cut up the gold articles that Solomon king of Israel had made for the temple of the LORD. He carried all Jerusalem into exile: all the officers and fighting men, and all the skilled workers and artisans—a total of ten thousand. Only the poorest people of the land were left.

Nebuchadnezzar took Jehoiachin captive to Babylon. He also took from Jerusalem to Babylon the king's mother, his wives, his officials and the prominent people of the land. The king of Babylon also deported to Babylon the entire force of seven thousand fighting men, strong and fit for war, and a thousand skilled workers and artisans. He made Mattaniah, Jehoiachin's uncle, king in his place and changed his name to Zedekiah.

God allowed the powerful King Nebuchadnezzar to begin crushing Jerusalem, Judah's last stronghold of promise and hope. Under Nebuchadnezzar's order, a second, larger group of Israelites was deported to Babylon in 597 BC. Among them was a young priest named Ezekiel, a man of keen intellect, immense literary giftedness and spiritual insight.

Ezekiel relayed to his fellow exiles the stern message of God's judgment. Jerusalem was still standing, but it was the beginning of the end. In a vision, Ezekiel received his marching orders and his prophetic message: unbelief leads to doom.

In my thirtieth year, in the fourth month on the fifth day, while I was among the exiles by the Kebar River, the heavens were opened and I saw visions of God.

I looked, and I saw a windstorm coming out of the north — an immense cloud with flashing lightning and surrounded by brilliant light. The center of the fire looked like glowing metal, and in the fire was what looked like four living creatures. In appearance their form was human, but each of them had four faces and four wings.

Spread out above the heads of the living creatures was what looked something like a vault, sparkling like crystal, and awesome. Under the vault their wings were stretched out one toward the other, and each had two wings covering its body. When the creatures moved, I heard the sound of their wings, like the roar of rushing waters, like the voice of the Almighty, like the tumult of an army. When they stood still, they lowered their wings.

Then there came a voice from above the vault over their heads as they stood with lowered wings. Above the vault over their heads was what looked like a throne of lapis lazuli, and high above on the throne was a figure like that of a man. I saw that from what appeared to be his waist up he looked like glowing metal, as if full of fire, and that from there down he looked like fire; and brilliant light surrounded him. Like the appearance of a rainbow in the clouds on a rainy day, so was the radiance around him.

This was the appearance of the likeness of the glory of the LORD. When I saw it, I fell facedown, and I heard the voice of one speaking.

He said to me, "Son of man, stand up on your feet and I will speak to you." As he spoke, the Spirit came into me and raised me to my feet, and I heard him speaking to me.

He said: "Son of man, I am sending you to the Israelites, to a rebellious nation that has rebelled against me; they and their ancestors have been in revolt against me to this very day. The people to whom I am sending you are obstinate and stubborn. Say to them, 'This is what the Sovereign LORD says.'

"And you, son of man, do not be afraid of them or their words. Do not be afraid, though briers and thorns are all around you and you live among scorpions. Do not be afraid of what they say or be terrified by them, though they are a rebellious people. You must speak my words to them, whether they listen or fail to listen, for they are rebellious."

The word of the LORD came to me: "Son of man, set your face against the mountains of Israel; prophesy against them and say: 'You mountains of Israel, hear the word of the Sovereign LORD. This is what the Sovereign LORD says to the mountains and hills, to the ravines and valleys: I am about to bring a sword against you, and I will destroy your high places. Your altars will be demolished and your incense altars will be smashed; and I will slay your people in front of your idols. I will lay the dead bodies of the Israelites in front of their idols, and I will scatter your bones around your altars. Wherever you live, the towns will be laid waste and the high places demolished, so that your altars will be laid waste and devastated, your idols smashed and ruined, your incense altars broken down, and what you have made wiped out. Your people will fall slain among you, and you will know that I am the LORD.

"'But I will spare some, for some of you will escape the sword when you are scattered among the lands and nations. Then in the nations where they have been carried captive, those who escape will remember me—how I have been grieved by their adulterous hearts, which have turned away from me, and by their eyes, which have lusted after their idols. They will loathe themselves for the evil they have done and for all their detestable practices. And they will know that I am the LORD; I did not threaten in vain to bring this calamity on them.'

"This is what the Sovereign LORD says:

> "'Disaster! Unheard-of disaster!
>   See, it comes!

> "'Doom has come upon you,
>   upon you who dwell in the land.
> The time has come! The day is near!
>   There is panic, not joy, on the mountains.
> I am about to pour out my wrath on you
>   and spend my anger against you.
> I will judge you according to your conduct
>   and repay you for all your detestable practices.'"

Back on the home front, things were going from bad to worse in Jerusalem. But God continued to pursue and warn his people. Another prophet, named Jeremiah, was called into service in a very interesting conversation with God.

The word of the LORD came to me, saying,

> "Before I formed you in the womb I knew you,
>   before you were born I set you apart;
>   I appointed you as a prophet to the nations."

"Alas, Sovereign LORD," I said, "I do not know how to speak; I am too young."

But the LORD said to me, "Do not say, 'I am too young.' You must go to everyone I send you to and say whatever I command you. Do not be afraid of them, for I am with you and will rescue you," declares the LORD.

Then the LORD reached out his hand and touched my mouth

and said to me, "I have put my words in your mouth. See, today I appoint you over nations and kingdoms to uproot and tear down, to destroy and overthrow, to build and to plant.

"Today I have made you a fortified city, an iron pillar and a bronze wall to stand against the whole land — against the kings of Judah, its officials, its priests and the people of the land. They will fight against you but will not overcome you, for I am with you and will rescue you," declares the LORD.

Knowing God was with him, Jeremiah shed his fears. Known as the "weeping prophet," Jeremiah felt deeply the burden of the people's sin and the coming judgment. It didn't help that his message was unwelcome and unwanted. He told of the coming destruction of Jerusalem, God's judgment for the people's sins of idolatry and pride.

But another truth Jeremiah also knew and told: God's mercy will never fail, though reprieve from punishment may seem distant. For all the crumbled buildings, lives lost in hapless battles and lives squandered pursuing pagan pleasure, still God's mercies endure — tender mercies that will be lavished on a nation that had forsaken him. With the God of majestic love, nothing is impossible.

Hear the word of the LORD, you descendants of Jacob,
    all you clans of Israel.

"Has a nation ever changed its gods?
    (Yet they are not gods at all.)
But my people have exchanged their glorious God
    for worthless idols.
Be appalled at this, you heavens,
    and shudder with great horror,"
                    declares the LORD.
"My people have committed two sins:
They have forsaken me,
    the spring of living water,

and have dug their own cisterns,
    broken cisterns that cannot hold water.

"Long ago you broke off your yoke
    and tore off your bonds;
    you said, 'I will not serve you!'

"I had planted you like a choice vine
    of sound and reliable stock.
How then did you turn against me
    into a corrupt, wild vine?
Although you wash yourself with soap
    and use an abundance of cleansing powder,
    the stain of your guilt is still before me,"
                    declares the Sovereign LORD.

"As a thief is disgraced when he is caught,
    so the people of Israel are disgraced —
they, their kings and their officials,
    their priests and their prophets.
They say to wood, 'You are my father,'
    and to stone, 'You gave me birth.'
They have turned their backs to me
    and not their faces;
yet when they are in trouble, they say,
    'Come and save us!'
Where then are the gods you made for yourselves?
    Let them come if they can save you
    when you are in trouble!
For you, Judah, have as many gods
    as you have towns.

"Announce in Judah and proclaim in Jerusalem and say:
    'Sound the trumpet throughout the land!'
Cry aloud and say:
    'Gather together!
    Let us flee to the fortified cities!'
Raise the signal to go to Zion!

Flee for safety without delay!
For I am bringing disaster from the north,
    even terrible destruction."

A lion has come out of his lair;
    a destroyer of nations has set out.
He has left his place
    to lay waste your land.
Your towns will lie in ruins
    without inhabitant.
So put on sackcloth,
    lament and wail,
for the fierce anger of the LORD
    has not turned away from us.

"Go up and down the streets of Jerusalem,
    look around and consider,
    search through her squares.
If you can find but one person
    who deals honestly and seeks the truth,
    I will forgive this city."

If you do not listen,
    I will weep in secret
    because of your pride;
my eyes will weep bitterly,
    overflowing with tears,
    because the LORD's flock will be taken captive.

Say to the king and to the queen mother,
    "Come down from your thrones,
for your glorious crowns
    will fall from your heads."
The cities in the Negev will be shut up,
    and there will be no one to open them.
All Judah will be carried into exile,
    carried completely away.

The words of Jeremiah were clear, but the kings who followed Josiah refused to listen. They grew increasingly brash, ignoring the prophet's warnings and wisdom. Their tactics of duplicity and greed were destined to fail. Finally, Judah's kings had to face Babylon's full military muscle, rock hard and set to kill.

The LORD, the God of their ancestors, sent word to them through his messengers again and again, because he had pity on his people and on his dwelling place. But they mocked God's messengers, despised his words and scoffed at his prophets until the wrath of the LORD was aroused against his people and there was no remedy.

Zedekiah was twenty-one years old when he became king, and he reigned in Jerusalem eleven years. He did evil in the eyes of the LORD his God and did not humble himself before Jeremiah the prophet, who spoke the word of the LORD. He also rebelled against King Nebuchadnezzar, who had made him take an oath in God's name. He became stiff-necked and hardened his heart and would not turn to the LORD, the God of Israel. Furthermore, all the leaders of the priests and the people became more and more unfaithful, following all the detestable practices of the nations and defiling the temple of the LORD, which he had consecrated in Jerusalem.

So in the ninth year of Zedekiah's reign, on the tenth day of the tenth month, Nebuchadnezzar king of Babylon marched against Jerusalem with his whole army. He encamped outside the city and built siege works all around it. The city was kept under siege until the eleventh year of King Zedekiah.

By the ninth day of the fourth month the famine in the city had become so severe that there was no food for the people to eat.

On the surface, it appeared that God had abandoned his people. Where was his mercy now? Zedekiah and his associates

wanted Jeremiah to step in and ask God for help. Instead, Jer-
emiah foretold defeat and death as the consequence of the
people's continued sin.

The word came to Jeremiah from the LORD when King
Zedekiah sent to him Pashhur son of Malkijah and the priest
Zephaniah son of Maaseiah. They said: "Inquire now of the LORD
for us because Nebuchadnezzar king of Babylon is attacking us.
Perhaps the LORD will perform wonders for us as in times past so
that he will withdraw from us."

But Jeremiah answered them, "Tell Zedekiah, 'This is what the
LORD, the God of Israel, says: I am about to turn against you the
weapons of war that are in your hands, which you are using to
fight the king of Babylon and the Babylonians who are outside the
wall besieging you. And I will gather them inside this city. I myself
will fight against you with an outstretched hand and a mighty
arm in furious anger and in great wrath. I will strike down those
who live in this city — both man and beast — and they will die of a
terrible plague. After that, declares the LORD, I will give Zedekiah
king of Judah, his officials and the people in this city who survive
the plague, sword and famine, into the hands of Nebuchadnezzar
king of Babylon and to their enemies who want to kill them. He
will put them to the sword; he will show them no mercy or pity or
compassion.'

"Furthermore, tell the people, 'This is what the LORD says:
See, I am setting before you the way of life and the way of death.
Whoever stays in this city will die by the sword, famine or plague.
But whoever goes out and surrenders to the Babylonians who are
besieging you will live; they will escape with their lives. I have
determined to do this city harm and not good, declares the LORD.
It will be given into the hands of the king of Babylon, and he will
destroy it with fire.'"

Then the city wall was broken through, and the whole army
fled at night through the gate between the two walls near the

king's garden, though the Babylonians were surrounding the city. They fled toward the Arabah, but the Babylonian army pursued the king and overtook him in the plains of Jericho. All his soldiers were separated from him and scattered, and he was captured.

He was taken to the king of Babylon at Riblah, where sentence was pronounced on him. They killed the sons of Zedekiah before his eyes. Then they put out his eyes, bound him with bronze shackles and took him to Babylon.

On the seventh day of the fifth month, in the nineteenth year of Nebuchadnezzar king of Babylon, Nebuzaradan commander of the imperial guard, an official of the king of Babylon, came to Jerusalem. He set fire to the temple of the LORD, the royal palace and all the houses of Jerusalem. Every important building he burned down. The whole Babylonian army under the commander of the imperial guard broke down the walls around Jerusalem. Nebuzaradan the commander of the guard carried into exile the people who remained in the city, along with the rest of the populace and those who had deserted to the king of Babylon. But the commander left behind some of the poorest people of the land to work the vineyards and fields.

So Judah went into captivity, away from her land.

Jerusalem had fallen. But the prophet Jeremiah was not deported. Rather, Nebuchadnezzar advised him to reside with the region's new governor, Gedaliah. Shortly thereafter, Gedaliah was assassinated. Many of the Jews still in Judah, afraid of Babylon's reprisal, fled to Egypt and forced Jeremiah to go with them. (Jewish tradition says Jeremiah was stoned to death while living in Egypt.) But Jeremiah's heart was always in the holy city of his homeland—once busy with trade and prayer, now empty and still. Jeremiah wept bitterly for his people.

> How deserted lies the city,
> once so full of people!

How like a widow is she,
　who once was great among the nations!
She who was queen among the provinces
　has now become a slave.

Bitterly she weeps at night,
　tears are on her cheeks.
Among all her lovers
　there is no one to comfort her.
All her friends have betrayed her;
　they have become her enemies.

After affliction and harsh labor,
　Judah has gone into exile.
She dwells among the nations;
　she finds no resting place.
All who pursue her have overtaken her
　in the midst of her distress.

The LORD has done what he planned;
　he has fulfilled his word,
　which he decreed long ago.
He has overthrown you without pity,
　he has let the enemy gloat over you,
　he has exalted the horn of your foes.

Yet this I call to mind
　and therefore I have hope:

Because of the LORD's great love we are not consumed,
　for his compassions never fail.
They are new every morning;
　great is your faithfulness.
I say to myself, "The LORD is my portion;
　therefore I will wait for him."

The LORD is good to those whose hope is in him,
　to the one who seeks him;

it is good to wait quietly
   for the salvation of the LORD.

Remember, LORD, what has happened to us;
   look, and see our disgrace.

Joy is gone from our hearts;
   our dancing has turned to mourning.
The crown has fallen from our head.
   Woe to us, for we have sinned!

You, LORD, reign forever;
   your throne endures from generation to generation.
Why do you always forget us?
   Why do you forsake us so long?
Restore us to yourself, LORD, that we may return;
   renew our days as of old.

Though Jeremiah was faced with sorrow and tragedy, he trusted in God's mercies—as did Ezekiel. Before Jerusalem fell to the Babylonians, the prophet Ezekiel warned the people of the destruction that was to come. And yet once Ezekiel and his fellow exiles in Babylon received the news that Jerusalem had fallen, his message turned to hope. Although the people had turned their backs on God, they would again receive an abundance of undeserved grace and mercy.

"Therefore say to the Israelites, 'This is what the Sovereign LORD says: It is not for your sake, people of Israel, that I am going to do these things, but for the sake of my holy name, which you have profaned among the nations where you have gone. I will show the holiness of my great name, which has been profaned among the nations, the name you have profaned among them. Then the nations will know that I am the LORD, declares the Sovereign LORD, when I am proved holy through you before their eyes.

"'For I will take you out of the nations; I will gather you from all the countries and bring you back into your own land. I will sprinkle clean water on you, and you will be clean; I will cleanse you from all your impurities and from all your idols. I will give you a new heart and put a new spirit in you; I will remove from you your heart of stone and give you a heart of flesh. And I will put my Spirit in you and move you to follow my decrees and be careful to keep my laws. Then you will live in the land I gave your ancestors; you will be my people, and I will be your God.

" 'This is what the Sovereign LORD says: On the day I cleanse you from all your sins, I will resettle your towns, and the ruins will be rebuilt. The desolate land will be cultivated instead of lying desolate in the sight of all who pass through it. They will say, "This land that was laid waste has become like the garden of Eden; the cities that were lying in ruins, desolate and destroyed, are now fortified and inhabited." Then the nations around you that remain will know that I the LORD have rebuilt what was destroyed and have replanted what was desolate. I the LORD have spoken, and I will do it.' "

The hand of the LORD was on me, and he brought me out by the Spirit of the LORD and set me in the middle of a valley; it was full of bones. He led me back and forth among them, and I saw a great many bones on the floor of the valley, bones that were very dry. He asked me, "Son of man, can these bones live?"

I said, "Sovereign LORD, you alone know."

Then he said to me, "Prophesy to these bones and say to them, 'Dry bones, hear the word of the LORD! This is what the Sovereign LORD says to these bones: I will make breath enter you, and you will come to life. I will attach tendons to you and make flesh come upon you and cover you with skin; I will put breath in you, and you will come to life. Then you will know that I am the LORD.' "

So I prophesied as I was commanded. And as I was prophesying, there was a noise, a rattling sound, and the bones came together, bone to bone. I looked, and tendons and flesh appeared on them and skin covered them, but there was no breath in them.

Then he said to me, "Prophesy to the breath; prophesy, son of man, and say to it, 'This is what the Sovereign Lord says: Come, breath, from the four winds and breathe into these slain, that they may live.'" So I prophesied as he commanded me, and breath entered them; they came to life and stood up on their feet — a vast army.

Then he said to me: "Son of man, these bones are the people of Israel. They say, 'Our bones are dried up and our hope is gone; we are cut off.' Therefore prophesy and say to them: 'This is what the Sovereign Lord says: My people, I am going to open your graves and bring you up from them; I will bring you back to the land of Israel. Then you, my people, will know that I am the Lord, when I open your graves and bring you up from them. I will put my Spirit in you and you will live, and I will settle you in your own land. Then you will know that I the Lord have spoken, and I have done it, declares the Lord.'"

18

Daniel in Exile

Daniel and three other young men were among those taken to Babylon in 605 BC as part of the first deportation of Jews prior to the fall of Jerusalem. These four have become the most well-known quartet of heroes in the Old Testament. They successfully adapted to the losses of home and family and survived the tough training in foreign etiquette. It's not hard to see how they quickly became the king's favorites.

THEN THE KING ORDERED ASHPENAZ, chief of his court officials, to bring into the king's service some of the Israelites from the royal family and the nobility — young men without any physical defect, handsome, showing aptitude for every kind of learning, well informed, quick to understand, and qualified to serve in the king's palace. He was to teach them the language and literature of the Babylonians. The king assigned them a daily amount of food and wine from the king's table. They were to be trained for three years, and after that they were to enter the king's service.

Among those who were chosen were some from Judah: Daniel, Hananiah, Mishael and Azariah. The chief official gave them new

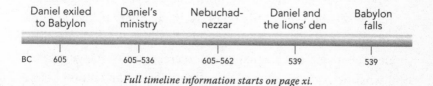

Daniel exiled to Babylon	Daniel's ministry	Nebuchad-nezzar	Daniel and the lions' den	Babylon falls
BC 605	605–536	605–562	539	539

Full timeline information starts on page xi.

names: to Daniel, the name Belteshazzar; to Hananiah, Shadrach; to Mishael, Meshach; and to Azariah, Abednego.

But Daniel resolved not to defile himself with the royal food and wine, and he asked the chief official for permission not to defile himself this way. Now God had caused the official to show favor and compassion to Daniel, but the official told Daniel, "I am afraid of my lord the king, who has assigned your food and drink. Why should he see you looking worse than the other young men your age? The king would then have my head because of you."

Daniel then said to the guard whom the chief official had appointed over Daniel, Hananiah, Mishael and Azariah, "Please test your servants for ten days: Give us nothing but vegetables to eat and water to drink. Then compare our appearance with that of the young men who eat the royal food, and treat your servants in accordance with what you see." So he agreed to this and tested them for ten days.

At the end of the ten days they looked healthier and better nourished than any of the young men who ate the royal food. So the guard took away their choice food and the wine they were to drink and gave them vegetables instead.

To these four young men God gave knowledge and understanding of all kinds of literature and learning. And Daniel could understand visions and dreams of all kinds.

At the end of the time set by the king to bring them into his service, the chief official presented them to Nebuchadnezzar. The king talked with them, and he found none equal to Daniel, Hananiah, Mishael and Azariah; so they entered the king's service. In every matter of wisdom and understanding about which the king questioned them, he found them ten times better than all the magicians and enchanters in his whole kingdom.

And Daniel remained there until the first year of King Cyrus.

In the second year of his reign, Nebuchadnezzar had dreams; his mind was troubled and he could not sleep. So the king summoned the magicians, enchanters, sorcerers and astrologers to tell him what he had dreamed. When they came in and stood before the king, he said to them, "I have had a dream that troubles me and I want to know what it means."

Then the astrologers answered the king, "May the king live forever! Tell your servants the dream, and we will interpret it."

The king replied to the astrologers, "This is what I have firmly decided: If you do not tell me what my dream was and interpret it, I will have you cut into pieces and your houses turned into piles of rubble. But if you tell me the dream and explain it, you will receive from me gifts and rewards and great honor. So tell me the dream and interpret it for me."

Once more they replied, "Let the king tell his servants the dream, and we will interpret it."

Then the king answered, "I am certain that you are trying to gain time, because you realize that this is what I have firmly decided: If you do not tell me the dream, there is only one penalty for you. You have conspired to tell me misleading and wicked things, hoping the situation will change. So then, tell me the dream, and I will know that you can interpret it for me."

The astrologers answered the king, "There is no one on earth who can do what the king asks! No king, however great and mighty, has ever asked such a thing of any magician or enchanter or astrologer. What the king asks is too difficult. No one can reveal it to the king except the gods, and they do not live among humans."

This made the king so angry and furious that he ordered the execution of all the wise men of Babylon. So the decree was issued to put the wise men to death, and men were sent to look for Daniel and his friends to put them to death.

When Arioch, the commander of the king's guard, had gone out to put to death the wise men of Babylon, Daniel spoke to him with wisdom and tact. He asked the king's officer, "Why did the king issue such a harsh decree?" Arioch then explained the matter to Daniel. At this, Daniel went in to the king and asked for time, so that he might interpret the dream for him.

Then Daniel returned to his house and explained the matter to his friends Hananiah, Mishael and Azariah. He urged them to plead for mercy from the God of heaven concerning this mystery, so that he and his friends might not be executed with the rest of the wise men of Babylon. During the night the mystery was revealed to Daniel in a vision. Then Daniel praised the God of heaven and said:

> "Praise be to the name of God for ever and ever;
>> wisdom and power are his.
> He changes times and seasons;
>> he deposes kings and raises up others.
> He gives wisdom to the wise
>> and knowledge to the discerning.
> He reveals deep and hidden things;
>> he knows what lies in darkness,
>> and light dwells with him.
> I thank and praise you, God of my ancestors:
>> You have given me wisdom and power,
> you have made known to me what we asked of you,
>> you have made known to us the dream of the king."

Then Daniel went to Arioch, whom the king had appointed to execute the wise men of Babylon, and said to him, "Do not execute the wise men of Babylon. Take me to the king, and I will interpret his dream for him."

Arioch took Daniel to the king at once and said, "I have found a man among the exiles from Judah who can tell the king what his dream means."

The king asked Daniel (also called Belteshazzar), "Are you able to tell me what I saw in my dream and interpret it?"

Daniel replied, "No wise man, enchanter, magician or diviner can explain to the king the mystery he has asked about, but there is a God in heaven who reveals mysteries. He has shown King Nebuchadnezzar what will happen in days to come. Your dream and the visions that passed through your mind as you were lying in bed are these:

"As Your Majesty was lying there, your mind turned to things to come, and the revealer of mysteries showed you what is going to happen. As for me, this mystery has been revealed to me, not because I have greater wisdom than anyone else alive, but so that Your Majesty may know the interpretation and that you may understand what went through your mind."

First, amazingly Daniel described the king's dream in every detail. His subsequent interpretation of Nebuchadnezzar's dream was a history lesson using the king's magnificent dream statue as a visual aid. The head of the statue was gold. The figure's chest and arms were silver, the belly and thighs bronze, the legs iron and the feet a mix of iron and baked clay. Each part of the statue represented an empire.

The statue's gold head represented Nebuchadnezzar himself and his empire. He was chief among chiefs, leader of the known world, dazzling and incomparable. But not, unfortunately, permanent. Babylon would someday give way to an inferior but momentarily stronger power, the Medo-Persians under Cyrus. They would also fall—to the Greeks led by Alexander the Great. And then the Romans would come. The statue's feet made partly from iron and partly from clay could point to a globalized world of shifting power bases as history spins forward, while some Bible interpreters have found in the ten toes symbolic clues to our own future at the end of history.

For Nebuchadnezzar, though, the message was clear and simple: God directs history, and Babylon's power, prestige and privilege formed only a short chapter in a much longer story. Such news at the height of an empire's influence was bound to create a strong response.

Then King Nebuchadnezzar fell prostrate before Daniel and paid him honor and ordered that an offering and incense be presented to him. The king said to Daniel, "Surely your God is the God of gods and the Lord of kings and a revealer of mysteries, for you were able to reveal this mystery."

Then the king placed Daniel in a high position and lavished

many gifts on him. He made him ruler over the entire province of Babylon and placed him in charge of all its wise men. Moreover, at Daniel's request the king appointed Shadrach, Meshach and Abednego administrators over the province of Babylon, while Daniel himself remained at the royal court.

Daniel was gifted to interpret the meaning of dream images, but neither he nor his three buddies were authorized to bow down before idols. There was one thing they refused to adapt to—foreign worship practices that violated their commitment to God. In that regard they were holdouts, malcontents and law-breakers. Nebuchadnezzar decided to erect a statue some 90 feet tall and 9 feet wide. When the people were ordered to bow low and worship the statue, three men stood tall and refused to comply. The king was not happy ...

King Nebuchadnezzar made an image of gold, sixty cubits high and six cubits wide, and set it up on the plain of Dura in the province of Babylon. He then summoned the satraps, prefects, governors, advisers, treasurers, judges, magistrates and all the other provincial officials to come to the dedication of the image he had set up. So the satraps, prefects, governors, advisers, treasurers, judges, magistrates and all the other provincial officials assembled for the dedication of the image that King Nebuchadnezzar had set up, and they stood before it.

Then the herald loudly proclaimed, "Nations and peoples of every language, this is what you are commanded to do: As soon as you hear the sound of the horn, flute, zither, lyre, harp, pipe and all kinds of music, you must fall down and worship the image of gold that King Nebuchadnezzar has set up. Whoever does not fall down and worship will immediately be thrown into a blazing furnace."

Therefore, as soon as they heard the sound of the horn, flute, zither, lyre, harp and all kinds of music, all the nations and peoples of every language fell down and worshiped the image of gold that King Nebuchadnezzar had set up.

At this time some astrologers came forward and denounced the Jews. They said to King Nebuchadnezzar, "May the king live forever! Your Majesty has issued a decree that everyone who hears the sound of the horn, flute, zither, lyre, harp, pipe and all kinds of music must fall down and worship the image of gold, and that who-ever does not fall down and worship will be thrown into a blazing furnace. But there are some Jews whom you have set over the affairs of the province of Babylon — Shadrach, Meshach and Abednego — who pay no attention to you, Your Majesty. They neither serve your gods nor worship the image of gold you have set up."

Furious with rage, Nebuchadnezzar summoned Shadrach, Meshach and Abednego. So these men were brought before the king, and Nebuchadnezzar said to them, "Is it true, Shadrach, Meshach and Abednego, that you do not serve my gods or worship the image of gold I have set up? Now when you hear the sound of the horn, flute, zither, lyre, harp, pipe and all kinds of music, if you are ready to fall down and worship the image I made, very good. But if you do not worship it, you will be thrown immediately into a blazing furnace. Then what god will be able to rescue you from my hand?"

Shadrach, Meshach and Abednego replied to him, "King Nebu-chadnezzar, we do not need to defend ourselves before you in this matter. If we are thrown into the blazing furnace, the God we serve is able to deliver us from it, and he will deliver us from Your Majesty's hand. But even if he does not, we want you to know, Your Majesty, that we will not serve your gods or worship the image of gold you have set up."

Then Nebuchadnezzar was furious with Shadrach, Meshach and Abednego, and his attitude toward them changed. He ordered the furnace heated seven times hotter than usual and commanded some of the strongest soldiers in his army to tie up Shadrach, Meshach and Abednego and throw them into the blazing fur-nace. So these men, wearing their robes, trousers, turbans and other clothes, were bound and thrown into the blazing furnace. The king's command was so urgent and the furnace so hot that the flames of the fire killed the soldiers who took up Shadrach, Meshach and Abednego, and these three men, firmly tied, fell into the blazing furnace.

Then King Nebuchadnezzar leaped to his feet in amazement and asked his advisers, "Weren't there three men that we tied up and threw into the fire?"

They replied, "Certainly, Your Majesty."

He said, "Look! I see four men walking around in the fire, unbound and unharmed, and the fourth looks like a son of the gods."

Nebuchadnezzar then approached the opening of the blazing furnace and shouted, "Shadrach, Meshach and Abednego, servants of the Most High God, come out! Come here!"

So Shadrach, Meshach and Abednego came out of the fire, and the satraps, prefects, governors and royal advisers crowded around them. They saw that the fire had not harmed their bodies, nor was a hair of their heads singed; their robes were not scorched, and there was no smell of fire on them.

Then Nebuchadnezzar said, "Praise be to the God of Shadrach, Meshach and Abednego, who has sent his angel and rescued his servants! They trusted in him and defied the king's command and were willing to give up their lives rather than serve or worship any god except their own God. Therefore I decree that the people of any nation or language who say anything against the God of Shadrach, Meshach and Abednego be cut into pieces and their houses be turned into piles of rubble, for no other god can save in this way."

Then the king promoted Shadrach, Meshach and Abednego in the province of Babylon.

Pride regularly precedes a fall, but few world leaders fall as far as Nebuchadnezzar and then recover their power. The king had another spectacular dream, this time of a tree. Daniel was called in again and informed Nebuchadnezzar that the great tree represented the king himself. In the dream a loud voice issues a command to cut down the tree, symbolizing that the king would lose everything, becoming so deranged that his behavior will resemble a beast in the wild. One year later, as words of arrogant pride were on his lips, Nebuchadnezzar was struck suddenly with a mental/behavioral disorder that caused the most severe forms of disorientation. He lived in the bush, eating grass and acting like a common animal. Then, miraculously he was healed—which he credited to Daniel's God—and returned to Babylon's palace a whole man.

Fast forward to the new king, Belshazzar, who ignored Daniel and dishonored Daniel's God. Once, at a gala party, Belshazzar poured his best wine into chalices taken from Jerusalem's holy temple, and his guests drank merrily in ridicule. At the height of the fun, suddenly a large and mysterious hand appeared and wrote something on the wall of the banquet chamber: Mene, Mene, Tekel, Parsin.

The king was frightened and called in Daniel to make sense of it. The meaning of the writing on the wall was, "You have been weighed on the scales and found wanting." The king was great now, but soon he and his kingdom would become weak, Daniel warned. That very night, as the party waned, invading Persians rode victoriously through Babylon's gates and killed King Belshazzar.

So Daniel served yet another king and empire with honor and distinction. He became a top administrator under "Darius" —likely either the Babylonian throne name of King Cyrus of Persia or a name given to Cyrus's newly appointed governor over Babylon. But what happens when you mix a new ruler, jealous colleagues and prayer?

It pleased Darius to appoint 120 satraps to rule throughout the kingdom, with three administrators over them, one of whom was Daniel. The satraps were made accountable to them so that the king might not suffer loss. Now Daniel so distinguished himself among the administrators and the satraps by his exceptional qualities that the king planned to set him over the whole kingdom. At this, the administrators and the satraps tried to find grounds for charges against Daniel in his conduct of government affairs, but they were unable to do so. They could find no corruption in him, because he was trustworthy and neither corrupt nor negligent. Finally these men said, "We will never find any basis for charges against this man Daniel unless it has something to do with the law of his God."

So these administrators and satraps went as a group to the king and said: "May King Darius live forever! The royal administrators, prefects, satraps, advisers and governors have all agreed that the king should issue an edict and enforce the decree that anyone who prays to any god or human being during the next thirty days, except to you, Your Majesty, shall be thrown into the lions' den. Now, Your Majesty, issue the decree and put it in writing so that it cannot be altered—in accordance with the law of the Medes and Persians, which cannot be repealed." So King Darius put the decree in writing.

Now when Daniel learned that the decree had been published, he went home to his upstairs room where the windows opened toward Jerusalem. Three times a day he got down on his knees and prayed, giving thanks to his God, just as he had done before. Then these men went as a group and found Daniel praying and asking God for help. So they went to the king and spoke to him about his royal decree: "Did you not publish a decree that during the next thirty days anyone who prays to any god or human being except to you, Your Majesty, would be thrown into the lions' den?"

The king answered, "The decree stands—in accordance with the law of the Medes and Persians, which cannot be repealed."

Then they said to the king, "Daniel, who is one of the exiles from Judah, pays no attention to you, Your Majesty, or to the decree you put in writing. He still prays three times a day." When the king heard this, he was greatly distressed; he was determined to rescue Daniel and made every effort until sundown to save him.

Then the men went as a group to King Darius and said to him, "Remember, Your Majesty, that according to the law of the

Medes and Persians no decree or edict that the king issues can be changed."

So the king gave the order, and they brought Daniel and threw him into the lions' den. The king said to Daniel, "May your God, whom you serve continually, rescue you!"

A stone was brought and placed over the mouth of the den, and the king sealed it with his own signet ring and with the rings of his nobles, so that Daniel's situation might not be changed. Then the king returned to his palace and spent the night without eating and without any entertainment being brought to him. And he could not sleep.

At the first light of dawn, the king got up and hurried to the lions' den. When he came near the den, he called to Daniel in an anguished voice, "Daniel, servant of the living God, has your God, whom you serve continually, been able to rescue you from the lions?"

Daniel answered, "May the king live forever! My God sent his angel, and he shut the mouths of the lions. They have not hurt me, because I was found innocent in his sight. Nor have I ever done any wrong before you, Your Majesty."

The king was overjoyed and gave orders to lift Daniel out of the den. And when Daniel was lifted from the den, no wound was found on him, because he had trusted in his God.

At the king's command, the men who had falsely accused Daniel were brought in and thrown into the lions' den, along with their wives and children. And before they reached the floor of the den, the lions overpowered them and crushed all their bones.

Then King Darius wrote to all the nations and peoples of every language in all the earth:

"May you prosper greatly!

"I issue a decree that in every part of my kingdom people must fear and reverence the God of Daniel.

"For he is the living God
and he endures forever;
his kingdom will not be destroyed,
his dominion will never end.
He rescues and he saves;
he performs signs and wonders
in the heavens and on the earth.
He has rescued Daniel
from the power of the lions."

Even in exile a remnant of God's faithful people was growing. The prophet Jeremiah was now dead, but perhaps his message still rang in their hearts—the message of God's ultimate compassion and the promise of returning to their homeland. Though Jeremiah had prophesied a cloud of gloom and doom, the "weeping prophet" of Judah had not ended the story in a minor key. Behind the pages of ruin and loss was one bright page of mercy, one last word of restoration that was bound up in the loving character of God. "This is what the Lord says ... I will save you."

"This is what the LORD, the God of Israel, says: 'Write in a book all the words I have spoken to you. The days are coming,' declares the LORD, 'when I will bring my people Israel and Judah back from captivity and restore them to the land I gave their ancestors to possess,' says the LORD.

"'In that day,' declares the LORD Almighty,
'I will break the yoke off their necks
and will tear off their bonds;
no longer will foreigners enslave them.

"'So do not be afraid, Jacob my servant;
do not be dismayed, Israel,'
declares the LORD.
'I will surely save you out of a distant place,
your descendants from the land of their exile.

> Jacob will again have peace and security,
>> and no one will make him afraid.
> I am with you and will save you,'
>> declares the LORD.
> 'Though I completely destroy all the nations
>> among which I scatter you,
>> I will not completely destroy you.
> I will discipline you but only in due measure;
>> I will not let you go entirely unpunished.'"

This is what the LORD Almighty, the God of Israel, says: "When I bring them back from captivity, the people in the land of Judah and in its towns will once again use these words: 'The LORD bless you, you prosperous city, you sacred mountain.' People will live together in Judah and all its towns — farmers and those who move about with their flocks. I will refresh the weary and satisfy the faint."

This is what the LORD says: "When seventy years are completed for Babylon, I will come to you and fulfill my good promise to bring you back to this place. For I know the plans I have for you," declares the LORD, "plans to prosper you and not to harm you, plans to give you hope and a future. Then you will call on me and come and pray to me, and I will listen to you. You will seek me and find me when you seek me with all your heart. I will be found by you," declares the LORD, "and will bring you back from captivity. I will gather you from all the nations and places where I have banished you," declares the LORD, "and will bring you back to the place from which I carried you into exile."

Jeremiah's words rang clear. Mighty Babylon did fall to Persian invaders in 539 BC. During the first year of his official reign over the kingdom, Cyrus, the great Persian overlord, issued a decree permitting Jewish exiles to return to Jerusalem. Thus, a little less than 70 years after the first deportations began in 605 BC, a caravan of deportees retraced their steps, praising God each step of the way for guiding history toward his good end. They were going home!

19

The Return Home

IN THE FIRST YEAR of Cyrus king of Persia, in order to fulfill the word of the LORD spoken by Jeremiah, the LORD moved the heart of Cyrus king of Persia to make a proclamation throughout his realm and also to put it in writing:

"This is what Cyrus king of Persia says:

"'The LORD, the God of heaven, has given me all the kingdoms of the earth and he has appointed me to build a temple for him at Jerusalem in Judah. Any of his people among you may go up to Jerusalem in Judah and build the temple of the LORD, the God of Israel, the God who is in Jerusalem, and may their God be with them. And in any locality where survivors may now be living, the people are to provide them with silver and gold, with goods and livestock, and with freewill offerings for the temple of God in Jerusalem.'"

Then the family heads of Judah and Benjamin, and the priests and Levites — everyone whose heart God had moved — prepared to go up and build the house of the LORD in Jerusalem. All their

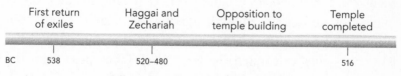

First return of exiles	Haggai and Zechariah	Opposition to temple building	Temple completed
BC 538	520–480		516

Full timeline information starts on page xi.

neighbors assisted them with articles of silver and gold, with goods and livestock, and with valuable gifts, in addition to all the freewill offerings.

Moreover, King Cyrus brought out the articles belonging to the temple of the LORD, which Nebuchadnezzar had carried away from Jerusalem and had placed in the temple of his god.

In all, there were 5,400 articles of gold and of silver. Sheshbazzar brought all these along with the exiles when they came up from Babylon to Jerusalem.

The whole company numbered 42,360, besides their 7,337 male and female slaves; and they also had 200 male and female singers. They had 736 horses, 245 mules, 435 camels and 6,720 donkeys.

The Babylonians appointed Zerubbabel, grandson of Jehoiachin, Judah's next-to-last king, as governor of Judah—making him the last of the line of David to be entrusted with political authority. Around 537 BC, Zerubbabel led these nearly 50,000 people back home to begin their rebuilding mission. With long, hard labor ahead of them, the people remembered to put first things first. With courage and conviction, they rebuilt the altar first, and then laid the foundation for the house of God. True worship was again a reality.

When the seventh month came and the Israelites had settled in their towns, the people assembled together as one in Jerusalem. Then Joshua son of Jozadak and his fellow priests and Zerubbabel son of Shealtiel and his associates began to build the altar of the God of Israel to sacrifice burnt offerings on it, in accordance with what is written in the Law of Moses the man of God. Despite their fear of the peoples around them, they built the altar on its foundation and sacrificed burnt offerings on it to the LORD, both the morning and evening sacrifices. Then in accordance with what is written, they celebrated the Festival of Tabernacles with the required number of burnt offerings prescribed for each day. After that, they presented the regular burnt offerings, the New Moon sacrifices and the sacrifices for all the appointed sacred festivals of the Lord, as well as those brought as freewill offerings to the Lord.

When the builders laid the foundation of the temple of the Lord, the priests in their vestments and with trumpets, and the Levites (the sons of Asaph) with cymbals, took their places to praise the Lord, as prescribed by David king of Israel. With praise and thanksgiving they sang to the Lord:

> "He is good;
> his love toward Israel endures forever."

And all the people gave a great shout of praise to the Lord, because the foundation of the house of the Lord was laid. But many of the older priests and Levites and family heads, who had seen the former temple, wept aloud when they saw the foundation of this temple being laid, while many others shouted for joy. No one could distinguish the sound of the shouts of joy from the sound of weeping, because the people made so much noise. And the sound was heard far away.

When the enemies of Judah and Benjamin heard that the exiles were building a temple for the Lord, the God of Israel, they came to Zerubbabel and to the heads of the families and said, "Let us help you build because, like you, we seek your God and have been sacrificing to him since the time of Esarhaddon king of Assyria, who brought us here."

But Zerubbabel, Joshua and the rest of the heads of the families of Israel answered, "You have no part with us in building a temple to our God. We alone will build it for the Lord, the God of Israel, as King Cyrus, the king of Persia, commanded us."

Then the peoples around them set out to discourage the people of Judah and make them afraid to go on building. They bribed officials to work against them and frustrate their plans during the entire reign of Cyrus king of Persia and down to the reign of Darius king of Persia.

Thus the work on the house of God in Jerusalem came to a standstill until the second year of the reign of Darius king of Persia.

The returnees' initial success alarmed the Samaritans and other neighbors who feared what a rebuilt temple in a thriving Jewish state might mean to the political stability of the area. They therefore opposed the project vigorously, hindering the work for about six years and stopping it completely for another ten years. Weary of the resistance and fighting, the Israelites began thinking that maybe this wasn't the right time to build the Lord's house after all. Instead, they concentrated on their own homes and settling down. But God had different plans. Once again intervening, he sent his prophets to jump-start the temple project. Haggai's message helped shake the people out of their complacency.

In the second year of King Darius, on the first day of the sixth month, the word of the LORD came through the prophet Haggai to Zerubbabel son of Shealtiel, governor of Judah, and to Joshua son of Jozadak, the high priest:

This is what the LORD Almighty says: "These people say, 'The time has not yet come to rebuild the LORD's house.'"

Then the word of the LORD came through the prophet Haggai: "Is it a time for you yourselves to be living in your paneled houses, while this house remains a ruin?"

Now this is what the LORD Almighty says: "Give careful thought to your ways. You have planted much, but harvested little. You eat, but never have enough. You drink, but never have your fill. You put on clothes, but are not warm. You earn wages, only to put them in a purse with holes in it."

This is what the LORD Almighty says: "Give careful thought to your ways. Go up into the mountains and bring down timber and build my house, so that I may take pleasure in it and be honored," says the LORD. "You expected much, but see, it turned out to be little. What you brought home, I blew away. Why?" declares the LORD Almighty. "Because of my house, which remains a ruin, while each of you is busy with your own house. Therefore, because of you the heavens have withheld their dew and the earth its crops. I called for a drought on the fields and the mountains, on the grain, the new wine, the olive oil and everything else the ground produces, on people and livestock, and on all the labor of your hands."

Then Zerubbabel son of Shealtiel, Joshua son of Jozadak, the high priest, and the whole remnant of the people obeyed the voice of the LORD their God and the message of the prophet Haggai, because the LORD their God had sent him. And the people feared the LORD.

Then Haggai, the LORD's messenger, gave this message of the LORD to the people: "I am with you," declares the LORD. So the LORD stirred up the spirit of Zerubbabel son of Shealtiel, governor of Judah, and the spirit of Joshua son of Jozadak, the high priest, and the spirit of the whole remnant of the people. They came and began to work on the house of the LORD Almighty, their God, on the twenty-fourth day of the sixth month.

Haggai continued his prophetic message of encouragement. God had not forgotten his covenant with Abraham, Isaac and Jacob, he said. And he hinted at a glorious future promise that sounded too good to be true—a promise that would ultimately be fulfilled when Jesus the Messiah visited this temple.

In the second year of King Darius, on the twenty-first day of the seventh month, the word of the LORD came through the prophet Haggai: "Speak to Zerubbabel son of Shealtiel, governor of Judah, to Joshua son of Jozadak, the high priest, and to the remnant of the people. Ask them, 'Who of you is left who saw this house in its former glory? How does it look to you now? Does it not seem to you like nothing? But now be strong, Zerubbabel,' declares the LORD. 'Be strong, Joshua son of Jozadak, the high priest. Be strong, all you people of the land,' declares the LORD, 'and work. For I am with you,' declares the LORD Almighty. 'This is what I covenanted with you when you came out of Egypt. And my Spirit remains among you. Do not fear.'

"This is what the LORD Almighty says: 'In a little while I will once more shake the heavens and the earth, the sea and the dry land. I will shake all nations, and what is desired by all nations will come, and I will fill this house with glory,' says the LORD Almighty. 'The silver is mine and the gold is mine,' declares the LORD Almighty. 'The glory of this present house will be greater than the glory of the former house,' says the LORD Almighty. 'And in this place I will grant peace,' declares the LORD Almighty."

Zechariah, a prophet and priest, began his work in Jerusalem in 520 BC, during the time of Haggai's ministry. Both men wanted to stimulate renewal in the temple rebuilding project. Like Haggai, Zechariah had a dual message: The temple is important, but it's a sign and symbol of something greater coming. Work on the temple; don't be afraid. But watch for the day when God will bless Jerusalem once again.

In the eighth month of the second year of Darius, the word of the LORD came to the prophet Zechariah son of Berekiah, the son of Iddo:

This is what the LORD Almighty says: "I am very jealous for Zion; I am burning with jealousy for her."

This is what the LORD says: "I will return to Zion and dwell in Jerusalem. Then Jerusalem will be called the Faithful City, and the mountain of the LORD Almighty will be called the Holy Mountain."

This is what the LORD Almighty says: "Once again men and women of ripe old age will sit in the streets of Jerusalem, each of them with cane in hand because of their age. The city streets will be filled with boys and girls playing there."

This is what the LORD Almighty says: "It may seem marvelous to the remnant of this people at that time, but will it seem marvelous to me?" declares the LORD Almighty.

This is what the LORD Almighty says: "I will save my people from the countries of the east and the west. I will bring them back to live in Jerusalem; they will be my people, and I will be faithful and righteous to them as their God."

This is what the LORD Almighty says: "Now hear these words, 'Let your hands be strong so that the temple may be built.' This is also what the prophets said who were present when the foundation was laid for the house of the LORD Almighty. Before that time there were no wages for people or hire for animals. No one could go about their business safely because of their enemies, since I had turned everyone against their neighbor. But now I will not deal with the remnant of this people as I did in the past," declares the LORD Almighty.

"The seed will grow well, the vine will yield its fruit, the ground will produce its crops, and the heavens will drop their dew. I will give all these things as an inheritance to the remnant of this people. Just as you, Judah and Israel, have been a curse among the nations, so I will save you, and you will be a blessing. Do not be afraid, but let your hands be strong."

This is what the LORD Almighty says: "Just as I had determined to bring disaster on you and showed no pity when your ancestors angered me," says the LORD Almighty, "so now I have determined to do good again to Jerusalem and Judah. Do not be afraid. These are the things you are to do: Speak the truth to each other, and render true and sound judgment in your courts; do not plot evil against each other, and do not love to swear falsely. I hate all this," declares the LORD.

The word of the LORD Almighty came to me.

This is what the LORD Almighty says: "The fasts of the fourth, fifth, seventh and tenth months will become joyful and glad occasions and happy festivals for Judah. Therefore love truth and peace."

This is what the LORD Almighty says: "Many peoples and the inhabitants of many cities will yet come, and the inhabitants of one city will go to another and say, 'Let us go at once to entreat the

LORD and seek the LORD Almighty. I myself am going.' And many peoples and powerful nations will come to Jerusalem to seek the LORD Almighty and to entreat him."

This is what the LORD Almighty says: "In those days ten people from all languages and nations will take firm hold of one Jew by the hem of his robe and say, 'Let us go with you, because we have heard that God is with you.'"

Thanks to Haggai's and Zechariah's encouragement, the people returned to their work on the temple. However, they were not the only ones back at work. So was their opposition, this time from Tattenai, the governor of the Trans-Euphrates region. But the people could not have anticipated what God would do next.

At that time Tattenai, governor of Trans-Euphrates, and Shethar-Bozenai and their associates went to them and asked, "Who authorized you to rebuild this temple and to finish it?" They also asked, "What are the names of those who are constructing this building?" But the eye of their God was watching over the elders of the Jews, and they were not stopped until a report could go to Darius and his written reply be received.

This is a copy of the letter that Tattenai, governor of Trans-Euphrates, and Shethar-Bozenai and their associates, the officials of Trans-Euphrates, sent to King Darius. The report they sent him read as follows:

To King Darius:

Cordial greetings.

The king should know that we went to the district of Judah, to the temple of the great God. The people are building it with large stones and placing the timbers in the walls. The work is being carried on with diligence and is making rapid progress under their direction.

We questioned the elders and asked them, "Who authorized you to rebuild this temple and to finish it?" We also asked them their names, so that we could write down the names of their leaders for your information.

This is the answer they gave us:

"We are the servants of the God of heaven and earth, and we are rebuilding the temple that was built many years ago, one that a great king of Israel built and finished. But because our ancestors angered the God of heaven, he gave them into the hands of Nebuchadnezzar the Chaldean, king of Babylon, who destroyed this temple and deported the people to Babylon.

"However, in the first year of Cyrus king of Babylon, King Cyrus issued a decree to rebuild this house of God. He even removed from the temple of Babylon the gold and silver articles of the house of God, which Nebuchadnezzar had taken from the temple in Jerusalem and brought to the temple in Babylon. Then King Cyrus gave them to a man named Sheshbazzar, whom he had appointed governor, and he told him, 'Take these articles and go and deposit them in the temple in Jerusalem. And rebuild the house of God on its site.'

"So this Sheshbazzar came and laid the foundations of the house of God in Jerusalem. From that day to the present it has been under construction but is not yet finished."

Now if it pleases the king, let a search be made in the royal archives of Babylon to see if King Cyrus did in fact issue a decree to rebuild this house of God in Jerusalem. Then let the king send us his decision in this matter.

King Darius then issued an order, and they searched in the archives stored in the treasury at Babylon. A scroll was found in the citadel of Ecbatana in the province of Media, and this was written on it:

Memorandum:

In the first year of King Cyrus, the king issued a decree concerning the temple of God in Jerusalem:

Let the temple be rebuilt as a place to present sacrifices, and let its foundations be laid. It is to be sixty cubits[1] high and sixty cubits wide, with three courses of large stones and one of timbers. The costs are to be paid by the royal treasury. Also, the gold and silver articles of the house of God, which Nebuchadnezzar took from the temple in Jerusalem and brought to Babylon, are to be returned to their places in the temple in Jerusalem; they are to be deposited in the house of God.

Now then, Tattenai, governor of Trans-Euphrates, and Shethar-Bozenai and you other officials of that province, stay away from there. Do not interfere with the work on this temple of God. Let the governor of the Jews and the Jewish elders rebuild this house of God on its site.

Moreover, I hereby decree what you are to do for these elders of the Jews in the construction of this house of God:

Their expenses are to be fully paid out of the royal treasury, from the revenues of Trans-Euphrates, so that the work will not stop. Whatever is needed — young bulls, rams, male lambs for burnt offerings to the God of heaven, and wheat, salt, wine and olive oil, as requested by the priests in Jerusalem — must be given them daily without fail, so that they may offer sacrifices pleasing to the God of heaven and pray for the well-being of the king and his sons.

Furthermore, I decree that if anyone defies this edict, a beam is to be pulled from their house and they are to be impaled on it. And for this crime their house is to be made a pile of rubble. May God, who has caused his Name to dwell there, overthrow any king or people who lifts a hand to change this decree or to destroy this temple in Jerusalem.

---

[1] **Sixty cubits:** That is, about 90 feet or 27 meters.

I Darius have decreed it. Let it be carried out with diligence.

Then, because of the decree King Darius had sent, Tattenai, governor of Trans-Euphrates, and Shethar-Bozenai and their associates carried it out with diligence. So the elders of the Jews continued to build and prosper under the preaching of Haggai the prophet and Zechariah, a descendant of Iddo. They finished building the temple according to the command of the God of Israel and the decrees of Cyrus, Darius and Artaxerxes, kings of Persia. The temple was completed on the third day of the month Adar, in the sixth year of the reign of King Darius.

So on March 12, 516 BC, almost 70 years after its destruction, the rebuilding of the temple was complete. Sustained work had continued on the project for three and a half years. Though not as large or spectacular as Solomon's temple, the rebuilt temple actually enjoyed a longer life.

Then the people of Israel — the priests, the Levites and the rest of the exiles — celebrated the dedication of the house of God with joy. For the dedication of this house of God they offered a hundred bulls, two hundred rams, four hundred male lambs and, as a sin offering for all Israel, twelve male goats, one for each of the tribes of Israel. And they installed the priests in their divisions and the Levites in their groups for the service of God at Jerusalem, according to what is written in the Book of Moses.

Many Jews chose not to return to Judah. One man, Mordecai, was living in the city of Susa — one of the four capitals of the Persian Empire — with his adopted daughter Hadassah, also known as Esther. Through a series of miraculous events, they both become involved in a web of circumstances that involved the king, a royal decree and a heinous plot of betrayal.

20

The Queen of Beauty and Courage

THIS IS WHAT HAPPENED during the time of Xerxes, the Xerxes who ruled over 127 provinces stretching from India to Cush: At that time King Xerxes reigned from his royal throne in the citadel of Susa, and in the third year of his reign he gave a banquet for all his nobles and officials. The military leaders of Persia and Media, the princes, and the nobles of the provinces were present.

For a full 180 days he displayed the vast wealth of his kingdom and the splendor and glory of his majesty. When these days were over, the king gave a banquet, lasting seven days, in the enclosed garden of the king's palace, for all the people from the least to the greatest who were in the citadel of Susa. The garden had hangings of white and blue linen, fastened with cords of white linen and purple material to silver rings on marble pillars. There were couches of gold and silver on a mosaic pavement of porphyry, marble, mother-of-pearl and other costly stones. Wine was served in goblets of gold, each one different from the other, and the royal wine was abundant, in keeping with the king's liberality. By the

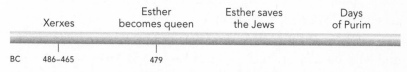

Xerxes	Esther becomes queen	Esther saves the Jews	Days of Purim

BC   486–465   479

Full timeline information starts on page xi.

king's command each guest was allowed to drink with no restrictions, for the king instructed all the wine stewards to serve each man what he wished.

Queen Vashti also gave a banquet for the women in the royal palace of King Xerxes.

On the seventh day, when King Xerxes was in high spirits from wine, he commanded the seven eunuchs who served him — Mehuman, Biztha, Harbona, Bigtha, Abagtha, Zethar and Karkas — to bring before him Queen Vashti, wearing her royal crown, in order to display her beauty to the people and nobles, for she was lovely to look at. But when the attendants delivered the king's command, Queen Vashti refused to come. Then the king became furious and burned with anger.

Since it was customary for the king to consult experts in matters of law and justice, he spoke with the wise men who understood the times and were closest to the king — Karshena, Shethar, Admatha, Tarshish, Meres, Marsena and Memukan, the seven nobles of Persia and Media who had special access to the king and were highest in the kingdom.

"According to law, what must be done to Queen Vashti?" he asked. "She has not obeyed the command of King Xerxes that the eunuchs have taken to her."

Then Memukan replied in the presence of the king and the nobles, "Queen Vashti has done wrong, not only against the king but also against all the nobles and the peoples of all the provinces of King Xerxes. For the queen's conduct will become known to all the women, and so they will despise their husbands and say, 'King Xerxes commanded Queen Vashti to be brought before him, but she would not come.' This very day the Persian and Median women of the nobility who have heard about the queen's conduct will respond to all the king's nobles in the same way. There will be no end of disrespect and discord.

"Therefore, if it pleases the king, let him issue a royal decree and let it be written in the laws of Persia and Media, which cannot be repealed, that Vashti is never again to enter the presence of

King Xerxes. Also let the king give her royal position to someone else who is better than she. Then when the king's edict is proclaimed throughout all his vast realm, all the women will respect their husbands, from the least to the greatest."

The king and his nobles were pleased with this advice, so the king did as Memukan proposed. He sent dispatches to all parts of the kingdom, to each province in its own script and to each people in their own language, proclaiming that every man should be ruler over his own household, using his native tongue.

Later when King Xerxes' fury had subsided, he remembered Vashti and what she had done and what he had decreed about her. Then the king's personal attendants proposed, "Let a search be made for beautiful young virgins for the king. Let the king appoint commissioners in every province of his realm to bring all these beautiful young women into the harem at the citadel of Susa. Let them be placed under the care of Hegai, the king's eunuch, who is in charge of the women; and let beauty treatments be given to them. Then let the young woman who pleases the king be queen instead of Vashti." This advice appealed to the king, and he followed it.

Vashti paid the price for her stand against the king. Although she was the rightful queen, she was deposed at the whim of her husband. Such was the precarious state of women — and men — in the royal court.

Women outside the court were also subject to the king's plans. His decree that girls from the kingdom be brought into his harem was irrefutable. The girls and their families had no say in the matter. If the king summoned, the family had no choice but to surrender their daughter to the king.

Now there was in the citadel of Susa a Jew of the tribe of Benjamin, named Mordecai son of Jair, the son of Shimei, the son of Kish, who had been carried into exile from Jerusalem by Nebuchadnezzar king of Babylon, among those taken captive with

Jehoiachin king of Judah. Mordecai had a cousin named Hadassah, whom he had brought up because she had neither father nor mother. This young woman, who was also known as Esther, had a lovely figure and was beautiful. Mordecai had taken her as his own daughter when her father and mother died.

When the king's order and edict had been proclaimed, many young women were brought to the citadel of Susa and put under the care of Hegai. Esther also was taken to the king's palace and entrusted to Hegai, who had charge of the harem. She pleased him and won his favor. Immediately he provided her with her beauty treatments and special food. He assigned to her seven female attendants selected from the king's palace and moved her and her attendants into the best place in the harem.

Esther had not revealed her nationality and family background, because Mordecai had forbidden her to do so. Every day he walked back and forth near the courtyard of the harem to find out how Esther was and what was happening to her.

Before a young woman's turn came to go in to King Xerxes, she had to complete twelve months of beauty treatments prescribed for the women, six months with oil of myrrh and six with perfumes and cosmetics. And this is how she would go to the king: Anything she wanted was given her to take with her from the harem to the king's palace. In the evening she would go there and in the morning return to another part of the harem to the care of Shaashgaz, the king's eunuch who was in charge of the concubines. She would not return to the king unless he was pleased with her and summoned her by name.

When the turn came for Esther (the young woman Mordecai had adopted, the daughter of his uncle Abihail) to go to the king, she asked for nothing other than what Hegai, the king's eunuch who was in charge of the harem, suggested. And Esther won the favor of everyone who saw her. She was taken to King Xerxes in the royal residence in the tenth month, the month of Tebeth, in the seventh year of his reign.

Now the king was attracted to Esther more than to any of the other women, and she won his favor and approval more than any of the other virgins. So he set a royal crown on her head and made her queen instead of Vashti. And the king gave a great banquet, Esther's banquet, for all his nobles and officials. He proclaimed a holiday throughout the provinces and distributed gifts with royal liberality.

When the virgins were assembled a second time, Mordecai was sitting at the king's gate. But Esther had kept secret her family background and nationality just as Mordecai had told her to do, for she continued to follow Mordecai's instructions as she had done when he was bringing her up.

During the time Mordecai was sitting at the king's gate, Bigthana and Teresh, two of the king's officers who guarded the doorway, became angry and conspired to assassinate King Xerxes. But Mordecai found out about the plot and told Queen Esther, who in turn reported it to the king, giving credit to Mordecai. And when the report was investigated and found to be true, the two officials were impaled on poles. All this was recorded in the book of the annals in the presence of the king.

Haman, a noble in the king's court, was not aware of Esther's background and Mordecai's loyalty to the king or he may not have plotted so openly against the Jews. However, Jewish tradition considers him to have been a descendant of the Amalekite king Agag, an enemy of Israel during Saul's reign. The Amalekites were ancient enemies of the Jews. So perhaps his confrontation with Mordecai and resulting decree against the Jews was inevitable.

After these events, King Xerxes honored Haman son of Hammedatha, the Agagite, elevating him and giving him a seat of honor higher than that of all the other nobles. All the royal officials at the king's gate knelt down and paid honor to Haman, for the king had commanded this concerning him. But Mordecai would not kneel down or pay him honor.

Then the royal officials at the king's gate asked Mordecai, "Why do you disobey the king's command?" Day after day they spoke to him but he refused to comply. Therefore they told Haman about it to see whether Mordecai's behavior would be tolerated, for he had told them he was a Jew.

When Haman saw that Mordecai would not kneel down or pay him honor, he was enraged. Yet having learned who Mordecai's people were, he scorned the idea of killing only Mordecai. Instead Haman looked for a way to destroy all Mordecai's people, the Jews, throughout the whole kingdom of Xerxes.

In the twelfth year of King Xerxes, in the first month, the month of Nisan, the *pur* (that is, the lot) was cast in the presence of Haman to select a day and month. And the lot fell on the twelfth month, the month of Adar.

Then Haman said to King Xerxes, "There is a certain people dispersed among the peoples in all the provinces of your kingdom who keep themselves separate. Their customs are different from those of all other people, and they do not obey the king's laws; it is not in the king's best interest to tolerate them. If it pleases the king, let a decree be issued to destroy them, and I will give ten thousand talents of silver to the king's administrators for the royal treasury."

So the king took his signet ring from his finger and gave it to Haman son of Hammedatha, the Agagite, the enemy of the Jews. "Keep the money," the king said to Haman, "and do with the people as you please."

Then on the thirteenth day of the first month the royal secretaries were summoned. They wrote out in the script of each province and in the language of each people all Haman's orders to the king's satraps, the governors of the various provinces and the nobles of the various peoples. These were written in the name of King Xerxes himself and sealed with his own ring. Dispatches were sent by couriers to all the king's provinces with the order to destroy, kill and annihilate all the Jews — young and old, women and children — on a single day, the thirteenth day of the twelfth month, the month of Adar, and to plunder their goods. A copy of the text of the edict was to be issued as law in every province and made known to the people of every nationality so they would be ready for that day.

The couriers went out, spurred on by the king's command, and the edict was issued in the citadel of Susa. The king and Haman sat down to drink, but the city of Susa was bewildered.

When Mordecai learned of all that had been done, he tore his clothes, put on sackcloth and ashes, and went out into the city, wailing loudly and bitterly. But he went only as far as the king's gate, because no one clothed in sackcloth was allowed to enter it. In every province to which the edict and order of the king came, there was great mourning among the Jews, with fasting, weeping and wailing. Many lay in sackcloth and ashes.

When Esther's eunuchs and female attendants came and told her about Mordecai, she was in great distress. She sent clothes for him to put on instead of his sackcloth, but he would not accept them. Then Esther summoned Hathak, one of the king's eunuchs assigned to attend her, and ordered him to find out what was troubling Mordecai and why.

So Hathak went out to Mordecai in the open square of the city in front of the king's gate. Mordecai told him everything that had happened to him, including the exact amount of money Haman had promised to pay into the royal treasury for the destruction of the Jews. He also gave him a copy of the text of the edict for their annihilation, which had been published in Susa, to show to Esther and explain it to her, and he told him to instruct her to go into the king's presence to beg for mercy and plead with him for her people.

Hathak went back and reported to Esther what Mordecai had said. Then she instructed him to say to Mordecai, "All the king's officials and the people of the royal provinces know that for any man or woman who approaches the king in the inner court without being summoned the king has but one law: that they be put to death unless the king extends the gold scepter to them and spares their lives. But thirty days have passed since I was called to go to the king."

When Esther's words were reported to Mordecai, he sent back this answer: "Do not think that because you are in the king's house you alone of all the Jews will escape. For if you remain silent at this time, relief and deliverance for the Jews will arise from another place, but you and your father's family will perish. And who knows but that you have come to your royal position for such a time as this?"

Then Esther sent this reply to Mordecai: "Go, gather together all the Jews who are in Susa, and fast for me. Do not eat or drink for three days, night or day. I and my attendants will fast as you do. When this is done, I will go to the king, even though it is against the law. And if I perish, I perish."

So Mordecai went away and carried out all of Esther's instructions.

Queen Vashti had earlier risked her life by refusing to appear before the king when summoned. As a result she lost her standing as queen. Now Esther risks her life by appearing before the same king uninvited.

On the third day Esther put on her royal robes and stood in the inner court of the palace, in front of the king's hall. The king was sitting on his royal throne in the hall, facing the entrance. When he saw Queen Esther standing in the court, he was pleased with her and held out to her the gold scepter that was in his hand. So Esther approached and touched the tip of the scepter.

Then the king asked, "What is it, Queen Esther? What is your request? Even up to half the kingdom, it will be given you."

"If it pleases the king," replied Esther, "let the king, together with Haman, come today to a banquet I have prepared for him."

"Bring Haman at once," the king said, "so that we may do what Esther asks."

So the king and Haman went to the banquet Esther had prepared. As they were drinking wine, the king again asked Esther,

"Now what is your petition? It will be given you. And what is your request? Even up to half the kingdom, it will be granted."

Esther replied, "My petition and my request is this: If the king regards me with favor and if it pleases the king to grant my petition and fulfill my request, let the king and Haman come tomorrow to the banquet I will prepare for them. Then I will answer the king's question."

Haman went out that day happy and in high spirits. But when he saw Mordecai at the king's gate and observed that he neither rose nor showed fear in his presence, he was filled with rage against Mordecai. Nevertheless, Haman restrained himself and went home.

Calling together his friends and Zeresh, his wife, Haman boasted to them about his vast wealth, his many sons, and all the ways the king had honored him and how he had elevated him above the other nobles and officials. "And that's not all," Haman added. "I'm the only person Queen Esther invited to accompany the king to the banquet she gave. And she has invited me along with the king tomorrow. But all this gives me no satisfaction as long as I see that Jew Mordecai sitting at the king's gate."

His wife Zeresh and all his friends said to him, "Have a pole set up, reaching to a height of fifty cubits,[1] and ask the king in the morning to have Mordecai impaled on it. Then go with the king to the banquet and enjoy yourself." This suggestion delighted Haman, and he had the pole set up.

That night the king could not sleep; so he ordered the book of the chronicles, the record of his reign, to be brought in and read to him. It was found recorded there that Mordecai had exposed Bigthana and Teresh, two of the king's officers who guarded the doorway, who had conspired to assassinate King Xerxes.

"What honor and recognition has Mordecai received for this?" the king asked.

"Nothing has been done for him," his attendants answered.

---

[1]**Fifty cubits:** That is, about 75 feet or about 22.5 meters.

The king said, "Who is in the court?" Now Haman had just entered the outer court of the palace to speak to the king about impaling Mordecai on the pole he had set up for him.

His attendants answered, "Haman is standing in the court."

"Bring him in," the king ordered.

When Haman entered, the king asked him, "What should be done for the man the king delights to honor?"

Now Haman thought to himself, "Who is there that the king would rather honor than me?" So he answered the king, "For the man the king delights to honor, have them bring a royal robe the king has worn and a horse the king has ridden, one with a royal crest placed on its head. Then let the robe and horse be entrusted to one of the king's most noble princes. Let them robe the man the king delights to honor, and lead him on the horse through the city streets, proclaiming before him, 'This is what is done for the man the king delights to honor!' "

"Go at once," the king commanded Haman. "Get the robe and the horse and do just as you have suggested for Mordecai the Jew, who sits at the king's gate. Do not neglect anything you have recommended."

So Haman got the robe and the horse. He robed Mordecai, and led him on horseback through the city streets, proclaiming before him, "This is what is done for the man the king delights to honor!"

Afterward Mordecai returned to the king's gate. But Haman rushed home, with his head covered in grief, and told Zeresh his wife and all his friends everything that had happened to him.

His advisers and his wife Zeresh said to him, "Since Mordecai, before whom your downfall has started, is of Jewish origin, you cannot stand against him — you will surely come to ruin!" While they were still talking with him, the king's eunuchs arrived and hurried Haman away to the banquet Esther had prepared.

So the king and Haman went to Queen Esther's banquet, and as they were drinking wine on the second day, the king again asked, "Queen Esther, what is your petition? It will be given you. What is your request? Even up to half the kingdom, it will be granted."

Then Queen Esther answered, "If I have found favor with you, Your Majesty, and if it pleases you, grant me my life — this is my petition. And spare my people — this is my request. For I and my people have been sold to be destroyed, killed and annihilated. If we had merely been sold as male and female slaves, I would have kept quiet, because no such distress would justify disturbing the king."

King Xerxes asked Queen Esther, "Who is he? Where is he — the man who has dared to do such a thing?"

Esther said, "An adversary and enemy! This vile Haman!"

Then Haman was terrified before the king and queen. The king got up in a rage, left his wine and went out into the palace garden. But Haman, realizing that the king had already decided his fate, stayed behind to beg Queen Esther for his life.

Just as the king returned from the palace garden to the banquet hall, Haman was falling on the couch where Esther was reclining.

The king exclaimed, "Will he even molest the queen while she is with me in the house?"

As soon as the word left the king's mouth, they covered Haman's face. Then Harbona, one of the eunuchs attending the king, said, "A pole reaching to a height of fifty cubits stands by Haman's house. He had it set up for Mordecai, who spoke up to help the king."

The king said, "Impale him on it!" So they impaled Haman on the pole he had set up for Mordecai. Then the king's fury subsided.

That same day King Xerxes gave Queen Esther the estate of Haman, the enemy of the Jews. And Mordecai came into the presence of the king, for Esther had told how he was related to her. The king took off his signet ring, which he had reclaimed from Haman, and presented it to Mordecai. And Esther appointed him over Haman's estate.

Esther and Mordecai are secure, but the irrevocable decree is still a threat to the rest of the Jews. Haman's overthrow and Mordecai's elevation could not give Esther comfort so long as Haman's decree against the Jews remained in force.

Esther again pleaded with the king, falling at his feet and weeping. She begged him to put an end to the evil plan of Haman the Agagite, which he had devised against the Jews. Then the king extended the gold scepter to Esther and she arose and stood before him.

"If it pleases the king," she said, "and if he regards me with favor and thinks it the right thing to do, and if he is pleased with me, let an order be written overruling the dispatches that Haman son of Hammedatha, the Agagite, devised and wrote to destroy the Jews in all the king's provinces. For how can I bear to see disaster fall on my people? How can I bear to see the destruction of my family?"

King Xerxes replied to Queen Esther and to Mordecai the Jew, "Because Haman attacked the Jews, I have given his estate to Esther, and they have impaled him on the pole he set up. Now write another decree in the king's name in behalf of the Jews as seems best to you, and seal it with the king's signet ring—for no document written in the king's name and sealed with his ring can be revoked."

At once the royal secretaries were summoned—on the twenty-third day of the third month, the month of Sivan. They wrote out all Mordecai's orders to the Jews, and to the satraps, governors and nobles of the 127 provinces stretching from India to Cush. These orders were written in the script of each province and the language of each people and also to the Jews in their own script and language. Mordecai wrote in the name of King Xerxes, sealed the dispatches with the king's signet ring, and sent them by mounted couriers, who rode fast horses especially bred for the king.

The king's edict granted the Jews in every city the right to assemble and protect themselves; to destroy, kill and annihilate the armed men of any nationality or province who might attack them and their women and children, and to plunder the property of their enemies. The day appointed for the Jews to do this in all the provinces of King Xerxes was the thirteenth day of the twelfth month, the month of Adar. A copy of the text of the edict was to be issued as law in every province and made known to the people of every nationality so that the Jews would be ready on that day to avenge themselves on their enemies.

The couriers, riding the royal horses, went out, spurred on by the king's command, and the edict was issued in the citadel of Susa.

When Mordecai left the king's presence, he was wearing royal garments of blue and white, a large crown of gold and a purple robe of fine linen. And the city of Susa held a joyous celebration. For the Jews it was a time of happiness and joy, gladness and honor. In every province and in every city to which the edict of the king came, there was joy and gladness among the Jews, with feasting and celebrating. And many people of other nationalities became Jews because fear of the Jews had seized them.

On the thirteenth day of the twelfth month, the month of Adar, the edict commanded by the king was to be carried out. On this day the enemies of the Jews had hoped to overpower them, but now the tables were turned and the Jews got the upper hand over those who hated them. The Jews assembled in their cities in all the provinces of King Xerxes to attack those determined to destroy them. No one could stand against them, because the people of all the other nationalities were afraid of them. And all the nobles of the provinces, the satraps, the governors and the king's administrators helped the Jews, because fear of Mordecai had seized them. Mordecai was prominent in the palace; his reputation spread throughout the provinces, and he became more and more powerful.

The Jews struck down all their enemies with the sword, killing and destroying them, and they did what they pleased to those who hated them. In the citadel of Susa, the Jews killed and destroyed five hundred men. They also killed Parshandatha, Dalphon, Aspatha, Poratha, Adalia, Aridatha, Parmashta, Arisai, Aridai and Vaizatha, the ten sons of Haman son of Hammedatha, the enemy of the Jews. But they did not lay their hands on the plunder.

The number of those killed in the citadel of Susa was reported to the king that same day. The king said to Queen Esther, "The Jews have killed and destroyed five hundred men and the ten sons of Haman in the citadel of Susa. What have they done in the rest of the king's provinces? Now what is your petition? It will be given you. What is your request? It will also be granted."

"If it pleases the king," Esther answered, "give the Jews in Susa permission to carry out this day's edict tomorrow also, and let Haman's ten sons be impaled on poles."

So the king commanded that this be done. An edict was issued in Susa, and they impaled the ten sons of Haman. The Jews in Susa came together on the fourteenth day of the month of Adar, and they put to death in Susa three hundred men, but they did not lay their hands on the plunder.

Meanwhile, the remainder of the Jews who were in the king's provinces also assembled to protect themselves and get relief from their enemies. They killed seventy-five thousand of them but did not lay their hands on the plunder. This happened on the thirteenth day of the month of Adar, and on the fourteenth they rested and made it a day of feasting and joy.

This story of Esther and Mordecai is also the story of the beginnings of one of the annual Jewish festivals, the festival of Purim. The story also keeps the memory alive of the great deliverance of the Jewish people during the reign of Xerxes.

Mordecai recorded these events, and he sent letters to all the Jews throughout the provinces of King Xerxes, near and far, to have them celebrate annually the fourteenth and fifteenth days of the month of Adar as the time when the Jews got relief from their enemies, and as the month when their sorrow was turned into joy and their mourning into a day of celebration. He wrote them to observe the days as days of feasting and joy and giving presents of food to one another and gifts to the poor.

So the Jews agreed to continue the celebration they had begun, doing what Mordecai had written to them. For Haman son of Hammedatha, the Agagite, the enemy of all the Jews, had plotted against the Jews to destroy them and had cast the *pur* (that is, the lot) for their ruin and destruction. But when the plot came to the king's attention, he issued written orders that the evil scheme Haman had devised against the Jews should come back onto his own head, and that he and his sons should be impaled on poles. (Therefore these days were called Purim, from the word *pur.*) Because of everything written in this letter and because of what they had seen and what had happened to them, the Jews took it on themselves to establish the custom that they and their descendants and all who join them should without fail observe these two days every year, in the way prescribed and at the time appointed. These days should be remembered and observed in every generation by every family, and in every province and in every city. And these days of Purim should never fail to be celebrated by the Jews — nor should the memory of these days die out among their descendants.

21

Rebuilding the Walls

God had promised the people that some day he would bring them back to their land. And, as promised, the people began to return to Judah. Once there, Zerubbabel and the prophets had spurred the people on to finish the temple, the Jews' central worship site in Jerusalem. Enter Ezra (half a century later), a respected priest and teacher of the Law living in Babylon, who took a serious interest in making sure that God's Law was heard and followed again now that the people had returned home.

DURING THE REIGN of Artaxerxes king of Persia, Ezra son of Seraiah, the son of Azariah, the son of Hilkiah, the son of Shallum, the son of Zadok, the son of Ahitub, the son of Amariah, the son of Azariah, the son of Meraioth, the son of Zerahiah, the son of Uzzi, the son of Bukki, the son of Abishua, the son of Phinehas, the son of Eleazar, the son of Aaron the chief priest — this Ezra came up from Babylon. He was a teacher well versed in the Law of Moses, which the LORD, the God of Israel, had given. The king had granted him everything he asked, for the hand of the LORD his God was on him. Some of the Israelites, including priests, Levites,

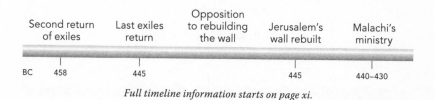

Second return of exiles	Last exiles return	Opposition to rebuilding the wall	Jerusalem's wall rebuilt	Malachi's ministry
BC 458	445		445	440–430

Full timeline information starts on page xi.

musicians, gatekeepers and temple servants, also came up to Jerusalem in the seventh year of King Artaxerxes.

Ezra arrived in Jerusalem in the fifth month of the seventh year of the king. He had begun his journey from Babylon on the first day of the first month, and he arrived in Jerusalem on the first day of the fifth month, for the gracious hand of his God was on him. For Ezra had devoted himself to the study and observance of the Law of the LORD, and to teaching its decrees and laws in Israel.

Ezra

Ezra son of Seraiah,

the son of Azariah,

the son of Hilkiah,

the son of Shallum,

the son of Zadok,

the son of Ahitub,

the son of Amariah,

the son of Azariah,

the son of Meraioth,

the son of Zerahiah,

the son of Uzzi,

the son of Bukki,

the son of Abishua,

the son of Phinehas,

the son of Eleazar,

the son of Aaron the chief priest.

This is a copy of the letter King Artaxerxes had given to Ezra the priest, a teacher of the Law, a man learned in matters concerning the commands and decrees of the LORD for Israel:

Artaxerxes, king of kings,

To Ezra the priest, teacher of the Law of the God of heaven:

Greetings.

Now I decree that any of the Israelites in my kingdom, including priests and Levites, who volunteer to go to Jerusalem with you, may go. You are sent by the king and his seven advisers to inquire about Judah and Jerusalem with regard to the Law of your God, which is in your hand. Moreover, you are to take with you the silver and gold that the king and his advisers have freely given to the God of Israel, whose dwelling is in Jerusalem, together with all the silver and gold you may obtain from the province of Babylon, as well as the freewill offerings of the people and priests for the temple of their God in Jerusalem. With this money be sure to buy bulls, rams and male lambs, together with their grain offerings and drink offerings, and sacrifice them on the altar of the temple of your God in Jerusalem.

You and your fellow Israelites may then do whatever seems best with the rest of the silver and gold, in accordance with the will of your God. Deliver to the God of Jerusalem all the articles entrusted to you for worship in the temple of your God. And anything else needed for the temple of your God that you are responsible to supply, you may provide from the royal treasury.

Now I, King Artaxerxes, decree that all the treasurers of Trans-Euphrates are to provide with diligence whatever Ezra the priest, the teacher of the Law of the God of heaven, may ask of you — up to a hundred talents of silver, a hundred cors of wheat, a hundred baths of wine, a hundred baths of olive oil, and salt without limit. Whatever the God of heaven has prescribed, let it be done with diligence for the temple of the God of heaven. Why should his wrath fall on the realm of the king and of his sons? You are also to know that you have no authority to impose taxes, tribute or duty on any of the priests, Levites, musicians, gatekeepers, temple servants or other workers at this house of God.

And you, Ezra, in accordance with the wisdom of your God, which you possess, appoint magistrates and judges to administer justice to all the people of Trans-Euphrates — all who know the laws of your God. And you are to teach any who do not know them. Whoever does not obey the law of your God and the law of the king must surely be punished by death, banishment, confiscation of property, or imprisonment.

Praise be to the LORD, the God of our ancestors, who has put it into the king's heart to bring honor to the house of the LORD in Jerusalem in this way and who has extended his good favor to me before the king and his advisers and all the king's powerful officials. Because the hand of the LORD my God was on me, I took courage and gathered leaders from Israel to go up with me.

Loaded down with the king's gifts and supplies, Ezra led several thousand fellow Israelites on a journey to Jerusalem. He found the temple in good order, but he also discovered that the people were intermarrying with neighboring cultures who worshiped other gods. God's Law clearly warned the people against such actions. Appalled, Ezra tore his clothes in grief and wept as he prayed, confessing the people's sin and asking for God's mercy. Convicted by Ezra's display of remorse, the people of Jerusalem repented.

About 13 years later, Nehemiah, cupbearer to the king of Persia (a position requiring the highest level of security clearance), received a visit from his brother who lived in Judah. Nehemiah was anxious to hear news of the city of Jerusalem. But as Ezra had discovered earlier, the news from home wasn't so good.

The words of Nehemiah son of Hakaliah:

In the month of Kislev in the twentieth year, while I was in the citadel of Susa, Hanani, one of my brothers, came from Judah with some other men, and I questioned them about the Jewish remnant that had survived the exile, and also about Jerusalem.

They said to me, "Those who survived the exile and are back in the province are in great trouble and disgrace. The wall of Jerusalem is broken down, and its gates have been burned with fire."

When I heard these things, I sat down and wept. For some days I mourned and fasted and prayed before the God of heaven. Then I said:

"Lord, the God of heaven, the great and awesome God, who keeps his covenant of love with those who love him and keep his commandments, let your ear be attentive and your eyes open to hear the prayer your servant is praying before you day and night for your servants, the people of Israel. I confess the sins we Israelites, including myself and my father's family, have committed against you.

"Lord, let your ear be attentive to the prayer of this your servant and to the prayer of your servants who delight in revering your name. Give your servant success today by granting him favor in the presence of this man."

The temple in Jerusalem was completed, but the wall of the city still lay in ruins. A city without a wall? Might as well just invite the pillagers to walk through the open doors. Nehemiah decided he would lead the people in rebuilding the city's walls.

A mission of this scope required permission from Artaxerxes, king of Persia. After praying for God's help, Nehemiah approached the king, who was pleased to send Nehemiah on his way with letters for safe-conduct and supplies. Hard work lay ahead, long days and restless nights, but Nehemiah packed and led his caravan toward Jerusalem.

I went to Jerusalem, and after staying there three days I set out during the night with a few others. I had not told anyone what my God had put in my heart to do for Jerusalem. There were no mounts with me except the one I was riding on.

By night I went out through the Valley Gate toward the Jackal Well and the Dung Gate, examining the walls of Jerusalem, which had been broken down, and its gates, which had been destroyed by fire. Then I moved on toward the Fountain Gate and the King's Pool, but there was not enough room for my mount to get through; so I went up the valley by night, examining the wall. Finally, I turned back and reentered through the Valley Gate. The officials did not know where I had gone or what I was doing, because as yet I had said nothing to the Jews or the priests or nobles or officials or any others who would be doing the work.

Then I said to them, "You see the trouble we are in: Jerusalem lies in ruins, and its gates have been burned with fire. Come, let us rebuild the wall of Jerusalem, and we will no longer be in disgrace." I also told them about the gracious hand of my God on me and what the king had said to me.

They replied, "Let us start rebuilding." So they began this good work.

Just as the Jews had received opposition from the neighboring peoples when they worked at rebuilding the temple a century earlier, they came under attack for trying to rebuild Jerusalem's walls. Sanballat, the governor of Samaria, and Tobiah, a leading official and perhaps governor of Transjordan, were undoubtedly particularly threatened by the fact that King Artaxerxes had not only provided for Nehemiah's journey to Jerusalem but had also appointed him governor of Judah.

When Sanballat heard that we were rebuilding the wall, he became angry and was greatly incensed. He ridiculed the Jews, and in the presence of his associates and the army of Samaria, he said, "What are those feeble Jews doing? Will they restore their wall? Will they offer sacrifices? Will they finish in a day? Can they bring the stones back to life from those heaps of rubble—burned as they are?"

Tobiah the Ammonite, who was at his side, said, "What they are building — even a fox climbing up on it would break down their wall of stones!"

Hear us, our God, for we are despised. Turn their insults back on their own heads. Give them over as plunder in a land of captivity. Do not cover up their guilt or blot out their sins from your sight, for they have thrown insults in the face of the builders.

So we rebuilt the wall till all of it reached half its height, for the people worked with all their heart.

But when Sanballat, Tobiah, the Arabs, the Ammonites and the people of Ashdod heard that the repairs to Jerusalem's walls had gone ahead and that the gaps were being closed, they were very angry. They all plotted together to come and fight against Jerusalem and stir up trouble against it. But we prayed to our God and posted a guard day and night to meet this threat.

Meanwhile, the people in Judah said, "The strength of the laborers is giving out, and there is so much rubble that we cannot rebuild the wall."

Also our enemies said, "Before they know it or see us, we will be right there among them and will kill them and put an end to the work."

Then the Jews who lived near them came and told us ten times over, "Wherever you turn, they will attack us."

Therefore I stationed some of the people behind the lowest points of the wall at the exposed places, posting them by families, with their swords, spears and bows. After I looked things over, I stood up and said to the nobles, the officials and the rest of the people, "Don't be afraid of them. Remember the LORD, who is great and awesome, and fight for your families, your sons and your daughters, your wives and your homes."

When our enemies heard that we were aware of their plot and that God had frustrated it, we all returned to the wall, each to our own work.

From that day on, half of my men did the work, while the other half were equipped with spears, shields, bows and armor. The officers posted themselves behind all the people of Judah who were building the wall. Those who carried materials did their work with one hand and held a weapon in the other, and each of the builders wore his sword at his side as he worked. But the man who sounded the trumpet stayed with me.

Then I said to the nobles, the officials and the rest of the people, "The work is extensive and spread out, and we are widely separated from each other along the wall. Wherever you hear the sound of the trumpet, join us there. Our God will fight for us!"

So we continued the work with half the men holding spears, from the first light of dawn till the stars came out. At that time I also said to the people, "Have every man and his helper stay inside Jerusalem at night, so they can serve us as guards by night and as workers by day." Neither I nor my brothers nor my men nor the guards with me took off our clothes; each had his weapon, even when he went for water.

Nehemiah showed steady persistence and grace under pressure. He moved ahead while every indicator showed trouble. He also showed a savvy perception of human nature, as he could smell a trap a mile away.

When word came to Sanballat, Tobiah, Geshem the Arab and the rest of our enemies that I had rebuilt the wall and not a gap was left in it — though up to that time I had not set the doors in the gates — Sanballat and Geshem sent me this message: "Come, let us meet together in one of the villages on the plain of Ono."

But they were scheming to harm me; so I sent messengers to them with this reply: "I am carrying on a great project and cannot go down. Why should the work stop while I leave it and go down to you?" Four times they sent me the same message, and each time I gave them the same answer.

Then, the fifth time, Sanballat sent his aide to me with the same message, and in his hand was an unsealed letter in which was written:

"It is reported among the nations — and Geshem says it is true — that you and the Jews are plotting to revolt, and therefore you are building the wall. Moreover, according to these reports you are about to become their king and have even appointed prophets to make this proclamation about you in Jerusalem: 'There is a king in Judah!' Now this report will get back to the king; so come, let us meet together."

I sent him this reply: "Nothing like what you are saying is happening; you are just making it up out of your head."

They were all trying to frighten us, thinking, "Their hands will get too weak for the work, and it will not be completed."

But I prayed, "Now strengthen my hands."

One day I went to the house of Shemaiah son of Delaiah, the son of Mehetabel, who was shut in at his home. He said, "Let us meet in the house of God, inside the temple, and let us close the temple doors, because men are coming to kill you — by night they are coming to kill you."

So the wall was completed on the twenty-fifth of Elul, in fifty-two days.

When all our enemies heard about this, all the surrounding nations were afraid and lost their self-confidence, because they realized that this work had been done with the help of our God.

First the temple and now the walls of the city were complete. But why build temples and walls if people's hearts were still wandering? Both Ezra and Nehemiah wanted to ensure that a pure system of worship was in place and to enforce the laws against intermarriage with people of ungodly nations. What better way than to let God's Word speak for itself?

After the wall had been rebuilt and I had set the doors in place, the gatekeepers, the musicians and the Levites were appointed. I put in charge of Jerusalem my brother Hanani, along with Hananiah the commander of the citadel, because he was a man of integrity and feared God more than most people do.

All the people came together as one in the square before the Water Gate. They told Ezra the teacher of the Law to bring out the Book of the Law of Moses, which the LORD had commanded for Israel.

So on the first day of the seventh month Ezra the priest brought the Law before the assembly, which was made up of men and women and all who were able to understand. He read it aloud from daybreak till noon as he faced the square before the Water Gate in the presence of the men, women and others who could understand. And all the people listened attentively to the Book of the Law.

Ezra opened the book. All the people could see him because he was standing above them; and as he opened it, the people all stood up. Ezra praised the LORD, the great God; and all the people lifted their hands and responded, "Amen! Amen!" Then they bowed down and worshiped the LORD with their faces to the ground.

The Levites — Jeshua, Bani, Sherebiah, Jamin, Akkub, Shabbethai, Hodiah, Maaseiah, Kelita, Azariah, Jozabad, Hanan and Pelaiah — instructed the people in the Law while the people were standing there. They read from the Book of the Law of God, making it clear and giving the meaning so that the people understood what was being read.

Then Nehemiah the governor, Ezra the priest and teacher of the Law, and the Levites who were instructing the people said to them all, "This day is holy to the LORD your God. Do not mourn or weep." For all the people had been weeping as they listened to the words of the Law.

Nehemiah said, "Go and enjoy choice food and sweet drinks,

and send some to those who have nothing prepared. This day is holy to our Lord. Do not grieve, for the joy of the LORD is your strength."

The Levites calmed all the people, saying, "Be still, for this is a holy day. Do not grieve."

Then all the people went away to eat and drink, to send portions of food and to celebrate with great joy, because they now understood the words that had been made known to them.

On the second day of the month, the heads of all the families, along with the priests and the Levites, gathered around Ezra the teacher to give attention to the words of the Law. They found written in the Law, which the LORD had commanded through Moses, that the Israelites were to live in temporary shelters during the festival of the seventh month and that they should proclaim this word and spread it throughout their towns and in Jerusalem: "Go out into the hill country and bring back branches from olive and wild olive trees, and from myrtles, palms and shade trees, to make temporary shelters" — as it is written.

So the people went out and brought back branches and built themselves temporary shelters on their own roofs, in their courtyards, in the courts of the house of God and in the square by the Water Gate and the one by the Gate of Ephraim. The whole company that had returned from exile built temporary shelters and lived in them. From the days of Joshua son of Nun until that day, the Israelites had not celebrated it like this. And their joy was very great.

Day after day, from the first day to the last, Ezra read from the Book of the Law of God. They celebrated the festival for seven days, and on the eighth day, in accordance with the regulation, there was an assembly.

The Israelites had indeed rebuilt the temple and were worshiping God again; yet many of the people and priests strayed from the faith. God called Malachi, the last of the Old Testament prophets, to offer a final word to the people. Malachi likely lived in the same period as Ezra and Nehemiah. Perhaps his prophecies came after Ezra's death and during the time when Nehemiah was called to return to the service of the king of Persia. Through Malachi, God issued his warnings against the people's hypocrisy, but also reminded them of his never-ending covenant promise.

A prophecy: The word of the LORD to Israel through Malachi.

"A son honors his father, and a slave his master. If I am a father, where is the honor due me? If I am a master, where is the respect due me?" says the LORD Almighty.

"It is you priests who show contempt for my name.

"But you ask, 'How have we shown contempt for your name?'

"By offering defiled food on my altar.

"But you ask, 'How have we defiled you?'

"By saying that the LORD's table is contemptible. When you offer blind animals for sacrifice, is that not wrong? When you sacrifice lame or diseased animals, is that not wrong? Try offering them to your governor! Would he be pleased with you? Would he accept you?" says the LORD Almighty.

"Now plead with God to be gracious to us. With such offerings from your hands, will he accept you?" — says the LORD Almighty.

"Oh, that one of you would shut the temple doors, so that you would not light useless fires on my altar! I am not pleased with you," says the LORD Almighty, "and I will accept no offering from your hands. My name will be great among the nations, from where the sun rises to where it sets. In every place incense and pure offerings will be brought to me, because my name will be great among the nations," says the LORD Almighty.

Another thing you do: You flood the LORD's altar with tears. You weep and wail because he no longer looks with favor on your offerings or accepts them with pleasure from your hands. You ask, "Why?" It is because the LORD is the witness between you and the wife of your youth. You have been unfaithful to her, though she is your partner, the wife of your marriage covenant.

Has not the one God made you? You belong to him in body and spirit. And what does the one God seek? Godly offspring. So be on your guard, and do not be unfaithful to the wife of your youth.

"The man who hates and divorces his wife," says the LORD, the God of Israel, "does violence to the one he should protect," says the LORD Almighty.

So be on your guard, and do not be unfaithful.

"I the LORD do not change. So you, the descendants of Jacob, are not destroyed. Ever since the time of your ancestors you have turned away from my decrees and have not kept them. Return to me, and I will return to you," says the LORD Almighty.

"But you ask, 'How are we to return?'

"Will a mere mortal rob God? Yet you rob me.

"But you ask, 'How are we robbing you?'

"In tithes and offerings. You are under a curse — your whole nation — because you are robbing me. Bring the whole tithe into the storehouse, that there may be food in my house. Test me in this," says the LORD Almighty, "and see if I will not throw open the floodgates of heaven and pour out so much blessing that there will not be room enough to store it. I will prevent pests from devouring your crops, and the vines in your fields will not drop their fruit before it is ripe," says the LORD Almighty. "Then all the nations will call you blessed, for yours will be a delightful land," says the LORD Almighty.

"You have spoken arrogantly against me," says the LORD.

"Yet you ask, 'What have we said against you?'

"You have said, 'It is futile to serve God. What do we gain by carrying out his requirements and going about like mourners before the LORD Almighty? But now we call the arrogant blessed. Certainly evildoers prosper, and even when they put God to the test, they get away with it.'"

Then those who feared the LORD talked with each other, and

the Lord listened and heard. A scroll of remembrance was written in his presence concerning those who feared the Lord and honored his name.

"On the day when I act," says the Lord Almighty, "they will be my treasured possession. I will spare them, just as a father has compassion and spares his son who serves him. And you will again see the distinction between the righteous and the wicked, between those who serve God and those who do not.

"Surely the day is coming; it will burn like a furnace. All the arrogant and every evildoer will be stubble, and the day that is coming will set them on fire," says the Lord Almighty. "Not a root or a branch will be left to them. But for you who revere my name, the sun of righteousness will rise with healing in its rays. And you will go out and frolic like well-fed calves. Then you will trample on the wicked; they will be ashes under the soles of your feet on the day when I act," says the Lord Almighty.

"Remember the law of my servant Moses, the decrees and laws I gave him at Horeb for all Israel.

"See, I will send the prophet Elijah to you before that great and dreadful day of the Lord comes. He will turn the hearts of the parents to their children, and the hearts of the children to their parents; or else I will come and strike the land with total destruction."

Holy Land in the Time of Jesus

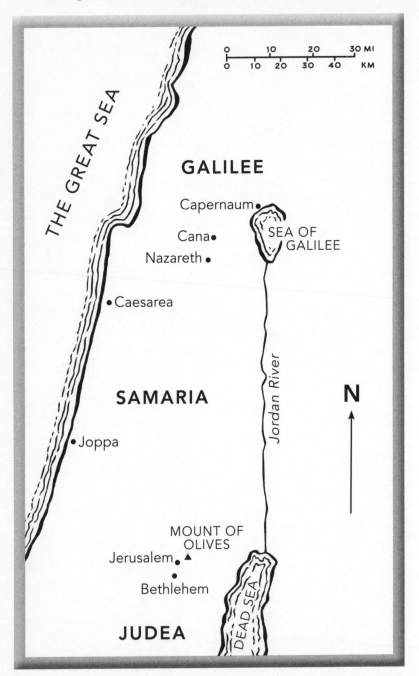

_F_OR 400 YEARS after Malachi's prophecies, no prophets or leaders rose to the level of inclusion in the record of Holy Scripture. For this reason, the period is sometimes referred to as the "silent years." In actuality, these years of social and political upheaval were anything but silent for the Jewish people.

The Maccabean revolt against the Seleucids during the second century BC was one of the most heroic eras of Jewish history. During these 400 years numerous significant writings were produced as well. The Qumran community copied the books of Isaiah, the Psalms, Deuteronomy and other sacred writings. These ancient manuscripts were discovered by a shepherd boy in AD 1947 near the Dead Sea and are known today as the "Dead Sea Scrolls."

The Deuterocanonical books, or books of the Apocrypha, accepted as Holy Scripture by the Roman and Eastern churches, were written in the years between the Old and New Testament. The Septuagint, the Greek translation of the Old Testament, was also an important product of the period. It became the Bible for Greek-speaking Jews outside Palestine and later for the early church.

But God's story wasn't finished. "When the set time had fully come," as the apostle Paul put it, God spoke again—this time in the person of Jesus the Messiah, the Son of God, whose birth, life, death and resurrection changed everything.

Now the prophets' ancient promises of a new Servant-King and kingdom of God, the promises anticipated for so many years, came to life in bold new ways. Now the people could see personified God's gracious, compassionate, unfailing love and dedication to restoring lost relationships through this carpenter and itinerant teacher, Jesus—the Messiah[1] come to set his people free. All the wisdom and purposes of God centered in Jesus' mission on planet Earth. He was God's final word. And this is how it happened . . .

---

[1]**Messiah:** A name of Jesus that emphasizes his role as God's chosen deliverer.

22

The Birth of the King

IN THE BEGINNING WAS THE WORD, and the Word was with God, and the Word was God. He was with God in the beginning. Through him all things were made; without him nothing was made that has been made. In him was life, and that life was the light of all mankind. The light shines in the darkness, and the darkness has not overcome it.

There was a man sent from God whose name was John. He came as a witness to testify concerning that light, so that through him all might believe. He himself was not the light; he came only as a witness to the light.

The true light that gives light to everyone was coming into the world. He was in the world, and though the world was made through him, the world did not recognize him. He came to that which was his own, but his own did not receive him. Yet to all who did receive him, to those who believed in his name, he gave the right to become children of God — children born not of natural descent, nor of human decision or a husband's will, but born of God.

The Word became flesh and made his dwelling among us. We

Jesus is born	Flight to Egypt	Jesus visits the temple
6/5 BC	5/4 BC	AD 7/8

Full timeline information starts on page xi.

have seen his glory, the glory of the one and only Son, who came from the Father, full of grace[1] and truth.

For the law was given through Moses; grace and truth came through Jesus Christ. No one has ever seen God, but the one and only Son, who is himself God and is in closest relationship with the Father, has made him known.

God sent the angel Gabriel to Nazareth, a town in Galilee, to a virgin pledged to be married to a man named Joseph, a descendant of David. The virgin's name was Mary. The angel went to her and said, "Greetings, you who are highly favored! The Lord is with you."

Mary was greatly troubled at his words and wondered what kind of greeting this might be. But the angel said to her, "Do not be afraid, Mary; you have found favor with God. You will conceive and give birth to a son, and you are to call him Jesus. He will be great and will be called the Son of the Most High. The Lord God will give him the throne of his father David, and he will reign over Jacob's descendants forever; his kingdom will never end."

"How will this be," Mary asked the angel, "since I am a virgin?"

The angel answered, "The Holy Spirit will come on you, and the power of the Most High will overshadow you. So the holy one to be born will be called the Son of God."

"I am the Lord's servant," Mary answered. "May your word to me be fulfilled." Then the angel left her.

And Mary said:

"My soul glorifies the Lord
    and my spirit rejoices in God my Savior,[2]

---

[1]**Grace:** Unmerited favor and blessing. In the New Testament, this term often refers to the undeserved pardon from sin through Jesus' death.

[2]**Savior:** One who rescues or heals. Jesus Christ is revealed as the Savior who rescues his people from sin and eternal punishment.

for he has been mindful
    of the humble state of his servant.
From now on all generations will call me blessed,
    for the Mighty One has done great things for me —
    holy is his name.
His mercy extends to those who fear him,
    from generation to generation.
He has performed mighty deeds with his arm;
    he has scattered those who are proud in their inmost
        thoughts.
He has brought down rulers from their thrones
    but has lifted up the humble.
He has filled the hungry with good things
    but has sent the rich away empty.
He has helped his servant Israel,
    remembering to be merciful
to Abraham and his descendants forever,
    just as he promised our ancestors."

How did Mary, a virgin, become pregnant? She and Joseph were engaged but had not had sexual relations. No medical doctor could answer this question, but such was the mysterious nature of Mary's conception and Jesus' birth — a miraculous beginning ordained by God's power alone. Imagine Mary's problem explaining this incredible experience! She couldn't understand it herself, much less explain it to her friends and family.

In that day and time, an engagement was considered as strong a commitment as marriage although Joseph and Mary were not officially married. Although he probably wanted to believe Mary, Joseph was in a difficult situation. Engaged and committed to a woman whom his family and friends would now despise, Joseph decided it was best to break off the engagement ... until an unusual visitor changed his perspective.

Because Joseph her husband was faithful to the law, and yet

did not want to expose her to public disgrace, he had in mind to divorce her quietly.

But after he had considered this, an angel of the Lord appeared to him in a dream and said, "Joseph son of David, do not be afraid to take Mary home as your wife, because what is conceived in her is from the Holy Spirit. She will give birth to a son, and you are to give him the name Jesus, because he will save his people from their sins."

All this took place to fulfill what the Lord had said through the prophet: "The virgin will conceive and give birth to a son, and they will call him Immanuel" (which means "God with us").

When Joseph woke up, he did what the angel of the Lord had commanded him and took Mary home as his wife.

In those days Caesar Augustus issued a decree that a census should be taken of the entire Roman world. (This was the first census that took place while Quirinius was governor of Syria.) And everyone went to their own town to register.

So Joseph also went up from the town of Nazareth in Galilee to Judea, to Bethlehem the town of David, because he belonged to the house and line of David. He went there to register with Mary, who was pledged to be married to him and was expecting a child. While they were there, the time came for the baby to be born, and she gave birth to her firstborn, a son. She wrapped him in cloths and placed him in a manger, because there was no guest room available for them.

And there were shepherds living out in the fields nearby, keeping watch over their flocks at night. An angel of the Lord appeared to them, and the glory of the Lord shone around them, and they were terrified. But the angel said to them, "Do not be afraid. I bring you good news[3] that will cause great joy for all the people. Today in the town of David a Savior has been born to you; he is the Messiah,

---

[3]**Good news:** The literal translation of the word *gospel*, this word refers to the message that Jesus has come to reconcile humanity to God. The good news is that each individual can accept this undeserved gift and enter into a relationship with him.

the Lord. This will be a sign to you: You will find a baby wrapped in cloths and lying in a manger."

Suddenly a great company of the heavenly host appeared with the angel, praising God and saying,

> "Glory to God in the highest heaven,
>   and on earth peace to those on whom his favor rests."

When the angels had left them and gone into heaven, the shepherds said to one another, "Let's go to Bethlehem and see this thing that has happened, which the Lord has told us about."

So they hurried off and found Mary and Joseph, and the baby, who was lying in the manger. When they had seen him, they spread the word concerning what had been told them about this child, and all who heard it were amazed at what the shepherds said to them. But Mary treasured up all these things and pondered them in her heart. The shepherds returned, glorifying and praising God for all the things they had heard and seen, which were just as they had been told.

Joseph and Mary decided to remain in Bethlehem after Jesus was born. Faithful to the Law of Moses, they had Jesus circumcised when he was eight days old. There the new family was greeted by two older saints, Simeon and Anna, to whom God gave the opportunity to see and recognize the Messiah before the end of their days. And these wouldn't be the last individuals to discern the special nature of the child Jesus.

After Jesus was born in Bethlehem in Judea, during the time of King Herod, Magi[4] from the east came to Jerusalem and asked, "Where is the one who has been born king of the Jews? We saw his star when it rose and have come to worship him."

When King Herod heard this he was disturbed, and all Jerusalem with him. When he had called together all the people's chief priests and teachers of the law, he asked them where the Messiah

---

[4]**Magi:** Traditionally *wise men*.

was to be born. "In Bethlehem in Judea," they replied, "for this is what the prophet has written:

> "'But you, Bethlehem, in the land of Judah,
>   are by no means least among the rulers of Judah;
> for out of you will come a ruler
>   who will shepherd my people Israel.'"

Then Herod called the Magi secretly and found out from them the exact time the star had appeared. He sent them to Bethlehem and said, "Go and search carefully for the child. As soon as you find him, report to me, so that I too may go and worship him."

After they had heard the king, they went on their way, and the star they had seen when it rose went ahead of them until it stopped over the place where the child was. When they saw the star, they were overjoyed. On coming to the house, they saw the child with his mother Mary, and they bowed down and worshiped him. Then they opened their treasures and presented him with gifts of gold, frankincense and myrrh. And having been warned in a dream not to go back to Herod, they returned to their country by another route.

When they had gone, an angel of the Lord appeared to Joseph in a dream. "Get up," he said, "take the child and his mother and escape to Egypt. Stay there until I tell you, for Herod is going to search for the child to kill him."

So he got up, took the child and his mother during the night and left for Egypt, where he stayed until the death of Herod. And so was fulfilled what the Lord had said through the prophet: "Out of Egypt I called my son."

When Herod realized that he had been outwitted by the Magi, he was furious, and he gave orders to kill all the boys in Bethlehem and its vicinity who were two years old and under, in accordance with the time he had learned from the Magi. Then what was said through the prophet Jeremiah was fulfilled:

> "A voice is heard in Ramah,
>   weeping and great mourning,

Rachel weeping for her children
and refusing to be comforted,
because they are no more."

After Herod died, an angel of the Lord appeared in a dream to Joseph in Egypt and said, "Get up, take the child and his mother and go to the land of Israel, for those who were trying to take the child's life are dead."

So he got up, took the child and his mother and went to the land of Israel. But when he heard that Archelaus was reigning in Judea in place of his father Herod, he was afraid to go there. Having been warned in a dream, he withdrew to the district of Galilee, and he went and lived in a town called Nazareth.

Nothing more is known about the boy Jesus until he appears in Jerusalem at age 12. Most likely he learned carpentry skills as a youngster from Joseph and studied in the synagogue. His mind grew strong, along with his body and soul. While still a youth, his agile mind was ready to engage in discussion with synagogue leaders. One time Jesus became so engrossed in learning and questioning that he lost track of time.

Every year Jesus' parents went to Jerusalem for the Festival of the Passover. When he was twelve years old, they went up to the festival, according to the custom. After the festival was over, while his parents were returning home, the boy Jesus stayed behind in Jerusalem, but they were unaware of it. Thinking he was in their company, they traveled on for a day. Then they began looking for him among their relatives and friends. When they did not find him, they went back to Jerusalem to look for him. After three days they found him in the temple courts, sitting among the teachers, listening to them and asking them questions. Everyone who heard him was amazed at his understanding and his answers. When his parents saw him, they were astonished. His mother said to him, "Son, why have you treated us like this? Your father and I have been anxiously searching for you."

"Why were you searching for me?" he asked. "Didn't you know I had to be in my Father's house?" But they did not understand what he was saying to them.

Then he went down to Nazareth with them and was obedient to them. But his mother treasured all these things in her heart. And Jesus grew in wisdom and stature, and in favor with God and man.

Who was this Jesus? A new prophet? A scholar destined to be a great rabbi? Perhaps a political leader with the charisma to finally send the oppressive Roman armies, who controlled Judea, back across the sea? None of these expectations turned out to describe him adequately. In fact, Jesus defied expectations as the people watched and wondered.

Jesus

This is the genealogy of Jesus the Messiah,
the son of David,
the son of Abraham:

Abraham was the father of Isaac,

Isaac the father of Jacob,

Jacob the father of Judah and his brothers,

Judah the father of Perez and Zerah,

whose mother was Tamar,

Perez the father of Hezron,

Hezron the father of Ram,

Ram the father of Amminadab,

Amminadab the father of Nahshon

Nahshon the father of Salmon,

Salmon the father of Boaz, whose mother was Rahab,

Boaz the father of Obed, whose mother was Ruth,

Obed the father of Jesse,

and Jesse the father of King David.

David was the father of Solomon,

whose mother had been Uriah's wife,

Solomon the father of Rehoboam,

Rehoboam the father of Abijah,

Abijah the father of Asa,

Asa the father of Jehoshaphat,

Jehoshaphat the father of Jehoram,

Jehoram the father of Uzziah,
Uzziah the father of Jotham,
Jotham the father of Ahaz,
Ahaz the father of Hezekiah,
Hezekiah the father of Manasseh,
Manasseh the father of Amon,
Amon the father of Josiah,
and Josiah the father of Jeconiah
and his brothers at the time of the exile to Babylon.
After the exile to Babylon:
Jeconiah was the father of Shealtiel,
Shealtiel the father of Zerubbabel,
Zerubbabel the father of Abiud,
Abiud the father of Eliakim,
Eliakim the father of Azor,
Azor the father of Zadok,
Zadok the father of Akim,
Akim the father of Eliud,
Eliud the father of Eleazar,
Eleazar the father of Matthan,
Matthan the father of Jacob,
and Jacob the father of Joseph,
the husband of Mary,
and Mary was the mother of Jesus
who is called the Messiah.

23

Jesus' Ministry Begins

Imagine if you were introducing the Savior of the world. Wouldn't you make it a gala event? Call in the media? Spotlight the attending celebs? Give the Savior the red-carpet treatment? Get people's attention?

God doesn't work that way. He planned his Son's introduction using a scruffy bohemian prophet called John the Baptist. John, the son of Mary's relative Elizabeth, was the one who had been foretold to precede the Messiah "in the spirit and power of Elijah." John was unique among the prophets. He lived outside of the mainstream religious culture, yet his message was more timely than any other.

IN THOSE DAYS John the Baptist came, preaching in the wilderness of Judea and saying, "Repent, for the kingdom of heaven has come near."

John's clothes were made of camel's hair, and he had a leather belt around his waist. His food was locusts and wild honey. People went out to him from Jerusalem and all Judea and the whole region

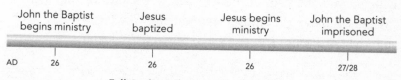

John the Baptist begins ministry	Jesus baptized	Jesus begins ministry	John the Baptist imprisoned
AD 26	26	26	27/28

Full timeline information starts on page xi.

of the Jordan. Confessing their sins, they were baptized[1] by him in the Jordan River.

Then Jesus came from Galilee to the Jordan to be baptized by John. But John tried to deter him, saying, "I need to be baptized by you, and do you come to me?"

Jesus replied, "Let it be so now; it is proper for us to do this to fulfill all righteousness." Then John consented.

As soon as Jesus was baptized, he went up out of the water. At that moment heaven was opened, and he saw the Spirit of God descending like a dove and alighting on him. And a voice from heaven said, "This is my Son, whom I love; with him I am well pleased."

Then Jesus was led by the Spirit into the wilderness to be tempted by the devil. After fasting forty days and forty nights, he was hungry. The tempter came to him and said, "If you are the Son of God, tell these stones to become bread."

Jesus answered, "It is written: 'Man shall not live on bread alone, but on every word that comes from the mouth of God.'"

Then the devil took him to the holy city and had him stand on the highest point of the temple. "If you are the Son of God," he said, "throw yourself down. For it is written:

> "'He will command his angels concerning you,
>   and they will lift you up in their hands,
>   so that you will not strike your foot against a stone.'"

Jesus answered him, "It is also written: 'Do not put the Lord your God to the test.'"

Again, the devil took him to a very high mountain and showed him all the kingdoms of the world and their splendor. "All this I will give you," he said, "if you will bow down and worship me."

Jesus said to him, "Away from me, Satan! For it is written: 'Worship the Lord your God, and serve him only.'"

---

[1]**Baptized, baptism:** A symbolic act demonstrating that new believers have abandoned their former ways and have embarked on new life.

Then the devil left him, and angels came and attended him.

Following the test in the wilderness, Jesus began his public ministry. John the Baptist continued to point to Jesus, claiming that everything God had promised centered on this one man. This was startling news to the religious elite, and John was asked to explain himself. Imagine skilled religious lawyers questioning this rough-hewn eccentric, a man without credentials or authorization. The interrogation began.

Now this was John's testimony when the Jewish leaders in Jerusalem sent priests and Levites to ask him who he was. He did not fail to confess, but confessed freely, "I am not the Messiah."

They asked him, "Then who are you? Are you Elijah?"

He said, "I am not."

"Are you the Prophet?"

He answered, "No."

Finally they said, "Who are you? Give us an answer to take back to those who sent us. What do you say about yourself?"

John replied in the words of Isaiah the prophet, "I am the voice of one calling in the wilderness, 'Make straight the way for the Lord.'"

Now the Pharisees[2] who had been sent questioned him, "Why then do you baptize if you are not the Messiah, nor Elijah, nor the Prophet?"

"I baptize with water," John replied, "but among you stands one you do not know. He is the one who comes after me, the straps of whose sandals I am not worthy to untie."

This all happened at Bethany on the other side of the Jordan, where John was baptizing.

The next day John saw Jesus coming toward him and said, "Look, the Lamb of God,[3] who takes away the sin of the world!

---

[2]**Pharisees:** The most powerful group of religious authorities within Judaism. The Pharisees were highly focused on their interpretation of the laws given by God, and they often challenged Jesus regarding these precepts.

[3]**Lamb of God:** One of the names of Jesus, which demonstrates the connection between Jesus' sacrificial death and the offerings of the Old Testament.

This is the one I meant when I said, 'A man who comes after me has surpassed me because he was before me.' I myself did not know him, but the reason I came baptizing with water was that he might be revealed to Israel."

Then John gave this testimony: "I saw the Spirit come down from heaven as a dove and remain on him. And I myself did not know him, but the one who sent me to baptize with water told me, 'The man on whom you see the Spirit come down and remain is the one who will baptize with the Holy Spirit.' I have seen and I testify that this is God's Chosen One."

The next day John was there again with two of his disciples.[4] When he saw Jesus passing by, he said, "Look, the Lamb of God!"

When the two disciples heard him say this, they followed Jesus. Turning around, Jesus saw them following and asked, "What do you want?"

They said, "Rabbi" (which means "Teacher"), "where are you staying?"

"Come," he replied, "and you will see."

So they went and saw where he was staying, and they spent that day with him. It was about four in the afternoon.

Andrew, Simon Peter's brother, was one of the two who heard what John had said and who had followed Jesus. The first thing Andrew did was to find his brother Simon and tell him, "We have found the Messiah" (that is, the Christ). And he brought him to Jesus.

Jesus looked at him and said, "You are Simon son of John. You will be called Cephas" (which, when translated, is Peter).[5]

The next day Jesus decided to leave for Galilee. Finding Philip, he said to him, "Follow me."

Philip, like Andrew and Peter, was from the town of Bethsaida. Philip found Nathanael and told him, "We have found the one Moses wrote about in the Law, and about whom the prophets also wrote — Jesus of Nazareth, the son of Joseph."

---

[4]**Disciples:** The followers of Jesus.
[5]**Peter:** *Cephas* (Aramaic) and *Peter* (Greek) both mean "rock."

"Nazareth! Can anything good come from there?" Nathanael asked.

"Come and see," said Philip.

When Jesus saw Nathanael approaching, he said of him, "Here truly is an Israelite in whom there is no deceit."

"How do you know me?" Nathanael asked.

Jesus answered, "I saw you while you were still under the fig tree before Philip called you."

Then Nathanael declared, "Rabbi, you are the Son of God; you are the king of Israel."

Jesus said, "You believe because I told you I saw you under the fig tree. You will see greater things than that." He then added, "Very truly I tell you, you will see 'heaven open, and the angels of God ascending and descending on' the Son of Man."[6]

On the third day a wedding took place at Cana in Galilee. Jesus' mother was there, and Jesus and his disciples had also been invited to the wedding. When the wine was gone, Jesus' mother said to him, "They have no more wine."

"Woman, why do you involve me?" Jesus replied. "My hour has not yet come."

His mother said to the servants, "Do whatever he tells you."

Nearby stood six stone water jars, the kind used by the Jews for ceremonial washing, each holding from twenty to thirty gallons.

Jesus said to the servants, "Fill the jars with water"; so they filled them to the brim.

Then he told them, "Now draw some out and take it to the master of the banquet."

They did so, and the master of the banquet tasted the water that had been turned into wine. He did not realize where it had come from, though the servants who had drawn the water knew. Then he called the bridegroom aside and said, "Everyone brings out the choice wine first and then the cheaper wine after the guests have had too much to drink; but you have saved the best till now."

---

[6]**Son of Man:** A name of Jesus that emphasizes his dual nature as both fully God and fully human.

What Jesus did here in Cana of Galilee was the first of the signs through which he revealed his glory; and his disciples believed in him.

Jesus began to reveal who he was, and he was like no other person anyone had known. Although he was fully human, he was also fully God. With his 12 disciples as interns, Jesus began his itinerant ministry of teaching and healing.

Soon he traveled to the city of Jerusalem to celebrate the Passover feast. It was in Jerusalem that political and religious decisions were made; power brokers set their agendas in this bustling town. Many people listened to Jesus' teachings and believed he was the Messiah. Others thought he was a trouble-maker. One inquisitive religious leader sought Jesus out privately, under cover of darkness. Jesus took the opportunity to summarize his mission by talking about being born ... again.

Now there was a Pharisee, a man named Nicodemus who was a member of the Jewish ruling council. He came to Jesus at night and said, "Rabbi, we know that you are a teacher who has come from God. For no one could perform the signs you are doing if God were not with him."

Jesus replied, "Very truly I tell you, no one can see the kingdom of God unless they are born again."[7]

"How can someone be born when they are old?" Nicodemus asked. "Surely they cannot enter a second time into their mother's womb to be born!"

Jesus answered, "Very truly I tell you, no one can enter the kingdom of God unless they are born of water and the Spirit. Flesh gives birth to flesh, but the Spirit gives birth to spirit. You should not be surprised at my saying, 'You must be born again.' The wind blows wherever it pleases. You hear its sound, but you cannot tell where it comes from or where it is going. So it is with everyone born of the Spirit."

---

[7]**Born again:** A term signifying the new spiritual life gained when one believes in Jesus Christ as the Son of God and accepts his death on the cross as a "free gift" that releases people from the penalty of sin.

"How can this be?" Nicodemus asked.

"You are Israel's teacher," said Jesus, "and do you not under-stand these things? Very truly I tell you, we speak of what we know, and we testify to what we have seen, but still you people do not accept our testimony. I have spoken to you of earthly things and you do not believe; how then will you believe if I speak of heav-enly things? No one has ever gone into heaven except the one who came from heaven — the Son of Man. Just as Moses lifted up the snake in the wilderness, so the Son of Man must be lifted up, that everyone who believes may have eternal life in him."

For God so loved the world that he gave his one and only Son, that whoever believes in him shall not perish but have eternal life. For God did not send his Son into the world to condemn the world, but to save the world through him. Whoever believes in him is not condemned, but whoever does not believe stands condemned already because they have not believed in the name of God's one and only Son.

The kind of claims Jesus made did not make him very popu-lar with the religious elite. But Jesus knew his purpose, and he spent much of his time with ordinary people who had ordinary human needs. One such person was a woman he met in the region of Samaria. Women were second-class citizens in the cul-ture of that day. In addition, there was a harsh rivalry between Jews and Samaritans, and most Jews would not associate in any way with Samaritans, let alone a woman. But once again, Jesus broke the mold.

Now he had to go through Samaria. So he came to a town in Samaria called Sychar, near the plot of ground Jacob had given to his son Joseph. Jacob's well was there, and Jesus, tired as he was from the journey, sat down by the well. It was about noon.

When a Samaritan woman came to draw water, Jesus said to her, "Will you give me a drink?" (His disciples had gone into the town to buy food.)

The Samaritan woman said to him, "You are a Jew and I am a Samaritan woman. How can you ask me for a drink?" (For Jews do not associate with Samaritans.)

Jesus answered her, "If you knew the gift of God and who it is that asks you for a drink, you would have asked him and he would have given you living water."

"Sir," the woman said, "you have nothing to draw with and the well is deep. Where can you get this living water? Are you greater than our father Jacob, who gave us the well and drank from it himself, as did also his sons and his livestock?"

Jesus answered, "Everyone who drinks this water will be thirsty again, but whoever drinks the water I give them will never thirst. Indeed, the water I give them will become in them a spring of water welling up to eternal life."

The woman said to him, "Sir, give me this water so that I won't get thirsty and have to keep coming here to draw water."

He told her, "Go, call your husband and come back."

"I have no husband," she replied.

Jesus said to her, "You are right when you say you have no husband. The fact is, you have had five husbands, and the man you now have is not your husband. What you have just said is quite true."

"Sir," the woman said, "I can see that you are a prophet. Our ancestors worshiped on this mountain, but you Jews claim that the place where we must worship is in Jerusalem."

"Woman," Jesus replied, "believe me, a time is coming when you will worship the Father neither on this mountain nor in Jerusalem. You Samaritans worship what you do not know; we worship what we do know, for salvation is from the Jews. Yet a time is coming and has now come when the true worshipers will worship the Father in the Spirit and in truth, for they are the kind of worshipers the Father seeks. God is spirit, and his worshipers must worship in the Spirit and in truth."

The woman said, "I know that Messiah" (called Christ) "is coming. When he comes, he will explain everything to us."

Then Jesus declared, "I, the one speaking to you — I am he."

Just then his disciples returned and were surprised to find him talking with a woman. But no one asked, "What do you want?" or "Why are you talking with her?"

Then, leaving her water jar, the woman went back to the town and said to the people, "Come, see a man who told me everything I ever did. Could this be the Messiah?" They came out of the town and made their way toward him.

Many of the Samaritans from that town believed in him because of the woman's testimony, "He told me everything I ever did." So when the Samaritans came to him, they urged him to stay with them, and he stayed two days. And because of his words many more became believers.

They said to the woman, "We no longer believe just because of what you said; now we have heard for ourselves, and we know that this man really is the Savior of the world."

After the two days he left for Galilee.

They went to Capernaum, and when the Sabbath came, Jesus went into the synagogue and began to teach. The people were amazed at his teaching, because he taught them as one who had authority, not as the teachers of the law. Just then a man in their synagogue who was possessed by an impure spirit cried out, "What do you want with us, Jesus of Nazareth? Have you come to destroy us? I know who you are — the Holy One of God!"

"Be quiet!" said Jesus sternly. "Come out of him!" The impure spirit shook the man violently and came out of him with a shriek.

The people were all so amazed that they asked each other, "What is this? A new teaching — and with authority! He even gives orders to impure spirits and they obey him." News about him spread quickly over the whole region of Galilee.

As soon as they left the synagogue, they went with James and John to the home of Simon and Andrew. Simon's mother-in-law was in bed with a fever, and they immediately told Jesus about her.

So he went to her, took her hand and helped her up. The fever left her and she began to wait on them.

That evening after sunset the people brought to Jesus all the sick and demon-possessed. The whole town gathered at the door, and Jesus healed many who had various diseases. He also drove out many demons, but he would not let the demons speak because they knew who he was.

Very early in the morning, while it was still dark, Jesus got up, left the house and went off to a solitary place, where he prayed. Simon and his companions went to look for him, and when they found him, they exclaimed: "Everyone is looking for you!"

Jesus replied, "Let us go somewhere else — to the nearby villages — so I can preach there also. That is why I have come." So he traveled throughout Galilee, preaching in their synagogues and driving out demons.

A man with leprosy came to him and begged him on his knees, "If you are willing, you can make me clean."

Jesus was indignant. He reached out his hand and touched the man. "I am willing," he said. "Be clean!" Immediately the leprosy left him and he was cleansed.

Jesus sent him away at once with a strong warning: "See that you don't tell this to anyone. But go, show yourself to the priest and offer the sacrifices that Moses commanded for your cleansing, as a testimony to them." Instead he went out and began to talk freely, spreading the news. As a result, Jesus could no longer enter a town openly but stayed outside in lonely places. Yet the people still came to him from everywhere.

A few days later, when Jesus again entered Capernaum, the people heard that he had come home. They gathered in such large numbers that there was no room left, not even outside the door, and he preached the word to them. Some men came, bringing to him a paralyzed man, carried by four of them. Since they could not get him to Jesus because of the crowd, they made an opening in the roof above Jesus by digging through it and then lowered the mat the man was lying on. When Jesus saw their faith, he said to the paralyzed man, "Son, your sins are forgiven."

Now some teachers of the law were sitting there, thinking to themselves, "Why does this fellow talk like that? He's blaspheming! Who can forgive sins but God alone?"

Immediately Jesus knew in his spirit that this was what they were thinking in their hearts, and he said to them, "Why are you thinking these things? Which is easier: to say to this paralyzed man, 'Your sins are forgiven,' or to say, 'Get up, take your mat and walk'? But I want you to know that the Son of Man has authority on earth to forgive sins." So he said to the man, "I tell you, get up, take your mat and go home." He got up, took his mat and walked out in full view of them all. This amazed everyone and they praised God, saying, "We have never seen anything like this!"

Once again Jesus went out beside the lake. A large crowd came to him, and he began to teach them. As he walked along, he saw Levi son of Alphaeus sitting at the tax collector's booth. "Follow me," Jesus told him, and Levi got up and followed him.

While Jesus was having dinner at Levi's house, many tax collectors and sinners were eating with him and his disciples, for there were many who followed him. When the teachers of the law who were Pharisees saw him eating with the sinners and tax collectors, they asked his disciples: "Why does he eat with tax collectors and sinners?"

On hearing this, Jesus said to them, "It is not the healthy who need a doctor, but the sick. I have not come to call the righteous, but sinners."

From the start, Jesus appeared to be a different kind of rabbi. He seemed to disregard the many customary laws that defined proper behavior for Jewish people. He put people before laws. His "new way" was forgiving and kind. Jesus didn't come off as a rabble-rouser but as a friend to people on the outside, people suspected of not being pure, people most religious leaders disliked.

Another time Jesus went into the synagogue, and a man with a shriveled hand was there. Some of them were looking for a reason to accuse Jesus, so they watched him closely to see if he would heal him on the Sabbath. Jesus said to the man with the shriveled hand, "Stand up in front of everyone."

Then Jesus asked them, "Which is lawful on the Sabbath: to do good or to do evil, to save life or to kill?" But they remained silent.

He looked around at them in anger and, deeply distressed at their stubborn hearts, said to the man, "Stretch out your hand." He stretched it out, and his hand was completely restored. Then the Pharisees went out and began to plot with the Herodians[8] how they might kill Jesus.

Jesus went throughout Galilee, teaching in their synagogues, proclaiming the good news of the kingdom, and healing every disease and sickness among the people. News about him spread all over Syria, and people brought to him all who were ill with various diseases, those suffering severe pain, the demon-possessed, those having seizures, and the paralyzed; and he healed them. Large crowds from Galilee, the Decapolis, Jerusalem, Judea and the region across the Jordan followed him.

Because of the crowd he told his disciples to have a small boat ready for him, to keep the people from crowding him. For he had healed many, so that those with diseases were pushing forward to touch him. Whenever the impure spirits saw him, they fell down before him and cried out, "You are the Son of God." But he gave them strict orders not to tell others about him.

The Jews were convinced that when the long-awaited Messiah came, he would free the people from political oppression. He would liberate them from the power of the Roman Empire. They were looking for an earthly king to bring their nation into power. But Jesus' purpose was much deeper, his intentions more sig-

---

[8]**Herodians:** A Jewish sect.

nificant, and his kingship infinitely more glorious than what the people were expecting. They had to learn the true meaning of the word "Messiah"—Anointed One. They had to discover who Jesus really was. Only then would they have his okay to spread the Good News.

Jesus went up on a mountainside and called to him those he wanted, and they came to him. He appointed twelve that they might be with him and that he might send them out to preach and to have authority to drive out demons. These are the twelve he appointed: Simon (to whom he gave the name Peter), James son of Zebedee and his brother John (to them he gave the name Boanerges, which means "sons of thunder"), Andrew, Philip, Bartholomew, Matthew, Thomas, James son of Alphaeus, Thaddaeus, Simon the Zealot and Judas Iscariot, who betrayed him.

After this, Jesus traveled about from one town and village to another, proclaiming the good news of the kingdom of God. The Twelve were with him, and also some women who had been cured of evil spirits and diseases: Mary (called Magdalene) from whom seven demons had come out; Joanna the wife of Chuza, the manager of Herod's household; Susanna; and many others. These women were helping to support them out of their own means.

Apparently even John the Baptist didn't really understand who Jesus was. John had announced Jesus as the coming Messiah, but Jesus' work hadn't brought the results John evidently expected. Added to John's disappointment was the fact that he had been languishing in prison for some time because he had publicly criticized Herod Antipas.

Herod Antipas was one of the sons of Herod the Great, who ruled at the time of Jesus' birth. Herod Antipas was the Roman puppet ruler over Galilee, and he had convinced his brother's wife to leave her husband and marry him, a violation of Jewish law. John had been locked up for pointing out Herod's sin.

When John, who was in prison, heard about the deeds of the Messiah, he sent his disciples to ask him, "Are you the one who is to come, or should we expect someone else?"

Jesus replied, "Go back and report to John what you hear and see: The blind receive sight, the lame walk, those who have leprosy are cleansed, the deaf hear, the dead are raised, and the good news is proclaimed to the poor. Blessed is anyone who does not stumble on account of me."

As John's disciples were leaving, Jesus began to speak to the crowd about John: "What did you go out into the wilderness to see? A reed swayed by the wind? If not, what did you go out to see? A man dressed in fine clothes? No, those who wear fine clothes are in kings' palaces. Then what did you go out to see? A prophet? Yes, I tell you, and more than a prophet. This is the one about whom it is written:

> "'I will send my messenger ahead of you,
>   who will prepare your way before you.'

Truly I tell you, among those born of women there has not risen anyone greater than John the Baptist; yet whoever is least in the kingdom of heaven is greater than he. From the days of John the Baptist until now, the kingdom of heaven has been subjected to violence, and violent people have been raiding it. For all the Prophets and the Law prophesied until John. And if you are willing to accept it, he is the Elijah who was to come."

Jesus' answer to John gave more insight into Jesus' role as Savior and the Messiah. Many people were intrigued by this prophet and teacher, and they wanted to hear more.

24

No Ordinary Man

AGAIN JESUS BEGAN TO TEACH by the lake. The crowd that gathered around him was so large that he got into a boat and sat in it out on the lake, while all the people were along the shore at the water's edge. He taught them many things by parables, and in his teaching said: "Listen! A farmer went out to sow his seed. As he was scattering the seed, some fell along the path, and the birds came and ate it up. Some fell on rocky places, where it did not have much soil. It sprang up quickly, because the soil was shallow. But when the sun came up, the plants were scorched, and they withered because they had no root. Other seed fell among thorns, which grew up and choked the plants, so that they did not bear grain. Still other seed fell on good soil. It came up, grew and produced a crop, some multiplying thirty, some sixty, some a hundred times."

Then Jesus said, "Whoever has ears to hear, let them hear."

When he was alone, the Twelve and the others around him asked him about the parables. He told them, "The secret of the kingdom of God has been given to you. But to those on the outside everything is said in parables so that,

Jesus begins ministry	Jesus gives Sermon on the Mount	Jesus sends disciples	John the Baptist dies	Jesus feeds 5,000 people	Jesus as the bread of life
AD 26	28	28	28/29	29	29

Full timeline information starts on page xi.

"'they may be ever seeing but never perceiving,
    and ever hearing but never understanding;
otherwise they might turn and be forgiven!'"

Then Jesus said to them, "Don't you understand this parable? How then will you understand any parable? The farmer sows the word. Some people are like seed along the path, where the word is sown. As soon as they hear it, Satan comes and takes away the word that was sown in them. Others, like seed sown on rocky places, hear the word and at once receive it with joy. But since they have no root, they last only a short time. When trouble or persecution comes because of the word, they quickly fall away. Still others, like seed sown among thorns, hear the word; but the worries of this life, the deceitfulness of wealth and the desires for other things come in and choke the word, making it unfruitful. Others, like seed sown on good soil, hear the word, accept it, and produce a crop — some thirty, some sixty, some a hundred times what was sown."

He said to them, "Do you bring in a lamp to put it under a bowl or a bed? Instead, don't you put it on its stand? For whatever is hidden is meant to be disclosed, and whatever is concealed is meant to be brought out into the open. If anyone has ears to hear, let them hear."

"Consider carefully what you hear," he continued. "With the measure you use, it will be measured to you — and even more. Whoever has will be given more; whoever does not have, even what they have will be taken from them."

He also said, "This is what the kingdom of God is like. A man scatters seed on the ground. Night and day, whether he sleeps or gets up, the seed sprouts and grows, though he does not know how. All by itself the soil produces grain — first the stalk, then the head, then the full kernel in the head. As soon as the grain is ripe, he puts the sickle to it, because the harvest has come."

Again he said, "What shall we say the kingdom of God is like, or what parable shall we use to describe it? It is like a mustard seed, which is the smallest of all seeds on earth. Yet when planted, it grows and becomes the largest of all garden plants, with such big branches that the birds can perch in its shade."

With many similar parables Jesus spoke the word to them, as much as they could understand. He did not say anything to them without using a parable. But when he was alone with his own disciples, he explained everything.

Jesus often used parables to teach the people. These stories, typically drawn from nature or everyday life, pointed out a central truth that called out an intended response from the listeners. On one occasion Jesus told three parables in response to the self-righteous complaints of the Pharisees and teachers of the law about the company Jesus kept.

Now the tax collectors and sinners were all gathering around to hear Jesus. But the Pharisees and the teachers of the law muttered, "This man welcomes sinners and eats with them."

Then Jesus told them this parable: "Suppose one of you has a hundred sheep and loses one of them. Doesn't he leave the ninety-nine in the open country and go after the lost sheep until he finds it? And when he finds it, he joyfully puts it on his shoulders and goes home. Then he calls his friends and neighbors together and says, 'Rejoice with me; I have found my lost sheep.' I tell you that in the same way there will be more rejoicing in heaven over one sinner who repents than over ninety-nine righteous persons who do not need to repent.

"Or suppose a woman has ten silver coins and loses one. Doesn't she light a lamp, sweep the house and search carefully until she finds it? And when she finds it, she calls her friends and neighbors together and says, 'Rejoice with me; I have found my lost coin.' In the same way, I tell you, there is rejoicing in the presence of the angels of God over one sinner who repents."

Jesus continued: "There was a man who had two sons. The

younger one said to his father, 'Father, give me my share of the estate.' So he divided his property between them.

"Not long after that, the younger son got together all he had, set off for a distant country and there squandered his wealth in wild living. After he had spent everything, there was a severe famine in that whole country, and he began to be in need. So he went and hired himself out to a citizen of that country, who sent him to his fields to feed pigs. He longed to fill his stomach with the pods that the pigs were eating, but no one gave him anything.

"When he came to his senses, he said, 'How many of my father's hired servants have food to spare, and here I am starving to death! I will set out and go back to my father and say to him: Father, I have sinned against heaven and against you. I am no longer worthy to be called your son; make me like one of your hired servants.' So he got up and went to his father.

"But while he was still a long way off, his father saw him and was filled with compassion for him; he ran to his son, threw his arms around him and kissed him.

"The son said to him, 'Father, I have sinned against heaven and against you. I am no longer worthy to be called your son.'

"But the father said to his servants, 'Quick! Bring the best robe and put it on him. Put a ring on his finger and sandals on his feet. Bring the fattened calf and kill it. Let's have a feast and celebrate. For this son of mine was dead and is alive again; he was lost and is found.' So they began to celebrate.

"Meanwhile, the older son was in the field. When he came near the house, he heard music and dancing. So he called one of the servants and asked him what was going on. 'Your brother has come,' he replied, 'and your father has killed the fattened calf because he has him back safe and sound.'

"The older brother became angry and refused to go in. So his father went out and pleaded with him. But he answered his father, 'Look! All these years I've been slaving for you and never disobeyed your orders. Yet you never gave me even a young goat so I could celebrate with my friends. But when this son of yours who has squandered your property with prostitutes comes home, you kill the fattened calf for him!'

"'My son,' the father said, 'you are always with me, and everything I have is yours. But we had to celebrate and be glad, because this brother of yours was dead and is alive again; he was lost and is found.'"

Another time Jesus used a parable when he was questioned by a religious leader.

On one occasion an expert in the law stood up to test Jesus. "Teacher," he asked, "what must I do to inherit eternal life?"

"What is written in the Law?" he replied. "How do you read it?"

He answered, "'Love the Lord your God with all your heart and with all your soul and with all your strength and with all your mind'; and, 'Love your neighbor as yourself.'"

"You have answered correctly," Jesus replied. "Do this and you will live."

But he wanted to justify himself, so he asked Jesus, "And who is my neighbor?"

In reply Jesus said: "A man was going down from Jerusalem to Jericho, when he was attacked by robbers. They stripped him of his clothes, beat him and went away, leaving him half dead. A priest happened to be going down the same road, and when he saw the man, he passed by on the other side. So too, a Levite, when he came to the place and saw him, passed by on the other side. But a Samaritan, as he traveled, came where the man was; and when he saw him, he took pity on him. He went to him and bandaged his wounds, pouring on oil and wine. Then he put the man on his own donkey, brought him to an inn and took care of him. The next day he took out two denarii[1] and gave them to the innkeeper. 'Look after him,' he said, 'and when I return, I will reimburse you for any extra expense you may have.'

---

[1]**Denarii:** A denarius was the daily wage of a day laborer.

"Which of these three do you think was a neighbor to the man who fell into the hands of robbers?"

The expert in the law replied, "The one who had mercy on him."

Jesus told him, "Go and do likewise."

Besides teaching in parables, Jesus also taught in a more direct style, as seen in what came to be known as the "Sermon on the Mount."

Now when Jesus saw the crowds, he went up on a mountainside and sat down. His disciples came to him, and he began to teach them.

He said:

> "Blessed are the poor in spirit,
>> for theirs is the kingdom of heaven.
> Blessed are those who mourn,
>> for they will be comforted.
> Blessed are the meek,
>> for they will inherit the earth.
> Blessed are those who hunger and thirst for
>> righteousness,
>> for they will be filled.
> Blessed are the merciful,
>> for they will be shown mercy.
> Blessed are the pure in heart,
>> for they will see God.
> Blessed are the peacemakers,
>> for they will be called children of God.
> Blessed are those who are persecuted because of
>> righteousness,
>> for theirs is the kingdom of heaven.

"Blessed are you when people insult you, persecute you and falsely say all kinds of evil against you because of me. Rejoice and be glad, because great is your reward in heaven, for in the same way they persecuted the prophets who were before you.

"You are the salt of the earth. But if the salt loses its saltiness, how can it be made salty again? It is no longer good for anything, except to be thrown out and trampled underfoot.

"You are the light of the world. A town built on a hill cannot be hidden. Neither do people light a lamp and put it under a bowl. Instead they put it on its stand, and it gives light to everyone in the house. In the same way, let your light shine before others, that they may see your good deeds and glorify your Father in heaven.

"And when you pray, do not be like the hypocrites, for they love to pray standing in the synagogues and on the street corners to be seen by others. Truly I tell you, they have received their reward in full. But when you pray, go into your room, close the door and pray to your Father, who is unseen. Then your Father, who sees what is done in secret, will reward you. And when you pray, do not keep on babbling like pagans, for they think they will be heard because of their many words. Do not be like them, for your Father knows what you need before you ask him.

"This, then, is how you should pray:

> "'Our Father in heaven,
> hallowed be your name,
> your kingdom come,
> your will be done,
>   on earth as it is in heaven.
> Give us today our daily bread.
> And forgive us our debts,
>   as we also have forgiven our debtors.
> And lead us not into temptation,
>   but deliver us from the evil one.'

For if you forgive other people when they sin against you, your heavenly Father will also forgive you. But if you do not forgive others their sins, your Father will not forgive your sins.

"Do not store up for yourselves treasures on earth, where moths and vermin destroy, and where thieves break in and steal. But store up for yourselves treasures in heaven, where moths and vermin do not destroy, and where thieves do not break in and steal. For where your treasure is, there your heart will be also.

"The eye is the lamp of the body. If your eyes are healthy, your whole body will be full of light. But if your eyes are unhealthy, your whole body will be full of darkness. If then the light within you is darkness, how great is that darkness!

"No one can serve two masters. Either you will hate the one and love the other, or you will be devoted to the one and despise the other. You cannot serve both God and money.

"Therefore I tell you, do not worry about your life, what you will eat or drink; or about your body, what you will wear. Is not life more than food, and the body more than clothes? Look at the birds of the air; they do not sow or reap or store away in barns, and yet your heavenly Father feeds them. Are you not much more valuable than they? Can any one of you by worrying add a single hour to your life?

"And why do you worry about clothes? See how the flowers of the field grow. They do not labor or spin. Yet I tell you that not even Solomon in all his splendor was dressed like one of these. If that is how God clothes the grass of the field, which is here today and tomorrow is thrown into the fire, will he not much more clothe you — you of little faith? So do not worry, saying, 'What shall we eat?' or 'What shall we drink?' or 'What shall we wear?' For the pagans run after all these things, and your heavenly Father knows that you need them. But seek first his kingdom and his righteousness, and all these things will be given to you as well. Therefore do not worry about tomorrow, for tomorrow will worry about itself. Each day has enough trouble of its own.

"Therefore everyone who hears these words of mine and puts them into practice is like a wise man who built his house on the rock. The rain came down, the streams rose, and the winds blew and beat against that house; yet it did not fall, because it had its foundation on the rock. But everyone who hears these words of mine and does not put them into practice is like a foolish man who built his house on sand. The rain came down, the streams rose, and the winds blew and beat against that house, and it fell with a great crash."

Jesus' teachings moved many people and changed lives. However, those who continually heard his parables and sermons were his disciples. At one point during their travels together, the disciples' trust in Jesus was put to the test when a violent storm overtook their boat.

That day when evening came, he said to his disciples, "Let us go over to the other side." Leaving the crowd behind, they took him along, just as he was, in the boat. There were also other boats with him. A furious squall came up, and the waves broke over the boat, so that it was nearly swamped. Jesus was in the stern, sleeping on a cushion. The disciples woke him and said to him, "Teacher, don't you care if we drown?"

He got up, rebuked the wind and said to the waves, "Quiet! Be still!" Then the wind died down and it was completely calm.

He said to his disciples, "Why are you so afraid? Do you still have no faith?"

They were terrified and asked each other, "Who is this? Even the wind and the waves obey him!"

They went across the lake to the region of the Gerasenes. When Jesus got out of the boat, a man with an impure spirit came from the tombs to meet him. This man lived in the tombs, and no one could bind him anymore, not even with a chain. For he had often been chained hand and foot, but he tore the chains apart and broke the irons on his feet. No one was strong enough to subdue him. Night and day among the tombs and in the hills he would cry out and cut himself with stones.

When he saw Jesus from a distance, he ran and fell on his knees in front of him. He shouted at the top of his voice, "What do you want with me, Jesus, Son of the Most High God? In God's name don't torture me!" For Jesus had said to him, "Come out of this man, you impure spirit!"

Then Jesus asked him, "What is your name?"

"My name is Legion," he replied, "for we are many." And he begged Jesus again and again not to send them out of the area.

A large herd of pigs was feeding on the nearby hillside. The demons begged Jesus, "Send us among the pigs; allow us to go into them." He gave them permission, and the impure spirits came out and went into the pigs. The herd, about two thousand in number, rushed down the steep bank into the lake and were drowned.

Those tending the pigs ran off and reported this in the town and countryside, and the people went out to see what had happened. When they came to Jesus, they saw the man who had been possessed by the legion of demons, sitting there, dressed and in his right mind; and they were afraid. Those who had seen it told the people what had happened to the demon-possessed man — and told about the pigs as well. Then the people began to plead with Jesus to leave their region.

As Jesus was getting into the boat, the man who had been demon-possessed begged to go with him. Jesus did not let him, but said, "Go home to your own people and tell them how much the Lord has done for you, and how he has had mercy on you." So the man went away and began to tell in the Decapolis how much Jesus had done for him. And all the people were amazed.

When Jesus had again crossed over by boat to the other side of the lake, a large crowd gathered around him while he was by the lake. Then one of the synagogue leaders, named Jairus, came, and when he saw Jesus, he fell at his feet. He pleaded earnestly with him, "My little daughter is dying. Please come and put your hands on her so that she will be healed and live." So Jesus went with him.

A large crowd followed and pressed around him. And a woman was there who had been subject to bleeding for twelve years. She had suffered a great deal under the care of many doctors and had spent all she had, yet instead of getting better she grew worse. When she heard about Jesus, she came up behind him in the crowd and touched his cloak, because she thought, "If I just touch his clothes, I will be healed." Immediately her bleeding stopped and she felt in her body that she was freed from her suffering.

At once Jesus realized that power had gone out from him. He turned around in the crowd and asked, "Who touched my clothes?"

"You see the people crowding against you," his disciples answered, "and yet you can ask, 'Who touched me?'"

But Jesus kept looking around to see who had done it. Then the woman, knowing what had happened to her, came and fell at his feet and, trembling with fear, told him the whole truth. He said to her, "Daughter, your faith has healed you. Go in peace and be freed from your suffering."

While Jesus was still speaking, some people came from the house of Jairus, the synagogue leader. "Your daughter is dead," they said. "Why bother the teacher anymore?"

Overhearing what they said, Jesus told him, "Don't be afraid; just believe."

He did not let anyone follow him except Peter, James and John the brother of James. When they came to the home of the synagogue leader, Jesus saw a commotion, with people crying and wailing loudly. He went in and said to them, "Why all this commotion and wailing? The child is not dead but asleep." But they laughed at him.

After he put them all out, he took the child's father and mother and the disciples who were with him, and went in where the child was. He took her by the hand and said to her, "*Talitha koum!*" (which means "Little girl, I say to you, get up!"). Immediately the girl stood up and began to walk around (she was twelve years old). At this they were completely astonished. He gave strict orders not to let anyone know about this, and told them to give her something to eat.

As Jesus went on from there, two blind men followed him, calling out, "Have mercy on us, Son of David!"

When he had gone indoors, the blind men came to him, and he asked them, "Do you believe that I am able to do this?"

"Yes, Lord," they replied.

Then he touched their eyes and said, "According to your faith let it be done to you"; and their sight was restored. Jesus warned them sternly, "See that no one knows about this." But they went out and spread the news about him all over that region.

While they were going out, a man who was demon-possessed and could not talk was brought to Jesus. And when the demon was driven out, the man who had been mute spoke. The crowd was amazed and said, "Nothing like this has ever been seen in Israel."

But the Pharisees said, "It is by the prince of demons that he drives out demons."

Jesus commissioned his closest followers, the 12 disciples, to spread out and tell people that the kingdom of God had come. He also gave them spiritual authority to heal people from sickness and demonic oppression.

This first band of preachers was sent out with almost no supplies in order to learn about faith and prayer. God performed many miracles through them, adding to the mounting excitement among the populace. A top official also heard the reports ... filtered through his guilty conscience.

King Herod heard about this, for Jesus' name had become well known. Some were saying, "John the Baptist has been raised from the dead, and that is why miraculous powers are at work in him."

Others said, "He is Elijah."

And still others claimed, "He is a prophet, like one of the prophets of long ago."

But when Herod heard this, he said, "John, whom I beheaded, has been raised from the dead!"

For Herod himself had given orders to have John arrested, and he had him bound and put in prison. He did this because of Herodias, his brother Philip's wife, whom he had married. For John had been saying to Herod, "It is not lawful for you to have your brother's wife." So Herodias nursed a grudge against John and wanted to kill him. But she was not able to, because Herod feared John and protected him, knowing him to be a righteous and holy man. When Herod heard John, he was greatly puzzled; yet he liked to listen to him.

Finally the opportune time came. On his birthday Herod gave a banquet for his high officials and military commanders and the leading men of Galilee. When the daughter of Herodias came in and danced, she pleased Herod and his dinner guests.

The king said to the girl, "Ask me for anything you want, and I'll give it to you." And he promised her with an oath, "Whatever you ask I will give you, up to half my kingdom."

She went out and said to her mother, "What shall I ask for?"

"The head of John the Baptist," she answered.

At once the girl hurried in to the king with the request: "I want you to give me right now the head of John the Baptist on a platter."

The king was greatly distressed, but because of his oaths and his dinner guests, he did not want to refuse her. So he immediately sent an executioner with orders to bring John's head. The man went, beheaded John in the prison, and brought back his head on a platter. He presented it to the girl, and she gave it to her mother. On hearing of this, John's disciples came and took his body and laid it in a tomb.

The apostles gathered around Jesus and reported to him all they had done and taught. Then, because so many people were coming and going that they did not even have a chance to eat, he said to them, "Come with me by yourselves to a quiet place and get some rest."

So they went away by themselves in a boat to a solitary place. But many who saw them leaving recognized them and ran on foot from all the towns and got there ahead of them. When Jesus landed and saw a large crowd, he had compassion on them, because they were like sheep without a shepherd. So he began teaching them many things.

By this time it was late in the day, so his disciples came to him. "This is a remote place," they said, "and it's already very late. Send the people away so that they can go to the surrounding country-side and villages and buy themselves something to eat."

But he answered, "You give them something to eat."

They said to him, "That would take more than half a year's wages! Are we to go and spend that much on bread and give it to them to eat?"

"How many loaves do you have?" he asked. "Go and see."

When they found out, they said, "Five — and two fish."

Then Jesus directed them to have all the people sit down in groups on the green grass. So they sat down in groups of hundreds and fifties. Taking the five loaves and the two fish and looking up to heaven, he gave thanks and broke the loaves. Then he gave them to his disciples to distribute to the people. He also divided the two fish among them all. They all ate and were satisfied, and the disciples picked up twelve basketfuls of broken pieces of bread and fish. The number of the men who had eaten was five thousand.

Immediately Jesus made the disciples get into the boat and go on ahead of him to the other side, while he dismissed the crowd. After he had dismissed them, he went up on a mountainside by himself to pray. Later that night, he was there alone, and the boat was already a considerable distance from land, buffeted by the waves because the wind was against it.

Shortly before dawn Jesus went out to them, walking on the lake. When the disciples saw him walking on the lake, they were terrified. "It's a ghost," they said, and cried out in fear.

But Jesus immediately said to them: "Take courage! It is I. Don't be afraid."

"Lord, if it's you," Peter replied, "tell me to come to you on the water."

"Come," he said.

Then Peter got down out of the boat, walked on the water and came toward Jesus. But when he saw the wind, he was afraid and, beginning to sink, cried out, "Lord, save me!"

Immediately Jesus reached out his hand and caught him. "You of little faith," he said, "why did you doubt?"

And when they climbed into the boat, the wind died down. Then those who were in the boat worshiped him, saying, "Truly you are the Son of God."

When they had crossed over, they landed at Gennesaret. And when the men of that place recognized Jesus, they sent word to all the surrounding country. People brought all their sick to him and begged him to let the sick just touch the edge of his cloak, and all who touched it were healed.

The next day the crowd that had stayed on the opposite shore of the lake realized that only one boat had been there, and that Jesus had not entered it with his disciples, but that they had gone away alone. Then some boats from Tiberias landed near the place where the people had eaten the bread after the Lord had given thanks. Once the crowd realized that neither Jesus nor his disciples were there, they got into the boats and went to Capernaum in search of Jesus.

When they found him on the other side of the lake, they asked him, "Rabbi, when did you get here?"

Jesus answered, "Very truly I tell you, you are looking for me, not because you saw the signs I performed but because you ate the loaves and had your fill. Do not work for food that spoils, but for food that endures to eternal life, which the Son of Man will give you. For on him God the Father has placed his seal of approval."

Then they asked him, "What must we do to do the works God requires?"

Jesus answered, "The work of God is this: to believe in the one he has sent."

So they asked him, "What sign then will you give that we may see it and believe you? What will you do? Our ancestors ate the manna in the wilderness; as it is written: 'He gave them bread from heaven to eat.'"

Jesus said to them, "Very truly I tell you, it is not Moses who has given you the bread from heaven, but it is my Father who gives you the true bread from heaven. For the bread of God is the bread that comes down from heaven and gives life to the world."

"Sir," they said, "always give us this bread."

Then Jesus declared, "I am the bread of life.[2] Whoever comes to me will never go hungry, and whoever believes in me will never be thirsty.

"Very truly I tell you, the one who believes has eternal life. I am the bread of life. Your ancestors ate the manna in the wilderness, yet they died. But here is the bread that comes down from heaven, which anyone may eat and not die. I am the living bread that came down from heaven. Whoever eats this bread will live forever. This bread is my flesh, which I will give for the life of the world."

Then the Jews began to argue sharply among themselves, "How can this man give us his flesh to eat?"

Jesus said to them, "Very truly I tell you, unless you eat the flesh of the Son of Man and drink his blood, you have no life in you. Whoever eats my flesh and drinks my blood has eternal life, and I will raise them up at the last day. For my flesh is real food and my blood is real drink. Whoever eats my flesh and drinks my blood remains in me, and I in them. Just as the living Father sent me and I live because of the Father, so the one who feeds on me will live because of me. This is the bread that came down from heaven. Your ancestors ate manna and died, but whoever feeds on this bread will live forever."

From this time many of his disciples turned back and no longer followed him.

"You do not want to leave too, do you?" Jesus asked the Twelve.

---

[2]**Bread of life:** By saying this, Jesus was proclaiming that he is the source of true fulfillment and satisfaction.

Simon Peter answered him, "Lord, to whom shall we go? You have the words of eternal life. We have come to believe and to know that you are the Holy One of God."

Then Jesus replied, "Have I not chosen you, the Twelve? Yet one of you is a devil!" (He meant Judas, the son of Simon Iscariot, who, though one of the Twelve, was later to betray him.)

Jesus could get very personal, in-your-face, below the surface. He had a rock-solid sense of who he was, and he wanted his followers to know him to the core. Listening to his teaching and admiring his character were not enough. To follow this rabbi, his followers needed to know him in a deeper way, a way that would change their hearts, pursuits and lives. He wanted to be the center, the joy, the "bread" and sustenance of their lives. As Jesus continued his ministry, he began to reveal more about who he was and why he had come.

25

Jesus, the Son of God

JESUS AND HIS DISCIPLES went on to the villages around Caesarea Philippi. On the way he asked them, "Who do people say I am?"

They replied, "Some say John the Baptist; others say Elijah; and still others, one of the prophets."

"But what about you?" he asked. "Who do you say I am?"

Peter answered, "You are the Messiah."

Jesus warned them not to tell anyone about him.

He then began to teach them that the Son of Man must suffer many things and be rejected by the elders, the chief priests and the teachers of the law, and that he must be killed and after three days rise again. He spoke plainly about this, and Peter took him aside and began to rebuke him.

But when Jesus turned and looked at his disciples, he rebuked Peter. "Get behind me, Satan!" he said. "You do not have in mind the concerns of God, but merely human concerns."

Then he called the crowd to him along with his disciples and said: "Whoever wants to be my disciple must deny themselves and take up their cross and follow me. For whoever wants to save their

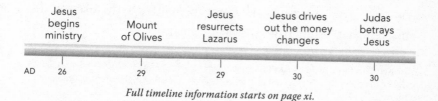

| Jesus begins ministry | Mount of Olives | Jesus resurrects Lazarus | Jesus drives out the money changers | Judas betrays Jesus |

AD   26   29   29   30   30

Full timeline information starts on page xi.

life will lose it, but whoever loses their life for me and for the gospel[1] will save it. What good is it for someone to gain the whole world, yet forfeit their soul? Or what can anyone give in exchange for their soul? If anyone is ashamed of me and my words in this adulterous and sinful generation, the Son of Man will be ashamed of them when he comes in his Father's glory with the holy angels."

After six days Jesus took with him Peter, James and John the brother of James, and led them up a high mountain by themselves. There he was transfigured before them. His face shone like the sun, and his clothes became as white as the light.

Two men, Moses and Elijah, appeared in glorious splendor, talking with Jesus. They spoke about his departure, which he was about to bring to fulfillment at Jerusalem.

Peter said to Jesus, "Rabbi, it is good for us to be here. Let us put up three shelters — one for you, one for Moses and one for Elijah." (He did not know what to say, they were so frightened.)

While he was still speaking, a bright cloud covered them, and a voice from the cloud said, "This is my Son, whom I love; with him I am well pleased. Listen to him!"

When the disciples heard this, they fell facedown to the ground, terrified. But Jesus came and touched them. "Get up," he said. "Don't be afraid." When they looked up, they saw no one except Jesus.

As they were coming down the mountain, Jesus gave them orders not to tell anyone what they had seen until the Son of Man had risen from the dead. They kept the matter to themselves, discussing what "rising from the dead" meant.

---

[1]**Gospel:** The message that Jesus has come to reconcile humanity to God and that each individual can accept this undeserved gift and enter into a relationship with him; synonymous with *Good News*.

When they came to the other disciples, they saw a large crowd around them and the teachers of the law arguing with them. As soon as all the people saw Jesus, they were overwhelmed with wonder and ran to greet him.

They left that place and passed through Galilee. Jesus did not want anyone to know where they were, because he was teaching his disciples. He said to them, "The Son of Man is going to be delivered into the hands of men. They will kill him, and after three days he will rise." But they did not understand what he meant and were afraid to ask him about it.

Remember King David and King Solomon? All the great kings of ancient Israel had been warriors, builders and diplomats. Little wonder that most people, if they believed at all in a coming Messiah, imagined the new king would be the greatest warrior, builder and deliverer of all. How odd, then, that Jesus seemed indifferent to regime change. His message was "Open your hearts to God." He did not gather a cache of weapons or train a commando platoon for toppling Roman rule. This unexpected focus, coupled with Jesus' insistence on genuine personal repentance, offended many in Jerusalem's religious establishment. Some educated Pharisees considered him a teacher of dangerous and misleading philosophy. In the midst of growing Jewish opposition and common-folk popularity, Jesus went to Jerusalem to celebrate one of the greatest of the Jewish holidays, the Festival of Tabernacles. He used the festival as a backdrop for revealing his authority, identity and mission.

Now at the festival the Jewish leaders were watching for Jesus and asking, "Where is he?"

Among the crowds there was widespread whispering about him. Some said, "He is a good man."

Others replied, "No, he deceives the people." But no one would say anything publicly about him for fear of the leaders.

Not until halfway through the festival did Jesus go up to the temple courts and begin to teach. The Jews there were amazed and asked, "How did this man get such learning without having been taught?"

At that point some of the people of Jerusalem began to ask, "Isn't this the man they are trying to kill? Here he is, speaking publicly, and they are not saying a word to him. Have the authorities really concluded that he is the Messiah? But we know where this man is from; when the Messiah comes, no one will know where he is from."

Then Jesus, still teaching in the temple courts, cried out, "Yes, you know me, and you know where I am from. I am not here on my own authority, but he who sent me is true. You do not know him, but I know him because I am from him and he sent me."

At this they tried to seize him, but no one laid a hand on him, because his hour had not yet come. Still, many in the crowd believed in him. They said, "When the Messiah comes, will he perform more signs than this man?"

On the last and greatest day of the festival, Jesus stood and said in a loud voice, "Let anyone who is thirsty come to me and drink. Whoever believes in me, as Scripture has said, rivers of living water will flow from within them." By this he meant the Spirit, whom those who believed in him were later to receive. Up to that time the Spirit had not been given, since Jesus had not yet been glorified.

On hearing his words, some of the people said, "Surely this man is the Prophet."

Others said, "He is the Messiah."

Still others asked, "How can the Messiah come from Galilee? Does not Scripture say that the Messiah will come from David's descendants and from Bethlehem, the town where David lived?" Thus the people were divided because of Jesus. Some wanted to seize him, but no one laid a hand on him.

When Jesus preached, he made many claims with which people took issue. He said he was the light—but only God himself is the source of light! He was from above—but only God claims residence in heaven! Jesus was setting out the clear and fateful choice: believe in him and know God's power in your life, or stay in spiritual darkness. This message would change everything.

When Jesus spoke again to the people, he said, "I am the light of the world. Whoever follows me will never walk in darkness, but will have the light of life."

The Pharisees challenged him, "Here you are, appearing as your own witness; your testimony is not valid."

Jesus answered, "Even if I testify on my own behalf, my testimony is valid, for I know where I came from and where I am going. But you have no idea where I come from or where I am going."

Once more Jesus said to them, "I am going away, and you will look for me, and you will die in your sin. Where I go, you cannot come."

This made the Jews ask, "Will he kill himself? Is that why he says, 'Where I go, you cannot come'?"

But he continued, "You are from below; I am from above. You are of this world; I am not of this world. I told you that you would die in your sins; if you do not believe that I am he, you will indeed die in your sins."

Even as he spoke, many believed in him.

To the Jews who had believed him, Jesus said, "If you hold to my teaching, you are really my disciples. Then you will know the truth, and the truth will set you free."

"Very truly I tell you, whoever obeys my word will never see death."

At this they exclaimed, "Now we know that you are demon-possessed! Abraham died and so did the prophets, yet you say that whoever obeys your word will never taste death. Are you greater than our father Abraham? He died, and so did the prophets. Who do you think you are?"

Jesus replied, "If I glorify myself, my glory means nothing. My Father, whom you claim as your God, is the one who glorifies me. Though you do not know him, I know him. If I said I did not, I would be a liar like you, but I do know him and obey his word. Your father Abraham rejoiced at the thought of seeing my day; he saw it and was glad."

"You are not yet fifty years old," they said to him, "and you have seen Abraham!"

"Very truly I tell you," Jesus answered, "before Abraham was born, I am!" At this, they picked up stones to stone him, but Jesus hid himself, slipping away from the temple grounds.

There it was. Jesus told the crowd that he existed before Abraham was even born. He told the crowd that his life was without beginning. He told the crowd he was God! The crowd turned into a lynch mob. Advisers might have urged Jesus to give the religious leaders time to cool off, but Jesus would not be stopped. He was driven by a passion to show people the glory of God, and even when a close friend was ill and near death, he used that experience as another example of God's power.

Now a man named Lazarus was sick. He was from Bethany, the village of Mary and her sister Martha. (This Mary, whose brother Lazarus now lay sick, was the same one who poured perfume on the Lord and wiped his feet with her hair.) So the sisters sent word to Jesus, "Lord, the one you love is sick."

When he heard this, Jesus said, "This sickness will not end in death. No, it is for God's glory so that God's Son may be glorified through it." Now Jesus loved Martha and her sister and Lazarus. So when he heard that Lazarus was sick, he stayed where he was two more days, and then he said to his disciples, "Let us go back to Judea."

"But Rabbi," they said, "a short while ago the Jews there tried to stone you, and yet you are going back?"

Jesus answered, "Are there not twelve hours of daylight? Anyone who walks in the daytime will not stumble, for they see by this world's light. It is when a person walks at night that they stumble, for they have no light."

After he had said this, he went on to tell them, "Our friend Lazarus has fallen asleep; but I am going there to wake him up."

His disciples replied, "Lord, if he sleeps, he will get better." Jesus had been speaking of his death, but his disciples thought he meant natural sleep.

So then he told them plainly, "Lazarus is dead, and for your sake I am glad I was not there, so that you may believe. But let us go to him."

Then Thomas (also known as Didymus) said to the rest of the disciples, "Let us also go, that we may die with him."

On his arrival, Jesus found that Lazarus had already been in the tomb for four days. Now Bethany was less than two miles from Jerusalem, and many Jews had come to Martha and Mary to comfort them in the loss of their brother. When Martha heard that Jesus was coming, she went out to meet him, but Mary stayed at home.

"Lord," Martha said to Jesus, "if you had been here, my brother would not have died. But I know that even now God will give you whatever you ask."

Jesus said to her, "Your brother will rise again."

Martha answered, "I know he will rise again in the resurrection at the last day."

Jesus said to her, "I am the resurrection and the life. The one who believes in me will live, even though they die; and whoever lives by believing in me will never die. Do you believe this?"

"Yes, Lord," she replied, "I believe that you are the Messiah, the Son of God, who is to come into the world."

After she had said this, she went back and called her sister Mary aside. "The Teacher is here," she said, "and is asking for you." When Mary heard this, she got up quickly and went to him. Now Jesus had not yet entered the village, but was still at the place where Martha had met him. When the Jews who had been with Mary in the house, comforting her, noticed how quickly she got up and went out, they followed her, supposing she was going to the tomb to mourn there.

When Mary reached the place where Jesus was and saw him, she fell at his feet and said, "Lord, if you had been here, my brother would not have died."

When Jesus saw her weeping, and the Jews who had come along with her also weeping, he was deeply moved in spirit and troubled. "Where have you laid him?" he asked.

"Come and see, Lord," they replied.

Jesus wept.

Then the Jews said, "See how he loved him!"

But some of them said, "Could not he who opened the eyes of the blind man have kept this man from dying?"

Jesus, once more deeply moved, came to the tomb. It was a cave with a stone laid across the entrance. "Take away the stone," he said.

"But, Lord," said Martha, the sister of the dead man, "by this time there is a bad odor, for he has been there four days."

Then Jesus said, "Did I not tell you that if you believe, you will see the glory of God?"

So they took away the stone. Then Jesus looked up and said, "Father, I thank you that you have heard me. I knew that you always hear me, but I said this for the benefit of the people standing here, that they may believe that you sent me."

When he had said this, Jesus called in a loud voice, "Lazarus, come out!" The dead man came out, his hands and feet wrapped with strips of linen, and a cloth around his face.

Jesus said to them, "Take off the grave clothes and let him go."

Therefore many of the Jews who had come to visit Mary, and had seen what Jesus did, believed in him. But some of them went to the Pharisees and told them what Jesus had done. Then the chief priests and the Pharisees called a meeting of the Sanhedrin.

"What are we accomplishing?" they asked. "Here is this man performing many signs. If we let him go on like this, everyone will believe in him, and then the Romans will come and take away both our temple and our nation."

Then one of them, named Caiaphas, who was high priest that year, spoke up, "You know nothing at all! You do not realize that it is better for you that one man die for the people than that the whole nation perish."

He did not say this on his own, but as high priest that year he prophesied that Jesus would die for the Jewish nation, and not only for that nation but also for the scattered children of God, to bring them together and make them one. So from that day on they plotted to take his life.

Usually, people try to avoid trouble, yet Jesus set his direction straight toward those who were plotting to kill him. Jerusalem was the site of the Passover Festival celebration. People there needed to hear his message. Time was short. Jesus soon would enter Jerusalem for the last time.

People were bringing little children to Jesus for him to place his hands on them, but the disciples rebuked them. When Jesus saw this, he was indignant. He said to them, "Let the little children come to me, and do not hinder them, for the kingdom of God belongs to such as these. Truly I tell you, anyone who will not receive the kingdom of God like a little child will never enter it." And he took the children in his arms, placed his hands on them and blessed them.

As Jesus started on his way, a man ran up to him and fell on his knees before him. "Good teacher," he asked, "what must I do to inherit eternal life?"

"Why do you call me good?" Jesus answered. "No one is good — except God alone. You know the commandments: 'You shall not murder, you shall not commit adultery, you shall not steal, you shall not give false testimony, you shall not defraud, honor your father and mother.'"

"Teacher," he declared, "all these I have kept since I was a boy."

Jesus looked at him and loved him. "One thing you lack," he said. "Go, sell everything you have and give to the poor, and you will have treasure in heaven. Then come, follow me."

At this the man's face fell. He went away sad, because he had great wealth.

Jesus looked around and said to his disciples, "How hard it is for the rich to enter the kingdom of God!"

The disciples were amazed at his words. But Jesus said again, "Children, how hard it is to enter the kingdom of God! It is easier for a camel to go through the eye of a needle than for someone who is rich to enter the kingdom of God."

The disciples were even more amazed, and said to each other, "Who then can be saved?"

Jesus looked at them and said, "With man this is impossible, but not with God; all things are possible with God."

Then Peter spoke up, "We have left everything to follow you!"

"Truly I tell you," Jesus replied, "no one who has left home or brothers or sisters or mother or father or children or fields for me and the gospel will fail to receive a hundred times as much in this present age: homes, brothers, sisters, mothers, children and fields — along with persecutions — and in the age to come eternal life. But many who are first will be last, and the last first."

They were on their way up to Jerusalem, with Jesus leading the way, and the disciples were astonished, while those who followed were afraid. Again he took the Twelve aside and told them what was going to happen to him. "We are going up to Jerusalem," he said, "and the Son of Man will be delivered over to the chief priests and the teachers of the law. They will condemn him to death and will hand him over to the Gentiles, who will mock him and spit on him, flog him and kill him. Three days later he will rise."

When it was almost time for the Jewish Passover, many went up from the country to Jerusalem for their ceremonial cleansing before the Passover. They kept looking for Jesus, and as they stood in the temple courts they asked one another, "What do you think? Isn't he coming to the festival at all?" But the chief priests and the Pharisees had given orders that anyone who found out where Jesus was should report it so that they might arrest him.

How many times had Jesus instructed his followers to hold back, to not tell who he was, to wait? And they had waited. Now the waiting was over. As Jesus entered Jerusalem, he let the crowds rejoice. He knew what this week would hold, but for the moment, those who loved him could cheer and celebrate.

As they approached Jerusalem and came to Bethphage and Bethany at the Mount of Olives, Jesus sent two of his disciples, saying to them, "Go to the village ahead of you, and just as you enter it, you will find a colt tied there, which no one has ever ridden. Untie it and bring it here. If anyone asks you, 'Why are you doing this?' say, 'The Lord needs it and will send it back here shortly.'"

They went and found a colt outside in the street, tied at a doorway. As they untied it, some people standing there asked, "What are you doing, untying that colt?" They answered as Jesus had told them to, and the people let them go. When they brought the colt to Jesus and threw their cloaks over it, he sat on it. Many people spread their cloaks on the road, while others spread branches they had cut in the fields. Those who went ahead and those who followed shouted,

> "Hosanna!"[2]

> "Blessed is he who comes in the name of the Lord!"

> "Blessed is the coming kingdom of our father David!"

> "Hosanna in the highest heaven!"

---

[2]**Hosanna:** A Hebrew expression meaning *Save!* which became an exclamation of praise.

When Jesus entered Jerusalem, the whole city was stirred and asked, "Who is this?"

The crowds answered, "This is Jesus, the prophet from Nazareth in Galilee."

Jesus entered the temple courts and drove out all who were buying and selling there. He overturned the tables of the money changers and the benches of those selling doves. "It is written," he said to them, "'My house will be called a house of prayer,' but you are making it 'a den of robbers.'"

The blind and the lame came to him at the temple, and he healed them. But when the chief priests and the teachers of the law saw the wonderful things he did and the children shouting in the temple courts, "Hosanna to the Son of David," they were indignant.

"Do you hear what these children are saying?" they asked him.

"Yes," replied Jesus, "have you never read,

> "'From the lips of children and infants
>   you, Lord, have called forth your praise'?"

And he left them and went out of the city to Bethany, where he spent the night.

Jesus spent much of his final week teaching at the temple. Rabbis commonly lectured in the temple or the synagogues. But this rabbi was different. This teacher changed everything by implying that the Messiah, the one greater even than David, was speaking to them. No one had talked like this before. No one had dared.

While Jesus was teaching in the temple courts, he asked, "Why do the teachers of the law say that the Messiah is the son of David? David himself, speaking by the Holy Spirit, declared:

> "'The Lord said to my Lord:
>   "Sit at my right hand

until I put your enemies
under your feet.”'

David himself calls him 'Lord.' How then can he be his son?”
The large crowd listened to him with delight.

The crowds liked Jesus, but the hatred of the religious leaders grew more intense. So human was Jesus that as his situation worsened, his heart was troubled. But Jesus faced his fear and refused to let it stop him from doing the will of God.

“Now my soul is troubled, and what shall I say? 'Father, save me from this hour'? No, it was for this very reason I came to this hour. Father, glorify your name!”

Then a voice came from heaven, “I have glorified it, and will glorify it again.” The crowd that was there and heard it said it had thundered; others said an angel had spoken to him.

Jesus said, “This voice was for your benefit, not mine. Now is the time for judgment on this world; now the prince of this world will be driven out. And I, when I am lifted up from the earth, will draw all people to myself.” He said this to show the kind of death he was going to die.

Even after Jesus had performed so many signs in their presence, they still would not believe in him.

Yet at the same time many even among the leaders believed in him. But because of the Pharisees they would not openly acknowledge their faith for fear they would be put out of the synagogue; for they loved human praise more than praise from God.

Then Jesus cried out, “Whoever believes in me does not believe in me only, but in the one who sent me. The one who looks at me is seeing the one who sent me. I have come into the world as a light, so that no one who believes in me should stay in darkness.

“If anyone hears my words but does not keep them, I do not

judge that person. For I did not come to judge the world, but to save the world. There is a judge for the one who rejects me and does not accept my words; the very words I have spoken will condemn them at the last day. For I did not speak on my own, but the Father who sent me commanded me to say all that I have spoken. I know that his command leads to eternal life. So whatever I say is just what the Father has told me to say."

Now the Passover and the Festival of Unleavened Bread were only two days away, and the chief priests and the teachers of the law were scheming to arrest Jesus secretly and kill him. "But not during the festival," they said, "or the people may riot."

Behind the scenes, under the radar of politics or religious courts, a dark power was brewing and waiting. That evil power found an opening among Jesus' intimate circle of followers. Just a touch of greed was all that power needed to accelerate the plot.

Then Satan entered Judas, called Iscariot, one of the Twelve. And Judas went to the chief priests and the officers of the temple guard and discussed with them how he might betray Jesus. They were delighted and agreed to give him money. He consented, and watched for an opportunity to hand Jesus over to them when no crowd was present.

26

The Hour of Darkness

ON THE FIRST DAY of the Festival of Unleavened Bread, when it was customary to sacrifice the Passover lamb, Jesus' disciples asked him, "Where do you want us to go and make preparations for you to eat the Passover?"

So he sent two of his disciples, telling them, "Go into the city, and a man carrying a jar of water will meet you. Follow him. Say to the owner of the house he enters, 'The Teacher asks: Where is my guest room, where I may eat the Passover with my disciples?' He will show you a large room upstairs, furnished and ready. Make preparations for us there."

The disciples left, went into the city and found things just as Jesus had told them. So they prepared the Passover.

When evening came, Jesus arrived with the Twelve.

Jesus knew that the hour had come for him to leave this world and go to the Father. Having loved his own who were in the world, he loved them to the end.

The evening meal was in progress, and the devil had already

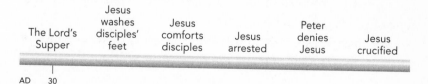

| The Lord's Supper | Jesus washes disciples' feet | Jesus comforts disciples | Jesus arrested | Peter denies Jesus | Jesus crucified |

AD 30

Full timeline information starts on page xi.

prompted Judas, the son of Simon Iscariot, to betray Jesus. Jesus knew that the Father had put all things under his power, and that he had come from God and was returning to God; so he got up from the meal, took off his outer clothing, and wrapped a towel around his waist. After that, he poured water into a basin and began to wash his disciples' feet, drying them with the towel that was wrapped around him.

He came to Simon Peter, who said to him, "Lord, are you going to wash my feet?"

Jesus replied, "You do not realize now what I am doing, but later you will understand."

"No," said Peter, "you shall never wash my feet."

Jesus answered, "Unless I wash you, you have no part with me."

"Then, Lord," Simon Peter replied, "not just my feet but my hands and my head as well!"

Jesus answered, "Those who have had a bath need only to wash their feet; their whole body is clean. And you are clean, though not every one of you." For he knew who was going to betray him, and that was why he said not every one was clean.

When he had finished washing their feet, he put on his clothes and returned to his place. "Do you understand what I have done for you?" he asked them. "You call me 'Teacher' and 'Lord,' and rightly so, for that is what I am. Now that I, your Lord and Teacher, have washed your feet, you also should wash one another's feet. I have set you an example that you should do as I have done for you. Very truly I tell you, no servant is greater than his master, nor is a messenger greater than the one who sent him. Now that you know these things, you will be blessed if you do them."

Jesus was troubled in spirit and testified, "Very truly I tell you, one of you is going to betray me."

His disciples stared at one another, at a loss to know which of them he meant. One of them, the disciple whom Jesus loved,[1] was

---

[1]**Disciple whom Jesus loved:** Probably John.

reclining next to him. Simon Peter motioned to this disciple and said, "Ask him which one he means."

Leaning back against Jesus, he asked him, "Lord, who is it?"

Jesus answered, "It is the one to whom I will give this piece of bread when I have dipped it in the dish." Then, dipping the piece of bread, he gave it to Judas, the son of Simon Iscariot. As soon as Judas took the bread, Satan entered into him.

So Jesus told him, "What you are about to do, do quickly." But no one at the meal understood why Jesus said this to him. Since Judas had charge of the money, some thought Jesus was telling him to buy what was needed for the festival, or to give something to the poor. As soon as Judas had taken the bread, he went out. And it was night.

After Judas left, Jesus gave the disciples a glimpse of what was to come. He foreshadowed the fact that he was going to be "broken" and "poured out"—he was going to take humanity's punishment for sin on himself.

While they were eating, Jesus took bread, and when he had given thanks, he broke it and gave it to his disciples, saying, "Take and eat; this is my body."

Then he took a cup, and when he had given thanks, he gave it to them, saying, "Drink from it, all of you. This is my blood of the covenant, which is poured out for many for the forgiveness of sins. I tell you, I will not drink from this fruit of the vine from now on until that day when I drink it new with you in my Father's kingdom."

Jesus warned his disciples that he would be with them only a little while longer. He went on to comfort his confused followers.

"Do not let your hearts be troubled. You believe in God; believe also in me. My Father's house has many rooms; if that were not so, would I have told you that I am going there to prepare a place for you? And if I go and prepare a place for you, I will come back and take you to be with me that you also may be where I am. You know the way to the place where I am going."

Thomas said to him, "Lord, we don't know where you are going, so how can we know the way?"

Jesus answered, "I am the way and the truth and the life. No one comes to the Father except through me. If you really know me, you will know my Father as well. From now on, you do know him and have seen him."

Philip said, "Lord, show us the Father and that will be enough for us."

Jesus answered: "Don't you know me, Philip, even after I have been among you such a long time? Anyone who has seen me has seen the Father. How can you say, 'Show us the Father'? Don't you believe that I am in the Father, and that the Father is in me? The words I say to you I do not speak on my own authority. Rather, it is the Father, living in me, who is doing his work. Believe me when I say that I am in the Father and the Father is in me; or at least believe on the evidence of the works themselves. Very truly I tell you, whoever believes in me will do the works I have been doing, and they will do even greater things than these, because I am going to the Father. And I will do whatever you ask in my name, so that the Father may be glorified in the Son. You may ask me for anything in my name, and I will do it.

"If you love me, keep my commands. And I will ask the Father, and he will give you another advocate to help you and be with you forever — the Spirit of truth. The world cannot accept him, because it neither sees him nor knows him. But you know him, for he lives with you and will be in you.

"I have much more to say to you, more than you can now bear. But when he, the Spirit of truth, comes, he will guide you into all the truth. He will not speak on his own; he will speak only what he hears, and he will tell you what is yet to come.

"A time is coming and in fact has come when you will be scattered, each to your own home. You will leave me all alone. Yet I am not alone, for my Father is with me.

"I have told you these things, so that in me you may have peace. In this world you will have trouble. But take heart! I have overcome the world."

After Jesus said this, he looked toward heaven and prayed:

"Father, the hour has come. Glorify your Son, that your Son may glorify you. For you granted him authority over all people that he might give eternal life to all those you have given him. Now this is eternal life: that they know you, the only true God, and Jesus Christ, whom you have sent. I have brought you glory on earth by finishing the work you gave me to do. And now, Father, glorify me in your presence with the glory I had with you before the world began.

"Father, I want those you have given me to be with me where I am, and to see my glory, the glory you have given me because you loved me before the creation of the world.

"Righteous Father, though the world does not know you, I know you, and they know that you have sent me. I have made you known to them, and will continue to make you known in order that the love you have for me may be in them and that I myself may be in them."

When they had sung a hymn, they went out to the Mount of Olives.

Perhaps they sang a hymn from Psalms 115–118, the traditional psalms sung as part of the Passover meal. "The Lord is gracious and righteous; our God is full of compassion . . . Give thanks to the Lord, for he is good; his love endures forever . . . Blessed is he who comes in the name of the Lord." What were the disciples thinking and feeling as they followed Jesus to the Mount of Olives? They had probably gone to this place with him many times before for prayer and conversation. But now, shadows too dark for them to comprehend were beginning to fall on their hopes and dreams.

Then Jesus told them, "This very night you will all fall away on account of me, for it is written:

> " 'I will strike the shepherd,
>   and the sheep of the flock will be scattered.'

But after I have risen, I will go ahead of you into Galilee."

Peter replied, "Even if all fall away on account of you, I never will."

"Truly I tell you," Jesus answered, "this very night, before the rooster crows, you will disown me three times."

But Peter declared, "Even if I have to die with you, I will never disown you." And all the other disciples said the same.

Then Jesus went with his disciples to a place called Gethsemane, and he said to them, "Sit here while I go over there and pray." He took Peter and the two sons of Zebedee along with him, and he began to be sorrowful and troubled. Then he said to them, "My soul is overwhelmed with sorrow to the point of death. Stay here and keep watch with me."

Going a little farther, he fell with his face to the ground and prayed, "My Father, if it is possible, may this cup be taken from me. Yet not as I will, but as you will."

Then he returned to his disciples and found them sleeping. "Couldn't you men keep watch with me for one hour?" he asked Peter. "Watch and pray so that you will not fall into temptation. The spirit is willing, but the flesh is weak."

He went away a second time and prayed, "My Father, if it is not possible for this cup to be taken away unless I drink it, may your will be done."

An angel from heaven appeared to him and strengthened him. And being in anguish, he prayed more earnestly, and his sweat was like drops of blood falling to the ground.

When he came back, he again found them sleeping, because their eyes were heavy. So he left them and went away once more and prayed the third time, saying the same thing.

Then he returned to the disciples and said to them, "Are you still sleeping and resting? Look, the hour has come, and the Son of Man is delivered into the hands of sinners. Rise! Let us go! Here comes my betrayer!"

While he was still speaking, Judas, one of the Twelve, arrived. With him was a large crowd armed with swords and clubs, sent from the chief priests and the elders of the people.

Jesus, knowing all that was going to happen to him, went out and asked them, "Who is it you want?"

"Jesus of Nazareth," they replied.

"I am he," Jesus said. (And Judas the traitor was standing there with them.) When Jesus said, "I am he," they drew back and fell to the ground.

Again he asked them, "Who is it you want?"

"Jesus of Nazareth," they said.

Jesus answered, "I told you that I am he. If you are looking for me, then let these men go." This happened so that the words he had spoken would be fulfilled: "I have not lost one of those you gave me."

Then Simon Peter, who had a sword, drew it and struck the high priest's servant, cutting off his right ear. (The servant's name was Malchus.)

Jesus commanded Peter, "Put your sword away! Shall I not drink the cup the Father has given me?"

And he touched the man's ear and healed him.

Then Jesus said to the chief priests, the officers of the temple guard, and the elders, who had come for him, "Am I leading a rebellion, that you have come with swords and clubs? Every day I was with you in the temple courts, and you did not lay a hand on me. But this is your hour — when darkness reigns."

Soldiers of the Jewish religious establishment had come to place Jesus under arrest, and Jesus gave himself up. He could topple his foes with a word. He had the power to call on vast armies of angels to rescue him, but instead he surrendered. The disciples knew something very bad was happening, and they ran away to save their own skins. Jesus was left alone with his captors.

Those who had arrested Jesus took him to Caiaphas the high priest, where the teachers of the law and the elders had assembled. But Peter followed him at a distance, right up to the courtyard of the high priest. He entered and sat down with the guards to see the outcome.

The chief priests and the whole Sanhedrin were looking for false evidence against Jesus so that they could put him to death. But they did not find any, though many false witnesses came forward.

Finally two came forward and declared, "This fellow said, 'I am able to destroy the temple of God and rebuild it in three days.'"

Then the high priest stood up and said to Jesus, "Are you not going to answer? What is this testimony that these men are bringing against you?" But Jesus remained silent.

The high priest said to him, "I charge you under oath by the living God: Tell us if you are the Messiah, the Son of God."

"You have said so," Jesus replied. "But I say to all of you: From now on you will see the Son of Man sitting at the right hand of the Mighty One and coming on the clouds of heaven."

Then the high priest tore his clothes and said, "He has spoken blasphemy! Why do we need any more witnesses? Look, now you have heard the blasphemy. What do you think?"

"He is worthy of death," they answered.

Then they spit in his face and struck him with their fists. Others slapped him and said, "Prophesy to us, Messiah. Who hit you?"

Peter was not the timid sort. His normal reaction to trouble was to wrestle it to the ground, not to run from it. Quite naturally,

*then, he was the one to follow the soldiers back to the high
priest's house and wait for the outcome. Maybe he was dream-
ing up "Plan B" when a few people took him by surprise.*

And when some there had kindled a fire in the middle of the
courtyard and had sat down together, Peter sat down with them.
A servant girl saw him seated there in the firelight. She looked
closely at him and said, "This man was with him."

But he denied it. "Woman, I don't know him," he said.

A little later someone else saw him and said, "You also are one
of them."

"Man, I am not!" Peter replied.

About an hour later another asserted, "Certainly this fellow
was with him, for he is a Galilean."

Peter replied, "Man, I don't know what you're talking about!"
Just as he was speaking, the rooster crowed. The Lord turned and
looked straight at Peter. Then Peter remembered the word the
Lord had spoken to him: "Before the rooster crows today, you will
disown me three times." And he went outside and wept bitterly.

Early in the morning, all the chief priests and the elders of the
people made their plans how to have Jesus executed. So they bound
him, led him away and handed him over to Pilate the governor.

When Judas, who had betrayed him, saw that Jesus was condemned, he was seized with remorse and returned the thirty
pieces of silver to the chief priests and the elders. "I have sinned,"
he said, "for I have betrayed innocent blood."

"What is that to us?" they replied. "That's your responsibility."

So Judas threw the money into the temple and left. Then he
went away and hanged himself.

*The Jewish leaders brought Jesus to Pilate, who had gov-
erned the region of Judea for Rome for four years. Historical
records reveal that he was no friend of the Jews. He frequently
ordered soldiers to beat and kill Jewish protestors, and he had*

no compunction about offending Jewish leaders by placing symbols of pagan Roman worship in Jerusalem. On this Friday morning of Passover week, the Jewish leaders asked him to judge Jesus as a subversive threat. Now Pilate was caught. If he refused to condemn Jesus, Jewish accusers would portray him as no friend of Caesar (a very dangerous public image). If he agreed to crucify Jesus, he'd be acting against his own judicial instincts and, perhaps worse, caving in to those he despised. He needed to question this prisoner himself.

Pilate then went back inside the palace, summoned Jesus and asked him, "Are you the king of the Jews?"

"Is that your own idea," Jesus asked, "or did others talk to you about me?"

"Am I a Jew?" Pilate replied. "Your own people and chief priests handed you over to me. What is it you have done?"

Jesus said, "My kingdom is not of this world. If it were, my servants would fight to prevent my arrest by the Jewish leaders. But now my kingdom is from another place."

"You are a king, then!" said Pilate.

Jesus answered, "You say that I am a king. In fact, the reason I was born and came into the world is to testify to the truth. Everyone on the side of truth listens to me."

"What is truth?" retorted Pilate. With this he went out again to the Jews gathered there and said, "I find no basis for a charge against him. But it is your custom for me to release to you one prisoner at the time of the Passover. Do you want me to release 'the king of the Jews'?"

They shouted back, "No, not him! Give us Barabbas!" Now Barabbas had taken part in an uprising.

Then Pilate took Jesus and had him flogged. The soldiers twisted together a crown of thorns and put it on his head. They clothed him in a purple robe and went up to him again and again, saying, "Hail, king of the Jews!" And they slapped him in the face.

Once more Pilate came out and said to the Jews gathered there,

"Look, I am bringing him out to you to let you know that I find no basis for a charge against him." When Jesus came out wearing the crown of thorns and the purple robe, Pilate said to them, "Here is the man!"

As soon as the chief priests and their officials saw him, they shouted, "Crucify! Crucify!"

But Pilate answered, "You take him and crucify him. As for me, I find no basis for a charge against him."

The Jewish leaders insisted, "We have a law, and according to that law he must die, because he claimed to be the Son of God."

When Pilate heard this, he was even more afraid, and he went back inside the palace. "Where do you come from?" he asked Jesus, but Jesus gave him no answer. "Do you refuse to speak to me?" Pilate said. "Don't you realize I have power either to free you or to crucify you?"

Jesus answered, "You would have no power over me if it were not given to you from above. Therefore the one who handed me over to you is guilty of a greater sin."

From then on, Pilate tried to set Jesus free, but the Jewish leaders kept shouting, "If you let this man go, you are no friend of Caesar. Anyone who claims to be a king opposes Caesar."

When Pilate heard this, he brought Jesus out and sat down on the judge's seat at a place known as the Stone Pavement (which in Aramaic is Gabbatha). It was the day of Preparation of the Passover; it was about noon.

"Here is your king," Pilate said to the Jews.

But they shouted, "Take him away! Take him away! Crucify him!"

"Shall I crucify your king?" Pilate asked.

"We have no king but Caesar," the chief priests answered.

Finally Pilate handed him over to them to be crucified.

So the soldiers took charge of Jesus.

As they were going out, they met a man from Cyrene, named Simon, and they forced him to carry the cross.

Roman crucifixion was a cruel punishment. Nailed to a wooden cross by wrists and feet, it was an excruciating, slow and very public way to die. The victim's groaning became a morning's entertainment for onlookers. Seeing the horrors of crucifixion was an effective deterrent for wrong-doers. For Jesus, this heinous death was undeserved. As he gave his life, he looked beyond it to God's bigger story of salvation that was being played out through his life and death.

Those who passed by hurled insults at him, shaking their heads and saying, "So! You who are going to destroy the temple and build it in three days, come down from the cross and save yourself!"

In the same way the chief priests and the teachers of the law mocked him among themselves. "He saved others," they said, "but he can't save himself! Let this Messiah, this king of Israel, come down now from the cross, that we may see and believe."

Two other men, both criminals, were also led out with him to be executed. When they came to the place called the Skull, they crucified him there, along with the criminals — one on his right, the other on his left. Jesus said, "Father, forgive them, for they do not know what they are doing." And they divided up his clothes by casting lots.

The people stood watching, and the rulers even sneered at him. They said, "He saved others; let him save himself if he is God's Messiah, the Chosen One."

The soldiers also came up and mocked him. They offered him wine vinegar and said, "If you are the king of the Jews, save yourself."

There was a written notice above him, which read: THIS IS THE KING OF THE JEWS.

One of the criminals who hung there hurled insults at him: "Aren't you the Messiah? Save yourself and us!"

But the other criminal rebuked him. "Don't you fear God," he said, "since you are under the same sentence? We are punished justly, for we are getting what our deeds deserve. But this man has done nothing wrong."

Then he said, "Jesus, remember me when you come into your kingdom."

Jesus answered him, "Truly I tell you, today you will be with me in paradise."

Near the cross of Jesus stood his mother, his mother's sister, Mary the wife of Clopas, and Mary Magdalene. When Jesus saw his mother there, and the disciple whom he loved standing nearby, he said to her, "Woman, here is your son," and to the disciple, "Here is your mother." From that time on, this disciple took her into his home.

For those made to suffer crucifixion, death itself was the only resolution. So Jesus waited that day, along with two other victims and a crowd of onlookers, for death to overcome him. Before that, however, a deeper pain was coming. A pain that went far beyond the nails in his feet and wrists, the labored breathing or the "crown" of thorns puncturing his brow. God poured out humanity's rightful punishment for sin upon his Son. And even the physical elements trembled.

It was now about noon, and darkness came over the whole land until three in the afternoon, for the sun stopped shining. And the curtain of the temple was torn in two.

About three in the afternoon Jesus cried out in a loud voice, *"Eli, Eli, lema sabachthani?"* (which means "My God, my God, why have you forsaken me?").

When some of those standing there heard this, they said, "He's calling Elijah."

Immediately one of them ran and got a sponge. He filled it with wine vinegar, put it on a staff, and offered it to Jesus to drink. The rest said, "Now leave him alone. Let's see if Elijah comes to save him."

When he had received the drink, Jesus said, "It is finished." With that, he bowed his head and gave up his spirit.

At that moment the curtain of the temple was torn in two from top to bottom. The earth shook, the rocks split and the tombs broke open. The bodies of many holy people who had died were raised to life. They came out of the tombs after Jesus' resurrection and went into the holy city and appeared to many people.

When the centurion and those with him who were guarding Jesus saw the earthquake and all that had happened, they were terrified, and exclaimed, "Surely he was the Son of God!"

When all the people who had gathered to witness this sight saw what took place, they beat their breasts and went away. But all those who knew him, including the women who had followed him from Galilee, stood at a distance, watching these things.

27

The Resurrection

Now it was the day of Preparation, and the next day was to be a special Sabbath. Because the Jewish leaders did not want the bodies left on the crosses during the Sabbath, they asked Pilate to have the legs broken and the bodies taken down. The soldiers therefore came and broke the legs of the first man who had been crucified with Jesus, and then those of the other. But when they came to Jesus and found that he was already dead, they did not break his legs. Instead, one of the soldiers pierced Jesus' side with a spear, bringing a sudden flow of blood and water. The man who saw it has given testimony, and his testimony is true. He knows that he tells the truth, and he testifies so that you also may believe. These things happened so that the scripture would be fulfilled: "Not one of his bones will be broken," and, as another scripture says, "They will look on the one they have pierced."

Later, Joseph of Arimathea asked Pilate for the body of Jesus. Now Joseph was a disciple of Jesus, but secretly because he feared the Jewish leaders. With Pilate's permission, he came and took the body away. He was accompanied by Nicodemus, the man who earlier had visited Jesus at night. Nicodemus brought a mixture of

Jesus buried	Jesus resurrected	Jesus appears to Mary Magdalene and the disciples

AD   30

Full timeline information starts on page xi.

myrrh and aloes, about seventy-five pounds. Taking Jesus' body, the two of them wrapped it, with the spices, in strips of linen. This was in accordance with Jewish burial customs. At the place where Jesus was crucified, there was a garden, and in the garden a new tomb, in which no one had ever been laid. Because it was the Jewish day of Preparation and since the tomb was nearby, they laid Jesus there.

The next day, the one after Preparation Day, the chief priests and the Pharisees went to Pilate. "Sir," they said, "we remember that while he was still alive that deceiver said, 'After three days I will rise again.' So give the order for the tomb to be made secure until the third day. Otherwise, his disciples may come and steal the body and tell the people that he has been raised from the dead. This last deception will be worse than the first."

"Take a guard," Pilate answered. "Go, make the tomb as secure as you know how." So they went and made the tomb secure by putting a seal on the stone and posting the guard.

Jesus died and was buried on Friday. The next day was the Jewish Sabbath, and a guard was posted to prevent any tampering with the body. Then on the first day of the week, Sunday, those who mourned Jesus came to pay their respects.

When the Sabbath was over, Mary Magdalene, Mary the mother of James, and Salome bought spices so that they might go to anoint Jesus' body. Very early on the first day of the week, just after sunrise, they were on their way to the tomb and they asked each other, "Who will roll the stone away from the entrance of the tomb?"

There was a violent earthquake, for an angel of the Lord came down from heaven and, going to the tomb, rolled back the stone and sat on it. His appearance was like lightning, and his clothes were white as snow. The guards were so afraid of him that they shook and became like dead men.

The angel said to the women, "Do not be afraid, for I know that you are looking for Jesus, who was crucified. He is not here; he has risen, just as he said. Come and see the place where he lay. Then go quickly and tell his disciples: 'He has risen from the dead and is going ahead of you into Galilee. There you will see him.' Now I have told you."

So the women hurried away from the tomb, afraid yet filled with joy, and ran to tell his disciples.

So Peter and the other disciple[1] started for the tomb. Both were running, but the other disciple outran Peter and reached the tomb first. He bent over and looked in at the strips of linen lying there but did not go in. Then Simon Peter came along behind him and went straight into the tomb. He saw the strips of linen lying there, as well as the cloth that had been wrapped around Jesus' head. The cloth was still lying in its place, separate from the linen. Finally the other disciple, who had reached the tomb first, also went inside. He saw and believed. (They still did not understand from Scripture that Jesus had to rise from the dead.) Then the disciples went back to where they were staying.

Now Mary[2] stood outside the tomb crying. As she wept, she bent over to look into the tomb and saw two angels in white, seated where Jesus' body had been, one at the head and the other at the foot.

They asked her, "Woman, why are you crying?"

"They have taken my Lord away," she said, "and I don't know where they have put him." At this, she turned around and saw Jesus standing there, but she did not realize that it was Jesus.

He asked her, "Woman, why are you crying? Who is it you are looking for?"

---

[1]**The other disciple:** Probably John.
[2]**Mary:** That is, Mary Magdalene.

Thinking he was the gardener, she said, "Sir, if you have carried him away, tell me where you have put him, and I will get him."

Jesus said to her, "Mary."

She turned toward him and cried out in Aramaic, "Rabboni!" (which means "Teacher").

Jesus said, "Do not hold on to me, for I have not yet ascended to the Father. Go instead to my brothers and tell them, 'I am ascending to my Father and your Father, to my God and your God.'"

Mary Magdalene went to the disciples with the news: "I have seen the Lord!" And she told them that he had said these things to her.

Now that same day two of them were going to a village called Emmaus, about seven miles from Jerusalem. They were talking with each other about everything that had happened. As they talked and discussed these things with each other, Jesus himself came up and walked along with them; but they were kept from recognizing him.

He asked them, "What are you discussing together as you walk along?"

They stood still, their faces downcast. One of them, named Cleopas, asked him, "Are you the only one visiting Jerusalem who does not know the things that have happened there in these days?"

"What things?" he asked.

"About Jesus of Nazareth," they replied. "He was a prophet, powerful in word and deed before God and all the people. The chief priests and our rulers handed him over to be sentenced to death, and they crucified him; but we had hoped that he was the one who was going to redeem Israel. And what is more, it is the third day since all this took place. In addition, some of our women amazed us. They went to the tomb early this morning but didn't find his body. They came and told us that they had seen a vision of angels, who said he was alive. Then some of our companions went to the tomb and found it just as the women had said, but they did not see Jesus."

He said to them, "How foolish you are, and how slow to believe all that the prophets have spoken! Did not the Messiah have to suffer these things and then enter his glory?" And beginning with Moses and all the Prophets, he explained to them what was said in all the Scriptures concerning himself.

As they approached the village to which they were going, Jesus continued on as if he were going farther. But they urged him strongly, "Stay with us, for it is nearly evening; the day is almost over." So he went in to stay with them.

When he was at the table with them, he took bread, gave thanks, broke it and began to give it to them. Then their eyes were opened and they recognized him, and he disappeared from their sight. They asked each other, "Were not our hearts burning within us while he talked with us on the road and opened the Scriptures to us?"

They got up and returned at once to Jerusalem. There they found the Eleven and those with them, assembled together and saying, "It is true! The Lord has risen and has appeared to Simon." Then the two told what had happened on the way, and how Jesus was recognized by them when he broke the bread.

While they were still talking about this, Jesus himself stood among them and said to them, "Peace be with you."

They were startled and frightened, thinking they saw a ghost. He said to them, "Why are you troubled, and why do doubts rise in your minds? Look at my hands and my feet. It is I myself! Touch me and see; a ghost does not have flesh and bones, as you see I have."

When he had said this, he showed them his hands and feet. And while they still did not believe it because of joy and amazement, he asked them, "Do you have anything here to eat?" They gave him a piece of broiled fish, and he took it and ate it in their presence.

He said to them, "This is what I told you while I was still with you: Everything must be fulfilled that is written about me in the Law of Moses, the Prophets and the Psalms."

Then he opened their minds so they could understand the Scriptures. He told them, "This is what is written: The Messiah will suffer and rise from the dead on the third day, and repentance for the forgiveness of sins will be preached in his name to all nations, beginning at Jerusalem. You are witnesses of these things. I am going to send you what my Father has promised; but stay in the city until you have been clothed with power from on high."

Now Thomas (also known as Didymus), one of the Twelve, was not with the disciples when Jesus came. So the other disciples told him, "We have seen the Lord!"

But he said to them, "Unless I see the nail marks in his hands and put my finger where the nails were, and put my hand into his side, I will not believe."

A week later his disciples were in the house again, and Thomas was with them. Though the doors were locked, Jesus came and stood among them and said, "Peace be with you!" Then he said to Thomas, "Put your finger here; see my hands. Reach out your hand and put it into my side. Stop doubting and believe."

Thomas said to him, "My Lord and my God!"

Then Jesus told him, "Because you have seen me, you have believed; blessed are those who have not seen and yet have believed."

Afterward Jesus appeared again to his disciples, by the Sea of Galilee. It happened this way: Simon Peter, Thomas (also known as Didymus), Nathanael from Cana in Galilee, the sons of Zebedee, and two other disciples were together. "I'm going out to fish," Simon Peter told them, and they said, "We'll go with you." So they went out and got into the boat, but that night they caught nothing.

Early in the morning, Jesus stood on the shore, but the disciples did not realize that it was Jesus.

He called out to them, "Friends, haven't you any fish?"

"No," they answered.

He said, "Throw your net on the right side of the boat and you will find some." When they did, they were unable to haul the net in because of the large number of fish.

Then the disciple whom Jesus loved[3] said to Peter, "It is the Lord!" As soon as Simon Peter heard him say, "It is the Lord," he wrapped his outer garment around him (for he had taken it off) and jumped into the water. The other disciples followed in the boat, towing the net full of fish, for they were not far from shore, about a hundred yards. When they landed, they saw a fire of burning coals there with fish on it, and some bread.

Jesus said to them, "Bring some of the fish you have just caught." Simon Peter climbed back into the boat and dragged the net ashore. It was full of large fish, 153, but even with so many the net was not torn. Jesus said to them, "Come and have breakfast." None of the disciples dared ask him, "Who are you?" They knew it was the Lord. Jesus came, took the bread and gave it to them, and did the same with the fish. This was now the third time Jesus appeared to his disciples after he was raised from the dead.

When they had finished eating, Jesus said to Simon Peter, "Simon son of John, do you love me more than these?"

"Yes, Lord," he said, "you know that I love you."

Jesus said, "Feed my lambs."

Again Jesus said, "Simon son of John, do you love me?"

He answered, "Yes, Lord, you know that I love you."

Jesus said, "Take care of my sheep."

The third time he said to him, "Simon son of John, do you love me?"

Peter was hurt because Jesus asked him the third time, "Do you love me?" He said, "Lord, you know all things; you know that I love you."

Jesus said, "Feed my sheep. Very truly I tell you, when you were younger you dressed yourself and went where you wanted; but when you are old you will stretch out your hands, and someone

---

[3]**The disciple whom Jesus loved:** Probably John.

else will dress you and lead you where you do not want to go." Jesus said this to indicate the kind of death by which Peter would glorify God. Then he said to him, "Follow me!"

Then the eleven disciples went to Galilee, to the mountain where Jesus had told them to go. When they saw him, they worshiped him; but some doubted. Then Jesus came to them and said, "All authority in heaven and on earth has been given to me. Therefore go and make disciples of all nations, baptizing them in the name of the Father and of the Son and of the Holy Spirit, and teaching them to obey everything I have commanded you. And surely I am with you always, to the very end of the age."

Jesus did many other things as well. If every one of them were written down, I suppose that even the whole world would not have room for the books that would be written.

But these are written that you may believe that Jesus is the Messiah, the Son of God, and that by believing you may have life in his name.

God had promised since Old Testament days that he would redeem and restore his people. He sent his Son, the Savior, who died and was raised to life so that people could be forgiven and brought into a relationship of peace and fellowship with God. What a story! But was Jesus' resurrection the end of the saga? What else could possibly happen? Luke, the author of the Gospel by that name, answers that question in his second work — the "Acts of the Apostles," better known simply as "Acts."

28

New Beginnings

IN MY FORMER BOOK, Theophilus, I wrote about all that Jesus began to do and to teach until the day he was taken up to heaven, after giving instructions through the Holy Spirit to the apostles he had chosen. After his suffering, he presented himself to them and gave many convincing proofs that he was alive. He appeared to them over a period of forty days and spoke about the kingdom of God. On one occasion, while he was eating with them, he gave them this command: "Do not leave Jerusalem, but wait for the gift my Father promised, which you have heard me speak about. For John baptized with water, but in a few days you will be baptized with the Holy Spirit."

Then they gathered around him and asked him, "Lord, are you at this time going to restore the kingdom to Israel?"

He said to them: "It is not for you to know the times or dates the Father has set by his own authority. But you will receive power when the Holy Spirit comes on you; and you will be my witnesses in Jerusalem, and in all Judea and Samaria, and to the ends of the earth."

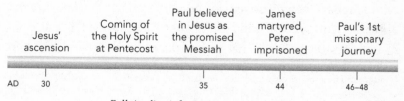

| Jesus' ascension | Coming of the Holy Spirit at Pentecost | Paul believed in Jesus as the promised Messiah | James martyred, Peter imprisoned | Paul's 1st missionary journey |
| AD 30 | | 35 | 44 | 46–48 |

Full timeline information starts on page xi.

After he said this, he was taken up before their very eyes, and a cloud hid him from their sight.

They were looking intently up into the sky as he was going, when suddenly two men dressed in white stood beside them. "Men of Galilee," they said, "why do you stand here looking into the sky? This same Jesus, who has been taken from you into heaven, will come back in the same way you have seen him go into heaven."

Jesus' ascension occurred 40 days after his resurrection. In the Jewish calendar, the harvest festival called Pentecost[1] came 50 days after the Sabbath of Passover week—coinciding with Jesus' crucifixion and resurrection. At this eventful Pentecost celebration, the Holy Spirit appeared like flames over the disciples' heads and endued them with the Holy Spirit's power and a new sense of God-with-us. During the 10 days between Jesus' ascension to heaven and the Festival of Pentecost, the 11 disciples chose a replacement for Judas, and then spent most of their time praying and waiting for Jesus' promise of the Holy Spirit to arrive. When the Holy Spirit came, the house rocked.

When the day of Pentecost came, they were all together in one place. Suddenly a sound like the blowing of a violent wind came from heaven and filled the whole house where they were sitting. They saw what seemed to be tongues of fire that separated and came to rest on each of them. All of them were filled with the Holy Spirit and began to speak in other tongues as the Spirit enabled them.

Now there were staying in Jerusalem God-fearing Jews from every nation under heaven. When they heard this sound, a crowd came together in bewilderment, because each one heard their own language being spoken. Utterly amazed, they asked: "Aren't all these who are speaking Galileans? Then how is it that each of us hears them in our native language? Parthians, Medes and

---

[1]**Pentecost:** The Jewish festival celebrated on the 50th day after Passover. Jesus' disciples were celebrating this festival in Jerusalem when God sent his Holy Spirit to empower them with new life and blessing.

Elamites; residents of Mesopotamia, Judea and Cappadocia, Pontus and Asia,[2] Phrygia and Pamphylia, Egypt and the parts of Libya near Cyrene; visitors from Rome (both Jews and converts to Judaism); Cretans and Arabs — we hear them declaring the wonders of God in our own tongues!" Amazed and perplexed, they asked one another, "What does this mean?"

Some, however, made fun of them and said, "They have had too much wine."

Then Peter stood up with the Eleven, raised his voice and addressed the crowd: "Fellow Jews and all of you who live in Jerusalem, let me explain this to you; listen carefully to what I say. These people are not drunk, as you suppose. It's only nine in the morning! No, this is what was spoken by the prophet Joel:

> "'In the last days, God says,
>> I will pour out my Spirit on all people.
> Your sons and daughters will prophesy,
>> your young men will see visions,
>> your old men will dream dreams.
> Even on my servants, both men and women,
>> I will pour out my Spirit in those days,
>> and they will prophesy.
> I will show wonders in the heavens above
>> and signs on the earth below,
>> blood and fire and billows of smoke.
> The sun will be turned to darkness
>> and the moon to blood
>> before the coming of the great and glorious day
>>> of the Lord.
> And everyone who calls
>> on the name of the Lord will be saved.'

"Fellow Israelites, listen to this: Jesus of Nazareth was a man accredited by God to you by miracles, wonders and signs, which God did among you through him, as you yourselves know. This

---

[2] **Asia:** That is, the Roman province by the same name.

man was handed over to you by God's deliberate plan and fore-knowledge; and you, with the help of wicked men, put him to death by nailing him to the cross. But God raised him from the dead, freeing him from the agony of death, because it was impossible for death to keep its hold on him.

"God has raised this Jesus to life, and we are all witnesses of it. Exalted to the right hand of God, he has received from the Father the promised Holy Spirit and has poured out what you now see and hear.

"Therefore let all Israel be assured of this: God has made this Jesus, whom you crucified, both Lord and Messiah."

When the people heard this, they were cut to the heart and said to Peter and the other apostles, "Brothers, what shall we do?"

Peter replied, "Repent and be baptized, every one of you, in the name of Jesus Christ for the forgiveness of your sins. And you will receive the gift of the Holy Spirit. The promise is for you and your children and for all who are far off — for all whom the Lord our God will call."

With many other words he warned them; and he pleaded with them, "Save yourselves from this corrupt generation." Those who accepted his message were baptized, and about three thousand were added to their number that day.

They devoted themselves to the apostles' teaching and to fel-lowship, to the breaking of bread and to prayer. Everyone was filled with awe at the many wonders and signs performed by the apostles. All the believers were together and had everything in common. They sold property and possessions to give to anyone who had need. Every day they continued to meet together in the temple courts. They broke bread in their homes and ate together with glad and sincere hearts, praising God and enjoying the favor of all the people. And the Lord added to their number daily those who were being saved.

One day Peter and John were going up to the temple at the

time of prayer — at three in the afternoon. Now a man who was lame from birth was being carried to the temple gate called Beautiful, where he was put every day to beg from those going into the temple courts. When he saw Peter and John about to enter, he asked them for money. Peter looked straight at him, as did John. Then Peter said, "Look at us!" So the man gave them his attention, expecting to get something from them.

Then Peter said, "Silver or gold I do not have, but what I do have I give you. In the name of Jesus Christ of Nazareth, walk." Taking him by the right hand, he helped him up, and instantly the man's feet and ankles became strong. He jumped to his feet and began to walk. Then he went with them into the temple courts, walking and jumping, and praising God. When all the people saw him walking and praising God, they recognized him as the same man who used to sit begging at the temple gate called Beautiful, and they were filled with wonder and amazement at what had happened to him.

While the man held on to Peter and John, all the people were astonished and came running to them in the place called Solomon's Colonnade. When Peter saw this, he said to them: "Fellow Israelites, why does this surprise you? Why do you stare at us as if by our own power or godliness we had made this man walk? The God of Abraham, Isaac and Jacob, the God of our fathers, has glorified his servant Jesus. You handed him over to be killed, and you disowned him before Pilate, though he had decided to let him go. You disowned the Holy and Righteous One and asked that a murderer be released to you. You killed the author of life, but God raised him from the dead. We are witnesses of this. By faith in the name of Jesus, this man whom you see and know was made strong. It is Jesus' name and the faith that comes through him that has completely healed him, as you can all see.

"Now, fellow Israelites, I know that you acted in ignorance, as did your leaders. But this is how God fulfilled what he had foretold through all the prophets, saying that his Messiah would suffer. Repent, then, and turn to God, so that your sins may be wiped out, that times of refreshing may come from the Lord, and that he may send the Messiah, who has been appointed for you — even Jesus.

The priests and the captain of the temple guard and the Sadducees[3] came up to Peter and John while they were speaking to the people. They were greatly disturbed because the apostles were teaching the people, proclaiming in Jesus the resurrection of the dead. They seized Peter and John and, because it was evening, they put them in jail until the next day. But many who heard the message believed; so the number of men who believed grew to about five thousand.

The next day the rulers, the elders and the teachers of the law met in Jerusalem. Annas the high priest was there, and so were Caiaphas, John, Alexander and others of the high priest's family. They had Peter and John brought before them and began to question them: "By what power or what name did you do this?"

Then Peter, filled with the Holy Spirit, said to them: "Rulers and elders of the people! If we are being called to account today for an act of kindness shown to a man who was lame and are being asked how he was healed, then know this, you and all the people of Israel: It is by the name of Jesus Christ of Nazareth, whom you crucified but whom God raised from the dead, that this man stands before you healed. Jesus is

> " 'the stone you builders rejected,
>   which has become the cornerstone.'

Salvation[4] is found in no one else, for there is no other name under heaven given to mankind by which we must be saved."

When they saw the courage of Peter and John and realized that they were unschooled, ordinary men, they were astonished and they took note that these men had been with Jesus. But since

---

[3]**Sadducees:** An upper-class group of Jewish leaders who oversaw the temple administration.
[4]**Salvation:** Rescue from death or destruction. In the Biblical sense, the term *salvation* expresses the release from the debt of sin owed to God and the experience of never-ending life with him in heaven. Also relevant to earthly life, *salvation* can refer to the transformation of people's daily lives when they believe in Jesus.

they could see the man who had been healed standing there with them, there was nothing they could say. So they ordered them to withdraw from the Sanhedrin and then conferred together. "What are we going to do with these men?" they asked. "Everyone living in Jerusalem knows they have performed a notable sign, and we cannot deny it. But to stop this thing from spreading any further among the people, we must warn them to speak no longer to anyone in this name."

Then they called them in again and commanded them not to speak or teach at all in the name of Jesus. But Peter and John replied, "Which is right in God's eyes: to listen to you, or to him? You be the judges! As for us, we cannot help speaking about what we have seen and heard."

After further threats they let them go. They could not decide how to punish them, because all the people were praising God for what had happened.

All the believers were one in heart and mind. No one claimed that any of their possessions was their own, but they shared everything they had. With great power the apostles continued to testify to the resurrection of the Lord Jesus. And God's grace was so powerfully at work in them all that there were no needy persons among them. For from time to time those who owned land or houses sold them, brought the money from the sales and put it at the apostles' feet, and it was distributed to anyone who had need.

The apostles performed many signs and wonders among the people. And all the believers used to meet together in Solomon's Colonnade. No one else dared join them, even though they were highly regarded by the people. Nevertheless, more and more men and women believed in the Lord and were added to their number. As a result, people brought the sick into the streets and laid them on beds and mats so that at least Peter's shadow might fall on some of them as he passed by. Crowds gathered also from the towns around Jerusalem, bringing their sick and those tormented by impure spirits, and all of them were healed.

Then the high priest and all his associates, who were members of the party of the Sadducees, were filled with jealousy. They arrested the apostles and put them in the public jail. But during the night an angel of the Lord opened the doors of the jail and brought them out. "Go, stand in the temple courts," he said, "and tell the people all about this new life."

At daybreak they entered the temple courts, as they had been told, and began to teach the people.

When the high priest and his associates arrived, they called together the Sanhedrin — the full assembly of the elders of Israel — and sent to the jail for the apostles. But on arriving at the jail, the officers did not find them there. So they went back and reported, "We found the jail securely locked, with the guards standing at the doors; but when we opened them, we found no one inside." On hearing this report, the captain of the temple guard and the chief priests were at a loss, wondering what this might lead to.

Then someone came and said, "Look! The men you put in jail are standing in the temple courts teaching the people." At that, the captain went with his officers and brought the apostles. They did not use force, because they feared that the people would stone them.

The apostles were brought in and made to appear before the Sanhedrin to be questioned by the high priest. "We gave you strict orders not to teach in this name," he said. "Yet you have filled Jerusalem with your teaching and are determined to make us guilty of this man's blood."

Peter and the other apostles replied: "We must obey God rather than human beings! The God of our ancestors raised Jesus from the dead — whom you killed by hanging him on a cross. God exalted him to his own right hand as Prince and Savior that he might bring Israel to repentance and forgive their sins. We are witnesses of these things, and so is the Holy Spirit, whom God has given to those who obey him."

When they heard this, they were furious and wanted to put them to death. But a Pharisee named Gamaliel, a teacher of the law, who was honored by all the people, stood up in the Sanhedrin and ordered that the men be put outside for a little while. Then he addressed the Sanhedrin: "Men of Israel, consider carefully what you intend to do to these men. Some time ago Theudas appeared, claiming to be somebody, and about four hundred men rallied to him. He was killed, all his followers were dispersed, and it all came to nothing. After him, Judas the Galilean appeared in the days of the census and led a band of people in revolt. He too was killed, and all his followers were scattered. Therefore, in the present case I advise you: Leave these men alone! Let them go! For if their purpose or activity is of human origin, it will fail. But if it is from God, you will not be able to stop these men; you will only find yourselves fighting against God."

His speech persuaded them. They called the apostles in and had them flogged. Then they ordered them not to speak in the name of Jesus, and let them go.

The apostles left the Sanhedrin, rejoicing because they had been counted worthy of suffering disgrace for the Name. Day after day, in the temple courts and from house to house, they never stopped teaching and proclaiming the good news that Jesus is the Messiah.

> Growing movements create logistical nightmares. As hundreds, then thousands, said yes to following the resurrected Jesus, they gathered together, full of joy and needs. So who would run the errands, distribute food, clean the dishes and make sure everyone had name tags? For these important service jobs, the 12 apostles chose a small corps of servers, considered to be the first "deacons." Among them was a man described as "full of God's grace and power." His name was Stephen.

Now Stephen, a man full of God's grace and power, performed great wonders and signs among the people. Opposition arose, however, from members of the Synagogue of the Freedmen (as it was called) — Jews of Cyrene and Alexandria as well as the provinces of Cilicia and Asia — who began to argue with Stephen. But they could not stand up against the wisdom the Spirit gave him as he spoke.

Then they secretly persuaded some men to say, "We have heard Stephen speak blasphemous words against Moses and against God."

So they stirred up the people and the elders and the teachers of the law. They seized Stephen and brought him before the Sanhedrin. They produced false witnesses, who testified, "This fellow never stops speaking against this holy place and against the law. For we have heard him say that this Jesus of Nazareth will destroy this place and change the customs Moses handed down to us."

All who were sitting in the Sanhedrin looked intently at Stephen, and they saw that his face was like the face of an angel.

Then the high priest asked Stephen, "Are these charges true?"

Stephen's answer to this question came in the form of a Jewish history lesson about God's great story of redemption. Then Stephen spoke of the "Righteous One," Jesus.

"You stiff-necked people! Your hearts and ears are still uncircumcised. You are just like your ancestors: You always resist the Holy Spirit! Was there ever a prophet your ancestors did not persecute? They even killed those who predicted the coming of the Righteous One. And now you have betrayed and murdered him — you who have received the law that was given through angels but have not obeyed it."

When the members of the Sanhedrin heard this, they were furious and gnashed their teeth at him. But Stephen, full of the Holy Spirit, looked up to heaven and saw the glory of God, and Jesus standing at the right hand of God. "Look," he said, "I see heaven open and the Son of Man standing at the right hand of God."

At this they covered their ears and, yelling at the top of their voices, they all rushed at him, dragged him out of the city and began to stone him. Meanwhile, the witnesses laid their coats at the feet of a young man named Saul.

While they were stoning him, Stephen prayed, "Lord Jesus, receive my spirit." Then he fell on his knees and cried out, "Lord, do not hold this sin against them." When he had said this, he fell asleep.

And Saul approved of their killing him.

On that day a great persecution broke out against the church in Jerusalem, and all except the apostles were scattered throughout Judea and Samaria. Godly men buried Stephen and mourned deeply for him. But Saul began to destroy the church. Going from house to house, he dragged off both men and women and put them in prison.

Those who had been scattered preached the word wherever they went. Philip went down to a city in Samaria and proclaimed the Messiah there. When the crowds heard Philip and saw the signs he performed, they all paid close attention to what he said. For with shrieks, impure spirits came out of many, and many who were paralyzed or lame were healed. So there was great joy in that city.

Meanwhile, Saul was still breathing out murderous threats against the Lord's disciples. He went to the high priest and asked him for letters to the synagogues in Damascus, so that if he found any there who belonged to the Way, whether men or women, he might take them as prisoners to Jerusalem. As he neared Damascus on his journey, suddenly a light from heaven flashed around him. He fell to the ground and heard a voice say to him, "Saul, Saul, why do you persecute me?"

"Who are you, Lord?" Saul asked.

"I am Jesus, whom you are persecuting," he replied. "Now get up and go into the city, and you will be told what you must do."

The men traveling with Saul stood there speechless; they heard the sound but did not see anyone. Saul got up from the ground, but when he opened his eyes he could see nothing. So they led him by the hand into Damascus. For three days he was blind, and did not eat or drink anything.

In Damascus there was a disciple named Ananias. The Lord called to him in a vision, "Ananias!"

"Yes, Lord," he answered.

The Lord told him, "Go to the house of Judas on Straight Street and ask for a man from Tarsus named Saul, for he is praying. In a vision he has seen a man named Ananias come and place his hands on him to restore his sight."

"Lord," Ananias answered, "I have heard many reports about this man and all the harm he has done to your holy people in Jerusalem. And he has come here with authority from the chief priests to arrest all who call on your name."

But the Lord said to Ananias, "Go! This man is my chosen instrument to proclaim my name to the Gentiles and their kings and to the people of Israel. I will show him how much he must suffer for my name."

Then Ananias went to the house and entered it. Placing his hands on Saul, he said, "Brother Saul, the Lord — Jesus, who appeared to you on the road as you were coming here — has sent me so that you may see again and be filled with the Holy Spirit." Immediately, something like scales fell from Saul's eyes, and he could see again. He got up and was baptized, and after taking some food, he regained his strength.

Saul spent several days with the disciples in Damascus. At once he began to preach in the synagogues that Jesus is the Son of God. All those who heard him were astonished and asked, "Isn't he the man who raised havoc in Jerusalem among those who call on this name? And hasn't he come here to take them as prisoners to the chief priests?" Yet Saul grew more and more powerful and baffled the Jews living in Damascus by proving that Jesus is the Messiah.

After many days had gone by, there was a conspiracy among the Jews to kill him, but Saul learned of their plan. Day and night they kept close watch on the city gates in order to kill him. But his followers took him by night and lowered him in a basket through an opening in the wall.

When he came to Jerusalem, he tried to join the disciples, but they were all afraid of him, not believing that he really was a disciple. But Barnabas took him and brought him to the apostles. He told them how Saul on his journey had seen the Lord and that the Lord had spoken to him, and how in Damascus he had preached fearlessly in the name of Jesus. So Saul stayed with them and moved about freely in Jerusalem, speaking boldly in the name of the Lord. He talked and debated with the Hellenistic Jews, but they tried to kill him. When the believers learned of this, they took him down to Caesarea and sent him off to Tarsus.

Then the church throughout Judea, Galilee and Samaria enjoyed a time of peace and was strengthened. Living in the fear of the Lord and encouraged by the Holy Spirit, it increased in numbers.

Most of the new Christians were Jewish, but God's story of Good News was for everyone. Things had to change.

At Caesarea there was a man named Cornelius, a centurion in what was known as the Italian Regiment. He and all his family were devout and God-fearing; he gave generously to those in need and prayed to God regularly. One day at about three in the afternoon he had a vision. He distinctly saw an angel of God, who came to him and said, "Cornelius!"

Cornelius stared at him in fear. "What is it, Lord?" he asked.

The angel answered, "Your prayers and gifts to the poor have come up as a memorial offering before God. Now send men to Joppa to bring back a man named Simon who is called Peter. He is staying with Simon the tanner, whose house is by the sea."

When the angel who spoke to him had gone, Cornelius called two of his servants and a devout soldier who was one of his attendants. He told them everything that had happened and sent them to Joppa.

About noon the following day as they were on their journey and approaching the city, Peter went up on the roof to pray. He became hungry and wanted something to eat, and while the meal was being prepared, he fell into a trance. He saw heaven opened and something like a large sheet being let down to earth by its four corners. It contained all kinds of four-footed animals, as well as reptiles and birds. Then a voice told him, "Get up, Peter. Kill and eat."

"Surely not, Lord!" Peter replied. "I have never eaten anything impure or unclean."

The voice spoke to him a second time, "Do not call anything impure that God has made clean."

This happened three times, and immediately the sheet was taken back to heaven.

While Peter was wondering about the meaning of the vision, the men sent by Cornelius found out where Simon's house was and stopped at the gate. They called out, asking if Simon who was known as Peter was staying there.

While Peter was still thinking about the vision, the Spirit said to him, "Simon, three men are looking for you. So get up and go downstairs. Do not hesitate to go with them, for I have sent them."

Peter went down and said to the men, "I'm the one you're looking for. Why have you come?"

The men replied, "We have come from Cornelius the centurion. He is a righteous and God-fearing man, who is respected by all the Jewish people. A holy angel told him to ask you to come to his house so that he could hear what you have to say." Then Peter invited the men into the house to be his guests.

The next day Peter started out with them, and some of the believers from Joppa went along. The following day he arrived in Caesarea. Cornelius was expecting them and had called together his relatives and close friends. As Peter entered the house, Cornelius met him and fell at his feet in reverence. But Peter made him get up. "Stand up," he said, "I am only a man myself."

While talking with him, Peter went inside and found a large gathering of people. He said to them: "You are well aware that it is against our law for a Jew to associate with or visit a Gentile. But God has shown me that I should not call anyone impure or unclean.

> Peter went on to say he realized that God doesn't show favoritism but invites people from every ethnic group and nation to accept the gospel through Jesus the Messiah. As Peter was explaining the gospel message and the first-ever Gentile audience was responding with faith and repentance, something amazing happened: the gift of the Holy Spirit was poured out on them just as it had been on the Jewish believers on the day of Pentecost.
>
> At the same time the church was growing, it was also facing persecution from Herod Agrippa I, the grandson of Herod the Great (who reigned when Jesus was born) and nephew of Herod Antipas (who had John the Baptist beheaded).

It was about this time that King Herod arrested some who belonged to the church, intending to persecute them. He had James, the brother of John, put to death with the sword. When he saw that this met with approval among the Jews, he proceeded to seize Peter also. This happened during the Festival of Unleavened Bread. After arresting him, he put him in prison, handing him over to be guarded by four squads of four soldiers each. Herod intended to bring him out for public trial after the Passover.

So Peter was kept in prison, but the church was earnestly praying to God for him.

The night before Herod was to bring him to trial, Peter was sleeping between two soldiers, bound with two chains, and sentries stood guard at the entrance. Suddenly an angel of the Lord appeared and a light shone in the cell. He struck Peter on the side and woke him up. "Quick, get up!" he said, and the chains fell off Peter's wrists.

Then the angel said to him, "Put on your clothes and sandals." And Peter did so. "Wrap your cloak around you and follow me," the angel told him. Peter followed him out of the prison, but he had no idea that what the angel was doing was really happening; he thought he was seeing a vision. They passed the first and second guards and came to the iron gate leading to the city. It opened for them by itself, and they went through it. When they had walked the length of one street, suddenly the angel left him.

Then Peter came to himself and said, "Now I know without a doubt that the Lord has sent his angel and rescued me from Herod's clutches and from everything the Jewish people were hoping would happen."

When this had dawned on him, he went to the house of Mary the mother of John, also called Mark, where many people had gathered and were praying. Peter knocked at the outer entrance, and a servant named Rhoda came to answer the door. When she recognized Peter's voice, she was so overjoyed she ran back without opening it and exclaimed, "Peter is at the door!"

"You're out of your mind," they told her. When she kept insisting that it was so, they said, "It must be his angel."

But Peter kept on knocking, and when they opened the door and saw him, they were astonished. Peter motioned with his hand for them to be quiet and described how the Lord had brought him out of prison. "Tell James and the other brothers and sisters about this," he said, and then he left for another place.

In the morning, there was no small commotion among the soldiers as to what had become of Peter. After Herod had a thorough search made for him and did not find him, he cross-examined the guards and ordered that they be executed.

Then Herod went from Judea to Caesarea and stayed there. He had been quarreling with the people of Tyre and Sidon; they now joined together and sought an audience with him. After securing the support of Blastus, a trusted personal servant of the king, they asked for peace, because they depended on the king's country for their food supply.

On the appointed day Herod, wearing his royal robes, sat on his throne and delivered a public address to the people. They shouted,

"This is the voice of a god, not of a man." Immediately, because Herod did not give praise to God, an angel of the Lord struck him down, and he was eaten by worms and died.

But the word of God continued to spread and flourish.

Saul and his mentor Barnabas spent a year ministering to the first largely Gentile church at Antioch, where the believers were first called "Christians." From there the Lord called them to missionary service. Saul and Barnabas, accompanied at first by John Mark—who was Barnabas's cousin and who would later write the Gospel of Mark—began traveling and proclaiming Jesus throughout Asia Minor. It was also during this time that Saul got a name change to "Paul." Because God's Spirit was leading them, Saul (Paul) and his colleagues boldly spoke about Jesus everywhere they went. Little did they know what they would have to endure for the Good News.

29

Paul's Mission

Now in the church at Antioch there were prophets and teachers: Barnabas, Simeon called Niger, Lucius of Cyrene, Manaen (who had been brought up with Herod the tetrarch) and Saul. While they were worshiping the Lord and fasting, the Holy Spirit said, "Set apart for me Barnabas and Saul for the work to which I have called them." So after they had fasted and prayed, they placed their hands on them and sent them off.

The two of them, sent on their way by the Holy Spirit, went down to Seleucia and sailed from there to Cyprus. When they arrived at Salamis, they proclaimed the word of God in the Jewish synagogues. John was with them as their helper.

They traveled through the whole island until they came to Paphos. There they met a Jewish sorcerer and false prophet named Bar-Jesus, who was an attendant of the proconsul, Sergius Paulus. The proconsul, an intelligent man, sent for Barnabas and Saul because he wanted to hear the word of God. But Elymas the sorcerer (for that is what his name means) opposed them and tried to turn the proconsul from the faith. Then Saul, who was also called

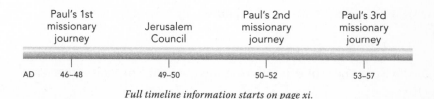

Paul's 1st missionary journey	Jerusalem Council	Paul's 2nd missionary journey	Paul's 3rd missionary journey
AD 46–48	49–50	50–52	53–57

Full timeline information starts on page xi.

Paul, filled with the Holy Spirit, looked straight at Elymas and said, "You are a child of the devil and an enemy of everything that is right! You are full of all kinds of deceit and trickery. Will you never stop perverting the right ways of the Lord? Now the hand of the Lord is against you. You are going to be blind for a time, not even able to see the light of the sun."

Immediately mist and darkness came over him, and he groped about, seeking someone to lead him by the hand. When the proconsul saw what had happened, he believed, for he was amazed at the teaching about the Lord.

From Paphos, Paul and his companions sailed to Perga in Pamphylia, where John left them to return to Jerusalem. From Perga they went on to Pisidian Antioch. On the Sabbath they entered the synagogue and sat down. After the reading from the Law and the Prophets, the leaders of the synagogue sent word to them, saying, "Brothers, if you have a word of exhortation for the people, please speak."

Standing up, Paul motioned with his hand and said: "Fellow Israelites and you Gentiles who worship God, listen to me!

"The people of Jerusalem and their rulers did not recognize Jesus, yet in condemning him they fulfilled the words of the prophets that are read every Sabbath. Though they found no proper ground for a death sentence, they asked Pilate to have him executed. When they had carried out all that was written about him, they took him down from the cross and laid him in a tomb. But God raised him from the dead, and for many days he was seen by those who had traveled with him from Galilee to Jerusalem. They are now his witnesses to our people.

"We tell you the good news: What God promised our ancestors he has fulfilled for us, their children, by raising up Jesus.

"Therefore, my friends, I want you to know that through Jesus the forgiveness of sins is proclaimed to you. Through him every-

one who believes is set free from every sin, a justification[1] you were
not able to obtain under the law of Moses."

As Paul and Barnabas were leaving the synagogue, the people
invited them to speak further about these things on the next Sabbath. When the congregation was dismissed, many of the Jews
and devout converts to Judaism followed Paul and Barnabas, who
talked with them and urged them to continue in the grace of God.

On the next Sabbath almost the whole city gathered to hear the
word of the Lord. When the Jews saw the crowds, they were filled
with jealousy. They began to contradict what Paul was saying and
heaped abuse on him.

Then Paul and Barnabas answered them boldly: "We had to
speak the word of God to you first. Since you reject it and do not
consider yourselves worthy of eternal life, we now turn to the Gentiles. For this is what the Lord has commanded us:

> "'I have made you a light for the Gentiles,
>   that you may bring salvation to the ends of the earth.'"

When the Gentiles heard this, they were glad and honored
the word of the Lord; and all who were appointed for eternal life
believed.

The word of the Lord spread through the whole region. But
the Jewish leaders incited the God-fearing women of high standing and the leading men of the city. They stirred up persecution
against Paul and Barnabas, and expelled them from their region.
So they shook the dust off their feet as a warning to them and
went to Iconium. And the disciples were filled with joy and with
the Holy Spirit.

When visiting a new city, Paul and Barnabas typically went first

---

[1]**Justified, justification:** The process by which one is made acceptable in the sight of God.
Justification occurs through faith that Jesus died to pay the price for human sin; thus, Jesus
himself justifies each person who believes in him.

to the Jewish synagogue. Not only did they feel that doing so was God's directed priority, but the synagogue's building and regularly scheduled meetings provided a convenient location and designated time for proclaiming the gospel. The Good News was often met with mixed results among the Jews — some gratefully embraced the message while others rejected it out of disbelief.

Within the mainstream Gentile community, some of the resistance to God's Good News was motivated by pure economics: each new follower of Jesus meant one less buyer of charms and idol merchandise, which was big business in many cities. Some of the opposition was political, as each convert subtracted from the number and clout of the leading religious groups. Much of it was personal, since believing in Jesus changed people and thus threatened the status quo.

At Iconium Paul and Barnabas went as usual into the Jewish synagogue. There they spoke so effectively that a great number of Jews and Greeks believed. But the Jews who refused to believe stirred up the other Gentiles and poisoned their minds against the brothers. So Paul and Barnabas spent considerable time there, speaking boldly for the Lord, who confirmed the message of his grace by enabling them to perform signs and wonders. The people of the city were divided; some sided with the Jews, others with the apostles. There was a plot afoot among both Gentiles and Jews, together with their leaders, to mistreat them and stone them. But they found out about it and fled to the Lycaonian cities of Lystra and Derbe and to the surrounding country, where they continued to preach the gospel.

In Lystra there sat a man who was lame. He had been that way from birth and had never walked. He listened to Paul as he was speaking. Paul looked directly at him, saw that he had faith to be healed and called out, "Stand up on your feet!" At that, the man jumped up and began to walk.

When the crowd saw what Paul had done, they shouted in the Lycaonian language, "The gods have come down to us in human form!" Barnabas they called Zeus, and Paul they called Hermes because he was the chief speaker. The priest of Zeus, whose temple was just outside the city, brought bulls and wreaths to the city gates because he and the crowd wanted to offer sacrifices to them.

But when the apostles Barnabas and Paul heard of this, they tore their clothes and rushed out into the crowd, shouting: "Friends, why are you doing this? We too are only human, like you. We are bringing you good news, telling you to turn from these worthless things to the living God, who made the heavens and the earth and the sea and everything in them. In the past, he let all nations go their own way. Yet he has not left himself without testimony: He has shown kindness by giving you rain from heaven and crops in their seasons; he provides you with plenty of food and fills your hearts with joy." Even with these words, they had difficulty keeping the crowd from sacrificing to them.

Paul felt the full weight of opposition as he challenged Gentiles and Jews to recognize Jesus as the long-promised Messiah and God's own Son. Shortly after being mistaken by the crowd of Gentiles in Lystra as a "god," some Jews were able to turn the tide of public opinion against the apostles. Paul was attacked by a mob, who stoned him and left him for dead. Christians gathered around him and prayed. Paul's strength was revived and he walked back into the city!

The next day Paul and Barnabas left for Derbe, the last city they would visit on this first missionary journey. After retracing their steps, encouraging the new churches they had founded earlier, they returned to their home base in Antioch. A year or so later, the developing Christian movement faced a critical issue. Some of the Jewish believers insisted that Gentile converts keep the Law of Moses, especially circumcision—the physical sign of God's promise to the Jews. A council of Christian leaders gathered in Jerusalem. Paul argued that Gentiles didn't need to become Jews in order to be saved, and eventually he (along with the support of Peter) persuaded the others.

After this, Paul and Barnabas had a sharp disagreement;

Barnabas wanted to reinstate John Mark to their team, but Paul didn't feel that was wise since Barnabas's young cousin had deserted them previously. Paul and Barnabas decided to part company. Silas joined Paul for the journey through Asia Minor, and Timothy joined them in Lystra. It was apparently at Troas, on the western coast of Asia Minor, that Luke—the author of both the Gospel of Luke and the book of Acts—joined the traveling missionaries. Also while at Troas, Paul had a vision of a man from Macedonia imploring them, "Come here, help us!" Believing that vision to be from God, Paul and his companions turned northwest across the Aegean Sea toward the city of Philippi, a Roman colony and leading Macedonian city. They soon were in trouble again.

On the Sabbath we went outside the city gate to the river, where we expected to find a place of prayer. We sat down and began to speak to the women who had gathered there. One of those listening was a woman from the city of Thyatira named Lydia, a dealer in purple cloth. She was a worshiper of God. The Lord opened her heart to respond to Paul's message. When she and the members of her household were baptized, she invited us to her home. "If you consider me a believer in the Lord," she said, "come and stay at my house." And she persuaded us.

Once when we were going to the place of prayer, we were met by a female slave who had a spirit by which she predicted the future. She earned a great deal of money for her owners by fortune-telling. She followed Paul and the rest of us, shouting, "These men are servants of the Most High God, who are telling you the way to be saved." She kept this up for many days. Finally Paul became so annoyed that he turned around and said to the spirit, "In the name of Jesus Christ I command you to come out of her!" At that moment the spirit left her.

When her owners realized that their hope of making money was gone, they seized Paul and Silas and dragged them into the marketplace to face the authorities. They brought them before the magistrates and said, "These men are Jews, and are throwing our city into an uproar by advocating customs unlawful for us Romans to accept or practice."

The crowd joined in the attack against Paul and Silas, and the magistrates ordered them to be stripped and beaten with rods. After they had been severely flogged, they were thrown into prison, and the jailer was commanded to guard them carefully. When he received these orders, he put them in the inner cell and fastened their feet in the stocks.

About midnight Paul and Silas were praying and singing hymns to God, and the other prisoners were listening to them. Suddenly there was such a violent earthquake that the foundations of the prison were shaken. At once all the prison doors flew open, and everyone's chains came loose. The jailer woke up, and when he saw the prison doors open, he drew his sword and was about to kill himself because he thought the prisoners had escaped. But Paul shouted, "Don't harm yourself! We are all here!"

The jailer called for lights, rushed in and fell trembling before Paul and Silas. He then brought them out and asked, "Sirs, what must I do to be saved?"

They replied, "Believe in the Lord Jesus, and you will be saved —you and your household." Then they spoke the word of the Lord to him and to all the others in his house. At that hour of the night the jailer took them and washed their wounds; then immediately he and all his household were baptized. The jailer brought them into his house and set a meal before them; he was filled with joy because he had come to believe in God—he and his whole household.

When it was daylight, the magistrates sent their officers to the jailer with the order: "Release those men." The jailer told Paul, "The magistrates have ordered that you and Silas be released. Now you can leave. Go in peace."

But Paul said to the officers: "They beat us publicly without a trial, even though we are Roman citizens, and threw us into prison.

And now do they want to get rid of us quietly? No! Let them come themselves and escort us out."

The officers reported this to the magistrates, and when they heard that Paul and Silas were Roman citizens, they were alarmed. They came to appease them and escorted them from the prison, requesting them to leave the city. After Paul and Silas came out of the prison, they went to Lydia's house, where they met with the brothers and sisters and encouraged them. Then they left.

> If the Good News about Jesus really was the answer to humanity's greatest questions, some people were not asking the right questions. Opposition showed up at every turn in the road. Paul's legal trump card, his Roman citizenship, certainly helped in some situations. But still there were mobs to face (or avoid), anger to contend with and bonds to post when "disturbing the peace" was the most convenient crime to hang around Paul's neck. None of this was easy, but Paul considered trouble an opportunity to trust God and never looked back.

When Paul and his companions had passed through Amphipolis and Apollonia, they came to Thessalonica, where there was a Jewish synagogue. As was his custom, Paul went into the synagogue, and on three Sabbath days he reasoned with them from the Scriptures, explaining and proving that the Messiah had to suffer and rise from the dead. "This Jesus I am proclaiming to you is the Messiah," he said. Some of the Jews were persuaded and joined Paul and Silas, as did a large number of God-fearing Greeks and quite a few prominent women.

But other Jews were jealous; so they rounded up some bad characters from the marketplace, formed a mob and started a riot in the city. They rushed to Jason's house in search of Paul and Silas in order to bring them out to the crowd. But when they did not find them, they dragged Jason and some other believers before the city officials, shouting: "These men who have caused trouble all over the world have now come here, and Jason has welcomed them into his house. They are all defying Caesar's decrees, saying that there is another king, one called Jesus." When they heard this, the crowd and the city officials were thrown into turmoil. Then they made Jason and the others post bond and let them go.

As soon as it was night, the believers sent Paul and Silas away to Berea. On arriving there, they went to the Jewish synagogue.

In Berea, Paul found an eager and receptive audience, although Jewish opponents stirred up the crowds against Paul once again. So he traveled on to Athens, where he confronted a not-so-receptive audience—the philosophical thinkers of the day. Seeing an altar dedicated "to an unknown god," Paul challenged his audience to consider the living God and Creator, who has spoken eloquently through the life of the risen Messiah. A few people politely nodded, some laughed and a few believed in Jesus. Paul's mission was to find key people in each city who could lead a new community of believers, a "church," and help those in need through their deeds of mercy and love. He went to Corinth and a new Christian community was soon born.

After this, Paul left Athens and went to Corinth. There he met a Jew named Aquila, a native of Pontus, who had recently come from Italy with his wife Priscilla, because Claudius[2] had ordered all Jews to leave Rome. Paul went to see them, and because he was a tentmaker as they were, he stayed and worked with them. Every Sabbath he reasoned in the synagogue, trying to persuade Jews and Greeks.

When Silas and Timothy came from Macedonia, Paul devoted himself exclusively to preaching, testifying to the Jews that Jesus was the Messiah. But when they opposed Paul and became abusive, he shook out his clothes in protest and said to them, "Your blood be on your own heads! I am innocent of it. From now on I will go to the Gentiles."

---

[2]**Claudius:** The emperor of Rome.

Then Paul left the synagogue and went next door to the house of Titius Justus, a worshiper of God. Crispus, the synagogue leader, and his entire household believed in the Lord; and many of the Corinthians who heard Paul believed and were baptized.

One night the Lord spoke to Paul in a vision: "Do not be afraid; keep on speaking, do not be silent. For I am with you, and no one is going to attack and harm you, because I have many people in this city." So Paul stayed in Corinth for a year and a half, teaching them the word of God.

As was the customary way of communicating, Paul composed letters on scrolls to the churches he had established. These "epistles" are collected in Bibles today as part of the New Testament. Christians read them still as inspired and reliable words of instruction on how to know and live for God.

While he was in Corinth, Paul wrote to believers in Thessalonica, probably around AD 51. Thessalonica was a bustling port city of 200,000 people (the largest population in Macedonia). With much emotion, Paul recalled the believers' response to him and the gospel message during his recent visit there, his longing to see them again and his encouragement when he received a good report about them from Timothy. Then Paul in turn encouraged them, in the midst of their trials and persecution, explaining that the living Messiah would return someday.

Paul, Silas and Timothy,

To the church of the Thessalonians in God the Father and the Lord Jesus Christ:

Grace and peace to you.

We always thank God for all of you and continually mention you in our prayers. We remember before our God and Father your work produced by faith, your labor prompted by love, and your endurance inspired by hope in our Lord Jesus Christ.

For we know, brothers and sisters loved by God, that he has chosen you, because our gospel came to you not simply with words but also with power, with the Holy Spirit and deep conviction. You know how we lived among you for your sake. You became imitators of us and of the Lord, for you welcomed the message in the midst of severe suffering with the joy given by the Holy Spirit. And so you became a model to all the believers in Macedonia and Achaia. The Lord's message rang out from you not only in Macedonia and Achaia—your faith in God has become known everywhere. Therefore we do not need to say anything about it, for they themselves report what kind of reception you gave us. They tell how you turned to God from idols to serve the living and true God, and to wait for his Son from heaven, whom he raised from the dead—Jesus, who rescues us from the coming wrath.

You know, brothers and sisters, that our visit to you was not without results. We had previously suffered and been treated outrageously in Philippi, as you know, but with the help of our God we dared to tell you his gospel in the face of strong opposition. For the appeal we make does not spring from error or impure motives, nor are we trying to trick you. On the contrary, we speak as those approved by God to be entrusted with the gospel. We are not trying to please people but God, who tests our hearts. You know we never used flattery, nor did we put on a mask to cover up greed—God is our witness. We were not looking for praise from people, not from you or anyone else, even though as apostles of Christ we could have asserted our authority. Instead, we were like young children among you.

Just as a nursing mother cares for her children, so we cared for you. Because we loved you so much, we were delighted to share with you not only the gospel of God but our lives as well.

But, brothers and sisters, when we were orphaned by being separated from you for a short time (in person, not in thought), out of our intense longing we made every effort to see you. For we wanted to come to you—certainly I, Paul, did, again and again—

but Satan blocked our way. For what is our hope, our joy, or the crown in which we will glory in the presence of our Lord Jesus when he comes? Is it not you? Indeed, you are our glory and joy.

So when we could stand it no longer, we thought it best to be left by ourselves in Athens. We sent Timothy, who is our brother and co-worker in God's service in spreading the gospel of Christ, to strengthen and encourage you in your faith, so that no one would be unsettled by these trials. For you know quite well that we are destined for them. In fact, when we were with you, we kept telling you that we would be persecuted. And it turned out that way, as you well know. For this reason, when I could stand it no longer, I sent to find out about your faith. I was afraid that in some way the tempter had tempted you and that our labors might have been in vain.

But Timothy has just now come to us from you and has brought good news about your faith and love. He has told us that you always have pleasant memories of us and that you long to see us, just as we also long to see you. Therefore, brothers and sisters, in all our distress and persecution we were encouraged about you because of your faith. For now we really live, since you are standing firm in the Lord. How can we thank God enough for you in return for all the joy we have in the presence of our God because of you? Night and day we pray most earnestly that we may see you again and supply what is lacking in your faith.

Now may our God and Father himself and our Lord Jesus clear the way for us to come to you. May the Lord make your love increase and overflow for each other and for everyone else, just as ours does for you. May he strengthen your hearts so that you will be blameless and holy in the presence of our God and Father when our Lord Jesus comes with all his holy ones.

For the Lord himself will come down from heaven, with a loud command, with the voice of the archangel and with the trumpet call of God, and the dead in Christ will rise first. After that, we who are still alive and are left will be caught up together with them in the clouds to meet the Lord in the air. And so we will be with the Lord forever. Therefore encourage one another with these words.

Rejoice always, pray continually, give thanks in all circumstances; for this is God's will for you in Christ Jesus.

Do not quench the Spirit. Do not treat prophecies with contempt but test them all; hold on to what is good, reject every kind of evil.

May God himself, the God of peace, sanctify[3] you through and through. May your whole spirit, soul and body be kept blameless at the coming of our Lord Jesus Christ. The one who calls you is faithful, and he will do it.

Brothers and sisters, pray for us. Greet all God's people with a holy kiss. I charge you before the Lord to have this letter read to all the brothers and sisters.

The grace of our Lord Jesus Christ be with you.

If ever a place was hostile to Jesus' way of holiness, faith and joy, it was the city of Corinth. Paganism owned this cosmopolitan city with its wild night-life and upscale markets. Yet Paul's message was steady and sure: once you've explored all the human wisdom collected by the best minds in Greece, there still remain problems only Jesus can answer. Paul's debating skills and encyclopedic knowledge of Roman and religious law helped him navigate past petty charges the Jewish leaders made against him. Whether standing in the synagogue or the public square, Paul spoke what he knew: Jesus, who died and rose again, is the key to peace with God; only he fills the God-shaped vacuum in every heart.

While Gallio was proconsul of Achaia, the Jews of Corinth

---

[3]**Sanctify, sanctification:** The process of growing continually closer to God and taking on his characteristics. Sanctification is essential to the Christian life as evidence of and an effect of the spiritual reality of justification.

made a united attack on Paul and brought him to the place of judgment. "This man," they charged, "is persuading the people to worship God in ways contrary to the law."

Just as Paul was about to speak, Gallio said to them, "If you Jews were making a complaint about some misdemeanor or serious crime, it would be reasonable for me to listen to you. But since it involves questions about words and names and your own law — settle the matter yourselves. I will not be a judge of such things." So he drove them off. Then the crowd there turned on Sosthenes the synagogue leader and beat him in front of the proconsul; and Gallio showed no concern whatever.

Paul stayed on in Corinth for some time. Then he left the brothers and sisters and sailed for Syria, accompanied by Priscilla and Aquila. Before he sailed, he had his hair cut off at Cenchreae because of a vow he had taken. They arrived at Ephesus, where Paul left Priscilla and Aquila. He himself went into the synagogue and reasoned with the Jews. When they asked him to spend more time with them, he declined. But as he left, he promised, "I will come back if it is God's will." Then he set sail from Ephesus. When he landed at Caesarea, he went up to Jerusalem and greeted the church and then went down to Antioch.

After spending some time in Antioch, Paul set out from there and traveled from place to place throughout the region of Galatia and Phrygia, strengthening all the disciples.

Meanwhile a Jew named Apollos, a native of Alexandria, came to Ephesus. He was a learned man, with a thorough knowledge of the Scriptures. He had been instructed in the way of the Lord, and he spoke with great fervor and taught about Jesus accurately, though he knew only the baptism of John. He began to speak boldly in the synagogue. When Priscilla and Aquila heard him, they invited him to their home and explained to him the way of God more adequately.

When Apollos wanted to go to Achaia, the brothers and sisters encouraged him and wrote to the disciples there to welcome him. When he arrived, he was a great help to those who by grace had believed. For he vigorously refuted his Jewish opponents in public debate, proving from the Scriptures that Jesus was the Messiah.

Everywhere Paul traveled, he saw God's power at work in people's lives. In some places he witnessed spiritual break-throughs when many people believed; in other places he was chased or beaten. He trusted that God would bring good out of it all. Although Paul was a tireless traveling missionary, he did settle into extended periods of ministry at a few strategic major cities. This had been the case at Antioch and Corinth. And now the apostle was about to spend more than two years at Ephesus — the leading commercial center of Asia Minor and the guardian of the temple of Artemis (the Greek name for the Roman goddess Diana), which was one of the seven wonders of the ancient world.

While Apollos was at Corinth, Paul took the road through the interior and arrived at Ephesus.

Paul entered the synagogue and spoke boldly there for three months, arguing persuasively about the kingdom of God. But some of them became obstinate; they refused to believe and publicly maligned the Way. So Paul left them. He took the disciples with him and had discussions daily in the lecture hall of Tyrannus. This went on for two years, so that all the Jews and Greeks who lived in the province of Asia heard the word of the Lord.

God did extraordinary miracles through Paul, so that even handkerchiefs and aprons that had touched him were taken to the sick, and their illnesses were cured and the evil spirits left them.

Some Jews who went around driving out evil spirits tried to invoke the name of the Lord Jesus over those who were demon-possessed. They would say, "In the name of the Jesus whom Paul preaches, I command you to come out." Seven sons of Sceva, a Jewish chief priest, were doing this. One day the evil spirit answered them, "Jesus I know, and Paul I know about, but who are you?"

Then the man who had the evil spirit jumped on them and overpowered them all. He gave them such a beating that they ran out of the house naked and bleeding.

When this became known to the Jews and Greeks living in Ephesus, they were all seized with fear, and the name of the Lord Jesus was held in high honor. Many of those who believed now came and openly confessed what they had done. A number who had practiced sorcery brought their scrolls together and burned them publicly. When they calculated the value of the scrolls, the total came to fifty thousand drachmas.[4] In this way the word of the Lord spread widely and grew in power.

About that time there arose a great disturbance about the Way. A silversmith named Demetrius, who made silver shrines of Artemis, brought in a lot of business for the craftsmen there. He called them together, along with the workers in related trades, and said: "You know, my friends, that we receive a good income from this business. And you see and hear how this fellow Paul has convinced and led astray large numbers of people here in Ephesus and in practically the whole province of Asia. He says that gods made by human hands are no gods at all. There is danger not only that our trade will lose its good name, but also that the temple of the great goddess Artemis will be discredited; and the goddess herself, who is worshiped throughout the province of Asia and the world, will be robbed of her divine majesty."

When they heard this, they were furious and began shouting: "Great is Artemis of the Ephesians!" Soon the whole city was in an uproar. The people seized Gaius and Aristarchus, Paul's traveling companions from Macedonia, and all of them rushed into the theater together. Paul wanted to appear before the crowd, but the disciples would not let him. Even some of the officials of the province, friends of Paul, sent him a message begging him not to venture into the theater.

---

[4]**Drachmas:** A drachma was a silver coin worth about a day's wages.

The assembly was in confusion: Some were shouting one thing, some another. Most of the people did not even know why they were there. The Jews in the crowd pushed Alexander to the front, and they shouted instructions to him. He motioned for silence in order to make a defense before the people. But when they realized he was a Jew, they all shouted in unison for about two hours: "Great is Artemis of the Ephesians!"

The city clerk quieted the crowd and said: "Fellow Ephesians, doesn't all the world know that the city of Ephesus is the guardian of the temple of the great Artemis and of her image, which fell from heaven? Therefore, since these facts are undeniable, you ought to calm down and not do anything rash. You have brought these men here, though they have neither robbed temples nor blasphemed our goddess. If, then, Demetrius and his fellow craftsmen have a grievance against anybody, the courts are open and there are proconsuls. They can press charges. If there is anything further you want to bring up, it must be settled in a legal assembly. As it is, we are in danger of being charged with rioting because of what happened today. In that case we would not be able to account for this commotion, since there is no reason for it." After he had said this, he dismissed the assembly.

When the uproar had ended, Paul sent for the disciples and, after encouraging them, said goodbye and set out for Macedonia.

Near the end of Paul's two-plus years in Ephesus, he wrote a very direct letter to the Christians in Corinth. Although this wasn't the first letter he had written them, we know it as "First Corinthians" because it's the first of two letters from Paul to the Corinthians found in the New Testament. In the city of Corinth, followers of Jesus had to work hard at keeping the faith. Idol worship was popular, as Corinth was home to at least a dozen pagan temples. At one time more than a thousand temple prostitutes "officiated" at Aphrodite's temple alone. Living out the truth was not easy. And, unfortunately, rather than facing the challenges of their culture as a united "body," the believers at

*Corinth were splintered into factions. Paul's letter spoke elo-
quently to issues they faced, concluding with a reminder that
Jesus has triumphed over death.*

Paul, called to be an apostle of Christ Jesus by the will of God,
and our brother Sosthenes,

To the church of God in Corinth, to those sanctified in Christ
Jesus and called to be his holy people, together with all those
everywhere who call on the name of our Lord Jesus Christ — their
Lord and ours:

Grace and peace to you from God our Father and the Lord
Jesus Christ.

I appeal to you, brothers and sisters, in the name of our Lord
Jesus Christ, that all of you agree with one another in what you
say and that there be no divisions among you, but that you be
perfectly united in mind and thought. My brothers and sisters,
some from Chloe's household have informed me that there are
quarrels among you. What I mean is this: One of you says, "I follow
Paul"; another, "I follow Apollos"; another, "I follow Cephas[5]"; still
another, "I follow Christ."
Is Christ divided? Was Paul crucified for you? Were you baptized in the name of Paul?

Brothers and sisters, I could not address you as people who live
by the Spirit but as people who are still worldly — mere infants in
Christ. I gave you milk, not solid food, for you were not yet ready for
it. Indeed, you are still not ready. You are still worldly. For since there
is jealousy and quarreling among you, are you not worldly? Are you
not acting like mere humans? For when one says, "I follow Paul," and
another, "I follow Apollos," are you not mere human beings?

---

[5]**Cephas:** That is, Peter.

What, after all, is Apollos? And what is Paul? Only servants, through whom you came to believe — as the Lord has assigned to each his task. I planted the seed, Apollos watered it, but God has been making it grow. So neither the one who plants nor the one who waters is anything, but only God, who makes things grow. The one who plants and the one who waters have one purpose, and they will each be rewarded according to their own labor. For we are co-workers in God's service; you are God's field, God's building.

By the grace God has given me, I laid a foundation as a wise builder, and someone else is building on it. But each one should build with care. For no one can lay any foundation other than the one already laid, which is Jesus Christ.

So then, no more boasting about human leaders! All things are yours, whether Paul or Apollos or Cephas or the world or life or death or the present or the future — all are yours, and you are of Christ, and Christ is of God.

I wrote to you in my letter not to associate with sexually immoral people — not at all meaning the people of this world who are immoral, or the greedy and swindlers, or idolaters. In that case you would have to leave this world. But now I am writing to you that you must not associate with anyone who claims to be a brother or sister but is sexually immoral or greedy, an idolater or slanderer, a drunkard or swindler. Do not even eat with such people.

What business is it of mine to judge those outside the church? Are you not to judge those inside? God will judge those outside.

Flee from sexual immorality. All other sins a person commits are outside the body, but whoever sins sexually, sins against their own body. Do you not know that your bodies are temples of the Holy Spirit, who is in you, whom you have received from God? You are not your own; you were bought at a price. Therefore honor God with your bodies.

My dear friends, flee from idolatry. I speak to sensible people; judge for yourselves what I say. Is not the cup of thanksgiving for which we give thanks a participation in the blood of Christ? And is not the bread that we break a participation in the body of Christ? Because there is one loaf, we, who are many, are one body, for we all share the one loaf.

Consider the people of Israel: Do not those who eat the sacrifices participate in the altar? Do I mean then that food sacrificed to an idol is anything, or that an idol is anything? No, but the sacrifices of pagans are offered to demons, not to God, and I do not want you to be participants with demons. You cannot drink the cup of the Lord and the cup of demons too; you cannot have a part in both the Lord's table and the table of demons.

Now about the gifts of the Spirit, brothers and sisters, I do not want you to be uninformed.

There are different kinds of gifts, but the same Spirit distributes them. There are different kinds of service, but the same Lord. There are different kinds of working, but in all of them and in everyone it is the same God at work.

Just as a body, though one, has many parts, but all its many parts form one body, so it is with Christ. For we were all baptized by one Spirit so as to form one body — whether Jews or Gentiles, slave or free — and we were all given the one Spirit to drink. Even so the body is not made up of one part but of many.

Now if the foot should say, "Because I am not a hand, I do not belong to the body," it would not for that reason stop being part of the body. And if the ear should say, "Because I am not an eye, I do not belong to the body," it would not for that reason stop being part of the body. If the whole body were an eye, where would the sense of hearing be? If the whole body were an ear, where would the sense of smell be? But in fact God has placed the parts in the body, every one of them, just as he wanted them to be.

Now you are the body of Christ, and each one of you is a part of it.

If I speak in the tongues of men or of angels, but do not have love, I am only a resounding gong or a clanging cymbal. If I have the gift of prophecy and can fathom all mysteries and all knowledge, and if I have a faith that can move mountains, but do not have love, I am nothing. If I give all I possess to the poor and give over my body to hardship that I may boast, but do not have love, I gain nothing.

Love is patient, love is kind. It does not envy, it does not boast, it is not proud. It does not dishonor others, it is not self-seeking, it is not easily angered, it keeps no record of wrongs. Love does not delight in evil but rejoices with the truth. It always protects, always trusts, always hopes, always perseveres.

Now, brothers and sisters, I want to remind you of the gospel I preached to you, which you received and on which you have taken your stand. By this gospel you are saved, if you hold firmly to the word I preached to you. Otherwise, you have believed in vain.

For what I received I passed on to you as of first importance: that Christ died for our sins according to the Scriptures, that he was buried, that he was raised on the third day according to the Scriptures, and that he appeared to Cephas, and then to the Twelve. After that, he appeared to more than five hundred of the brothers and sisters at the same time, most of whom are still living, though some have fallen asleep. Then he appeared to James, then to all the apostles, and last of all he appeared to me also, as to one abnormally born.[6]

For I am the least of the apostles and do not even deserve to be called an apostle, because I persecuted the church of God. But by the grace of God I am what I am, and his grace to me was not without effect. No, I worked harder than all of them — yet not I,

---

[6]**One abnormally born:** That is, Paul was not part of the original group of apostles and had not lived with Christ as the others had.

but the grace of God that was with me. Whether, then, it is I or they, this is what we preach, and this is what you believed.

But if it is preached that Christ has been raised from the dead, how can some of you say that there is no resurrection of the dead? If there is no resurrection of the dead, then not even Christ has been raised. And if Christ has not been raised, our preaching is useless and so is your faith. More than that, we are then found to be false witnesses about God, for we have testified about God that he raised Christ from the dead. But he did not raise him if in fact the dead are not raised. For if the dead are not raised, then Christ has not been raised either. And if Christ has not been raised, your faith is futile; you are still in your sins. Then those also who have fallen asleep in Christ are lost. If only for this life we have hope in Christ, we are of all people most to be pitied.

But Christ has indeed been raised from the dead, the firstfruits of those who have fallen asleep. For since death came through a man, the resurrection of the dead comes also through a man. For as in Adam all die, so in Christ all will be made alive. But each in turn: Christ, the firstfruits; then, when he comes, those who belong to him. Then the end will come, when he hands over the kingdom to God the Father after he has destroyed all dominion, authority and power. For he must reign until he has put all his enemies under his feet.

Listen, I tell you a mystery: We will not all sleep, but we will all be changed — in a flash, in the twinkling of an eye, at the last trumpet. For the trumpet will sound, the dead will be raised imperishable, and we will be changed. For the perishable must clothe itself with the imperishable, and the mortal with immortality. When the perishable has been clothed with the imperishable, and the mortal with immortality, then the saying that is written will come true: "Death has been swallowed up in victory."

"Where, O death, is your victory?
Where, O death, is your sting?"

The sting of death is sin, and the power of sin is the law. But thanks be to God! He gives us the victory through our Lord Jesus Christ.

Therefore, my dear brothers and sisters, stand firm. Let nothing move you. Always give yourselves fully to the work of the Lord, because you know that your labor in the Lord is not in vain.

The churches in the province of Asia send you greetings. Aquila and Priscilla greet you warmly in the Lord, and so does the church that meets at their house. All the brothers and sisters here send you greetings. Greet one another with a holy kiss.

I, Paul, write this greeting in my own hand.

If anyone does not love the Lord, let that person be cursed! Come, Lord!

The grace of the Lord Jesus be with you.

My love to all of you in Christ Jesus. Amen.

How does a person please God? Many religions teach that one must appease God/gods with offerings or superstitious rituals. Yet God's story abolishes our religious to-do lists. Faith in Jesus is God's way for us, and delight in Jesus is what God asks of us. When religious people become followers of Jesus, they are freed from sin and legalistic rituals.

The Christians in Galatia were coming under the influence of Jewish Christians who believed that a number of the ceremonial practices of Judaism remained obligatory for followers of Jesus. Paul wrote to the churches in this part of Asia Minor to warn them that they were in reality deserting God and turning to a false gospel. He forcefully proclaimed that people cannot be saved by performing good works in general or by adhering to the Law of Moses in particular. We must come to God trusting in Jesus alone. Only then will we experience freedom.

Paul, an apostle — sent not from men nor by a man, but by Jesus Christ and God the Father, who raised him from the dead — and all the brothers and sisters with me,

To the churches in Galatia:

Grace and peace to you from God our Father and the Lord Jesus Christ, who gave himself for our sins to rescue us from the present evil age, according to the will of our God and Father, to whom be glory for ever and ever. Amen.

I am astonished that you are so quickly deserting the one who called you to live in the grace of Christ and are turning to a different gospel — which is really no gospel at all. Evidently some people are throwing you into confusion and are trying to pervert the gospel of Christ. But even if we or an angel from heaven should preach a gospel other than the one we preached to you, let them be under God's curse! As we have already said, so now I say again: If anybody is preaching to you a gospel other than what you accepted, let them be under God's curse!

You foolish Galatians! Who has bewitched you? Before your very eyes Jesus Christ was clearly portrayed as crucified. I would like to learn just one thing from you: Did you receive the Spirit by the works of the law, or by believing what you heard? Are you so foolish? After beginning by means of the Spirit, are you now trying to finish by means of the flesh? Have you experienced so much in vain — if it really was in vain? So again I ask, does God give you his Spirit and work miracles among you by the works of the law, or by your believing what you heard?

All who rely on the works of the law are under a curse, as it is written: "Cursed is everyone who does not continue to do everything written in the Book of the Law." Clearly no one who relies on the law is justified before God, because "the righteous will live by faith."

Before the coming of this faith, we were held in custody under the law, locked up until the faith that was to come would be revealed. So the law was our guardian until Christ came that we might be justified by faith. Now that this faith has come, we are no longer under a guardian.

So in Christ Jesus you are all children of God through faith, for all of you who were baptized into Christ have clothed yourselves with Christ. There is neither Jew nor Gentile, neither slave nor free, nor is there male and female, for you are all one in Christ Jesus.

It is for freedom that Christ has set us free. Stand firm, then, and do not let yourselves be burdened again by a yoke of slavery.

You, my brothers and sisters, were called to be free. But do not use your freedom to indulge the flesh; rather, serve one another humbly in love.

The acts of the flesh are obvious: sexual immorality, impurity and debauchery; idolatry and witchcraft; hatred, discord, jealousy, fits of rage, selfish ambition, dissensions, factions and envy; drunkenness, orgies, and the like. I warn you, as I did before, that those who live like this will not inherit the kingdom of God.

But the fruit of the Spirit is love, joy, peace, forbearance, kindness, goodness, faithfulness, gentleness and self-control. Against such things there is no law. Those who belong to Christ Jesus have crucified the flesh with its passions and desires. Since we live by the Spirit, let us keep in step with the Spirit. Let us not become conceited, provoking and envying each other.

The grace of our Lord Jesus Christ be with your spirit, brothers and sisters. Amen.

Paul had never visited the church in Rome, which included both Jewish and Gentile Christians, though Gentiles comprised the majority. Around AD 57, he wrote them an amazing letter to stabilize their understanding of God's story of Jesus the Messiah and to give them courage under pressure. This brilliant letter mapped out foundational truths of Christianity and answered tough questions about sin, grace, the Jewish law and the never-ending power of God's love.

Paul, a servant of Christ Jesus, called to be an apostle and set apart for the gospel of God — the gospel he promised beforehand through his prophets in the Holy Scriptures regarding his Son, who as to his earthly life was a descendant of David, and who through the Spirit of holiness was appointed the Son of God in power by his resurrection from the dead: Jesus Christ our Lord.

To all in Rome who are loved by God and called to be his holy people:

Grace and peace to you from God our Father and from the Lord Jesus Christ.

I am not ashamed of the gospel, because it is the power of God that brings salvation to everyone who believes: first to the Jew, then to the Gentile. For in the gospel the righteousness of God is revealed — a righteousness that is by faith from first to last, just as it is written: "The righteous will live by faith."

Now we know that whatever the law says, it says to those who are under the law, so that every mouth may be silenced and the whole world held accountable to God. Therefore no one will be declared righteous in God's sight by the works of the law; rather, through the law we become conscious of our sin.

But now apart from the law the righteousness of God has been made known, to which the Law and the Prophets testify. This righteousness is given through faith in Jesus Christ to all who believe. There is no difference between Jew and Gentile, for all have sinned and fall short of the glory of God, and all are justified freely by his grace through the redemption[7] that came by Christ Jesus. God

---

[7]**Redemption:** The release of humanity from the debt owed to God for disobedience and the resulting restoration of a relationship with him.

presented Christ as a sacrifice of atonement,[8] through the shedding of his blood — to be received by faith. He did this to demonstrate his righteousness, because in his forbearance he had left the sins committed beforehand unpunished — he did it to demonstrate his righteousness at the present time, so as to be just and the one who justifies those who have faith in Jesus.

Where, then, is boasting? It is excluded. Because of what law? The law that requires works? No, because of the law that requires faith. For we maintain that a person is justified by faith apart from the works of the law.

What then shall we say that Abraham, our forefather according to the flesh, discovered in this matter? If, in fact, Abraham was justified by works, he had something to boast about — but not before God. What does Scripture say? "Abraham believed God, and it was credited to him as righteousness."

Now to the one who works, wages are not credited as a gift but as an obligation. However, to the one who does not work but trusts God who justifies the ungodly, their faith is credited as righteousness. David says the same thing when he speaks of the blessedness of the one to whom God credits righteousness apart from works:

> "Blessed are those
>   whose transgressions are forgiven,
>   whose sins are covered.
> Blessed is the one
>   whose sin the Lord will never count against them."

Therefore, since we have been justified through faith, we have peace with God through our Lord Jesus Christ, through whom we have gained access by faith into this grace in which we now stand. And we boast in the hope of the glory of God. Not only so, but we also glory in our sufferings, because we know that suffering

---

[8]**Atonement:** To make amends to God for wrongdoing (sin) through a sacrifice. In the Old Testament, crops or livestock were offered or sacrificed for atonement; in the New Testament, the death of Jesus was the sacrifice that pays for the sins of his people.

produces perseverance; perseverance, character; and character, hope. And hope does not put us to shame, because God's love has been poured out into our hearts through the Holy Spirit, who has been given to us.

You see, at just the right time, when we were still powerless, Christ died for the ungodly. Very rarely will anyone die for a righteous person, though for a good person someone might possibly dare to die. But God demonstrates his own love for us in this: While we were still sinners, Christ died for us.

Since we have now been justified by his blood, how much more shall we be saved from God's wrath through him! For if, while we were God's enemies, we were reconciled to him through the death of his Son, how much more, having been reconciled, shall we be saved through his life! Not only is this so, but we also boast in God through our Lord Jesus Christ, through whom we have now received reconciliation.

For the wages of sin is death, but the gift of God is eternal life in Christ Jesus our Lord.

Therefore, there is now no condemnation for those who are in Christ Jesus, because through Christ Jesus the law of the Spirit who gives life has set you free from the law of sin and death. For what the law was powerless to do because it was weakened by the flesh, God did by sending his own Son in the likeness of sinful flesh to be a sin offering. And so he condemned sin in the flesh, in order that the righteous requirement of the law might be fully met in us, who do not live according to the flesh but according to the Spirit.

Therefore, brothers and sisters, we have an obligation — but it is not to the flesh, to live according to it. For if you live according to the flesh, you will die; but if by the Spirit you put to death the misdeeds of the body, you will live.

For those who are led by the Spirit of God are the children of God. The Spirit you received does not make you slaves, so that you live in fear again; rather, the Spirit you received brought about your adoption to sonship. And by him we cry, "*Abba*,[9] Father." The Spirit himself testifies with our spirit that we are God's children. Now if we are children, then we are heirs — heirs of God and co-heirs with Christ, if indeed we share in his sufferings in order that we may also share in his glory.

I consider that our present sufferings are not worth comparing with the glory that will be revealed in us.

And we know that in all things God works for the good of those who love him, who have been called according to his purpose.

What, then, shall we say in response to these things? If God is for us, who can be against us? He who did not spare his own Son, but gave him up for us all — how will he not also, along with him, graciously give us all things? Who will bring any charge against those whom God has chosen? It is God who justifies. Who then is the one who condemns? No one. Christ Jesus who died — more than that, who was raised to life — is at the right hand of God and is also interceding for us. Who shall separate us from the love of Christ? Shall trouble or hardship or persecution or famine or nakedness or danger or sword? As it is written:

> "For your sake we face death all day long;
>   we are considered as sheep to be slaughtered."

No, in all these things we are more than conquerors through him who loved us. For I am convinced that neither death nor life, neither angels nor demons, neither the present nor the future, nor any powers, neither height nor depth, nor anything else in all creation, will be able to separate us from the love of God that is in Christ Jesus our Lord.

---

[9]**Abba:** Aramaic for *Father*.

Therefore, I urge you, brothers and sisters, in view of God's mercy, to offer your bodies as a living sacrifice, holy and pleasing to God—this is your true and proper worship. Do not conform to the pattern of this world, but be transformed by the renewing of your mind. Then you will be able to test and approve what God's will is—his good, pleasing and perfect will.

For by the grace given me I say to every one of you: Do not think of yourself more highly than you ought, but rather think of yourself with sober judgment, in accordance with the faith God has distributed to each of you. For just as each of us has one body with many members, and these members do not all have the same function, so in Christ we, though many, form one body, and each member belongs to all the others. We have different gifts, according to the grace given to each of us. If your gift is prophesying, then prophesy in accordance with your faith; if it is serving, then serve; if it is teaching, then teach; if it is to encourage, then give encouragement; if it is giving, then give generously; if it is to lead, do it diligently; if it is to show mercy, do it cheerfully.

Since I have been longing for many years to visit you, I plan to do so when I go to Spain. I hope to see you while passing through and to have you assist me on my journey there, after I have enjoyed your company for a while. Now, however, I am on my way to Jerusalem in the service of the Lord's people there. For Macedonia and Achaia were pleased to make a contribution for the poor among the Lord's people in Jerusalem. They were pleased to do it, and indeed they owe it to them. For if the Gentiles have shared in the Jews' spiritual blessings, they owe it to the Jews to share with them their material blessings. So after I have completed this task and have made sure that they have received this contribution, I will go to Spain and visit you on the way. I know that when I come to you, I will come in the full measure of the blessing of Christ.

I urge you, brothers and sisters, by our Lord Jesus Christ and by the love of the Spirit, to join me in my struggle by praying to God for me. Pray that I may be kept safe from the unbelievers in Judea and that the contribution I take to Jerusalem may be favorably received by the Lord's people there, so that I may come to you with joy, by God's will, and in your company be refreshed. The God of peace be with you all. Amen.

After traveling through Macedonia and encouraging many people there, Paul set his sights on Jerusalem. He felt urgently compelled by God to return there, even though he had an inkling that hardship awaited him. Luke the physician was traveling with Paul at this time and recorded in the book of Acts a breathtaking first-person account of their final shared experiences.

30

Paul's Final Days

WE WENT ON AHEAD to the ship and sailed for Assos, where we were going to take Paul aboard. He had made this arrangement because he was going there on foot. When he met us at Assos, we took him aboard and went on to Mitylene. The next day we set sail from there and arrived off Chios. The day after that we crossed over to Samos, and on the following day arrived at Miletus. Paul had decided to sail past Ephesus to avoid spending time in the province of Asia, for he was in a hurry to reach Jerusalem, if possible, by the day of Pentecost.

From Miletus, Paul sent to Ephesus for the elders of the church. When they arrived, he said to them: "You know how I lived the whole time I was with you, from the first day I came into the province of Asia. I served the Lord with great humility and with tears and in the midst of severe testing by the plots of my Jewish opponents. You know that I have not hesitated to preach anything that would be helpful to you but have taught you publicly and from house to house. I have declared to both Jews and Greeks that they must turn to God in repentance and have faith in our Lord Jesus.

"And now, compelled by the Spirit, I am going to Jerusalem, not

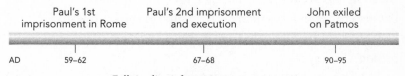

Paul's 1st imprisonment in Rome	Paul's 2nd imprisonment and execution	John exiled on Patmos
AD 59–62	67–68	90–95

Full timeline information starts on page xi.

knowing what will happen to me there. I only know that in every city the Holy Spirit warns me that prison and hardships are facing me. However, I consider my life worth nothing to me; my only aim is to finish the race and complete the task the Lord Jesus has given me — the task of testifying to the good news of God's grace.

"Now I know that none of you among whom I have gone about preaching the kingdom will ever see me again. Therefore, I declare to you today that I am innocent of the blood of any of you. For I have not hesitated to proclaim to you the whole will of God. Keep watch over yourselves and all the flock of which the Holy Spirit has made you overseers. Be shepherds of the church of God, which he bought with his own blood.

When Paul had finished speaking, he knelt down with all of them and prayed. They all wept as they embraced him and kissed him. What grieved them most was his statement that they would never see his face again. Then they accompanied him to the ship.

We continued our voyage from Tyre and landed at Ptolemais, where we greeted the brothers and sisters and stayed with them for a day. Leaving the next day, we reached Caesarea and stayed at the house of Philip the evangelist, one of the Seven. He had four unmarried daughters who prophesied.

After we had been there a number of days, a prophet named Agabus came down from Judea. Coming over to us, he took Paul's belt, tied his own hands and feet with it and said, "The Holy Spirit says, 'In this way the Jewish leaders in Jerusalem will bind the owner of this belt and will hand him over to the Gentiles.'"

When we heard this, we and the people there pleaded with Paul not to go up to Jerusalem. Then Paul answered, "Why are you weeping and breaking my heart? I am ready not only to be bound, but also to die in Jerusalem for the name of the Lord Jesus." When he would not be dissuaded, we gave up and said, "The Lord's will be done."

After this, we started on our way up to Jerusalem.

In the face of a warning as strong as the prophetic word through Agabus, most people would seek shelter far from the antici-pated danger. Yet Paul had a calling and would not flinch. His sense of personal safety was vested in God alone. Arriving in Jerusalem, Paul was warmly received by the believers there, and they were excited to hear what God had done among the Gen-tiles through Paul's ministry. Paul then went to the temple, and his enemies saw their chance. Paul took the opportunity to tell his story once again—that Jesus was alive and had appeared to him in a miraculous vision on the Damascus road.

Some Jews from the province of Asia saw Paul at the temple. They stirred up the whole crowd and seized him, shouting, "Fellow Israelites, help us! This is the man who teaches everyone every-where against our people and our law and this place. And besides, he has brought Greeks into the temple and defiled this holy place." (They had previously seen Trophimus the Ephesian in the city with Paul and assumed that Paul had brought him into the temple.)

The whole city was aroused, and the people came running from all directions. Seizing Paul, they dragged him from the temple, and immediately the gates were shut. While they were trying to kill him, news reached the commander of the Roman troops that the whole city of Jerusalem was in an uproar. He at once took some officers and soldiers and ran down to the crowd. When the rioters saw the commander and his soldiers, they stopped beating Paul.

The commander came up and arrested him and ordered him to be bound with two chains. Then he asked who he was and what he had done. Some in the crowd shouted one thing and some another, and since the commander could not get at the truth because of the uproar, he ordered that Paul be taken into the barracks. When Paul reached the steps, the violence of the mob was so great he had to be carried by the soldiers. The crowd that followed kept shouting, "Get rid of him!"

As the soldiers were about to take Paul into the barracks, he asked the commander, "May I say something to you?"

"Do you speak Greek?" he replied. "Aren't you the Egyptian who started a revolt and led four thousand terrorists out into the wilderness some time ago?"

Paul answered, "I am a Jew, from Tarsus in Cilicia, a citizen of no ordinary city. Please let me speak to the people."

After receiving the commander's permission, Paul stood on the steps and motioned to the crowd. When they were all silent, he said to them in Aramaic: "Brothers and fathers, listen now to my defense."

When they heard him speak to them in Aramaic, they became very quiet.

Then Paul said: "I am a Jew, born in Tarsus of Cilicia, but brought up in this city. I studied under Gamaliel and was thoroughly trained in the law of our ancestors. I was just as zealous for God as any of you are today. I persecuted the followers of this Way to their death, arresting both men and women and throwing them into prison, as the high priest and all the Council can themselves testify. I even obtained letters from them to their associates in Damascus, and went there to bring these people as prisoners to Jerusalem to be punished.

"About noon as I came near Damascus, suddenly a bright light from heaven flashed around me. I fell to the ground and heard a voice say to me, 'Saul! Saul! Why do you persecute me?'

" 'Who are you, Lord?' I asked.

" 'I am Jesus of Nazareth, whom you are persecuting,' he replied. My companions saw the light, but they did not understand the voice of him who was speaking to me.

" 'What shall I do, Lord?' I asked.

" 'Get up,' the Lord said, 'and go into Damascus. There you will be told all that you have been assigned to do.' My companions led me by the hand into Damascus, because the brilliance of the light had blinded me.

"A man named Ananias came to see me. He was a devout observer of the law and highly respected by all the Jews living there. He stood beside me and said, 'Brother Saul, receive your sight!' And at that very moment I was able to see him.

"Then he said: 'The God of our ancestors has chosen you to know his will and to see the Righteous One and to hear words from his mouth. You will be his witness to all people of what you have seen and heard. And now what are you waiting for? Get up, be baptized and wash your sins away, calling on his name.'

"When I returned to Jerusalem and was praying at the temple, I fell into a trance and saw the Lord speaking to me. 'Quick!' he said. 'Leave Jerusalem immediately, because the people here will not accept your testimony about me.'

"'Lord,' I replied, 'these people know that I went from one synagogue to another to imprison and beat those who believe in you. And when the blood of your martyr Stephen was shed, I stood there giving my approval and guarding the clothes of those who were killing him.'

"Then the Lord said to me, 'Go; I will send you far away to the Gentiles.'"

The crowd listened to Paul until he said this. Then they raised their voices and shouted, "Rid the earth of him! He's not fit to live!"

As they were shouting and throwing off their cloaks and flinging dust into the air, the commander ordered that Paul be taken into the barracks. He directed that he be flogged and interrogated in order to find out why the people were shouting at him like this. As they stretched him out to flog him, Paul said to the centurion standing there, "Is it legal for you to flog a Roman citizen who hasn't even been found guilty?"

When the centurion heard this, he went to the commander and reported it. "What are you going to do?" he asked. "This man is a Roman citizen."

The commander went to Paul and asked, "Tell me, are you a Roman citizen?"

"Yes, I am," he answered.

Then the commander said, "I had to pay a lot of money for my citizenship."

"But I was born a citizen," Paul replied.

Those who were about to interrogate him withdrew immediately. The commander himself was alarmed when he realized that he had put Paul, a Roman citizen, in chains.

The commander wanted to find out exactly why Paul was being accused by the Jews. So the next day he released him and ordered the chief priests and all the members of the Sanhedrin to assemble. Then he brought Paul and had him stand before them.

Paul looked straight at the Sanhedrin and said, "My brothers, I have fulfilled my duty to God in all good conscience to this day." At this the high priest Ananias ordered those standing near Paul to strike him on the mouth. Then Paul said to him, "God will strike you, you whitewashed wall! You sit there to judge me according to the law, yet you yourself violate the law by commanding that I be struck!"

Those who were standing near Paul said, "How dare you insult God's high priest!"

Paul replied, "Brothers, I did not realize that he was the high priest; for it is written: 'Do not speak evil about the ruler of your people.'"

Then Paul, knowing that some of them were Sadducees and the others Pharisees, called out in the Sanhedrin, "My brothers, I am a Pharisee, descended from Pharisees. I stand on trial because of the hope of the resurrection of the dead." When he said this, a dispute broke out between the Pharisees and the Sadducees, and the assembly was divided. (The Sadducees say that there is no resurrection, and that there are neither angels nor spirits, but the Pharisees believe all these things.)

There was a great uproar, and some of the teachers of the law who were Pharisees stood up and argued vigorously. "We find nothing wrong with this man," they said. "What if a spirit or an angel has spoken to him?" The dispute became so violent that the commander was afraid Paul would be torn to pieces by them. He ordered the troops to go down and take him away from them by force and bring him into the barracks.

The following night the Lord stood near Paul and said, "Take courage! As you have testified about me in Jerusalem, so you must also testify in Rome."

The next morning some Jews formed a conspiracy and bound themselves with an oath not to eat or drink until they had killed Paul. More than forty men were involved in this plot. They went to the chief priests and the elders and said, "We have taken a solemn oath not to eat anything until we have killed Paul. Now then, you and the Sanhedrin petition the commander to bring him before you on the pretext of wanting more accurate information about his case. We are ready to kill him before he gets here."

But when the son of Paul's sister heard of this plot, he went into the barracks and told Paul.

Then Paul called one of the centurions and said, "Take this young man to the commander; he has something to tell him." So he took him to the commander.

The centurion said, "Paul, the prisoner, sent for me and asked me to bring this young man to you because he has something to tell you."

The commander took the young man by the hand, drew him aside and asked, "What is it you want to tell me?"

He said: "Some Jews have agreed to ask you to bring Paul before the Sanhedrin tomorrow on the pretext of wanting more accurate information about him. Don't give in to them, because more than forty of them are waiting in ambush for him. They have taken an oath not to eat or drink until they have killed him. They are ready now, waiting for your consent to their request."

The commander dismissed the young man with this warning: "Don't tell anyone that you have reported this to me."

Then he called two of his centurions and ordered them, "Get ready a detachment of two hundred soldiers, seventy horsemen and two hundred spearmen to go to Caesarea at nine tonight. Provide horses for Paul so that he may be taken safely to Governor Felix."

He wrote a letter as follows:

Claudius Lysias,

To His Excellency, Governor Felix:

Greetings.

This man was seized by the Jews and they were about to kill him, but I came with my troops and rescued him, for I had learned that he is a Roman citizen. I wanted to know why they were accusing him, so I brought him to their Sanhedrin. I found that the accusation had to do with questions about their law, but there was no charge against him that deserved death or imprisonment. When I was informed of a plot to be carried out against the man, I sent him to you at once. I also ordered his accusers to present to you their case against him.

So the soldiers, carrying out their orders, took Paul with them during the night and brought him as far as Antipatris. The next day they let the cavalry go on with him, while they returned to the barracks. When the cavalry arrived in Caesarea, they delivered the letter to the governor and handed Paul over to him. The governor read the letter and asked what province he was from. Learning that he was from Cilicia, he said, "I will hear your case when your accusers get here." Then he ordered that Paul be kept under guard in Herod's palace.

Paul's arrest resulted from anything but criminal behavior, and the years he spent waiting for Roman justice would have broken most people. None of the officials he faced could find legal fault with him (the charge was sedition), yet no one would release him for fear of political repercussions. The Roman governor Felix held Paul in custody at Caesarea for two years, sending for him frequently in hope that Paul would offer him a bribe. Finally Felix was recalled to Rome for failing, among other things, to control local insurrection.

The Jewish leaders immediately asked the new governor, Festus, to transfer Paul from Caesarea to Jerusalem. Paul, a Roman citizen, was forced to exercise his right of appeal to Caesar in order to avoid the grave danger of going to Jerusalem. Next, Paul appeared before King Herod Agrippa II. Agrippa and Festus agreed that Paul wasn't guilty of any crime. But Paul had made an appeal to Caesar, so the Roman Imperial Court would finally get the privilege of disposing of his case.

Paul's defense before these authorities was more a continuation of his life work than a defendant's plea for justice. Paul tried to show them how important faith in Jesus was—for them and everyone! They refused to respond and placed Paul on a ship to Rome.

When it was decided that we would sail for Italy, Paul and some other prisoners were handed over to a centurion named Julius, who belonged to the Imperial Regiment. We boarded a ship from Adramyttium about to sail for ports along the coast of the province of Asia, and we put out to sea. Aristarchus, a Macedonian from Thessalonica, was with us.

The next day we landed at Sidon; and Julius, in kindness to Paul, allowed him to go to his friends so they might provide for his needs. From there we put out to sea again and passed to the lee of Cyprus because the winds were against us. When we had sailed across the open sea off the coast of Cilicia and Pamphylia, we landed at Myra in Lycia. There the centurion found an Alexandrian ship sailing for Italy and put us on board. We made slow headway for many days and had difficulty arriving off Cnidus. When the wind did not allow us to hold our course, we sailed to the lee of Crete, opposite Salmone. We moved along the coast with difficulty and came to a place called Fair Havens, near the town of Lasea.

Much time had been lost, and sailing had already become dangerous because by now it was after the Day of Atonement. So Paul warned them, "Men, I can see that our voyage is going to be disastrous and bring great loss to ship and cargo, and to our own lives also." But the centurion, instead of listening to what Paul said, followed the advice of the pilot and of the owner of the ship. Since the harbor was unsuitable to winter in, the majority decided that we should sail on, hoping to reach Phoenix and winter there. This was a harbor in Crete, facing both southwest and northwest.

When a gentle south wind began to blow, they saw their opportunity; so they weighed anchor and sailed along the shore of Crete. Before very long, a wind of hurricane force, called the Northeaster, swept down from the island. The ship was caught by the storm and could not head into the wind; so we gave way to it and were driven along. As we passed to the lee of a small island called Cauda, we were hardly able to make the lifeboat secure, so the men hoisted it aboard. Then they passed ropes under the ship itself to hold it together. Because they were afraid they would run aground on the sandbars of Syrtis, they lowered the sea anchor and let the ship be driven along. We took such a violent battering from the storm that the next day they began to throw the cargo overboard. On the third day, they threw the ship's tackle overboard with their own hands. When neither sun nor stars appeared for many days and the storm continued raging, we finally gave up all hope of being saved.

After they had gone a long time without food, Paul stood up before them and said: "Men, you should have taken my advice not to sail from Crete; then you would have spared yourselves this damage and loss. But now I urge you to keep up your courage, because not one of you will be lost; only the ship will be destroyed. Last night an angel of the God to whom I belong and whom I serve stood beside me and said, 'Do not be afraid, Paul. You must stand trial before Caesar; and God has graciously given you the lives of all who sail with you.' So keep up your courage, men, for I have faith in God that it will happen just as he told me. Nevertheless, we must run aground on some island."

On the fourteenth night we were still being driven across the

Adriatic[1] Sea, when about midnight the sailors sensed they were approaching land. They took soundings and found that the water was a hundred and twenty feet deep. A short time later they took soundings again and found it was ninety feet deep. Fearing that we would be dashed against the rocks, they dropped four anchors from the stern and prayed for daylight. In an attempt to escape from the ship, the sailors let the lifeboat down into the sea, pretending they were going to lower some anchors from the bow. Then Paul said to the centurion and the soldiers, "Unless these men stay with the ship, you cannot be saved." So the soldiers cut the ropes that held the lifeboat and let it drift away.

Just before dawn Paul urged them all to eat. "For the last fourteen days," he said, "you have been in constant suspense and have gone without food—you haven't eaten anything. Now I urge you to take some food. You need it to survive. Not one of you will lose a single hair from his head." After he said this, he took some bread and gave thanks to God in front of them all. Then he broke it and began to eat. They were all encouraged and ate some food themselves. Altogether there were 276 of us on board. When they had eaten as much as they wanted, they lightened the ship by throwing the grain into the sea.

When daylight came, they did not recognize the land, but they saw a bay with a sandy beach, where they decided to run the ship aground if they could. Cutting loose the anchors, they left them in the sea and at the same time untied the ropes that held the rudders. Then they hoisted the foresail to the wind and made for the beach. But the ship struck a sandbar and ran aground. The bow stuck fast and would not move, and the stern was broken to pieces by the pounding of the surf.

The soldiers planned to kill the prisoners to prevent any of them from swimming away and escaping. But the centurion wanted to spare Paul's life and kept them from carrying out their plan. He ordered those who could swim to jump overboard first and get to

---

[1]**Adriatic:** In ancient times the name referred to an area extending well south of Italy.

land. The rest were to get there on planks or on other pieces of the ship. In this way everyone reached land safely.

Once safely on shore, we found out that the island was called Malta. The islanders showed us unusual kindness. They built a fire and welcomed us all because it was raining and cold. Paul gathered a pile of brushwood and, as he put it on the fire, a viper, driven out by the heat, fastened itself on his hand. When the islanders saw the snake hanging from his hand, they said to each other, "This man must be a murderer; for though he escaped from the sea, the goddess Justice has not allowed him to live." But Paul shook the snake off into the fire and suffered no ill effects. The people expected him to swell up or suddenly fall dead; but after waiting a long time and seeing nothing unusual happen to him, they changed their minds and said he was a god.

There was an estate nearby that belonged to Publius, the chief official of the island. He welcomed us to his home and showed us generous hospitality for three days. His father was sick in bed, suffering from fever and dysentery. Paul went in to see him and, after prayer, placed his hands on him and healed him. When this had happened, the rest of the sick on the island came and were cured. They honored us in many ways; and when we were ready to sail, they furnished us with the supplies we needed.

After three months we put out to sea in a ship that had wintered in the island — it was an Alexandrian ship with the figurehead of the twin gods Castor and Pollux. We put in at Syracuse and stayed there three days. From there we set sail and arrived at Rhegium. The next day the south wind came up, and on the following day we reached Puteoli. There we found some brothers and sisters who invited us to spend a week with them. And so we came to Rome. The brothers and sisters there had heard that we were coming, and they traveled as far as the Forum of Appius and the Three Taverns to meet us. At the sight of these people Paul thanked God and was encouraged. When we got to Rome, Paul was allowed to live by himself, with a soldier to guard him.

Three days later he called together the local Jewish leaders. When they had assembled, Paul said to them: "My brothers, although I have done nothing against our people or against the customs of our ancestors, I was arrested in Jerusalem and handed over to the Romans. They examined me and wanted to release me, because I was not guilty of any crime deserving death. The Jews objected, so I was compelled to make an appeal to Caesar. I certainly did not intend to bring any charge against my own people. For this reason I have asked to see you and talk with you. It is because of the hope of Israel that I am bound with this chain."

They replied, "We have not received any letters from Judea concerning you, and none of our people who have come from there has reported or said anything bad about you. But we want to hear what your views are, for we know that people everywhere are talking against this sect."

They arranged to meet Paul on a certain day, and came in even larger numbers to the place where he was staying. He witnessed to them from morning till evening, explaining about the kingdom of God, and from the Law of Moses and from the Prophets he tried to persuade them about Jesus. Some were convinced by what he said, but others would not believe. They disagreed among themselves and began to leave after Paul had made this final statement: "The Holy Spirit spoke the truth to your ancestors when he said through Isaiah the prophet:

> "'Go to this people and say,
> "You will be ever hearing but never understanding;
>   you will be ever seeing but never perceiving."
> For this people's heart has become calloused;
>   they hardly hear with their ears,
>   and they have closed their eyes.
> Otherwise they might see with their eyes,
>   hear with their ears,
>   understand with their hearts
> and turn, and I would heal them.'

"Therefore I want you to know that God's salvation has been sent to the Gentiles, and they will listen!"

For two whole years Paul stayed there in his own rented house and welcomed all who came to see him. He proclaimed the kingdom of God and taught about the Lord Jesus Christ — with all boldness and without hindrance!

While Paul was under house arrest in Rome, awaiting his trial before Caesar, he penned a letter to his beloved friends in Ephesus. This letter was probably intended to be circulated and read in several churches in addition to the one at Ephesus. It was a passionate review of God's love through Jesus and a call for all believers to live in unity. As Paul's life was nearing an end, his heart overflowed with joy and praise at God's wonderful story of redemption in Jesus the Messiah.

Paul, an apostle of Christ Jesus by the will of God,

To God's holy people in Ephesus, the faithful in Christ Jesus:

Grace and peace to you from God our Father and the Lord Jesus Christ.

Praise be to the God and Father of our Lord Jesus Christ, who has blessed us in the heavenly realms with every spiritual blessing in Christ. For he chose us in him before the creation of the world to be holy and blameless in his sight. In love he predestined us for adoption to sonship through Jesus Christ, in accordance with his pleasure and will — to the praise of his glorious grace, which he has freely given us in the One he loves. In him we have redemption through his blood, the forgiveness of sins, in accordance with the riches of God's grace that he lavished on us. With all wisdom and understanding, he made known to us the mystery of his will according to his good pleasure, which he purposed in Christ, to be put into effect when the times reach their fulfillment — to bring unity to all things in heaven and on earth under Christ.

I have not stopped giving thanks for you, remembering you in my prayers. I keep asking that the God of our Lord Jesus Christ, the glorious Father, may give you the Spirit of wisdom and revelation, so that you may know him better. I pray that the eyes of your heart may be enlightened in order that you may know the hope to which he has called you, the riches of his glorious inheritance in his holy people, and his incomparably great power for us who believe. That power is the same as the mighty strength he exerted when he raised Christ from the dead and seated him at his right hand in the heavenly realms, far above all rule and authority, power and dominion, and every name that is invoked, not only in the present age but also in the one to come. And God placed all things under his feet and appointed him to be head over everything for the church, which is his body, the fullness of him who fills everything in every way.

As for you, you were dead in your transgressions and sins, in which you used to live when you followed the ways of this world and of the ruler of the kingdom of the air, the spirit who is now at work in those who are disobedient. All of us also lived among them at one time, gratifying the cravings of our flesh and following its desires and thoughts. Like the rest, we were by nature deserving of wrath. But because of his great love for us, God, who is rich in mercy, made us alive with Christ even when we were dead in transgressions — it is by grace you have been saved. And God raised us up with Christ and seated us with him in the heavenly realms in Christ Jesus, in order that in the coming ages he might show the incomparable riches of his grace, expressed in his kindness to us in Christ Jesus. For it is by grace you have been saved, through faith — and this is not from yourselves, it is the gift of God — not by works, so that no one can boast. For we are God's handiwork, created in Christ Jesus to do good works, which God prepared in advance for us to do.

Therefore, remember that formerly you who are Gentiles by birth and called "uncircumcised" by those who call themselves "the circumcision" (which is done in the body by human hands) —

remember that at that time you were separate from Christ, excluded from citizenship in Israel and foreigners to the covenants of the promise, without hope and without God in the world. But now in Christ Jesus you who once were far away have been brought near by the blood of Christ.

For he himself is our peace, who has made the two groups one and has destroyed the barrier, the dividing wall of hostility, by setting aside in his flesh the law with its commands and regulations. His purpose was to create in himself one new humanity out of the two, thus making peace, and in one body to reconcile both of them to God through the cross, by which he put to death their hostility. He came and preached peace to you who were far away and peace to those who were near. For through him we both have access to the Father by one Spirit.

Consequently, you are no longer foreigners and strangers, but fellow citizens with God's people and also members of his household, built on the foundation of the apostles and prophets, with Christ Jesus himself as the chief cornerstone. In him the whole building is joined together and rises to become a holy temple in the Lord. And in him you too are being built together to become a dwelling in which God lives by his Spirit.

For this reason I kneel before the Father, from whom every family in heaven and on earth derives its name. I pray that out of his glorious riches he may strengthen you with power through his Spirit in your inner being, so that Christ may dwell in your hearts through faith. And I pray that you, being rooted and established in love, may have power, together with all the Lord's holy people, to grasp how wide and long and high and deep is the love of Christ, and to know this love that surpasses knowledge — that you may be filled to the measure of all the fullness of God.

Now to him who is able to do immeasurably more than all we ask or imagine, according to his power that is at work within us, to him be glory in the church and in Christ Jesus throughout all generations, for ever and ever! Amen.

As a prisoner for the Lord, then, I urge you to live a life worthy of the calling you have received. Be completely humble and gentle; be patient, bearing with one another in love. Make every effort to keep the unity of the Spirit through the bond of peace. There is one body and one Spirit, just as you were called to one hope when you were called; one Lord, one faith, one baptism; one God and Father of all, who is over all and through all and in all.

Submit to one another out of reverence for Christ.

Wives, submit yourselves to your own husbands as you do to the Lord. For the husband is the head of the wife as Christ is the head of the church, his body, of which he is the Savior. Now as the church submits to Christ, so also wives should submit to their husbands in everything.

Husbands, love your wives, just as Christ loved the church and gave himself up for her to make her holy, cleansing her by the washing with water through the word, and to present her to himself as a radiant church, without stain or wrinkle or any other blemish, but holy and blameless. In this same way, husbands ought to love their wives as their own bodies. He who loves his wife loves himself. After all, no one ever hated their own body, but they feed and care for their body, just as Christ does the church — for we are members of his body. "For this reason a man will leave his father and mother and be united to his wife, and the two will become one flesh." This is a profound mystery — but I am talking about Christ and the church. However, each one of you also must love his wife as he loves himself, and the wife must respect her husband.

Children, obey your parents in the Lord, for this is right. "Honor your father and mother" — which is the first commandment with a promise — "so that it may go well with you and that you may enjoy long life on the earth."

Fathers, do not exasperate your children; instead, bring them up in the training and instruction of the Lord.

Peace to the brothers and sisters, and love with faith from God the Father and the Lord Jesus Christ. Grace to all who love our Lord Jesus Christ with an undying love.

It appears that Paul was released from house arrest in Rome in AD 62 and embarked on a final missionary journey to Asia Minor, Crete, Greece and perhaps Spain. He was imprisoned again in Rome, but this time he languished in a cold dungeon, chained like a common criminal. Paul was martyred during the reign of the emperor Nero in AD 67 or 68. During his final days, he wrote one last letter—a personal letter to Timothy, his coworker and "son in the faith." To distinguish it from Paul's earlier letter to Timothy, this letter is known as "Second Timothy" in the New Testament. Here, the beloved apostle pours out his heart with a mixture of loneliness, tenacious faith and concern for his fellow believers during this time of persecution under Nero.

Paul, an apostle of Christ Jesus by the will of God, in keeping with the promise of life that is in Christ Jesus,

To Timothy, my dear son:

Grace, mercy and peace from God the Father and Christ Jesus our Lord.

I thank God, whom I serve, as my ancestors did, with a clear conscience, as night and day I constantly remember you in my prayers. Recalling your tears, I long to see you, so that I may be filled with joy. I am reminded of your sincere faith, which first lived in your grandmother Lois and in your mother Eunice and, I am persuaded, now lives in you also.

Do not be ashamed of the testimony about our Lord or of me his prisoner. Rather, join with me in suffering for the gospel, by the power of God. He has saved us and called us to a holy life — not because of anything we have done but because of his own purpose and grace. This grace was given us in Christ Jesus before the beginning of time, but it has now been revealed through the appearing of our Savior, Christ Jesus, who has destroyed death and has brought life and immortality to light through the gospel. And of this gospel I was appointed a herald and an apostle and a teacher. That is why I am suffering as I am. Yet this is no cause for shame, because I know whom I have believed, and am convinced that he is able to guard what I have entrusted to him until that day.

You then, my son, be strong in the grace that is in Christ Jesus. And the things you have heard me say in the presence of many witnesses entrust to reliable people who will also be qualified to teach others. Join with me in suffering, like a good soldier of Christ Jesus. No one serving as a soldier gets entangled in civilian affairs, but rather tries to please his commanding officer. Similarly, anyone who competes as an athlete does not receive the victor's crown except by competing according to the rules. The hardworking farmer should be the first to receive a share of the crops. Reflect on what I am saying, for the Lord will give you insight into all this.

Remember Jesus Christ, raised from the dead, descended from David. This is my gospel, for which I am suffering even to the point of being chained like a criminal. But God's word is not chained.

You, however, know all about my teaching, my way of life, my purpose, faith, patience, love, endurance, persecutions, sufferings — what kinds of things happened to me in Antioch, Iconium and Lystra, the persecutions I endured. Yet the Lord rescued me from all of them. In fact, everyone who wants to live a godly life in Christ Jesus will be persecuted, while evildoers and impostors will go from bad to worse, deceiving and being deceived. But as for you, continue in what you have learned and have become convinced of, because you know those from whom you learned it, and how from infancy you have known the Holy Scriptures, which are able to make you wise for salvation through faith in Christ Jesus. All Scripture is God-breathed and is useful for teaching, rebuking, correcting and training in righteousness, so that the servant of God may be thoroughly equipped for every good work.

For I am already being poured out like a drink offering, and the time for my departure is near. I have fought the good fight, I have finished the race, I have kept the faith. Now there is in store for me the crown of righteousness, which the Lord, the righteous Judge, will award to me on that day — and not only to me, but also to all who have longed for his appearing.

Do your best to come to me quickly, for Demas, because he loved this world, has deserted me and has gone to Thessalonica. Crescens has gone to Galatia, and Titus to Dalmatia. Only Luke is with me. Get Mark and bring him with you, because he is helpful to me in my ministry. I sent Tychicus to Ephesus. When you come, bring the cloak that I left with Carpus at Troas, and my scrolls, especially the parchments.

Paul wasn't the only apostle to be martyred. Tradition says that John, the author of a lofty and mysterious vision called "Revelation," was the oldest and last surviving member of Jesus' original disciples. By the time he wrote this book, it's likely that the other disciples had been killed (according to tradition, Peter was crucified upside down) or had wandered into regions where news of them was lost to distance and time. John was exiled to the island of Patmos, where he wrote of the vision and revelation he received.

31

The End of Time

THE REVELATION FROM JESUS CHRIST, which God gave him to show his servants what must soon take place. He made it known by sending his angel to his servant John, who testifies to everything he saw — that is, the word of God and the testimony of Jesus Christ. Blessed is the one who reads aloud the words of this prophecy, and blessed are those who hear it and take to heart what is written in it, because the time is near.

John,

To the seven churches in the province of Asia:

Grace and peace to you from him who is, and who was, and who is to come, and from the seven spirits before his throne, and from Jesus Christ, who is the faithful witness, the firstborn from the dead, and the ruler of the kings of the earth.

To him who loves us and has freed us from our sins by his blood, and has made us to be a kingdom and priests to serve his

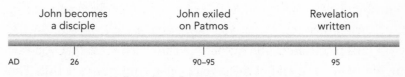

John becomes a disciple	John exiled on Patmos	Revelation written
AD 26	90–95	95

Full timeline information starts on page xi.

God and Father — to him be glory and power for ever and ever!
Amen.

> "Look, he is coming with the clouds,"
>   and "every eye will see him,
> even those who pierced him";
>   and all peoples on earth "will mourn because of him."
>   So shall it be! Amen.

"I am the Alpha and the Omega," says the Lord God, "who is,
and who was, and who is to come, the Almighty."

I, John, your brother and companion in the suffering and kingdom and patient endurance that are ours in Jesus, was on the
island of Patmos because of the word of God and the testimony
of Jesus. On the Lord's Day I was in the Spirit, and I heard behind
me a loud voice like a trumpet, which said: "Write on a scroll what
you see and send it to the seven churches: to Ephesus, Smyrna,
Pergamum, Thyatira, Sardis, Philadelphia and Laodicea."

I turned around to see the voice that was speaking to me.
And when I turned I saw seven golden lampstands, and among
the lampstands was someone like a son of man, dressed in a robe
reaching down to his feet and with a golden sash around his chest.
The hair on his head was white like wool, as white as snow, and his
eyes were like blazing fire. His feet were like bronze glowing in a
furnace, and his voice was like the sound of rushing waters. In his
right hand he held seven stars, and coming out of his mouth was
a sharp, double-edged sword. His face was like the sun shining in
all its brilliance.

When I saw him, I fell at his feet as though dead. Then he
placed his right hand on me and said: "Do not be afraid. I am the
First and the Last. I am the Living One; I was dead, and now look, I
am alive for ever and ever! And I hold the keys of death and Hades.

"Write, therefore, what you have seen, what is now and what
will take place later. The mystery of the seven stars that you saw
in my right hand and of the seven golden lampstands is this: The

seven stars are the angels of the seven churches, and the seven lampstands are the seven churches.

> This blazing Living One, the risen Lord Jesus, then dictated letters to seven individual churches throughout Asia Minor, warning of problems and pitfalls in their faith. The letters imply that we live in a morally accountable universe, and those accounts will be "called in" at the end of history. God, firmly in control of his story, has set a day when patience will give way to a final judgment.

"To the angel of the church in Ephesus write:

"These are the words of him who holds the seven stars in his right hand and walks among the seven golden lampstands. I know your deeds, your hard work and your perseverance. I know that you cannot tolerate wicked people, that you have tested those who claim to be apostles but are not, and have found them false. You have persevered and have endured hardships for my name, and have not grown weary.

Yet I hold this against you: You have forsaken the love you had at first. Consider how far you have fallen! Repent and do the things you did at first. If you do not repent, I will come to you and remove your lampstand from its place. But you have this in your favor: You hate the practices of the Nicolaitans, which I also hate.

"Whoever has ears, let them hear what the Spirit says to the churches. To the one who is victorious, I will give the right to eat from the tree of life, which is in the paradise of God.

"To the angel of the church in Sardis write:

"These are the words of him who holds the seven spirits of God and the seven stars. I know your deeds; you have a reputation of being alive, but you are dead. Wake up! Strengthen what remains and is about to die, for I have found your deeds unfinished in the sight of my God. Remember, therefore, what you have received and heard; hold it fast, and repent. But if you do not wake up, I will come like a thief, and you will not know at what time I will come to you.

"Yet you have a few people in Sardis who have not soiled their clothes. They will walk with me, dressed in white, for they are worthy. The one who is victorious will, like them, be dressed in white. I will never blot out the name of that person from the book of life, but will acknowledge that name before my Father and his angels. Whoever has ears, let them hear what the Spirit says to the churches.

"To the angel of the church in Laodicea write:

"These are the words of the Amen, the faithful and true witness, the ruler of God's creation. I know your deeds, that you are neither cold nor hot. I wish you were either one or the other! So, because you are lukewarm — neither hot nor cold — I am about to spit you out of my mouth. You say, 'I am rich; I have acquired wealth and do not need a thing.' But you do not realize that you are wretched, pitiful, poor, blind and naked. I counsel you to buy from me gold refined in the fire, so you can become rich; and white clothes to wear, so you can cover your shameful nakedness; and salve to put on your eyes, so you can see.

"Those whom I love I rebuke and discipline. So be earnest and repent. Here I am! I stand at the door and knock. If anyone hears my voice and opens the door, I will come in and eat with that person, and they with me.

"To the one who is victorious, I will give the right to sit with me on my throne, just as I was victorious and sat down with my Father on his throne. Whoever has ears, let them hear what the Spirit says to the churches."

Now John's Revelation takes a turn from an exhortation of the seven churches to a series of mysterious and symbolic scenes.

The curtains of heaven are rolled back, and John gets a glimpse of spiritual realities—including the final days of history when the utterly astounding glory of God and his plan for the world will be revealed.

After this I looked, and there before me was a door standing open in heaven. And the voice I had first heard speaking to me like a trumpet said, "Come up here, and I will show you what must take place after this." At once I was in the Spirit, and there before me was a throne in heaven with someone sitting on it. And the one who sat there had the appearance of jasper and ruby. A rainbow that shone like an emerald encircled the throne. Surrounding the throne were twenty-four other thrones, and seated on them were twenty-four elders. They were dressed in white and had crowns of gold on their heads. From the throne came flashes of lightning, rumblings and peals of thunder. In front of the throne, seven lamps were blazing. These are the seven spirits of God. Also in front of the throne there was what looked like a sea of glass, clear as crystal.

In the center, around the throne, were four living creatures, and they were covered with eyes, in front and in back. The first living creature was like a lion, the second was like an ox, the third had a face like a man, the fourth was like a flying eagle. Each of the four living creatures had six wings and was covered with eyes all around, even under its wings. Day and night they never stop saying:

> " 'Holy, holy, holy
> is the Lord God Almighty,'
> who was, and is, and is to come."

Whenever the living creatures give glory, honor and thanks to him who sits on the throne and who lives for ever and ever, the twenty-four elders fall down before him who sits on the throne and worship him who lives for ever and ever. They lay their crowns before the throne and say:

> "You are worthy, our Lord and God,
>> to receive glory and honor and power,
> for you created all things,
>> and by your will they were created
>> and have their being."

Then I saw in the right hand of him who sat on the throne a scroll with writing on both sides and sealed with seven seals. And I saw a mighty angel proclaiming in a loud voice, "Who is worthy to break the seals and open the scroll?" But no one in heaven or on earth or under the earth could open the scroll or even look inside it. I wept and wept because no one was found who was worthy to open the scroll or look inside. Then one of the elders said to me, "Do not weep! See, the Lion of the tribe of Judah, the Root of David, has triumphed. He is able to open the scroll and its seven seals."

Then I saw a Lamb, looking as if it had been slain, standing at the center of the throne, encircled by the four living creatures and the elders. The Lamb had seven horns and seven eyes, which are the seven spirits of God sent out into all the earth. He went and took the scroll from the right hand of him who sat on the throne. And when he had taken it, the four living creatures and the twenty-four elders fell down before the Lamb. Each one had a harp and they were holding golden bowls full of incense, which are the prayers of God's people. And they sang a new song, saying:

> "You are worthy to take the scroll
>> and to open its seals,
> because you were slain,
>> and with your blood you purchased for God
>> persons from every tribe and language and people
>>> and nation.
> You have made them to be a kingdom and priests
>> to serve our God,
>> and they will reign on the earth."

Then I looked and heard the voice of many angels, numbering thousands upon thousands, and ten thousand times ten thousand. They encircled the throne and the living creatures and the elders. In a loud voice they were saying:

> "Worthy is the Lamb, who was slain,
>> to receive power and wealth and wisdom and strength
>> and honor and glory and praise!"

Then I heard every creature in heaven and on earth and under the earth and on the sea, and all that is in them, saying:

> "To him who sits on the throne and to the Lamb
>> be praise and honor and glory and power,
>>> for ever and ever!"

The four living creatures said, "Amen," and the elders fell down and worshiped.

Then a voice came from the throne, saying:

> "Praise our God,
>> all you his servants,
> you who fear him,
>> both great and small!"

Then I heard what sounded like a great multitude, like the roar of rushing waters and like loud peals of thunder, shouting:

> "Hallelujah!
>> For our Lord God Almighty reigns.
> Let us rejoice and be glad
>> and give him glory!
> For the wedding of the Lamb has come,
>> and his bride has made herself ready.
> Fine linen, bright and clean,
>> was given her to wear."

(Fine linen stands for the righteous acts of God's holy people.)

Then the angel said to me, "Write this: Blessed are those who are invited to the wedding supper of the Lamb!" And he added, "These are the true words of God."

At this I fell at his feet to worship him. But he said to me, "Don't do that! I am a fellow servant with you and with your brothers and sisters who hold to the testimony of Jesus. Worship God! For it is the Spirit of prophecy who bears testimony to Jesus."

I saw heaven standing open and there before me was a white horse, whose rider is called Faithful and True. With justice he judges and wages war. His eyes are like blazing fire, and on his head are many crowns. He has a name written on him that no one knows but he himself. He is dressed in a robe dipped in blood, and his name is the Word of God. The armies of heaven were following him, riding on white horses and dressed in fine linen, white and clean. Coming out of his mouth is a sharp sword with which to strike down the nations. "He will rule them with an iron scepter." He treads the winepress of the fury of the wrath of God Almighty. On his robe and on his thigh he has this name written:

KING OF KINGS AND LORD OF LORDS.

Soon after this story opened in the book of Genesis, God's battle against evil became evident in the Garden of Eden. Here at the end, the final battle will be engaged. When it's over, all the oppression, injustice and grief caused by Satan's side will be wrapped up and consigned to a place far from God's home. All the world's destruction and brokenness will give way to Jesus' promise of a new creation, a new environment, a new city of peace and freedom. It is here that Christians will forever enjoy the glory and holiness of God himself. This is very good news to God's children, but it will be a time of unspeakable horror for those who turn away from God.

Then I saw a great white throne and him who was seated on it. The earth and the heavens fled from his presence, and there was no place for them. And I saw the dead, great and small, standing before the throne, and books were opened. Another book was opened, which is the book of life. The dead were judged according to what they had done as recorded in the books. The sea gave up the dead that were in it, and death and Hades gave up the dead that were in them, and each person was judged according to what they had done. Then death and Hades were thrown into the lake of fire. The lake of fire is the second death. Anyone whose name was not found written in the book of life was thrown into the lake of fire.

Then I saw "a new heaven and a new earth," for the first heaven and the first earth had passed away, and there was no longer any sea. I saw the Holy City, the new Jerusalem, coming down out of heaven from God, prepared as a bride beautifully dressed for her husband. And I heard a loud voice from the throne saying, "Look! God's dwelling place is now among the people, and he will dwell with them. They will be his people, and God himself will be with them and be their God. 'He will wipe every tear from their eyes. There will be no more death' or mourning or crying or pain, for the old order of things has passed away."

He who was seated on the throne said, "I am making everything new!" Then he said, "Write this down, for these words are trustworthy and true."

He said to me: "It is done. I am the Alpha and the Omega, the Beginning and the End. To the thirsty I will give water without cost from the spring of the water of life. Those who are victorious will inherit all this, and I will be their God and they will be my children. But the cowardly, the unbelieving, the vile, the murderers, the sexually immoral, those who practice magic arts, the idolaters and all liars — they will be consigned to the fiery lake of burning sulfur. This is the second death."

One of the seven angels who had the seven bowls full of the seven last plagues came and said to me, "Come, I will show you the bride, the wife of the Lamb." And he carried me away in the Spirit to a mountain great and high, and showed me the Holy City, Jerusalem, coming down out of heaven from God. It shone with the glory of God, and its brilliance was like that of a very precious jewel, like a jasper, clear as crystal. It had a great, high wall with twelve gates, and with twelve angels at the gates. On the gates were written the names of the twelve tribes of Israel. There were three gates on the east, three on the north, three on the south and three on the west. The wall of the city had twelve foundations, and on them were the names of the twelve apostles of the Lamb.

The angel who talked with me had a measuring rod of gold to measure the city, its gates and its walls. The city was laid out like a square, as long as it was wide. He measured the city with the rod and found it to be 12,000 stadia in length, and as wide and high as it is long. The angel measured the wall using human measurement, and it was 144 cubits thick. The wall was made of jasper, and the city of pure gold, as pure as glass. The foundations of the city walls were decorated with every kind of precious stone. The first foundation was jasper, the second sapphire, the third agate, the fourth emerald, the fifth onyx, the sixth ruby, the seventh chrysolite, the eighth beryl, the ninth topaz, the tenth turquoise, the eleventh jacinth, and the twelfth amethyst. The twelve gates were twelve pearls, each gate made of a single pearl. The great street of the city was of gold, as pure as transparent glass.

I did not see a temple in the city, because the Lord God Almighty and the Lamb are its temple. The city does not need the sun or the moon to shine on it, for the glory of God gives it light, and the Lamb is its lamp. The nations will walk by its light, and the kings of the earth will bring their splendor into it. On no day will its gates ever be shut, for there will be no night there. The glory and honor of the nations will be brought into it. Nothing impure will ever enter it, nor will anyone who does what is shameful or deceitful, but only those whose names are written in the Lamb's book of life.

Then the angel showed me the river of the water of life, as clear as crystal, flowing from the throne of God and of the Lamb down the middle of the great street of the city. On each side of the river stood the tree of life, bearing twelve crops of fruit, yielding its fruit every month. And the leaves of the tree are for the healing of the nations. No longer will there be any curse. The throne of God and of the Lamb will be in the city, and his servants will serve him. They will see his face, and his name will be on their foreheads. There will be no more night. They will not need the light of a lamp or the light of the sun, for the Lord God will give them light. And they will reign for ever and ever.

The angel said to me, "These words are trustworthy and true. The Lord, the God who inspires the prophets, sent his angel to show his servants the things that must soon take place."

"Look, I am coming soon! Blessed is the one who keeps the words of the prophecy written in this scroll."

I, John, am the one who heard and saw these things. And when I had heard and seen them, I fell down to worship at the feet of the angel who had been showing them to me. But he said to me, "Don't do that! I am a fellow servant with you and with your fellow prophets and with all who keep the words of this scroll. Worship God!"

Then he told me, "Do not seal up the words of the prophecy of this scroll, because the time is near. Let the one who does wrong continue to do wrong; let the vile person continue to be vile; let the one who does right continue to do right; and let the holy person continue to be holy."

"Look, I am coming soon! My reward is with me, and I will give to each person according to what they have done. I am the Alpha and the Omega, the First and the Last, the Beginning and the End.

"Blessed are those who wash their robes, that they may have the right to the tree of life and may go through the gates into the city. Outside are the dogs, those who practice magic arts, the sexually immoral, the murderers, the idolaters and everyone who loves and practices falsehood.

"I, Jesus, have sent my angel to give you this testimony for the churches. I am the Root and the Offspring of David, and the bright Morning Star."

The Spirit and the bride say, "Come!" And let the one who hears say, "Come!" Let the one who is thirsty come; and let the one who wishes take the free gift of the water of life.

I warn everyone who hears the words of the prophecy of this scroll: If anyone adds anything to them, God will add to that person the plagues described in this scroll. And if anyone takes words away from this scroll of prophecy, God will take away from that person any share in the tree of life and in the Holy City, which are described in this scroll.

He who testifies to these things says, "Yes, I am coming soon." Amen. Come, Lord Jesus.

The grace of the Lord Jesus be with God's people. Amen.

Epilogue

THE STORY HAS COME TO AN END, and God's message rings loud and clear:

I have opened the door; I have made a way—come to me and have life!

The Good News has gone out to the world. Jesus has come to provide salvation for us all! All of God's story has led up to this ultimate news that we can experience and share with others. It has survived for thousands of years, marching forth to all cultures and peoples, leaving behind an incredible wake of transformation and change. Many have tried to put out its fire, but God's words have proven to be true, "My word ... will accomplish what I desire and achieve the purpose for which I sent it."

And now God's triumphant Word has found its way to you. You've read *The Story*. You've heard the truth. You've come face to face with the most important message you will ever hear: Jesus, God's Son, came, lived, died and rose again.

So now the question remains ...

What will *you* do with *The Story*?

Will you turn away and dismiss it as an interesting tale? Will you block out the light that shines so brightly? Or will you take a step down the narrow path that leads to unimaginable glory? Jesus tells us, "Enter through the narrow gate ... small is the gate and narrow the road that leads to life, and only a few find it." Will you be one of the few?

The chapter bearing your name is about to be written.

Discussion Questions

1 Creation: The Beginning of Life as We Know It

1. In what ways was life in the original creation different from life as we know it today?

2. Why did God create humans in his own image? What does this mean?

3. What was the root cause of Adam and Eve's sin against God?

4. Why did God put the tree of the knowledge of good and evil in the garden?

5. Why did God bring the flood upon the earth?

6. What does this act of judgment tell you about God?

2 God Builds a Nation

1. Abraham left his homeland and family to follow God. What did God say his reward would be?

2. What might God be asking you to give up to follow him?

3. What made Abraham righteous in God's sight? How is this fact relevant to your life?

4. Why did God ask Abraham to sacrifice his son Isaac? What did Abraham — and Isaac — learn from this experience?

5. Because Jacob had shrewdly acquired Esau's birthright and stolen their father's blessing, Jacob feared his brother's revenge. How did Jacob prepare for his meeting with Esau?

6. What attitude did Jacob have when he wrestled with the "man" who Jacob eventually realized was actually God?

3 Joseph: From Slave to Deputy Pharaoh

1. Why did Joseph's brothers want to get rid of him?

2. Why does God allow hurtful things to happen to people?

3. What were the positive effects of Joseph's being sold into slavery?

4. What does Joseph's statement to his brothers, "You intended to harm me, but God intended it for good," tell you about God?

5. In what ways have you seen God work through the most bleak and hopeless situations to cause a greater good?

6. Why can God be trusted at all times?

4 Deliverance

1. What was significant about Moses' birth?

2. How did God display his concern and love for his people after hearing their cries and groaning?

3. In what ways was Moses qualified to lead the people? In what ways did he feel he was not qualified?

4. Have you ever felt unqualified or unable to do something, as Moses did? How did you handle it?

5. *The Story* notes several amazing miracles in the deliverance of the people from Egypt. Do you believe God performs miracles today? Why or why not?

6. What can you learn about the character of God from the story of the Israelites' deliverance from slavery?

5 New Commands and a New Covenant

1. How were the people to prepare themselves to meet with God?

2. What does this story of the giving of these new commands tell you about the character of God?

3. What was the purpose of the Ten Commandments?

4. How can God be both the merciful forgiver of sin and the punisher of the guilty?

5. The Israelites became impatient and finally made a golden idol in the shape of a calf for themselves. What are some false gods/idols worshiped in our society today?

6. The Lord spoke to Moses "as one speaks to a friend." What steps can you take to gain a deeper understanding of who God is?

6 Wandering

1. What do you think was the root cause of most of the Israelites' problems? Why?

2. How did God respond to the people's lack of faith?

3. Why is God so radically opposed to sin?

4. What do you learn from Moses' leadership throughout this difficult period? How did he display frustration and faith?

5. Have you ever felt as if you were "wandering in the wilderness" — spiritually or emotionally? Explain.

6. How can having faith in what God has promised help you in difficult times?

7 The Battle Begins

1. How could Joshua be "strong and courageous" in such intimidating situations?

2. What do you learn about God from the story of the salvation of Rahab the prostitute?

3. What do the string of amazing battle victories the people experienced as they entered the land reveal about who is really in charge of history?

4. Why did God order the Israelites to go to war against others? How was this war justified?

5. How did Joshua challenge the people in his final speech?

6. Why do you think God lavished blessings on Joshua and all the Israelites, who, like Joshua, trusted God?

7. What practical steps can you take to gain a deeper faith in God?

8 A Few Good Men ... and Women

1. What does God's choice of Deborah as judge during this time reveal about God's view of women?

2. Why does God often use weak and uncertain people like Gideon to do his work?

3. If you ever feel uncertain about your gifts and abilities, how could the story of Gideon encourage and strengthen you?

4. What reasons can you give for why the Israelites kept repeating their downward cycle of sin?

5. What was the root cause of Samson's fall? What was the result?

6. What are the strongest temptations that you face? How do you fight such temptations?

9 The Faith of a Foreign Woman

1. What does Ruth's story reveal about the love of God?

2. What does Ruth's story reveal about how God views all people groups? What does that mean for you?

3. Both Ruth and Naomi suffered tremendous loss. Why does a good and gracious God allow tragedy to come upon those who love him?

4. When difficult times come, what causes you to continue to hope in God?

5. Ruth left her home to follow Naomi and to follow God. How is God asking you to follow him?

6. In what way do Ruth's actions and responses challenge you? Encourage you?

7. What steps can you take to become a more selfless, loving person?

10 Standing Tall, Falling Hard

1. What do you learn about prayer from Hannah?

2. How did Samuel show his faith in God?

3. Why was it wrong for the Israelites to ask for a king?

4. What factors led to King Saul's demise?

5. How did Saul respond when confronted with his sin? How do you respond when confronted with your own shortcomings?

6. What instances of God's grace do you see in this chapter?

11 From Shepherd to King

1. Why was David chosen to be the next king of Israel?

2. What obstacles did David face to become the king he was anointed to be?

3. How was David able to face a giant when so many others gave way to fear?

4. Why did David spare Saul when he had the chance to be free of Saul's attempts to kill him? What would you have done?

5. David had a single goal (that the God of Israel would be glorified) because he had a single love (the God of Israel). What can you do to cultivate a heart like David's?

12 The Trials of a King

1. What were some factors that led to David's sin with Bathsheba?

2. Both Saul and David sinned against God, yet how did their responses differ? What was the result of their responses?

3. How did David's sins affect the future of his family?

4. David was allowed to plan the temple, but God told him that his son would be the one to actually build it. How do think David felt about that? How did David respond?

5. Do you, like David, give God credit and praise for your successes and accomplishments?

13 The King Who Had It All

1. Why was Solomon's request for wisdom and discernment so pleasing to the Lord?

2. How is wisdom different from mere knowledge and intellect?

3. Why is it vital to become wise?

4. What can you do to gain more wisdom?

5. How did pride and lust contribute to Solomon's fall?

6. What can you do to guard yourself against these sins?

14 A Kingdom Torn in Two

1. What caused the kingdom of Israel to be divided?

2. How did Rehoboam and Jeroboam both make mistakes?

3. What observations do you make about God's character and what is important to God, based on this chapter?

4. Why is it important to always remain loyal to God?

5. When have you strayed from God? What caused the straying?

6. In what ways has God been kind to you even when you didn't deserve it?

15 God's Messengers

1. What do you learn about faith from Elijah's ups (victory over the prophets of Baal) and his downs (depression in the desert)?

2. God revealed himself to Elijah in a gentle whisper. What does this tell you about God's character and methods of communication?

3. What steps can you take to hear the gentle whisper of God?

4. In what ways did the prophet Elisha live a life of faith?

5. Identify the ways God was faithful to Elisha.

6. How has God been faithful to you?

7. What specific message of social justice and spiritual faithfulness do you think the prophets Amos and Hosea would proclaim today?

16 The Beginning of the End (of the Kingdom of Israel)

1. Why did Hezekiah experience so many difficulties? Does obedience to God guarantee prosperity?

2. When Hezekiah received an intimidating letter from his enemies, he "went up to the temple of the LORD and spread it out before the LORD." When have you reacted to an attack or urgent problem with a similar attitude?

3. What were some of the main themes in Isaiah's prophecies?

4. How could God be merciful to his people in light of their actions toward him?

5. How has God shown mercy to you?

6. Isaiah foretold the rise and fall of nations. Is God still in control of world events in our day?

17 The Kingdoms' Fall

1. Why did disaster come upon God's people?

2. What negative effects of sin have you seen in your life?

3. What were some of the main themes of the prophets' messages during this time?

4. Can you relate to Jeremiah as the "weeping prophet" who felt deeply the burden of God's people's sin?

5. How does God's promise of restoration for his people still give you hope today?

18 Daniel in Exile

1. In what ways do you see Daniel exhibit his faith in God?

2. What enabled Daniel's three friends to stand against the king's orders?

3. Why did God choose to punish Nebuchadnezzar the way that he did? What was the result of this punishment?

4. Why did Daniel prosper under the kings of Babylon and Persia?

5. What can you learn about prayer from Daniel?

6. What steps can you take to become more devoted to prayer?

19 The Return Home

1. Why did God rescue the Israelites again?

2. In what ways have you seen or experienced the rescuing power of God?

3. What did the Israelites do to deserve the mercy they received?

4. What reason does God have for being merciful to you?

5. The Jews returned home to rebuild the temple, the dwelling place of God on earth. Why was it important for them to do this?

6. Where does God dwell on earth today?

20 The Queen of Beauty and Courage

1. What does this chapter of *The Story* teach about God's work behind the scenes of history?

2. How did Mordecai respond when faced with disaster?

3. What character qualities do you observe in Queen Esther?

4. When was the last time you faced a threatening situation? What was your reaction?

5. In what ways have you experienced God's faithfulness in your life?

6. What steps can you take to show that you trust in the faithfulness of God?

21 Rebuilding the Walls

1. What was Ezra's role when he arrived in Jerusalem?

2. In what ways do you see God's faithfulness in this chapter?

3. Why was Nehemiah able to rebuild the city walls amidst such severe opposition?

4. What can you do to gain a greater dependence on God in difficult circumstances?

5. According to the prophet Malachi, what did the Israelites do (or not do) that displeased the Lord? Why were these things so evil?

6. Are there areas of your life displeasing to the Lord? What can you do to make your relationship right again?

22 The Birth of the King

1. Why did God send Jesus into the world?

2. What can you learn from Mary's reaction to her surprising and somewhat disturbing news?

3. Why was Jesus born into such humble circumstances?

4. What does this chapter reveal about who Jesus is?

5. What impact has the birth of Christ had on your life?

6. Why should you be thankful that God sent his Son into the world?

23 Jesus' Ministry Begins

1. What purposes did Jesus' baptism and temptation serve?

2. How would you sum up the main message that Jesus had for the people?

3. Why did so many people have a deep hatred for Jesus?

4. Jesus said that we must be "born again" to enter the kingdom of God. What does it mean to be born again?

5. What kind of people did Jesus typically reach out to? What kind of people did he oppose? Why?

6. Jesus stated that "whoever drinks the water I give them will never thirst. Indeed, the water I give them will become in them a spring of water welling up to eternal life." What do you think this statement means?

24 No Ordinary Man

1. Why might Jesus have used parables as a way to teach people?

2. What can you learn from Jesus' parables that you can use in your own life?

3. If you would have heard Jesus' sermon, what do you think you would have done? Would you have followed him?

4. Why did Jesus' teaching bother some of the religious leaders?

5. Jesus explained that he is the "bread of life" — the source of sustenance and satisfaction. What can you do to gain a deeper satisfaction in your relationship with Jesus?

25 Jesus, the Son of God

1. How would you respond to someone who asked, "Who is Jesus?"

2. What was Jesus' primary mission during his life?

3. What character qualities do you see in Jesus?

4. What changes do you need to make to bring your life into conformity with Jesus' values and priorities?

5. In what ways did Jesus' words and actions reveal the fact that he is equal with God?

6. How would you respond to the question, "How can you be sure that Jesus is God?"

7. What can you do to gain a deeper love for Jesus? Why is this important?

26 The Hour of Darkness

1. What did Jesus predict at the last supper with his disciples?

2. Why did Jesus have to die?

3. How did Jesus' followers respond to the tragic events?

4. What implications does Jesus' death on the cross for the sins of humanity have for your life?

5. What can you learn about God's love through these events?

6. In what way has Jesus' life and death affected the way you live your life from day to day?

27 The Resurrection

1. After Jesus died, why did some of his followers come to the tomb? What does this tell you about friendship and loyalty among Jesus' companions?

2. Do you believe that Jesus rose from the dead? Why?

3. When Jesus appeared to people after his resurrection, how do you think their lives were changed?

4. What does Jesus' resurrection from the dead reveal about God's power over death and sin?

5. What difference can or does it make in your life knowing that Jesus is alive today?

6. Before Jesus ascended to heaven, he commanded his followers to "go and make disciples of all nations." If you are a believer, when was the last time you talked to someone else about your faith in Jesus?

28 New Beginnings

1. Why was Peter's sermon on the day of Pentecost so effective?

2. Why did the Jewish religious leaders dislike the early Christians?

3. What examples of Christian love and fellowship do you see in this chapter?

4. What factors helped the Good News of Jesus Christ to spread quickly?

5. How were the early Christians able to remain faithful even in the midst of extremely difficult circumstances?

6. What practical steps can you take to increase your faith?

7. How do you explain the drastic change in Saul's (Paul's) life?

29 Paul's Mission

1. After Paul found the Lord, what was Paul's passion and mission in life?

2. What is your passion and mission in life?

3. When in a new city, why did Paul invariably begin his outreach at the Jewish synagogue?

4. How would you define "the gospel"?

5. What impact does the gospel have on your life?

6. What would have happened to Christianity if the Jewish believers who insisted that Gentiles become Jews prevailed?

7. What does Paul's letter to the Romans reveal to us about salvation?

30 Paul's Final Days

1. How was Paul able to endure the pain and trials that he suffered for his beliefs?

2. What can you learn from Paul's life about how to face difficult circumstances?

3. Why was Paul willing to walk into the face of danger?

4. What character qualities do you see in Paul?

5. What practical steps can you take to cultivate character qualities that resemble Paul's?

6. How would you sum up Paul's message?

31 The End of Time

1. What was John's response when he saw Jesus in the vision? Why did he respond this way?

2. What were the warnings Jesus gave to the churches? In what way do these warnings apply to your life?

3. What do you learn about God from his actions and descriptions in this chapter?

4. What does this chapter reveal about what heaven will be like?

5. Why is it important to think about and set your hope on heaven?

6. What steps can you take to set your hope more fully on what you know about eternity from this chapter?

Characters

Adam: The first man, husband of Eve. Created by God out of dust. Adam sinned when he ate fruit from the tree of the knowledge of good and evil.

Eve: The first woman, wife of Adam. Created by God from Adam's rib. Eve sinned when she ate fruit from the tree of the knowledge of good and evil.

Noah: At God's command, Noah built an ark to save himself, his family and the animals from a flood sent to wipe out humanity.

Abraham: The founding father of Israel. He was a model of faith in God, who promised him the land of Canaan and the legacy of being the father of a great nation.

Sarah: The wife of Abraham. She was infertile, but God enabled her to give birth to Isaac in her old age.

Isaac: One of the patriarchs of Israel. His birth was miraculous because his mother, Sarah, had been infertile and was 90 years old. His children were Jacob and Esau.

Rebekah: A member of Abraham's extended family. She married Isaac and had twin boys: Jacob and Esau.

Jacob: Also called "Israel," Jacob was another patriarch of the Israelite nation. He had 12 sons, whose descendants formed the 12 tribes of Israel.

Leah: Unloved wife of Jacob and sister of Rachel. She struggled with her situation, but came to trust in God as she gave birth to six sons and a daughter.

Rachel: Beloved wife of Jacob and sister of Leah. Her infertility caused strife between her and her sister. However, God eventually blessed her with two sons: Joseph and Benjamin.

Joseph: Jacob's favorite son. His jealous brothers sold him into slavery, but he rose to prominence in Egypt and brought his family to live there during a famine.

Moses: Used by God to deliver the Israelites from slavery in Egypt. Moses was God's spokesman to the people and gave them the Law.

Joshua: Succeeded Moses and led the Israelites' conquest of Canaan.

Deborah: One of Israel's judges (leaders who brought deliverance from foreign oppressors). She ordered Barak to move against Sisera's army but predicted that Sisera himself would be killed by a woman.

Gideon: One of Israel's judges. Using unorthodox tactics commanded by God, he reluctantly led the Israelites to victory against their Midianite oppressors.

Samson: One of Israel's judges. God gave him superhuman strength. He had a lifelong rivalry with the Philistines, whom he defeated at the cost of his own life.

Ruth: A Moabite woman during the time of the judges. After her Israelite husband died, she left her homeland to return to Bethlehem with her mother-in-law, Naomi. She became the great-grandmother of King David.

Samuel: A great prophet and the last judge of Israel. He anointed Saul and David as Israel's kings.

Saul: The first king of Israel. His repeated disobedience to God during his reign led to its ignominious end. He was succeeded by David, whom he repeatedly tried to kill.

David: The second king of Israel, father of Solomon. David was devoted to God, and Israel flourished under him, but his reign was marred by his adultery with Bathsheba.

Nathan: A prophet during David's rule. Nathan supported David but confronted him about his adultery with Bathsheba.

Bathsheba: David committed adultery with her and then murdered her husband, Uriah. Bathsheba then married David, and later she gave birth to Solomon.

Solomon: Son of David. He was the third king of Israel and the world's wisest man. He built an extraordinary temple but then strayed into idolatry. After his reign, the kingdom divided.

Rehoboam: Son of Solomon. He was the first king of Judah during the Divided Kingdom era. His oppressive policies prompted the northern tribes, led by Jeroboam, to rebel.

Jeroboam: The first king of Israel during the Divided Kingdom era. In fulfillment of God's predicted punishment of Solomon's idolatry, Jeroboam rebelled against Rehoboam and split the kingdom.

Ahab: A king of Israel, husband of Jezebel. He was weak as a king, opposed Elijah and died after being wounded by a random arrow in battle.

Jezebel: Queen of Israel and Ahab's wife. She encouraged idolatry in the kingdom and threatened Elijah's life after he challenged the prophets of Baal.

Elijah: A prophet of Israel during the Divided Kingdom era. His chief opponents were Ahab, Jezebel and the prophets of Baal. Instead of dying, he ascended to heaven in a whirlwind.

Elisha: Elijah's successor. Astonishing miracles characterized his ministry. The king he appointed, Jehu, killed Jezebel and the remaining prophets of Baal.

Amos: A shepherd and prophet in Israel during the reign of Jeroboam II. He foretold disaster for the nation because the people refused to return to God.

Hosea: A prophet in Israel just after Amos. God had Hosea marry an adulterous woman named Gomer. The drama of their relationship mirrored Israel's unfaithfulness to God.

Hoshea: The last king of Israel. The king of Assyria arrested him and invaded the whole land of Israel because Hoshea had stopped paying him tribute.

Hezekiah: A king of Judah. He reigned at the same time as Hoshea but trusted in God and was able to resist Assyria's army.

Isaiah: A prophet in Judah. He supported Hezekiah's struggle against Assyria and foretold both the exile of Judah to Babylon and its return.

Jeremiah: A prophet to Judah just before the Babylonian captivity. He foretold the exile and a return after 70 years; he also witnessed Jerusalem's destruction.

Nebuchadnezzar: The king of Babylon who invaded Judah and laid siege to Jerusalem. He plundered Solomon's temple, destroyed Jerusalem and removed Judah's population to Babylon.

Zedekiah: The last king of Judah. He rebelled against Babylon. Following his capture, his sons were killed before his eyes and then his eyes were put out. He was taken to Babylon where he died.

Ezekiel: A prophet to Judah before and during the Babylonian captivity. He prophesied the destruction of Jerusalem and the eventual return from exile.

Daniel: A prophet during the exile and a high-ranking administrator under both the Babylonians and Persians. He prophesied about the future of Babylon and the empires that would follow. God delivered him from his enemies' dramatic opposition.

Cyrus: The king of Persia who overthrew Babylon. He permitted the exiles to return to Judah and ordered the temple to be rebuilt.

Zerubbabel: A member of Judah's royal family who led the first group of exiles back to Judah and eventually led the successful effort to rebuild the temple.

Ezra: A priest who led the second group of exiles back to Judah and renewed the people's faithfulness to God's Word.

Haggai: A prophet during the return from the exile. Haggai motivated the people to rebuild the temple.

Zechariah: A prophet during the return from the exile. Like Haggai, he motivated the people to rebuild the temple. He also prophesied the restoration and prosperity of God's people.

Esther: The Jewish queen of the Persian Empire during the reign of Xerxes. She exposed a plot to kill the Jews.

Mordecai: Esther's cousin. Mordecai raised Esther, guided her when she became queen and uncovered a conspiracy to assassinate the king.

Nehemiah: Appointed governor of Judah by the king of Persia, he directed the rebuilding of the wall around Jerusalem, countering opposition from the rulers of surrounding regions.

Malachi: The last prophet of the Old Testament era. He preached judgment and repentance to Judah, and prophesied the return, in a sense, of Elijah — fulfilled by John the Baptist.

Mary: The mother of Jesus. Jesus' birth was miraculous because Mary was still a virgin when she conceived. She was also present at Jesus' crucifixion.

Joseph: Jesus' adoptive father. At the command of an angel in a dream, he married Mary despite the scandal of her out-of-wedlock pregnancy.

Jesus: The promised Messiah and Son of God. He carried out a three-year ministry of preaching and miracle-working, traveling with his disciples. He was executed by crucifixion but rose to life three days later.

John the Baptist: The prophet who prepared the Jews for Jesus' ministry. He preached repentance and baptized people in the Jordan River. John was imprisoned and later beheaded for criticizing Herod.

Peter: One of Jesus' disciples. Peter was outspoken and fiercely devoted to Jesus, though during Jesus' trial Peter denied knowing him. After Jesus' resurrection, Peter was the key leader of the church in Jerusalem.

James and John: Two brothers who were disciples of Jesus. They were part of Jesus' inner circle and were close friends of Jesus.

They both continued to work to spread the Good News after the death and resurrection of Jesus.

Mary and Martha: Sisters and supporters of Jesus and his ministry. Their brother was Lazarus.

Lazarus: Friend and supporter of Jesus. He died of an illness, but Jesus raised him back to life after four days.

Judas Iscariot: The disciple who betrayed Jesus. He led the temple guards to Jesus the night before his crucifixion. Judas later committed suicide.

Pilate: The Roman governor who sentenced Jesus to death.

Stephen: The first Christian martyr. The Jewish authorities stoned Stephen for allegedly speaking against the Law of Moses and the temple. His death sparked a rash of persecution against the church.

Barnabas: One of Paul's missionary partners. When Paul began to follow Jesus, Barnabas was one of his first supporters. He accompanied Paul on his first missionary journey.

Paul: Paul persecuted the church until he became a believer when Jesus dramatically appeared to him. He became a missionary and the apostle to the Gentiles. Paul wrote much of the New Testament.

Chart of References

1 **Creation: The Beginning of Life as We Know It:** Genesis 1 – 4; 6 – 9

2 **God Builds a Nation:** Genesis 12 – 13; 15 – 17; 21 – 22; 32 – 33; 35; Romans 4; Hebrews 11

3 **Joseph: From Slave to Deputy Pharaoh:** Genesis 37; 39; 41 – 48; 50

4 **Deliverance:** Exodus 1 – 7; 10 – 17

5 **New Commands and a New Covenant:** Exodus 19 – 20; 24 – 25; 32 – 34; 40

6 **Wandering:** Numbers 10 – 14; 20 – 21; 25; 27; Deuteronomy 1 – 2; 4; 6; 8 – 9; 29 – 32; 34

7 **The Battle Begins:** Joshua 1 – 2; 6; 8; 10 – 11; 23 – 24

8 **A Few Good Men ... and Women:** Judges 2 – 4; 6 – 8; 13 – 16

9 **The Faith of a Foreign Woman:** Ruth 1 – 4

10 **Standing Tall, Falling Hard:** 1 Samuel 1 – 4; 8 – 13; 15

11 **From Shepherd to King:** 1 Samuel 16 – 18; 24; 31; 2 Samuel 6; 22; 1 Chronicles 17; Psalm 59

12 **The Trials of a King:** 2 Samuel 11 – 12; 18 – 19; 1 Chronicles 22; 29; Psalms 23; 32; 51

13 **The King Who Had It All:** 1 Kings 1 – 8; 10 – 11; 2 Chronicles 5 – 7; Proverbs 1 – 3; 6; 20 – 21

14 **A Kingdom Torn in Two:** 1 Kings 12 – 16

15 **God's Messengers:** 1 Kings 17 – 19; 2 Kings 2; 4; 6; Hosea 4 – 5; 8 – 9; 14; Amos 1; 3 – 5; 9

16 **The Beginning of the End:** 2 Kings 17 – 19; Isaiah 3; 6; 13 – 14; 49; 53

17 **The Kingdoms' Fall:** 2 Kings 21; 23 – 25; 2 Chronicles 33; 36; Jeremiah 1 – 2; 4 – 5; 13; 21; Lamentations 1 – 3; 5; Ezekiel 1 – 2; 6 – 7; 36 – 37

18 **Daniel in Exile:** Daniel 1 – 3; 6; Jeremiah 29 – 31

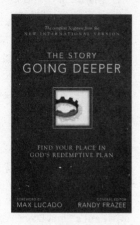

Rome

ITALY

Sicily

IONIAN
SEA

MACEDONIA

Philippi

Thessalonica

Athens

Corinth

ACHAIA

Crete

N

THE GREAT S

CYRENAICA

| 0 | 100 | 200 MI |
| 0 | 100 | 200 | 300 KM |